C Programming
A Modern Approach

Second Edition

C Programming
A Modern Approach

Second Edition

K. N. KING
Department of Computer Science
Georgia State University

W • W • Norton & Company

New York • London

In memory of my father, Paul Ellsworth King

Copyright © 2008, 1996 by W. W. Norton & Company, Inc.

Editors: Fred McFarland and Aaron Javsicas
Managing Editor, College: Marian Johnson
Associate Managing Editor, College: Kim Yi
Copy Editor: Mary Kelly
Production Manager: Roy Tedoff
Editorial Assistants: Alexis Hilts and Carly Fraser

Composition by K. N. King.
Manufacturing by LSC Communications, Crawfordsville.
Book design by K. N. King.

Library of Congress Cataloging-in-Publication Data

King, K. N. (Kim N.)
    C programming : a modern approach / K.N. King. — 2nd ed.
        p.   cm.
    Includes bibliographical references and index.

    ISBN 978-0-393-97950-3 (pbk.)

    1. C (Computer program language) I. Title.

QA76.73.C15K49 2008
005.13'3—dc22   2007049425

W. W. Norton & Company, Inc., 500 Fifth Avenue, New York, NY 10110
www.wwnorton.com

W. W. Norton & Company Ltd., 15 Carlisle Street, London W1D 3BS

6 7 8 9 0

BRIEF CONTENTS

CONTENTS

PREFACE

In computing, turning the obvious into the useful
is a living definition of the word "frustration."

In the years since the first edition of *C Programming: A Modern Approach* was published, a host of new C-based languages have sprung up—Java and C# foremost among them—and related languages such as C++ and Perl have achieved greater prominence. Still, C remains as popular as ever, plugging away in the background, quietly powering much of the world's software. It remains the *lingua franca* of the computer universe, as it was in 1996.

But even C must change with the times. The need for a new edition of *C Programming: A Modern Approach* became apparent when the C99 standard was published. Moreover, the first edition, with its references to DOS and 16-bit processors, was becoming dated. The second edition is fully up-to-date and has been improved in many other ways as well.

What's New in the Second Edition

Here's a list of new features and improvements in the second edition:

- **Complete coverage of both the C89 standard and the C99 standard.** The biggest difference between the first and second editions is coverage of the C99 standard. My goal was to cover every significant difference between C89 and C99, including all the language features and library functions added in C99. Each C99 change is clearly marked, either with "C99" in the heading of a section or—in the case of shorter discussions—with a special icon in the left margin. I did this partly to draw attention to the changes and partly so that readers who aren't interested in C99 or don't have access to a C99 compiler will know what to skip. Many of the C99 additions are of interest only to a specialized audience, but some of the new features will be of use to nearly all C programmers.

- *Includes a quick reference to all C89 and C99 library functions.* Appendix D in the first edition described all C89 standard library functions. In this edition, the appendix covers all C89 and C99 library functions.

- *Expanded coverage of GCC.* In the years since the first edition, use of GCC (originally the GNU C Compiler, now the GNU Compiler Collection) has spread. GCC has some significant advantages, including high quality, low (i.e., no) cost, and portability across a variety of hardware and software platforms. In recognition of its growing importance, I've included more information about GCC in this edition, including discussions of how to use it as well as common GCC error messages and warnings.

- *New coverage of abstract data types.* In the first edition, a significant portion of Chapter 19 was devoted to C++. This material seems less relevant today, since students may already have learned C++, Java, or C# before reading this book. In this edition, coverage of C++ has been replaced by a discussion of how to set up abstract data types in C.

- *Expanded coverage of international features.* Chapter 25, which is devoted to C's international features, is now much longer and more detailed. Information about the Unicode/UCS character set and its encodings is a highlight of the expanded coverage.

- *Updated to reflect today's CPUs and operating systems.* When I wrote the first edition, 16-bit architectures and the DOS operating system were still relevant to many readers, but such is not the case today. I've updated the discussion to focus more on 32-bit and 64-bit architectures. The rise of Linux and other versions of UNIX has dictated a stronger focus on that family of operating systems, although aspects of Windows and the Mac OS operating system that affect C programmers are mentioned as well.

- *More exercises and programming projects.* The first edition of this book contained 311 exercises. This edition has nearly 500 (498, to be exact), divided into two groups: exercises and programming projects.

- *Solutions to selected exercises and programming projects.* The most frequent request I received from readers of the first edition was to provide answers to the exercises. In response to this request, I've put the answers to roughly one-third of the exercises and programming projects on the web at *knking.com/books/c2*. This feature is particularly useful for readers who aren't enrolled in a college course and need a way to check their work. Exercises and projects for which answers are provided are marked with a **W** icon (the "W" stands for "answer available on the Web").

- *Password-protected instructor website.* For this edition, I've built a new instructor resource site (accessible through *knking.com/books/c2*) containing solutions to the remaining exercises and projects, plus PowerPoint presentations for most chapters. Faculty may contact me at *cbook@knking.com* for a password. Please use your campus email address and include a link to your department's website so that I can verify your identity.

I've also taken the opportunity to improve wording and explanations throughout the book. The changes are extensive and painstaking: every sentence has been checked and—if necessary—rewritten.

Although much has changed in this edition, I've tried to retain the original chapter and section numbering as much as possible. Only one chapter (the last one) is entirely new, but many chapters have additional sections. In a few cases, existing sections have been renumbered. One appendix (C syntax) has been dropped, but a new appendix that compares C99 with C89 has been added.

Goals

The goals of this edition remain the same as those of the first edition:

- **Be clear, readable, and possibly even entertaining.** Many C books are too concise for the average reader. Others are badly written or just plain dull. I've tried to give clear, thorough explanations, leavened with enough humor to hold the reader's interest.

- **Be accessible to a broad range of readers.** I assume that the reader has at least a little previous programming experience, but I don't assume knowledge of a particular language. I've tried to keep jargon to a minimum and to define the terms that I use. I've also attempted to separate advanced material from more elementary topics, so that the beginner won't get discouraged.

- **Be authoritative without being pedantic.** To avoid arbitrarily deciding what to include and what not to include, I've tried to cover all the features of the C language and library. At the same time, I've tried to avoid burdening the reader with unnecessary detail.

- **Be organized for easy learning.** My experience in teaching C underscores the importance of presenting the features of C gradually. I use a spiral approach, in which difficult topics are introduced briefly, then revisited one or more times later in the book with details added each time. Pacing is deliberate, with each chapter building gradually on what has come before. For most students, this is probably the best approach: it avoids the extremes of boredom on the one hand, or "information overload" on the other.

- **Motivate language features.** Instead of just describing each feature of the language and giving a few simple examples of how the feature is used, I've tried to motivate each feature and discuss how it's used in practical situations.

- **Emphasize style.** It's important for every C programmer to develop a consistent style. Rather than dictating what this style should be, though, I usually describe a few possibilities and let the reader choose the one that's most appealing. Knowing alternative styles is a big help when reading other people's programs (which programmers often spend a great deal of time doing).

- **Avoid dependence on a particular machine, compiler, or operating system.** Since C is available on such a wide variety of platforms, I've tried to avoid dependence on any particular machine, compiler, or operating system. All programs are designed to be portable to a wide variety of platforms.

■ *Use illustrations to clarify key concepts.* I've tried to put in as many figures as I could, since I think these are crucial for understanding many aspects of C. In particular, I've tried to "animate" algorithms whenever possible by showing snapshots of data at different points in the computation.

What's So Modern about *A Modern Approach?*

One of my most important goals has been to take a "modern approach" to C. Here are some of the ways I've tried to achieve this goal:

■ *Put C in perspective.* Instead of treating C as the only programming language worth knowing, I treat it as one of many useful languages. I discuss what kind of applications C is best suited for; I also show how to capitalize on C's strengths while minimizing its weaknesses.

■ *Emphasize standard versions of C.* I pay minimal attention to versions of the language prior to the C89 standard. There are just a few scattered references to K&R C (the 1978 version of the language described in the first edition of Brian Kernighan and Dennis Ritchie's book, *The C Programming Language*). Appendix C lists the major differences between C89 and K&R C.

■ *Debunk myths.* Today's compilers are often at odds with commonly held assumptions about C. I don't hesitate to debunk some of the myths about C or challenge beliefs that have long been part of the C folklore (for example, the belief that pointer arithmetic is always faster than array subscripting). I've reexamined the old conventions of C, keeping the ones that are still helpful.

■ *Emphasize software engineering.* I treat C as a mature software engineering tool, emphasizing how to use it to cope with issues that arise during programming-in-the-large. I stress making programs readable, maintainable, reliable, and portable, and I put special emphasis on information hiding.

■ *Postpone C's low-level features.* These features, although handy for the kind of systems programming originally done in C, are not as relevant now that C is used for a great variety of applications. Instead of introducing them in the early chapters, as many C books do, I postpone them until Chapter 20.

■ *De-emphasize "manual optimization."* Many books teach the reader to write tricky code in order to gain small savings in program efficiency. With today's abundance of optimizing C compilers, these techniques are often no longer necessary; in fact, they can result in programs that are less efficient.

Q&A Sections

Each chapter ends with a "Q&A section"—a series of questions and answers related to material covered in the chapter. Topics addressed in these sections include:

- *Frequently asked questions.* I've tried to answer questions that come up frequently in my own courses, in other books, and on newsgroups related to C.

- *Additional discussion and clarification of tricky issues.* Although readers with experience in a variety of languages may be satisfied with a brief explanation and a couple of examples, readers with less experience need more.

- *Side issues that don't belong in the main flow.* Some questions raise technical issues that won't be of interest to all readers.

- *Material too advanced or too esoteric to interest the average reader.* Questions of this nature are marked with an asterisk (*). Curious readers with a fair bit of programming experience may wish to delve into these questions immediately; others should definitely skip them on a first reading. *Warning:* These questions often refer to topics covered in later chapters.

- *Common differences among C compilers.* I discuss some frequently used (but nonstandard) features provided by particular compilers.

Q&A Some questions in Q&A sections relate directly to specific places in the chapter; these places are marked by a special icon to signal the reader that additional information is available.

Other Features

In addition to Q&A sections, I've included a number of useful features, many of which are marked with simple but distinctive icons (shown at left).

- **Warnings** alert readers to common pitfalls. C is famous for its traps; documenting them all is a hopeless—if not impossible—task. I've tried to pick out the pitfalls that are most common and/or most important.

cross-references ➤ *Preface*

- **Cross-references** provide a hypertext-like ability to locate information. Although many of these are pointers to topics covered later in the book, some point to previous topics that the reader may wish to review.

idiom

- **Idioms**—code patterns frequently seen in C programs—are marked for quick reference.

portability tip

- **Portability tips** give hints for writing programs that are independent of a particular machine, compiler, or operating system.

- **Sidebars** cover topics that aren't strictly part of C but that every knowledgeable C programmer should be aware of. (See "Source Code" on the next page for an example of a sidebar.)

- **Appendices** provide valuable reference information.

Programs

Choosing illustrative programs isn't an easy job. If programs are too brief and artificial, readers won't get any sense of how the features are used in the real world. On the other hand, if a program is *too* realistic, its point can easily be lost in a forest of details. I've chosen a middle course, using small, simple examples to make concepts clear when they're first introduced, then gradually building up to complete programs. I haven't included programs of great length; it's been my experience that instructors don't have the time to cover them and students don't have the patience to read them. I don't ignore the issues that arise in the creation of large programs, though—Chapter 15 (Writing Large Programs) and Chapter 19 (Program Design) cover them in detail.

I've resisted the urge to rewrite programs to take advantage of the features of C99, since not every reader may have access to a C99 compiler or wish to use C99. I have, however, used C99's `<stdbool.h>` header in a few programs, because it conveniently defines macros named `bool`, `true`, and `false`. If your compiler doesn't support the `<stdbool.h>` header, you'll need to provide your own definitions for these names.

The programs in this edition have undergone one very minor change. The `main` function now has the form `int main(void) { ... }` in most cases. This change reflects recommended practice and is compatible with C99, which requires an explicit return type for each function.

Source Code

Source code for all programs is available at *knking.com/books/c2*. Updates, corrections, and news about the book can also be found at this site.

Audience

This book is designed as a primary text for a C course at the undergraduate level. Previous programming experience in a high-level language or assembler is helpful but not necessary for a computer-literate reader (an "adept beginner," as one of my former editors put it).

Since the book is self-contained and usable for reference as well as learning, it makes an excellent companion text for a course in data structures, compiler design, operating systems, computer graphics, embedded systems, or other courses that use C for project work. Thanks to its Q&A sections and emphasis on practical problems, the book will also appeal to readers who are enrolled in a training class or who are learning C by self-study.

Organization

The book is divided into four parts:

- *Basic Features of C.* Chapters 1–10 cover enough of C to allow the reader to write single-file programs using arrays and functions.
- *Advanced Features of C.* Chapters 11–20 build on the material in the earlier chapters. The topics become a little harder in these chapters, which provide in-

depth coverage of pointers, strings, the preprocessor, structures, unions, enumerations, and low-level features of C. In addition, two chapters (15 and 19) offer guidance on program design.

■ ***The Standard C Library.*** Chapters 21–27 focus on the C library, a large collection of functions that come with every compiler. These chapters are most likely to be used as reference material, although portions are suitable for lectures.

■ ***Reference.*** Appendix A gives a complete list of C operators. Appendix B describes the major differences between C99 and C89, and Appendix C covers the differences between C89 and K&R C. Appendix D is an alphabetical listing of all functions in the C89 and C99 standard libraries, with a thorough description of each. Appendix E lists the ASCII character set. An annotated bibliography points the reader toward other sources of information.

A full-blown course on C should cover Chapters 1–20 in sequence, with topics from Chapters 21–27 added as needed. (Chapter 22, which includes coverage of file input/output, is the most important chapter of this group.) A shorter course can omit the following topics without losing continuity: Section 8.3 (variable-length arrays), Section 9.6 (recursion), Section 12.4 (pointers and multidimensional arrays), Section 12.5 (pointers and variable-length arrays), Section 14.5 (miscellaneous directives), Section 17.7 (pointers to functions), Section 17.8 (restricted pointers), Section 17.9 (flexible array members), Section 18.6 (inline functions), Chapter 19 (program design), Section 20.2 (bit-fields in structures), and Section 20.3 (other low-level techniques).

Exercises and Programming Projects

Having a variety of good problems is obviously essential for a textbook. This edition of the book contains both exercises (shorter problems that don't require writing a full program) and programming projects (problems that require writing or modifying an entire program).

A few exercises have nonobvious answers (some individuals uncharitably call these "trick questions"—the nerve!). Since C programs often contain abundant examples of such code, I feel it's necessary to provide some practice. However, I'll play fair by marking these exercises with an asterisk (*). Be careful with a starred exercise: either pay close attention and think hard or skip it entirely.

Errors, Lack of (?)

I've taken great pains to ensure the accuracy of this book. Inevitably, however, any book of this size contains a few errors. If you spot one, please contact me at *cbook@knking.com*. I'd also appreciate hearing about which features you found especially helpful, which ones you could do without, and what you'd like to see added.

Acknowledgments

First, I'd like to thank my editors at Norton, Fred McFarland and Aaron Javsicas. Fred got the second edition underway and Aaron stepped in with brisk efficiency to bring it to completion. I'd also like to thank associate managing editor Kim Yi, copy editor Mary Kelly, production manager Roy Tedoff, and editorial assistant Carly Fraser.

I owe a huge debt to the following colleagues, who reviewed some or all of the manuscript for the second edition:

Markus Bussmann, University of Toronto
Jim Clarke, University of Toronto
Karen Reid, University of Toronto
Peter Seebach, moderator of *comp.lang.c.moderated*

Jim and Peter deserve special mention for their detailed reviews, which saved me from a number of embarrassing slips. The reviewers for the first edition, in alphabetical order, were: Susan Anderson-Freed, Manuel E. Bermudez, Lisa J. Brown, Steven C. Cater, Patrick Harrison, Brian Harvey, Henry H. Leitner, Darrell Long, Arthur B. Maccabe, Carolyn Rosner, and Patrick Terry.

I received many useful comments from readers of the first edition; I thank everyone who took the time to write. Students and colleagues at Georgia State University also provided valuable feedback. Ed Bullwinkel and his wife Nancy were kind enough to read much of the manuscript. I'm particularly grateful to my department chair, Yi Pan, who was very supportive of the project.

My wife, Susan Cole, was a pillar of strength as always. Our cats, Dennis, Pounce, and Tex, were also instrumental in the completion of the book. Pounce and Tex were happy to contribute the occasional catfight to help keep me awake while I was working late at night.

Finally, I'd like to acknowledge the late Alan J. Perlis, whose epigrams appear at the beginning of each chapter. I had the privilege of studying briefly under Alan at Yale in the mid-70s. I think he'd be amused at finding his epigrams in a C book.

1 Introducing C

*When someone says "I want a programming language in which
I need only say what I wish done," give him a lollipop.**

What is C? The simple answer—a widely used programming language developed
in the early 1970s at Bell Laboratories—conveys little of C's special flavor. Before
we become immersed in the details of the language, let's take a look at where C
came from, what it was designed for, and how it has changed over the years (Section 1.1). We'll also discuss C's strengths and weaknesses and see how to get the
most out of the language (Section 1.2).

1.1 History of C

Let's take a quick look at C's history, from its origins, to its coming of age as a
standardized language, to its influence on recent languages.

Origins

C is a by-product of the UNIX operating system, which was developed at Bell Laboratories by Ken Thompson, Dennis Ritchie, and others. Thompson single-hand-
edly wrote the original version of UNIX, which ran on the DEC PDP-7 computer,
an early minicomputer with only 8K words of main memory (this was 1969, after
all!).

Like other operating systems of the time, UNIX was written in assembly language. Programs written in assembly language are usually painful to debug and
hard to enhance; UNIX was no exception. Thompson decided that a higher-level

---

*The epigrams at the beginning of each chapter are from "Epigrams on Programming" by Alan J. Perlis
(*ACM SIGPLAN Notices* (September, 1982): 7–13).

1

language was needed for the further development of UNIX, so he designed a small language named B. Thompson based B on BCPL, a systems programming language developed in the mid-1960s. BCPL, in turn, traces its ancestry to Algol 60, one of the earliest (and most influential) programming languages.

Ritchie soon joined the UNIX project and began programming in B. In 1970, Bell Labs acquired a PDP-11 for the UNIX project. Once B was up and running on the PDP-11, Thompson rewrote a portion of UNIX in B. By 1971, it became apparent that B was not well-suited to the PDP-11, so Ritchie began to develop an extended version of B. He called his language NB ("New B") at first, and then, as it began to diverge more from B, he changed the name to C. The language was stable enough by 1973 that UNIX could be rewritten in C. The switch to C provided an important benefit: portability. By writing C compilers for other computers at Bell Labs, the team could get UNIX running on those machines as well.

Standardization

C continued to evolve during the 1970s, especially between 1977 and 1979. It was during this period that the first book on C appeared. *The C Programming Language*, written by Brian Kernighan and Dennis Ritchie and published in 1978, quickly became the bible of C programmers. In the absence of an official standard for C, this book—known as K&R or the "White Book" to aficionados—served as a de facto standard.

During the 1970s, there were relatively few C programmers, and most of them were UNIX users. By the 1980s, however, C had expanded beyond the narrow confines of the UNIX world. C compilers became available on a variety of machines running under different operating systems. In particular, C began to establish itself on the fast-growing IBM PC platform.

With C's increasing popularity came problems. Programmers who wrote new C compilers relied on K&R as a reference. Unfortunately, K&R was fuzzy about some language features, so compilers often treated these features differently. Also, K&R failed to make a clear distinction between which features belonged to C and which were part of UNIX. To make matters worse, C continued to change after K&R was published, with new features being added and a few older features removed. The need for a thorough, precise, and up-to-date description of the language soon became apparent. Without such a standard, numerous dialects would have arisen, threatening the portability of C programs, one of the language's major strengths.

The development of a U.S. standard for C began in 1983 under the auspices of the American National Standards Institute (ANSI). After many revisions, the standard was completed in 1988 and formally approved in December 1989 as ANSI standard X3.159-1989. In 1990, it was approved by the International Organization for Standardization (ISO) as international standard ISO/IEC 9899:1990. This version of the language is usually referred to as C89 or C90, to distinguish it from the original version of C, often called K&R C. Appendix C summarizes the major differences between C89 and K&R C.

The language underwent a few changes in 1995 (described in a document known as Amendment 1). More significant changes occurred with the publication of a new standard, ISO/IEC 9899:1999, in 1999. The language described in this standard is commonly known as C99. The terms "ANSI C," "ANSI/ISO C," and "ISO C"—once used to describe C89—are now ambiguous, thanks to the existence of two standards.

 Because C99 isn't yet universal, and because of the need to maintain millions (if not billions) of lines of code written in older versions of C, I'll use a special icon (shown in the left margin) to mark discussions of features that were added in C99. A compiler that doesn't recognize these features isn't "C99-compliant." If history is any guide, it will be some years before all C compilers are C99-compliant, if they ever are. Appendix B lists the major differences between C99 and C89.

C-Based Languages

C has had a huge influence on modern-day programming languages, many of which borrow heavily from it. Of the many C-based languages, several are especially prominent:

- **C++** includes all the features of C, but adds classes and other features to support object-oriented programming.

- **Java** is based on C++ and therefore inherits many C features.

- **C#** is a more recent language derived from C++ and Java.

- **Perl** was originally a fairly simple scripting language; over time it has grown and adopted many of the features of C.

Considering the popularity of these newer languages, it's logical to ask whether it's worth the trouble to learn C. I think it is, for several reasons. First, learning C can give you greater insight into the features of C++, Java, C#, Perl, and the other C-based languages. Programmers who learn one of these languages first often fail to master basic features that were inherited from C. Second, there are a lot of older C programs around; you may find yourself needing to read and maintain this code. Third, C is still widely used for developing new software, especially in situations where memory or processing power is limited or where the simplicity of C is desired.

If you haven't already used one of the newer C-based languages, you'll find that this book is excellent preparation for learning these languages. It emphasizes data abstraction, information hiding, and other principles that play a large role in object-oriented programming. C++ includes all the features of C, so you'll be able to use everything you learn from this book if you later tackle C++. Many of the features of C can be found in the other C-based languages as well.

1.2 Strengths and Weaknesses of C

Like any other programming language, C has strengths and weaknesses. Both stem from the language's original use (writing operating systems and other systems software) and its underlying philosophy:

- ***C is a low-level language.*** To serve as a suitable language for systems programming, C provides access to machine-level concepts (bytes and addresses, for example) that other programming languages try to hide. C also provides operations that correspond closely to a computer's built-in instructions, so that programs can be fast. Since application programs rely on it for input/output, storage management, and numerous other services, an operating system can't afford to be slow.

- ***C is a small language.*** C provides a more limited set of features than many languages. (The reference manual in the second edition of K&R covers the entire language in 49 pages.) To keep the number of features small, C relies heavily on a "library" of standard functions. (A "function" is similar to what other programming languages might call a "procedure," "subroutine," or "method.")

- ***C is a permissive language.*** C assumes that you know what you're doing, so it allows you a wider degree of latitude than many languages. Moreover, C doesn't mandate the detailed error-checking found in other languages.

Strengths

C's strengths help explain why the language has become so popular:

- ***Efficiency.*** Efficiency has been one of C's advantages from the beginning. Because C was intended for applications where assembly language had traditionally been used, it was crucial that C programs could run quickly and in limited amounts of memory.

- ***Portability.*** Although program portability wasn't a primary goal of C, it has turned out to be one of the language's strengths. When a program must run on computers ranging from PCs to supercomputers, it is often written in C. One reason for the portability of C programs is that—thanks to C's early association with UNIX and the later ANSI/ISO standards—the language hasn't splintered into incompatible dialects. Another is that C compilers are small and easily written, which has helped make them widely available. Finally, C itself has features that support portability (although there's nothing to prevent programmers from writing nonportable programs).

- ***Power.*** C's large collection of data types and operators help make it a powerful language. In C, it's often possible to accomplish quite a bit with just a few lines of code.

- *Flexibility.* Although C was originally designed for systems programming, it has no inherent restrictions that limit it to this arena. C is now used for applications of all kinds, from embedded systems to commercial data processing. Moreover, C imposes very few restrictions on the use of its features; operations that would be illegal in other languages are often permitted in C. For example, C allows a character to be added to an integer value (or, for that matter, a floating-point number). This flexibility can make programming easier, although it may allow some bugs to slip through.

- *Standard library.* One of C's great strengths is its standard library, which contains hundreds of functions for input/output, string handling, storage allocation, and other useful operations.

- *Integration with UNIX.* C is particularly powerful in combination with UNIX (including the popular variant known as Linux). In fact, some UNIX tools assume that the user knows C.

Weaknesses

C's weaknesses arise from the same source as many of its strengths: C's closeness to the machine. Here are a few of C's most notorious problems:

- *C programs can be error-prone.* C's flexibility makes it an error-prone language. Programming mistakes that would be caught in many other languages can't be detected by a C compiler. In this respect, C is a lot like assembly language, where most errors aren't detected until the program is run. To make matters worse, C contains a number of pitfalls for the unwary. In later chapters, we'll see how an extra semicolon can create an infinite loop or a missing & symbol can cause a program crash.

- *C programs can be difficult to understand.* Although C is a small language by most measures, it has a number of features that aren't found in all programming languages (and that consequently are often misunderstood). These features can be combined in a great variety of ways, many of which—although obvious to the original author of a program—can be hard for others to understand. Another problem is the terse nature of C programs. C was designed at a time when interactive communication with computers was tedious at best. As a result, C was purposefully kept terse to minimize the time required to enter and edit programs. C's flexibility can also be a negative factor; programmers who are too clever for their own good can make programs almost impossible to understand.

- *C programs can be difficult to modify.* Large programs written in C can be hard to change if they haven't been designed with maintenance in mind. Modern programming languages usually provide features such as classes and packages that support the division of a large program into more manageable pieces. C, unfortunately, lacks such features.

Obfuscated C

Even C's most ardent admirers admit that C code can be hard to read. The annual International Obfuscated C Code Contest actually encourages contestants to write the most confusing C programs possible. The winners are truly baffling, as 1990's "Best Small Program" shows:

```
v,i,j,k,l,s,a[99];
main()
{
  for(scanf("%d",&s);*a-s;v=a[j*=v]-a[i],k=i<s,j+=(v=j<s&&
(!k&&!!printf(2+"\n\n%c"-(!l<<!j)," #Q"[l^v?(l^j)&1:2])&&
++l||a[i]<s&&v&&v-i+j&&v+i-j))&&!(l%=s),v||(i==j?a[i+=k]=0:
++a[i])>=s*k&&++a[--i]))
    ;
}
```

This program, written by Doron Osovlanski and Baruch Nissenbaum, prints all solutions to the Eight Queens problem (the problem of placing eight queens on a chessboard in such a way that no queen attacks any other queen). In fact, it works for any number of queens between four and 99. For more winning programs, visit *www.ioccc.org*, the contest's web site.

Effective Use of C

Using C effectively requires taking advantage of C's strengths while avoiding its weaknesses. Here are a few suggestions:

- ***Learn how to avoid C pitfalls.*** Hints for avoiding pitfalls are scattered throughout this book—just look for the ⚠ symbol. For a more extensive list of pitfalls, see Andrew Koenig's *C Traps and Pitfalls* (Reading, Mass.: Addison-Wesley, 1989). Modern compilers will detect common pitfalls and issue warnings, but no compiler spots them all.

- ***Use software tools to make programs more reliable.*** C programmers are prolific tool builders (and users). One of the most famous C tools is named lint. lint, which is traditionally provided with UNIX, can subject a program to a more extensive error analysis than most C compilers. If lint (or a similar program) is available, it's a good idea to use it. Another useful tool is a debugger. Because of the nature of C, many bugs can't be detected by a C compiler; these show up instead in the form of run-time errors or incorrect output. Consequently, using a good debugger is practically mandatory for C programmers.

- ***Take advantage of existing code libraries.*** One of the benefits of using C is that so many other people also use it; it's a good bet that they've written code you can employ in your own programs. C code is often bundled into libraries (collections of functions); obtaining a suitable library is a good way to reduce errors—and save considerable programming effort. Libraries for common tasks, including user-interface development, graphics, communications, database management, and networking, are readily available. Some libraries are in the public domain, some are open source, and some are sold commercially.

■ *Adopt a sensible set of coding conventions.* A coding convention is a style rule that a programmer has decided to adopt even though it's not enforced by the language. Well-chosen conventions help make programs more uniform, easier to read, and easier to modify. Conventions are important when using any programming language, but especially so with C. As noted above, C's highly flexible nature makes it possible for programmers to write code that is all but unreadable. The programming examples in this book follow one set of conventions, but there are other, equally valid, conventions in use. (We'll discuss some of the alternatives from time to time.) Which set you use is less important than adopting *some* conventions and sticking to them.

■ *Avoid "tricks" and overly complex code.* C encourages programming tricks. There are usually several ways to accomplish a given task in C; programmers are often tempted to choose the method that's most concise. Don't get carried away; the shortest solution is often the hardest to comprehend. In this book, I'll illustrate a style that's reasonably concise but still understandable.

■ *Stick to the standard.* Most C compilers provide language features and library functions that aren't part of the C89 or C99 standards. For portability, it's best to avoid using nonstandard features and libraries unless they're absolutely necessary.

Q & A

Q: What is this Q&A section anyway?

A: Glad you asked. The Q&A section, which appears at the end of each chapter, serves several purposes.

   The primary purpose of Q&A is to tackle questions that are frequently asked by students learning C. Readers can participate in a dialogue (more or less) with the author, much the same as if they were attending one of my C classes.

   Another purpose of Q&A is to provide additional information about topics covered in the chapter. Readers of this book will likely have widely varying backgrounds. Some will be experienced in other programming languages, whereas others will be learning to program for the first time. Readers with experience in a variety of languages may be satisfied with a brief explanation and a couple of examples, but readers with less experience may need more. The bottom line: If you find the coverage of a topic to be sketchy, check Q&A for more details.

   On occasion, Q&A will discuss common differences among C compilers. For example, we'll cover some frequently used (but nonstandard) features that are provided by particular compilers.

Q: What does `lint` do? [p. 6]

A: `lint` checks a C program for a host of potential errors, including—but not limited to—suspicious combinations of types, unused variables, unreachable code, and nonportable code. It produces a list of diagnostic messages, which the programmer must then sift through. The advantage of using `lint` is that it can detect errors that are missed by the compiler. On the other hand, you've got to remember to use `lint`; it's all too easy to forget about it. Worse still, `lint` can produce messages by the hundreds, of which only a fraction refer to actual errors.

Q: Where did `lint` get its name?

A: Unlike the names of many other UNIX tools, `lint` isn't an acronym; it got its name from the way it picks up pieces of "fluff" from a program.

Q: How do I get a copy of `lint`?

A: `lint` is a standard UNIX utility; if you rely on another operating system, then you probably don't have `lint`. Fortunately, versions of `lint` are available from third parties. An enhanced version of `lint` known as `splint` (Secure Programming Lint) is included in many Linux distributions and can be downloaded for free from *www.splint.org*.

Q: Is there some way to force a compiler to do a more thorough job of error-checking, without having to use `lint`?

A: Yes. Most compilers will do a more thorough check of a program if asked to. In addition to checking for errors (undisputed violations of the rules of C), most compilers also produce warning messages, indicating potential trouble spots. Some compilers have more than one "warning level"; selecting a higher level causes the compiler to check for more problems than choosing a lower level. If your compiler supports warning levels, it's a good idea to select the highest level, causing the compiler to perform the most thorough job of checking that it's capable of. Error-checking options for the GCC compiler, which is distributed with Linux, are discussed in the Q&A section at the end of Chapter 2.

GCC ➤*2.1*

*Q: I'm interested in making my program as reliable as possible. Are there any other tools available besides `lint` and debuggers?

A: Yes. Other common tools include "bounds-checkers" and "leak-finders." C doesn't require that array subscripts be checked; a bounds-checker adds this capability. A leak-finder helps locate "memory leaks": blocks of memory that are dynamically allocated but never deallocated.

---

*Starred questions cover material too advanced or too esoteric to interest the average reader, and often refer to topics covered in later chapters. Curious readers with a fair bit of programming experience may wish to delve into these questions immediately; others should definitely skip them on a first reading.

2 C Fundamentals

One man's constant is another man's variable.

This chapter introduces several basic concepts, including preprocessing directives, functions, variables, and statements, that we'll need in order to write even the simplest programs. Later chapters will cover these topics in much greater detail.

To start off, Section 2.1 presents a small C program and describes how to compile and link it. Section 2.2 then discusses how to generalize the program, and Section 2.3 shows how to add explanatory remarks, known as comments. Section 2.4 introduces variables, which store data that may change during the execution of a program, and Section 2.5 shows how to use the scanf function to read data into variables. Constants—data that won't change during program execution—can be given names, as Section 2.6 shows. Finally, Section 2.7 explains C's rules for creating names (identifiers) and Section 2.8 gives the rules for laying out a program.

2.1 Writing a Simple Program

In contrast to programs written in some languages, C programs require little "boilerplate"—a complete program can be as short as a few lines.

PROGRAM **Printing a Pun**

The first program in Kernighan and Ritchie's classic *The C Programming Language* is extremely short; it does nothing but write the message hello, world. Unlike other C authors, I won't use this program as my first example. I will, however, uphold another C tradition: the bad pun. Here's the pun:

```
To C, or not to C: that is the question.
```

The following program, which we'll name `pun.c`, displays this message each time it is run.

pun.c

```
#include <stdio.h>

int main(void)
{
  printf("To C, or not to C: that is the question.\n");
  return 0;
}
```

Section 2.2 explains the form of this program in some detail. For now, I'll just make a few brief observations. The line

```
#include <stdio.h>
```

is necessary to "include" information about C's standard I/O (input/output) library. The program's executable code goes inside `main`, which represents the "main" program. The only line inside `main` is a command to display the desired message. `printf` is a function from the standard I/O library that can produce nicely formatted output. The `\n` code tells `printf` to advance to the next line after printing the message. The line

```
return 0;
```

indicates that the program "returns" the value 0 to the operating system when it terminates.

Compiling and Linking

Despite its brevity, getting `pun.c` to run is more involved than you might expect. First, we need to create a file named `pun.c` containing the program (any text editor will do). The name of the file doesn't matter, but the `.c` extension is often required by compilers.

Next, we've got to convert the program to a form that the machine can execute. For a C program, that usually involves three steps:

- ***Preprocessing.*** The program is first given to a ***preprocessor***, which obeys commands that begin with # (known as ***directives***). A preprocessor is a bit like an editor; it can add things to the program and make modifications.

- ***Compiling.*** The modified program now goes to a ***compiler***, which translates it into machine instructions (***object code***). The program isn't quite ready to run yet, however.

- ***Linking.*** In the final step, a ***linker*** combines the object code produced by the compiler with any additional code needed to yield a complete executable program. This additional code includes library functions (like `printf`) that are used in the program.

Fortunately, this process is often automated, so you won't find it too onerous. In fact, the preprocessor is usually integrated with the compiler, so you probably won't even notice it at work.

The commands necessary to compile and link vary, depending on the compiler and operating system. Under UNIX, the C compiler is usually named cc. To compile and link the pun.c program, enter the following command in a terminal or command-line window:

```
% cc pun.c
```

(The % character is the UNIX prompt, not something that you need to enter.) Linking is automatic when using cc; no separate link command is necessary.

After compiling and linking the program, cc leaves the executable program in a file named a.out by default. cc has many options; one of them (the -o option) allows us to choose the name of the file containing the executable program. For example, if we want the executable version of pun.c to be named pun, we would enter the following command:

```
% cc -o pun pun.c
```

The GCC Compiler

One of the most popular C compilers is the GCC compiler, which is supplied with Linux but is available for many other platforms as well. Using this compiler is similar to using the traditional UNIX cc compiler. For example, to compile the pun.c program, we would use the following command:

```
% gcc -o pun pun.c
```

Q&A The Q&A section at the end of the chapter provides more information about GCC.

Integrated Development Environments

So far, we've assumed the use of a "command-line" compiler that's invoked by entering a command in a special window provided by the operating system. The alternative is to use an *integrated development environment (IDE),* a software package that allows us to edit, compile, link, execute, and even debug a program without leaving the environment. The components of an IDE are designed to work together. For example, when the compiler detects an error in a program, it can arrange for the editor to highlight the line that contains the error. There's a great deal of variation among IDEs, so I won't discuss them further in this book. However, I would recommend checking to see which IDEs are available for your platform.

2.2 The General Form of a Simple Program

Let's take a closer look at pun.c and see how we can generalize it a bit. Simple C programs have the form

directives

```
int main(void)
{
    statements
}
```

In this template, and in similar templates elsewhere in this book, items printed in Courier would appear in a C program exactly as shown; items in *italics* represent text to be supplied by the programmer.

Notice how the braces show where main begins and ends. C uses { and } in much the same way that some other languages use words like begin and end. This illustrates a general point about C: it relies heavily on abbreviations and special symbols, one reason that C programs are concise (or—less charitably—cryptic).

Q&A

Even the simplest C programs rely on three key language features: directives (editing commands that modify the program prior to compilation), functions (named blocks of executable code, of which main is an example), and statements (commands to be performed when the program is run). We'll take a closer look at these features now.

Directives

Before a C program is compiled, it is first edited by a preprocessor. Commands intended for the preprocessor are called directives. Chapters 14 and 15 discuss directives in detail. For now, we're interested only in the #include directive.

The pun.c program begins with the line

```
#include <stdio.h>
```

headers ➤ 15.2

This directive states that the information in <stdio.h> is to be "included" into the program before it is compiled. <stdio.h> contains information about C's standard I/O library. C has a number of **headers** like <stdio.h>; each contains information about some part of the standard library. The reason we're including <stdio.h> is that C, unlike some programming languages, has no built-in "read" and "write" commands. The ability to perform input and output is provided instead by functions in the standard library.

Directives always begin with a # character, which distinguishes them from other items in a C program. By default, directives are one line long; there's no semicolon or other special marker at the end of a directive.

Functions

Functions are like "procedures" or "subroutines" in other programming languages—they're the building blocks from which programs are constructed. In fact, a C program is little more than a collection of functions. Functions fall into two categories: those written by the programmer and those provided as part of the C implementation. I'll refer to the latter as **library functions**, since they belong to a "library" of functions that are supplied with the compiler.

The term "function" comes from mathematics, where a function is a rule for computing a value when given one or more arguments:

$$f(x) = x + 1$$
$$g(y, z) = y^2 - z^2$$

C uses the term "function" more loosely. In C, a function is simply a series of statements that have been grouped together and given a name. Some functions compute a value; some don't. A function that computes a value uses the `return` statement to specify what value it "returns." For example, a function that adds 1 to its argument might execute the statement

```
return x + 1;
```

while a function that computes the difference of the squares of its arguments might execute the statement

```
return y * y - z * z;
```

Although a C program may consist of many functions, only the `main` function is mandatory. `main` is special: it gets called automatically when the program is executed. Until Chapter 9, where we'll learn how to write other functions, `main` will be the only function in our programs.

 The name `main` is critical; it can't be `begin` or `start` or even `MAIN`.

If `main` is a function, does it return a value? Yes: it returns a status code that is given to the operating system when the program terminates. Let's take another look at the `pun.c` program:

```
#include <stdio.h>

int main(void)
{
  printf("To C, or not to C: that is the question.\n");
  return 0;
}
```

The word `int` just before `main` indicates that the `main` function returns an integer value. The word `void` in parentheses indicates that `main` has no arguments.

The statement

```
return 0;
```

has two effects: it causes the `main` function to terminate (thus ending the program) and it indicates that the `main` function returns a value of 0. We'll have more to say about `main`'s return value in a later chapter. For now, we'll always have `main` return the value 0, which indicates normal program termination.

return value of `main` ➤*9.5*

If there's no `return` statement at the end of the `main` function, the program will still terminate. However, many compilers will produce a warning message (because the function was supposed to return an integer but failed to).

Statements

A *statement* is a command to be executed when the program runs. We'll explore statements later in the book, primarily in Chapters 5 and 6. The `pun.c` program uses only two kinds of statements. One is the `return` statement; the other is the *function call*. Asking a function to perform its assigned task is known as *calling* the function. The `pun.c` program, for example, calls the `printf` function to display a string on the screen:

```
printf("To C, or not to C: that is the question.\n");
```

compound statement ➤ *5.2* C requires that each statement end with a semicolon. (As with any good rule, there's one exception: the compound statement, which we'll encounter later.) The semicolon shows the compiler where the statement ends; since statements can continue over several lines, it's not always obvious where they end. Directives, on the other hand, are normally one line long, and they *don't* end with a semicolon.

Printing Strings

`printf` is a powerful function that we'll examine in Chapter 3. So far, we've only used `printf` to display a *string literal*—a series of characters enclosed in double quotation marks. When `printf` displays a string literal, it doesn't show the quotation marks.

`printf` doesn't automatically advance to the next output line when it finishes printing. To instruct `printf` to advance one line, we must include \n (the *new-line character*) in the string to be printed. Writing a new-line character terminates the current output line; subsequent output goes onto the next line. To illustrate this point, consider the effect of replacing the statement

```
printf("To C, or not to C: that is the question.\n");
```

by two calls of `printf`:

```
printf("To C, or not to C: ");
printf("that is the question.\n");
```

The first call of `printf` writes To C, or not to C: . The second call writes that is the question. and advances to the next line. The net effect is the same as the original `printf`—the user can't tell the difference.

The new-line character can appear more than once in a string literal. To display the message

```
Brevity is the soul of wit.
  --Shakespeare
```

we could write

```
printf("Brevity is the soul of wit.\n  --Shakespeare\n");
```

2.3 Comments

Our `pun.c` program still lacks something important: documentation. Every program should contain identifying information: the program name, the date written, the author, the purpose of the program, and so forth. In C, this information is placed in *comments*. The symbol `/*` marks the beginning of a comment and the symbol `*/` marks the end:

```
/* This is a comment */
```

Comments may appear almost anywhere in a program, either on separate lines or on the same lines as other program text. Here's what `pun.c` might look like with comments added at the beginning:

```
/* Name: pun.c                */
/* Purpose: Prints a bad pun. */
/* Author: K. N. King         */

#include <stdio.h>

int main(void)
{
  printf("To C, or not to C: that is the question.\n");
  return 0;
}
```

Comments may extend over more than one line; once it has seen the `/*` symbol, the compiler reads (and ignores) whatever follows until it encounters the `*/` symbol. If we like, we can combine a series of short comments into one long comment:

```
/* Name: pun.c
   Purpose: Prints a bad pun.
   Author: K. N. King */
```

A comment like this can be hard to read, though, because it's not easy to see where the comment ends. Putting `*/` on a line by itself helps:

```
/* Name: pun.c
   Purpose: Prints a bad pun.
   Author: K. N. King
*/
```

Even better, we can form a "box" around the comment to make it stand out:

```
/************************************************************
 * Name: pun.c                                             *
 * Purpose: Prints a bad pun.                              *
 * Author: K. N. King                                      *
 ************************************************************/
```

Programmers often simplify boxed comments by omitting three of the sides:

```
/*
 * Name: pun.c
 * Purpose: Prints a bad pun.
 * Author: K. N. King
 */
```

A short comment can go on the same line with other program code:

```
int main(void)    /* Beginning of main program */
```

A comment like this is sometimes called a "winged comment."

Forgetting to terminate a comment may cause the compiler to ignore part of your program. Consider the following example:

```
printf("My ");     /* forgot to close this comment...
printf("cat ");
printf("has ");    /* so it ends here */
printf("fleas");
```

Because we've neglected to terminate the first comment, the compiler ignores the middle two statements, and the example prints My fleas.

C99 provides a second kind of comment, which begins with `//` (two adjacent slashes):

```
// This is a comment
```

This style of comment ends automatically at the end of a line. To create a comment that's more than one line long, we can either use the older comment style (`/* ... */`) or else put `//` at the beginning of each comment line:

```
// Name: pun.c
// Purpose: Prints a bad pun.
// Author: K. N. King
```

The newer comment style has a couple of important advantages. First, because a comment automatically ends at the end of a line, there's no chance that an unterminated comment will accidentally consume part of a program. Second, multiline comments stand out better, thanks to the `//` that's required at the beginning of each line.

2.4   Variables and Assignment

Few programs are as simple as the one in Section 2.1. Most programs need to perform a series of calculations before producing output, and thus need a way to store data temporarily during program execution. In C, as in most programming languages, these storage locations are called *variables*.

Types

Every variable must have a *type*, which specifies what kind of data it will hold. C has a wide variety of types. For now, we'll limit ourselves to just two: `int` and `float`. Choosing the proper type is critical, since the type affects how the variable is stored and what operations can be performed on the variable. The type of a numeric variable determines the largest and smallest numbers that the variable can store; it also determines whether or not digits are allowed after the decimal point.

range of `int` values ►*7.1*

A variable of type `int` (short for *integer*) can store a whole number such as 0, 1, 392, or –2553. The range of possible values is limited, though. The largest `int` value is typically 2,147,483,647 but can be as small as 32,767.

A variable of type `float` (short for *floating-point*) can store much larger numbers than an `int` variable. Furthermore, a `float` variable can store numbers with digits after the decimal point, like 379.125. `float` variables have drawbacks, however. Arithmetic on `float` numbers may be slower than arithmetic on `int` numbers. Most significantly, the value of a `float` variable is often just an approximation of the number that was stored in it. If we store 0.1 in a `float` variable, we may later find that the variable has a value such as 0.09999999999999987, thanks to rounding error.

Declarations

Variables must be *declared*—described for the benefit of the compiler—before they can be used. To declare a variable, we first specify the *type* of the variable, then its *name*. (Variable names are chosen by the programmer, subject to the rules described in Section 2.7.) For example, we might declare variables `height` and `profit` as follows:

```
int height;
float profit;
```

The first declaration states that `height` is a variable of type `int`, meaning that `height` can store an integer value. The second declaration says that `profit` is a variable of type `float`.

If several variables have the same type, their declarations can be combined:

```
int height, length, width, volume;
float profit, loss;
```

Notice that each complete declaration ends with a semicolon.

Our first template for `main` didn't include declarations. When `main` contains declarations, these must precede statements:

```
int main(void)
{
    declarations
    statements
}
```

 As we'll see in Chapter 9, this is true of functions in general, as well as blocks (statements that contain embedded declarations). As a matter of style, it's a good idea to leave a blank line between the declarations and the statements.

C99 In C99, declarations don't have to come before statements. For example, `main` might contain a declaration, then a statement, and then another declaration. For compatibility with older compilers, the programs in this book don't take advantage of this rule. However, it's common in C++ and Java programs not to declare variables until they're first needed, so this practice can be expected to become popular in C99 programs as well.

Assignment

A variable can be given a value by means of *assignment*. For example, the statements

```
height = 8;
length = 12;
width = 10;
```

assign values to `height`, `length`, and `width`. The numbers 8, 12, and 10 are said to be *constants.*

Before a variable can be assigned a value—or used in any other way, for that matter—it must first be declared. Thus, we could write

```
int height;
height = 8;
```

but not

```
height = 8;    /*** WRONG ***/
int height;
```

A constant assigned to a float variable usually contains a decimal point. For example, if profit is a float variable, we might write

```
profit = 2150.48;
```

 It's best to append the letter f (for "float") to a constant that contains a decimal point if the number is assigned to a float variable:

```
profit = 2150.48f;
```

Failing to include the f may cause a warning from the compiler.

An int variable is normally assigned a value of type int, and a float variable is normally assigned a value of type float. Mixing types (such as assigning an int value to a float variable or assigning a float value to an int variable) is possible but not always safe, as we'll see in Section 4.2.

Once a variable has been assigned a value, it can be used to help compute the value of another variable:

```
height = 8;
length = 12;
width = 10;
volume = height * length * width;    /* volume is now 960 */
```

In C, * represents the multiplication operator, so this statement multiplies the values stored in height, length, and width, then assigns the result to the variable volume. In general, the right side of an assignment can be a formula (or *expression*, in C terminology) involving constants, variables, and operators.

Printing the Value of a Variable

We can use printf to display the current value of a variable. For example, to write the message

```
Height: h
```

where *h* is the current value of the height variable, we'd use the following call of printf:

```
printf("Height: %d\n", height);
```

%d is a placeholder indicating where the value of height is to be filled in during printing. Note the placement of \n just after %d, so that printf will advance to the next line after printing the value of height.

%d works only for int variables; to print a float variable, we'd use %f instead. By default, %f displays a number with six digits after the decimal point. To force %f to display *p* digits after the decimal point, we can put .*p* between % and f. For example, to print the line

```
Profit: $2150.48
```

we'd call `printf` as follows:

```
printf("Profit: $%.2f\n", profit);
```

There's no limit to the number of variables that can be printed by a single call of `printf`. To display the values of both the `height` and `length` variables, we could use the following call of `printf`:

```
printf("Height: %d  Length: %d\n", height, length);
```

PROGRAM **Computing the Dimensional Weight of a Box**

Shipping companies don't especially like boxes that are large but very light, since they take up valuable space in a truck or airplane. In fact, companies often charge extra for such a box, basing the fee on its volume instead of its weight. In the United States, the usual method is to divide the volume by 166 (the allowable number of cubic inches per pound). If this number—the box's "dimensional" or "volumetric" weight—exceeds its actual weight, the shipping fee is based on the dimensional weight. (The 166 divisor is for international shipments; the dimensional weight of a domestic shipment is typically calculated using 194 instead.)

Let's say that you've been hired by a shipping company to write a program that computes the dimensional weight of a box. Since you're new to C, you decide to start off by writing a program that calculates the dimensional weight of a particular box that's $12'' \times 10'' \times 8''$. Division is represented by / in C, so the obvious way to compute the dimensional weight would be

```
weight = volume / 166;
```

where `weight` and `volume` are integer variables representing the box's weight and volume. Unfortunately, this formula isn't quite what we need. In C, when one integer is divided by another, the answer is "truncated": all digits after the decimal point are lost. The volume of a $12'' \times 10'' \times 8''$ box will be 960 cubic inches. Dividing by 166 gives the answer 5 instead of 5.783, so we have in effect rounded *down* to the next lowest pound; the shipping company expects us to round *up*. One solution is to add 165 to the volume before dividing by 166:

```
weight = (volume + 165) / 166;
```

A volume of 166 would give a weight of 331/166, or 1, while a volume of 167 would yield 332/166, or 2. Calculating the weight in this fashion gives us the following program.

dweight.c
```
/* Computes the dimensional weight of a 12" x 10" x 8" box */

#include <stdio.h>

int main(void)
{
```

```
    int height, length, width, volume, weight;

    height = 8;
    length = 12;
    width = 10;
    volume = height * length * width;
    weight = (volume + 165) / 166;

    printf("Dimensions: %dx%dx%d\n", length, width, height);
    printf("Volume (cubic inches): %d\n", volume);
    printf("Dimensional weight (pounds): %d\n", weight);

    return 0;
}
```

The output of the program is

```
Dimensions: 12x10x8
Volume (cubic inches): 960
Dimensional weight (pounds): 6
```

Initialization

variable initialization ➤ 18.5 Some variables are automatically set to zero when a program begins to execute, but most are not. A variable that doesn't have a default value and hasn't yet been assigned a value by the program is said to be *uninitialized.*

 Attempting to access the value of an uninitialized variable (for example, by displaying the variable using `printf` or using it in an expression) may yield an unpredictable result such as 2568, –30891, or some equally strange number. With some compilers, worse behavior—even a program crash—may occur.

We can always give a variable an initial value by using assignment, of course. But there's an easier way: put the initial value of the variable in its declaration. For example, we can declare the `height` variable and initialize it in one step:

```
int height = 8;
```

In C jargon, the value 8 is said to be an *initializer.*

Any number of variables can be initialized in the same declaration:

```
int height = 8, length = 12, width = 10;
```

Notice that each variable requires its own initializer. In the following example, the initializer 10 is good only for the variable `width`, not for `height` or `length` (which remain uninitialized):

```
int height, length, width = 10;
```

Printing Expressions

`printf` isn't limited to displaying numbers stored in variables; it can display the value of *any* numeric expression. Taking advantage of this property can simplify a program and reduce the number of variables. For instance, the statements

```
volume = height * length * width;
printf("%d\n", volume);
```

could be replaced by

```
printf("%d\n", height * length * width);
```

`printf`'s ability to print expressions illustrates one of C's general principles: *Wherever a value is needed, any expression of the same type will do.*

2.5   Reading Input

Because the `dweight.c` program calculates the dimensional weight of just one box, it isn't especially useful. To improve the program, we'll need to allow the user to enter the dimensions.

To obtain input, we'll use the `scanf` function, the C library's counterpart to `printf`. The f in `scanf`, like the f in `printf`, stands for "formatted"; both `scanf` and `printf` require the use of a *format string* to specify the appearance of the input or output data. `scanf` needs to know what form the input data will take, just as `printf` needs to know how to display output data.

To read an `int` value, we'd use `scanf` as follows:

```
scanf("%d", &i);    /* reads an integer; stores into i */
```

The `"%d"` string tells `scanf` to read input that represents an integer; i is an `int` variable into which we want `scanf` to store the input. The & symbol is hard to explain at this point; for now, I'll just note that it is usually (but not always) required when using `scanf`.

& operator ➤ 11.2

Reading a `float` value requires a slightly different call of `scanf`:

```
scanf("%f", &x);    /* reads a float value; stores into x */
```

`%f` works only with variables of type `float`, so I'm assuming that x is a `float` variable. The `"%f"` string tells `scanf` to look for an input value in `float` format (the number may contain a decimal point, but doesn't have to).

PROGRAM   ### Computing the Dimensional Weight of a Box (Revisited)

Here's an improved version of the dimensional weight program in which the user enters the dimensions. Note that each call of `scanf` is immediately preceded by a call of printf. That way, the user will know when to enter input and what input to enter.

dweight2.c

```
/* Computes the dimensional weight of a
   box from input provided by the user */

#include <stdio.h>

int main(void)
{
  int height, length, width, volume, weight;

  printf("Enter height of box: ");
  scanf("%d", &height);
  printf("Enter length of box: ");
  scanf("%d", &length);
  printf("Enter width of box: ");
  scanf("%d", &width);
  volume = height * length * width;
  weight = (volume + 165) / 166;

  printf("Volume (cubic inches): %d\n", volume);
  printf("Dimensional weight (pounds): %d\n", weight);

  return 0;
}
```

The output of the program has the following appearance (input entered by the user is underlined):

```
Enter height of box: 8
Enter length of box: 12
Enter width of box: 10
Volume (cubic inches): 960
Dimensional weight (pounds): 6
```

A message that asks the user to enter input (a ***prompt***) normally shouldn't end with a new-line character, because we want the user to enter input on the same line as the prompt itself. When the user presses the Enter key, the cursor automatically moves to the next line—the program doesn't need to display a new-line character to terminate the current line.

The dweight2.c program suffers from one problem: it doesn't work correctly if the user enters nonnumeric input. Section 3.2 discusses this issue in more detail.

2.6   Defining Names for Constants

When a program contains constants, it's often a good idea to give them names. The dweight.c and dweight2.c programs rely on the constant 166, whose meaning may not be at all clear to someone reading the program later. Using a feature known as *macro definition*, we can name this constant:

```
#define INCHES_PER_POUND 166
```

`#define` is a preprocessing directive, just as `#include` is, so there's no semicolon at the end of the line.

When a program is compiled, the preprocessor replaces each macro by the value that it represents. For example, the statement

```
weight = (volume + INCHES_PER_POUND - 1) / INCHES_PER_POUND;
```

will become

```
weight = (volume + 166 - 1) / 166;
```

giving the same effect as if we'd written the latter statement in the first place.

The value of a macro can be an expression:

```
#define RECIPROCAL_OF_PI (1.0f / 3.14159f)
```

parentheses in macros ➤ *14.3* If it contains operators, the expression should be enclosed in parentheses.

Notice that we've used only upper-case letters in macro names. This is a convention that most C programmers follow, not a requirement of the language. (Still, C programmers have been doing this for decades; you wouldn't want to be the first to deviate.)

PROGRAM **Converting from Fahrenheit to Celsius**

The following program prompts the user to enter a Fahrenheit temperature; it then prints the equivalent Celsius temperature. The output of the program will have the following appearance (as usual, input entered by the user is underlined):

```
Enter Fahrenheit temperature: 212
Celsius equivalent: 100.0
```

The program will allow temperatures that aren't integers; that's why the Celsius temperature is displayed as `100.0` instead of `100`. Let's look first at the entire program, then see how it's put together.

celsius.c
```
/* Converts a Fahrenheit temperature to Celsius */

#include <stdio.h>

#define FREEZING_PT 32.0f
#define SCALE_FACTOR (5.0f / 9.0f)

int main(void)
{
  float fahrenheit, celsius;

  printf("Enter Fahrenheit temperature: ");
```

```
    scanf("%f", &fahrenheit);

    celsius = (fahrenheit - FREEZING_PT) * SCALE_FACTOR;

    printf("Celsius equivalent: %.1f\n", celsius);

    return 0;
}
```

The statement

```
celsius = (fahrenheit - FREEZING_PT) * SCALE_FACTOR;
```

converts the Fahrenheit temperature to Celsius. Since `FREEZING_PT` stands for `32.0f` and `SCALE_FACTOR` stands for `(5.0f / 9.0f)`, the compiler sees this statement as

```
celsius = (fahrenheit - 32.0f) * (5.0f / 9.0f);
```

Defining `SCALE_FACTOR` to be `(5.0f / 9.0f)` instead of `(5 / 9)` is important, because C truncates the result when two integers are divided. The value of `(5 / 9)` would be 0, which definitely isn't what we want.

The call of `printf` writes the Celsius temperature:

```
printf("Celsius equivalent: %.1f\n", celsius);
```

Notice the use of `%.1f` to display `celsius` with just one digit after the decimal point.

2.7 Identifiers

As we're writing a program, we'll have to choose names for variables, functions, macros, and other entities. These names are called *identifiers*. In C, an identifier may contain letters, digits, and underscores, but must begin with a letter or underscore. (In C99, identifiers may contain certain "universal character names" as well.)

universal character names ▶25.4

Here are some examples of legal identifiers:

```
times10  get_next_char  _done
```

The following are *not* legal identifiers:

```
10times  get-next-char
```

The symbol `10times` begins with a digit, not a letter or underscore. `get-next-char` contains minus signs, not underscores.

C is *case-sensitive:* it distinguishes between upper-case and lower-case letters in identifiers. For example, the following identifiers are all different:

```
job  joB  jOb  jOB  Job  JoB  JOb  JOB
```

These eight identifiers could all be used simultaneously, each for a completely different purpose. (Talk about obfuscation!) Sensible programmers try to make identifiers look different unless they're somehow related.

Since case matters in C, many programmers follow the convention of using only lower-case letters in identifiers (other than macros), with underscores inserted when necessary for legibility:

```
symbol_table    current_page    name_and_address
```

Other programmers avoid underscores, instead using an upper-case letter to begin each word within an identifier:

```
symbolTable    currentPage    nameAndAddress
```

(The first letter is sometimes capitalized as well.) Although the former style is common in traditional C, the latter style is becoming more popular thanks to its widespread use in Java and C# (and, to a lesser extent, C++). Other reasonable conventions exist; just be sure to capitalize an identifier the same way each time it appears in a program.

C places no limit on the maximum length of an identifier, so don't be afraid to use long, descriptive names. A name such as `current_page` is a lot easier to understand than a name like `cp`.

Keywords

The *keywords* in Table 2.1 have special significance to C compilers and therefore can't be used as identifiers. Note that five keywords were added in C99.

Table 2.1
Keywords

auto	enum	restrict[†]	unsigned
break	extern	return	void
case	float	short	volatile
char	for	signed	while
const	goto	sizeof	_Bool[†]
continue	if	static	_Complex[†]
default	inline[†]	struct	_Imaginary[†]
do	int	switch	
double	long	typedef	
else	register	union	

[†]C99 only

Because of C's case-sensitivity, keywords must appear in programs exactly as shown in Table 2.1, with all letters in lower case. Names of functions in the standard library (such as `printf`) contain only lower-case letters also. Avoid the plight of the unfortunate programmer who enters an entire program in upper case, only to find that the compiler can't recognize keywords and calls of library functions.

restrictions on identifiers ➤*21.1*

Watch out for other restrictions on identifiers. Some compilers treat certain identifiers (asm, for example) as additional keywords. Identifiers that belong to the standard library are restricted as well. Accidentally using one of these names can cause an error during compilation or linking. Identifiers that begin with an underscore are also restricted.

2.8 Layout of a C Program

We can think of a C program as a series of *tokens:* groups of characters that can't be split up without changing their meaning. Identifiers and keywords are tokens. So are operators like + and -, punctuation marks such as the comma and semicolon, and string literals. For example, the statement

```
printf("Height: %d\n", height);
```

consists of seven tokens:

```
printf    (    "Height: %d\n"    ,    height   )    ;
  ①       ②          ③          ④      ⑤      ⑥    ⑦
```

Tokens ① and ⑤ are identifiers, token ③ is a string literal, and tokens ②, ④, ⑥, and ⑦ are punctuation.

 The amount of space between tokens in a program isn't critical in most cases. At one extreme, tokens can be crammed together with no space between them at all, except where this would cause two tokens to merge into a third token. For example, we could delete most of the space in the celsius.c program of Section 2.6, provided that we leave space between tokens such as int and main and between float and fahrenheit:

```
/* Converts a Fahrenheit temperature to Celsius */
#include <stdio.h>
#define FREEZING_PT 32.0f
#define SCALE_FACTOR (5.0f/9.0f)
int main(void){float fahrenheit,celsius;printf(
"Enter Fahrenheit temperature: ");scanf("%f", &fahrenheit);
celsius=(fahrenheit-FREEZING_PT)*SCALE_FACTOR;
printf("Celsius equivalent: %.1f\n", celsius);return 0;}
```

In fact, if the page were wider, we could put the entire main function on a single line. We can't put the whole *program* on one line, though, because each preprocessing directive requires a separate line.

 Compressing programs in this fashion isn't a good idea. In fact, adding spaces and blank lines to a program can make it easier to read and understand. Fortunately,

C allows us to insert any amount of space—blanks, tabs, and new-line characters—between tokens. This rule has several important consequences for program layout:

- *Statements can be divided* over any number of lines. The following statement, for example, is so long that it would be hard to squeeze it onto a single line:

```
printf("Dimensional weight (pounds): %d\n",
    (volume + INCHES_PER_POUND - 1) / INCHES_PER_POUND);
```

- *Space between tokens* makes it easier for the eye to separate them. For this reason, I usually put a space before and after each operator:

```
volume = height * length * width;
```

I also put a space after each comma. Some programmers go even further, putting spaces around parentheses and other punctuation.

- *Indentation* can make nesting easier to spot. For example, we should indent declarations and statements to make it clear that they're nested inside `main`.

Q&A

- *Blank lines* can divide a program into logical units, making it easier for the reader to discern the program's structure. A program with no blank lines is as hard to read as a book with no chapters.

The `celsius.c` program of Section 2.6 illustrates several of these guidelines. Let's take a closer look at the `main` function in that program:

```
int main(void)
{
  float fahrenheit, celsius;

  printf("Enter Fahrenheit temperature: ");
  scanf("%f", &fahrenheit);

  celsius = (fahrenheit - FREEZING_PT) * SCALE_FACTOR;

  printf("Celsius equivalent: %.1f\n", celsius);

  return 0;
}
```

First, observe how the space around `=`, `-`, and `*` makes these operators stand out. Second, notice how the indentation of declarations and statements makes it obvious that they all belong to `main`. Finally, note how blank lines divide `main` into five parts: (1) declaring the `fahrenheit` and `celsius` variables; (2) obtaining the Fahrenheit temperature; (3) calculating the value of `celsius`; (4) printing the Celsius temperature; and (5) returning to the operating system.

While we're on the subject of program layout, notice how I've placed the `{` token underneath `main()` and put the matching `}` on a separate line, aligned with `{`. Putting `}` on a separate line lets us insert or delete statements at the end of the function; aligning it with `{` makes it easy to spot the end of `main`.

A final note: Although extra spaces can be added *between* tokens, it's not possible to add space *within* a token without changing the meaning of the program or causing an error. Writing

```
fl oat fahrenheit, celsius;   /*** WRONG ***/
```

or

```
fl
oat fahrenheit, celsius;      /*** WRONG ***/
```

produces an error when the program is compiled. Putting a space inside a string literal is allowed, although it changes the meaning of the string. However, putting a new-line character in a string (in other words, splitting the string over two lines) is illegal:

```
printf("To C, or not to C:
that is the question.\n");   /*** WRONG ***/
```

Continuing a string from one line to the next requires a special technique that we'll learn in a later chapter.

continuing a string ➤ *13.1*

Q & A

Q: **What does GCC stand for? [p. 11]**

A: GCC originally stood for "G̲NU C̲ c̲ompiler." It now stands for "G̲NU C̲ompiler C̲ollection," because the current version of GCC compiles programs written in a variety of languages, including Ada, C, C++, Fortran, Java, and Objective-C.

Q: **OK, so what does GNU stand for?**

A: GNU stands for "G̲NU's N̲ot U̲NIX!" (and is pronounced *guh-NEW*, by the way). GNU is a project of the Free Software Foundation, an organization set up by Richard M. Stallman as a protest against the restrictions of licensed UNIX software. According to its web site, the Free Software Foundation believes that users should be free to "run, copy, distribute, study, change and improve" software. The GNU Project has rewritten much traditional UNIX software from scratch and made it publicly available at no charge.

GCC and other GNU software are crucial to Linux. Linux itself is only the "kernel" of an operating system (the part that handles program scheduling and basic I/O services); the GNU software is necessary to have a fully functional operating system.

For more information on the GNU Project, visit *www.gnu.org*.

Q: **What's the big deal about GCC, anyway?**

A: GCC is significant for many reasons, not least the fact that it's free and capable of compiling a number of languages. It runs under many operating systems and generates code for many different CPUs, including all the widely used ones. GCC is the primary compiler for many UNIX-based operating systems, including Linux, BSD, and Mac OS X, and it's used extensively for commercial software development. For more information about GCC, visit *gcc.gnu.org*.

Q: How good is GCC at finding errors in programs?

A: GCC has various command-line options that control how thoroughly it checks programs. When these options are used, GCC is quite good at finding potential trouble spots in a program. Here are some of the more popular options:

`-Wall`	Causes the compiler to produce warning messages when it detects possible errors. (`-W` can be followed by codes for specific warnings; `-Wall` means "all `-W` options.") Should be used in conjunction with `-O` for maximum effect.
`-W`	Issues additional warning messages beyond those produced by `-Wall`.
`-pedantic`	Issues all warnings required by the C standard. Causes programs that use nonstandard features to be rejected.
`-ansi`	Turns off features of GCC that aren't standard C and enables a few standard features that are normally disabled.
`-std=c89`	
`-std=c99`	Specifies which version of C the compiler should use to check the program.

These options are often used in combination:

```
% gcc -O -Wall -W -pedantic -ansi -std=c99 -o pun pun.c
```

Q: Why is C so terse? It seems as though programs would be more readable if C used `begin` and `end` instead of `{` and `}`, `integer` instead of `int`, and so forth. [p. 12]

A: Legend has it that the brevity of C programs is due to the environment that existed in Bell Labs at the time the language was developed. The first C compiler ran on a DEC PDP-11 (an early minicomputer); programmers used a teletype—essentially a typewriter connected to a computer—to enter programs and print listings. Because teletypes were very slow (they could print only 10 characters per second), minimizing the number of characters in a program was clearly advantageous.

Q: In some C books, the `main` function ends with `exit(0)` instead of `return 0`. Are these the same? [p. 14]

A: When they appear inside `main`, these statements are indeed equivalent: both terminate the program, returning the value 0 to the operating system. Which one to use is mostly a matter of taste.

Q: What happens if a program reaches the end of the `main` function without executing a `return` statement? [p. 14]

A: The `return` statement isn't mandatory; if it's missing, the program will still terminate. In C89, the value returned to the operating system is undefined. In C99, if `main` is declared to return an `int` (as in our examples), the program returns 0 to the operating system; otherwise, the program returns an unspecified value.

Q: **Does the compiler remove a comment entirely or replace it with blank space?**

A: Some old C compilers deleted all the characters in each comment, making it possible to write

```
a/**/b = 0;
```

and have the compiler interpret it as

```
ab = 0;
```

According to the C standard, however, the compiler must replace each comment by a single space character, so this trick doesn't work. Instead, we'd end up with the following (illegal) statement:

```
a b = 0;
```

Q: **How can I tell if my program has an unterminated comment?**

A: If you're lucky, the program won't compile because the comment has rendered the program illegal. If the program does compile, there are several techniques that you can use. Stepping through the program line by line with a debugger will reveal if any lines are being skipped. Some IDEs display comments in a distinctive color to distinguish them from surrounding code. If you're using such an environment, you can easily spot unterminated comments, since program text will have a different color if it's accidentally included in a comment. A program such as `lint` can also help.

`lint ➤1.2`

Q: **Is it legal to nest one comment inside another?**

A: Old-style comments (`/* ... */`) can't be nested. For instance, the following code is illegal:

```
/*
   /*** WRONG ***/
*/
```

The `*/` symbol on the second line matches the `/*` symbol on the first line, so the compiler will flag the `*/` symbol on the third line as an error.

C's prohibition against nested comments can sometimes be a problem. Suppose we've written a long program containing many short comments. To disable a portion of the program temporarily (during testing, say), our first impulse is to "comment out" the offending lines with `/*` and `*/`. Unfortunately, this method won't work if the lines contain old-style comments. C99 comments (those beginning with `//`) can be nested inside old-style comments, however—another advantage to using this kind of comment.

In any event, there's a better way to disable portions of a program, as we'll see

disabling code ➤ 14.4 later.

Q: Where does the `float` type get its name? [p. 17]

A: `float` is short for "floating-point," a technique for storing numbers in which the decimal point "floats." A `float` value is usually stored in two parts: the fraction (or mantissa) and the exponent. The number 12.0 might be stored as 1.5×2^3, for example, where 1.5 is the fraction and 3 is the exponent. Some programming languages call this type `real` instead of `float`.

Q: Why do floating-point constants need to end with the letter f? [p. 19]

A: For the full explanation, see Chapter 7. Here's the short answer: a constant that contains a decimal point but doesn't end with f has type `double` (short for "double precision"). `double` values are stored more accurately than `float` values. Moreover, `double` values can be larger than `float` values, which is why we need to add the letter f when assigning to a `float` variable. Without the f, a warning may be generated about the possibility of a number being stored into a `float` variable that exceeds the capacity of the variable.

*Q: Is it really true that there's no limit on the length of an identifier? [p. 26]

A: Yes and no. The C89 standard says that identifiers may be arbitrarily long. However, compilers are only required to remember the first 31 characters (63 characters

 in C99). Thus, if two names begin with the same 31 characters, a compiler might be unable to distinguish between them.

external linkage ➤ 18.2 To make matters even more complicated, there are special rules for identifiers with external linkage; most function names fall into this category. Since these names must be made available to the linker, and since some older linkers can handle only short names, only the first six characters are significant in C89. Moreover, the case of letters may not matter. As a result, `ABCDEFG` and `abcdefh` might be treated as the same name. (In C99, the first 31 characters are significant, and the case of letters is taken into account.)

Most compilers and linkers are more generous than the standard, so these rules aren't a problem in practice. Don't worry about making identifiers too long—worry about making them too short.

Q: How many spaces should I use for indentation? [p. 28]

A: That's a tough question. Leave too little space, and the eye has trouble detecting indentation. Leave too much, and lines run off the screen (or page). Many C programmers indent nested statements eight spaces (one tab stop), which is probably too much. Studies have shown that the optimum amount of indentation is three spaces, but many programmers feel uncomfortable with numbers that aren't a power of two. Although I normally prefer to indent three or four spaces, I'll use two spaces in this book so that my programs will fit within the margins.

Exercises

Section 2.1

1. Create and run Kernighan and Ritchie's famous "hello, world" program:

```
#include <stdio.h>

int main(void)
{
    printf("hello, world\n");
}
```

Do you get a warning message from the compiler? If so, what's needed to make it go away?

Section 2.2   Ⓦ 2. Consider the following program:

```
#include <stdio.h>

int main(void)
{
    printf("Parkinson's Law:\nWork expands so as to ");
    printf("fill the time\n");
    printf("available for its completion.\n");
    return 0;
}
```

(a) Identify the directives and statements in this program.
(b) What output does the program produce?

Section 2.4   Ⓦ 3. Condense the dweight.c program by (1) replacing the assignments to height, length, and width with initializers and (2) removing the weight variable, instead calculating (volume + 165) / 166 within the last printf.

Ⓦ 4. Write a program that declares several int and float variables—without initializing them—and then prints their values. Is there any pattern to the values? (Usually there isn't.)

Section 2.7   Ⓦ 5. Which of the following are not legal C identifiers?

(a) 100_bottles
(b) _100_bottles
(c) one__hundred__bottles
(d) bottles_by_the_hundred_

6. Why is it not a good idea for an identifier to contain more than one adjacent underscore (as in current___balance, for example)?

7. Which of the following are keywords in C?

(a) for
(b) If
(c) main
(d) printf
(e) while

Ⓦ Answer available on the Web at *knking.com/books/c2*.

Section 2.8   Ⓦ 8. How many tokens are there in the following statement?

```
answer=(3*q-p*p)/3;
```

   9. Insert spaces between the tokens in Exercise 8 to make the statement easier to read.

  10. In the `dweight.c` program (Section 2.4), which spaces are essential?

Programming Projects

1. Write a program that uses `printf` to display the following picture on the screen:

```
    *
   *
  *
 *   *
* *
 *
```

2. Write a program that computes the volume of a sphere with a 10-meter radius, using the formula $v = 4/3\pi r^3$. Write the fraction 4/3 as `4.0f/3.0f`. (Try writing it as `4/3`. What happens?) *Hint:* C doesn't have an exponentiation operator, so you'll need to multiply r by itself twice to compute r^3.

3. Modify the program of Programming Project 2 so that it prompts the user to enter the radius of the sphere.

Ⓦ 4. Write a program that asks the user to enter a dollars-and-cents amount, then displays the amount with 5% tax added:

```
Enter an amount: 100.00
With tax added: $105.00
```

5. Write a program that asks the user to enter a value for x and then displays the value of the following polynomial:

$$3x^5 + 2x^4 - 5x^3 - x^2 + 7x - 6$$

Hint: C doesn't have an exponentiation operator, so you'll need to multiply x by itself repeatedly in order to compute the powers of x. (For example, `x * x * x` is x cubed.)

6. Modify the program of Programming Project 5 so that the polynomial is evaluated using the following formula:

$$((((3x + 2)x - 5)x - 1)x + 7)x - 6$$

Note that the modified program performs fewer multiplications. This technique for evaluating polynomials is known as ***Horner's Rule***.

7. Write a program that asks the user to enter a U.S. dollar amount and then shows how to pay that amount using the smallest number of $20, $10, $5, and $1 bills:

```
Enter a dollar amount: 93

$20 bills: 4
$10 bills: 1
 $5 bills: 0
 $1 bills: 3
```

Hint: Divide the amount by 20 to determine the number of $20 bills needed, and then reduce the amount by the total value of the $20 bills. Repeat for the other bill sizes. Be sure to use integer values throughout, not floating-point numbers.

8. Write a program that calculates the remaining balance on a loan after the first, second, and third monthly payments:

```
Enter amount of loan: 20000.00
Enter interest rate: 6.0
Enter monthly payment: 386.66

Balance remaining after first payment: $19713.34
Balance remaining after second payment: $19425.25
Balance remaining after third payment: $19135.71
```

Display each balance with two digits after the decimal point. *Hint:* Each month, the balance is decreased by the amount of the payment, but increased by the balance times the monthly interest rate. To find the monthly interest rate, convert the interest rate entered by the user to a percentage and divide it by 12.

3 Formatted Input/Output

In seeking the unattainable, simplicity only gets in the way.

`scanf` and `printf`, which support formatted reading and writing, are two of the most frequently used functions in C. As this chapter shows, both are powerful but tricky to use properly. Section 3.1 describes `printf`, and Section 3.2 covers `scanf`. Neither section gives complete details, which will have to wait until Chapter 22.

3.1 The `printf` Function

The `printf` function is designed to display the contents of a string, known as the *format string,* with values possibly inserted at specified points in the string. When it's called, `printf` must be supplied with the format string, followed by any values that are to be inserted into the string during printing:

`printf` (*string*, *expr*$_1$, *expr*$_2$, ...);

The values displayed can be constants, variables, or more complicated expressions. There's no limit on the number of values that can be printed by a single call of `printf`.

The format string may contain both ordinary characters and *conversion specifications*, which begin with the % character. A conversion specification is a placeholder representing a value to be filled in during printing. The information that follows the % character *specifies* how the value is *converted* from its internal form (binary) to printed form (characters)—that's where the term "conversion specification" comes from. For example, the conversion specification %d specifies that `printf` is to convert an `int` value from binary to a string of decimal digits, while %f does the same for a `float` value.

Ordinary characters in a format string are printed exactly as they appear in the string; conversion specifications are replaced by the values to be printed. Consider the following example:

```
int i, j;
float x, y;

i = 10;
j = 20;
x = 43.2892f;
y = 5527.0f;

printf("i = %d, j = %d, x = %f, y = %f\n", i, j, x, y);
```

This call of `printf` produces the following output:

```
i = 10, j = 20, x = 43.289200, y = 5527.000000
```

The ordinary characters in the format string are simply copied to the output line. The four conversion specifications are replaced by the values of the variables i, j, x, and y, in that order.

C compilers aren't required to check that the number of conversion specifications in a format string matches the number of output items. The following call of `printf` has more conversion specifications than values to be printed:

```
printf("%d %d\n", i);    /*** WRONG ***/
```

`printf` will print the value of i correctly, then print a second (meaningless) integer value. A call with too few conversion specifications has similar problems:

```
printf("%d\n", i, j);    /*** WRONG ***/
```

In this case, `printf` prints the value of i but doesn't show the value of j.

Furthermore, compilers aren't required to check that a conversion specification is appropriate for the type of item being printed. If the programmer uses an incorrect specification, the program will simply produce meaningless output. Consider the following call of `printf`, in which the `int` variable i and the `float` variable x are in the wrong order:

```
printf("%f %d\n", i, x);    /*** WRONG ***/
```

Since `printf` must obey the format string, it will dutifully display a `float` value, followed by an `int` value. Unfortunately, both will be meaningless.

Conversion Specifications

Conversion specifications give the programmer a great deal of control over the appearance of output. On the other hand, they can be complicated and hard to read. In fact, describing conversion specifications in complete detail is too arduous a task to tackle this early in the book. Instead, we'll just take a brief look at some of their more important capabilities.

In Chapter 2, we saw that a conversion specification can include formatting information. In particular, we used `%.1f` to display a `float` value with one digit after the decimal point. More generally, a conversion specification can have the form `%m.pX` or `%-m.pX`, where m and p are integer constants and X is a letter. Both m and p are optional; if p is omitted, the period that separates m and p is also dropped. In the conversion specification `%10.2f`, m is 10, p is 2, and X is `f`. In the specification `%10f`, m is 10 and p (along with the period) is missing, but in the specification `%.2f`, p is 2 and m is missing.

The **minimum field width**, m, specifies the minimum number of characters to print. If the value to be printed requires fewer than m characters, the value is right-justified within the field. (In other words, extra spaces precede the value.) For example, the specification `%4d` would display the number 123 as •123. (In this chapter, I'll use • to represent the space character.) If the value to be printed requires more than m characters, the field width automatically expands to the necessary size. Thus, the specification `%4d` would display the number 12345 as 12345—no digits are lost. Putting a minus sign in front of m causes left justification; the specification `%-4d` would display 123 as 123•.

The meaning of the **precision**, p, isn't as easily described, since it depends on the choice of X, the **conversion specifier**. X indicates which conversion should be applied to the value before it's printed. The most common conversion specifiers for numbers are:

Q&A

- `d` — Displays an integer in decimal (base 10) form. p indicates the minimum number of digits to display (extra zeros are added to the beginning of the number if necessary); if p is omitted, it is assumed to have the value 1. (In other words, `%d` is the same as `%.1d`.)

- `e` — Displays a floating-point number in exponential format (scientific notation). p indicates how many digits should appear after the decimal point (the default is 6). If p is 0, the decimal point is not displayed.

- `f` — Displays a floating-point number in "fixed decimal" format, without an exponent. p has the same meaning as for the `e` specifier.

- `g` — Displays a floating-point number in either exponential format or fixed decimal format, depending on the number's size. p indicates the maximum number of significant digits (*not* digits after the decimal point) to be displayed. Unlike the `f` conversion, the `g` conversion won't show trailing zeros. Furthermore, if the value to be printed has no digits after the decimal point, `g` doesn't display the decimal point.

The `g` specifier is especially useful for displaying numbers whose size can't be predicted when the program is written or that tend to vary widely in size. When used to print a moderately large or moderately small number, the `g` specifier uses fixed decimal format. But when used to print a very large or very small number, the `g` specifier switches to exponential format so that the number will require fewer characters.

specifiers for integers ➤ 7.1
specifiers for floats ➤ 7.2
specifiers for characters ➤ 7.3
specifiers for strings ➤ 13.3

There are many other specifiers besides %d, %e, %f, and %g. I'll gradually introduce many of them in subsequent chapters. For the full list, and for a complete explanation of the other capabilities of conversion specifications, consult Section 22.3.

PROGRAM   ## Using `printf` to Format Numbers

The following program illustrates the use of `printf` to print integers and floating-point numbers in various formats.

tprintf.c
```c
/* Prints int and float values in various formats */

#include <stdio.h>

int main(void)
{
  int i;
  float x;

  i = 40;
  x = 839.21f;

  printf("|%d|%5d|%-5d|%5.3d|\n", i, i, i, i);
  printf("|%10.3f|%10.3e|%-10g|\n", x, x, x);

  return 0;
}
```

The | characters in the `printf` format strings are there merely to help show how much space each number occupies when printed; unlike % or \, the | character has no special significance to `printf`. The output of this program is:

```
|40|   40|40   |  040|
|   839.210| 8.392e+02|839.21    |
```

Let's take a closer look at the conversion specifications used in this program:

- %d — Displays i in decimal form, using a minimum amount of space.

- %5d — Displays i in decimal form, using a minimum of five characters. Since i requires only two characters, three spaces were added.

- %-5d — Displays i in decimal form, using a minimum of five characters; since the value of i doesn't require five characters, the spaces are added afterward (that is, i is left-justified in a field of length five).

- %5.3d — Displays i in decimal form, using a minimum of five characters overall and a minimum of three digits. Since i is only two digits long, an extra zero was added to guarantee three digits. The resulting number is only three characters long, so two spaces were added, for a total of five characters (i is right-justified).

- %10.3f — Displays x in fixed decimal form, using 10 characters overall, with three digits after the decimal point. Since x requires only seven characters (three before the decimal point, three after the decimal point, and one for the decimal point itself), three spaces precede x.

- `%10.3e` — Displays x in exponential form, using 10 characters overall, with three digits after the decimal point. x requires nine characters altogether (including the exponent), so one space precedes x.

- `%-10g` — Displays x in either fixed decimal form or exponential form, using 10 characters overall. In this case, `printf` chose to display x in fixed decimal form. The presence of the minus sign forces left justification, so x is followed by four spaces.

Escape Sequences

escape sequences ➤7.3

The `\n` code that we often use in format strings is called an *escape sequence*. Escape sequences enable strings to contain characters that would otherwise cause problems for the compiler, including nonprinting (control) characters and characters that have a special meaning to the compiler (such as `"`). We'll provide a complete list of escape sequences later; for now, here's a sample:

Alert (bell)	`\a`
Backspace	`\b`
New line	`\n`
Horizontal tab	`\t`

When they appear in `printf` format strings, these escape sequences represent actions to perform upon printing. Printing `\a` causes an audible beep on most machines. Printing `\b` moves the cursor back one position. Printing `\n` advances the cursor to the beginning of the next line. Printing `\t` moves the cursor to the next tab stop.

Q&A

A string may contain any number of escape sequences. Consider the following `printf` example, in which the format string contains six escape sequences:

```
printf("Item\tUnit\tPurchase\n\tPrice\tDate\n");
```

Executing this statement prints a two-line heading:

```
Item    Unit    Purchase
        Price   Date
```

Another common escape sequence is `\"`, which represents the `"` character. Since the `"` character marks the beginning and end of a string, it can't appear within a string without the use of this escape sequence. Here's an example:

```
printf("\"Hello!\"");
```

This statement produces the following output:

```
"Hello!"
```

Incidentally, you can't just put a single \ character in a string; the compiler will assume that it's the beginning of an escape sequence. To print a single \ character, put two \ characters in the string:

```
printf("\\");    /* prints one \ character */
```

3.2 The `scanf` Function

Just as `printf` prints output in a specified format, `scanf` reads input according to a particular format. A `scanf` format string, like a `printf` format string, may contain both ordinary characters and conversion specifications. The conversions allowed with `scanf` are essentially the same as those used with `printf`.

In many cases, a `scanf` format string will contain only conversion specifications, as in the following example:

```
int i, j;
float x, y;

scanf("%d%d%f%f", &i, &j, &x, &y);
```

Suppose that the user enters the following input line:

```
1 -20 .3 -4.0e3
```

`scanf` will read the line, converting its characters to the numbers they represent, and then assign 1, –20, 0.3, and –4000.0 to `i`, `j`, `x`, and `y`, respectively. "Tightly packed" format strings like `"%d%d%f%f"` are common in `scanf` calls. `printf` format strings are less likely to have adjacent conversion specifications.

`scanf`, like `printf`, contains several traps for the unwary. When using `scanf`, the programmer must check that the number of conversion specifications matches the number of input variables and that each conversion is appropriate for the corresponding variable—as with `printf`, the compiler isn't required to check for a possible mismatch. Another trap involves the `&` symbol, which normally precedes each variable in a `scanf` call. The `&` is usually (but not always) required, and it's the programmer's responsibility to remember to use it.

Forgetting to put the `&` symbol in front of a variable in a call of `scanf` will have unpredictable—and possibly disastrous—results. A program crash is a common outcome. At the very least, the value that is read from the input won't be stored in the variable; instead, the variable will retain its old value (which may be meaningless if the variable wasn't given an initial value). Omitting the `&` is an extremely common error—be careful! Some compilers can spot this error and produce a warning message such as *"format argument is not a pointer."* (The term *pointer* is defined in Chapter 11; the `&` symbol is used to create a pointer to a variable.) If you get a warning, check for a missing `&`.

Calling `scanf` is a powerful but unforgiving way to read data. Many professional C programmers avoid `scanf`, instead reading all data in character form and converting it to numeric form later. We'll use `scanf` quite a bit, especially in the early chapters of this book, because it provides a simple way to read numbers. Be aware, however, that many of our programs won't behave properly if the user enters unexpected input. As we'll see later, it's possible to have a program test whether `scanf` successfully read the requested data (and attempt to recover if it didn't). Such tests are impractical for the programs in this book—they would add too many statements and obscure the point of the examples.

detecting errors in `scanf` ➤*22.3*

How `scanf` Works

`scanf` can actually do much more than I've indicated so far. It is essentially a "pattern-matching" function that tries to match up groups of input characters with conversion specifications.

Like the `printf` function, `scanf` is controlled by the format string. When it is called, `scanf` begins processing the information in the string, starting at the left. For each conversion specification in the format string, `scanf` tries to locate an item of the appropriate type in the input data, skipping blank space if necessary. `scanf` then reads the item, stopping when it encounters a character that can't possibly belong to the item. If the item was read successfully, `scanf` continues processing the rest of the format string. If any item is not read successfully, `scanf` returns immediately without looking at the rest of the format string (or the remaining input data).

As it searches for the beginning of a number, `scanf` ignores ***white-space characters*** (the space, horizontal and vertical tab, form-feed, and new-line characters). As a result, numbers can be put on a single line or spread out over several lines. Consider the following call of `scanf`:

```
scanf("%d%d%f%f", &i, &j, &x, &y);
```

Suppose that the user enters three lines of input:

```
  1
-20    .3
    -4.0e3
```

`scanf` sees one continuous stream of characters:

```
••1¤-20•••.3¤•••-4.0e3¤
```

(I'm using • to represent the space character and ¤ to represent the new-line character.) Since it skips over white-space characters as it looks for the beginning of each number, `scanf` will be able to read the numbers successfully. In the following diagram, an *s* under a character indicates that it was skipped, and an *r* indicates it was read as part of an input item:

```
••1¤-20•••.3¤•••-4.0e3¤
ssrsrrrsssrrssssrrrrrr
```

scanf "peeks" at the final new-line character without actually reading it. This new-line will be the first character read by the next call of scanf.

What rules does scanf follow to recognize an integer or a floating-point number? When asked to read an integer, scanf first searches for a digit, a plus sign, or a minus sign; it then reads digits until it reaches a nondigit. When asked to read a floating-point number, scanf looks for

> a plus or minus sign (optional), followed by
>
> a series of digits (possibly containing a decimal point), followed by
>
> an exponent (optional). An exponent consists of the letter e (or E), an optional sign, and one or more digits.

The %e, %f, and %g conversions are interchangeable when used with scanf; all three follow the same rules for recognizing a floating-point number.

Q&A When scanf encounters a character that can't be part of the current item, the character is "put back" to be read again during the scanning of the next input item or during the next call of scanf. Consider the following (admittedly pathological) arrangement of our four numbers:

```
1-20.3-4.0e3¤
```

Let's use the same call of scanf as before:

```
scanf("%d%d%f%f", &i, &j, &x, &y);
```

Here's how scanf would process the new input:

- Conversion specification: %d. The first nonblank input character is 1; since integers can begin with 1, scanf then reads the next character, -. Recognizing that - can't appear inside an integer, scanf stores 1 into i and puts the - character back.

- Conversion specification: %d. scanf then reads the characters -, 2, 0, and . (period). Since an integer can't contain a decimal point, scanf stores –20 into j and puts the . character back.

- Conversion specification: %f. scanf reads the characters ., 3, and -. Since a floating-point number can't contain a minus sign after a digit, scanf stores 0.3 into x and puts the - character back.

- Conversion specification: %f. Lastly, scanf reads the characters -, 4, ., 0, e, 3, and ¤ (new-line). Since a floating-point number can't contain a new-line character, scanf stores -4.0×10^3 into y and puts the new-line character back.

In this example, scanf was able to match every conversion specification in the format string with an input item. Since the new-line character wasn't read, it will be left for the next call of scanf.

Ordinary Characters in Format Strings

The concept of pattern-matching can be taken one step further by writing format strings that contain ordinary characters in addition to conversion specifications. The action that scanf takes when it processes an ordinary character in a format string depends on whether or not it's a white-space character.

- *White-space characters.* When it encounters one or more consecutive white-space characters in a format string, scanf repeatedly reads white-space characters from the input until it reaches a non-white-space character (which is "put back"). The number of white-space characters in the format string is irrelevant; one white-space character in the format string will match any number of white-space characters in the input. (Incidentally, putting a white-space character in a format string doesn't force the input to contain white-space characters. A white-space character in a format string matches *any* number of white-space characters in the input, including none.)

- *Other characters.* When it encounters a non-white-space character in a format string, scanf compares it with the next input character. If the two characters match, scanf discards the input character and continues processing the format string. If the characters don't match, scanf puts the offending character back into the input, then aborts without further processing the format string or reading characters from the input.

    For example, suppose that the format string is "%d/%d". If the input is

●5/●96

scanf skips the first space while looking for an integer, matches %d with 5, matches / with /, skips a space while looking for another integer, and matches %d with 96. On the other hand, if the input is

●5●/●96

scanf skips one space, matches %d with 5, then attempts to match the / in the format string with a space in the input. There's no match, so scanf puts the space back; the ● / ● 96 characters remain to be read by the next call of scanf. To allow spaces after the first number, we should use the format string "%d /%d" instead.

Confusing printf with scanf

Although calls of scanf and printf may appear similar, there are significant differences between the two functions; ignoring these differences can be hazardous to the health of your program.

One common mistake is to put & in front of variables in a call of printf:

```
printf("%d %d\n", &i, &j);    /*** WRONG ***/
```

Fortunately, this mistake is fairly easy to spot: `printf` will display a couple of odd-looking numbers instead of the values of `i` and `j`.

Since `scanf` normally skips white-space characters when looking for data items, there's often no need for a format string to include characters other than conversion specifications. Incorrectly assuming that `scanf` format strings should resemble `printf` format strings—another common error—may cause `scanf` to behave in unexpected ways. Let's see what happens when the following call of `scanf` is executed:

```
scanf("%d, %d", &i, &j);
```

`scanf` will first look for an integer in the input, which it stores in the variable `i`. `scanf` will then try to match a comma with the next input character. If the next input character is a space, not a comma, `scanf` will terminate without reading a value for `j`.

Although `printf` format strings often end with `\n`, putting a new-line character at the end of a `scanf` format string is usually a bad idea. To `scanf`, a new-line character in a format string is equivalent to a space; both cause `scanf` to advance to the next non-white-space character. For example, if the format string is `"%d\n"`, `scanf` will skip white space, read an integer, then skip to the next non-white-space character. A format string like this can cause an interactive program to "hang" until the user enters a nonblank character.

PROGRAM   **Adding Fractions**

To illustrate `scanf`'s ability to match patterns, consider the problem of reading a fraction entered by the user. Fractions are customarily written in the form *numerator/denominator*. Instead of having the user enter the numerator and denominator of a fraction as separate integers, `scanf` makes it possible to read the entire fraction. The following program, which adds two fractions, illustrates this technique.

addfrac.c
```
/* Adds two fractions */

#include <stdio.h>

int main(void)
{
    int num1, denom1, num2, denom2, result_num, result_denom;

    printf("Enter first fraction: ");
    scanf("%d/%d", &num1, &denom1);

    printf("Enter second fraction: ");
    scanf("%d/%d", &num2, &denom2);

    result_num = num1 * denom2 + num2 * denom1;
```

```
    result_denom = denom1 * denom2;
    printf("The sum is %d/%d\n", result_num, result_denom);

    return 0;
}
```

A session with this program might have the following appearance:

```
Enter first fraction: 5/6
Enter second fraction: 3/4
The sum is 38/24
```

Note that the resulting fraction isn't reduced to lowest terms.

▓▓▓▓▓▓▓▓▓▓▓▓▓▓▓▓▓

Q & A

*Q: **I've seen the `%i` conversion used to read and write integers. What's the difference between `%i` and `%d`? [p. 39]**

   A: In a `printf` format string, there's no difference between the two. In a `scanf` format string, however, `%d` can only match an integer written in decimal (base 10) form, while `%i` can match an integer expressed in octal (base 8), decimal, or hexadecimal (base 16). If an input number has a 0 prefix (as in 056), `%i` treats it as an octal number; if it has a 0x or 0X prefix (as in 0x56), `%i` treats it as a hex number. Using `%i` instead of `%d` to read a number can have surprising results if the user should accidentally put 0 at the beginning of the number. Because of this trap, I recommend sticking with `%d`.

octal numbers ➤7.1
hexadecimal numbers ➤7.1

   Q: **If `printf` treats `%` as the beginning of a conversion specification, how can I print the `%` character?**

   A: If `printf` encounters two consecutive `%` characters in a format string, it prints a single `%` character. For example, the statement

```
printf("Net profit: %d%%\n", profit);
```

might print

```
Net profit: 10%
```

   Q: **The `\t` escape is supposed to cause `printf` to advance to the next tab stop. How do I know how far apart tab stops are? [p. 41]**

   A: You don't. The effect of printing `\t` isn't defined in C; it depends on what your operating system does when asked to print a tab character. Tab stops are typically eight characters apart, but C makes no guarantee.

   Q: **What does `scanf` do if it's asked to read a number but the user enters nonnumeric input?**

A: Let's look at the following example:

```
printf("Enter a number: ");
scanf("%d", &i);
```

Suppose that the user enters a valid number, followed by nonnumeric characters:

Enter a number: 23foo

In this case, `scanf` reads the 2 and the 3, storing 23 in `i`. The remaining characters (`foo`) are left to be read by the next call of `scanf` (or some other input function). On the other hand, suppose that the input is invalid from the beginning:

Enter a number: foo

In this case, the value of `i` is undefined and `foo` is left for the next `scanf`.

What can we do about this sad state of affairs? Later, we'll see how to test whether a call of `scanf` has succeeded. If the call fails, we can have the program either terminate or try to recover, perhaps by discarding the offending input and asking the user to try again. (Ways to discard bad input are discussed in the Q&A section at the end of Chapter 22.)

detecting errors in scanf ►22.3

Q: **I don't understand how `scanf` can "put back" characters and read them again later. [p. 44]**

A: As it turns out, programs don't read user input as it is typed. Instead, input is stored in a hidden buffer, to which `scanf` has access. It's easy for `scanf` to put characters back into the buffer for subsequent reading. Chapter 22 discusses input buffering in more detail.

Q: **What does `scanf` do if the user puts punctuation marks (commas, for example) between numbers?**

A: Let's look at a simple example. Suppose that we try to read a pair of integers using `scanf`:

```
printf("Enter two numbers: ");
scanf("%d%d", &i, &j);
```

If the user enters

4,28

`scanf` will read the 4 and store it in `i`. As it searches for the beginning of the second number, `scanf` encounters the comma. Since numbers can't begin with a comma, `scanf` returns immediately. The comma and the second number are left for the next call of `scanf`.

Of course, we can easily solve the problem by adding a comma to the format string if we're sure that the numbers will *always* be separated by a comma:

```
printf("Enter two numbers, separated by a comma: ");
scanf("%d,%d", &i, &j);
```

Exercises

Section 3.1

1. What output do the following calls of `printf` produce?

   (a) `printf("%6d,%4d", 86, 1040);`

   (b) `printf("%12.5e", 30.253);`

   (c) `printf("%.4f", 83.162);`

   (d) `printf("%-6.2g", .0000009979);`

Ⓦ 2. Write calls of `printf` that display a `float` variable x in the following formats.

   (a) Exponential notation; left-justified in a field of size 8; one digit after the decimal point.

   (b) Exponential notation; right-justified in a field of size 10; six digits after the decimal point.

   (c) Fixed decimal notation; left-justified in a field of size 8; three digits after the decimal point.

   (d) Fixed decimal notation; right-justified in a field of size 6; no digits after the decimal point.

Section 3.2

3. For each of the following pairs of `scanf` format strings, indicate whether or not the two strings are equivalent. If they're not, show how they can be distinguished.

   (a) `"%d"`   versus `" %d"`

   (b) `"%d-%d-%d"` versus `"%d -%d -%d"`

   (c) `"%f"`   versus `"%f "`

   (d) `"%f,%f"`   versus `"%f, %f"`

*4. Suppose that we call `scanf` as follows:

   `scanf("%d%f%d", &i, &x, &j);`

   If the user enters

   `10.3 5 6`

   what will be the values of i, x, and j after the call? (Assume that i and j are `int` variables and x is a `float` variable.)

Ⓦ *5. Suppose that we call `scanf` as follows:

   `scanf("%f%d%f", &x, &i, &y);`

   If the user enters

   `12.3 45.6 789`

   what will be the values of x, i, and y after the call? (Assume that x and y are `float` variables and i is an `int` variable.)

6. Show how to modify the `addfrac.c` program of Section 3.2 so that the user is allowed to enter fractions that contain spaces before and after each / character.

---

*Starred exercises are tricky—the correct answer is usually not the obvious one. Read the question thoroughly, review the relevant section if necessary, and be careful!

Programming Projects

1. Write a program that accepts a date from the user in the form *mm/dd/yyyy* and then displays it in the form *yyyymmdd*:

   ```
   Enter a date (mm/dd/yyyy): 2/17/2011
   You entered the date 20110217
   ```

2. Write a program that formats product information entered by the user. A session with the program should look like this:

   ```
   Enter item number: 583
   Enter unit price: 13.5
   Enter purchase date (mm/dd/yyyy): 10/24/2010

   Item            Unit            Purchase
                   Price           Date
   583             $  13.50        10/24/2010
   ```

   The item number and date should be left justified; the unit price should be right justified. Allow dollar amounts up to $9999.99. *Hint:* Use tabs to line up the columns.

3. Books are identified by an International Standard Book Number (ISBN). ISBNs assigned after January 1, 2007 contain 13 digits, arranged in five groups, such as 978-0-393-97950-3. (Older ISBNs use 10 digits.) The first group (the *GS1 prefix*) is currently either 978 or 979. The *group identifier* specifies the language or country of origin (for example, 0 and 1 are used in English-speaking countries). The *publisher code* identifies the publisher (393 is the code for W. W. Norton). The *item number* is assigned by the publisher to identify a specific book (97950 is the code for this book). An ISBN ends with a *check digit* that's used to verify the accuracy of the preceding digits. Write a program that breaks down an ISBN entered by the user:

   ```
   Enter ISBN: 978-0-393-97950-3
   GS1 prefix: 978
   Group identifier: 0
   Publisher code: 393
   Item number: 97950
   Check digit: 3
   ```

   Note: The number of digits in each group may vary; you can't assume that groups have the lengths shown in this example. Test your program with actual ISBN values (usually found on the back cover of a book and on the copyright page).

4. Write a program that prompts the user to enter a telephone number in the form (xxx) xxx-xxxx and then displays the number in the form xxx.xxx.xxx:

   ```
   Enter phone number [(xxx) xxx-xxxx]: (404) 817-6900
   You entered 404.817.6900
   ```

5. Write a program that asks the user to enter the numbers from 1 to 16 (in any order) and then displays the numbers in a 4 by 4 arrangement, followed by the sums of the rows, columns, and diagonals:

   ```
   Enter the numbers from 1 to 16 in any order:
   16 3 2 13 5 10 11 8 9 6 7 12 4 15 14 1
   ```

```
16   3   2 13
 5  10  11   8
 9   6   7  12
 4  15  14   1
```

```
Row sums: 34 34 34 34
Column sums: 34 34 34 34
Diagonal sums: 34 34
```

If the row, column, and diagonal sums are all the same (as they are in this example), the numbers are said to form a *magic square*. The magic square shown here appears in a 1514 engraving by artist and mathematician Albrecht Dürer. (Note that the middle numbers in the last row give the date of the engraving.)

6. Modify the addfrac.c program of Section 3.2 so that the user enters both fractions at the same time, separated by a plus sign:

```
Enter two fractions separated by a plus sign: 5/6+3/4
The sum is 38/24
```

4 Expressions

One does not learn computing by using a hand calculator, but one can forget arithmetic.

One of C's distinguishing characteristics is its emphasis on expressions—formulas that show how to compute a value—rather than statements. The simplest expressions are variables and constants. A variable represents a value to be computed as the program runs; a constant represents a value that doesn't change. More complicated expressions apply operators to operands (which are themselves expressions). In the expression a + (b * c), the + operator is applied to the operands a and (b * c), both of which are expressions in their own right.

Operators are the basic tools for building expressions, and C has an unusually rich collection of them. To start off, C provides the rudimentary operators that are found in most programming languages:

- Arithmetic operators, including addition, subtraction, multiplication, and division.
- Relational operators to perform comparisons such as "i is *greater than* 0."
- Logical operators to build conditions such as "i is greater than 0 *and* i is less than 10."

But C doesn't stop here; it goes on to provide dozens of other operators. There are so many operators, in fact, that we'll need to introduce them gradually over the first twenty chapters of this book. Mastering so many operators can be a chore, but it's essential to becoming proficient at C.

In this chapter, we'll cover some of C's most fundamental operators: the arithmetic operators (Section 4.1), the assignment operators (Section 4.2), and the increment and decrement operators (Section 4.3). Section 4.1 also explains operator precedence and associativity, which are important for expressions that contain more than one operator. Section 4.4 describes how C expressions are evaluated. Finally, Section 4.5 introduces the expression statement, an unusual feature that allows any expression to serve as a statement.

4.1 Arithmetic Operators

The *arithmetic operators*—operators that perform addition, subtraction, multiplication, and division—are the workhorses of many programming languages, including C. Table 4.1 shows C's arithmetic operators.

Table 4.1
Arithmetic Operators

Unary	Binary	
	Additive	Multiplicative
+ unary plus - unary minus	+ addition - subtraction	* multiplication / division % remainder

The additive and multiplicative operators are said to be *binary* because they require *two* operands. The *unary* operators require *one* operand:

```
i = +1;   /* + used as a unary operator */
j = -i;   /* - used as a unary operator */
```

The unary + operator does nothing; in fact, it didn't even exist in K&R C. It's used primarily to emphasize that a numeric constant is positive.

The binary operators probably look familiar. The only one that might not is %, the remainder operator. The value of i % j is the remainder when i is divided by j. For example, the value of 10 % 3 is 1, and the value of 12 % 4 is 0.

The binary operators in Table 4.1—with the exception of %—allow either integer or floating-point operands, with mixing allowed. When int and float operands are mixed, the result has type float. Thus, 9 + 2.5f has the value 11.5, and 6.7f / 2 has the value 3.35.

The / and % operators require special care:

- The / operator can produce surprising results. When both of its operands are integers, the / operator "truncates" the result by dropping the fractional part. Thus, the value of 1 / 2 is 0, not 0.5.

- The % operator requires integer operands; if either operand is not an integer, the program won't compile.

undefined behavior ➤4.4

- Using zero as the right operand of either / or % causes undefined behavior.

Q&A

- Describing the result when / and % are used with negative operands is tricky. The C89 standard states that if either operand is negative, the result of a division can be rounded either up or down. (For example, the value of -9 / 7 could be either –1 or –2). If i or j is negative, the sign of i % j in C89 depends on the implementation. (For example, the value of -9 % 7 could be either –2 or 5). In C99, on the other hand, the result of a division is always truncated toward zero (so -9 / 7 has the value –1) and the value of i % j has the same sign as i (hence the value of -9 % 7 is –2).

C99

Implementation-Defined Behavior

The term ***implementation-defined*** will arise often enough that it's worth taking a moment to discuss it. The C standard deliberately leaves parts of the language unspecified, with the understanding that an "implementation"—the software needed to compile, link, and execute programs on a particular platform—will fill in the details. As a result, the behavior of the program may vary somewhat from one implementation to another. The behavior of the / and % operators for negative operands in C89 is an example of implementation-defined behavior.

Leaving parts of the language unspecified may seem odd or even dangerous, but it reflects C's philosophy. One of the language's goals is efficiency, which often means matching the way that hardware behaves. Some CPUs yield –1 when –9 is divided by 7, while others produce –2; the C89 standard simply reflects this fact of life.

It's best to avoid writing programs that depend on implementation-defined behavior. If that's not possible, at least check the manual carefully—the C standard requires that implementation-defined behavior be documented.

Operator Precedence and Associativity

When an expression contains more than one operator, its interpretation may not be immediately clear. For example, does i + j * k mean "add i and j, then multiply the result by k," or does it mean "multiply j and k, then add i"? One solution to this problem is to add parentheses, writing either (i + j) * k or i + (j * k). As a general rule, C allows the use of parentheses for grouping in all expressions.

What if we don't use parentheses, though? Will the compiler interpret i + j * k as (i + j) * k or i + (j * k)? Like many other languages, C uses *operator precedence* rules to resolve this potential ambiguity. The arithmetic operators have the following relative precedence:

```
Highest:  +   -  (unary)
          *   /   %
Lowest:   +   -  (binary)
```

Operators listed on the same line (such as + and -) have equal precedence.

When two or more operators appear in the same expression, we can determine how the compiler will interpret the expression by repeatedly putting parentheses around subexpressions, starting with high-precedence operators and working down to low-precedence operators. The following examples illustrate the result:

```
i + j * k     is equivalent to   i + (j * k)
-i * -j       is equivalent to   (-i) * (-j)
+i + j / k    is equivalent to   (+i) + (j / k)
```

Operator precedence rules alone aren't enough when an expression contains two or more operators at the same level of precedence. In this situation, the *associativity* of the operators comes into play. An operator is said to be ***left associative*** if it groups from left to right. The binary arithmetic operators (*, /, %, +, and -) are all left associative, so

```
i - j - k      is equivalent to   (i - j) - k
i * j / k      is equivalent to   (i * j) / k
```

An operator is ***right associative*** if it groups from right to left. The unary arithmetic operators (+ and -) are both right associative, so

```
- + i              is equivalent to   -(+i)
```

Precedence and associativity rules are important in many languages, but especially so in C. However, C has so many operators (almost fifty!) that few programmers bother to memorize the precedence and associativity rules. Instead, they consult a table of operators when in doubt or just use plenty of parentheses.

table of operators ➤ *Appendix A*

PROGRAM   **Computing a UPC Check Digit**

For a number of years, manufacturers of goods sold in U.S. and Canadian stores have put a bar code on each product. This code, known as a Universal Product Code (UPC), identifies both the manufacturer and the product. Each bar code represents a twelve-digit number, which is usually printed underneath the bars. For example, the following bar code comes from a package of Stouffer's French Bread Pepperoni Pizza:

The digits

```
0   13800 15173   5
```

appear underneath the bar code. The first digit identifies the type of item (0 or 7 for most items, 2 for items that must be weighed, 3 for drugs and health-related merchandise, and 5 for coupons). The first group of five digits identifies the manufacturer (13800 is the code for Nestlé USA's Frozen Food Division). The second group of five digits identifies the product (including package size). The final digit is a "check digit," whose only purpose is to help identify an error in the preceding digits. If the UPC is scanned incorrectly, the first 11 digits probably won't be consistent with the last digit, and the store's scanner will reject the entire code.

Here's one method of computing the check digit:

Add the first, third, fifth, seventh, ninth, and eleventh digits.
Add the second, fourth, sixth, eighth, and tenth digits.

Multiply the first sum by 3 and add it to the second sum.
Subtract 1 from the total.
Compute the remainder when the adjusted total is divided by 10.
Subtract the remainder from 9.

Using the Stouffer's example, we get $0 + 3 + 0 + 1 + 1 + 3 = 8$ for the first sum and $1 + 8 + 0 + 5 + 7 = 21$ for the second sum. Multiplying the first sum by 3 and adding the second yields 45. Subtracting 1 gives 44. The remainder upon dividing by 10 is 4. When the remainder is subtracted from 9, the result is 5. Here are a couple of other UPCs, in case you want to try your hand at computing the check digit (raiding the kitchen cabinet for the answer is *not* allowed):

Jif Creamy Peanut Butter (18 oz.):		0	51500 24128	?
Ocean Spray Jellied Cranberry Sauce (8 oz.):	0	31200 01005		?

The answers appear at the bottom of the page.

Let's write a program that calculates the check digit for an arbitrary UPC. We'll ask the user to enter the first 11 digits of the UPC, then we'll display the corresponding check digit. To avoid confusion, we'll ask the user to enter the number in three parts: the single digit at the left, the first group of five digits, and the second group of five digits. Here's what a session with the program will look like:

```
Enter the first (single) digit: 0
Enter first group of five digits: 13800
Enter second group of five digits: 15173
Check digit: 5
```

Instead of reading each digit group as a *five*-digit number, we'll read it as five *one*-digit numbers. Reading the numbers as single digits is more convenient; also, we won't have to worry that one of the five-digit numbers is too large to store in an `int` variable. (Some older compilers limit the maximum value of an `int` variable to 32,767.) To read single digits, we'll use `scanf` with the `%1d` conversion specification, which matches a one-digit integer.

upc.c   ```
/* Computes a Universal Product Code check digit */

#include <stdio.h>

int main(void)
{
  int d, i1, i2, i3, i4, i5, j1, j2, j3, j4, j5,
      first_sum, second_sum, total;

  printf("Enter the first (single) digit: ");
  scanf("%1d", &d);
  printf("Enter first group of five digits: ");
  scanf("%1d%1d%1d%1d%1d", &i1, &i2, &i3, &i4, &i5);
  printf("Enter second group of five digits: ");
  scanf("%1d%1d%1d%1d%1d", &j1, &j2, &j3, &j4, &j5);
```

---

The missing check digits are 8 (Jif) and 6 (Ocean Spray).
```

```
first_sum = d + i2 + i4 + j1 + j3 + j5;
second_sum = i1 + i3 + i5 + j2 + j4;
total = 3 * first_sum + second_sum;

printf("Check digit: %d\n", 9 - ((total - 1) % 10));

return 0;
}
```

Note that the expression 9 - ((total - 1) % 10) could have been written as 9 - (total - 1) % 10, but the extra set of parentheses makes it easier to understand.

4.2   Assignment Operators

Once the value of an expression has been computed, we'll often need to store it in a variable for later use. C's = (*simple assignment*) operator is used for that purpose. For updating a value already stored in a variable, C provides an assortment of compound assignment operators.

Simple Assignment

The effect of the assignment *v = e* is to evaluate the expression *e* and copy its value into *v*. As the following examples show, *e* can be a constant, a variable, or a more complicated expression:

```
i = 5;              /* i is now 5  */
j = i;              /* j is now 5  */
k = 10 * i + j;     /* k is now 55 */
```

If *v* and *e* don't have the same type, then the value of *e* is converted to the type of *v* as the assignment takes place:

```
int i;
float f;

i = 72.99f;    /* i is now 72 */
f = 136;       /* f is now 136.0 */
```

conversion during assignment ➤7.4   We'll return to the topic of type conversion later.

In many programming languages, assignment is a *statement*; in C, however, assignment is an *operator*, just like +. In other words, the act of assignment produces a result, just as adding two numbers produces a result. The value of an assignment *v = e* is the value of *v* *after* the assignment. Thus, the value of i = 72.99f is 72 (not 72.99).

Side Effects

We don't normally expect operators to modify their operands, since operators in mathematics don't. Writing `i + j` doesn't modify either `i` or `j`; it simply computes the result of adding `i` and `j`.

Most C operators don't modify their operands, but some do. We say that these operators have **side effects**, since they do more than just compute a value. The simple assignment operator is the first operator we've seen that has side effects; it modifies its left operand. Evaluating the expression `i = 0` produces the result 0 and—as a side effect—assigns 0 to `i`.

Since assignment is an operator, several assignments can be chained together:

```
i = j = k = 0;
```

The = operator is right associative, so this assignment is equivalent to

```
i = (j = (k = 0));
```

The effect is to assign 0 first to `k`, then to `j`, and finally to `i`.

Watch out for unexpected results in chained assignments as a result of type conversion:

```
int i;
float f;

f = i = 33.3f;
```

`i` is assigned the value 33, then `f` is assigned 33.0 (not 33.3, as you might think).

In general, an assignment of the form $v = e$ is allowed wherever a value of type v would be permitted. In the following example, the expression `j = i` copies `i` to `j`; the new value of `j` is then added to `1`, producing the new value of `k`:

```
i = 1;
k = 1 + (j = i);
printf("%d %d %d\n", i, j, k);   /* prints "1 1 2" */
```

Using the assignment operator in this fashion usually isn't a good idea. For one thing, "embedded assignments" can make programs hard to read. They can also be a source of subtle bugs, as we'll see in Section 4.4.

Lvalues

Most C operators allow their operands to be variables, constants, or expressions containing other operators. The assignment operator, however, requires an **lvalue** as its left operand. An lvalue (pronounced "L-value") represents an object stored in computer memory, not a constant or the result of a computation. Variables are lvalues; expressions such as `10` or `2 * i` are not. At this point, variables are the only lvalues that we know about; other kinds of lvalues will appear in later chapters.

Since the assignment operator requires an lvalue as its left operand, it's illegal to put any other kind of expression on the left side of an assignment expression:

```
12 = i;        /*** WRONG ***/
i + j = 0;     /*** WRONG ***/
-i = j;        /*** WRONG ***/
```

The compiler will detect errors of this nature, and you'll get an error message such as *"invalid lvalue in assignment."*

Compound Assignment

Assignments that use the old value of a variable to compute its new value are common in C programs. The following statement, for example, adds 2 to the value stored in `i`:

```
i = i + 2;
```

C's **compound assignment** operators allow us to shorten this statement and others like it. Using the `+=` operator, we simply write:

```
i += 2;    /* same as i = i + 2; */
```

The `+=` operator adds the value of the right operand to the variable on the left.

There are nine other compound assignment operators, including the following:

```
-=    *=    /=    %=
```

other assignment operators ➤20.1 (We'll cover the remaining compound assignment operators in a later chapter.) All compound assignment operators work in much the same way:

> v `+=` e adds v to e, storing the result in v
> v `-=` e subtracts e from v, storing the result in v
> v `*=` e multiplies v by e, storing the result in v
> v `/=` e divides v by e, storing the result in v
> v `%=` e computes the remainder when v is divided by e, storing the result in v

Note that I've been careful not to say that v `+=` e is "equivalent" to $v = v + e$. One problem is operator precedence: `i *= j + k` isn't the same as `i = i * j + k`. There are also rare cases in which v `+=` e differs from $v = v + e$ because v itself has a side effect. Similar remarks apply to the other compound assignment operators.

Q&A

When using the compound assignment operators, be careful not to switch the two characters that make up the operator. Switching the characters may yield an expression that is acceptable to the compiler but that doesn't have the intended meaning. For example, if you meant to write `i += j` but typed `i =+ j` instead, the

program will still compile. Unfortunately, the latter expression is equivalent to
i = (+j), which merely copies the value of j into i.

The compound assignment operators have the same properties as the = operator. In particular, they're right associative, so the statement

```
i += j += k;
```

means

```
i += (j += k);
```

4.3 Increment and Decrement Operators

Two of the most common operations on a variable are "incrementing" (adding 1) and "decrementing" (subtracting 1). We can, of course, accomplish these tasks by writing

```
i = i + 1;
j = j - 1;
```

The compound assignment operators allow us to condense these statements a bit:

```
i += 1;
j -= 1;
```

Q&A
But C allows increments and decrements to be shortened even further, using the ++ (*increment*) and -- (*decrement*) operators.

At first glance, the increment and decrement operators are simplicity itself: ++ adds 1 to its operand, whereas -- subtracts 1. Unfortunately, this simplicity is misleading—the increment and decrement operators can be tricky to use. One complication is that ++ and -- can be used as *prefix* operators (++i and --i, for example) or *postfix* operators (i++ and i--). The correctness of a program may hinge on picking the proper version.

Another complication is that, like the assignment operators, ++ and -- have side effects: they modify the values of their operands. Evaluating the expression ++i (a "pre-increment") yields i + 1 and—as a side effect—increments i:

```
i = 1;
printf("i is %d\n", ++i);    /* prints "i is 2" */
printf("i is %d\n", i);      /* prints "i is 2" */
```

Evaluating the expression i++ (a "post-increment") produces the result i, but causes i to be incremented afterwards:

```
i = 1;
printf("i is %d\n", i++);    /* prints "i is 1" */
printf("i is %d\n", i);      /* prints "i is 2" */
```

The first `printf` shows the original value of i, before it is incremented. The second `printf` shows the new value. As these examples illustrate, `++i` means "increment i immediately," while `i++` means "use the old value of i for now, but increment i later." How much later? The C standard doesn't specify a precise time, but it's safe to assume that i will be incremented before the next statement is executed.

Q&A

The `--` operator has similar properties:

```
i = 1;
printf("i is %d\n", --i);    /* prints "i is 0" */
printf("i is %d\n", i);      /* prints "i is 0" */

i = 1;
printf("i is %d\n", i--);    /* prints "i is 1" */
printf("i is %d\n", i);      /* prints "i is 0" */
```

When `++` or `--` is used more than once in the same expression, the result can often be hard to understand. Consider the following statements:

```
i = 1;
j = 2;
k = ++i + j++;
```

What are the values of i, j, and k after these statements are executed? Since i is incremented *before* its value is used, but j is incremented *after* it is used, the last statement is equivalent to

```
i = i + 1;
k = i + j;
j = j + 1;
```

so the final values of i, j, and k are 2, 3, and 4, respectively. In contrast, executing the statements

```
i = 1;
j = 2;
k = i++ + j++;
```

will give i, j, and k the values 2, 3, and 3, respectively.

For the record, the postfix versions of `++` and `--` have higher precedence than unary plus and minus and are left associative. The prefix versions have the same precedence as unary plus and minus and are right associative.

4.4 Expression Evaluation

Table 4.2 summarizes the operators we've seen so far. (Appendix A has a similar table that shows *all* operators.) The first column shows the precedence of each

Table 4.2
A Partial List of
C Operators

Precedence	Name	Symbol(s)	Associativity
1	increment (postfix) decrement (postfix)	++ --	left
2	increment (prefix) decrement (prefix) unary plus unary minus	++ -- + -	right
3	multiplicative	* / %	left
4	additive	+ -	left
5	assignment	= *= /= %= += -=	right

operator relative to the other operators in the table (the highest precedence is 1; the lowest is 5). The last column shows the associativity of each operator.

Table 4.2 (or its larger cousin in Appendix A) has a variety of uses. Let's look at one of these. Suppose that we run across a complicated expression such as

```
a = b += c++ - d + --e / -f
```

as we're reading someone's program. This expression would be easier to understand if there were parentheses to show how the expression is constructed from subexpressions. With the help of Table 4.2, adding parentheses to an expression is easy: after examining the expression to find the operator with highest precedence, we put parentheses around the operator and its operands, indicating that it should be treated as a single operand from that point onwards. We then repeat the process until the expression is fully parenthesized.

In our example, the operator with highest precedence is ++, used here as a postfix operator, so we put parentheses around ++ and its operand:

```
a = b += (c++) - d + --e / -f
```

We now spot a prefix -- operator and a unary minus operator (both precedence 2) in the expression:

```
a = b += (c++) - d + (--e) / (-f)
```

Note that the other minus sign has an operand to its immediate left, so it must be a subtraction operator, not a unary minus operator.

Next, we notice the / operator (precedence 3):

```
a = b += (c++) - d + ((--e) / (-f))
```

The expression contains two operators with precedence 4, subtraction and addition. Whenever two operators with the same precedence are adjacent to an operand, we've got to be careful about associativity. In our example, - and + are both adjacent to d, so associativity rules apply. The - and + operators group from left to right, so parentheses go around the subtraction first, then the addition:

```
a = b += (((c++) - d) + ((--e) / (-f)))
```

The only remaining operators are = and +=. Both operators are adjacent to b, so we must take associativity into account. Assignment operators group from right to left, so parentheses go around the += expression first, then the = expression:

```
(a = (b += (((c++) - d) + ((--e) / (-f)))))
```

The expression is now fully parenthesized.

Order of Subexpression Evaluation

The rules of operator precedence and associativity allow us to break any C expression into subexpressions—to determine uniquely where the parentheses would go if the expression were fully parenthesized. Paradoxically, these rules don't always allow us to determine the value of the expression, which may depend on the order in which its subexpressions are evaluated.

logical *and* and *or* operators ➤*5.1*

conditional operator ➤*5.2*

comma operator ➤*6.3*

C doesn't define the order in which subexpressions are evaluated (with the exception of subexpressions involving the logical *and*, logical *or*, conditional, and comma operators). Thus, in the expression (a + b) * (c - d) we don't know whether (a + b) will be evaluated before (c - d).

Most expressions have the same value regardless of the order in which their subexpressions are evaluated. However, this may not be true when a subexpression modifies one of its operands. Consider the following example:

```
a = 5;
c = (b = a + 2) - (a = 1);
```

The effect of executing the second statement is undefined; the C standard doesn't say what will happen. With most compilers, the value of c will be either 6 or 2. If the subexpression (b = a + 2) is evaluated first, b is assigned the value 7 and c is assigned 6. But if (a = 1) is evaluated first, b is assigned 3 and c is assigned 2.

 Avoid writing expressions that access the value of a variable and also modify the variable elsewhere in the expression. The expression (b = a + 2) - (a = 1) accesses the value of a (in order to compute a + 2) and also modifies the value of a (by assigning it 1). Some compilers may produce a warning message such as *"operation on 'a' may be undefined"* when they encounter such an expression.

To prevent problems, it's a good idea to avoid using the assignment operators in subexpressions; instead, use a series of separate assignments. For example, the statements above could be rewritten as

```
a = 5;
b = a + 2;
a = 1;
c = b - a;
```

The value of c will always be 6 after these statements are executed.

Besides the assignment operators, the only operators that modify their operands are increment and decrement. When using these operators, be careful that your expressions don't depend on a particular order of evaluation. In the following example, j may be assigned one of two values:

```
i = 2;
j = i * i++;
```

It's natural to assume that j is assigned the value 4. However, the effect of executing the statement is undefined, and j could just as well be assigned 6 instead. Here's the scenario: (1) The second operand (the original value of i) is fetched, then i is incremented. (2) The first operand (the new value of i) is fetched. (3) The new and old values of i are multiplied, yielding 6. "Fetching" a variable means to retrieve the value of the variable from memory. A later change to the variable won't affect the fetched value, which is typically stored in a special location registers ➤ *18.2* (known as a ***register***) inside the CPU.

Undefined Behavior

According to the C standard, statements such as c = (b = a + 2) - (a = 1); and j = i * i++; cause ***undefined behavior,*** which is different from implementation-defined behavior (see Section 4.1). When a program ventures into the realm of undefined behavior, all bets are off. The program may behave differently when compiled with different compilers. But that's not the only thing that can happen. The program may not compile in the first place, if it compiles it may not run, and if it does run, it may crash, behave erratically, or produce meaningless results. In other words, undefined behavior should be avoided like the plague.

4.5 Expression Statements

C has the unusual rule that *any* expression can be used as a statement. That is, any expression—regardless of its type or what it computes—can be turned into a statement by appending a semicolon. For example, we could turn the expression ++i into a statement:

```
++i;
```

When this statement is executed, i is first incremented, then the new value of i is fetched (as though it were to be used in an enclosing expression). However, since **Q&A** ++i isn't part of a larger expression, its value is discarded and the next statement executed. (The change to i is permanent, of course.)

Since its value is discarded, there's little point in using an expression as a statement unless the expression has a side effect. Let's look at three examples. In the first example, 1 is stored into i, then the new value of i is fetched but not used:

```
i = 1;
```

In the second example, the value of i is fetched but not used; however, i is decremented afterwards:

```
i--;
```

In the third example, the value of the expression i * j - 1 is computed and then discarded:

```
i * j - 1;
```

Since i and j aren't changed, this statement has no effect and therefore serves no purpose.

 A slip of the finger can easily create a "do-nothing" expression statement. For example, instead of entering

```
i = j;
```

we might accidentally type

```
i + j;
```

(This kind of error is more common than you might expect, since the = and + characters usually occupy the same key.) Some compilers can detect meaningless expression statements; you'll get a warning such as *"statement with no effect."*

Q & A

Q: I notice that C has no exponentiation operator. How can I raise a number to a power?

A: Raising an integer to a small positive integer power is best done by repeated multiplication (i * i * i is i cubed). To raise a number to a noninteger power, call the

pow function ▸23.3   pow function.

Q: I want to apply the % operator to a floating-point operand, but my program won't compile. What can I do? [p. 54]

fmod function ▸23.3   A: The % operator requires integer operands. Try the fmod function instead.

Q: Why are the rules for using the / and % operators with negative operands so complicated? [p. 54]

A: The rules aren't as complicated as they may first appear. In both C89 and C99, the goal is to ensure that the value of (a / b) * b + a % b will always be equal to a (and indeed, both standards guarantee that this is the case, provided that the value of a / b is "representable"). The problem is that there are two ways for a / b and a % b to satisfy this equality if either a or b is negative, as seen in C89, where either -9 / 7 is –1 and -9 % 7 is –2, or -9 / 7 is –2 and -9 % 7 is 5. In the first case, (-9 / 7) * 7 + -9 % 7 has the value $-1 \times 7 + -2 = -9$, and in the second case, (-9 / 7) * 7 + -9 % 7 has the value $-2 \times 7 + 5 = -9$. By the time C99 rolled around, most CPUs were designed to truncate the result of division toward zero, so this was written into the standard as the only allowable outcome.

Q: **If C has lvalues, does it also have rvalues? [p. 59]**

A: Yes, indeed. An *l*value is an expression that can appear on the *left* side of an assignment; an *r*value is an expression that can appear on the *right* side. Thus, an rvalue could be a variable, constant, or more complex expression. In this book, as in the C standard, we'll use the term "expression" instead of "rvalue."

*Q: **You said that v += e isn't equivalent to $v = v + e$ if v has a side effect. Can you explain? [p. 60]**

A: Evaluating v += e causes v to be evaluated only once; evaluating $v = v + e$ causes v to be evaluated twice. Any side effect caused by evaluating v will occur twice in the latter case. In the following example, i is incremented once:

```
a[i++] += 2;
```

If we use = instead of +=, here's what the statement will look like:

```
a[i++] = a[i++] + 2;
```

The value of i is modified as well as used elsewhere in the statement, so the effect of executing the statement is undefined. It's likely that i will be incremented twice, but we can't say with certainty what will happen.

Q: **Why does C provide the ++ and -- operators? Are they faster than other ways of incrementing and decrementing, or they are just more convenient? [p. 61]**

A: C inherited ++ and -- from Ken Thompson's earlier B language. Thompson apparently created these operators because his B compiler could generate a more compact translation for ++i than for i = i + 1. These operators have become a deeply ingrained part of C (in fact, many of C's most famous idioms rely on them). With modern compilers, using ++ and -- won't make a compiled program any smaller or faster; the continued popularity of these operators stems mostly from their brevity and convenience.

Q: **Do ++ and -- work with `float` variables?**

A: Yes; the increment and decrement operations can be applied to floating-point numbers as well as integers. In practice, however, it's fairly rare to increment or decrement a `float` variable.

*Q: **When I use the postfix version of ++ or - -, just when is the increment or decrement performed? [p. 62]**

A: That's an excellent question. Unfortunately, it's also a difficult one to answer. The C standard introduces the concept of "sequence point" and says that "updating the stored value of the operand shall occur between the previous and the next sequence point." There are various kinds of sequence points in C; the end of an expression statement is one example. By the end of an expression statement, all increments and decrements within the statement must have been performed; the next statement can't begin to execute until this condition has been met.

Certain operators that we'll encounter in later chapters (logical *and*, logical *or*, conditional, and comma) also impose sequence points. So do function calls: the arguments in a function call must be fully evaluated before the call can be performed. If an argument happens to be an expression containing a ++ or - - operator, the increment or decrement must occur before the call can take place.

Q: **What do you mean when you say that the value of an expression statement is discarded? [p. 65]**

A: By definition, an expression represents a value. If i has the value 5, for example, then evaluating i + 1 produces the value 6. Let's turn i + 1 into a statement by putting a semicolon after it:

```
i + 1;
```

When this statement is executed, the value of i + 1 is computed. Since we have failed to save this value—or at least use it in some way—it is lost.

Q: **But what about statements like i = 1;? I don't see what is being discarded.**

A: Don't forget that = is an operator in C and produces a value just like any other operator. The assignment

```
i = 1;
```

assigns 1 to i. The value of the entire expression is 1, which is discarded. Discarding the expression's value is no great loss, since the reason for writing the statement in the first place was to modify i.

Exercises

Section 4.1

1.   Show the output produced by each of the following program fragments. Assume that i, j, and k are int variables.

(a) ```i = 5; j = 3;
    printf("%d %d", i / j, i % j);```
(b) ```i = 2; j = 3;
    printf("%d", (i + 10) % j);```
(c) ```i = 7; j = 8; k = 9;
    printf("%d", (i + 10) % k / j);```

(d) ` i = 1; j = 2; k = 3;`
     ` printf("%d", (i + 5) % (j + 2) / k);`

Ⓦ *2. If `i` and `j` are positive integers, does `(-i)/j` always have the same value as `-(i/j)`? Justify your answer.

3. What is the value of each of the following expressions in C89? (Give all possible values if an expression may have more than one value.)

   (a) ` 8 / 5`
   (b) ` -8 / 5`
   (c) ` 8 / -5`
   (d) ` -8 / -5`

4. Repeat Exercise 3 for C99.

5. What is the value of each of the following expressions in C89? (Give all possible values if an expression may have more than one value.)

   (a) ` 8 % 5`
   (b) ` -8 % 5`
   (c) ` 8 % -5`
   (d) ` -8 % -5`

6. Repeat Exercise 5 for C99.

7. The algorithm for computing the UPC check digit ends with the following steps:

   Subtract 1 from the total.
   Compute the remainder when the adjusted total is divided by 10.
   Subtract the remainder from 9.

   It's tempting to try to simplify the algorithm by using these steps instead:

   Compute the remainder when the total is divided by 10.
   Subtract the remainder from 10.

   Why doesn't this technique work?

8. Would the `upc.c` program still work if the expression `9 - ((total - 1) % 10)` were replaced by `(10 - (total % 10)) % 10`?

Section 4.2 Ⓦ 9. Show the output produced by each of the following program fragments. Assume that `i`, `j`, and `k` are `int` variables.

   (a) ` i = 7; j = 8;`
       ` i *= j + 1;`
       ` printf("%d %d", i, j);`
   (b) ` i = j = k = 1;`
       ` i += j += k;`
       ` printf("%d %d %d", i, j, k);`
   (c) ` i = 1; j = 2; k = 3;`
       ` i -= j -= k;`
       ` printf("%d %d %d", i, j, k);`
   (d) ` i = 2; j = 1; k = 0;`
       ` i *= j *= k;`
       ` printf("%d %d %d", i, j, k);`

10. Show the output produced by each of the following program fragments. Assume that `i` and `j` are `int` variables.

```
(a) i = 6;
    j = i += i;
    printf("%d %d", i, j);
(b) i = 5;
    j = (i -= 2) + 1;
    printf("%d %d", i, j);
(c) i = 7;
    j = 6 + (i = 2.5);
    printf("%d %d", i, j);
(d) i = 2; j = 8;
    j = (i = 6) + (j = 3);
    printf("%d %d", i, j);
```

Section 4.3   *11. Show the output produced by each of the following program fragments. Assume that `i`, `j`, and `k` are `int` variables.

```
(a) i = 1;
    printf("%d ", i++ - 1);
    printf("%d", i);
(b) i = 10; j = 5;
    printf("%d ", i++ - ++j);
    printf("%d %d", i, j);
(c) i = 7; j = 8;
    printf("%d ", i++ - --j);
    printf("%d %d", i, j);
(d) i = 3; j = 4; k = 5;
    printf("%d ", i++ - j++ + --k);
    printf("%d %d %d", i, j, k);
```

12. Show the output produced by each of the following program fragments. Assume that `i` and `j` are `int` variables.

```
(a) i = 5;
    j = ++i * 3 - 2;
    printf("%d %d", i, j);
(b) i = 5;
    j = 3 - 2 * i++;
    printf("%d %d", i, j);
(c) i = 7;
    j = 3 * i-- + 2;
    printf("%d %d", i, j);
(d) i = 7;
    j = 3 + --i * 2;
    printf("%d %d", i, j);
```

Ⓦ 13. Only one of the expressions `++i` and `i++` is exactly the same as `(i += 1)`; which is it? Justify your answer.

Section 4.4   14. Supply parentheses to show how a C compiler would interpret each of the following expressions.

```
(a) a * b - c * d + e
(b) a / b % c / d
(c) - a - b + c - + d
(d) a * - b / c - d
```

Section 4.5   15.   Give the values of i and j after each of the following expression statements has been executed. (Assume that i has the value 1 initially and j has the value 2.)

    (a) `i += j;`
    (b) `i--;`
    (c) `i * j / i;`
    (d) `i % ++j;`

Programming Projects

1.   Write a program that asks the user to enter a two-digit number, then prints the number with its digits reversed. A session with the program should have the following appearance:

```
Enter a two-digit number: 28
The reversal is: 82
```

Read the number using %d, then break it into two digits. *Hint:* If n is an integer, then n % 10 is the last digit in n and n / 10 is n with the last digit removed.

2.   Extend the program in Programming Project 1 to handle *three*-digit numbers.

3.   Rewrite the program in Programming Project 2 so that it prints the reversal of a three-digit number without using arithmetic to split the number into digits. *Hint:* See the upc.c program of Section 4.1.

4.   Write a program that reads an integer entered by the user and displays it in octal (base 8):

```
Enter a number between 0 and 32767: 1953
In octal, your number is: 03641
```

The output should be displayed using five digits, even if fewer digits are sufficient. *Hint:* To convert the number to octal, first divide it by 8; the remainder is the last digit of the octal number (1, in this case). Then divide the original number by 8 and repeat the process to arrive at the next-to-last digit. (printf is capable of displaying numbers in base 8, as we'll see in Chapter 7, so there's actually an easier way to write this program.)

5.   Rewrite the upc.c program of Section 4.1 so that the user enters 11 digits at one time, instead of entering one digit, then five digits, and then another five digits.

```
Enter the first 11 digits of a UPC: 01380015173
Check digit: 5
```

6.   European countries use a 13-digit code, known as a European Article Number (EAN) instead of the 12-digit Universal Product Code (UPC) found in North America. Each EAN ends with a check digit, just as a UPC does. The technique for calculating the check digit is also similar:

    Add the second, fourth, sixth, eighth, tenth, and twelfth digits.
    Add the first, third, fifth, seventh, ninth, and eleventh digits.
    Multiply the first sum by 3 and add it to the second sum.

Subtract 1 from the total.
Compute the remainder when the adjusted total is divided by 10.
Subtract the remainder from 9.

For example, consider Güllüoglu Turkish Delight Pistachio & Coconut, which has an EAN of 8691484260008. The first sum is $6 + 1 + 8 + 2 + 0 + 0 = 17$, and the second sum is $8 + 9 + 4 + 4 + 6 + 0 = 31$. Multiplying the first sum by 3 and adding the second yields 82. Subtracting 1 gives 81. The remainder upon dividing by 10 is 1. When the remainder is subtracted from 9, the result is 8, which matches the last digit of the original code. Your job is to modify the upc.c program of Section 4.1 so that it calculates the check digit for an EAN. The user will enter the first 12 digits of the EAN as a single number:

```
Enter the first 12 digits of an EAN: 869148426000
Check digit: 8
```

5 Selection Statements

Programmers are not to be measured by their ingenuity and their logic but by the completeness of their case analysis.

return statement ➤2.2
expression statement ➤4.5

Although C has many operators, it has relatively few statements. We've encountered just two so far: the `return` statement and the expression statement. Most of C's remaining statements fall into three categories, depending on how they affect the order in which statements are executed:

- **Selection statements.** The `if` and `switch` statements allow a program to select a particular execution path from a set of alternatives.

- **Iteration statements.** The `while`, `do`, and `for` statements support iteration (looping).

- **Jump statements.** The `break`, `continue`, and `goto` statements cause an unconditional jump to some other place in the program. (The `return` statement belongs in this category, as well.)

The only other statements in C are the compound statement, which groups several statements into a single statement, and the null statement, which performs no action.

This chapter discusses the selection statements and the compound statement. (Chapter 6 covers the iteration statements, the jump statements, and the null statement.) Before we can write `if` statements, we'll need logical expressions: conditions that `if` statements can test. Section 5.1 explains how logical expressions are built from the relational operators (`<`, `<=`, `>`, and `>=`), the equality operators (`==` and `!=`), and the logical operators (`&&`, `||`, and `!`). Section 5.2 covers the `if` statement and compound statement, as well as introducing the conditional operator (`?:`), which can test a condition within an expression. Section 5.3 describes the `switch` statement.

5.1 Logical Expressions

Several of C's statements, including the if statement, must test the value of an expression to see if it is "true" or "false." For example, an if statement might need to test the expression i < j; a true value would indicate that i is less than j. In many programming languages, an expression such as i < j would have a special "Boolean" or "logical" type. Such a type would have only two values, *false* and *true*. In C, however, a comparison such as i < j yields an integer: either 0 (false) or 1 (true). With this in mind, let's look at the operators that are used to build logical expressions.

Relational Operators

C's **relational operators** (Table 5.1) correspond to the <, >, ≤, and ≥ operators of mathematics, except that they produce 0 (false) or 1 (true) when used in expressions. For example, the value of 10 < 11 is 1; the value of 11 < 10 is 0.

Table 5.1
Relational Operators

Symbol	Meaning
<	less than
>	greater than
<=	less than or equal to
>=	greater than or equal to

The relational operators can be used to compare integers and floating-point numbers, with operands of mixed types allowed. Thus, 1 < 2.5 has the value 1, while 5.6 < 4 has the value 0.

The precedence of the relational operators is lower than that of the arithmetic operators; for example, i + j < k - 1 means (i + j) < (k - 1). The relational operators are left associative.

The expression

```
i < j < k
```

is legal in C, but doesn't have the meaning that you might expect. Since the < operator is left associative, this expression is equivalent to

```
(i < j) < k
```

In other words, the expression first tests whether i is less than j; the 1 or 0 produced by this comparison is then compared to k. The expression does *not* test whether j lies between i and k. (We'll see later in this section that the correct expression would be i < j && j < k.)

Equality Operators

Although the relational operators are denoted by the same symbols as in many other programming languages, the *equality operators* have a unique appearance (Table 5.2). The "equal to" operator is two adjacent = characters, not one, since a single = character represents the assignment operator. The "not equal to" operator is also two characters: ! and =.

Table 5.2
Equality Operators

Symbol	Meaning
==	equal to
!=	not equal to

Like the relational operators, the equality operators are left associative and produce either 0 (false) or 1 (true) as their result. However, the equality operators have *lower* precedence than the relational operators. For example, the expression

```
i < j == j < k
```

is equivalent to

```
(i < j) == (j < k)
```

which is true if i < j and j < k are both true or both false.

Clever programmers sometimes exploit the fact that the relational and equality operators return integer values. For example, the value of the expression (i >= j) + (i == j) is either 0, 1, or 2, depending on whether i is less than, greater than, or equal to j, respectively. Tricky coding like this generally isn't a good idea, however; it makes programs hard to understand.

Logical Operators

More complicated logical expressions can be built from simpler ones by using the *logical operators: and, or,* and *not* (Table 5.3). The ! operator is unary, while && and || are binary.

Table 5.3
Logical Operators

Symbol	Meaning
!	logical negation
&&	logical *and*
||	logical *or*

The logical operators produce either 0 or 1 as their result. Often, the operands will have values of 0 or 1, but this isn't a requirement; the logical operators treat any nonzero operand as a true value and any zero operand as a false value.

The logical operators behave as follows:

- !*expr* has the value 1 if *expr* has the value 0.
- *expr1* && *expr2* has the value 1 if the values of *expr1* and *expr2* are both nonzero.

- *expr1* || *expr2* has the value 1 if either *expr1* or *expr2* (or both) has a nonzero value.

In all other cases, these operators produce the value 0.

Both && and || perform "short-circuit" evaluation of their operands. That is, these operators first evaluate the left operand, then the right operand. If the value of the expression can be deduced from the value of the left operand alone, then the right operand isn't evaluated. Consider the following expression:

```
(i != 0) && (j / i > 0)
```

To find the value of this expression, we must first evaluate (i != 0). If i isn't equal to 0, then we'll need to evaluate (j / i > 0) to determine whether the entire expression is true or false. However, if i is equal to 0, then the entire expression must be false, so there's no need to evaluate (j / i > 0). The advantage of short-circuit evaluation is apparent—without it, evaluating the expression would have caused a division by zero.

Be wary of side effects in logical expressions. Thanks to the short-circuit nature of the && and || operators, side effects in operands may not always occur. Consider the following expression:

```
i > 0 && ++j > 0
```

Although j is apparently incremented as a side effect of evaluating the expression, that isn't always the case. If i > 0 is false, then ++j > 0 is not evaluated, so j isn't incremented. The problem can be fixed by changing the condition to ++j > 0 && i > 0 or, even better, by incrementing j separately.

The ! operator has the same precedence as the unary plus and minus operators. The precedence of && and || is lower than that of the relational and equality operators; for example, i < j && k == m means (i < j) && (k == m). The ! operator is right associative; && and || are left associative.

5.2 The if Statement

The if statement allows a program to choose between two alternatives by testing the value of an expression. In its simplest form, the if statement has the form

if statement

> if (*expression*) *statement*

Notice that the parentheses around the expression are mandatory; they're part of the if statement, not part of the expression. Also note that the word then doesn't come after the parentheses, as it would in some programming languages.

When an `if` statement is executed, the expression in the parentheses is evaluated; if the value of the expression is nonzero—which C interprets as true—the statement after the parentheses is executed. Here's an example:

```
if (line_num == MAX_LINES)
  line_num = 0;
```

The statement `line_num = 0;` is executed if the condition `line_num == MAX_LINES` is true (has a nonzero value).

Don't confuse `==` (equality) with `=` (assignment). The statement

```
if (i == 0) …
```

tests whether `i` is equal to 0. However, the statement

```
if (i = 0) …
```

assigns 0 to `i`, then tests whether the *result* is nonzero. In this case, the test always fails.

Confusing `==` with `=` is perhaps the most common C programming error, probably because `=` means "is equal to" in mathematics (and in certain programming languages). Some compilers issue a warning if they notice `=` where `==` would normally appear.

Q&A

Often the expression in an `if` statement will test whether a variable falls within a range of values. To test whether $0 \leq i < n$, for example, we'd write

idiom   `if (0 <= i && i < n) …`

To test the *opposite* condition (`i` is outside the range), we'd write

idiom   `if (i < 0 || i >= n) …`

Note the use of the `||` operator instead of the `&&` operator.

Compound Statements

In our `if` statement template, notice that *statement* is singular, not plural:

`if ( ` *expression* ` ) ` *statement*

What if we want an `if` statement to control *two* or more statements? That's where the **compound statement** comes in. A compound statement has the form

compound statement

$$\{ \ statements \ \}$$

By putting braces around a group of statements, we can force the compiler to treat it as a single statement.

Here's an example of a compound statement:

```
{ line_num = 0; page_num++; }
```

For clarity, I'll usually put a compound statement on several lines, with one statement per line:

```
{
  line_num = 0;
  page_num++;
}
```

Notice that each inner statement still ends with a semicolon, but the compound statement itself does not.

Here's what a compound statement would look like when used inside an `if` statement:

```
if (line_num == MAX_LINES) {
  line_num = 0;
  page_num++;
}
```

Compound statements are also common in loops and other places where the syntax of C requires a single statement, but we want more than one.

The `else` Clause

An `if` statement may have an `else` clause:

`if` statement with `else` clause

> `if ( ` *expression* ` ) ` *statement* ` else ` *statement*

The statement that follows the word `else` is executed if the expression in parentheses has the value 0.

Here's an example of an `if` statement with an `else` clause:

```
if (i > j)
  max = i;
else
  max = j;
```

Notice that both "inner" statements end with a semicolon.

When an `if` statement contains an `else` clause, a layout issue arises: where should the `else` be placed? Many C programmers align it with the `if` at the beginning of the statement, as in the previous example. The inner statements are usually indented, but if they're short they can be put on the same line as the `if` and `else`:

```
if (i > j) max = i;
else max = j;
```

There are no restrictions on what kind of statements can appear inside an `if` statement. In fact, it's not unusual for `if` statements to be nested inside other `if` statements. Consider the following `if` statement, which finds the largest of the numbers stored in `i`, `j`, and `k` and stores that value in `max`:

```
if (i > j)
  if (i > k)
    max = i;
  else
    max = k;
else
  if (j > k)
    max = j;
  else
    max = k;
```

`if` statements can be nested to any depth. Notice how aligning each `else` with the matching `if` makes the nesting easier to see. If you still find the nesting confusing, don't hesitate to add braces:

```
if (i > j) {
  if (i > k)
    max = i;
  else
    max = k;
} else {
  if (j > k)
    max = j;
  else
    max = k;
}
```

Adding braces to statements—even when they're not necessary—is like using parentheses in expressions: both techniques help make a program more readable while at the same time avoiding the possibility that the compiler won't understand the program the way we thought it did.

Some programmers use as many braces as possible inside `if` statements (and iteration statements as well). A programmer who adopts this convention would include a pair of braces for every `if` clause and every `else` clause:

```
if (i > j) {
  if (i > k) {
    max = i;
  } else {
    max = k;
  }
} else {
  if (j > k) {
    max = j;
  } else {
    max = k;
  }
}
```

Using braces even when they're not required has two advantages. First, the program becomes easier to modify, because more statements can easily be added to any if or else clause. Second, it helps avoid errors that can result from forgetting to use braces when adding statements to an if or else clause.

Cascaded if Statements

We'll often need to test a series of conditions, stopping as soon as one of them is true. A "cascaded" if statement is often the best way to write such a series of tests. For example, the following cascaded if statement tests whether n is less than 0, equal to 0, or greater than 0:

```
if (n < 0)
  printf("n is less than 0\n");
else
  if (n == 0)
    printf("n is equal to 0\n");
  else
    printf("n is greater than 0\n");
```

Although the second if statement is nested inside the first, C programmers don't usually indent it. Instead, they align each else with the original if:

```
if (n < 0)
  printf("n is less than 0\n");
else if (n == 0)
  printf("n is equal to 0\n");
else
  printf("n is greater than 0\n");
```

This arrangement gives the cascaded if a distinctive appearance:

```
if ( expression )
  statement
else if ( expression )
  statement
...
else if ( expression )
  statement
else
  statement
```

The last two lines (else *statement*) aren't always present, of course. This way of indenting the cascaded if statement avoids the problem of excessive indentation when the number of tests is large. Moreover, it assures the reader that the statement is nothing more than a series of tests.

Keep in mind that a cascaded if statement isn't some new kind of statement; it's just an ordinary if statement that happens to have another if statement as its else clause (and *that* if statement has another if statement as its else clause, *ad infinitum*).

PROGRAM **Calculating a Broker's Commission**

When stocks are sold or purchased through a broker, the broker's commission is often computed using a sliding scale that depends upon the value of the stocks traded. Let's say that a broker charges the amounts shown in the following table:

Transaction size	Commission rate
Under $2,500	$30 + 1.7%
$2,500–$6,250	$56 + 0.66%
$6,250–$20,000	$76 + 0.34%
$20,000–$50,000	$100 + 0.22%
$50,000–$500,000	$155 + 0.11%
Over $500,000	$255 + 0.09%

The minimum charge is $39. Our next program asks the user to enter the amount of the trade, then displays the amount of the commission:

```
Enter value of trade: 30000
Commission: $166.00
```

The heart of the program is a cascaded `if` statement that determines which range the trade falls into.

broker.c
```c
/* Calculates a broker's commission */

#include <stdio.h>

int main(void)
{
  float commission, value;

  printf("Enter value of trade: ");
  scanf("%f", &value);

  if (value < 2500.00f)
    commission = 30.00f + .017f * value;
  else if (value < 6250.00f)
    commission = 56.00f + .0066f * value;
  else if (value < 20000.00f)
    commission = 76.00f + .0034f * value;
  else if (value < 50000.00f)
    commission = 100.00f + .0022f * value;
  else if (value < 500000.00f)
    commission = 155.00f + .0011f * value;
  else
    commission = 255.00f + .0009f * value;

  if (commission < 39.00f)
    commission = 39.00f;

  printf("Commission: $%.2f\n", commission);

  return 0;
}
```

The cascaded `if` statement could have been written this way instead (the changes are indicated in **bold**):

```
if (value < 2500.00f)
  commission = 30.00f + .017f * value;
else if (value >= 2500.00f && value < 6250.00f)
  commission = 56.00f + .0066f * value;
else if (value >= 6250.00f && value < 20000.00f)
  commission = 76.00f + .0034f * value;
...
```

Although the program will still work, the added conditions aren't necessary. For example, the first `if` clause tests whether `value` is less than 2500 and, if so, computes the commission. When we reach the second `if` test (`value >= 2500.00f && value < 6250.00f`), we know that `value` can't be less than 2500 and therefore must be greater than or equal to 2500. The condition `value >= 2500.00f` will always be true, so there's no point in checking it.

The "Dangling `else`" Problem

When `if` statements are nested, we've got to watch out for the notorious "dangling `else`" problem. Consider the following example:

```
if (y != 0)
  if (x != 0)
    result = x / y;
else
  printf("Error: y is equal to 0\n");
```

To which `if` statement does the `else` clause belong? The indentation suggests that it belongs to the outer `if` statement. However, C follows the rule that an `else` clause belongs to the nearest `if` statement that hasn't already been paired with an `else`. In this example, the `else` clause actually belongs to the inner `if` statement, so a correctly indented version would look like this:

```
if (y != 0)
  if (x != 0)
    result = x / y;
  else
    printf("Error: y is equal to 0\n");
```

To make the `else` clause part of the outer `if` statement, we can enclose the inner `if` statement in braces:

```
if (y != 0) {
  if (x != 0)
    result = x / y;
} else
    printf("Error: y is equal to 0\n");
```

This example illustrates the value of braces; if we'd used them in the original `if` statement, we wouldn't have gotten into this situation in the first place.

Conditional Expressions

C's if statement allows a program to perform one of two actions depending on the value of a condition. C also provides an *operator* that allows an expression to produce one of two *values* depending on the value of a condition.

The ***conditional operator*** consists of two symbols (? and :), which must be used together in the following way:

**conditional
expression**

$$\mathit{expr1} \ ? \ \mathit{expr2} \ : \ \mathit{expr3}$$

expr1, *expr2*, and *expr3* can be expressions of any type. The resulting expression is said to be a ***conditional expression***. The conditional operator is unique among C operators in that it requires *three* operands instead of one or two. For this reason, it is often referred to as a ***ternary*** operator.

The conditional expression *expr1* ? *expr2* : *expr3* should be read "if *expr1* then *expr2* else *expr3*." The expression is evaluated in stages: *expr1* is evaluated first; if its value isn't zero, then *expr2* is evaluated, and its value is the value of the entire conditional expression. If the value of *expr1* is zero, then the value of *expr3* is the value of the conditional.

The following example illustrates the conditional operator:

```
int i, j, k;

i = 1;
j = 2;
k = i > j ? i : j;          /* k is now 2 */
k = (i >= 0 ? i : 0) + j;   /* k is now 3 */
```

The conditional expression i > j ? i : j in the first assignment to k returns the value of either i or j, depending on which one is larger. Since i has the value 1 and j has the value 2, the i > j comparison fails, and the value of the conditional is 2, which is assigned to k. In the second assignment to k, the i >= 0 comparison succeeds; the conditional expression (i >= 0 ? i : 0) has the value 1, which is then added to j to produce 3. The parentheses are necessary, by the way; the precedence of the conditional operator is less than that of the other operators we've discussed so far, with the exception of the assignment operators.

Conditional expressions tend to make programs shorter but harder to understand, so it's probably best to avoid them. There are, however, a few places in which they're tempting; one is the return statement. Instead of writing

```
if (i > j)
  return i;
else
  return j;
```

many programmers would write

```
return i > j ? i : j;
```

Calls of `printf` can sometimes benefit from condition expressions. Instead of

```
if (i > j)
  printf("%d\n", i);
else
  printf("%d\n", j);
```

we could simply write

```
printf("%d\n", i > j ? i : j);
```

macro definitions ➤ 14.3   Conditional expressions are also common in certain kinds of macro definitions.

Boolean Values in C89

For many years, the C language lacked a proper Boolean type, and there is none defined in the C89 standard. This omission is a minor annoyance, since many programs need variables that can store either *false* or *true*. One way to work around this limitation of C89 is to declare an `int` variable and then assign it either 0 or 1:

```
int flag;

flag = 0;
...
flag = 1;
```

Although this scheme works, it doesn't contribute much to program readability. It's not obvious that `flag` is to be assigned only Boolean values and that 0 and 1 represent false and true.

To make programs more understandable, C89 programmers often define macros with names such as TRUE and FALSE:

```
#define TRUE 1
#define FALSE 0
```

Assignments to `flag` now have a more natural appearance:

```
flag = FALSE;
...
flag = TRUE;
```

To test whether `flag` is true, we can write

```
if (flag == TRUE) ...
```

or just

```
if (flag) ...
```

The latter form is better, not only because it's more concise, but also because it will still work correctly if `flag` has a value other than 0 or 1.

To test whether `flag` is false, we can write

```
if (flag == FALSE) ...
```

or

```
if (!flag) …
```

Carrying this idea one step further, we might even define a macro that can be used as a type:

```
#define BOOL int
```

BOOL can take the place of int when declaring Boolean variables:

```
BOOL flag;
```

It's now clear that flag isn't an ordinary integer variable, but instead represents a Boolean condition. (The compiler still treats flag as an int variable, of course.) In later chapters, we'll discover better ways to set up a Boolean type in C89 by using type definitions and enumerations.

type definitions ➤ 7.5
enumerations ➤ 16.5

C99   Boolean Values in C99

Q&A

The longstanding lack of a Boolean type has been remedied in C99, which provides the _Bool type. In this version of C, a Boolean variable can be declared by writing

```
_Bool flag;
```

unsigned integer types ➤ 7.1

_Bool is an integer type (more precisely, an *unsigned* integer type), so a _Bool variable is really just an integer variable in disguise. Unlike an ordinary integer variable, however, a _Bool variable can only be assigned 0 or 1. In general, attempting to store a nonzero value into a _Bool variable will cause the variable to be assigned 1:

```
flag = 5;   /* flag is assigned 1 */
```

It's legal (although not advisable) to perform arithmetic on _Bool variables; it's also legal to print a _Bool variable (either 0 or 1 will be displayed). And, of course, a _Bool variable can be tested in an if statement:

```
if (flag)   /* tests whether flag is 1 */
   …
```

<stdbool.h> header ➤ 21.5

In addition to defining the _Bool type, C99 also provides a new header, <stdbool.h>, that makes it easier to work with Boolean values. This header provides a macro, bool, that stands for _Bool. If <stdbool.h> is included, we can write

```
bool flag;   /* same as _Bool flag; */
```

The <stdbool.h> header also supplies macros named true and false, which stand for 1 and 0, respectively, making it possible to write

```
flag = false;
...
flag = true;
```

Because the `<stdbool.h>` header is so handy, I'll use it in subsequent programs whenever Boolean variables are needed.

5.3 The `switch` Statement

In everyday programming, we'll often need to compare an expression against a series of values to see which one it currently matches. We saw in Section 5.2 that a cascaded `if` statement can be used for this purpose. For example, the following cascaded `if` statement prints the English word that corresponds to a numerical grade:

```
if (grade == 4)
  printf("Excellent");
else if (grade == 3)
  printf("Good");
else if (grade == 2)
  printf("Average");
else if (grade == 1)
  printf("Poor");
else if (grade == 0)
  printf("Failing");
else
  printf("Illegal grade");
```

As an alternative to this kind of cascaded `if` statement, C provides the `switch` statement. The following `switch` is equivalent to our cascaded `if`:

```
switch (grade) {
  case 4:  printf("Excellent");
           break;
  case 3:  printf("Good");
           break;
  case 2:  printf("Average");
           break;
  case 1:  printf("Poor");
           break;
  case 0:  printf("Failing");
           break;
  default: printf("Illegal grade");
           break;
}
```

When this statement is executed, the value of the variable `grade` is tested against 4, 3, 2, 1, and 0. If it matches 4, for example, the message `Excellent` is printed, break statement ▶6.4 then the `break` statement transfers control to the statement following the `switch`. If the value of `grade` doesn't match any of the choices listed, the `default` case applies, and the message `Illegal grade` is printed.

A `switch` statement is often easier to read than a cascaded `if` statement. Moreover, `switch` statements are often faster than `if` statements, especially when there are more than a handful of cases.

Q&A

In its most common form, the `switch` statement has the form

`switch` statement

```
switch ( expression ) {
    case constant-expression : statements
    ...
    case constant-expression : statements
    default : statements
}
```

The `switch` statement is fairly complex; let's look at its components one by one:

- ■ ***Controlling expression.*** The word `switch` must be followed by an integer expression in parentheses. Characters are treated as integers in C and thus can be tested in `switch` statements. Floating-point numbers and strings don't qualify, however.

  characters ➤7.3

- ■ ***Case labels.*** Each case begins with a label of the form

  `case` *constant-expression* :

  A ***constant expression*** is much like an ordinary expression except that it can't contain variables or function calls. Thus, 5 is a constant expression, and 5 + 10 is a constant expression, but n + 10 isn't a constant expression (unless n is a macro that represents a constant). The constant expression in a case label must evaluate to an integer (characters are also acceptable).

- ■ ***Statements.*** After each case label comes any number of statements. No braces are required around the statements. (Enjoy it—this is one of the few places in C where braces aren't required.) The last statement in each group is normally `break`.

Duplicate case labels aren't allowed. The order of the cases doesn't matter; in particular, the `default` case doesn't need to come last.

Only one constant expression may follow the word `case`; however, several case labels may precede the same group of statements:

```
switch (grade) {
  case 4:
  case 3:
  case 2:
  case 1:  printf("Passing");
           break;
  case 0:  printf("Failing");
           break;
  default: printf("Illegal grade");
           break;
}
```

To save space, programmers sometimes put several case labels on the same line:

```
switch (grade) {
  case 4: case 3: case 2: case 1:
          printf("Passing");
          break;
  case 0:  printf("Failing");
          break;
  default: printf("Illegal grade");
          break;
}
```

Unfortunately, there's no way to write a case label that specifies a range of values, as there is in some programming languages.

A `switch` statement isn't required to have a `default` case. If `default` is missing and the value of the controlling expression doesn't match any of the case labels, control simply passes to the next statement after the `switch`.

The Role of the `break` Statement

Now, let's take a closer look at the mysterious `break` statement. As we've seen, executing a `break` statement causes the program to "break" out of the `switch` statement; execution continues at the next statement after the `switch`.

The reason that we need `break` has to do with the fact that the `switch` statement is really a form of "computed jump." When the controlling expression is evaluated, control jumps to the case label matching the value of the `switch` expression. A case label is nothing more than a marker indicating a position within the `switch`. When the last statement in the case has been executed, control "falls through" to the first statement in the following case; the case label for the next case is ignored. Without `break` (or some other jump statement), control will flow from one case into the next. Consider the following `switch` statement:

```
switch (grade) {
  case 4:  printf("Excellent");
  case 3:  printf("Good");
  case 2:  printf("Average");
  case 1:  printf("Poor");
  case 0:  printf("Failing");
  default: printf("Illegal grade");
}
```

If the value of `grade` is 3, the message printed is

```
GoodAveragePoorFailingIllegal grade
```

 Forgetting to use `break` is a common error. Although omitting `break` is sometimes done intentionally to allow several cases to share code, it's usually just an oversight.

Since deliberately falling through from one case into the next is rare, it's a good idea to point out any deliberate omission of `break`:

```
switch (grade) {
  case 4: case 3: case 2: case 1:
          num_passing++;
          /* FALL THROUGH */
  case 0:  total_grades++;
          break;
}
```

Without the comment, someone might later fix the "error" by adding an unwanted `break` statement.

Although the last case in a `switch` statement never needs a `break` statement, it's common practice to put one there anyway to guard against a "missing `break`" problem if cases should later be added.

PROGRAM   **Printing a Date in Legal Form**

Contracts and other legal documents are often dated in the following way:

Dated this _____ day of _____ , 20__ .

Let's write a program that displays dates in this form. We'll have the user enter the date in month/day/year form, then we'll display the date in "legal" form:

```
Enter date (mm/dd/yy): 7/19/14
Dated this 19th day of July, 2014.
```

We can get `printf` to do most of the formatting. However, we're left with two problems: how to add "th" (or "st" or "nd" or "rd") to the day, and how to print the month as a word instead of a number. Fortunately, the `switch` statement is ideal for both situations; we'll have one `switch` print the day suffix and another print the month name.

date.c
```
/* Prints a date in legal form */

#include <stdio.h>

int main(void)
{
  int month, day, year;

  printf("Enter date (mm/dd/yy): ");
  scanf("%d /%d /%d", &month, &day, &year);

  printf("Dated this %d", day);
  switch (day) {
    case 1: case 21: case 31:
      printf("st"); break;
    case 2: case 22:
      printf("nd"); break;
```

```
      case 3: case 23:
        printf("rd"); break;
      default: printf("th"); break;
  }
  printf(" day of ");

  switch (month) {
    case 1:  printf("January");   break;
    case 2:  printf("February");  break;
    case 3:  printf("March");     break;
    case 4:  printf("April");     break;
    case 5:  printf("May");       break;
    case 6:  printf("June");      break;
    case 7:  printf("July");      break;
    case 8:  printf("August");    break;
    case 9:  printf("September"); break;
    case 10: printf("October");   break;
    case 11: printf("November");  break;
    case 12: printf("December");  break;
  }

  printf(", 20%.2d.\n", year);
  return 0;
}
```

Note the use of `%.2d` to display the last two digits of the year. If we had used `%d` instead, single-digit years would be displayed incorrectly (2005 would be printed as `205`).

Q & A

Q: My compiler doesn't give a warning when I use = instead of ==. Is there some way to force the compiler to notice the problem? [p. 77]

A: Here's a trick that some programmers use: instead of writing

```
if (i == 0) …
```

they habitually write

```
if (0 == i) …
```

Now suppose that the `==` operator is accidentally written as `=`:

```
if (0 = i) …
```

The compiler will produce an error message, since it's not possible to assign a value to 0. I don't use this trick, because I think it makes programs look unnatural. Also, it can be used only when one of the operands in the test condition isn't an lvalue.

Fortunately, many compilers are capable of checking for suspect uses of the `=` operator in `if` conditions. The GCC compiler, for example, will perform this check if the -Wparentheses option is used or if -Wall (all warnings) is selected. GCC allows the programmer to suppress the warning in a particular case by enclosing the if condition in a second set of parentheses:

```
if ((i = j)) …
```

Q: **C books seem to use several different styles of indentation and brace placement for compound statements. Which style is best?**

A: According to *The New Hacker's Dictionary* (Cambridge, Mass.: MIT Press, 1996), there are four common styles of indentation and brace placement:

- The *K&R style*, used in Kernighan and Ritchie's *The C Programming Language*, is the one I've chosen for the programs in this book. In the K&R style, the left brace appears at the end of a line:

```
if (line_num == MAX_LINES) {
  line_num = 0;
  page_num++;
}
```

  The K&R style keeps programs compact by not putting the left brace on a line by itself. A disadvantage: the left brace can be hard to find. (I don't consider this a problem, since the indentation of the inner statements makes it clear where the left brace should be.) The K&R style is the one most often used in Java, by the way.

- The *Allman style*, named after Eric Allman (the author of sendmail and other UNIX utilities), puts the left brace on a separate line:

```
if (line_num == MAX_LINES)
{
  line_num = 0;
  page_num++;
}
```

  This style makes it easy to check that braces come in matching pairs.

- The *Whitesmiths style*, popularized by the Whitesmiths C compiler, dictates that braces be indented:

```
if (line_num == MAX_LINES)
  {
  line_num = 0;
  page_num++;
  }
```

- The *GNU style*, used in software developed by the GNU Project, indents the braces, then further indents the inner statements:

```
if (line_num == MAX_LINES)
  {
    line_num = 0;
    page_num++;
  }
```

Which style you use is mainly a matter of taste; there's no proof that one style is clearly better than the others. In any event, choosing the right style is less important than applying it consistently.

Q: **If i is an int variable and f is a float variable, what is the type of the conditional expression (i > 0 ? i : f)?**

A: When int and float values are mixed in a conditional expression, as they are here, the expression has type float. If i > 0 is true, the value of the expression will be the value of i after conversion to float type.

Q: **Why doesn't C99 have a better name for its Boolean type? [p. 85]**

A: _Bool isn't a very elegant name, is it? More common names, such as bool or boolean, weren't chosen because existing C programs might already define these names, causing older code not to compile.

C99

Q: **OK, so why wouldn't the name _Bool break older programs as well?**

A: The C89 standard specifies that names beginning with an underscore followed by an uppercase letter are reserved for future use and should not be used by programmers.

*Q: **The template given for the switch statement described it as the "most common form." Are there other forms? [p. 87]**

A: The switch statement is a bit more general than described in this chapter, although the description given here is general enough for virtually all programs. For example, a switch statement can contain labels that aren't preceded by the word case, which leads to an amusing (?) trap. Suppose that we accidentally misspell the word default:

labels ►6.4

```
switch (…) {
    …
  defualt: …
}
```

The compiler may not detect the error, since it assumes that defualt is an ordinary label.

Q: **I've seen several methods of indenting the switch statement. Which way is best?**

A: There are at least two common methods. One is to put the statements in each case *after* the case label:

```
switch (coin) {
  case 1:  printf("Cent");
           break;
  case 5:  printf("Nickel");
           break;
  case 10: printf("Dime");
           break;
```

```
      case 25: printf("Quarter");
               break;
}
```

If each case consists of a single action (a call of `printf`, in this example), the `break` statement could even go on the same line as the action:

```
switch (coin) {
  case 1:  printf("Cent"); break;
  case 5:  printf("Nickel"); break;
  case 10: printf("Dime"); break;
  case 25: printf("Quarter"); break;
}
```

The other method is to put the statements *under* the case label, indenting the statements to make the case label stand out:

```
switch (coin) {
  case 1:
    printf("Cent");
    break;
  case 5:
    printf("Nickel");
    break;
  case 10:
    printf("Dime");
    break;
  case 25:
    printf("Quarter");
    break;
}
```

In one variation of this scheme, each case label is aligned under the word `switch`.

The first method is fine when the statements in each case are short and there are relatively few of them. The second method is better for large `switch` statements in which the statements in each case are complex and/or numerous.

Exercises

Section 5.1   1.   The following program fragments illustrate the relational and equality operators. Show the output produced by each, assuming that `i`, `j`, and `k` are `int` variables.

(a) `i = 2; j = 3;`
    `k = i * j == 6;`
    `printf("%d", k);`
(b) `i = 5; j = 10; k = 1;`
    `printf("%d", k > i < j);`
(c) `i = 3; j = 2; k = 1;`
    `printf("%d", i < j == j < k);`
(d) `i = 3; j = 4; k = 5;`
    `printf("%d", i % j + i < k);`

Ⓦ 2.   The following program fragments illustrate the logical operators. Show the output produced by each, assuming that i, j, and k are int variables.

(a) `i = 10; j = 5;`
    `printf("%d", !i < j);`

(b) `i = 2; j = 1;`
    `printf("%d", !!i + !j);`

(c) `i = 5; j = 0; k = -5;`
    `printf("%d", i && j || k);`

(d) `i = 1; j = 2; k = 3;`
    `printf("%d", i < j || k);`

*3. The following program fragments illustrate the short-circuit behavior of logical expressions. Show the output produced by each, assuming that i, j, and k are int variables.

(a) `i = 3; j = 4; k = 5;`
    `printf("%d ", i < j || ++j < k);`
    `printf("%d %d %d", i, j, k);`

(b) `i = 7; j = 8; k = 9;`
    `printf("%d ", i - 7 && j++ < k);`
    `printf("%d %d %d", i, j, k);`

(c) `i = 7; j = 8; k = 9;`
    `printf("%d ", (i = j) || (j = k));`
    `printf("%d %d %d", i, j, k);`

(d) `i = 1; j = 1; k = 1;`
    `printf("%d ", ++i || ++j && ++k);`
    `printf("%d %d %d", i, j, k);`

Ⓦ *4. Write a single expression whose value is either –1, 0, or +1, depending on whether i is less than, equal to, or greater than j, respectively.

Section 5.2   *5. Is the following if statement legal?

```
if (n >= 1 <= 10)
   printf("n is between 1 and 10\n");
```

If so, what does it do when n is equal to 0?

Ⓦ *6. Is the following if statement legal?

```
if (n == 1-10)
   printf("n is between 1 and 10\n");
```

If so, what does it do when n is equal to 5?

7. What does the following statement print if i has the value 17? What does it print if i has the value –17?

```
printf("%d\n", i >= 0 ? i : -i);
```

8. The following if statement is unnecessarily complicated. Simplify it as much as possible. (*Hint:* The entire statement can be replaced by a single assignment.)

```
if (age >= 13)
  if (age <= 19)
    teenager = true;
  else
    teenager = false;
else if (age < 13)
  teenager = false;
```

9. Are the following if statements equivalent? If not, why not?

```
if (score >= 90)              if (score < 60)
  printf("A");                   printf("F");
else if (score >= 80)         else if (score < 70)
  printf("B");                   printf("D");
else if (score >= 70)         else if (score < 80)
  printf("C");                   printf("C");
else if (score >= 60)         else if (score < 90)
  printf("D");                   printf("B");
else                          else
  printf("F");                   printf("A");
```

Section 5.3   Ⓦ*10. What output does the following program fragment produce? (Assume that i is an integer variable.)

```
i = 1;
switch (i % 3) {
  case 0: printf("zero");
  case 1: printf("one");
  case 2: printf("two");
}
```

11. The following table shows telephone area codes in the state of Georgia along with the largest city in each area:

Area code	Major city
229	Albany
404	Atlanta
470	Atlanta
478	Macon
678	Atlanta
706	Columbus
762	Columbus
770	Atlanta
912	Savannah

Write a switch statement whose controlling expression is the variable area_code. If the value of area_code is in the table, the switch statement will print the corresponding city name. Otherwise, the switch statement will display the message "Area code not recognized". Use the techniques discussed in Section 5.3 to make the switch statement as simple as possible.

Programming Projects

1. Write a program that calculates how many digits a number contains:

```
Enter a number: 374
The number 374 has 3 digits
```

You may assume that the number has no more than four digits. *Hint:* Use if statements to test the number. For example, if the number is between 0 and 9, it has one digit. If the number is between 10 and 99, it has two digits.

Ⓦ 2. Write a program that asks the user for a 24-hour time, then displays the time in 12-hour form:

```
Enter a 24-hour time: 21:11
Equivalent 12-hour time: 9:11 PM
```

Be careful not to display 12:00 as 0:00.

3. Modify the broker.c program of Section 5.2 by making both of the following changes:

(a) Ask the user to enter the number of shares and the price per share, instead of the value of the trade.

(b) Add statements that compute the commission charged by a rival broker ($33 plus 3¢ per share for fewer than 2000 shares; $33 plus 2¢ per share for 2000 shares or more). Display the rival's commission as well as the commission charged by the original broker.

Ⓦ 4. Here's a simplified version of the Beaufort scale, which is used to estimate wind force:

Speed (knots)	*Description*
Less than 1	Calm
1–3	Light air
4–27	Breeze
28–47	Gale
48–63	Storm
Above 63	Hurricane

Write a program that asks the user to enter a wind speed (in knots), then displays the corresponding description.

5. In one state, single residents are subject to the following income tax:

Income	*Amount of tax*	
Not over $750	1% of income	
$750–$2,250	$7.50	plus 2% of amount over $750
$2,250–$3,750	$37.50	plus 3% of amount over $2,250
$3,750–$5,250	$82.50	plus 4% of amount over $3,750
$5,250–$7,000	$142.50	plus 5% of amount over $5,250
Over $7,000	$230.00	plus 6% of amount over $7,000

Write a program that asks the user to enter the amount of taxable income, then displays the tax due.

Ⓦ 6. Modify the upc.c program of Section 4.1 so that it checks whether a UPC is valid. After the user enters a UPC, the program will display either VALID or NOT VALID.

7. Write a program that finds the largest and smallest of four integers entered by the user:

```
Enter four integers: 21 43 10 35
Largest: 43
Smallest: 10
```

Use as few if statements as possible. *Hint:* Four if statements are sufficient.

8. The following table shows the daily flights from one city to another:

Departure time	*Arrival time*
8:00 a.m.	10:16 a.m.
9:43 a.m.	11:52 a.m.
11:19 a.m.	1:31 p.m.
12:47 p.m.	3:00 p.m.

2:00 p.m.	4:08 p.m.
3:45 p.m.	5:55 p.m.
7:00 p.m.	9:20 p.m.
9:45 p.m.	11:58 p.m.

Write a program that asks user to enter a time (expressed in hours and minutes, using the 24-hour clock). The program then displays the departure and arrival times for the flight whose departure time is closest to that entered by the user:

```
Enter a 24-hour time: 13:15
Closest departure time is 12:47 p.m., arriving at 3:00 p.m.
```

Hint: Convert the input into a time expressed in minutes since midnight, and compare it to the departure times, also expressed in minutes since midnight. For example, 13:15 is 13 × 60 + 15 = 795 minutes since midnight, which is closer to 12:47 p.m. (767 minutes since midnight) than to any of the other departure times.

9. Write a program that prompts the user to enter two dates and then indicates which date comes earlier on the calendar:

```
Enter first date (mm/dd/yy): 3/6/08
Enter second date (mm/dd/yy): 5/17/07
5/17/07 is earlier than 3/6/08
```

Ⓦ 10. Using the `switch` statement, write a program that converts a numerical grade into a letter grade:

```
Enter numerical grade: 84
Letter grade: B
```

Use the following grading scale: A = 90–100, B = 80–89, C = 70–79, D = 60–69, F = 0–59. Print an error message if the grade is larger than 100 or less than 0. *Hint:* Break the grade into two digits, then use a `switch` statement to test the ten's digit.

11. Write a program that asks the user for a two-digit number, then prints the English word for the number:

```
Enter a two-digit number: 45
You entered the number forty-five.
```

Hint: Break the number into two digits. Use one `switch` statement to print the word for the first digit ("twenty," "thirty," and so forth). Use a second `switch` statement to print the word for the second digit. Don't forget that the numbers between 11 and 19 require special treatment.

6 Loops

A program without a loop and a structured variable isn't worth writing.

Chapter 5 covered C's selection statements, `if` and `switch`. This chapter introduces C's iteration statements, which allow us to set up loops.

A *loop* is a statement whose job is to repeatedly execute some other statement (the *loop body*). In C, every loop has a *controlling expression*. Each time the loop body is executed (an *iteration* of the loop), the controlling expression is evaluated; if the expression is true—has a value that's not zero—the loop continues to execute.

C provides three iteration statements: `while`, `do`, and `for`, which are covered in Sections 6.1, 6.2, and 6.3, respectively. The `while` statement is used for loops whose controlling expression is tested *before* the loop body is executed. The `do` statement is used if the expression is tested *after* the loop body is executed. The `for` statement is convenient for loops that increment or decrement a counting variable. Section 6.3 also introduces the comma operator, which is used primarily in `for` statements.

The last two sections of this chapter are devoted to C features that are used in conjunction with loops. Section 6.4 describes the `break`, `continue`, and `goto` statements. `break` jumps out of a loop and transfers control to the next statement after the loop, `continue` skips the rest of a loop iteration, and `goto` jumps to any statement within a function. Section 6.5 covers the null statement, which can be used to create loops with empty bodies.

6.1 The `while` Statement

Of all the ways to set up loops in C, the `while` statement is the simplest and most fundamental. The `while` statement has the form

while statement

while (*expression*) *statement*

The expression inside the parentheses is the controlling expression; the statement after the parentheses is the loop body. Here's an example:

```
while (i < n)    /* controlling expression */
  i = i * 2;     /* loop body */
```

Note that the parentheses are mandatory and that nothing goes between the right parenthesis and the loop body. (Some languages require the word do.)

When a while statement is executed, the controlling expression is evaluated first. If its value is nonzero (true), the loop body is executed and the expression is tested again. The process continues in this fashion—first testing the controlling expression, then executing the loop body—until the controlling expression eventually has the value zero.

The following example uses a while statement to compute the smallest power of 2 that is greater than or equal to a number n:

```
i = 1;
while (i < n)
  i = i * 2;
```

Suppose that n has the value 10. The following trace shows what happens when the while statement is executed:

```
i = 1;       i is now 1.
Is i < n?    Yes; continue.
i = i * 2;   i is now 2.
Is i < n?    Yes; continue.
i = i * 2;   i is now 4.
Is i < n?    Yes; continue.
i = i * 2;   i is now 8.
Is i < n?    Yes; continue.
i = i * 2;   i is now 16.
Is i < n?    No; exit from loop.
```

Notice how the loop keeps going as long as the controlling expression (i < n) is true. When the expression is false, the loop terminates, and i is greater than or equal to n, as desired.

Although the loop body must be a single statement, that's merely a technicality. If we want more than one statement, we can just use braces to create a single compound statement:

compound statements ➤5.2

```
while (i > 0) {
  printf("T minus %d and counting\n", i);
  i--;
}
```

Some programmers always use braces, even when they're not strictly necessary:

```
while (i < n) {    /* braces allowed, but not required */
  i = i * 2;
}
```

As a second example, let's trace the execution of the following statements, which display a series of "countdown" messages:

```
i = 10;
while (i > 0) {
  printf("T minus %d and counting\n", i);
  i--;
}
```

Before the `while` statement is executed, the variable `i` is assigned the value 10. Since 10 is greater than 0, the loop body is executed, causing the message T minus 10 and counting to be printed and `i` to be decremented. The condition `i > 0` is then tested again. Since 9 is greater than 0, the loop body is executed once more. This process continues until the message T minus 1 and counting is printed and `i` becomes 0. The test `i > 0` then fails, causing the loop to terminate.

The countdown example leads us to make several observations about the `while` statement:

- The controlling expression is false when a `while` loop terminates. Thus, when a loop controlled by the expression `i > 0` terminates, `i` must be less than or equal to 0. (Otherwise, we'd still be executing the loop!)

- The body of a `while` loop may not be executed at all. Since the controlling expression is tested *before* the loop body is executed, it's possible that the body isn't executed even once. If `i` has a negative or zero value when the countdown loop is first entered, the loop will do nothing.

- A `while` statement can often be written in a variety of ways. For example, we could make the countdown loop more concise by decrementing `i` inside the call of `printf`:

Q&A
```
while (i > 0)
  printf("T minus %d and counting\n", i--);
```

Infinite Loops

A `while` statement won't terminate if the controlling expression always has a nonzero value. In fact, C programmers sometimes deliberately create an ***infinite loop*** by using a nonzero constant as the controlling expression:

idiom   `while (1) ...`

A `while` statement of this form will execute forever unless its body contains a statement that transfers control out of the loop (`break`, `goto`, `return`) or calls a function that causes the program to terminate.

PROGRAM   **Printing a Table of Squares**

Let's write a program that prints a table of squares. The program will first prompt the user to enter a number *n*. It will then print *n* lines of output, with each line containing a number between 1 and *n* together with its square:

```
This program prints a table of squares.
Enter number of entries in table: 5
         1         1
         2         4
         3         9
         4        16
         5        25
```

Let's have the program store the desired number of squares in a variable named n. We'll need a loop that repeatedly prints a number i and its square, starting with i equal to 1. The loop will repeat as long as i is less than or equal to n. We'll have to make sure to add 1 to i each time through the loop.

We'll write the loop as a while statement. (Frankly, we haven't got much choice, since the while statement is the only kind of loop we've covered so far.) Here's the finished program:

square.c
```c
/* Prints a table of squares using a while statement */

#include <stdio.h>

int main(void)
{
  int i, n;

  printf("This program prints a table of squares.\n");
  printf("Enter number of entries in table: ");
  scanf("%d", &n);

  i = 1;
  while (i <= n) {
    printf("%10d%10d\n", i, i * i);
    i++;
  }

  return 0;
}
```

Note how square.c displays numbers in neatly aligned columns. The trick is to use a conversion specification like %10d instead of just %d, taking advantage of the fact that printf right-justifies numbers when a field width is specified.

PROGRAM   **Summing a Series of Numbers**

As a second example of the while statement, let's write a program that sums a series of integers entered by the user. Here's what the user will see:

```
This program sums a series of integers.
Enter integers (0 to terminate): 8 23 71 5 0
The sum is: 107
```

Clearly we'll need a loop that uses `scanf` to read a number and then adds the number to a running total.

Letting n represent the number just read and `sum` the total of all numbers previously read, we end up with the following program:

sum.c

```c
/* Sums a series of numbers */

#include <stdio.h>

int main(void)
{
  int n, sum = 0;

  printf("This program sums a series of integers.\n");
  printf("Enter integers (0 to terminate): ");

  scanf("%d", &n);
  while (n != 0) {
    sum += n;
    scanf("%d", &n);
  }
  printf("The sum is: %d\n", sum);

  return 0;
}
```

Notice that the condition n != 0 is tested just after a number is read, allowing the loop to terminate as soon as possible. Also note that there are two identical calls of `scanf`, which is often hard to avoid when using `while` loops.

6.2 The do Statement

The do statement is closely related to the `while` statement; in fact, the do statement is essentially just a `while` statement whose controlling expression is tested *after* each execution of the loop body. The do statement has the form

do statement

> do *statement* while (*expression*) ;

As with the `while` statement, the body of a do statement must be one statement (possibly compound, of course) and the controlling expression must be enclosed within parentheses.

When a do statement is executed, the loop body is executed first, then the controlling expression is evaluated. If the value of the expression is nonzero, the loop body is executed again and then the expression is evaluated once more. Execution of the do statement terminates when the controlling expression has the value 0 *after* the loop body has been executed.

Let's rewrite the countdown example of Section 6.1, using a do statement this time:

```
i = 10;
do {
  printf("T minus %d and counting\n", i);
  --i;
} while (i > 0);
```

When the do statement is executed, the loop body is first executed, causing the message T minus 10 and counting to be printed and i to be decremented. The condition i > 0 is now tested. Since 9 is greater than 0, the loop body is executed a second time. This process continues until the message T minus 1 and counting is printed and i becomes 0. The test i > 0 now fails, causing the loop to terminate. As this example shows, the do statement is often indistinguishable from the while statement. The difference between the two is that the body of a do statement is always executed at least once; the body of a while statement is skipped entirely if the controlling expression is 0 initially.

Incidentally, it's a good idea to use braces in *all* do statements, whether or not they're needed, because a do statement without braces can easily be mistaken for a while statement:

```
do
  printf("T minus %d and counting\n", i--);
while (i > 0);
```

A careless reader might think that the word while was the beginning of a while statement.

PROGRAM   **Calculating the Number of Digits in an Integer**

Although the while statement appears in C programs much more often than the do statement, the latter is handy for loops that must execute at least once. To illustrate this point, let's write a program that calculates the number of digits in an integer entered by the user:

```
Enter a nonnegative integer: 60
The number has 2 digit(s).
```

Our strategy will be to divide the user's input by 10 repeatedly until it becomes 0; the number of divisions performed is the number of digits. Clearly we'll need some kind of loop, since we don't know how many divisions it will take to reach 0. But should we use a while statement or a do statement? The do statement turns out to be more attractive, because every integer—even 0—has at least *one* digit. Here's the program:

numdigits.c   `/* Calculates the number of digits in an integer */`

```
#include <stdio.h>

int main(void)
{
  int digits = 0, n;

  printf("Enter a nonnegative integer: ");
  scanf("%d", &n);

  do {
    n /= 10;
    digits++;
  } while (n > 0);

  printf("The number has %d digit(s).\n", digits);

  return 0;
}
```

To see why the do statement is the right choice, let's see what would happen if we were to replace the do loop by a similar while loop:

```
while (n > 0) {
  n /= 10;
  digits++;
}
```

If n is 0 initially, this loop won't execute at all, and the program would print

```
The number has 0 digit(s).
```

6.3 The `for` Statement

We now come to the last of C's loops: the for statement. Don't be discouraged by the for statement's apparent complexity; it's actually the best way to write many loops. The for statement is ideal for loops that have a "counting" variable, but it's versatile enough to be used for other kinds of loops as well.

The for statement has the form

for statement

> for (*expr1* ; *expr2* ; *expr3*) *statement*

where *expr1*, *expr2*, and *expr3* are expressions. Here's an example:

```
for (i = 10; i > 0; i--)
  printf("T minus %d and counting\n", i);
```

When this for statement is executed, the variable i is initialized to 10, then i is tested to see if it's greater than 0. Since it is, the message T minus 10 and counting is printed, then i is decremented. The condition i > 0 is then tested again. The loop body will be executed 10 times in all, with i varying from 10 down to 1.

The for statement is closely related to the while statement. In fact, except in a few rare cases, a for loop can always be replaced by an equivalent while loop:

Q&A

```
expr1;
while ( expr2 ) {
  statement
  expr3;
}
```

As this pattern shows, *expr1* is an initialization step that's performed only once, before the loop begins to execute, *expr2* controls loop termination (the loop continues executing as long as the value of *expr2* is nonzero), and *expr3* is an operation to be performed at the end of each loop iteration. Applying this pattern to our previous for loop example, we arrive at the following:

```
i = 10;
while (i > 0) {
  printf("T minus %d and counting\n", i);
  i--;
}
```

Studying the equivalent while statement can help us understand the fine points of a for statement. For example, suppose that we replace i-- by --i in our for loop example:

```
for (i = 10; i > 0; --i)
  printf("T minus %d and counting\n", i);
```

How does this change affect the loop? Looking at the equivalent while loop, we see that it has no effect:

```
i = 10;
while (i > 0) {
  printf("T minus %d and counting\n", i);
  --i;
}
```

Since the first and third expressions in a for statement are executed as statements, their values are irrelevant—they're useful only for their side effects. Consequently, these two expressions are usually assignments or increment/decrement expressions.

for Statement Idioms

The for statement is usually the best choice for loops that "count up" (increment a variable) or "count down" (decrement a variable). A for statement that counts up or down a total of n times will usually have one of the following forms:

■ *Counting up from* 0 *to* n–1*:*

idiom
```
for (i = 0; i < n; i++) …
```

■ *Counting up from* 1 *to* n*:*

idiom
```
for (i = 1; i <= n; i++) …
```

■ *Counting down from* n–1 *to* 0*:*

idiom
```
for (i = n - 1; i >= 0; i--) …
```

■ *Counting down from* n *to* 1*:*

idiom
```
for (i = n; i > 0; i--) …
```

Imitating these patterns will help you avoid some of the following errors, which beginning C programmers often make:

■ Using < instead of > (or vice versa) in the controlling expression. Notice that "counting up" loops use the < or <= operator, while "counting down" loops rely on > or >=.

■ Using == in the controlling expression instead of <, <=, >, or >=. A controlling expression needs to be true at the beginning of the loop, then later become false so that the loop can terminate. A test such as i == n doesn't make much sense, because it won't be true initially.

■ "Off-by-one" errors such as writing the controlling expression as i <= n instead of i < n.

Omitting Expressions in a for Statement

The for statement is even more flexible than we've seen so far. Some for loops may not need all three of the expressions that normally control the loop, so C allows us to omit any or all of the expressions.

If the *first* expression is omitted, no initialization is performed before the loop is executed:

```
i = 10;
for (; i > 0; --i)
  printf("T minus %d and counting\n", i);
```

In this example, i has been initialized by a separate assignment, so we've omitted the first expression in the for statement. (Notice that the semicolon between the first and second expressions remains. The two semicolons must always be present, even when we've omitted some of the expressions.)

If we omit the *third* expression in a for statement, the loop body is responsible for ensuring that the value of the second expression eventually becomes false. Our for statement example could be written like this:

```
for (i = 10; i > 0;)
  printf("T minus %d and counting\n", i--);
```

To compensate for omitting the third expression, we've arranged for i to be decremented inside the loop body.

When the *first* and *third* expressions are both omitted, the resulting loop is nothing more than a while statement in disguise. For example, the loop

```
for (; i > 0;)
  printf("T minus %d and counting\n", i--);
```

is the same as

```
while (i > 0)
  printf("T minus %d and counting\n", i--);
```

The while version is clearer and therefore preferable.

If the *second* expression is missing, it defaults to a true value, so the for statement doesn't terminate (unless stopped in some other fashion). For example, some programmers use the following for statement to establish an infinite loop:

Q&A

idiom   for (;;) …

C99   **for Statements in C99**

In C99, the first expression in a for statement can be replaced by a declaration. This feature allows the programmer to declare a variable for use by the loop:

```
for (int i = 0; i < n; i++)
  …
```

The variable i need not have been declared prior to this statement. (In fact, if a declaration of i already exists, this statement creates a *new* version of i that will be used solely within the loop.)

A variable declared by a for statement can't be accessed outside the body of the loop (we say that it's not *visible* outside the loop):

```
for (int i = 0; i < n; i++) {
  …
  printf("%d", i);   /* legal; i is visible inside loop */
  …
}
printf("%d", i);     /*** WRONG ***/
```

Having a for statement declare its own control variable is usually a good idea: it's convenient and it can make programs easier to understand. However, if the program needs to access the variable after loop termination, it's necessary to use the older form of the for statement.

Incidentally, a for statement may declare more than one variable, provided that all variables have the same type:

```
for (int i = 0, j = 0; i < n; i++)
  …
```

The Comma Operator

On occasion, we might like to write a for statement with two (or more) initialization expressions or one that increments several variables each time through the loop. We can do this by using a ***comma expression*** as the first or third expression in the for statement.

A comma expression has the form

comma expression

$$expr1 \ , \ expr2$$

where *expr1* and *expr2* are any two expressions. A comma expression is evaluated in two steps: First, *expr1* is evaluated and its value discarded. Second, *expr2* is evaluated; its value is the value of the entire expression. Evaluating *expr1* should always have a side effect; if it doesn't, then *expr1* serves no purpose.

For example, suppose that i and j have the values 1 and 5, respectively. When the comma expression ++i, i + j is evaluated, i is first incremented, then i + j is evaluated, so the value of the expression is 7. (And, of course, i now has the value 2.) The precedence of the comma operator is less than that of all other operators, by the way, so there's no need to put parentheses around ++i and i + j.

Occasionally, we'll need to chain together a series of comma expressions, just as we sometimes chain assignments together. The comma operator is left associative, so the compiler interprets

```
i = 1, j = 2, k = i + j
```

as

```
((i = 1), (j = 2)), (k = (i + j))
```

Since the left operand in a comma expression is evaluated before the right operand, the assignments i = 1, j = 2, and k = i + j will be performed from left to right.

The comma operator is provided for situations where C requires a single expression, but we'd like to have two or more expressions. In other words, the comma operator allows us to "glue" two expressions together to form a single expression. (Note the similarity to the compound statement, which allows us to treat a group of statements as a single statement.)

The need to glue expressions together doesn't arise that often. Certain macro definitions can benefit from the comma operator, as we'll see in a later chapter. The for statement is the only other place where the comma operator is likely to be found. For example, suppose that we want to initialize two variables when entering a for statement. Instead of writing

macro definitions ➤ 14.3

```
sum = 0;
for (i = 1; i <= N; i++)
  sum += i;
```

we can write

```
for (sum = 0, i = 1; i <= N; i++)
  sum += i;
```

The expression sum = 0, i = 1 first assigns 0 to sum, then assigns 1 to i. With additional commas, the for statement could initialize more than two variables.

PROGRAM   **Printing a Table of Squares (Revisited)**

The square.c program (Section 6.1) can be improved by converting its while loop to a for loop:

square2.c

```
/* Prints a table of squares using a for statement */

#include <stdio.h>

int main(void)
{
  int i, n;

  printf("This program prints a table of squares.\n");
  printf("Enter number of entries in table: ");
  scanf("%d", &n);

  for (i = 1; i <= n; i++)
    printf("%10d%10d\n", i, i * i);

  return 0;
}
```

We can use this program to illustrate an important point about the for statement: C places no restrictions on the three expressions that control its behavior. Although these expressions usually initialize, test, and update the same variable, there's no requirement that they be related in any way. Consider the following version of the same program:

square3.c

```
/* Prints a table of squares using an odd method */

#include <stdio.h>

int main(void)
{
  int i, n, odd, square;

  printf("This program prints a table of squares.\n");
  printf("Enter number of entries in table: ");
  scanf("%d", &n);

  i = 1;
  odd = 3;
  for (square = 1; i <= n; odd += 2) {
    printf("%10d%10d\n", i, square);
    ++i;
```

```
    square += odd;
  }

  return 0;
}
```

The `for` statement in this program initializes one variable (`square`), tests another (`i`), and increments a third (`odd`). `i` is the number to be squared, `square` is the square of `i`, and `odd` is the odd number that must be added to the current square to get the next square (allowing the program to compute consecutive squares without performing any multiplications).

linked lists ➤ *17.5* The tremendous flexibility of the `for` statement can sometimes be useful; we'll find it to be a great help when working with linked lists. The `for` statement can easily be misused, though, so don't go overboard. The `for` loop in `square3.c` would be a lot clearer if we rearranged its pieces so that the loop is clearly controlled by `i`.

6.4 Exiting from a Loop

We've seen how to write loops that have an exit point before the loop body (using `while` and `for` statements) or after it (using `do` statements). Occasionally, however, we'll need a loop with an exit point in the middle. We may even want a loop to have more than one exit point. The `break` statement makes it possible to write either kind of loop.

After we've examined the `break` statement, we'll look at a couple of related statements: `continue` and `goto`. The `continue` statement makes it possible to skip part of a loop iteration without jumping out of the loop. The `goto` statement allows a program to jump from one statement to another. Thanks to the availability of statements such as `break` and `continue`, the `goto` statement is rarely used.

The `break` Statement

We've already discussed how a `break` statement can transfer control out of a `switch` statement. The `break` statement can also be used to jump out of a `while`, `do`, or `for` loop.

Suppose that we're writing a program that checks whether a number `n` is prime. Our plan is to write a `for` statement that divides `n` by the numbers between 2 and `n` − 1. We should break out of the loop as soon as any divisor is found; there's no need to try the remaining possibilities. After the loop has terminated, we can use an `if` statement to determine whether termination was premature (hence `n` isn't prime) or normal (`n` is prime):

```
for (d = 2; d < n; d++)
  if (n % d == 0)
    break;
```

```
if (d < n)
  printf("%d is divisible by %d\n", n, d);
else
  printf("%d is prime\n", n);
```

The break statement is particularly useful for writing loops in which the exit point is in the middle of the body rather than at the beginning or end. Loops that read user input, terminating when a particular value is entered, often fall into this category:

```
for (;;) {
  printf("Enter a number (enter 0 to stop): ");
  scanf("%d", &n);
  if (n == 0)
    break;
  printf("%d cubed is %d\n", n, n * n * n);
}
```

A break statement transfers control out of the *innermost* enclosing while, do, for, or switch statement. Thus, when these statements are nested, the break statement can escape only one level of nesting. Consider the case of a switch statement nested inside a while statement:

```
while (…) {
  switch (…) {
    …
    break;
    …
  }
}
```

The break statement transfers control out of the switch statement, but not out of the while loop. I'll return to this point later.

The continue Statement

The continue statement doesn't really belong here, because it doesn't exit from a loop. It's similar to break, though, so its inclusion in this section isn't completely arbitrary. break transfers control just *past* the end of a loop, while continue transfers control to a point just *before* the end of the loop body. With break, control leaves the loop; with continue, control remains inside the loop. There's another difference between break and continue: break can be used in switch statements and loops (while, do, and for), whereas continue is limited to loops.

The following example, which reads a series of numbers and computes their sum, illustrates a simple use of continue. The loop terminates when 10 nonzero numbers have been read. Whenever the number 0 is read, the continue statement is executed, skipping the rest of the loop body (the statements sum += i; and n++;) but remaining inside the loop.

```
n = 0;
sum = 0;
while (n < 10) {
  scanf("%d", &i);
  if (i == 0)
    continue;
  sum += i;
  n++;
  /* continue jumps to here */
}
```

If `continue` were not available, we could have written the example as follows:

```
n = 0;
sum = 0;
while (n < 10) {
  scanf("%d", &i);
  if (i != 0) {
    sum += i;
    n++;
  }
}
```

The `goto` Statement

`break` and `continue` are jump statements that transfer control from one point in the program to another. Both are restricted: the target of a `break` is a point just *beyond* the end of the enclosing loop, while the target of a `continue` is a point just *before* the end of the loop. The `goto` statement, on the other hand, is capable of jumping to *any* statement in a function, provided that the statement has a *label*. (C99 places an additional restriction on the `goto` statement: it can't be used to bypass the declaration of a variable-length array.)

variable-length arrays ➤8.3

A label is just an identifier placed at the beginning of a statement:

labeled statement

> *identifier* : *statement*

A statement may have more than one label. The `goto` statement itself has the form

goto statement

> `goto` *identifier* `;`

Executing the statement `goto L;` transfers control to the statement that follows the label *L*, which must be in the same function as the `goto` statement itself.

If C didn't have a `break` statement, here's how we might use a `goto` statement to exit prematurely from a loop:

```
for (d = 2; d < n; d++)
  if (n % d == 0)
    goto done;
```

```
done:
if (d < n)
  printf("%d is divisible by %d\n", n, d);
else
  printf("%d is prime\n", n);
```

Q&A

exit function ➤9.5

The `goto` statement, a staple of older programming languages, is rarely needed in everyday C programming. The `break`, `continue`, and `return` statements—which are essentially restricted `goto` statements—and the `exit` function are sufficient to handle most situations that might require a `goto` in other languages.

Nonetheless, the `goto` statement can be helpful once in a while. Consider the problem of exiting a loop from within a `switch` statement. As we saw earlier, the `break` statement doesn't quite have the desired effect: it exits from the `switch`, but not from the loop. A `goto` statement solves the problem:

```
while (…) {
  switch (…) {
    …
    goto loop_done;    /* break won't work here */
    …
  }
}
loop_done: …
```

The `goto` statement is also useful for exiting from nested loops.

PROGRAM   **Balancing a Checkbook**

Many simple interactive programs are menu-based: they present the user with a list of commands to choose from. Once the user has selected a command, the program performs the desired action, then prompts the user for another command. This process continues until the user selects an "exit" or "quit" command.

The heart of such a program will obviously be a loop. Inside the loop will be statements that prompt the user for a command, read the command, then decide what action to take:

```
for (;;) {
  prompt user to enter command;
  read command;
  execute command;
}
```

Executing the command will require a `switch` statement (or cascaded `if` statement):

```
for (;;) {
  prompt user to enter command;
  read command;
  switch (command) {
    case command₁: perform operation₁; break;
```

```
     case command₂: perform operation₂; break;
       .
       .
       .
     case commandₙ: perform operationₙ; break;
     default: print error message; break;
   }
 }
```

To illustrate this arrangement, let's develop a program that maintains a check-book balance. The program will offer the user a menu of choices: clear the account balance, credit money to the account, debit money from the account, display the current balance, and exit the program. The choices are represented by the integers 0, 1, 2, 3, and 4, respectively. Here's what a session with the program will look like:

```
*** ACME checkbook-balancing program ***
Commands: 0=clear, 1=credit, 2=debit, 3=balance, 4=exit

Enter command: 1
Enter amount of credit: 1042.56
Enter command: 2
Enter amount of debit: 133.79
Enter command: 1
Enter amount of credit: 1754.32
Enter command: 2
Enter amount of debit: 1400
Enter command: 2
Enter amount of debit: 68
Enter command: 2
Enter amount of debit: 50
Enter command: 3
Current balance: $1145.09
Enter command: 4
```

When the user enters the command 4 (exit), the program needs to exit from the switch statement *and* the surrounding loop. The break statement won't help, and we'd prefer not to use a goto statement. Instead, we'll have the program execute a return statement, which will cause the main function to return to the operating system.

checking.c
```
/* Balances a checkbook */

#include <stdio.h>

int main(void)
{
  int cmd;
  float balance = 0.0f, credit, debit;

  printf("*** ACME checkbook-balancing program ***\n");
  printf("Commands: 0=clear, 1=credit, 2=debit, ");
  printf("3=balance, 4=exit\n\n");
```

```
for (;;) {
  printf("Enter command: ");
  scanf("%d", &cmd);
  switch (cmd) {
    case 0:
      balance = 0.0f;
      break;
    case 1:
      printf("Enter amount of credit: ");
      scanf("%f", &credit);
      balance += credit;
      break;
    case 2:
      printf("Enter amount of debit: ");
      scanf("%f", &debit);
      balance -= debit;
      break;
    case 3:
      printf("Current balance: $%.2f\n", balance);
      break;
    case 4:
      return 0;
    default:
      printf("Commands: 0=clear, 1=credit, 2=debit, ");
      printf("3=balance, 4=exit\n\n");
      break;
  }
}
```

Note that the `return` statement is not followed by a `break` statement. A `break` immediately following a `return` can never be executed, and many compilers will issue a warning message.

6.5 The Null Statement

A statement can be **null**—devoid of symbols except for the semicolon at the end. Here's an example:

```
i = 0; ; j = 1;
```

This line contains three statements: an assignment to `i`, a null statement, and an assignment to `j`.

Q&A
The null statement is primarily good for one thing: writing loops whose bodies are empty. As an example, recall the prime-finding loop of Section 6.4:

```
for (d = 2; d < n; d++)
  if (n % d == 0)
    break;
```

If we move the n % d == 0 condition into the loop's controlling expression, the body of the loop becomes empty:

```
for (d = 2; d < n && n % d != 0; d++)
  /* empty loop body */ ;
```

Each time through the loop, the condition d < n is tested first; if it's false, the loop terminates. Otherwise, the condition n % d != 0 is tested, and if that's false, the loop terminates. (In the latter case, n % d == 0 must be true; in other words, we've found a divisor of n.)

Note how we've put the null statement on a line by itself, instead of writing

```
for (d = 2; d < n && n % d != 0; d++);
```

Q&A C programmers customarily put the null statement on a line by itself. Otherwise, someone reading the program might get confused about whether the statement after the `for` was actually its body:

```
for (d = 2; d < n && n % d != 0; d++);
if (d < n)
  printf("%d is divisible by %d\n", n, d);
```

Converting an ordinary loop into one with an empty body doesn't buy much: the new loop is often more concise but usually no more efficient. In a few cases, though, a loop with an empty body is clearly superior to the alternatives. For example, we'll find these loops to be handy for reading character data.

reading characters ▶7.3

Accidentally putting a semicolon after the parentheses in an `if`, `while`, or `for` statement creates a null statement, thus ending the `if`, `while`, or `for` prematurely.

■ In an `if` statement, putting a semicolon after the parentheses creates an `if` statement that apparently performs the same action regardless of the value of its controlling expression:

```
if (d == 0);                              /*** WRONG ***/
  printf("Error: Division by zero\n");
```

The call of `printf` isn't inside the `if` statement, so it's performed regardless of whether d is equal to 0.

■ In a `while` statement, putting a semicolon after the parentheses may create an infinite loop:

```
i = 10;
while (i > 0);                            /*** WRONG ***/
{
  printf("T minus %d and counting\n", i);
  --i;
}
```

Another possibility is that the loop terminates, but the statement that should be the loop body is executed only once, after the loop has terminated:

```
i = 11;
while (--i > 0);                                    /*** WRONG ***/
  printf("T minus %d and counting\n", i);
```

This example prints the message

```
T minus 0 and counting
```

■ In a `for` statement, putting a semicolon after the parentheses causes the statement that should be the loop body to be executed only once:

```
for (i = 10; i > 0; i--);                           /*** WRONG ***/
  printf("T minus %d and counting\n", i);
```

This example also prints the message

```
T minus 0 and counting
```

Q & A

Q: The following loop appears in Section 6.1:

```
while (i > 0)
  printf("T minus %d and counting\n", i--);
```

Why not shorten the loop even more by removing the "> 0" test?

```
while (i)
  printf("T minus %d and counting\n", i--);
```

This version will stop when i reaches 0, so it should be just as good as the original. [p. 101]

A: The new version is certainly more concise, and many C programmers would write the loop in just this way. It does have drawbacks, though.

First, the new loop is not as easy to read as the original. It's clear that the loop will terminate when i reaches 0, but it's not obvious whether we're counting up or down. In the original loop, that information can be deduced from the controlling expression, i > 0.

Second, the new loop behaves differently than the original if i should happen to have a negative value when the loop begins to execute. The original loop terminates immediately, but the new loop doesn't.

Q: Section 6.3 says that, except in rare cases, `for` loops can be converted to `while` loops using a standard pattern. Can you give an example of such a case? [p. 106]

A: When the body of a for loop contains a continue statement, the while pattern shown in Section 6.3 is no longer valid. Consider the following example from Section 6.4:

```
n = 0;
sum = 0;
while (n < 10) {
  scanf("%d", &i);
  if (i == 0)
    continue;
  sum += i;
  n++;
}
```

At first glance, it looks as though we could convert the while loop into a for loop:

```
sum = 0;
for (n = 0; n < 10; n++) {
  scanf("%d", &i);
  if (i == 0)
    continue;
  sum += i;
}
```

Unfortunately, this loop isn't equivalent to the original. When i is equal to 0, the original loop doesn't increment n, but the new loop does.

Q: Which form of infinite loop is preferable, while (1) or for (;;)? [p. 108]

A: C programmers have traditionally preferred for (;;) for reasons of efficiency; older compilers would often force programs to test the 1 condition each time through the while loop. With modern compilers, however, there should be no difference in performance.

Q: I've heard that programmers should never use the continue statement. Is this true?

A: It's true that continue statements are rare. Still, continue is handy once in a while. Suppose we're writing a loop that reads some input data, checks that it's valid, and, if so, processes the input in some way. If there are a number of validity tests, or if they're complex, continue can be helpful. The loop would look something like this:

```
for (;;) {
  read data;
  if (data fails first test)
    continue;
  if (data fails second test)
    continue;
  .
  .
  .
```

```
    if (data fails last test)
        continue;
    process data;
}
```

Q: **What's so bad about the goto statement? [p. 114]**

A: The goto statement isn't inherently evil; it's just that we usually have better alternatives. Programs that use more than a few goto statements can quickly degenerate into "spaghetti code," with control blithely jumping from here to there. Spaghetti code is hard to understand and hard to modify.

goto statements make programs hard to read because they can jump either forward or backward. (In contrast, break and continue only jump forward.) A program that contains goto statements often requires the reader to jump back and forth in an attempt to follow the flow of control.

goto statements can make programs hard to modify, since they make it possible for a section of code to serve more than one purpose. For example, a statement that is preceded by a label might be reachable either by "falling through" from the previous statement or by executing one of several goto statements.

Q: **Does the null statement have any uses besides indicating that the body of a loop is empty? [p. 116]**

A: Very few. Since the null statement can appear wherever a statement is allowed, there are many *potential* uses for the null statement. In practice, however, there's only one other use of the null statement, and it's rare.

Suppose that we need to put a label at the end of a compound statement. A label can't stand alone; it must always be followed by a statement. Putting a null statement after the label solves the problem:

```
{
    …
    goto end_of_stmt;
    …
    end_of_stmt: ;
}
```

Q: **Are there any other ways to make an empty loop body stand out besides putting the null statement on a line by itself? [p. 117]**

A: Some programmers use a dummy continue statement:

```
for (d = 2; d < n && n % d != 0; d++)
    continue;
```

Others use an empty compound statement:

```
for (d = 2; d < n && n % d != 0; d++)
    {}
```

Exercises

Section 6.1

1. What output does the following program fragment produce?

```
i = 1;
while (i <= 128) {
  printf("%d ", i);
  i *= 2;
}
```

Section 6.2

2. What output does the following program fragment produce?

```
i = 9384;
do {
  printf("%d ", i);
  i /= 10;
} while (i > 0);
```

Section 6.3

*3. What output does the following `for` statement produce?

```
for (i = 5, j = i - 1; i > 0, j > 0; --i, j = i - 1)
  printf("%d ", i);
```

Ⓦ 4. Which one of the following statements is not equivalent to the other two (assuming that the loop bodies are the same)?
   (a) `for (i = 0; i < 10; i++)` …
   (b) `for (i = 0; i < 10; ++i)` …
   (c) `for (i = 0; i++ < 10; )` …

5. Which one of the following statements is not equivalent to the other two (assuming that the loop bodies are the same)?
   (a) `while (i < 10) {…}`
   (b) `for (; i < 10;) {…}`
   (c) `do {…} while (i < 10);`

6. Translate the program fragment of Exercise 1 into a single `for` statement.

7. Translate the program fragment of Exercise 2 into a single `for` statement.

*8. What output does the following `for` statement produce?

```
for (i = 10; i >= 1; i /= 2)
  printf("%d ", i++);
```

9. Translate the `for` statement of Exercise 8 into an equivalent `while` statement. You will need one statement in addition to the `while` loop itself.

Section 6.4

Ⓦ 10. Show how to replace a `continue` statement by an equivalent `goto` statement.

11. What output does the following program fragment produce?

```
sum = 0;
for (i = 0; i < 10; i++) {
  if (i % 2)
    continue;
  sum += i;
}
printf("%d\n", sum);
```

W 12. The following "prime-testing" loop appeared in Section 6.4 as an example:

```
for (d = 2; d < n; d++)
  if (n % d == 0)
    break;
```

This loop isn't very efficient. It's not necessary to divide n by all numbers between 2 and n − 1 to determine whether it's prime. In fact, we need only check divisors up to the square root of n. Modify the loop to take advantage of this fact. *Hint:* Don't try to compute the square root of n; instead, compare d * d with n.

Section 6.5   *13.   Rewrite the following loop so that its body is empty:

```
for (n = 0; m > 0; n++)
  m /= 2;
```

W*14.   Find the error in the following program fragment and fix it.

```
if (n % 2 == 0);
  printf("n is even\n");
```

Programming Projects

1.   Write a program that finds the largest in a series of numbers entered by the user. The program must prompt the user to enter numbers one by one. When the user enters 0 or a negative number, the program must display the largest nonnegative number entered:

```
Enter a number: 60
Enter a number: 38.3
Enter a number: 4.89
Enter a number: 100.62
Enter a number: 75.2295
Enter a number: 0

The largest number entered was 100.62
```

Notice that the numbers aren't necessarily integers.

W 2.   Write a program that asks the user to enter two integers, then calculates and displays their greatest common divisor (GCD):

```
Enter two integers: 12 28
Greatest common divisor: 4
```

Hint: The classic algorithm for computing the GCD, known as Euclid's algorithm, goes as follows: Let m and n be variables containing the two numbers. If n is 0, then stop: m contains the GCD. Otherwise, compute the remainder when m is divided by n. Copy n into m and copy the remainder into n. Then repeat the process, starting with testing whether n is 0.

3. Write a program that asks the user to enter a fraction, then reduces the fraction to lowest terms:

```
Enter a fraction: 6/12
In lowest terms: 1/2
```

Hint: To reduce a fraction to lowest terms, first compute the GCD of the numerator and denominator. Then divide both the numerator and denominator by the GCD.

Ⓦ 4. Add a loop to the `broker.c` program of Section 5.2 so that the user can enter more than one trade and the program will calculate the commission on each. The program should terminate when the user enters 0 as the trade value:

```
Enter value of trade: 30000
Commission: $166.00

Enter value of trade: 20000
Commission: $144.00

Enter value of trade: 0
```

5. Programming Project 1 in Chapter 4 asked you to write a program that displays a two-digit number with its digits reversed. Generalize the program so that the number can have one, two, three, or more digits. *Hint:* Use a do loop that repeatedly divides the number by 10, stopping when it reaches 0.

Ⓦ 6. Write a program that prompts the user to enter a number *n*, then prints all even squares between 1 and *n*. For example, if the user enters 100, the program should print the following:

```
4
16
36
64
100
```

7. Rearrange the `square3.c` program so that the for loop initializes i, tests i, and increments i. Don't rewrite the program; in particular, don't use any multiplications.

Ⓦ 8. Write a program that prints a one-month calendar. The user specifies the number of days in the month and the day of the week on which the month begins:

```
Enter number of days in month: 31
Enter starting day of the week (1=Sun, 7=Sat): 3

          1  2  3  4  5
 6  7  8  9 10 11 12
13 14 15 16 17 18 19
20 21 22 23 24 25 26
27 28 29 30 31
```

Hint: This program isn't as hard as it looks. The most important part is a for statement that uses a variable i to count from 1 to n, where n is the number of days in the month, printing each value of i. Inside the loop, an if statement tests whether i is the last day in a week; if so, it prints a new-line character.

9. Programming Project 8 in Chapter 2 asked you to write a program that calculates the remaining balance on a loan after the first, second, and third monthly payments. Modify the program so that it also asks the user to enter the number of payments and then displays the balance remaining after each of these payments.

10. Programming Project 9 in Chapter 5 asked you to write a program that determines which of two dates comes earlier on the calendar. Generalize the program so that the user may enter any number of dates. The user will enter 0/0/0 to indicate that no more dates will be entered:

```
Enter a date (mm/dd/yy): 3/6/08
Enter a date (mm/dd/yy): 5/17/07
Enter a date (mm/dd/yy): 6/3/07
Enter a date (mm/dd/yy): 0/0/0
5/17/07 is the earliest date
```

11. The value of the mathematical constant e can be expressed as an infinite series:

$$e = 1 + 1/1! + 1/2! + 1/3! + \ldots$$

Write a program that approximates e by computing the value of

$$1 + 1/1! + 1/2! + 1/3! + \ldots + 1/n!$$

where n is an integer entered by the user.

12. Modify Programming Project 11 so that the program continues adding terms until the current term becomes less than ε, where ε is a small (floating-point) number entered by the user.

7 Basic Types

Make no mistake about it: Computers process numbers—
not symbols. We measure our understanding (and control)
by the extent to which we can arithmetize an activity.

So far, we've used only two of C's *basic* (built-in) *types:* int and float. (We've also seen _Bool, which is a basic type in C99.) This chapter describes the rest of the basic types and discusses important issues about types in general. Section 7.1 reveals the full range of integer types, which include long integers, short integers, and unsigned integers. Section 7.2 introduces the double and long double types, which provide a larger range of values and greater precision than float. Section 7.3 covers the char type, which we'll need in order to work with character data. Section 7.4 tackles the thorny topic of converting a value of one type to an equivalent value of another. Section 7.5 shows how to use typedef to define new type names. Finally, Section 7.6 describes the sizeof operator, which measures the amount of storage required for a type.

7.1 Integer Types

C supports two fundamentally different kinds of numeric types: integer types and floating types. Values of an *integer type* are whole numbers, while values of a floating type can have a fractional part as well. The integer types, in turn, are divided into two categories: signed and unsigned.

Signed and Unsigned Integers

The leftmost bit of a *signed* integer (known as the *sign bit*) is 0 if the number is positive or zero, 1 if it's negative. Thus, the largest 16-bit integer has the binary representation

0111111111111111

which has the value 32,767 ($2^{15} - 1$). The largest 32-bit integer is

01111111111111111111111111111111

which has the value 2,147,483,647 ($2^{31} - 1$). An integer with no sign bit (the left-most bit is considered part of the number's magnitude) is said to be ***unsigned***. The largest 16-bit unsigned integer is 65,535 ($2^{16} - 1$), and the largest 32-bit unsigned integer is 4,294,967,295 ($2^{32} - 1$).

By default, integer variables are signed in C—the leftmost bit is reserved for the sign. To tell the compiler that a variable has no sign bit, we declare it to be `unsigned`. Unsigned numbers are primarily useful for systems programming and low-level, machine-dependent applications. We'll discuss typical applications for unsigned numbers in Chapter 20; until then, we'll generally avoid them.

C's integer types come in different sizes. The `int` type is usually 32 bits, but may be 16 bits on older CPUs. Since some programs require numbers that are too large to store in `int` form, C also provides ***long*** integers. At times, we may need to conserve memory by instructing the compiler to store a number in less space than normal; such a number is called a ***short*** integer.

To construct an integer type that exactly meets our needs, we can specify that a variable is `long` or `short`, `signed` or `unsigned`. We can even combine specifiers (e.g., `long unsigned int`). However, only the following six combinations actually produce different types:

```
short int
unsigned short int

int
unsigned int

long int
unsigned long int
```

Other combinations are synonyms for one of these six types. (For example, `long signed int` is the same as `long int`, since integers are always signed unless otherwise specified.) Incidentally, the order of the specifiers doesn't matter; `unsigned short int` is the same as `short unsigned int`.

C allows us to abbreviate the names of integer types by dropping the word `int`. For example, `unsigned short int` may be abbreviated to `unsigned short`, and `long int` may be abbreviated to just `long`. Omitting `int` is a widespread practice among C programmers, and some newer C-based languages (including Java) actually require the programmer to write `short` or `long` rather than `short int` or `long int`. For these reasons, I'll often omit the word `int` when it's not strictly necessary.

The range of values represented by each of the six integer types varies from one machine to another. However, there are a couple of rules that all compilers must obey. First, the C standard requires that `short int`, `int`, and `long int` each cover a certain minimum range of values (see Section 23.2 for details). Second, the standard requires that `int` not be shorter than `short int`, and `long int` not be shorter than `int`. However, it's possible that `short int` represents the same range of values as `int`; also, `int` may have the same range as `long int`.

Table 7.1 shows the usual range of values for the integer types on a 16-bit machine; note that `short int` and `int` have identical ranges.

Table 7.1

Integer Types on a
16-bit Machine

Type	Smallest Value	Largest Value
short int	−32,768	32,767
unsigned short int	0	65,535
int	−32,768	32,767
unsigned int	0	65,535
long int	−2,147,483,648	2,147,483,647
unsigned long int	0	4,294,967,295

Table 7.2 shows the usual ranges on a 32-bit machine; here `int` and `long int` have identical ranges.

Table 7.2

Integer Types on a
32-bit Machine

Type	Smallest Value	Largest Value
short int	−32,768	32,767
unsigned short int	0	65,535
int	−2,147,483,648	2,147,483,647
unsigned int	0	4,294,967,295
long int	−2,147,483,648	2,147,483,647
unsigned long int	0	4,294,967,295

In recent years, 64-bit CPUs have become more common. Table 7.3 shows typical ranges for the integer types on a 64-bit machine (especially under UNIX).

Table 7.3

Integer Types on a
64-bit Machine

Type	Smallest Value	Largest Value
short int	−32,768	32,767
unsigned short int	0	65,535
int	−2,147,483,648	2,147,483,647
unsigned int	0	4,294,967,295
long int	−9,223,372,036,854,775,808	9,223,372,036,854,775,807
unsigned long int	0	18,446,744,073,709,551,615

Once more, let me emphasize that the ranges shown in Tables 7.1, 7.2, and 7.3 aren't mandated by the C standard and may vary from one compiler to another. One way to determine the ranges of the integer types for a particular implementa-

<limits.h> header ➤23.2   tion is to check the <limits.h> header, which is part of the standard library. This header defines macros that represent the smallest and largest values of each integer type.

Integer Types in C99

C99 provides two additional standard integer types, `long long int` and `unsigned long long int`. These types were added because of the growing need for very large integers and the ability of newer processors to support 64-bit arithmetic. Both `long long` types are required to be at least 64 bits wide, so the range of `long long int` values is typically -2^{63} ($-9{,}223{,}372{,}036{,}854{,}775{,}808$) to $2^{63} - 1$ ($9{,}223{,}372{,}036{,}854{,}775{,}807$), and range of `unsigned long long int` values is usually 0 to $2^{64} - 1$ ($18{,}446{,}744{,}073{,}709{,}551{,}615$).

signed char type ➤7.3

unsigned char type ➤7.3

_Bool type ➤5.2

The `short int`, `int`, `long int`, and `long long int` types (along with the `signed char` type) are called ***standard signed integer types*** in C99. The `unsigned short int`, `unsigned int`, `unsigned long int`, and `unsigned long long int` types (along with the `unsigned char` type and the `_Bool` type) are called ***standard unsigned integer types.***

In addition to the standard integer types, the C99 standard allows implementation-defined ***extended integer types,*** both signed and unsigned. For example, a compiler might provide signed and unsigned 128-bit integer types.

Integer Constants

Let's turn our attention to ***constants***—numbers that appear in the text of a program, not numbers that are read, written, or computed. C allows integer constants to be written in decimal (base 10), octal (base 8), or hexadecimal (base 16).

Octal and Hexadecimal Numbers

An octal number is written using only the digits 0 through 7. Each position in an octal number represents a power of 8 (just as each position in a decimal number represents a power of 10). Thus, the octal number 237 represents the decimal number $2 \times 8^2 + 3 \times 8^1 + 7 \times 8^0 = 128 + 24 + 7 = 159$.

A hexadecimal (or hex) number is written using the digits 0 through 9 plus the letters A through F, which stand for 10 through 15, respectively. Each position in a hex number represents a power of 16; the hex number 1AF has the decimal value $1 \times 16^2 + 10 \times 16^1 + 15 \times 16^0 = 256 + 160 + 15 = 431$.

- ***Decimal*** constants contain digits between 0 and 9, but must not begin with a zero:

  ```
  15   255   32767
  ```

- ***Octal*** constants contain only digits between 0 and 7, and *must* begin with a zero:

  ```
  017   0377   077777
  ```

- **Hexadecimal** constants contain digits between 0 and 9 and letters between a and f, and always begin with 0x:

```
0xf   0xff   0x7fff
```

The letters in a hexadecimal constant may be either upper or lower case:

```
0xff   0xfF   0xFf   0xFF   0Xff   0XfF   0XFf   0XFF
```

Keep in mind that octal and hexadecimal are nothing more than an alternative way of writing numbers; they have no effect on how the numbers are actually stored. (Integers are always stored in binary, regardless of what notation we've used to express them.) We can switch from one notation to another at any time, and even mix them: 10 + 015 + 0x20 has the value 55 (decimal). Octal and hex are most convenient for writing low-level programs; we won't use these notations much until Chapter 20.

The type of a *decimal* integer constant is normally int. However, if the value of the constant is too large to store as an int, the constant has type long int instead. In the unlikely case that the constant is too large to store as a long int, the compiler will try unsigned long int as a last resort. The rules for determining the type of an *octal* or *hexadecimal* constant are slightly different: the compiler will go through the types int, unsigned int, long int, and unsigned long int until it finds one capable of representing the constant.

To force the compiler to treat a constant as a long integer, just follow it with the letter L (or l):

```
15L   0377L   0x7fffL
```

To indicate that a constant is unsigned, put the letter U (or u) after it:

```
15U   0377U   0x7fffU
```

L and U may be used in combination to show that a constant is both long *and* unsigned: 0xffffffffUL. (The order of the L and U doesn't matter, nor does their case.)

ⓒ99 Integer Constants in C99

In C99, integer constants that end with either LL or ll (the case of the two letters must match) have type long long int. Adding the letter U (or u) before or after the LL or ll denotes a constant of type unsigned long long int.

C99's general rules for determining the type of an integer constant are a bit different from those in C89. The type of a decimal constant with no suffix (U, u, L, l, LL, or ll) is the "smallest" of the types int, long int, or long long int that can represent the value of that constant. For an octal or hexadecimal constant, however, the list of possible types is int, unsigned int, long int, unsigned long int, long long int, and unsigned long long int, in that order. Any suffix at the end of a constant changes the list of possible types. For example, a constant that ends with U (or u) must have one of the types unsigned int, unsigned long int, or unsigned long long int. A decimal constant that ends with L (or l) must have one of the types long int or long long int. There's also a provision for a constant to have an extended integer type if it's too large to represent using one of the standard integer types.

Integer Overflow

When arithmetic operations are performed on integers, it's possible that the result will be too large to represent. For example, when an arithmetic operation is performed on two int values, the result must be able to be represented as an int. If the result can't be represented as an int (because it requires too many bits), we say that *overflow* has occurred.

The behavior when integer overflow occurs depends on whether the operands were signed or unsigned. When overflow occurs during an operation on *signed* integers, the program's behavior is undefined. Recall from Section 4.4 that the consequences of undefined behavior may vary. Most likely the result of the operation will simply be wrong, but the program could crash or exhibit other undesirable behavior.

When overflow occurs during an operation on *unsigned* integers, though, the result *is* defined: we get the correct answer modulo 2^n, where n is the number of bits used to store the result. For example, if we add 1 to the unsigned 16-bit number 65,535, the result is guaranteed to be 0.

Reading and Writing Integers

Suppose that a program isn't working because one of its int variables is overflowing. Our first thought is to change the type of the variable from int to long int. But we're not done yet; we need to see how the change will affect the rest of the program. In particular, we must check whether the variable is used in a call of printf or scanf. If so, the format string in the call will need to be changed, since the %d conversion works only for the int type.

Reading and writing unsigned, short, and long integers requires several new conversion specifiers:

Q&A   ■ When reading or writing an *unsigned* integer, use the letter u, o, or x instead of d in the conversion specification. If the u specifier is present, the number is read (or written) in decimal notation; o indicates octal notation, and x indicates hexadecimal notation.

```
unsigned int u;

scanf("%u", &u);    /* reads  u in base 10 */
printf("%u", u);    /* writes u in base 10 */
scanf("%o", &u);    /* reads  u in base  8 */
printf("%o", u);    /* writes u in base  8 */
```

```
scanf("%x", &u);   /* reads  u in base 16 */
printf("%x", u);   /* writes u in base 16 */
```

- When reading or writing a *short* integer, put the letter h in front of d, o, u, or x:

```
short s;

scanf("%hd", &s);
printf("%hd", s);
```

- When reading or writing a *long* integer, put the letter l ("ell," not "one") in front of d, o, u, or x:

```
long l;

scanf("%ld", &l);
printf("%ld", l);
```

 - When reading or writing a *long long* integer (C99 only), put the letters ll in front of d, o, u, or x:

```
long long ll;

scanf("%lld", &ll);
printf("%lld", ll);
```

PROGRAM **Summing a Series of Numbers (Revisited)**

In Section 6.1, we wrote a program that sums a series of integers entered by the user. One problem with this program is that the sum (or one of the input numbers) might exceed the largest value allowed for an int variable. Here's what might happen if the program is run on a machine whose integers are 16 bits long:

```
This program sums a series of integers.
Enter integers (0 to terminate): 10000 20000 30000 0
The sum is: -5536
```

The sum was 60,000, which wouldn't fit in an int variable, so overflow occurred. When overflow occurs with signed numbers, the outcome is undefined. In this case, we got an apparently meaningless number. To improve the program, let's switch to long variables.

sum2.c
```
/* Sums a series of numbers (using long variables) */

#include <stdio.h>

int main(void)
{
  long n, sum = 0;

  printf("This program sums a series of integers.\n");
```

```
    printf("Enter integers (0 to terminate): ");

    scanf("%ld", &n);
    while (n != 0) {
      sum += n;
      scanf("%ld", &n);
    }
    printf("The sum is: %ld\n", sum);

    return 0;
}
```

The change was fairly simple: we declared n and sum to be long variables instead of int variables, then we changed the conversion specifications in scanf and printf to %ld instead of %d.

7.2 Floating Types

The integer types aren't suitable for all applications. Sometimes we'll need variables that can store numbers with digits after the decimal point, or numbers that are exceedingly large or small. Numbers like these are stored in floating-point format (so called because the decimal point "floats"). C provides three *floating types*, corresponding to different floating-point formats:

float	Single-precision floating-point
double	Double-precision floating-point
long double	Extended-precision floating-point

float is suitable when the amount of precision isn't critical (calculating temperatures to one decimal point, for example). double provides greater precision—enough for most programs. long double, which supplies the ultimate in precision, is rarely used.

The C standard doesn't state how much precision the float, double, and long double types provide, since different computers may store floating-point numbers in different ways. Most modern computers follow the specifications in IEEE Standard 754 (also known as IEC 60559), so we'll use it as an example.

The IEEE Floating-Point Standard

IEEE Standard 754, developed by the Institute of Electrical and Electronics Engineers, provides two primary formats for floating-point numbers: single precision (32 bits) and double precision (64 bits). Numbers are stored in a form of scientific notation, with each number having three parts: a *sign*, an *exponent*, and a *fraction*. The number of bits reserved for the exponent determines how large (or small) numbers can be, while the number of bits in the fraction determines the precision. In single-precision format, the exponent is 8 bits long, while the fraction occupies 23 bits. As a result, a single-precision number has a maximum value of approximately 3.40×10^{38}, with a precision of about 6 decimal digits.

The IEEE standard also describes two other formats, single extended precision and double extended precision. The standard doesn't specify the number of bits in these formats, although it requires that the single extended type occupy at least 43 bits and the double extended type at least 79 bits. For more information about the IEEE standard and floating-point arithmetic in general, see "What every computer scientist should know about floating-point arithmetic" by David Goldberg (*ACM Computing Surveys*, vol. 23, no. 1 (March 1991): 5–48).

subnormal numbers ➤*23.4*

Table 7.4 shows the characteristics of the floating types when implemented according to the IEEE standard. (The table shows the smallest positive *normalized* values. Subnormal numbers can be smaller.) The `long double` type isn't shown in the table, since its length varies from one machine to another, with 80 bits and 128 bits being the most common sizes.

Table 7.4
Floating Type
Characteristics
(IEEE Standard)

Type	*Smallest Positive Value*	*Largest Value*	*Precision*
`float`	1.17549×10^{-38}	3.40282×10^{38}	6 digits
`double`	2.22507×10^{-308}	1.79769×10^{308}	15 digits

On computers that don't follow the IEEE standard, Table 7.4 won't be valid. In fact, on some machines, `float` may have the same set of values as `double`, or `double` may have the same values as `long double`. Macros that define the characteristics of the floating types can be found in the `<float.h>` header.

`<float.h>` header ➤*23.1*

In C99, the floating types are divided into two categories. The `float`, `double`, and `long double` types fall into one category, called the *real floating types.* Floating types also include the *complex types* (`float _Complex`, `double _Complex`, and `long double _Complex`), which are new in C99.

complex types ➤*27.3*

Floating Constants

Floating constants can be written in a variety of ways. The following constants, for example, are all valid ways of writing the number 57.0:

```
57.0  57.  57.0e0  57E0  5.7e1  5.7e+1  .57e2  570.e-1
```

A floating constant must contain a decimal point and/or an exponent; the exponent indicates the power of 10 by which the number is to be scaled. If an exponent is present, it must be preceded by the letter E (or e). An optional + or - sign may appear after the E (or e).

By default, floating constants are stored as double-precision numbers. In other words, when a C compiler finds the constant 57.0 in a program, it arranges for the number to be stored in memory in the same format as a `double` variable. This rule generally causes no problems, since `double` values are converted automatically to `float` when necessary.

On occasion, it may be necessary to force the compiler to store a floating constant in float or long double format. To indicate that only single precision is desired, put the letter F (or f) at the end of the constant (for example, 57.0F). To indicate that a constant should be stored in long double format, put the letter L (or l) at the end (57.0L).

C99 has a provision for writing floating constants in hexadecimal. Such a constant begins with 0x or 0X (like a hexadecimal integer constant). This feature is rarely used.

Reading and Writing Floating-Point Numbers

As we've discussed, the conversion specifications %e, %f, and %g are used for reading and writing single-precision floating-point numbers. Values of types double and long double require slightly different conversions:

- When *reading* a value of type double, put the letter l in front of e, f, or g:

```
double d;

scanf("%lf", &d);
```

Note: Use l only in a scanf format string, not a printf string. In a printf format string, the e, f, and g conversions can be used to write either float or double values. (C99 legalizes the use of %le, %lf, and %lg in calls of printf, although the l has no effect.)

- When reading or writing a value of type long double, put the letter L in front of e, f, or g:

```
long double ld;

scanf("%Lf", &ld);
printf("%Lf", ld);
```

7.3 Character Types

The only remaining basic type is char, the character type. The values of type char can vary from one computer to another, because different machines may have different underlying character sets.

Character Sets

ASCII character set ➤ Appendix E

Today's most popular character set is ***ASCII*** (American Standard Code for Information Interchange), a 7-bit code capable of representing 128 characters. In ASCII, the digits 0 to 9 are represented by the codes 0110000–0111001, and the uppercase letters A to Z are represented by 1000001–1011010. ASCII is often extended to a 256-character code known as *Latin-1* that provides the characters necessary for Western European and many African languages.

A variable of type `char` can be assigned any single character:

```
char ch;

ch = 'a';    /* lower-case a */
ch = 'A';    /* upper-case A */
ch = '0';    /* zero         */
ch = ' ';    /* space        */
```

Notice that character constants are enclosed in single quotes, not double quotes.

Operations on Characters

Working with characters in C is simple, because of one fact: *C treats characters as small integers.* After all, characters are encoded in binary, and it doesn't take much imagination to view these binary codes as integers. In ASCII, for example, character codes range from 0000000 to 1111111, which we can think of as the integers from 0 to 127. The character `'a'` has the value 97, `'A'` has the value 65, `'0'` has the value 48, and `' '` has the value 32. The connection between characters and integers in C is so strong that character constants actually have `int` type rather than `char` type (an interesting fact, but not one that will often matter to us).

When a character appears in a computation, C simply uses its integer value. Consider the following examples, which assume the ASCII character set:

```
char ch;
int i;

i = 'a';        /* i is now 97   */
ch = 65;        /* ch is now 'A' */
ch = ch + 1;    /* ch is now 'B' */
ch++;           /* ch is now 'C' */
```

Characters can be compared, just as numbers can. The following `if` statement checks whether `ch` contains a lower-case letter; if so, it converts `ch` to upper case.

```
if ('a' <= ch && ch <= 'z')
  ch = ch - 'a' + 'A';
```

Comparisons such as `'a' <= ch` are done using the integer values of the characters involved. These values depend on the character set in use, so programs that use `<`, `<=`, `>`, and `>=` to compare characters may not be portable.

The fact that characters have the same properties as numbers has some advantages. For example, we can easily write a `for` statement whose control variable steps through all the upper-case letters:

```
for (ch = 'A'; ch <= 'Z'; ch++) …
```

On the other hand, treating characters as numbers can lead to various programming errors that won't be caught by the compiler, and lets us write meaningless expressions such as `'a' * 'b' / 'c'`. It can also hamper portability, since our programs may be based on assumptions about the underlying character set. (Our `for` loop, for example, assumes that the letters from A to Z have consecutive codes.)

Signed and Unsigned Characters

Since C allows characters to be used as integers, it shouldn't be surprising that the `char` type—like the integer types—exists in both signed and unsigned versions. Signed characters normally have values between –128 and 127, while unsigned characters have values between 0 and 255.

The C standard doesn't specify whether ordinary `char` is a signed or an unsigned type; some compilers treat it as a signed type, while others treat it as an unsigned type. (Some even allow the programmer to select, via a compiler option, whether `char` should be signed or unsigned.)

Q&A

Most of the time, we don't really care whether `char` is signed or unsigned. Once in a while, though, we do, especially if we're using a character variable to store a small integer. For this reason, C allows the use of the words `signed` and `unsigned` to modify `char`:

```
signed char sch;
unsigned char uch;
```

portability tip

Don't assume that `char` is either signed or unsigned by default. If it matters, use `signed char` or `unsigned char` instead of `char`.

enumerated types ➤ 16.5

In light of the close relationship between characters and integers, C89 uses the term ***integral types*** to refer to both the integer types and the character types. Enumerated types are also integral types.

C99

C99 doesn't use the term "integral types." Instead, it expands the meaning of "integer types" to include the character types and the enumerated types. C99's

_Bool type ➤ 5.2

`_Bool` type is considered to be an unsigned integer type.

Arithmetic Types

The integer types and floating types are collectively known as ***arithmetic types.*** Here's a summary of the arithmetic types in C89, divided into categories and subcategories:

- Integral types
  - `char`
  - Signed integer types (`signed char`, `short int`, `int`, `long int`)
  - Unsigned integer types (`unsigned char`, `unsigned short int`, `unsigned int`, `unsigned long int`)

- ● Enumerated types
- ■ Floating types (`float`, `double`, `long double`)

C99 C99 has a more complicated hierarchy for its arithmetic types:

- ■ Integer types
  - ● `char`
  - ● Signed integer types, both standard (`signed char`, `short int`, `int`, `long int`, `long long int`) and extended
  - ● Unsigned integer types, both standard (`unsigned char`, `unsigned short int`, `unsigned int`, `unsigned long int`, `unsigned long long int`, `_Bool`) and extended
  - ● Enumerated types
- ■ Floating types
  - ● Real floating types (`float`, `double`, `long double`)
  - ● Complex types (`float _Complex`, `double _Complex`, `long double _Complex`)

Escape Sequences

A character constant is usually one character enclosed in single quotes, as we've seen in previous examples. However, certain special characters—including the new-line character—can't be written in this way, because they're invisible (non-printing) or because they can't be entered from the keyboard. So that programs can deal with every character in the underlying character set, C provides a special notation, the *escape sequence*.

There are two kinds of escape sequences: *character escapes* and *numeric escapes*. We saw a partial list of character escapes in Section 3.1; Table 7.5 gives the complete set.

Table 7.5
Character Escapes

Name	Escape Sequence
Alert (bell)	`\a`
Backspace	`\b`
Form feed	`\f`
New line	`\n`
Carriage return	`\r`
Horizontal tab	`\t`
Vertical tab	`\v`
Backslash	`\\`
Question mark	`\?`
Single quote	`\'`
Double quote	`\"`

Q&A The `\a`, `\b`, `\f`, `\r`, `\t`, and `\v` escapes represent common ASCII control characters. The `\n` escape represents the ASCII line-feed character. The `\\` escape allows a character constant or string to contain the `\` character. The `\'` escape

Q&A allows a character constant to contain the ' character, while the \ " escape allows a string to contain the " character. The \ ? escape is rarely used.

Character escapes are handy, but they have a problem: the list of character escapes doesn't include all the nonprinting ASCII characters, just the most common. Character escapes are also useless for representing characters beyond the basic 128 ASCII characters. Numeric escapes, which can represent *any* character, are the solution to this problem.

To write a numeric escape for a particular character, first look up the character's octal or hexadecimal value in a table like the one in Appendix E. For example, the ASCII escape character (decimal value: 27) has the value 33 in octal and 1B in hex. Either of these codes can be used to write an escape sequence:

- An *octal escape sequence* consists of the \ character followed by an octal number with at most three digits. (This number must be representable as an unsigned character, so its maximum value is normally 377 octal.) For example, the escape character could be written \33 or \033. Octal numbers in escape sequences—unlike octal constants—don't have to begin with 0.

- A *hexadecimal escape sequence* consists of \x followed by a hexadecimal number. Although C places no limit on the number of digits in the hexadecimal number, it must be representable as an unsigned character (hence it can't exceed FF if characters are eight bits long). Using this notation, the escape character would be written \x1b or \x1B. The x must be in lower case, but the hex digits (such as b) can be upper or lower case.

When used as a character constant, an escape sequence must be enclosed in single quotes. For example, a constant representing the escape character would be written '\33' (or '\x1b'). Escape sequences tend to get a bit cryptic, so it's often a good idea to give them names using #define:

```
#define ESC '\33'    /* ASCII escape character */
```

Escape sequences can be embedded in strings as well, as we saw in Section 3.1.

Escape sequences aren't the only special notations for representing characters. Trigraph sequences provide a way to represent the characters #, [, \,], ^, {, |, }, and ~, which may not be available on keyboards in some countries. C99 adds universal character names, which resemble escape sequences. Unlike escape sequences, however, universal character names are allowed in identifiers.

trigraph sequences ➤25.3

universal character names ➤25.4

Character-Handling Functions

Earlier in this section, we saw how to write an if statement that converts a lower-case letter to upper-case:

```
if ('a' <= ch && ch <= 'z')
  ch = ch - 'a' + 'A';
```

This isn't the best method, though. A faster—and more portable—way to convert case is to call C's toupper library function:

```
ch = toupper(ch);    /* converts ch to upper case */
```

When it's called, `toupper` checks whether its argument (`ch` in this case) is a lower-case letter. If so, it returns the corresponding upper-case letter. Otherwise, `toupper` returns the value of the argument. In our example, we've used the assignment operator to store the return value of `toupper` back into the `ch` variable, although we could just as easily have done something else with it—stored it in another variable, say, or tested it in an `if` statement:

```
if (toupper(ch) == 'A') …
```

Programs that call `toupper` need to have the following `#include` directive at the top:

```
#include <ctype.h>
```

`toupper` isn't the only useful character-handling function in the C library. Section 23.5 describes them all and gives examples of their use.

Reading and Writing Characters using `scanf` and `printf`

The `%c` conversion specification allows `scanf` and `printf` to read and write single characters:

```
char ch;

scanf("%c", &ch);    /* reads a single character */
printf("%c", ch);    /* writes a single character */
```

`scanf` doesn't skip white-space characters before reading a character. If the next unread character is a space, then the variable `ch` in the previous example will contain a space after `scanf` returns. To force `scanf` to skip white space before reading a character, put a space in its format string just before `%c`:

```
scanf(" %c", &ch);    /* skips white space, then reads ch */
```

Recall from Section 3.2 that a blank in a `scanf` format string means "skip zero or more white-space characters."

Since `scanf` doesn't normally skip white space, it's easy to detect the end of an input line: check to see if the character just read is the new-line character. For example, the following loop will read and ignore all remaining characters in the current input line:

```
do {
  scanf("%c", &ch);
} while (ch != '\n');
```

When `scanf` is called the next time, it will read the first character on the next input line.

Reading and Writing Characters using `getchar` and `putchar`

C provides other ways to read and write single characters. In particular, we can use the `getchar` and `putchar` functions instead of calling `scanf` and `printf`. `putchar` writes a single character:

```
putchar(ch);
```

Each time `getchar` is called, it reads one character, which it returns. In order to save this character, we must use assignment to store it in a variable:

```
ch = getchar();   /* reads a character and stores it in ch */
```

`getchar` actually returns an `int` value rather than a `char` value (the reason will be discussed in later chapters). As a result, it's not unusual for a variable to have type `int` rather than `char` if it will be used to store a character read by `getchar`. Like `scanf`, `getchar` doesn't skip white-space characters as it reads.

Using `getchar` and `putchar` (rather than `scanf` and `printf`) saves time when the program is executed. `getchar` and `putchar` are fast for two reasons. First, they're much simpler than `scanf` and `printf`, which are designed to read and write many kinds of data in a variety of formats. Second, `getchar` and *macros ➤ 14.3* `putchar` are usually implemented as macros for additional speed.

`getchar` has another advantage over `scanf`: because it returns the character that it reads, `getchar` lends itself to various C idioms, including loops that search for a character or skip over all occurrences of a character. Consider the `scanf` loop that we used to skip the rest of an input line:

```
do {
  scanf("%c", &ch);
} while (ch != '\n');
```

Rewriting this loop using `getchar` gives us the following:

```
do {
  ch = getchar();
} while (ch != '\n');
```

Moving the call of `getchar` into the controlling expression allows us to condense the loop:

```
while ((ch = getchar()) != '\n')
  ;
```

This loop reads a character, stores it into the variable `ch`, then tests if `ch` is not equal to the new-line character. If the test succeeds, the loop body (which is empty) is executed, then the loop test is performed once more, causing a new character to be read. Actually, we don't even need the `ch` variable; we can just compare the return value of `getchar` with the new-line character:

idiom
```
while (getchar() != '\n')    /* skips rest of line */
    ;
```

The resulting loop is a well-known C idiom that's cryptic but worth learning.

getchar is useful in loops that skip characters as well as loops that search for characters. Consider the following statement, which uses getchar to skip an indefinite number of blank characters:

idiom
```
while ((ch = getchar()) == ' ')    /* skips blanks */
    ;
```

When the loop terminates, ch will contain the first nonblank character that getchar encountered.

 Be careful if you mix getchar and scanf in the same program. scanf has a tendency to leave behind characters that it has "peeked" at but not read, including the new-line character. Consider what happens if we try to read a number first, then a character:

```
printf("Enter an integer: ");
scanf("%d", &i);
printf("Enter a command: ");
command = getchar();
```

The call of scanf will leave behind any characters that weren't consumed during the reading of i, including (but not limited to) the new-line character. getchar will fetch the first leftover character, which wasn't what we had in mind.

PROGRAM **Determining the Length of a Message**

To illustrate how characters are read, let's write a program that calculates the length of a message. After the user enters the message, the program displays the length:

```
Enter a message: Brevity is the soul of wit.
Your message was 27 character(s) long.
```

The length includes spaces and punctuation, but not the new-line character at the end of the message.

We'll need a loop whose body reads a character and increments a counter. The loop will terminate as soon as a new-line character turns up. We could use either scanf or getchar to read characters; most C programmers would choose getchar. Using a straightforward while loop, we might end up with the following program.

length.c   `/* Determines the length of a message */`

```
#include <stdio.h>

int main(void)
{
  char ch;
  int len = 0;

  printf("Enter a message: ");
  ch = getchar();
  while (ch != '\n') {
    len++;
    ch = getchar();
  }
  printf("Your message was %d character(s) long.\n", len);

  return 0;
}
```

Recalling our discussion of idioms involving `while` loops and `getchar`, we realize that the program can be shortened:

length2.c   `/* Determines the length of a message */`

```
#include <stdio.h>

int main(void)
{
  int len = 0;

  printf("Enter a message: ");
  while (getchar() != '\n')
    len++;
  printf("Your message was %d character(s) long.\n", len);

  return 0;
}
```

7.4 Type Conversion

Computers tend to be more restrictive than C when it comes to arithmetic. For a computer to perform an arithmetic operation, the operands must usually be of the same size (the same number of bits) and be stored in the same way. A computer may be able to add two 16-bit integers directly, but not a 16-bit integer and a 32-bit integer or a 32-bit integer and a 32-bit floating-point number.

C, on the other hand, allows the basic types to be mixed in expressions. We can combine integers, floating-point numbers, and even characters in a single expression. The C compiler may then have to generate instructions that convert some operands to different types so that the hardware will be able to evaluate the expression. If we add a 16-bit `short` and a 32-bit `int`, for example, the compiler will arrange for the `short` value to be converted to 32 bits. If we add an `int` and a `float`, the compiler will arrange for the `int` to be converted to `float` format. This conversion is a little more complicated, since `int` and `float` values are stored in different ways.

Because the compiler handles these conversions automatically, without the programmer's involvement, they're known as *implicit conversions*. C also allows the programmer to perform *explicit conversions*, using the cast operator. I'll discuss implicit conversions first, postponing explicit conversions until later in the section. Unfortunately, the rules for performing implicit conversions are somewhat complex, primarily because C has so many different arithmetic types.

Implicit conversions are performed in the following situations:

- When the operands in an arithmetic or logical expression don't have the same type. (C performs what are known as the *usual arithmetic conversions*.)
- When the type of the expression on the right side of an assignment doesn't match the type of the variable on the left side.
- When the type of an argument in a function call doesn't match the type of the corresponding parameter.
- When the type of the expression in a `return` statement doesn't match the function's return type.

We'll discuss the first two cases now and save the others for Chapter 9.

The Usual Arithmetic Conversions

The usual arithmetic conversions are applied to the operands of most binary operators, including the arithmetic, relational, and equality operators. For example, let's say that f has type `float` and i has type `int`. The usual arithmetic conversions will be applied to the operands in the expression f + i, because their types aren't the same. Clearly it's safer to convert i to type `float` (matching f's type) rather than convert f to type `int` (matching i's type). An integer can always be converted to `float`; the worst that can happen is a minor loss of precision. Converting a floating-point number to `int`, on the other hand, would cost us the fractional part of the number. Worse still, we'd get a completely meaningless result if the original number were larger than the largest possible integer or smaller than the smallest integer.

The strategy behind the usual arithmetic conversions is to convert operands to the "narrowest" type that will safely accommodate both values. (Roughly speaking, one type is narrower than another if it requires fewer bytes to store.) The types of the operands can often be made to match by converting the operand of the narrower type to the type of the other operand (this act is known as *promotion*). Among the most common promotions are the *integral promotions*, which convert a character or short integer to type `int` (or to `unsigned int` in some cases).

Q&A

We can divide the rules for performing the usual arithmetic conversions into two cases:

- **The type of either operand is a floating type.** Use the following diagram to promote the operand whose type is narrower:

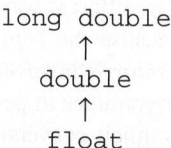

long double
↑
double
↑
float

  That is, if one operand has type long double, then convert the other operand to type long double. Otherwise, if one operand has type double, convert the other operand to type double. Otherwise, if one operand has type float, convert the other operand to type float. Note that these rules cover mixtures of integer and floating types: if one operand has type long int, for example, and the other has type double, the long int operand is converted to double.

- **Neither operand type is a floating type.** First perform integral promotion on both operands (guaranteeing that neither operand will be a character or short integer). Then use the following diagram to promote the operand whose type is narrower:

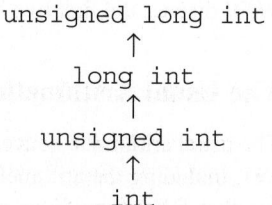

unsigned long int
↑
long int
↑
unsigned int
↑
int

There's one special case, but it occurs only when long int and unsigned int have the same length (32 bits, say). Under these circumstances, if one operand has type long int and the other has type unsigned int, both are converted to unsigned long int.

When a signed operand is combined with an unsigned operand, the signed operand is converted to an unsigned value. The conversion involves adding or subtracting a multiple of $n + 1$, where n is the largest representable value of the unsigned type. This rule can cause obscure programming errors.

Suppose that the int variable i has the value −10 and the unsigned int variable u has the value 10. If we compare i and u using the < operator, we might expect to get the result 1 (true). Before the comparison, however, i is converted to unsigned int. Since a negative number can't be represented as an unsigned integer, the converted value won't be −10. Instead, the value 4,294,967,296 is added (assuming that 4,294,967,295 is the largest unsigned int value), giving a converted value of 4,294,967,286. The comparison i < u will therefore produce 0. Some compilers produce a warning message such as *"comparison between signed and unsigned"* when a program attempts to compare a signed number with an unsigned number.

Because of traps like this one, it's best to use unsigned integers as little as possible and, especially, never mix them with signed integers.

The following example shows the usual arithmetic conversions in action:

```
char c;
short int s;
int i;
unsigned int u;
long int l;
unsigned long int ul;
float f;
double d;
long double ld;

i = i + c;      /* c is converted to int                  */
i = i + s;      /* s is converted to int                  */
u = u + i;      /* i is converted to unsigned int         */
l = l + u;      /* u is converted to long int             */
ul = ul + l;    /* l is converted to unsigned long int    */
f = f + ul;     /* ul is converted to float               */
d = d + f;      /* f is converted to double               */
ld = ld + d;    /* d is converted to long double          */
```

Conversion During Assignment

The usual arithmetic conversions don't apply to assignment. Instead, C follows the simple rule that the expression on the right side of the assignment is converted to the type of the variable on the left side. If the variable's type is at least as "wide" as the expression's, this will work without a snag. For example:

```
char c;
int i;
float f;
double d;

i = c;   /* c is converted to int   */
f = i;   /* i is converted to float */
d = f;   /* f is converted to double */
```

Other cases are problematic. Assigning a floating-point number to an integer variable drops the fractional part of the number:

```
int i;

i = 842.97;    /* i is now 842 */
i = -842.97;   /* i is now -842 */
```

Q&A Moreover, assigning a value to a variable of a narrower type will give a meaningless result (or worse) if the value is outside the range of the variable's type:

```
c = 10000;    /*** WRONG ***/
i = 1.0e20;   /*** WRONG ***/
f = 1.0e100;  /*** WRONG ***/
```

A "narrowing" assignment may elicit a warning from the compiler or from tools such as lint.

It's a good idea to append the f suffix to a floating-point constant if it will be assigned to a float variable, as we've been doing since Chapter 2:

```
f = 3.14159f;
```

Without the suffix, the constant 3.14159 would have type double, possibly causing a warning message.

C99 ## Implicit Conversions in C99

_Bool type ►5.2 The rules for implicit conversions in C99 are somewhat different from the rules in C89, primarily because C99 has additional types (_Bool, long long types, extended integer types, and complex types).

For the purpose of defining conversion rules, C99 gives each integer type an "integer conversion rank." Here are the ranks from highest to lowest:

1. long long int, unsigned long long int
2. long int, unsigned long int
3. int, unsigned int
4. short int, unsigned short int
5. char, signed char, unsigned char
6. _Bool

For simplicity, I'm ignoring extended integer types and enumerated types.

In place of C89's integral promotions, C99 has "integer promotions," which involve converting any type whose rank is less than int and unsigned int to int (provided that all values of the type can be represented using int) or else to unsigned int.

As in C89, the C99 rules for performing the usual arithmetic conversions can be divided into two cases:

- *The type of either operand is a floating type.* As long as neither operand has a complex type, the rules are the same as before. (The conversion rules for complex types will be discussed in Section 27.3.)

- *Neither operand type is a floating type.* First perform integer promotion on both operands. If the types of the two operands are now the same, the process ends. Otherwise, use the following rules, stopping at the first one that applies:

  - If both operands have signed types or both have unsigned types, convert the operand whose type has lesser integer conversion rank to the type of the operand with greater rank.

- If the unsigned operand has rank greater or equal to the rank of the type of the signed operand, convert the signed operand to the type of the unsigned operand.
- If the type of the signed operand can represent all of the values of the type of the unsigned operand, convert the unsigned operand to the type of the signed operand.
- Otherwise, convert both operands to the unsigned type corresponding to the type of the signed operand.

Incidentally, all arithmetic types can be converted to `_Bool` type. The result of the conversion is 0 if the original value is 0; otherwise, the result is 1.

Casting

Although C's implicit conversions are convenient, we sometimes need a greater degree of control over type conversion. For this reason, C provides *casts*. A cast expression has the form

cast expression

> (*type-name*) *expression*

type-name specifies the type to which the expression should be converted.

The following example shows how to use a cast expression to compute the fractional part of a `float` value:

```
float f, frac_part;

frac_part = f - (int) f;
```

The cast expression `(int) f` represents the result of converting the value of f to type `int`. C's usual arithmetic conversions then require that `(int) f` be converted back to type `float` before the subtraction can be performed. The difference between f and `(int) f` is the fractional part of f, which was dropped during the cast.

Cast expressions enable us to document type conversions that would take place anyway:

```
i = (int) f;    /* f is converted to int */
```

They also enable us to overrule the compiler and force it to do conversions that we want. Consider the following example:

```
float quotient;
int dividend, divisor;

quotient = dividend / divisor;
```

As it's now written, the result of the division—an integer—will be converted to float form before being stored in quotient. We probably want dividend and divisor converted to float *before* the division, though, so that we get a more exact answer. A cast expression will do the trick:

```
quotient = (float) dividend / divisor;
```

divisor doesn't need a cast, since casting dividend to float forces the compiler to convert divisor to float also.

Incidentally, C regards (*type-name*) as a unary operator. Unary operators have higher precedence than binary operators, so the compiler interprets

```
(float) dividend / divisor
```

as

```
((float) dividend) / divisor
```

If you find this confusing, note that there are other ways to accomplish the same effect:

```
quotient = dividend / (float) divisor;
```

or

```
quotient = (float) dividend / (float) divisor;
```

Casts are sometimes necessary to avoid overflow. Consider the following example:

```
long i;
int j = 1000;

i = j * j;   /* overflow may occur */
```

At first glance, this statement looks fine. The value of j * j is 1,000,000, and i is a long, so it can easily store values of this size, right? The problem is that when two int values are multiplied, the result will have int type. But j * j is too large to represent as an int on some machines, causing an overflow. Fortunately, using a cast avoids the problem:

```
i = (long) j * j;
```

Since the cast operator takes precedence over *, the first j is converted to long type, forcing the second j to be converted as well. Note that the statement

```
i = (long) (j * j);   /*** WRONG ***/
```

wouldn't work, since the overflow would already have occurred by the time of the cast.

7.5 Type Definitions

In Section 5.2, we used the `#define` directive to create a macro that could be used as a Boolean type:

```
#define BOOL int
```

 There's a better way to set up a Boolean type, though, using a feature known as a *type definition:*

```
typedef int Bool;
```

Notice that the name of the type being defined comes *last*. Note also that I've capitalized the word `Bool`. Capitalizing the first letter of a type name isn't required; it's just a convention that some C programmers employ.

Using `typedef` to define `Bool` causes the compiler to add `Bool` to the list of type names that it recognizes. `Bool` can now be used in the same way as the built-in type names—in variable declarations, cast expressions, and elsewhere. For example, we might use `Bool` to declare variables:

```
Bool flag;   /* same as int flag; */
```

The compiler treats `Bool` as a synonym for `int`; thus, `flag` is really nothing more than an ordinary `int` variable.

Advantages of Type Definitions

Type definitions can make a program more understandable (assuming that the programmer has been careful to choose meaningful type names). For example, suppose that the variables `cash_in` and `cash_out` will be used to store dollar amounts. Declaring `Dollars` as

```
typedef float Dollars;
```

and then writing

```
Dollars cash_in, cash_out;
```

is more informative than just writing

```
float cash_in, cash_out;
```

Type definitions can also make a program easier to modify. If we later decide that `Dollars` should really be defined as `double`, all we need do is change the type definition:

```
typedef double Dollars;
```

The declarations of Dollars variables need not be changed. Without the type definition, we would need to locate all float variables that store dollar amounts (not necessarily an easy task) and change their declarations.

Type Definitions and Portability

Type definitions are an important tool for writing portable programs. One of the problems with moving a program from one computer to another is that types may have different ranges on different machines. If i is an int variable, an assignment like

```
i = 100000;
```

is fine on a machine with 32-bit integers, but will fail on a machine with 16-bit integers.

portability tip   *For greater portability, consider using* typedef *to define new names for integer types.*

Suppose that we're writing a program that needs variables capable of storing product quantities in the range 0–50,000. We could use long variables for this purpose (since they're guaranteed to be able to hold numbers up to at least 2,147,483,647), but we'd rather use int variables, since arithmetic on int values may be faster than operations on long values; also, int variables may take up less space.

Instead of using the int type to declare quantity variables, we can define our own "quantity" type:

```
typedef int Quantity;
```

and use this type to declare variables:

```
Quantity q;
```

When we transport the program to a machine with shorter integers, we'll change the definition of Quantity:

```
typedef long Quantity;
```

This technique doesn't solve all our problems, unfortunately, since changing the definition of Quantity may affect the way Quantity variables are used. At the very least, calls of printf and scanf that use Quantity variables will need to be changed, with %d conversion specifications replaced by %ld.

The C library itself uses typedef to create names for types that can vary from one C implementation to another; these types often have names that end with _t, such as ptrdiff_t, size_t, and wchar_t. The exact definitions of these types will vary, but here are some typical examples:

```
typedef long int ptrdiff_t;
typedef unsigned long int size_t;
typedef int wchar_t;
```

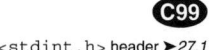

<stdint.h> header ➤27.1

In C99, the <stdint.h> header uses typedef to define names for integer types with a particular number of bits. For example, int32_t is a signed integer type with exactly 32 bits. Using these types is an effective way to make programs more portable.

7.6 The sizeof Operator

The sizeof operator allows a program to determine how much memory is required to store values of a particular type. The value of the expression

sizeof expression

> sizeof (*type-name*)

is an unsigned integer representing the number of bytes required to store a value belonging to *type-name*. sizeof(char) is always 1, but the sizes of the other types may vary. On a 32-bit machine, sizeof(int) is normally 4. Note that sizeof is a rather unusual operator, since the compiler itself can usually determine the value of a sizeof expression.

The sizeof operator can also be applied to constants, variables, and expressions in general. If i and j are int variables, then sizeof(i) is 4 on a 32-bit machine, as is sizeof(i + j). When applied to an expression—as opposed to a type—sizeof doesn't require parentheses; we could write sizeof i instead of sizeof(i). However, parentheses may be needed anyway because of operator precedence. The compiler would interpret sizeof i + j as (sizeof i) + j, because sizeof—a unary operator—takes precedence over the binary + operator. To avoid problems, I always use parentheses in sizeof expressions.

Printing a sizeof value requires care, because the type of a sizeof expression is an implementation-defined type named size_t. In C89, it's best to convert the value of the expression to a known type before printing it. size_t is guaranteed to be an unsigned integer type, so it's safest to cast a sizeof expression to unsigned long (the largest of C89's unsigned types) and then print it using the %lu conversion:

```
printf("Size of int: %lu\n", (unsigned long) sizeof(int));
```

In C99, the size_t type can be larger than unsigned long. However, the printf function in C99 is capable of displaying size_t values directly, without needing a cast. The trick is to use the letter z in the conversion specification, followed by one of the usual integer codes (typically u):

```
printf("Size of int: %zu\n", sizeof(int));    /* C99 only */
```

Q & A

Q: **Section 7.1 says that %o and %x are used to write unsigned integers in octal and hex notation. How do I write ordinary (signed) integers in octal or hex? [p. 130]**

A: You can use %o and %x to print a signed integer as long as its value isn't negative. These conversions cause printf to treat a signed integer as though it were unsigned; in other words, printf will assume that the sign bit is part of the number's magnitude. As long as the sign bit is 0, there's no problem. If the sign bit is 1, printf will print an unexpectedly large number.

Q: **But what if the number *is* negative? How can I write it in octal or hex?**

A: There's no direct way to print a negative number in octal or hex. Fortunately, the need to do so is pretty rare. You can, of course, test whether the number is negative and print a minus sign yourself:

```
if (i < 0)
  printf("-%x", -i);
else
  printf("%x", i);
```

Q: **Why are floating constants stored in double form rather than float form? [p. 133]**

A: For historical reasons, C gives preference to the double type; float is treated as a second-class citizen. Consider, for instance, the discussion of float in Kernighan and Ritchie's *The C Programming Language*: "The main reason for using float is to save storage in large arrays, or, less often, to save time on machines where double-precision arithmetic is particularly expensive." C originally mandated that all floating-point arithmetic be done in double precision. (C89 and C99 have no such requirement.)

*Q: **What do hexadecimal floating constants look like, and what are they good for? [p. 134]**

A: A hexadecimal floating constant begins with 0x or 0X and must contain an exponent, which is preceded by the letter P (or p). The exponent may have a sign, and the constant may end with f, F, l, or L. The exponent is expressed in decimal, but represents a power of 2, not a power of 10. For example, 0x1.Bp3 represents the number $1.6875 \times 2^3 = 13.5$. The hex digit B corresponds to the bit pattern 1011. The B occurs to the right of the period, so each 1 bit represents a negative power of 2. Summing these powers of 2 $(2^{-1} + 2^{-3} + 2^{-4})$ yields .6875.

Hexadecimal floating constants are primarily useful for specifying constants that require great precision (including mathematical constants such as e and π). Hex numbers have a precise binary representation, whereas a constant written in decimal may be subject to a tiny rounding error when converted to binary. Hexadecimal numbers are also useful for defining constants with extreme values, such as the values of the macros in the <float.h> header. These constants are easy to write in hex but difficult to write in decimal.

*Q: **Why do we use `%lf` to read a `double` value but `%f` to print it? [p. 134]**

A: This is a tough question to answer. First, notice that scanf and printf are unusual functions in that they aren't restricted to a fixed number of arguments. We say that scanf and printf have variable-length argument lists. When functions with variable-length argument lists are called, the compiler arranges for float arguments to be converted automatically to type double. As a result, printf can't distinguish between float and double arguments. This explains why %f works for both float and double arguments in calls of printf.

variable-length argument lists
➤26.1

scanf, on the other hand, is passed a *pointer* to a variable. %f tells scanf to store a float value at the address passed to it, while %lf tells scanf to store a double value at that address. The distinction between float and double is crucial here. If given the wrong conversion specification, scanf will likely store the wrong number of bytes (not to mention the fact that the bit pattern for a float isn't the same as that for a double).

Q: **What's the proper way to pronounce `char`? [p. 134]**

A: There's no universally accepted pronunciation. Some people pronounce char in the same way as the first syllable of "character." Others say "char," as in

```
char broiled;
```

Q: **When does it matter whether a character variable is signed or unsigned? [p. 136]**

A: If we store only 7-bit characters in the variable, it doesn't matter, since the sign bit will be zero. If we plan to store 8-bit characters, however, we'll probably want the variable to have unsigned char type. Consider the following example:

```
ch = '\xdb';
```

If ch has been declared to have type char, the compiler may choose to treat it as a signed character (many compilers do). As long as ch is used only as a character, there won't be any problem. But if ch is ever used in a context that requires the compiler to convert its value to an integer, we're likely to have trouble: the resulting integer will be negative, since ch's sign bit is 1.

Here's another situation: In some kinds of programs, it's customary to use char variables to store one-byte integers. If we're writing such a program, we'll have to decide whether each variable should be signed char or unsigned char, just as we must decide whether ordinary integer variables should have type int or unsigned int.

Q: **I don't understand how the new-line character can be the ASCII line-feed character. When a user enters input and presses the Enter key, doesn't the program read this as a carriage-return character or a carriage return plus a line feed? [p. 137]**

A: Nope. As part of C's UNIX heritage, it always regards the end of a line as being marked by a single line-feed character. (In UNIX text files, a single line-feed character—but no carriage return—appears at the end of each line.) The C library takes care of translating the user's keypress into a line-feed character. When a program reads from a file, the I/O library translates the file's end-of-line marker (whatever it may be) into a single line-feed character. The same transformations occur—in reverse—when output is written to the screen or to a file. (See Section 22.1 for details.)

Although these translations may seem confusing, they serve an important purpose: insulating programs from details that may vary from one operating system to another.

*Q: What's the purpose of the \? escape sequence? [p. 138]

A: The \? escape is related to trigraph sequences, which begin with ??. If you should
trigraph sequences ▸25.3   put ?? in a string, there's a possibility that the compiler will mistake it for the beginning of a trigraph. Replacing the second ? by \? fixes the problem.

Q: If `getchar` is faster, why would we ever want to use `scanf` to read individual characters? [p. 140]

A: Although it's not as fast as `getchar`, the `scanf` function is more flexible. As we saw previously, the `"%c"` format string causes `scanf` to read the next input character; `" %c"` causes it to read the next non-white-space character. Also, `scanf` is good at reading characters that are mixed in with other kinds of data. Let's say that our input data consists of an integer, then a single nonnumeric character, then another integer. By using the format string `"%d%c%d"`, we can get `scanf` to read all three items.

*Q: Under what circumstances do the integral promotions convert a character or short integer to `unsigned int`? [p. 143]

A: The integral promotions yield an `unsigned int` if the `int` type isn't large enough to include all possible values of the original type. Since characters are usually eight bits long, they are almost always converted to `int`, which is guaranteed to be at least 16 bits long. Signed short integers can always be converted to `int` as well. Unsigned short integers are problematic. If short integers have the same length as ordinary integers (as they do on a 16-bit machine), then unsigned short integers will have to be converted to `unsigned int`, since the largest unsigned short integer (65,535 on a 16-bit machine) is larger than the largest `int` (32,767).

Q: Exactly what happens if I assign a value to a variable that's not large enough to hold it? [p. 146]

A: Roughly speaking, if the value is of an integral type and the variable is of an unsigned type, the extra bits are thrown away; if the variable has a signed type, the result is implementation-defined. Assigning a floating-point number to a variable—integer or floating—that's too small to hold it produces undefined behavior: anything can happen, including program termination.

*Q: **Why does C bother to provide type definitions? Isn't defining a `BOOL` macro just as good as defining a `Bool` type using `typedef`? [p. 149]***

A: There are two important differences between type definitions and macro definitions. First, type definitions are more powerful than macro definitions. In particular, array and pointer types can't be defined as macros. Suppose that we try to use a macro to define a "pointer to integer" type:

```
#define PTR_TO_INT int *
```

The declaration

```
PTR_TO_INT p, q, r;
```

will become

```
int * p, q, r;
```

after preprocessing. Unfortunately, only p is a pointer; q and r are ordinary integer variables. Type definitions don't have this problem.

Second, `typedef` names are subject to the same scope rules as variables; a `typedef` name defined inside a function body wouldn't be recognized outside the function. Macro names, on the other hand, are replaced by the preprocessor wherever they appear.

*Q: **You said that compilers "can usually determine the value of a `sizeof` expression." Can't a compiler *always* determine the value of a `sizeof` expression? [p. 151]***

A: In C89, yes. In C99, however, there's one exception. The compiler can't determine the size of a variable-length array, because the number of elements in the array may change during the execution of the program.

variable-length arrays ➤8.3

Exercises

Section 7.1

1. Give the decimal value of each of the following integer constants.

   (a) `077`
   (b) `0x77`
   (c) `0XABC`

Section 7.2

2. Which of the following are not legal constants in C? Classify each legal constant as either integer or floating-point.

   (a) `010E2`
   (b) `32.1E+5`
   (c) `0790`
   (d) `100_000`
   (e) `3.978e-2`

Ⓦ 3. Which of the following are not legal types in C?

(a) `short unsigned int`
(b) `short float`
(c) `long double`
(d) `unsigned long`

Section 7.3   Ⓦ 4. If `c` is a variable of type `char`, which one of the following statements is illegal?

(a) `i += c;    /* i has type int */`
(b) `c = 2 * c - 1;`
(c) `putchar(c);`
(d) `printf(c);`

5. Which one of the following is not a legal way to write the number 65? (Assume that the character set is ASCII.)

(a) `'A'`
(b) `0b1000001`
(c) `0101`
(d) `0x41`

6. For each of the following items of data, specify which one of the types `char`, `short`, `int`, or `long` is the smallest one guaranteed to be large enough to store the item.

(a) Days in a month
(b) Days in a year
(c) Minutes in a day
(d) Seconds in a day

7. For each of the following character escapes, give the equivalent octal escape. (Assume that the character set is ASCII.) You may wish to consult Appendix E, which lists the numerical codes for ASCII characters.

(a) `\b`
(b) `\n`
(c) `\r`
(d) `\t`

8. Repeat Exercise 7, but give the equivalent hexadecimal escape.

Section 7.4   9. Suppose that `i` and `j` are variables of type `int`. What is the type of the expression `i / j + 'a'`?

Ⓦ 10. Suppose that `i` is a variable of type `int`, `j` is a variable of type `long`, and `k` is a variable of type `unsigned int`. What is the type of the expression `i + (int) j * k`?

11. Suppose that `i` is a variable of type `int`, `f` is a variable of type `float`, and `d` is a variable of type `double`. What is the type of the expression `i * f / d`?

Ⓦ 12. Suppose that `i` is a variable of type `int`, `f` is a variable of type `float`, and `d` is a variable of type `double`. Explain what conversions take place during the execution of the following statement:

`d = i + f;`

13. Assume that a program contains the following declarations:

```
char c = '\1';
short s = 2;
int i = -3;
long m = 5;
float f = 6.5f;
double d = 7.5;
```

Give the value and the type of each expression listed below.

(a) c * i   (c) f / c   (e) f - d
(b) s + m   (d) d / s   (f) (int) f

Ⓦ 14. Does the following statement always compute the fractional part of f correctly (assuming that f and `frac_part` are `float` variables)?

```
frac_part = f - (int) f;
```

If not, what's the problem?

Section 7.5   15. Use `typedef` to create types named `Int8`, `Int16`, and `Int32`. Define the types so that they represent 8-bit, 16-bit, and 32-bit integers on your machine.

Programming Projects

Ⓦ 1. The `square2.c` program of Section 6.3 will fail (usually by printing strange answers) if i * i exceeds the maximum `int` value. Run the program and determine the smallest value of n that causes failure. Try changing the type of i to `short` and running the program again. (Don't forget to update the conversion specifications in the call of `printf`!) Then try `long`. From these experiments, what can you conclude about the number of bits used to store integer types on your machine?

Ⓦ 2. Modify the `square2.c` program of Section 6.3 so that it pauses after every 24 squares and displays the following message:

```
Press Enter to continue...
```

After displaying the message, the program should use `getchar` to read a character. `getchar` won't allow the program to continue until the user presses the Enter key.

3. Modify the `sum2.c` program of Section 7.1 to sum a series of `double` values.

4. Write a program that translates an alphabetic phone number into numeric form:

```
Enter phone number: CALLATT
2255288
```

(In case you don't have a telephone nearby, here are the letters on the keys: 2=ABC, 3=DEF, 4=GHI, 5=JKL, 6=MNO, 7=PRS, 8=TUV, 9=WXY.) If the original phone number contains nonalphabetic characters (digits or punctuation, for example), leave them unchanged:

```
Enter phone number: 1-800-COL-LECT
1-800-265-5328
```

You may assume that any letters entered by the user are upper case.

(W) 5.   In the SCRABBLE Crossword Game, players form words using small tiles, each containing a letter and a face value. The face value varies from one letter to another, based on the letter's rarity. (Here are the face values: 1: AEILNORSTU, 2: DG, 3: BCMP, 4: FHVWY, 5: K, 8: JX, 10: QZ.) Write a program that computes the value of a word by summing the values of its letters:

```
Enter a word: pitfall
Scrabble value: 12
```

Your program should allow any mixture of lower-case and upper-case letters in the word. *Hint:* Use the `toupper` library function.

(W) 6.   Write a program that prints the values of `sizeof(int)`, `sizeof(short)`, `sizeof(long)`, `sizeof(float)`, `sizeof(double)` and `sizeof(long double)`.

7.   Modify Programming Project 6 from Chapter 3 so that the user may add, subtract, multiply, or divide two fractions (by entering either +, -, *, or / between the fractions).

8.   Modify Programming Project 8 from Chapter 5 so that the user enters a time using the 12-hour clock. The input will have the form *hours* : *minutes* followed by either A, P, AM, or PM (either lower-case or upper-case). White space is allowed (but not required) between the numerical time and the AM/PM indicator. Examples of valid input:

```
1:15P
1:15PM
1:15p
1:15pm
1:15 P
1:15 PM
1:15 p
1:15 pm
```

You may assume that the input has one of these forms; there is no need to test for errors.

9.   Write a program that asks the user for a 12-hour time, then displays the time in 24-hour form:

```
Enter a 12-hour time: 9:11 PM
Equivalent 24-hour time: 21:11
```

See Programming Project 8 for a description of the input format.

10.   Write a program that counts the number of vowels (*a, e, i, o,* and *u*) in a sentence:

```
Enter a sentence: And that's the way it is.
Your sentence contains 6 vowels.
```

11.   Write a program that takes a first name and last name entered by the user and displays the last name, a comma, and the first initial, followed by a period:

```
Enter a first and last name: Lloyd Fosdick
Fosdick, L.
```

The user's input may contain extra spaces before the first name, between the first and last names, and after the last name.

12.   Write a program that evaluates an expression:

```
Enter an expression: 1+2.5*3
Value of expression: 10.5
```

The operands in the expression are floating-point numbers; the operators are +, -, *, and /. The expression is evaluated from left to right (no operator takes precedence over any other operator).

13. Write a program that calculates the average word length for a sentence:

```
Enter a sentence: It was deja vu all over again.
Average word length: 3.4
```

For simplicity, your program should consider a punctuation mark to be part of the word to which it is attached. Display the average word length to one decimal place.

14. Write a program that uses Newton's method to compute the square root of a positive floating-point number:

```
Enter a positive number: 3
Square root: 1.73205
```

Let x be the number entered by the user. Newton's method requires an initial guess y for the square root of x (we'll use $y = 1$). Successive guesses are found by computing the average of y and x/y. The following table shows how the square root of 3 would be found:

x	y	x/y	Average of y and x/y
3	1	3	2
3	2	1.5	1.75
3	1.75	1.71429	1.73214
3	1.73214	1.73196	1.73205
3	1.73205	1.73205	1.73205

Note that the values of y get progressively closer to the true square root of x. For greater accuracy, your program should use variables of type `double` rather than `float`. Have the program terminate when the absolute value of the difference between the old value of y and the new value of y is less than the product of .00001 and y. *Hint:* Call the `fabs` function to find the absolute value of a `double`. (You'll need to include the `<math.h>` header at the beginning of your program in order to use `fabs`.)

15. Write a program that computes the factorial of a positive integer:

```
Enter a positive integer: 6
Factorial of 6: 720
```

(a) Use a `short` variable to store the value of the factorial. What is the largest value of n for which the program correctly prints the factorial of n?
(b) Repeat part (a), using an `int` variable instead.
(c) Repeat part (a), using a `long` variable instead.
(d) Repeat part (a), using a `long long` variable instead (if your compiler supports the `long long` type).
(e) Repeat part (a), using a `float` variable instead.
(f) Repeat part (a), using a `double` variable instead.
(g) Repeat part (a), using a `long double` variable instead.

In cases (e)–(g), the program will display a close approximation of the factorial, not necessarily the exact value.

8 Arrays

*If a program manipulates a large amount of data,
it does so in a small number of ways.*

So far, the only variables we've seen are **scalar:** capable of holding a single data item. C also supports **aggregate** variables, which can store collections of values. There are two kinds of aggregates in C: arrays and structures. This chapter shows how to declare and use arrays, both one-dimensional (Section 8.1) and multidimensional (Section 8.2). Section 8.3 covers C99's variable-length arrays. The focus of the chapter is on one-dimensional arrays, which play a much bigger role in C than do multidimensional arrays. Later chapters (Chapter 12 in particular) provide additional information about arrays; Chapter 16 covers structures.

8.1 One-Dimensional Arrays

An **array** is a data structure containing a number of data values, all of which have the same type. These values, known as **elements**, can be individually selected by their position within the array.

The simplest kind of array has just one dimension. The elements of a one-dimensional array are conceptually arranged one after another in a single row (or column, if you prefer). Here's how we might visualize a one-dimensional array named a:

To declare an array, we must specify the *type* of the array's elements and the *number* of elements. For example, to declare that the array a has 10 elements of type int, we would write

```
int a[10];
```

The elements of an array may be of any type; the length of the array can be specified by any (integer) constant expression. Since array lengths may need to be
adjusted when the program is later changed, using a macro to define the length of
an array is an excellent practice:

constant expressions ➤5.3

```
#define N 10
…
int a[N];
```

Array Subscripting

To access a particular element of an array, we write the array name followed by an
integer value in square brackets (this is referred to as *subscripting* or *indexing* the
array). Array elements are always numbered starting from 0, so the elements of an
array of length *n* are indexed from 0 to *n* – 1. For example, if a is an array with 10
elements, they're designated by a[0], a[1], ..., a[9], as the following figure
shows:

Q&A

a[0] a[1] a[2] a[3] a[4] a[5] a[6] a[7] a[8] a[9]

lvalues ➤4.2

Expressions of the form a[i] are lvalues, so they can be used in the same way as
ordinary variables:

```
a[0] = 1;
printf("%d\n", a[5]);
++a[i];
```

In general, if an array contains elements of type *T*, then each element of the array is
treated as if it were a variable of type *T*. In this example, the elements a[0],
a[5], and a[i] behave like int variables.

Arrays and for loops go hand-in-hand. Many programs contain for loops
whose job is to perform some operation on every element in an array. Here are a
few examples of typical operations on an array a of length N:

idiom
```
for (i = 0; i < N; i++)
    a[i] = 0;                /* clears a */
```

idiom
```
for (i = 0; i < N; i++)
    scanf("%d", &a[i]);      /* reads data into a */
```

idiom
```
for (i = 0; i < N; i++)
    sum += a[i];             /* sums the elements of a */
```

Notice that we must use the & symbol when calling scanf to read an array element, just as we would with an ordinary variable.

C doesn't require that subscript bounds be checked; if a subscript goes out of range, the program's behavior is undefined. One cause of a subscript going out of bounds: forgetting that an array with n elements is indexed from 0 to $n - 1$, not 1 to n. (As one of my professors liked to say, "In this business, you're always off by one." He was right, of course.) The following example illustrates a bizarre effect that can be caused by this common blunder:

```c
int a[10], i;

for (i = 1; i <= 10; i++)
  a[i] = 0;
```

With some compilers, this innocent-looking `for` statement causes an infinite loop! When i reaches 10, the program stores 0 into a[10]. But a[10] doesn't exist, so 0 goes into memory immediately after a[9]. If the variable i happens to follow a[9] in memory—as might be the case—then i will be reset to 0, causing the loop to start over.

An array subscript may be any integer expression:

```c
a[i+j*10] = 0;
```

The expression can even have side effects:

```c
i = 0;
while (i < N)
  a[i++] = 0;
```

Let's trace this code. After i is set to 0, the `while` statement checks whether i is less than N. If it is, 0 is assigned to a[0], i is incremented, and the loop repeats. Note that a[++i] wouldn't be right, because 0 would be assigned to a[1] during the first loop iteration.

 Be careful when an array subscript has a side effect. For example, the following loop—which is supposed to copy the elements of the array b into the array a—may not work properly:

```c
i = 0;
while (i < N)
  a[i] = b[i++];
```

The expression a[i] = b[i++] accesses the value of i and also modifies i elsewhere in the expression, which—as we saw in Section 4.4—causes undefined behavior. Of course, we can easily avoid the problem by removing the increment from the subscript:

```c
for (i = 0; i < N; i++)
  a[i] = b[i];
```

PROGRAM   **Reversing a Series of Numbers**

Our first array program prompts the user to enter a series of numbers, then writes the numbers in reverse order:

```
Enter 10 numbers: 34 82 49 102 7 94 23 11 50 31
In reverse order: 31 50 11 23 94 7 102 49 82 34
```

Our strategy will be to store the numbers in an array as they're read, then go through the array backwards, printing the elements one by one. In other words, we won't actually reverse the elements in the array, but we'll make the user think we did.

reverse.c   ```
/* Reverses a series of numbers */

#include <stdio.h>

#define N 10

int main(void)
{
  int a[N], i;

  printf("Enter %d numbers: ", N);
  for (i = 0; i < N; i++)
    scanf("%d", &a[i]);

  printf("In reverse order:");
  for (i = N - 1; i >= 0; i--)
    printf(" %d", a[i]);
  printf("\n");

  return 0;
}
```

This program shows just how useful macros can be in conjunction with arrays. The macro `N` is used four times in the program: in the declaration of `a`, in the `printf` that displays a prompt, and in both `for` loops. Should we later decide to change the size of the array, we need only edit the definition of `N` and recompile the program. Nothing else will need to be altered; even the prompt will still be correct.

**Array Initialization**

An array, like any other variable, can be given an initial value at the time it's declared. The rules are somewhat tricky, though, so we'll cover some of them now initializers ➤18.5    and save others until later.

The most common form of *array initializer* is a list of constant expressions enclosed in braces and separated by commas:

```
int a[10] = {1, 2, 3, 4, 5, 6, 7, 8, 9, 10};
```
```

If the initializer is *shorter* than the array, the remaining elements of the array are given the value 0:

```
int a[10] = {1, 2, 3, 4, 5, 6};
  /* initial value of a is {1, 2, 3, 4, 5, 6, 0, 0, 0, 0} */
```

Using this feature, we can easily initialize an array to all zeros:

```
int a[10] = {0};
  /* initial value of a is {0, 0, 0, 0, 0, 0, 0, 0, 0, 0} */
```

It's illegal for an initializer to be completely empty, so we've put a single 0 inside the braces. It's also illegal for an initializer to be *longer* than the array it initializes.

If an initializer is present, the length of the array may be omitted:

```
int a[] = {1, 2, 3, 4, 5, 6, 7, 8, 9, 10};
```

The compiler uses the length of the initializer to determine how long the array is. The array still has a fixed number of elements (10, in this example), just as if we had specified the length explicitly.

C99 **Designated Initializers**

It's often the case that relatively few elements of an array need to be initialized explicitly; the other elements can be given default values. Consider the following example:

```
int a[15] = {0, 0, 29, 0, 0, 0, 0, 0, 0, 7, 0, 0, 0, 0, 48};
```

We want element 2 of the array to be 29, element 9 to be 7, and element 14 to be 48, but the other values are just zero. For a large array, writing an initializer in this fashion is tedious and error-prone (what if there were 200 zeros between two of the nonzero values?).

C99's *designated initializers* can be used to solve this problem. Here's how we could redo the previous example using a designated initializer:

```
int a[15] = {[2] = 29, [9] = 7, [14] = 48};
```

Each number in brackets is said to be a *designator.*

Besides being shorter and easier to read (at least for some arrays), designated initializers have another advantage: the order in which the elements are listed no longer matters. Thus, our previous example could also be written in the following way:

```
int a[15] = {[14] = 48, [9] = 7, [2] = 29};
```

Designators must be integer constant expressions. If the array being initialized has length n, each designator must be between 0 and $n - 1$. However, if the length of the array is omitted, a designator can be any nonnegative integer. In the latter case, the compiler will deduce the length of the array from the largest designator.

In the following example, the fact that 23 appears as a designator will force the array to have length 24:

```
int b[] = {[5] = 10, [23] = 13, [11] = 36, [15] = 29};
```

An initializer may use both the older (element-by-element) technique and the newer (designated) technique:

```
int c[10] = {5, 1, 9, [4] = 3, 7, 2, [8] = 6};
```

Q&A This initializer specifies that the array's first three elements will be 5, 1, and 9. Element 4 will have the value 3. The two elements after element 4 will be 7 and 2. Finally, element 8 will have the value 6. All elements for which no value is specified will default to zero.

PROGRAM ### Checking a Number for Repeated Digits

Our next program checks whether any of the digits in a number appear more than once. After the user enters a number, the program prints either Repeated digit or No repeated digit:

```
Enter a number: 28212
Repeated digit
```

The number 28212 has a repeated digit (2); a number like 9357 doesn't.

The program uses an array of Boolean values to keep track of which digits appear in a number. The array, named digit_seen, is indexed from 0 to 9 to correspond to the 10 possible digits. Initially, every element of the array is false. (The initializer for digit_seen is {false}, which only initializes the first element of the array. However, the compiler will automatically make the remaining elements zero, which is equivalent to false.)

When given a number n, the program examines n's digits one at a time, storing each into the digit variable and then using it as an index into digit_seen. If digit_seen[digit] is true, then digit appears at least twice in n. On the other hand, if digit_seen[digit] is false, then digit has not been seen before, so the program sets digit_seen[digit] to true and keeps going.

repdigit.c
```
/* Checks numbers for repeated digits */

#include <stdbool.h>    /* C99 only */
#include <stdio.h>

int main(void)
{
  bool digit_seen[10] = {false};
  int digit;
  long n;

  printf("Enter a number: ");
  scanf("%ld", &n);
```

```
  while (n > 0) {
    digit = n % 10;
    if (digit_seen[digit])
      break;
    digit_seen[digit] = true;
    n /= 10;
  }

  if (n > 0)
    printf("Repeated digit\n");
  else
    printf("No repeated digit\n");

  return 0;
}
```

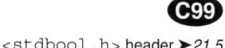

<stdbool.h> header ➤21.5

This program uses the names bool, true, and false, which are defined in C99's <stdbool.h> header. If your compiler doesn't support this header, you'll need to define these names yourself. One way to do so is to put the following lines above the main function:

```
#define true 1
#define false 0
typedef int bool;
```

Notice that n has type long, allowing the user to enter numbers up to 2,147,483,647 (or more, on some machines).

Using the sizeof Operator with Arrays

The sizeof operator can determine the size of an array (in bytes). If a is an array of 10 integers, then sizeof(a) is typically 40 (assuming that each integer requires four bytes).

We can also use sizeof to measure the size of an array element, such as a[0]. Dividing the array size by the element size gives the length of the array:

```
sizeof(a) / sizeof(a[0])
```

Some programmers use this expression when the length of the array is needed. To clear the array a, for example, we could write

```
for (i = 0; i < sizeof(a) / sizeof(a[0]); i++)
  a[i] = 0;
```

With this technique, the loop doesn't have to be modified if the array length should change at a later date. Using a macro to represent the array length has the same advantage, of course, but the sizeof technique is slightly better, since there's no macro name to remember (and possibly get wrong).

One minor annoyance is that some compilers produce a warning message for the expression i < sizeof(a) / sizeof(a[0]). The variable i probably has type int (a signed type), whereas sizeof produces a value of type size_t (an unsigned type). We know from Section 7.4 that comparing a signed integer with an unsigned integer is a dangerous practice, although in this case it's safe because both i and sizeof(a) / sizeof(a[0]) have nonnegative values. To avoid a warning, we can add a cast that converts sizeof(a) / sizeof(a[0]) to a signed integer:

```
for (i = 0; i < (int) (sizeof(a) / sizeof(a[0])); i++)
  a[i] = 0;
```

Writing (int) (sizeof(a) / sizeof(a[0])) is a bit unwieldy; defining a macro that represents it is often helpful:

```
#define SIZE ((int) (sizeof(a) / sizeof(a[0])))

for (i = 0; i < SIZE; i++)
  a[i] = 0;
```

If we're back to using a macro, though, what's the advantage of sizeof? We'll answer that question in a later chapter (the trick is to add a parameter to the macro).

parameterized macros ➤ 14.3

PROGRAM   **Computing Interest**

Our next program prints a table showing the value of $100 invested at different rates of interest over a period of years. The user will enter an interest rate and the number of years the money will be invested. The table will show the value of the money at one-year intervals—at that interest rate and the next four higher rates—assuming that interest is compounded once a year. Here's what a session with the program will look like:

```
Enter interest rate: 6
Enter number of years: 5

Years      6%      7%      8%      9%     10%
  1      106.00 107.00 108.00 109.00 110.00
  2      112.36 114.49 116.64 118.81 121.00
  3      119.10 122.50 125.97 129.50 133.10
  4      126.25 131.08 136.05 141.16 146.41
  5      133.82 140.26 146.93 153.86 161.05
```

Clearly, we can use a for statement to print the first row. The second row is a little trickier, since its values depend on the numbers in the first row. Our solution is to store the first row in an array as it's computed, then use the values in the array to compute the second row. Of course, this process can be repeated for the third and later rows. We'll end up with two for statements, one nested inside the other. The outer loop will count from 1 to the number of years requested by the user. The inner loop will increment the interest rate from its lowest value to its highest value.

interest.c

```c
/* Prints a table of compound interest */

#include <stdio.h>

#define NUM_RATES ((int) (sizeof(value) / sizeof(value[0])))
#define INITIAL_BALANCE 100.00

int main(void)
{
  int i, low_rate, num_years, year;
  double value[5];

  printf("Enter interest rate: ");
  scanf("%d", &low_rate);
  printf("Enter number of years: ");
  scanf("%d", &num_years);

  printf("\nYears");
  for (i = 0; i < NUM_RATES; i++) {
    printf("%6d%%", low_rate + i);
    value[i] = INITIAL_BALANCE;
  }
  printf("\n");

  for (year = 1; year <= num_years; year++) {
    printf("%3d    ", year);
    for (i = 0; i < NUM_RATES; i++) {
      value[i] += (low_rate + i) / 100.0 * value[i];
      printf("%7.2f", value[i]);
    }
    printf("\n");
  }

  return 0;
}
```

Note the use of NUM_RATES to control two of the `for` loops. If we later change the size of the `value` array, the loops will adjust automatically.

8.2 Multidimensional Arrays

An array may have any number of dimensions. For example, the following declaration creates a two-dimensional array (a *matrix*, in mathematical terminology):

```c
int m[5][9];
```

The array m has 5 rows and 9 columns. Both rows and columns are indexed from 0, as the following figure shows:

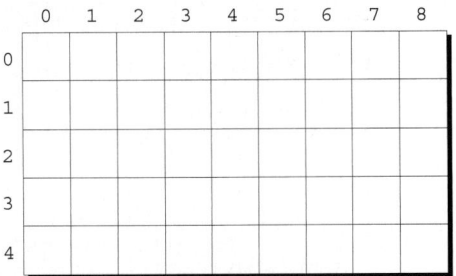

To access the element of m in row i, column j, we must write m[i][j]. The expression m[i] designates row i of m, and m[i][j] then selects element j in this row.

comma operator ➤6.3

Resist the temptation to write m[i,j] instead of m[i][j]. C treats the comma as an operator in this context, so m[i,j] is the same as m[j].

Although we visualize two-dimensional arrays as tables, that's not the way they're actually stored in computer memory. C stores arrays in **row-major order,** with row 0 first, then row 1, and so forth. For example, here's how the m array is stored:

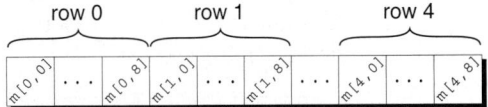

We'll usually ignore this detail, but sometimes it will affect our code.

Just as for loops go hand-in-hand with one-dimensional arrays, nested for loops are ideal for processing multidimensional arrays. Consider, for example, the problem of initializing an array for use as an identity matrix. (In mathematics, an *identity matrix* has 1's on the main diagonal, where the row and column index are the same, and 0's everywhere else.) We'll need to visit each element in the array in some systematic fashion. A pair of nested for loops—one that steps through every row index and one that steps through each column index—is perfect for the job:

```
#define N 10

double ident[N][N];
int row, col;

for (row = 0; row < N; row++)
  for (col = 0; col < N; col++)
    if (row == col)
      ident[row][col] = 1.0;
    else
      ident[row][col] = 0.0;
```

Multidimensional arrays play a lesser role in C than in many other programming languages, primarily because C provides a more flexible way to store multidimensional data: arrays of pointers.

arrays of pointers ➤13.7

Initializing a Multidimensional Array

We can create an initializer for a two-dimensional array by nesting one-dimensional initializers:

```
int m[5][9] = {{1, 1, 1, 1, 1, 0, 1, 1, 1},
               {0, 1, 0, 1, 0, 1, 0, 1, 0},
               {0, 1, 0, 1, 1, 0, 0, 1, 0},
               {1, 1, 0, 1, 0, 0, 0, 1, 0},
               {1, 1, 0, 1, 0, 0, 1, 1, 1}};
```

Each inner initializer provides values for one row of the matrix. Initializers for higher-dimensional arrays are constructed in a similar fashion.

C provides a variety of ways to abbreviate initializers for multidimensional arrays:

- If an initializer isn't large enough to fill a multidimensional array, the remaining elements are given the value 0. For example, the following initializer fills only the first three rows of m; the last two rows will contain zeros:

```
int m[5][9] = {{1, 1, 1, 1, 1, 0, 1, 1, 1},
               {0, 1, 0, 1, 0, 1, 0, 1, 0},
               {0, 1, 0, 1, 1, 0, 0, 1, 0}};
```

- If an inner list isn't long enough to fill a row, the remaining elements in the row are initialized to 0:

```
int m[5][9] = {{1, 1, 1, 1, 1, 0, 1, 1, 1},
               {0, 1, 0, 1, 0, 1, 0, 1},
               {0, 1, 0, 1, 1, 0, 0, 1},
               {1, 1, 0, 1, 0, 0, 0, 1},
               {1, 1, 0, 1, 0, 0, 1, 1, 1}};
```

- We can even omit the inner braces:

```
int m[5][9] = {1, 1, 1, 1, 1, 0, 1, 1, 1,
               0, 1, 0, 1, 0, 1, 0, 1, 0,
               0, 1, 0, 1, 1, 0, 0, 1, 0,
               1, 1, 0, 1, 0, 0, 0, 1, 0,
               1, 1, 0, 1, 0, 0, 1, 1, 1};
```

Once the compiler has seen enough values to fill one row, it begins filling the next.

 Omitting the inner braces in a multidimensional array initializer can be risky, since an extra element (or even worse, a missing element) will affect the rest of the initializer. Leaving out the braces causes some compilers to produce a warning message such as *"missing braces around initializer."*

 C99's designated initializers work with multidimensional arrays. For example, we could create a 2 × 2 identity matrix as follows:

```
double ident[2][2] = {[0][0] = 1.0, [1][1] = 1.0};
```

As usual, all elements for which no value is specified will default to zero.

Constant Arrays

Any array, whether one-dimensional or multidimensional, can be made "constant" by starting its declaration with the word `const`:

```
const char hex_chars[] =
  {'0', '1', '2', '3', '4', '5', '6', '7', '8', '9',
   'A', 'B', 'C', 'D', 'E', 'F'};
```

An array that's been declared `const` should not be modified by the program; the compiler will detect direct attempts to modify an element.

Declaring an array to be `const` has a couple of primary advantages. It documents that the program won't change the array, which can be valuable information for someone reading the code later. It also helps the compiler catch errors, by informing it that we don't intend to modify the array.

const type qualifier ➤18.3

`const` isn't limited to arrays; it works with any variable, as we'll see later. However, `const` is particularly useful in array declarations, because arrays may contain reference information that won't change during program execution.

PROGRAM

Dealing a Hand of Cards

Our next program illustrates both two-dimensional arrays and constant arrays. The program deals a random hand from a standard deck of playing cards. (In case you haven't had time to play games recently, each card in a standard deck has a *suit*—clubs, diamonds, hearts, or spades—and a *rank*—two, three, four, five, six, seven, eight, nine, ten, jack, queen, king, or ace.) We'll have the user specify how many cards should be in the hand:

```
Enter number of cards in hand: 5
Your hand: 7c 2s 5d as 2h
```

It's not immediately obvious how we'd write such a program. How do we pick cards randomly from the deck? And how do we avoid picking the same card twice? Let's tackle these problems separately.

time function ➤26.3

To pick cards randomly, we'll use several C library functions. The `time` function (from `<time.h>`) returns the current time, encoded in a single number. The `srand` function (from `<stdlib.h>`) initializes C's random number generator.

srand function ➤26.2

Passing the return value of `time` to `srand` prevents the program from dealing the same cards every time we run it. The `rand` function (also from `<stdlib.h>`)

rand function ➤26.2

produces an apparently random number each time it's called. By using the `%` operator, we can scale the return value from `rand` so that it falls between 0 and 3 (for suits) or between 0 and 12 (for ranks).

To avoid picking the same card twice, we'll need to keep track of which cards have already been chosen. For that purpose, we'll use an array named `in_hand` that has four rows (one for each suit) and 13 columns (one for each rank). In other words, each element in the array corresponds to one of the 52 cards in the deck. All elements of the array will be false to start with. Each time we pick a card at random, we'll check whether the element of in_hand corresponding to that card is true or false. If it's true, we'll have to pick another card. If it's false, we'll store `true` in that card's array element to remind us later that this card has already been picked.

Once we've verified that a card is "new"—not already selected—we'll need to translate its numerical rank and suit into characters and then display the card. To translate the rank and suit to character form, we'll set up two arrays of characters—one for the rank and one for the suit—and then use the numbers to subscript the arrays. These arrays won't change during program execution, so we may as well declare them to be `const`.

deal.c

```
/* Deals a random hand of cards */

#include <stdbool.h>    /* C99 only */
#include <stdio.h>
#include <stdlib.h>
#include <time.h>

#define NUM_SUITS 4
#define NUM_RANKS 13

int main(void)
{
  bool in_hand[NUM_SUITS][NUM_RANKS] = {false};
  int num_cards, rank, suit;
  const char rank_code[] = {'2','3','4','5','6','7','8',
                            '9','t','j','q','k','a'};
  const char suit_code[] = {'c','d','h','s'};

  srand((unsigned) time(NULL));

  printf("Enter number of cards in hand: ");
  scanf("%d", &num_cards);

  printf("Your hand:");
  while (num_cards > 0) {
    suit = rand() % NUM_SUITS;        /* picks a random suit */
    rank = rand() % NUM_RANKS;        /* picks a random rank */
    if (!in_hand[suit][rank]) {
      in_hand[suit][rank] = true;
      num_cards--;
      printf(" %c%c", rank_code[rank], suit_code[suit]);
    }
  }
  printf("\n");

  return 0;
}
```

Notice the initializer for the `in_hand` array:

```
bool in_hand[NUM_SUITS][NUM_RANKS] = {false};
```

Even though `in_hand` is a two-dimensional array, we can use a single pair of braces (at the risk of possibly incurring a warning from the compiler). Also, we've supplied only one value in the initializer, knowing that the compiler will fill in 0 (false) for the other elements.

8.3 Variable-Length Arrays (C99)

Section 8.1 stated that the length of an array variable must be specified by a constant expression. In C99, however, it's sometimes possible to use an expression that's *not* constant. The following modification of the `reverse.c` program (Section 8.1) illustrates this ability:

reverse2.c
```
/* Reverses a series of numbers using a variable-length
   array - C99 only */

#include <stdio.h>

int main(void)
{
  int i, n;

  printf("How many numbers do you want to reverse? ");
  scanf("%d", &n);

  int a[n];    /* C99 only - length of array depends on n */

  printf("Enter %d numbers: ", n);
  for (i = 0; i < n; i++)
    scanf("%d", &a[i]);

  printf("In reverse order:");
  for (i = n - 1; i >= 0; i--)
    printf(" %d", a[i]);
  printf("\n");

  return 0;
}
```

The array a in this program is an example of a *variable-length array* (or *VLA* for short). The length of a VLA is computed when the program is executed, not when the program is compiled. The chief advantage of a VLA is that the programmer doesn't have to pick an arbitrary length when declaring an array; instead, the program itself can calculate exactly how many elements are needed. If the programmer makes the choice, it's likely that the array will be too long (wasting memory) or too short (causing the program to fail). In the `reverse2.c` program, the number entered by the user determines the length of a; the programmer doesn't have to choose a fixed length, unlike in the original version of the program.

The length of a VLA doesn't have to be specified by a single variable. Arbitrary expressions, possibly containing operators, are also legal. For example:

```
int a[3*i+5];
int b[j+k];
```

Like other arrays, VLAs can be multidimensional:

```
int c[m][n];
```

static storage duration ➤ *18.2*

The primary restriction on VLAs is that they can't have static storage duration. (We haven't yet seen any arrays with this property.) Another restriction is that a VLA may not have an initializer.

Variable-length arrays are most often seen in functions other than main. One big advantage of a VLA that belongs to a function f is that it can have a different length each time f is called. We'll explore this feature in Section 9.3.

Q & A

Q: **Why do array subscripts start at 0 instead of 1? [p. 162]**

A: Having subscripts begin at 0 simplifies the compiler a bit. Also, it can make array subscripting marginally faster.

Q: **What if I want an array with subscripts that go from 1 to 10 instead of 0 to 9?**

A: Here's a common trick: declare the array to have 11 elements instead of 10. The subscripts will go from 0 to 10, but you can just ignore element 0.

Q: **Is it possible to use a character as an array subscript?**

A: Yes, because C treats characters as integers. You'll probably need to "scale" the character before you use it as a subscript, though. Let's say that we want the letter_count array to keep track of a count for each letter in the alphabet. The array will need 26 elements, so we'd declare it in the following way:

```
int letter_count[26];
```

However, we can't use letters to subscript letter_count directly, because their integer values don't fall between 0 and 25. To scale a lower-case letter to the proper range, we can simply subtract 'a'; to scale an upper-case letter, we'll subtract 'A'. For example, if ch contains a lower-case letter, we'd write

```
letter_count[ch-'a'] = 0;
```

to clear the count that corresponds to ch. A minor caveat: this technique isn't completely portable, because it assumes that letters have consecutive codes. However, it works with most character sets, including ASCII.

Q: **It seems like a designated initializer could end up initializing an array element more than once. Consider the following array declaration:**

```
int a[] = {4, 9, 1, 8, [0] = 5, 7};
```

Is this declaration legal, and if so, what is the length of the array? [p. 166]

A: Yes, the declaration is legal. Here's how it works: as it processes an initializer list, the compiler keeps track of which array element is to be initialized next. Normally, the next element is the one following the element that was last initialized. However, when a designator appears in the list, it forces the next element be the one represented by the designator, *even if that element has already been initialized.*

Here's a step-by-step look at how the compiler will process the initializer for the array a:

The 4 initializes element 0; the next element to be initialized is element 1.
The 9 initializes element 1; the next element to be initialized is element 2.
The 1 initializes element 2; the next element to be initialized is element 3.
The 8 initializes element 3; the next element to be initialized is element 4.
The [0] designator causes the next element to become 0, so the 5 initializes element 0 (replacing the 4 previously stored there). The next element to be initialized is element 1.
The 7 initializes element 1 (replacing the 9 previously stored there). The next element to be initialized is element 2 (which is irrelevant since we're at the end of the list).

The net effect is the same as if we had written

```
int a[] = {5, 7, 1, 8};
```

Thus, the length of this array is four.

Q: **The compiler gives me an error message if I try to copy one array into another by using the assignment operator. What's wrong?**

A: Although it looks quite plausible, the assignment

```
a = b;    /* a and b are arrays */
```

is indeed illegal. The reason for its illegality isn't obvious; it has to do with the peculiar relationship between arrays and pointers in C, a topic we'll explore in Chapter 12.

The simplest way to copy one array into another is to use a loop that copies the elements, one by one:

```
for (i = 0; i < N; i++)
  a[i] = b[i];
```

memcpy function ▸*23.6*   Another possibility is to use the memcpy ("memory copy") function from the <string.h> header. memcpy is a low-level function that simply copies bytes from one place to another. To copy the array b into the array a, use memcpy as follows:

```
memcpy(a, b, sizeof(a));
```

Many programmers prefer `memcpy`, especially for large arrays, because it's potentially faster than an ordinary loop.

*Q: **Section 6.4 mentioned that C99 doesn't allow a `goto` statement to bypass the declaration of a variable-length array. What's the reason for this restriction?**

A: The memory used to store a variable-length array is usually allocated when the declaration of the array is reached during program execution. Bypassing the declaration using a `goto` statement could result in a program accessing the elements of an array that was never allocated.

Exercises

Section 8.1

Ⓦ 1. We discussed using the expression `sizeof(a) / sizeof(a[0])` to calculate the number of elements in an array. The expression `sizeof(a) / sizeof(t)`, where *t* is the type of a's elements, would also work, but it's considered an inferior technique. Why?

Ⓦ 2. The Q&A section shows how to use a *letter* as an array subscript. Describe how to use a *digit* (in character form) as a subscript.

3. Write a declaration of an array named `weekend` containing seven `bool` values. Include an initializer that makes the first and last values `true`; all other values should be `false`.

4. (C99) Repeat Exercise 3, but this time use a designated initializer. Make the initializer as short as possible.

5. The Fibonacci numbers are 0, 1, 1, 2, 3, 5, 8, 13, ..., where each number is the sum of the two preceding numbers. Write a program fragment that declares an array named `fib_numbers` of length 40 and fills the array with the first 40 Fibonacci numbers. *Hint:* Fill in the first two numbers individually, then use a loop to compute the remaining numbers.

Section 8.2

6. Calculators, watches, and other electronic devices often rely on seven-segment displays for numerical output. To form a digit, such devices "turn on" some of the seven segments while leaving others "off":

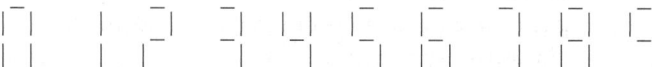

Suppose that we want to set up an array that remembers which segments should be "on" for each digit. Let's number the segments as follows:

$$5\left|\frac{0}{6}\right|1$$
$$4\left|\frac{}{3}\right|2$$

Here's what the array might look like, with each row representing one digit:

```
const int segments[10][7] = {{1, 1, 1, 1, 1, 1, 0}, …};
```

I've given you the first row of the initializer; fill in the rest.

W 7. Using the shortcuts described in Section 8.2, shrink the initializer for the `segments` array (Exercise 6) as much as you can.

8. Write a declaration for a two-dimensional array named `temperature_readings` that stores one month of hourly temperature readings. (For simplicity, assume that a month has 30 days.) The rows of the array should represent days of the month; the columns should represent hours of the day.

9. Using the array of Exercise 8, write a program fragment that computes the average temperature for a month (averaged over all days of the month and all hours of the day).

10. Write a declaration for an 8×8 `char` array named `chess_board`. Include an initializer that puts the following data into the array (one character per array element):

```
r n b q k b n r
p p p p p p p p
  .   .   .   .
.   .   .   .
  .   .   .   .
.   .   .   .
P P P P P P P P
R N B Q K B N R
```

11. Write a program fragment that declares an 8×8 `char` array named `checker_board` and then uses a loop to store the following data into the array (one character per array element):

```
B R B R B R B R
R B R B R B R B
B R B R B R B R
R B R B R B R B
B R B R B R B R
R B R B R B R B
B R B R B R B R
R B R B R B R B
```

Hint: The element in row i, column j, should be the letter B if $i + j$ is an even number.

Programming Projects

1. Modify the `repdigit.c` program of Section 8.1 so that it shows which digits (if any) were repeated:

```
Enter a number: 939577
Repeated digit(s): 7 9
```

W 2. Modify the `repdigit.c` program of Section 8.1 so that it prints a table showing how many times each digit appears in the number:

```
Enter a number: 41271092
Digit:        0  1  2  3  4  5  6  7  8  9
Occurrences:  1  2  2  0  1  0  0  1  0  1
```

3. Modify the `repdigit.c` program of Section 8.1 so that the user can enter more than one number to be tested for repeated digits. The program should terminate when the user enters a number that's less than or equal to 0.

4. Modify the `reverse.c` program of Section 8.1 to use the expression `(int)` `(sizeof(a) / sizeof(a[0]))` (or a macro with this value) for the array length.

Ⓦ 5. Modify the `interest.c` program of Section 8.1 so that it compounds interest *monthly* instead of *annually*. The form of the output shouldn't change; the balance should still be shown at annual intervals.

6. The prototypical Internet newbie is a fellow named B1FF, who has a unique way of writing messages. Here's a typical B1FF communiqué:

```
H3Y DUD3, C 15 R1LLY C00L!!!!!!!!!!!
```

Write a "B1FF filter" that reads a message entered by the user and translates it into B1FF-speak:

```
Enter message: Hey dude, C is rilly cool
In B1FF-speak: H3Y DUD3, C 15 R1LLY C00L!!!!!!!!!!!
```

Your program should convert the message to upper-case letters, substitute digits for certain letters (A→4, B→8, E→3, I→1, O→0, S→5), and then append 10 or so exclamation marks. *Hint:* Store the original message in an array of characters, then go back through the array, translating and printing characters one by one.

7. Write a program that reads a 5 × 5 array of integers and then prints the row sums and the column sums:

```
Enter row 1: 8 3 9 0 10
Enter row 2: 3 5 17 1 1
Enter row 3: 2 8 6 23 1
Enter row 4: 15 7 3 2 9
Enter row 5: 6 14 2 6 0

Row totals: 30 27 40 36 28
Column totals: 34 37 37 32 21
```

Ⓦ 8. Modify Programming Project 7 so that it prompts for five quiz grades for each of five students, then computes the total score and average score for each *student*, and the average score, high score, and low score for each *quiz*.

9. Write a program that generates a "random walk" across a 10 × 10 array. The array will contain characters (all `'.'` initially). The program must randomly "walk" from element to element, always going up, down, left, or right by one element. The elements visited by the program will be labeled with the letters A through Z, in the order visited. Here's an example of the desired output:

```
A . . . . . . . . .
B C D . . . . . . .
. F E . . . . . . .
H G . . . . . . . .
I . . . . . . . . .
J . . . . . . Z . .
K . . R S T U V Y .
L M P Q . . . W X .
. N O . . . . . . .
. . . . . . . . . .
```

Hint: Use the `srand` and `rand` functions (see `deal.c`) to generate random numbers. After generating a number, look at its remainder when divided by 4. There are four possible values for the remainder—0, 1, 2, and 3—indicating the direction of the next move. Before performing a move, check that (a) it won't go outside the array, and (b) it doesn't take us to an element that already has a letter assigned. If either condition is violated, try moving in another direction. If all four directions are blocked, the program must terminate. Here's an example of premature termination:

```
A B G H I . . . . .
. C F . J K . . . .
. D E . M L . . . .
. . . . N O . . . .
. . W X Y P Q . . .
. . V U T S R . . .
. . . . . . . . . .
. . . . . . . . . .
. . . . . . . . . .
. . . . . . . . . .
```

Y is blocked on all four sides, so there's no place to put Z.

10.   Modify Programming Project 8 from Chapter 5 so that the departure times are stored in an array and the arrival times are stored in a second array. (The times are integers, representing the number of minutes since midnight.) The program will use a loop to search the array of departure times for the one closest to the time entered by the user.

11.   Modify Programming Project 4 from Chapter 7 so that the program labels its output:

```
Enter phone number: 1-800-COL-LECT
In numeric form: 1-800-265-5328
```

The program will need to store the phone number (either in its original form or in its numeric form) in an array of characters until it can be printed. You may assume that the phone number is no more than 15 characters long.

12.   Modify Programming Project 5 from Chapter 7 so that the SCRABBLE values of the letters are stored in an array. The array will have 26 elements, corresponding to the 26 letters of the alphabet. For example, element 0 of the array will store 1 (because the SCRABBLE value of the letter A is 1), element 1 of the array will store 3 (because the SCRABBLE value of the letter B is 3), and so forth. As each character of the input word is read, the program will use the array to determine the SCRABBLE value of that character. Use an array initializer to set up the array.

13.   Modify Programming Project 11 from Chapter 7 so that the program labels its output:

```
Enter a first and last name: Lloyd Fosdick
You entered the name: Fosdick, L.
```

The program will need to store the last name (but not the first name) in an array of characters until it can be printed. You may assume that the last name is no more than 20 characters long.

14.   Write a program that reverses the words in a sentence:

```
Enter a sentence: you can cage a swallow can't you?
Reversal of sentence: you can't swallow a cage can you?
```

Hint: Use a loop to read the characters one by one and store them in a one-dimensional `char` array. Have the loop stop at a period, question mark, or exclamation point (the "terminating character"), which is saved in a separate `char` variable. Then use a second loop to search backward through the array for the beginning of the last word. Print the last word, then search backward for the next-to-last word. Repeat until the beginning of the array is reached. Finally, print the terminating character.

15.   One of the oldest known encryption techniques is the Caesar cipher, attributed to Julius Caesar. It involves replacing each letter in a message with another letter that is a fixed number of

positions later in the alphabet. (If the replacement would go past the letter Z, the cipher "wraps around" to the beginning of the alphabet. For example, if each letter is replaced by the letter two positions after it, then *Y* would be replaced by *A*, and *Z* would be replaced by *B*.) Write a program that encrypts a message using a Caesar cipher. The user will enter the message to be encrypted and the shift amount (the number of positions by which letters should be shifted):

```
Enter message to be encrypted: Go ahead, make my day.
Enter shift amount (1-25): 3
Encrypted message: Jr dkhdg, pdnh pb gdb.
```

Notice that the program can decrypt a message if the user enters 26 minus the original key:

```
Enter message to be encrypted: Jr dkhdg, pdnh pb gdb.
Enter shift amount (1-25): 23
Encrypted message: Go ahead, make my day.
```

You may assume that the message does not exceed 80 characters. Characters other than letters should be left unchanged. Lower-case letters remain lower-case when encrypted, and upper-case letters remain upper-case. *Hint:* To handle the wrap-around problem, use the expression `((ch - 'A') + n) % 26 + 'A'` to calculate the encrypted version of an upper-case letter, where `ch` stores the letter and `n` stores the shift amount. (You'll need a similar expression for lower-case letters.)

16.   Write a program that tests whether two words are anagrams (permutations of the same letters):

```
Enter first word: smartest
Enter second word: mattress
The words are anagrams.

Enter first word: dumbest
Enter second word: stumble
The words are not anagrams.
```

Write a loop that reads the first word, character by character, using an array of 26 integers to keep track of how many times each letter has been seen. (For example, after the word *smartest* has been read, the array should contain the values 1 0 0 0 1 0 0 0 0 0 0 0 1 0 0 0 0 1 2 2 0 0 0 0 0 0, reflecting the fact that *smartest* contains one *a*, one *e*, one *m*, one *r*, two *s*'s and two *t*'s.) Use another loop to read the second word, except this time decrementing the corresponding array element as each letter is read. Both loops should ignore any characters that aren't letters, and both should treat upper-case letters in the same way as lower-case letters. After the second word has been read, use a third loop to check whether all the elements in the array are zero. If so, the words are anagrams. *Hint:* You may wish to use functions from `<ctype.h>`, such as `isalpha` and `tolower`.

17.   Write a program that prints an $n \times n$ magic square (a square arrangement of the numbers 1, 2, ..., n^2 in which the sums of the rows, columns, and diagonals are all the same). The user will specify the value of *n*:

```
This program creates a magic square of a specified size.
The size must be an odd number between 1 and 99.
Enter size of magic square: 5
    17   24    1    8   15
    23    5    7   14   16
     4    6   13   20   22
    10   12   19   21    3
    11   18   25    2    9
```

Store the magic square in a two-dimensional array. Start by placing the number 1 in the middle of row 0. Place each of the remaining numbers 2, 3, …, n^2 by moving up one row and over one column. Any attempt to go outside the bounds of the array should "wrap around" to the opposite side of the array. For example, instead of storing the next number in row −1, we would store it in row $n - 1$ (the last row). Instead of storing the next number in column n, we would store it in column 0. If a particular array element is already occupied, put the number directly below the previously stored number. If your compiler supports variable-length arrays, declare the array to have n rows and n columns. If not, declare the array to have 99 rows and 99 columns.

9 Functions

If you have a procedure with ten
parameters, you probably missed some.

We saw in Chapter 2 that a function is simply a series of statements that have been grouped together and given a name. Although the term "function" comes from mathematics, C functions don't always resemble math functions. In C, a function doesn't necessarily have arguments, nor does it necessarily compute a value. (In some programming languages, a "function" returns a value, whereas a "procedure" doesn't. C lacks this distinction.)

Functions are the building blocks of C programs. Each function is essentially a small program, with its own declarations and statements. Using functions, we can divide a program into small pieces that are easier for us—and others—to understand and modify. Functions can take some of the tedium out of programming by allowing us to avoid duplicating code that's used more than once. Moreover, functions are reusable: we can take a function that was originally part of one program and use it in others.

Our programs so far have consisted of just the `main` function. In this chapter, we'll see how to write functions other than `main`, and we'll learn more about `main` itself. Section 9.1 shows how to define and call functions. Section 9.2 then discusses function declarations and how they differ from function definitions. Next, Section 9.3 examines how arguments are passed to functions. The remainder of the chapter covers the `return` statement (Section 9.4), the related issue of program termination (Section 9.5), and recursion (Section 9.6).

9.1 Defining and Calling Functions

Before we go over the formal rules for defining a function, let's look at three simple programs that define functions.

PROGRAM   **Computing Averages**

Suppose we often need to compute the average of two `double` values. The C library doesn't have an "average" function, but we can easily define our own. Here's what it would look like:

```
double average(double a, double b)
{
  return (a + b) / 2;
}
```

The word `double` at the beginning is `average`'s ***return type:*** the type of data that the function returns each time it's called. The identifiers a and b (the function's ***parameters***) represent the two numbers that will be supplied when `average` is called. Each parameter must have a type (just like every variable has a type); in this example, both a and b have type `double`. (It may look odd, but the word `double` must appear twice, once for a and once for b.) A function parameter is essentially a variable whose initial value will be supplied later, when the function is called.

Every function has an executable part, called the ***body***, which is enclosed in braces. The body of `average` consists of a single `return` statement. Executing this statement causes the function to "return" to the place from which it was called; the value of `(a + b) / 2` will be the value returned by the function.

To call a function, we write the function name, followed by a list of ***arguments***. For example, `average(x, y)` is a call of the `average` function. Arguments are used to supply information to a function; in this case, `average` needs to know which two numbers to average. The effect of the call `average(x, y)` is to copy the values of x and y into the parameters a and b, and then execute the body of `average`. An argument doesn't have to be a variable; any expression of a compatible type will do, allowing us to write `average(5.1, 8.9)` or `average(x/2, y/3)`.

We'll put the call of `average` in the place where we need to use the return value. For example, we could write

```
printf("Average: %g\n", average(x, y));
```

to compute the average of x and y and then print it. This statement has the following effect:

1. The `average` function is called with x and y as arguments.
2. x and y are copied into a and b.
3. `average` executes its `return` statement, returning the average of a and b.
4. `printf` prints the value that `average` returns. (The return value of `average` becomes one of `printf`'s arguments.)

Note that the return value of `average` isn't saved anywhere; the program prints it and then discards it. If we had needed the return value later in the program, we could have captured it in a variable:

```
avg = average(x, y);
```

This statement calls `average`, then saves its return value in the variable `avg`.

Now, let's use the `average` function in a complete program. The following program reads three numbers and computes their averages, one pair at a time:

```
Enter three numbers: 3.5 9.6 10.2
Average of 3.5 and 9.6: 6.55
Average of 9.6 and 10.2: 9.9
Average of 3.5 and 10.2: 6.85
```

Among other things, this program shows that a function can be called as often as we need.

average.c

```
/* Computes pairwise averages of three numbers */

#include <stdio.h>

double average(double a, double b)
{
  return (a + b) / 2;
}

int main(void)
{
  double x, y, z;

  printf("Enter three numbers: ");
  scanf("%lf%lf%lf", &x, &y, &z);
  printf("Average of %g and %g: %g\n", x, y, average(x, y));
  printf("Average of %g and %g: %g\n", y, z, average(y, z));
  printf("Average of %g and %g: %g\n", x, z, average(x, z));

  return 0;
}
```

Notice that I've put the definition of `average` before `main`. We'll see in Section 9.2 that putting `average` after `main` causes problems.

PROGRAM   **Printing a Countdown**

Not every function returns a value. For example, a function whose job is to produce output may not need to return anything. To indicate that a function has no return value, we specify that its return type is `void`. (`void` is a type with no values.) Consider the following function, which prints the message `T minus` *n* and `counting`, where *n* is supplied when the function is called:

```
void print_count(int n)
{
  printf("T minus %d and counting\n", n);
}
```

`print_count` has one parameter, n, of type `int`. It returns nothing, so I've specified `void` as the return type and omitted the `return` statement. Since `print_count` doesn't return a value, we can't call it in the same way we call `average`. Instead, a call of `print_count` must appear in a statement by itself:

```
print_count(i);
```

Here's a program that calls `print_count` 10 times inside a loop:

countdown.c

```
/* Prints a countdown */

#include <stdio.h>

void print_count(int n)
{
  printf("T minus %d and counting\n", n);
}

int main(void)
{
  int i;

  for (i = 10; i > 0; --i)
    print_count(i);

  return 0;
}
```

Initially, i has the value 10. When `print_count` is called for the first time, i is copied into n, so that n takes on the value 10 as well. As a result, the first call of `print_count` will print

```
T minus 10 and counting
```

`print_count` then returns to the point at which it was called, which happens to be the body of a `for` statement. The `for` statement resumes where it left off, decrementing i to 9 and testing whether it's greater than 0. It is, so `print_count` is called again, this time printing

```
T minus 9 and counting
```

Each time `print_count` is called, i is different, so `print_count` will print 10 different messages.

PROGRAM   **Printing a Pun (Revisited)**

Some functions have no parameters at all. Consider `print_pun`, which prints a bad pun each time it's called:

```
void print_pun(void)
{
  printf("To C, or not to C: that is the question.\n");
}
```

The word `void` in parentheses indicates that `print_pun` has no arguments. (This time, we're using `void` as a placeholder that means "nothing goes here.")

To call a function with no arguments, we write the function's name, followed by parentheses:

```
print_pun();
```

The parentheses *must* be present, even though there are no arguments.

Here's a tiny program that tests the `print_pun` function:

pun2.c

```
/* Prints a bad pun */

#include <stdio.h>

void print_pun(void)
{
  printf("To C, or not to C: that is the question.\n");
}

int main(void)
{
  print_pun();
  return 0;
}
```

The execution of this program begins with the first statement in `main`, which happens to be a call of `print_pun`. When `print_pun` begins to execute, it in turn calls `printf` to display a string. When `printf` returns, `print_pun` returns to `main`.

Function Definitions

Now that we've seen several examples, let's look at the general form of a *function definition:*

function definition

> *return-type function-name (parameters)*
> {
>   *declarations*
>   *statements*
> }

The return type of a function is the type of value that the function returns. The following rules govern the return type:

- Functions may not return arrays, but there are no other restrictions on the return type.
- Specifying that the return type is `void` indicates that the function doesn't return a value.

- If the return type is omitted in C89, the function is presumed to return a value of type int. In C99, it's illegal to omit the return type of a function.

As a matter of style, some programmers put the return type *above* the function name:

```
double
average(double a, double b)
{
  return (a + b) / 2;
}
```

Putting the return type on a separate line is especially useful if the return type is lengthy, like unsigned long int.

After the function name comes a list of parameters. Each parameter is preceded by a specification of its type; parameters are separated by commas. If the function has no parameters, the word void should appear between the parentheses. *Note:* A separate type must be specified for each parameter, even when several parameters have the same type:

```
double average(double a, b)    /*** WRONG ***/
{
  return (a + b) / 2;
}
```

The body of a function may include both declarations and statements. For example, the average function could be written

```
double average(double a, double b)
{
  double sum;      /* declaration */

  sum = a + b;     /* statement */
  return sum / 2;  /* statement */
}
```

Variables declared in the body of a function belong exclusively to that function; they can't be examined or modified by other functions. In C89, variable declarations must come first, before all statements in the body of a function. In C99, variable declarations and statements can be mixed, as long as each variable is declared prior to the first statement that uses the variable. (Some pre-C99 compilers also allow mixing of declarations and statements.)

The body of a function whose return type is void (which I'll call a "void function") can be empty:

```
void print_pun(void)
{
}
```

Leaving the body empty may make sense during program development; we can leave room for the function without taking the time to complete it, then come back later and write the body.

Function Calls

A function call consists of a function name followed by a list of arguments, enclosed in parentheses:

```
average(x, y)
print_count(i)
print_pun()
```

If the parentheses are missing, the function won't get called:

```
print_pun;   /*** WRONG ***/
```

The result is a legal (albeit meaningless) expression statement that looks correct, but has no effect. Some compilers issue a warning such as *"statement with no effect."*

A call of a `void` function is always followed by a semicolon to turn it into a statement:

```
print_count(i);
print_pun();
```

A call of a non-`void` function, on the other hand, produces a value that can be stored in a variable, tested, printed, or used in some other way:

```
avg = average(x, y);
if (average(x, y) > 0)
  printf("Average is positive\n");
printf("The average is %g\n", average(x, y));
```

The value returned by a non-`void` function can always be discarded if it's not needed:

```
average(x, y);   /* discards return value */
```

expression statements ➤ 4.5   This call of `average` is an example of an expression statement: a statement that evaluates an expression but then discards the result.

Ignoring the return value of `average` is an odd thing to do, but for some functions it makes sense. The `printf` function, for example, returns the number of characters that it prints. After the following call, `num_chars` will have the value 9:

```
num_chars = printf("Hi, Mom!\n");
```

Since we're probably not interested in the number of characters printed, we'll normally discard `printf`'s return value:

```
printf("Hi, Mom!\n");   /* discards return value */
```

To make it clear that we're deliberately discarding the return value of a function, C allows us to put `(void)` before the call:

```
(void) printf("Hi, Mom!\n");
```

casting ►7.4   What we're doing is casting (converting) the return value of `printf` to type `void`. (In C, "casting to `void`" is a polite way of saying "throwing away.") Using `(void)` makes it clear to others that you deliberately discarded the return value, not just forgot that there was one. Unfortunately, there are a great many functions in the C library whose values are routinely ignored; using `(void)` when calling them all can get tiresome, so I haven't done so in this book.

PROGRAM   **Testing Whether a Number Is Prime**

To see how functions can make programs easier to understand, let's write a program that tests whether a number is prime. The program will prompt the user to enter a number, then respond with a message indicating whether or not the number is prime:

```
Enter a number: 34
Not prime
```

Instead of putting the prime-testing details in `main`, we'll define a separate function that returns `true` if its parameter is a prime number and `false` if it isn't. When given a number n, the `is_prime` function will divide n by each of the numbers between 2 and the square root of n; if the remainder is ever 0, we know that n isn't prime.

prime.c
```c
/* Tests whether a number is prime */

#include <stdbool.h>    /* C99 only */
#include <stdio.h>

bool is_prime(int n)
{
  int divisor;

  if (n <= 1)
    return false;
  for (divisor = 2; divisor * divisor <= n; divisor++)
    if (n % divisor == 0)
      return false;
  return true;
}

int main(void)
{
  int n;

  printf("Enter a number: ");
  scanf("%d", &n);
  if (is_prime(n))
    printf("Prime\n");
  else
    printf("Not prime\n");
```

```
    return 0;
}
```

Notice that `main` contains a variable named n even though is_prime's parameter is also named n. In general, a function may declare a variable with the same name as a variable in another function. The two variables represent different locations in memory, so assigning a new value to one variable doesn't change the other. (This property extends to parameters as well.) Section 10.1 discusses this point in more detail.

As is_prime demonstrates, a function may have more than one `return` statement. However, we can execute just one of these statements during a given call of the function, because reaching a `return` statement causes the function to return to where it was called. We'll learn more about the `return` statement in Section 9.4.

9.2 Function Declarations

In the programs in Section 9.1, the definition of each function was always placed *above* the point at which it was called. In fact, C doesn't require that the definition of a function precede its calls. Suppose that we rearrange the `average.c` program by putting the definition of `average` *after* the definition of `main`:

```
#include <stdio.h>

int main(void)
{
  double x, y, z;

  printf("Enter three numbers: ");
  scanf("%lf%lf%lf", &x, &y, &z);
  printf("Average of %g and %g: %g\n", x, y, average(x, y));
  printf("Average of %g and %g: %g\n", y, z, average(y, z));
  printf("Average of %g and %g: %g\n", x, z, average(x, z));

  return 0;
}

double average(double a, double b)
{
  return (a + b) / 2;
}
```

When the compiler encounters the first call of `average` in `main`, it has no information about `average`: it doesn't know how many parameters `average` has, what the types of these parameters are, or what kind of value `average` returns. Instead of producing an error message, though, the compiler assumes that `average` returns an `int` value (recall from Section 9.1 that the return type of a function is `int` by default). We say that the compiler has created an ***implicit declaration*** of the function. The compiler is unable to check that we're passing `average` the right number of arguments and that the arguments have the proper type. Instead, it performs the default argument promotions and hopes for the best. When it encounters the definition of `average` later in the program, the compiler notices that the function's return type is actually `double`, not `int`, and so we get an error message.

default argument promotions ➤*9.3*

One way to avoid the problem of call-before-definition is to arrange the program so that the definition of each function precedes all its calls. Unfortunately, such an arrangement doesn't always exist, and even when it does, it may make the program harder to understand by putting its function definitions in an unnatural order.

Fortunately, C offers a better solution: declare each function before calling it. A ***function declaration*** provides the compiler with a brief glimpse at a function whose full definition will appear later. A function declaration resembles the first line of a function definition with a semicolon added at the end:

function declaration

> *return-type function-name (parameters) ;*

Needless to say, the declaration of a function must be consistent with the function's definition.

Q&A

Here's how our program would look with a declaration of `average` added:

```
#include <stdio.h>

double average(double a, double b);    /* DECLARATION */

int main(void)
{
  double x, y, z;

  printf("Enter three numbers: ");
  scanf("%lf%lf%lf", &x, &y, &z);
  printf("Average of %g and %g: %g\n", x, y, average(x, y));
  printf("Average of %g and %g: %g\n", y, z, average(y, z));
  printf("Average of %g and %g: %g\n", x, z, average(x, z));

  return 0;
}

double average(double a, double b)    /* DEFINITION */
{
  return (a + b) / 2;
}
```

Q&A

Function declarations of the kind we've been discussing are known as ***function prototypes*** to distinguish them from an older style of function declaration in which the parentheses are left empty. A prototype provides a complete description of how to call a function: how many arguments to supply, what their types should be, and what type of result will be returned.

Incidentally, a function prototype doesn't have to specify the *names* of the function's parameters, as long as their *types* are present:

```
double average(double, double);
```

It's usually best not to omit parameter names, since they help document the purpose of each parameter and remind the programmer of the order in which arguments must appear when the function is called. However, there are legitimate reasons for omitting parameter names, and some programmers prefer to do so.

C99 has adopted the rule that either a declaration or a definition of a function must be present prior to any call of the function. Calling a function for which the compiler has not yet seen a declaration or definition is an error.

9.3 Arguments

Let's review the difference between a parameter and an argument. *Parameters* appear in function *definitions;* they're dummy names that represent values to be supplied when the function is called. *Arguments* are expressions that appear in function *calls*. When the distinction between *argument* and *parameter* isn't important, I'll sometimes use *argument* to mean either.

In C, arguments are ***passed by value:*** when a function is called, each argument is evaluated and its value assigned to the corresponding parameter. Since the parameter contains a copy of the argument's value, any changes made to the parameter during the execution of the function don't affect the argument. In effect, each parameter behaves like a variable that's been initialized to the value of the matching argument.

The fact that arguments are passed by value has both advantages and disadvantages. Since a parameter can be modified without affecting the corresponding argument, we can use parameters as variables within the function, thereby reducing the number of genuine variables needed. Consider the following function, which raises a number x to a power n:

```
int power(int x, int n)
{
  int i, result = 1;

  for (i = 1; i <= n; i++)
    result = result * x;

  return result;
}
```

Since n is a *copy* of the original exponent, we can modify it inside the function, thus removing the need for i:

```
int power(int x, int n)
{
  int result = 1;

  while (n-- > 0)
    result = result * x;

  return result;
}
```

Unfortunately, C's requirement that arguments be passed by value makes it difficult to write certain kinds of functions. For example, suppose that we need a function that will decompose a `double` value into an integer part and a fractional part. Since a function can't *return* two numbers, we might try passing a pair of variables to the function and having it modify them:

```
void decompose(double x, long int_part, double frac_part)
{
  int_part = (long) x;    /* drops the fractional part of x */
  frac_part = x - int_part;
}
```

Suppose that we call the function in the following way:

```
decompose(3.14159, i, d);
```

At the beginning of the call, 3.14159 is copied into `x`, `i`'s value is copied into `int_part`, and `d`'s value is copied into `frac_part`. The statements inside decompose then assign 3 to `int_part` and .14159 to `frac_part`, and the function returns. Unfortunately, `i` and `d` weren't affected by the assignments to `int_part` and `frac_part`, so they have the same values after the call as they did before the call. With a little extra effort, `decompose` can be made to work, as we'll see in Section 11.4. However, we'll need to cover more of C's features first.

Argument Conversions

C allows function calls in which the types of the arguments don't match the types of the parameters. The rules governing how the arguments are converted depend on whether or not the compiler has seen a prototype for the function (or the function's full definition) prior to the call:

- **The compiler has encountered a prototype prior to the call.** The value of each argument is implicitly converted to the type of the corresponding parameter as if by assignment. For example, if an `int` argument is passed to a function that was expecting a `double`, the argument is converted to `double` automatically.

- **The compiler has not encountered a prototype prior to the call.** The compiler performs the *default argument promotions:* (1) `float` arguments are converted to `double`. (2) The integral promotions are performed, causing `char` and `short` arguments to be converted to `int`. (In C99, the integer promotions are performed.)

Relying on the default argument promotions is dangerous. Consider the following program:

```
#include <stdio.h>

int main(void)
{
  double x = 3.0;
  printf("Square: %d\n", square(x));

  return 0;
}

int square(int n)
{
  return n * n;
}
```

At the time `square` is called, the compiler hasn't seen a prototype yet, so it doesn't know that `square` expects an argument of type `int`. Instead, the compiler performs the default argument promotions on `x`, with no effect. Since it's expecting an argument of type `int` but has been given a `double` value instead, the effect of calling `square` is undefined. The problem can be fixed by casting `square`'s argument to the proper type:

```
printf("Square: %d\n", square((int) x));
```

Of course, a much better solution is to provide a prototype for `square` before calling it. In C99, calling `square` without first providing a declaration or definition of the function is an error.

Array Arguments

Arrays are often used as arguments. When a function parameter is a one-dimensional array, the length of the array can be (and is normally) left unspecified:

```
int f(int a[])    /* no length specified */
{
  ...
}
```

The argument can be any one-dimensional array whose elements are of the proper type. There's just one problem: how will `f` know how long the array is? Unfortunately, C doesn't provide any easy way for a function to determine the length of an array passed to it. Instead, we'll have to supply the length—if the function needs it—as an additional argument.

Although we can use the `sizeof` operator to help determine the length of an array *variable*, it doesn't give the correct answer for an array *parameter:*

```
int f(int a[])
{
  int len = sizeof(a) / sizeof(a[0]);
    /*** WRONG: not the number of elements in a ***/
  ...
}
```

Section 12.3 explains why.

The following function illustrates the use of one-dimensional array arguments. When given an array a of `int` values, `sum_array` returns the sum of the elements in a. Since `sum_array` needs to know the length of a, we must supply it as a second argument.

```
int sum_array(int a[], int n)
{
  int i, sum = 0;

  for (i = 0; i < n; i++)
    sum += a[i];

  return sum;
}
```

The prototype for `sum_array` has the following appearance:

```
int sum_array(int a[], int n);
```

As usual, we can omit the parameter names if we wish:

```
int sum_array(int [], int);
```

When `sum_array` is called, the first argument will be the name of an array, and the second will be its length. For example:

```
#define LEN 100

int main(void)
{
  int b[LEN], total;
  ...
  total = sum_array(b, LEN);
  ...
}
```

Notice that we don't put brackets after an array name when passing it to a function:

```
total = sum_array(b[], LEN);   /*** WRONG ***/
```

An important point about array arguments: A function has no way to check that we've passed it the correct array length. We can exploit this fact by telling the function that the array is smaller than it really is. Suppose that we've only stored 50 numbers in the b array, even though it can hold 100. We can sum just the first 50 elements by writing

```
total = sum_array(b, 50);    /* sums first 50 elements */
```

sum_array will ignore the other 50 elements. (Indeed, it won't know that they even exist!)

Be careful not to tell a function that an array argument is *larger* than it really is:

```
total = sum_array(b, 150);   /*** WRONG ***/
```

In this example, sum_array will go past the end of the array, causing undefined behavior.

Another important thing to know is that a function is allowed to change the elements of an array parameter, and the change is reflected in the corresponding argument. For example, the following function modifies an array by storing zero into each of its elements:

```
void store_zeros(int a[], int n)
{
  int i;

  for (i = 0; i < n; i++)
    a[i] = 0;
}
```

The call

```
store_zeros(b, 100);
```

will store zero into the first 100 elements of the array b. This ability to modify the elements of an array argument may seem to contradict the fact that C passes arguments by value. In fact, there's no contradiction, but I won't be able to explain why until Section 12.3.

Q&A   If a parameter is a multidimensional array, only the length of the first dimension may be omitted when the parameter is declared. For example, if we revise the sum_array function so that a is a two-dimensional array, we must specify the number of columns in a, although we don't have to indicate the number of rows:

```
#define LEN 10

int sum_two_dimensional_array(int a[][LEN], int n)
{
  int i, j, sum = 0;
```

```
for (i = 0; i < n; i++)
    for (j = 0; j < LEN; j++)
        sum += a[i][j];

return sum;
}
```

Not being able to pass multidimensional arrays with an arbitrary number of columns can be a nuisance. Fortunately, we can often work around this difficulty by using arrays of pointers. C99's variable-length array parameters provide an even better solution to the problem.

arrays of pointers ➤ 13.7

C99 Variable-Length Array Parameters

C99 adds several new twists to array arguments. The first has to do with variable-length arrays (VLAs), a feature of C99 that allows the length of an array to be specified using a non-constant expression. Variable-length arrays can also be parameters, as it turns out.

variable-length arrays ➤ 8.3

Consider the sum_array function discussed earlier in this section. Here's the definition of sum_array, with the body omitted:

```
int sum_array(int a[], int n)
{
    ...
}
```

As it stands now, there's no direct link between n and the length of the array a. Although the function body treats n as a's length, the actual length of the array could in fact be larger than n (or smaller, in which case the function won't work correctly).

Using a variable-length array parameter, we can explicitly state that a's length is n:

```
int sum_array(int n, int a[n])
{
    ...
}
```

The value of the first parameter (n) specifies the length of the second parameter (a). Note that the order of the parameters has been switched; order is important when variable-length array parameters are used.

The following version of sum_array is illegal:

```
int sum_array(int a[n], int n)    /*** WRONG ***/
{
    ...
}
```

The compiler will issue an error message at int a[n], because it hasn't yet seen n.

There are several ways to write the prototype for our new version of sum_array. One possibility is to make it look exactly like the function definition:

```
int sum_array(int n, int a[n]);   /* Version 1 */
```

Another possibility is to replace the array length by an asterisk (*):

```
int sum_array(int n, int a[*]);   /* Version 2a */
```

The reason for using the * notation is that parameter names are optional in function declarations. If the name of the first parameter is omitted, it wouldn't be possible to specify that the length of the array is n, but the * provides a clue that the length of the array is related to parameters that come earlier in the list:

```
int sum_array(int, int [*]);      /* Version 2b */
```

It's also legal to leave the brackets empty, as we normally do when declaring an array parameter:

```
int sum_array(int n, int a[]);    /* Version 3a */
int sum_array(int, int []);       /* Version 3b */
```

Leaving the brackets empty isn't a good choice, because it doesn't expose the relationship between n and a.

In general, the length of a variable-length array parameter can be any expression. For example, suppose that we were to write a function that concatenates two arrays a and b by copying the elements of a, followed by the elements of b, into a third array named c:

```
int concatenate(int m, int n, int a[m], int b[n], int c[m+n])
{
   ...
}
```

The length of c is the sum of the lengths of a and b. The expression used to specify the length of c involves two other parameters, but in general it could refer to variables outside the function or even call other functions.

Variable-length array parameters with a single dimension—as in all our examples so far—have limited usefulness. They make a function declaration or definition more descriptive by stating the desired length of an array argument. However, no additional error-checking is performed; it's still possible for an array argument to be too long or too short.

It turns out that variable-length array parameters are most useful for multidimensional arrays. Earlier in this section, we tried to write a function that sums the elements in a two-dimensional array. Our original function was limited to arrays with a fixed number of columns. If we use a variable-length array parameter, we can generalize the function to any number of columns:

```
int sum_two_dimensional_array(int n, int m, int a[n][m])
{
  int i, j, sum = 0;

  for (i = 0; i < n; i++)
    for (j = 0; j < m; j++)
      sum += a[i][j];

  return sum;
}
```

Prototypes for this function include the following:

```
int sum_two_dimensional_array(int n, int m, int a[n][m]);
int sum_two_dimensional_array(int n, int m, int a[*][*]);
int sum_two_dimensional_array(int n, int m, int a[][m]);
int sum_two_dimensional_array(int n, int m, int a[][*]);
```

C99 Using `static` in Array Parameter Declarations

C99 allows the use of the keyword `static` in the declaration of array parameters. (The keyword itself existed before C99. Section 18.2 discusses its traditional uses.)

In the following example, putting `static` in front of the number 3 indicates that the length of a is guaranteed to be at least 3:

```
int sum_array(int a[static 3], int n)
{
  ...
}
```

Using `static` in this way has no effect on the behavior of the program. The presence of `static` is merely a "hint" that may allow a C compiler to generate faster instructions for accessing the array. (If the compiler knows that an array will always have a certain minimum length, it can arrange to "prefetch" these elements from memory when the function is called, before the elements are actually needed by statements within the function.)

One last note about `static`: If an array parameter has more than one dimension, `static` can be used only in the first dimension (for example, when specifying the number of rows in a two-dimensional array).

C99 Compound Literals

Let's return to the original `sum_array` function one last time. When `sum_array` is called, the first argument is usually the name of an array (the one whose elements are to be summed). For example, we might call `sum_array` in the following way:

```
int b[] = {3, 0, 3, 4, 1};
total = sum_array(b, 5);
```

The only problem with this arrangement is that b must be declared as a variable and then initialized prior to the call. If b isn't needed for any other purpose, it can be mildly annoying to create it solely for the purpose of calling sum_array.

In C99, we can avoid this annoyance by using a **compound literal:** an unnamed array that's created "on the fly" by simply specifying which elements it contains. The following call of sum_array has a compound literal (shown in **bold**) as its first argument:

```
total = sum_array((int []){3, 0, 3, 4, 1}, 5);
```

In this example, the compound literal creates an array containing the five integers 3, 0, 3, 4, and 1. We didn't specify the length of the array, so it's determined by the number of elements in the literal. We also have the option of specifying a length explicitly: (int [4]){1, 9, 2, 1} is equivalent to (int []){1, 9, 2, 1}.

In general, a compound literal consists of a type name within parentheses, followed by a set of values enclosed by braces. A compound literal resembles a cast applied to an initializer. In fact, compound literals and initializers obey the same rules. A compound literal may contain designators, just like a designated initializer, and it may fail to provide full initialization (in which case any uninitialized elements default to zero). For example, the literal (int [10]){8, 6} has 10 elements; the first two have the values 8 and 6, and the remaining elements have the value 0.

designated initializers ➤8.1

Compound literals created inside a function may contain arbitrary expressions, not just constants. For example, we could write

```
total = sum_array((int []){2 * i, i + j, j * k}, 3);
```

where i, j, and k are variables. This aspect of compound literals greatly enhances their usefulness.

lvalues ➤4.2

A compound literal is an lvalue, so the values of its elements can be changed. If desired, a compound literal can be made "read-only" by adding the word const to its type, as in (const int []){5, 4}.

9.4 The return Statement

A non-void function must use the return statement to specify what value it will return. The return statement has the form

return statement

> return *expression* ;

The expression is often just a constant or variable:

```
return 0;
return status;
```

conditional operator ➤5.2   More complex expressions are possible. For example, it's not unusual to see the conditional operator used in a return expression:

```
return n >= 0 ? n : 0;
```

When this statement is executed, the expression `n >= 0 ? n : 0` is evaluated first. The statement returns the value of `n` if it's not negative; otherwise, it returns 0.

If the type of the expression in a `return` statement doesn't match the function's return type, the expression will be implicitly converted to the return type. For example, if a function is declared to return an `int`, but the `return` statement contains a `double` expression, the value of the expression is converted to `int`.

`return` statements may appear in functions whose return type is `void`, provided that no expression is given:

```
return;    /* return in a void function */
```

Q&A   Putting an expression in such a `return` statement will get you a compile-time error. In the following example, the `return` statement causes the function to return immediately when given a negative argument:

```
void print_int(int i)
{
  if (i < 0)
    return;
  printf("%d", i);
}
```

If `i` is less than 0, `print_int` will return without calling `printf`.

A `return` statement may appear at the end of a `void` function:

```
void print_pun(void)
{
  printf("To C, or not to C: that is the question.\n");
  return;    /* OK, but not needed */
}
```

Using `return` is unnecessary, though, since the function will return automatically after its last statement has been executed.

If a non-`void` function reaches the end of its body—that is, it fails to execute a `return` statement—the behavior of the program is undefined if it attempts to use the value returned by the function. Some compilers will issue a warning such as *"control reaches end of non-void function"* if they detect the possibility of a non-`void` function "falling off" the end of its body.

9.5 Program Termination

Since `main` is a function, it must have a return type. Normally, the return type of `main` is `int`, which is why the programs we've seen so far have defined `main` in the following way:

```
int main(void)
{
    ...
}
```

Older C programs often omit `main`'s return type, taking advantage of the fact that it traditionally defaults to `int`:

```
main()
{
    ...
}
```

 Omitting the return type of a function isn't legal in C99, so it's best to avoid this practice. Omitting the word `void` in `main`'s parameter list remains legal, but—as a matter of style—it's best to be explicit about the fact that `main` has no parameters. (We'll see later that `main` sometimes *does* have two parameters, usually named `argc` and `argv`.)

argc and argv ➤ 13.7

The value returned by `main` is a status code that—in some operating systems—can be tested when the program terminates. `main` should return 0 if the program terminates normally; to indicate abnormal termination, `main` should return a value other than 0. (Actually, there's no rule to prevent us from using the return value for other purposes.) It's good practice to make sure that every C program returns a status code, even if there are no plans to use it, since someone running the program later may decide to test it.

The `exit` Function

Executing a `return` statement in `main` is one way to terminate a program. Another is calling the `exit` function, which belongs to `<stdlib.h>`. The argument passed to `exit` has the same meaning as `main`'s return value: both indicate the program's status at termination. To indicate normal termination, we'd pass 0:

<stdlib.h> header ➤ 26.2

```
exit(0);                /* normal termination */
```

Since 0 is a bit cryptic, C allows us to pass `EXIT_SUCCESS` instead (the effect is the same):

```
exit(EXIT_SUCCESS);     /* normal termination */
```

Passing `EXIT_FAILURE` indicates abnormal termination:

```
exit(EXIT_FAILURE);     /* abnormal termination */
```

`EXIT_SUCCESS` and `EXIT_FAILURE` are macros defined in `<stdlib.h>`. The values of `EXIT_SUCCESS` and `EXIT_FAILURE` are implementation-defined; typical values are 0 and 1, respectively.

As methods of terminating a program, `return` and `exit` are closely related. In fact, the statement

```
return expression;
```

in `main` is equivalent to

```
exit(expression);
```

The difference between `return` and `exit` is that `exit` causes program termination regardless of which function calls it. The `return` statement causes program termination only when it appears in the `main` function. Some programmers use `exit` exclusively to make it easier to locate all exit points in a program.

9.6 Recursion

A function is **recursive** if it calls itself. For example, the following function computes $n!$ recursively, using the formula $n! = n \times (n - 1)!$:

```
int fact(int n)
{
  if (n <= 1)
    return 1;
  else
    return n * fact(n - 1);
}
```

Some programming languages rely heavily on recursion, while others don't even allow it. C falls somewhere in the middle: it allows recursion, but most C programmers don't use it that often.

To see how recursion works, let's trace the execution of the statement

```
i = fact(3);
```

Here's what happens:

> `fact(3)` finds that 3 is not less than or equal to 1, so it calls
> > `fact(2)`, which finds that 2 is not less than or equal to 1, so it calls
> > > `fact(1)`, which finds that 1 *is* less than or equal to 1, so it returns 1, causing
> > `fact(2)` to return $2 \times 1 = 2$, causing
> `fact(3)` to return $3 \times 2 = 6$.

Notice how the unfinished calls of `fact` "pile up" until `fact` is finally passed 1. At that point, the old calls of `fact` begin to "unwind" one by one, until the original call—`fact(3)`—finally returns with the answer, 6.

Here's another example of recursion: a function that computes x^n, using the formula $x^n = x \times x^{n-1}$.

```
int power(int x, int n)
{
  if (n == 0)
    return 1;
  else
    return x * power(x, n - 1);
}
```

The call power(5, 3) would be executed as follows:

> power(5, 3) finds that 3 is not equal to 0, so it calls
>> power(5, 2), which finds that 2 is not equal to 0, so it calls
>>> power(5, 1), which finds that 1 is not equal to 0, so it calls
>>>> power(5, 0), which finds that 0 *is* equal to 0, so it returns 1, causing
>>> power(5, 1) to return $5 \times 1 = 5$, causing
>> power(5, 2) to return $5 \times 5 = 25$, causing
> power(5, 3) to return $5 \times 25 = 125$.

Incidentally, we can condense the power function a bit by putting a conditional expression in the return statement:

```
int power(int x, int n)
{
  return n == 0 ? 1 : x * power(x, n - 1);
}
```

Both fact and power are careful to test a "termination condition" as soon as they're called. When fact is called, it immediately checks whether its parameter is less than or equal to 1. When power is called, it first checks whether its second parameter is equal to 0. All recursive functions need some kind of termination condition in order to prevent infinite recursion.

The Quicksort Algorithm

At this point, you may wonder why we're bothering with recursion; after all, neither fact nor power really needs it. Well, you've got a point. Neither function makes much of a case for recursion, because each calls itself just once. Recursion is much more helpful for sophisticated algorithms that require a function to call itself two or more times.

In practice, recursion often arises naturally as a result of an algorithm design technique known as ***divide-and-conquer***, in which a large problem is divided into smaller pieces that are then tackled by the same algorithm. A classic example of the divide-and-conquer strategy can be found in the popular sorting algorithm known as ***Quicksort***. The Quicksort algorithm goes as follows (for simplicity, we'll assume that the array being sorted is indexed from 1 to *n*):

1. Choose an array element *e* (the "partitioning element"), then rearrange the array so that elements 1, ..., *i* – 1 are less than or equal to *e*, element *i* contains *e*, and elements *i* + 1, ..., *n* are greater than or equal to *e*.
2. Sort elements 1, ..., *i* – 1 by using Quicksort recursively.
3. Sort elements *i* + 1, ..., *n* by using Quicksort recursively.

After step 1, the element *e* is in its proper location. Since the elements to the left of *e* are all less than or equal to it, they'll be in their proper places once they've been sorted in step 2; similar reasoning applies to the elements to the right of *e*.

Step 1 of the Quicksort algorithm is obviously critical. There are various methods to partition an array, some much better than others. We'll use a technique that's easy to understand but not particularly efficient. I'll first describe the partitioning algorithm informally; later, we'll translate it into C code.

The algorithm relies on two "markers" named *low* and *high*, which keep track of positions within the array. Initially, *low* points to the first element of the array and *high* points to the last element. We start by copying the first element (the partitioning element) into a temporary location elsewhere, leaving a "hole" in the array. Next, we move *high* across the array from right to left until it points to an element that's smaller than the partitioning element. We then copy the element into the hole that *low* points to, which creates a new hole (pointed to by *high*). We now move *low* from left to right, looking for an element that's larger than the partitioning element. When we find one, we copy it into the hole that *high* points to. The process repeats, with *low* and *high* taking turns, until they meet somewhere in the middle of the array. At that time, both will point to a hole; all we need do is copy the partitioning element into the hole. The following diagrams illustrate how Quicksort would sort an array of integers:

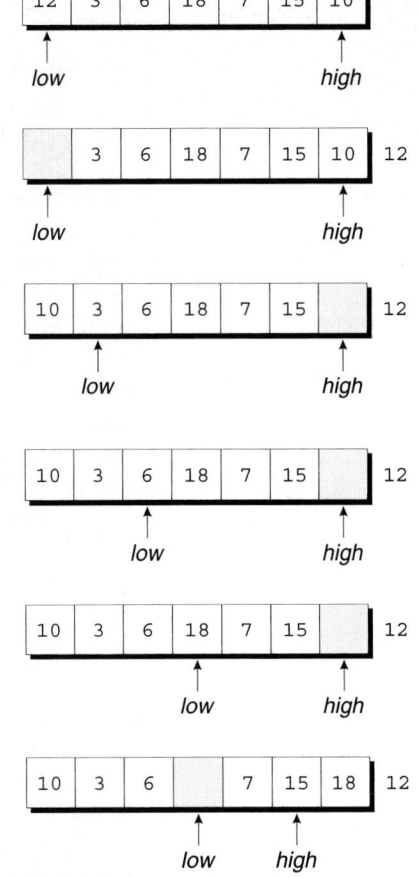

Let's start with an array containing seven elements. *low* points to the first element; *high* points to the last one.

The first element, 12, is the partitioning element. Copying it somewhere else leaves a hole at the beginning of the array.

We now compare the element pointed to by *high* with 12. Since 10 is smaller than 12, it's on the wrong side of the array, so we move it to the hole and shift *low* to the right.

low points to the number 3, which is less than 12 and therefore doesn't need to be moved. We shift *low* to the right instead.

Since 6 is also less than 12, we shift *low* again.

low now points to 18, which is larger than 12 and therefore out of position. After moving 18 to the hole, we shift *high* to the left.

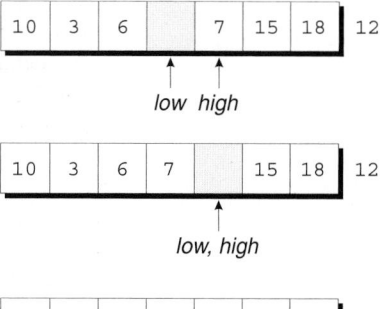

high points to 15, which is greater than 12 and thus doesn't need to be moved. We shift *high* to the left and continue.

high points to 7, which is out of position. After moving 7 to the hole, we shift *low* to the right.

low and *high* are now equal, so we move the partitioning element to the hole.

At this point, we've accomplished our objective: all elements to the left of the partitioning element are less than or equal to 12, and all elements to the right are greater than or equal to 12. Now that the array has been partitioned, we can use Quicksort recursively to sort the first four elements of the array (10, 3, 6, and 7) and the last two (15 and 18).

PROGRAM **Quicksort**

Let's develop a recursive function named `quicksort` that uses the Quicksort algorithm to sort an array of integers. To test the function, we'll have `main` read 10 numbers into an array, call `quicksort` to sort the array, then print the elements in the array:

```
Enter 10 numbers to be sorted: 9 16 47 82 4 66 12 3 25 51
In sorted order: 3 4 9 12 16 25 47 51 66 82
```

Since the code for partitioning the array is a bit lengthy, I'll put it in a separate function named `split`.

qsort.c

```c
/* Sorts an array of integers using Quicksort algorithm */

#include <stdio.h>

#define N 10

void quicksort(int a[], int low, int high);
int split(int a[], int low, int high);

int main(void)
{
  int a[N], i;

  printf("Enter %d numbers to be sorted: ", N);
  for (i = 0; i < N; i++)
    scanf("%d", &a[i]);
```

```
      quicksort(a, 0, N - 1);

      printf("In sorted order: ");
      for (i = 0; i < N; i++)
        printf("%d ", a[i]);
      printf("\n");

      return 0;
    }

    void quicksort(int a[], int low, int high)
    {
      int middle;

      if (low >= high) return;
      middle = split(a, low, high);
      quicksort(a, low, middle - 1);
      quicksort(a, middle + 1, high);
    }

    int split(int a[], int low, int high)
    {
      int part_element = a[low];

      for (;;) {
        while (low < high && part_element <= a[high])
          high--;
        if (low >= high) break;
        a[low++] = a[high];

        while (low < high && a[low] <= part_element)
          low++;
        if (low >= high) break;
        a[high--] = a[low];
      }

      a[high] = part_element;
      return high;
    }
```

Although this version of Quicksort works, it's not the best. There are numerous ways to improve the program's performance, including:

- *Improving the partitioning algorithm.* Our method isn't the most efficient. Instead of choosing the first element in the array as the partitioning element, it's better to take the median of the first element, the middle element, and the last element. The partitioning process itself can also be sped up. In particular, it's possible to avoid the low < high tests in the two while loops.

- *Using a different method to sort small arrays.* Instead of using Quicksort recursively all the way down to arrays with one element, it's better to use a simpler method for small arrays (those with fewer than, say, 25 elements).

■ *Making Quicksort nonrecursive.* Although Quicksort is a recursive algorithm by nature—and is easiest to understand in recursive form—it's actually more efficient if the recursion is removed.

For details about improving Quicksort, consult a book on algorithm design, such as Robert Sedgewick's *Algorithms in C, Parts 1–4: Fundamentals, Data Structures, Sorting, Searching,* Third Edition (Boston, Mass.: Addison-Wesley, 1998).

Q & A

Q: **Some C books appear to use terms other than *parameter* and *argument*. Is there any standard terminology? [p. 184]**

A: As with many other aspects of C, there's no general agreement on terminology, although the C89 and C99 standards use *parameter* and *argument*. The following table should help you translate:

This book:	*Other books:*
parameter	formal argument, formal parameter
argument	actual argument, actual parameter

Keep in mind that—when no confusion would result—I sometimes deliberately blur the distinction between the two terms, using *argument* to mean either.

Q: **I've seen programs in which parameter types are specified in separate declarations after the parameter list, as in the following example:**

```
double average(a, b)
double a, b;
{
  return (a + b) / 2;
}
```

Is this practice legal? [p. 188]

A: This method of defining functions comes from K&R C, so you may encounter it in older books and programs. C89 and C99 support this style so that older programs will still compile. I'd avoid using it in new programs, however, for a couple of reasons.

First, functions that are defined in the older way aren't subject to the same degree of error-checking. When a function is defined in the older way—and no prototype is present—the compiler won't check that the function is called with the right number of arguments, nor will it check that the arguments have the proper types. Instead, it will perform the default argument promotions.

default argument promotions ➤9.3

Second, the C standard says that the older style is "obsolescent," meaning that its use is discouraged and that it may be dropped from C eventually.

Q: **Some programming languages allow procedures and functions to be nested within each other. Does C allow function definitions to be nested?**

A: No. C does not permit the definition of one function to appear in the body of another. Among other things, this restriction simplifies the compiler.

*Q: **Why does the compiler allow the use of function names that aren't followed by parentheses? [p. 189]**

pointers to functions ➤ 17.7

A: We'll see in a later chapter that the compiler treats a function name not followed by parentheses as a *pointer* to the function. Pointers to functions have legitimate uses, so the compiler can't automatically assume that a function name without parentheses is an error. The statement

```
print_pun;
```

expression statements ➤ 4.5

is legal because the compiler treats `print_pun` as a pointer and therefore an expression, making this a valid (although pointless) expression statement.

*Q: **In the function call `f(a, b)`, how does the compiler know whether the comma is punctuation or whether it's an operator?**

A: It turns out that the arguments in a function call can't be arbitrary expressions. Instead, they must be "assignment expressions," which can't contain commas used as operators unless they're enclosed in parentheses. In other words, in the call `f(a, b)` the comma is punctuation; in the call `f((a, b))` it's an operator.

Q: **Do the names of parameters in a function prototype have to match the names given later in the function's definition? [p. 192]**

A: No. Some programmers take advantage of this fact by giving long names to parameters in the prototype, then using shorter names in the actual definition. Or a French-speaking programmer might use English names in prototypes, then switch to more familiar French names in function definitions.

Q: **I still don't understand why we bother with function prototypes. If we just put definitions of all the functions before `main`, we're covered, right?**

A: Wrong. First, you're assuming that only `main` calls the other functions, which is unrealistic. In practice, some of the functions will call each other. If we put all function definitions above `main`, we'll have to watch their order carefully. Calling a function that hasn't been defined yet can lead to big problems.

But that's not all. Suppose that two functions call each other (which isn't as far-fetched as it may sound). No matter which function we define first, it will end up calling a function that hasn't been defined yet.

But there's still more! Once programs reach a certain size, it won't be feasible to put all the functions in one file anymore. When we reach that point, we'll need prototypes to tell the compiler about functions in other files.

Q: **I've seen function declarations that omit all information about parameters:**

```
double average();
```

Is this practice legal? [p. 192]

A: Yes. This declaration informs the compiler that `average` returns a `double` value but provides no information about the number and types of its parameters. (Leaving the parentheses empty doesn't necessarily mean that `average` has no parameters.)

In K&R C, this form of function declaration is the only one allowed; the form that we've been using—the function prototype, in which parameter information *is* included—was introduced in C89. The older kind of function declaration is now obsolescent, although still allowed.

Q: **Why would a programmer deliberately omit parameter names in a function prototype? Isn't it easier to just leave the names? [p. 193]**

A: Omitting parameter names in prototypes is typically done for defensive purposes. If a macro happens to have the same name as a parameter, the parameter name will be replaced during preprocessing, thereby damaging the prototype in which it appears. This isn't likely to be a problem in a small program written by one person but can occur in large applications written by many people.

Q: **Is it legal to put a function declaration inside the body of another function?**

A: Yes. Here's an example:

```
int main(void)
{
  double average(double a, double b);
  ...
}
```

This declaration of `average` is valid only for the body of `main`; if other functions need to call `average`, they'll each have to declare it.

The advantage of this practice is that it's clearer to the reader which functions call which other functions. (In this example, we see that `main` will be calling `average`.) On the other hand, it can be a nuisance if several functions need to call the same function. Even worse, trying to add and remove declarations during program maintenance can be a real pain. For these reasons, I'll always put function declarations outside function bodies.

Q: **If several functions have the same return type, can their declarations be combined? For example, since both `print_pun` and `print_count` have `void` as their return type, is the following declaration legal?**

```
void print_pun(void), print_count(int n);
```

A: Yes. In fact, C even allows us to combine function declarations with variable declarations:

```
double x, y, average(double a, double b);
```

Combining declarations in this way usually isn't a good idea, though; it can easily cause confusion.

Q: What happens if I specify a length for a one-dimensional array parameter? [p. 195]

A: The compiler ignores it. Consider the following example:

```
double inner_product(double v[3], double w[3]);
```

Other than documenting that `inner_product`'s arguments are supposed to be arrays of length 3, specifying a length doesn't buy us much. The compiler won't check that the arguments actually have length 3, so there's no added security. In fact, the practice is misleading in that it suggests that `inner_product` can only be passed arrays of length 3, when in fact we can pass arrays of arbitrary length.

*Q: Why can the first dimension in an array parameter be left unspecified, but not the other dimensions? [p. 197]

A: First, we need to discuss how arrays are passed in C. As Section 12.3 explains, when an array is passed to a function, the function is given a *pointer* to the first element in the array.

Next, we need to know how the subscripting operator works. Suppose that `a` is a one-dimensional array passed to a function. When we write

```
a[i] = 0;
```

the compiler generates instructions that compute the address of `a[i]` by multiplying `i` by the size of an array element and adding the result to the address that `a` represents (the pointer passed to the function). This calculation doesn't depend on the length of `a`, which explains why we can omit it when defining the function.

What about multidimensional arrays? Recall that C stores arrays in row-major order, with the elements in row 0 stored first, then the elements in row 1, and so forth. Suppose that `a` is a two-dimensional array parameter and we write

```
a[i][j] = 0;
```

The compiler generates instructions to do the following: (1) multiply `i` by the size of a single row of `a`; (2) add this result to the address that `a` represents; (3) multiply `j` by the size of an array element; and (4) add this result to the address computed in step 2. To generate these instructions, the compiler must know the size of a row in the array, which is determined by the number of columns. The bottom line: the programmer must declare the number of columns in `a`.

Q: Why do some programmers put parentheses around the expression in a `return` statement?

A: The examples in the first edition of Kernighan and Ritchie's *The C Programming Language* always have parentheses in `return` statements, even though they aren't required. Programmers (and authors of subsequent books) picked up the habit from K&R. I don't use these parentheses, since they're unnecessary and contribute nothing to readability. (Kernighan and Ritchie apparently agree: the return statements in the second edition of *The C Programming Language* lack parentheses.)

Q: **What happens if a non-void function attempts to execute a return statement that has no expression? [p. 202]**

A: That depends on the version of C. In C89, executing a return statement without an expression in a non-void function causes undefined behavior (but only if the program attempts to use the value returned by the function). In C99, such a statement is illegal and should be detected as an error by the compiler.

Q: **How can I test main's return value to see if a program has terminated normally? [p. 203]**

A: That depends on your operating system. Many operating systems allow this value to be tested within a "batch file" or "shell script" that contains commands to run several programs. For example, the line

```
if errorlevel 1 command
```

in a Windows batch file will execute *command* if the last program terminated with a status code greater than or equal to 1.

In UNIX, each shell has its own method for testing the status code. In the Bourne shell, the variable $? contains the status of the last program run. The C shell has a similar variable, but its name is $status.

Q: **Why does my compiler produce a** *"control reaches end of non-void function"* **warning when it compiles main?**

A: The compiler has noticed that main, despite having int as its return type, doesn't have a return statement. Putting the statement

```
return 0;
```

at the end of main will keep the compiler happy. Incidentally, this is good practice even if your compiler doesn't object to the lack of a return statement.

When a program is compiled using a C99 compiler, this warning shouldn't occur. In C99, it's OK to "fall off" the end of main without returning a value; the standard states that main automatically returns 0 in this situation.

Q: **With regard to the previous question: Why not just define main's return type to be void?**

A: Although this practice is fairly common, it's illegal according to the C89 standard. Even if it weren't illegal, it wouldn't be a good idea, since it presumes that no one will ever test the program's status upon termination.

C99 opens the door to legalizing this practice, by allowing main to be declared "in some other implementation-defined manner" (with a return type other than int or parameters other than those specified by the standard). However, any such usage isn't portable, so it's best to declare main's return type to be int.

Q: Is it legal for a function f1 to call a function f2, which then calls f1?

A: Yes. This is just an indirect form of recursion in which one call of f1 leads to another. (But make sure that either f1 or f2 eventually terminates!)

Exercises

Section 9.1

1.   The following function, which computes the area of a triangle, contains two errors. Locate the errors and show how to fix them. (*Hint:* There are no errors in the formula.)

```
double triangle_area(double base, height)
double product;
{
    product = base * height;
    return product / 2;
}
```

Ⓦ 2.   Write a function check(x, y, n) that returns 1 if both x and y fall between 0 and n – 1, inclusive. The function should return 0 otherwise. Assume that x, y, and n are all of type int.

3.   Write a function gcd(m, n) that calculates the greatest common divisor of the integers m and n. (Programming Project 2 in Chapter 6 describes Euclid's algorithm for computing the GCD.)

Ⓦ 4.   Write a function day_of_year(month, day, year) that returns the day of the year (an integer between 1 and 366) specified by the three arguments.

5.   Write a function num_digits(n) that returns the number of digits in n (a positive integer). *Hint:* To determine the number of digits in a number *n*, divide it by 10 repeatedly. When *n* reaches 0, the number of divisions indicates how many digits *n* originally had.

Ⓦ 6.   Write a function digit(n, k) that returns the kth digit (from the right) in n (a positive integer). For example, digit(829, 1) returns 9, digit(829, 2) returns 2, and digit(829, 3) returns 8. If k is greater than the number of digits in n, have the function return 0.

7.   Suppose that the function f has the following definition:

```
int f(int a, int b) { ... }
```

Which of the following statements are legal? (Assume that i has type int and x has type double.)

(a) i = f(83, 12);
(b) x = f(83, 12);
(c) i = f(3.15, 9.28);
(d) x = f(3.15, 9.28);
(e) f(83, 12);

Section 9.2   Ⓦ 8.   Which of the following would be valid prototypes for a function that returns nothing and has one double parameter?

(a) void f(double x);

(b) `void f(double);`

(c) `void f(x);`

(d) `f(double x);`

Section 9.3   *9.   What will be the output of the following program?

```
#include <stdio.h>

void swap(int a, int b);

int main(void)
{
   int i = 1, j = 2;

   swap(i, j);
   printf("i = %d, j = %d\n", i, j);
   return 0;
}

void swap(int a, int b)
{
   int temp = a;
   a = b;
   b = temp;
}
```

Ⓦ 10.   Write functions that return the following values. (Assume that `a` and `n` are parameters, where `a` is an array of `int` values and `n` is the length of the array.)

(a) The largest element in `a`.

(b) The average of all elements in `a`.

(c) The number of positive elements in `a`.

11.   Write the following function:

`float compute_GPA(char grades[], int n);`

The `grades` array will contain letter grades (A, B, C, D, or F, either upper-case or lower-case); n is the length of the array. The function should return the average of the grades (assume that A = 4, B = 3, C = 2, D = 1, and F = 0).

12.   Write the following function:

`double inner_product(double a[], double b[], int n);`

The function should return `a[0] * b[0] + a[1] * b[1] + ... + a[n-1] * b[n-1]`.

13.   Write the following function, which evaluates a chess position:

`int evaluate_position(char board[8][8]);`

`board` represents a configuration of pieces on a chessboard, where the letters K, Q, R, B, N, P represent White pieces, and the letters k, q, r, b, n, and p represent Black pieces. `evaluate_position` should sum the values of the White pieces (Q = 9, R = 5, B = 3, N = 3, P = 1). It should also sum the values of the Black pieces (done in a similar way). The function will return the difference between the two numbers. This value will be positive if White has an advantage in material and negative if Black has an advantage.

Section 9.4   14.   The following function is supposed to return `true` if any element of the array `a` has the value 0 and `false` if all elements are nonzero. Sadly, it contains an error. Find the error and show how to fix it:

```
bool has_zero(int a[], int n)
{
  int i;

  for (i = 0; i < n; i++)
    if (a[i] == 0)
      return true;
    else
      return false;
}
```

W 15. The following (rather confusing) function finds the median of three numbers. Rewrite the function so that it has just one `return` statement.

```
double median(double x, double y, double z)
{
  if (x <= y)
    if (y <= z) return y;
    else if (x <= z) return z;
    else return x;
  if (z <= y) return y;
  if (x <= z) return x;
  return z;
}
```

Section 9.6   16. Condense the `fact` function in the same way we condensed `power`.

W 17. Rewrite the `fact` function so that it's no longer recursive.

18. Write a recursive version of the `gcd` function (see Exercise 3). Here's the strategy to use for computing `gcd(m, n)`: If n is 0, return m. Otherwise, call `gcd` recursively, passing n as the first argument and m % n as the second.

W*19. Consider the following "mystery" function:

```
void pb(int n)
{
  if (n != 0) {
    pb(n / 2);
    putchar('0' + n % 2);
  }
}
```

Trace the execution of the function by hand. Then write a program that calls the function, passing it a number entered by the user. What does the function do?

Programming Projects

1. Write a program that asks the user to enter a series of integers (which it stores in an array), then sorts the integers by calling the function `selection_sort`. When given an array with *n* elements, `selection_sort` must do the following:

   1. Search the array to find the largest element, then move it to the last position in the array.

   2. Call itself recursively to sort the first *n* – 1 elements of the array.

2. Modify Programming Project 5 from Chapter 5 so that it uses a function to compute the amount of income tax. When passed an amount of taxable income, the function will return the tax due.

3. Modify Programming Project 9 from Chapter 8 so that it includes the following functions:

```
void generate_random_walk(char walk[10][10]);
void print_array(char walk[10][10]);
```

main first calls generate_random_walk, which initializes the array to contain '.' characters and then replaces some of these characters by the letters A through Z, as described in the original project. main then calls print_array to display the array on the screen.

4. Modify Programming Project 16 from Chapter 8 so that it includes the following functions:

```
void read_word(int counts[26]);
bool equal_array(int counts1[26], int counts2[26]);
```

main will call read_word twice, once for each of the two words entered by the user. As it reads a word, read_word will use the letters in the word to update the counts array, as described in the original project. (main will declare two arrays, one for each word. These arrays are used to track how many times each letter occurs in the words.) main will then call equal_array, passing it the two arrays. equal_array will return true if the elements in the two arrays are identical (indicating that the words are anagrams) and false otherwise.

5. Modify Programming Project 17 from Chapter 8 so that it includes the following functions:

```
void create_magic_square(int n, char magic_square[n][n]);
void print_magic_square(int n, char magic_square[n][n]);
```

After obtaining the number n from the user, main will call create_magic_square, passing it an $n \times n$ array that is declared inside main. create_magic_square will fill the array with the numbers 1, 2, ..., n^2 as described in the original project. main will then call print_magic_square, which will display the array in the format described in the original project. *Note:* If your compiler doesn't support variable-length arrays, declare the array in main to be 99×99 instead of $n \times n$ and use the following prototypes instead:

```
void create_magic_square(int n, char magic_square[99][99]);
void print_magic_square(int n, char magic_square[99][99]);
```

6. Write a function that computes the value of the following polynomial:

$$3x^5 + 2x^4 - 5x^3 - x^2 + 7x - 6$$

Write a program that asks the user to enter a value for x, calls the function to compute the value of the polynomial, and then displays the value returned by the function.

7. The power function of Section 9.6 can be made faster by having it calculate x^n in a different way. We first notice that if n is a power of 2, then x^n can be computed by squaring. For example, x^4 is the square of x^2, so x^4 can be computed using only two multiplications instead of three. As it happens, this technique can be used even when n is not a power of 2. If n is even, we use the formula $x^n = (x^{n/2})^2$. If n is odd, then $x^n = x \times x^{n-1}$. Write a recursive function that computes x^n. (The recursion ends when $n = 0$, in which case the function returns 1.) To test your function, write a program that asks the user to enter values for x and n, calls power to compute x^n, and then displays the value returned by the function.

8. Write a program that simulates the game of craps, which is played with two dice. On the first roll, the player wins if the sum of the dice is 7 or 11. The player loses if the sum is 2, 3,

or 12. Any other roll is called the "point" and the game continues. On each subsequent roll, the player wins if he or she rolls the point again. The player loses by rolling 7. Any other roll is ignored and the game continues. At the end of each game, the program will ask the user whether or not to play again. When the user enters a response other than y or Y, the program will display the number of wins and losses and then terminate.

```
You rolled: 8
Your point is 8
You rolled: 3
You rolled: 10
You rolled: 8
You win!

Play again? y

You rolled: 6
Your point is 6
You rolled: 5
You rolled: 12
You rolled: 3
You rolled: 7
You lose!

Play again? y

You rolled: 11
You win!

Play again? n

Wins: 2  Losses: 1
```

Write your program as three functions: `main`, `roll_dice`, and `play_game`. Here are the prototypes for the latter two functions:

```
int roll_dice(void);
bool play_game(void);
```

`roll_dice` should generate two random numbers, each between 1 and 6, and return their sum. `play_game` should play one craps game (calling `roll_dice` to determine the outcome of each dice roll); it will return `true` if the player wins and `false` if the player loses. `play_game` is also responsible for displaying messages showing the results of the player's dice rolls. `main` will call `play_game` repeatedly, keeping track of the number of wins and losses and displaying the "you win" and "you lose" messages. *Hint:* Use the `rand` function to generate random numbers. See the `deal.c` program in Section 8.2 for an example of how to call `rand` and the related `srand` function.

10 Program Organization

As Will Rogers would have said, "There is no such thing as a free variable."

Having covered functions in Chapter 9, we're ready to confront several issues that arise when a program contains more than one function. The chapter begins with a discussion of the differences between local variables (Section 10.1) and external variables (Section 10.2). Section 10.3 then considers blocks (compound statements containing declarations). Section 10.4 tackles the scope rules that apply to local names, external names, and names declared in blocks. Finally, Section 10.5 suggests a way to organize function prototypes, function definitions, variable declarations, and the other parts of a C program.

10.1 Local Variables

A variable declared in the body of a function is said to be *local* to the function. In the following function, sum is a local variable:

```c
int sum_digits(int n)
{
  int sum = 0;   /* local variable */

  while (n > 0) {
    sum += n % 10;
    n /= 10;
  }

  return sum;
}
```

By default, local variables have the following properties:

- **Automatic storage duration.** The **storage duration** (or **extent**) of a variable is the portion of program execution during which storage for the variable exists. Storage for a local variable is "automatically" allocated when the enclosing function is called and deallocated when the function returns, so the variable is said to have **automatic storage duration.** A local variable doesn't retain its value when its enclosing function returns. When the function is called again, there's no guarantee that the variable will still have its old value.

- **Block scope.** The **scope** of a variable is the portion of the program text in which the variable can be referenced. A local variable has **block scope:** it is visible from its point of declaration to the end of the enclosing function body. Since the scope of a local variable doesn't extend beyond the function to which it belongs, other functions can use the same name for other purposes.

Section 18.2 covers these and other related concepts in more detail.

 Since C99 doesn't require variable declarations to come at the beginning of a function, it's possible for a local variable to have a very small scope. In the following example, the scope of i doesn't begin until the line on which it's declared, which could be near the end of the function body:

```
void f(void)
{
    ...
    int i; ⎤
    ...     ⎬ scope of i
}         ⎦
```

Static Local Variables

Putting the word static in the declaration of a local variable causes it to have **static storage duration** instead of automatic storage duration. A variable with static storage duration has a permanent storage location, so it retains its value throughout the execution of the program. Consider the following function:

```
void f(void)
{
    static int i;   /* static local variable */
    ...
}
```

Since the local variable i has been declared static, it occupies the same memory location throughout the execution of the program. When f returns, i won't lose its value.

A static local variable still has block scope, so it's not visible to other functions. In a nutshell, a static variable is a place to hide data from other functions but retain it for future calls of the same function.

Parameters

Parameters have the same properties—automatic storage duration and block scope—as local variables. In fact, the only real difference between parameters and local variables is that each parameter is initialized automatically when a function is called (by being assigned the value of the corresponding argument).

10.2 External Variables

Passing arguments is one way to transmit information to a function. Functions can also communicate through *external variables*—variables that are declared outside the body of any function.

The properties of external variables (or *global variables,* as they're sometimes called) are different from those of local variables:

- *Static storage duration.* External variables have static storage duration, just like local variables that have been declared `static`. A value stored in an external variable will stay there indefinitely.

- *File scope.* An external variable has *file scope:* it is visible from its point of declaration to the end of the enclosing file. As a result, an external variable can be accessed (and potentially modified) by all functions that follow its declaration.

Example: Using External Variables to Implement a Stack

To illustrate how external variables might be used, let's look at a data structure known as a *stack*. (Stacks are an abstract concept, not a C feature; they can be implemented in most programming languages.) A stack, like an array, can store multiple data items of the same type. However, the operations on a stack are limited: we can either *push* an item onto the stack (add it to one end—the "stack top") or *pop* it from the stack (remove it from the same end). Examining or modifying an item that's not at the top of the stack is forbidden.

One way to implement a stack in C is to store its items in an array, which we'll call `contents`. A separate integer variable named `top` marks the position of the stack top. When the stack is empty, `top` has the value 0. To push an item on the stack, we simply store the item in `contents` at the position indicated by `top`, then increment `top`. Popping an item requires decrementing `top`, then using it as an index into `contents` to fetch the item that's being popped.

Based on this outline, here's a program fragment (not a complete program) that declares the `contents` and `top` variables for a stack and provides a set of functions that represent operations on the stack. All five functions need access to the `top` variable, and two functions need access to `contents`, so we'll make `contents` and `top` external.

```
#include <stdbool.h>    /* C99 only */

#define STACK_SIZE 100

/* external variables */
int contents[STACK_SIZE];
int top = 0;

void make_empty(void)
{
  top = 0;
}

bool is_empty(void)
{
  return top == 0;
}

bool is_full(void)
{
  return top == STACK_SIZE;
}

void push(int i)
{
  if (is_full())
    stack_overflow();
  else
    contents[top++] = i;
}

int pop(void)
{
  if (is_empty())
    stack_underflow();
  else
    return contents[--top];
}
```

Pros and Cons of External Variables

External variables are convenient when many functions must share a variable or when a few functions share a large number of variables. In most cases, however, it's better for functions to communicate through parameters rather than by sharing variables. Here's why:

- If we change an external variable during program maintenance (by altering its type, say), we'll need to check every function in the same file to see how the change affects it.

- If an external variable is assigned an incorrect value, it may be difficult to identify the guilty function. It's like trying to solve a murder committed at a crowded party—there's no easy way to narrow the list of suspects.

- Functions that rely on external variables are hard to reuse in other programs. A function that depends on external variables isn't self-contained; to reuse the function, we'll have to drag along any external variables that it needs.

Many C programmers rely far too much on external variables. One common abuse: using the same external variable for different purposes in different functions. Suppose that several functions need a variable named i to control a `for` statement. Instead of declaring i in each function that uses it, some programmers declare it at the top of the program, thereby making the variable visible to all functions. This practice is poor not only for the reasons listed earlier, but also because it's misleading; someone reading the program later may think that the uses of the variable are related, when in fact they're not.

When you use external variables, make sure they have meaningful names. (Local variables don't always need meaningful names: it's often hard to think of a better name than i for the control variable in a `for` loop.) If you find yourself using names like i and `temp` for external variables, that's a clue that perhaps they should really be local variables.

 Making variables external when they should be local can lead to some rather frustrating bugs. Consider the following example, which is supposed to display a 10 × 10 arrangement of asterisks:

```c
int i;

void print_one_row(void)
{
  for (i = 1; i <= 10; i++)
    printf("*");
}

void print_all_rows(void)
{
  for (i = 1; i <= 10; i++) {
    print_one_row();
    printf("\n");
  }
}
```

Instead of printing 10 rows, `print_all_rows` prints only one row. When `print_one_row` returns after being called the first time, i will have the value 11. The `for` statement in `print_all_rows` then increments i and tests whether it's less than or equal to 10. It's not, so the loop terminates and the function returns.

PROGRAM   **Guessing a Number**

To get more experience with external variables, we'll write a simple game-playing program. The program generates a random number between 1 and 100, which the user attempts to guess in as few tries as possible. Here's what the user will see when the program is run:

```
Guess the secret number between 1 and 100.

A new number has been chosen.
Enter guess: 55
Too low; try again.
Enter guess: 65
Too high; try again.
Enter guess: 60
Too high; try again.
Enter guess: 58
You won in 4 guesses!

Play again? (Y/N) y

A new number has been chosen.
Enter guess: 78
Too high; try again.
Enter guess: 34
You won in 2 guesses!

Play again? (Y/N) n
```

This program will need to carry out several different tasks: initializing the random number generator, choosing a secret number, and interacting with the user until the correct number is picked. If we write a separate function to handle each task, we might end up with the following program.

guess.c
```
/* Asks user to guess a hidden number */

#include <stdio.h>
#include <stdlib.h>
#include <time.h>

#define MAX_NUMBER 100

/* external variable */
int secret_number;

/* prototypes */
void initialize_number_generator(void);
void choose_new_secret_number(void);
void read_guesses(void);

int main(void)
{
  char command;
```

```
    printf("Guess the secret number between 1 and %d.\n\n",
           MAX_NUMBER);
    initialize_number_generator();
    do {
      choose_new_secret_number();
      printf("A new number has been chosen.\n");
      read_guesses();
      printf("Play again? (Y/N) ");
      scanf(" %c", &command);
      printf("\n");
    } while (command == 'y' || command == 'Y');

    return 0;
  }

  /**********************************************************
   * initialize_number_generator: Initializes the random   *
   *                               number generator using   *
   *                               the time of day.         *
   **********************************************************/
  void initialize_number_generator(void)
  {
    srand((unsigned) time(NULL));
  }

  /**********************************************************
   * choose_new_secret_number: Randomly selects a number    *
   *                           between 1 and MAX_NUMBER and *
   *                           stores it in secret_number.  *
   **********************************************************/
  void choose_new_secret_number(void)
  {
    secret_number = rand() % MAX_NUMBER + 1;
  }

  /**********************************************************
   * read_guesses: Repeatedly reads user guesses and tells  *
   *               the user whether each guess is too low,  *
   *               too high, or correct. When the guess is  *
   *               correct, prints the total number of      *
   *               guesses and returns.                     *
   **********************************************************/
  void read_guesses(void)
  {
    int guess, num_guesses = 0;

    for (;;) {
      num_guesses++;
      printf("Enter guess: ");
      scanf("%d", &guess);
      if (guess == secret_number) {
        printf("You won in %d guesses!\n\n", num_guesses);
        return;
      } else if (guess < secret_number)
```

```
                      printf("Too low; try again.\n");
                   else
                      printf("Too high; try again.\n");
               }
         }
```

time function ➤26.3
srand function ➤26.2
rand function ➤26.2

For random number generation, the guess.c program relies on the time, srand, and rand functions, which we first used in deal.c (Section 8.2). This time, we're scaling the return value of rand so that it falls between 1 and MAX_NUMBER.

Although guess.c works fine, it relies on an external variable. We made secret_number external so that both choose_new_secret_number and read_guesses could access it. If we alter choose_new_secret_number and read_guesses just a little, we should be able to move secret_number into the main function. We'll modify choose_new_secret_number so that it returns the new number, and we'll rewrite read_guesses so that secret_number can be passed to it as an argument.

Here's our new program, with changes in **bold**:

guess2.c

```
/* Asks user to guess a hidden number */

#include <stdio.h>
#include <stdlib.h>
#include <time.h>

#define MAX_NUMBER 100

/* prototypes */
void initialize_number_generator(void);
int new_secret_number(void);
void read_guesses(int secret_number);

int main(void)
{
  char command;
  int secret_number;

  printf("Guess the secret number between 1 and %d.\n\n",
         MAX_NUMBER);
  initialize_number_generator();
  do {
    secret_number = new_secret_number();
    printf("A new number has been chosen.\n");
    read_guesses(secret_number);
    printf("Play again? (Y/N) ");
    scanf(" %c", &command);
    printf("\n");
  } while (command == 'y' || command == 'Y');

  return 0;
}
```

```
/***********************************************************
 * initialize_number_generator: Initializes the random    *
 *                              number generator using     *
 *                              the time of day.           *
 ***********************************************************/
void initialize_number_generator(void)
{
  srand((unsigned) time(NULL));
}

/***********************************************************
 * new_secret_number: Returns a randomly chosen number     *
 *                    between 1 and MAX_NUMBER.             *
 ***********************************************************/
int new_secret_number(void)
{
  return rand() % MAX_NUMBER + 1;
}

/***********************************************************
 * read_guesses: Repeatedly reads user guesses and tells   *
 *               the user whether each guess is too low,    *
 *               too high, or correct. When the guess is    *
 *               correct, prints the total number of        *
 *               guesses and returns.                       *
 ***********************************************************/
void read_guesses(int secret_number)
{
  int guess, num_guesses = 0;

  for (;;) {
    num_guesses++;
    printf("Enter guess: ");
    scanf("%d", &guess);
    if (guess == secret_number) {
      printf("You won in %d guesses!\n\n", num_guesses);
      return;
    } else if (guess < secret_number)
      printf("Too low; try again.\n");
    else
      printf("Too high; try again.\n");
  }
}
```

10.3 Blocks

In Section 5.2, we encountered compound statements of the form

    { *statements* }

It turns out that C allows compound statements to contain declarations as well:

block

$$\{ \ \textit{declarations} \quad \textit{statements} \ \}$$

I'll use the term **block** to describe such a compound statement. Here's an example of a block:

```
if (i > j) {
  /* swap values of i and j */
  int temp = i;
  i = j;
  j = temp;
}
```

By default, the storage duration of a variable declared in a block is automatic: storage for the variable is allocated when the block is entered and deallocated when the block is exited. The variable has block scope; it can't be referenced outside the block. A variable that belongs to a block can be declared `static` to give it static storage duration.

The body of a function is a block. Blocks are also useful inside a function body when we need variables for temporary use. In our last example, we needed a variable temporarily so that we could swap the values of i and j. Putting temporary variables in blocks has two advantages: (1) It avoids cluttering the declarations at the beginning of the function body with variables that are used only briefly. (2) It reduces name conflicts. In our example, the name `temp` can be used elsewhere in the same function for different purposes—the `temp` variable is strictly local to the block in which it's declared.

 C99 allows variables to be declared anywhere within a block, just as it allows variables to be declared anywhere within a function.

10.4 Scope

In a C program, the same identifier may have several different meanings. C's scope rules enable the programmer (and the compiler) to determine which meaning is relevant at a given point in the program.

Here's the most important scope rule: When a declaration inside a block names an identifier that's already visible (because it has file scope or because it's declared in an enclosing block), the new declaration temporarily "hides" the old one, and the identifier takes on a new meaning. At the end of the block, the identifier regains its old meaning.

Consider the (somewhat extreme) example at the top of the next page, in which the identifier i has four different meanings:

- In Declaration 1, i is a variable with static storage duration and file scope.

```
int (i) ;              /* Declaration 1 */

void f(int (i) )       /* Declaration 2 */
{
    i = 1;
}

void g(void)
{
    int (i) = 2;       /* Declaration 3 */

    if (i > 0) {
        int (i) ;      /* Declaration 4 */

        i = 3;
    }

    i = 4;
}

void h(void)
{
    i = 5;
}
```

- In Declaration 2, i is a parameter with block scope.
- In Declaration 3, i is an automatic variable with block scope.
- In Declaration 4, i is also automatic and has block scope.

i is used five times. C's scope rules allow us to determine the meaning of i in each case:

- The i = 1 assignment refers to the parameter in Declaration 2, not the variable in Declaration 1, since Declaration 2 hides Declaration 1.
- The i > 0 test refers to the variable in Declaration 3, since Declaration 3 hides Declaration 1 and Declaration 2 is out of scope.
- The i = 3 assignment refers to the variable in Declaration 4, which hides Declaration 3.
- The i = 4 assignment refers to the variable in Declaration 3. It can't refer to Declaration 4, which is out of scope.
- The i = 5 assignment refers to the variable in Declaration 1.

10.5 Organizing a C Program

Now that we've seen the major elements that make up a C program, it's time to develop a strategy for their arrangement. For now, we'll assume that a program always fits into a single file. Chapter 15 shows how to organize a program that's split over several files.

So far, we've seen that a program may contain the following:

Preprocessing directives such as `#include` and `#define`
Type definitions
Declarations of external variables
Function prototypes
Function definitions

C imposes only a few rules on the order of these items: A preprocessing directive doesn't take effect until the line on which it appears. A type name can't be used until it's been defined. A variable can't be used until it's declared. Although C isn't as picky about functions, I strongly recommend that every function be defined or declared prior to its first call. (C99 makes this a requirement anyway.)

There are several ways to organize a program so that these rules are obeyed. Here's one possible ordering:

`#include` directives
`#define` directives
Type definitions
Declarations of external variables
Prototypes for functions other than `main`
Definition of `main`
Definitions of other functions

It makes sense to put `#include` directives first, since they bring in information that will likely be needed in several places within the program. `#define` directives create macros, which are generally used throughout the program. Putting type definitions above the declarations of external variables is logical, since the declarations of these variables may refer to the type names just defined. Declaring external variables next makes them available to all the functions that follow. Declaring all functions except for `main` avoids the problems that arise when a function is called before the compiler has seen its prototype. This practice also makes it possible to arrange the function definitions in any order whatsoever: alphabetically by function name or with related functions grouped together, for example. Defining `main` before the other functions makes it easier for a reader to locate the program's starting point.

A final suggestion: Precede each function definition by a boxed comment that gives the name of the function, explains its purpose, discusses the meaning of each parameter, describes its return value (if any), and lists any side effects it has (such as modifying external variables).

PROGRAM   **Classifying a Poker Hand**

To show how a C program might be organized, let's attempt a program that's a little more complex than our previous examples. The program will read and classify a poker hand. Each card in the hand will have both a *suit* (clubs, diamonds, hearts, or spades) and a *rank* (two, three, four, five, six, seven, eight, nine, ten, jack, queen, king, or ace). We won't allow the use of jokers, and we'll assume that aces are high. The program will read a hand of five cards, then classify the hand into one of the following categories (listed in order from best to worst):

> straight flush (both a straight and a flush)
> four-of-a-kind (four cards of the same rank)
> full house (a three-of-a-kind and a pair)
> flush (five cards of the same suit)
> straight (five cards with consecutive ranks)
> three-of-a-kind (three cards of the same rank)
> two pairs
> pair (two cards of the same rank)
> high card (any other hand)

If a hand falls into two or more categories, the program will choose the best one.

For input purposes, we'll abbreviate ranks and suits as follows (letters may be either upper- or lower-case):

> Ranks: 2 3 4 5 6 7 8 9 t j q k a
> Suits: c d h s

If the user enters an illegal card or tries to enter the same card twice, the program will ignore the card, issue an error message, and then request another card. Entering the number 0 instead of a card will cause the program to terminate.

A session with the program will have the following appearance:

```
Enter a card: 2s
Enter a card: 5s
Enter a card: 4s
Enter a card: 3s
Enter a card: 6s
Straight flush

Enter a card: 8c
Enter a card: as
Enter a card: 8c
Duplicate card; ignored.
Enter a card: 7c
Enter a card: ad
Enter a card: 3h
Pair

Enter a card: 6s
Enter a card: d2
Bad card; ignored.
Enter a card: 2d
Enter a card: 9c
Enter a card: 4h
Enter a card: ts
```

```
High card

Enter a card: 0
```

From this description of the program, we see that it has three tasks:

Read a hand of five cards.
Analyze the hand for pairs, straights, and so forth.
Print the classification of the hand.

We'll divide the program into three functions—read_cards, analyze_hand, and print_result—that perform these three tasks. main does nothing but call these functions inside an endless loop. The functions will need to share a fairly large amount of information, so we'll have them communicate through external variables. read_cards will store information about the hand into several external variables. analyze_hand will then examine these variables, storing its findings into other external variables for the benefit of print_result.

Based on this preliminary design, we can begin to sketch an outline of the program:

```
/* #include directives go here */

/* #define directives go here */

/* declarations of external variables go here */

/* prototypes */
void read_cards(void);
void analyze_hand(void);
void print_result(void);

/**************************************************************
 * main: Calls read_cards, analyze_hand, and print_result *
 *       repeatedly.                                        *
 **************************************************************/
int main(void)
{
  for (;;) {
    read_cards();
    analyze_hand();
    print_result();
  }
}

/**************************************************************
 * read_cards:  Reads the cards into external variables;   *
 *              checks for bad cards and duplicate cards.   *
 **************************************************************/
void read_cards(void)
{
  ...
}
```

```
/**************************************************************
 * analyze_hand: Determines whether the hand contains a      *
 *               straight, a flush, four-of-a-kind,          *
 *               and/or three-of-a-kind; determines the      *
 *               number of pairs; stores the results into    *
 *               external variables.                         *
 **************************************************************/
void analyze_hand(void)
{
  ...
}

/**************************************************************
 * print_result: Notifies the user of the result, using     *
 *               the external variables set by               *
 *               analyze_hand.                               *
 **************************************************************/
void print_result(void)
{
  ...
}
```

The most pressing question that remains is how to represent the hand of cards. Let's see what operations read_cards and analyze_hand will perform on the hand. During the analysis of the hand, analyze_hand will need to know how many cards are in each rank and each suit. This suggests that we use two arrays, num_in_rank and num_in_suit. The value of num_in_rank[r] will be the number of cards with rank r, and the value of num_in_suit[s] will be the number of cards with suit s. (We'll encode ranks as numbers between 0 and 12, and suits as numbers between 0 and 3.) We'll also need a third array, card_exists, so that read_cards can detect duplicate cards. Each time read_cards reads a card with rank r and suit s, it checks whether the value of card_exists[r][s] is true. If so, the card was previously entered; if not, read_cards assigns true to card_exists[r][s].

Both the read_cards function and the analyze_hand function will need access to the num_in_rank and num_in_suit arrays, so I'll make them external variables. The card_exists array is used only by read_cards, so it can be local to that function. As a rule, variables should be made external only if necessary.

Having decided on the major data structures, we can now finish the program:

poker.c
```
/* Classifies a poker hand */

#include <stdbool.h>    /* C99 only */
#include <stdio.h>
#include <stdlib.h>

#define NUM_RANKS 13
#define NUM_SUITS 4
#define NUM_CARDS 5
```

```
                 /* external variables */
                 int num_in_rank[NUM_RANKS];
                 int num_in_suit[NUM_SUITS];
                 bool straight, flush, four, three;
                 int pairs;    /* can be 0, 1, or 2 */

                 /* prototypes */
                 void read_cards(void);
                 void analyze_hand(void);
                 void print_result(void);

                 /****************************************************************
                  * main: Calls read_cards, analyze_hand, and print_result *
                  *       repeatedly.                                       *
                  ****************************************************************/
                 int main(void)
                 {
                   for (;;) {
                     read_cards();
                     analyze_hand();
                     print_result();
                   }
                 }

                 /****************************************************************
                  * read_cards: Reads the cards into the external          *
                  *             variables num_in_rank and num_in_suit;     *
                  *             checks for bad cards and duplicate cards.   *
                  ****************************************************************/
                 void read_cards(void)
                 {
                   bool card_exists[NUM_RANKS][NUM_SUITS];
                   char ch, rank_ch, suit_ch;
                   int rank, suit;
                   bool bad_card;
                   int cards_read = 0;

                   for (rank = 0; rank < NUM_RANKS; rank++) {
                     num_in_rank[rank] = 0;
                     for (suit = 0; suit < NUM_SUITS; suit++)
                       card_exists[rank][suit] = false;
                   }

                   for (suit = 0; suit < NUM_SUITS; suit++)
                     num_in_suit[suit] = 0;

                   while (cards_read < NUM_CARDS) {
                     bad_card = false;

                     printf("Enter a card: ");

                     rank_ch = getchar();
                     switch (rank_ch) {
```

```
          case '0':               exit(EXIT_SUCCESS);
          case '2':               rank = 0; break;
          case '3':               rank = 1; break;
          case '4':               rank = 2; break;
          case '5':               rank = 3; break;
          case '6':               rank = 4; break;
          case '7':               rank = 5; break;
          case '8':               rank = 6; break;
          case '9':               rank = 7; break;
          case 't': case 'T': rank = 8; break;
          case 'j': case 'J': rank = 9; break;
          case 'q': case 'Q': rank = 10; break;
          case 'k': case 'K': rank = 11; break;
          case 'a': case 'A': rank = 12; break;
          default:                bad_card = true;
        }

        suit_ch = getchar();
        switch (suit_ch) {
          case 'c': case 'C': suit = 0; break;
          case 'd': case 'D': suit = 1; break;
          case 'h': case 'H': suit = 2; break;
          case 's': case 'S': suit = 3; break;
          default:                bad_card = true;
        }

        while ((ch = getchar()) != '\n')
          if (ch != ' ') bad_card = true;

        if (bad_card)
          printf("Bad card; ignored.\n");
        else if (card_exists[rank][suit])
          printf("Duplicate card; ignored.\n");
        else {
          num_in_rank[rank]++;
          num_in_suit[suit]++;
          card_exists[rank][suit] = true;
          cards_read++;
        }
    }
  }
}

/**************************************************************
 * analyze_hand: Determines whether the hand contains a      *
 *               straight, a flush, four-of-a-kind,          *
 *               and/or three-of-a-kind; determines the      *
 *               number of pairs; stores the results into    *
 *               the external variables straight, flush,     *
 *               four, three, and pairs.                     *
 **************************************************************/
void analyze_hand(void)
{
  int num_consec = 0;
  int rank, suit;
```

```
    straight = false;
    flush = false;
    four = false;
    three = false;
    pairs = 0;

    /* check for flush */
    for (suit = 0; suit < NUM_SUITS; suit++)
      if (num_in_suit[suit] == NUM_CARDS)
        flush = true;

    /* check for straight */
    rank = 0;
    while (num_in_rank[rank] == 0) rank++;
    for (; rank < NUM_RANKS && num_in_rank[rank] > 0; rank++)
      num_consec++;
    if (num_consec == NUM_CARDS) {
      straight = true;
      return;
    }

    /* check for 4-of-a-kind, 3-of-a-kind, and pairs */
    for (rank = 0; rank < NUM_RANKS; rank++) {
      if (num_in_rank[rank] == 4) four = true;
      if (num_in_rank[rank] == 3) three = true;
      if (num_in_rank[rank] == 2) pairs++;
    }
}

/**************************************************************
 * print_result: Prints the classification of the hand,     *
 *               based on the values of the external        *
 *               variables straight, flush, four, three,    *
 *               and pairs.                                  *
 **************************************************************/
void print_result(void)
{
  if (straight && flush) printf("Straight flush");
  else if (four)         printf("Four of a kind");
  else if (three &&
           pairs == 1)   printf("Full house");
  else if (flush)        printf("Flush");
  else if (straight)     printf("Straight");
  else if (three)        printf("Three of a kind");
  else if (pairs == 2)   printf("Two pairs");
  else if (pairs == 1)   printf("Pair");
  else                   printf("High card");

  printf("\n\n");
}
```

    Notice the use of the exit function in read_cards (in case '0' of the first
switch statement). exit is convenient for this program because of its ability to
terminate execution from anywhere in the program.

Q & A

Q: **What impact do local variables with static storage duration have on recursive functions? [p. 220]**

A: When a function is called recursively, fresh copies are made of its automatic variables for each call. This doesn't occur for static variables, though. Instead, all calls of the function share the *same* static variables.

Q: **In the following example, j is initialized to the same value as i, but there are two variables named i:**

```
int i = 1;

void f(void)
{
  int j = i;
  int i = 2;
  ...
}
```

Is this code legal? If so, what is j's initial value, 1 or 2?

A: The code is indeed legal. The scope of a local variable doesn't begin until its declaration. Therefore, the declaration of j refers to the external variable named i. The initial value of j will be 1.

Exercises

Section 10.4 **Ⓦ** 1. The following program outline shows only function definitions and variable declarations.

```
int a;

void f(int b)
{
  int c;
}

void g(void)
{
  int d;
  {
    int e;
  }
}

int main(void)
{
  int f;
}
```

For each of the following scopes, list all variable and parameter names visible in that scope:

(a) The f function
(b) The g function
(c) The block in which e is declared
(d) The main function

2. The following program outline shows only function definitions and variable declarations.

```
int b, c;

void f(void)
{
  int b, d;
}

void g(int a)
{
  int c;
  {
    int a, d;
  }
}

int main(void)
{
  int c, d;
}
```

For each of the following scopes, list all variable and parameter names visible in that scope. If there's more than one variable or parameter with the same name, indicate which one is visible.

(a) The f function
(b) The g function
(c) The block in which a and d are declared
(d) The main function

*3. Suppose that a program has only one function (main). How many different variables named i could this program contain?

Programming Projects

1. Modify the stack example of Section 10.2 so that it stores characters instead of integers. Next, add a main function that asks the user to enter a series of parentheses and/or braces, then indicates whether or not they're properly nested:

```
Enter parentheses and/or braces: (() {}{() })
Parentheses/braces are nested properly
```

Hint: As the program reads characters, have it push each left parenthesis or left brace. When it reads a right parenthesis or brace, have it pop the stack and check that the item popped is a matching parenthesis or brace. (If not, the parentheses/braces aren't nested properly.) When the program reads the new-line character, have it check whether the stack is empty; if so, the parentheses/braces are matched. If the stack *isn't* empty (or if stack_underflow is ever called), the parentheses/braces aren't matched. If `stack_overflow` is called, have the program print the message `Stack overflow` and terminate immediately.

2. Modify the `poker.c` program of Section 10.5 by moving the `num_in_rank` and `num_in_suit` arrays into `main`, which will pass them as arguments to `read_cards` and `analyze_hand`.

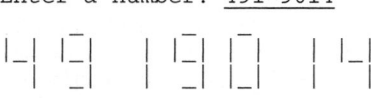 3. Remove the `num_in_rank`, `num_in_suit`, and `card_exists` arrays from the `poker.c` program of Section 10.5. Have the program store the cards in a 5 × 2 array instead. Each row of the array will represent a card. For example, if the array is named `hand`, then `hand[0][0]` will store the rank of the first card and `hand[0][1]` will store the suit of the first card.

4. Modify the `poker.c` program of Section 10.5 by having it recognize an additional category, "royal flush" (ace, king, queen, jack, ten of the same suit). A royal flush ranks higher than all other hands.

5. Modify the `poker.c` program of Section 10.5 by allowing "ace-low" straights (ace, two, three, four, five).

6. Some calculators (notably those from Hewlett-Packard) use a system of writing mathematical expressions known as Reverse Polish Notation (RPN). In this notation, operators are placed *after* their operands instead of *between* their operands. For example, 1 + 2 would be written 1 2 + in RPN, and 1 + 2 * 3 would be written 1 2 3 * +. RPN expressions can easily be evaluated using a stack. The algorithm involves reading the operators and operands in an expression from left to right, performing the following actions:

When an operand is encountered, push it onto the stack.

When an operator is encountered, pop its operands from the stack, perform the operation on those operands, and then push the result onto the stack.

Write a program that evaluates RPN expressions. The operands will be single-digit integers. The operators are +, −, *, /, and =. The = operator causes the top stack item to be displayed; afterwards, the stack is cleared and the user is prompted to enter another expression. The process continues until the user enters a character that is not an operator or operand:

```
Enter an RPN expression: 1 2 3 * + =
Value of expression: 7
Enter an RPN expression: 5 8 * 4 9 - / =
Value of expression: -8
Enter an RPN expression: q
```

If the stack overflows, the program will display the message `Expression is too complex` and terminate. If the stack underflows (because of an expression such as 1 2 + +), the program will display the message `Not enough operands in expression` and terminate. *Hints:* Incorporate the stack code from Section 10.2 into your program. Use `scanf(" %c", &ch)` to read the operators and operands.

7. Write a program that prompts the user for a number and then displays the number, using characters to simulate the effect of a seven-segment display:

```
Enter a number: 491-9014
```

```
 _|  |_|     _   _       |  |_
 |   |_|     |   _|  |_|  |   |
       |     |   _|  |_|  |   |
```

Characters other than digits should be ignored. Write the program so that the maximum number of digits is controlled by a macro named `MAX_DIGITS`, which has the value 10. If the number contains more than this number of digits, the extra digits are ignored. *Hints:* Use two external arrays. One is the segments array (see Exercise 6 in Chapter 8), which stores data representing the correspondence between digits and segments. The other array, digits, will be an array of characters with 4 rows (since each segmented digit is four characters high) and MAX_DIGITS * 4 columns (digits are three characters wide, but a space is needed between digits for readability). Write your program as four functions: main, clear_digits_array, process_digit, and print_digits_array. Here are the prototypes for the latter three functions:

```
void clear_digits_array(void);
void process_digit(int digit, int position);
void print_digits_array(void);
```

clear_digits_array will store blank characters into all elements of the digits array. process_digit will store the seven-segment representation of digit into a specified position in the digits array (positions range from 0 to MAX_DIGITS − 1). print_digits_array will display the rows of the digits array, each on a single line, producing output such as that shown in the example.

11 Pointers

The 11th commandment was "Thou Shalt Compute"
or "Thou Shalt Not Compute"—I forget which.

Pointers are one of C's most important—and most often misunderstood—features. Because of their importance, we'll devote three chapters to pointers. In this chapter, we'll concentrate on the basics; Chapters 12 and 17 cover more advanced uses of pointers.

We'll start with a discussion of memory addresses and their relationship to pointer variables (Section 11.1). Section 11.2 then introduces the address and indirection operators. Section 11.3 covers pointer assignment. Section 11.4 explains how to pass pointers to functions, while Section 11.5 discusses returning pointers from functions.

11.1 Pointer Variables

The first step in understanding pointers is visualizing what they represent at the machine level. In most modern computers, main memory is divided into *bytes*, with each byte capable of storing eight bits of information:

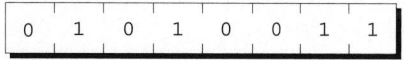

Each byte has a unique *address* to distinguish it from the other bytes in memory. If there are n bytes in memory, we can think of addresses as numbers that range from 0 to $n - 1$ (see the figure at the top of the next page).

An executable program consists of both code (machine instructions corresponding to statements in the original C program) and data (variables in the original program). Each variable in the program occupies one or more bytes of memory;

241

Address   Contents

Address	Contents
0	01010011
1	01110101
2	01110011
3	01100001
4	01101110
:	:
n-1	01000011

the address of the first byte is said to be the address of the variable. In the following figure, the variable i occupies the bytes at addresses 2000 and 2001, so i's address is 2000:

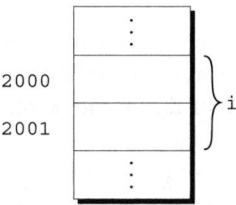

Here's where pointers come in. Although addresses are represented by numbers, their range of values may differ from that of integers, so we can't necessarily store them in ordinary integer variables. We can, however, store them in special *pointer variables*. When we store the address of a variable i in the pointer variable p, we say that p "points to" i. In other words, a pointer is nothing more than an address, and a pointer variable is just a variable that can store an address.

Q&A

Instead of showing addresses as numbers in our examples, I'll use a simpler notation. To indicate that a pointer variable p stores the address of a variable i, I'll show the contents of p as an arrow directed toward i:

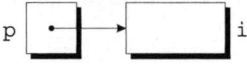

Declaring Pointer Variables

A pointer variable is declared in much the same way as an ordinary variable. The only difference is that the name of a pointer variable must be preceded by an asterisk:

```
int *p;
```

This declaration states that p is a pointer variable capable of pointing to **objects** of type int. I'm using the term *object* instead of *variable* since—as we'll see in Chapter 17—p might point to an area of memory that doesn't belong to a variable. (Be aware that "object" will have a different meaning when we discuss program design in Chapter 19.)

abstract objects ➤ 19.1

Pointer variables can appear in declarations along with other variables:

```
int i, j, a[10], b[20], *p, *q;
```

In this example, i and j are ordinary integer variables, a and b are arrays of integers, and p and q are pointers to integer objects.

C requires that every pointer variable point only to objects of a particular type (the **referenced type**):

```
int *p;      /* points only to integers   */
double *q;   /* points only to doubles    */
char *r;     /* points only to characters */
```

There are no restrictions on what the referenced type may be. In fact, a pointer variable can even point to another pointer.

pointers to pointers ➤ 17.6

11.2   The Address and Indirection Operators

C provides a pair of operators designed specifically for use with pointers. To find the address of a variable, we use the & (address) operator. If x is a variable, then &x is the address of x in memory. To gain access to the object that a pointer points to, we use the * (*indirection*) operator. If p is a pointer, then *p represents the object to which p currently points.

The Address Operator

Declaring a pointer variable sets aside space for a pointer but doesn't make it point to an object:

```
int *p;   /* points nowhere in particular */
```

It's crucial to initialize p before we use it. One way to initialize a pointer variable is to assign it the address of some variable—or, more generally, lvalue—using the & operator:

lvalues ➤ 4.2

```
int i, *p;
…
p = &i;
```

By assigning the address of i to the variable p, this statement makes p point to i:

It's also possible to initialize a pointer variable at the time we declare it:

Q&A

```
int i;
int *p = &i;
```

We can even combine the declaration of i with the declaration of p, provided that i is declared first:

```
int i, *p = &i;
```

The Indirection Operator

Once a pointer variable points to an object, we can use the * (indirection) operator to access what's stored in the object. If p points to i, for example, we can print the value of i as follows:

```
printf("%d\n", *p);
```

Q&A

printf will display the *value* of i, not the *address* of i.

The mathematically inclined reader may wish to think of * as the inverse of &. Applying & to a variable produces a pointer to the variable; applying * to the pointer takes us back to the original variable:

```
j = *&i;    /* same as j = i; */
```

As long as p points to i, *p is an **alias** for i. Not only does *p have the same value as i, but changing the value of *p also changes the value of i. (*p is an lvalue, so assignment to it is legal.) The following example illustrates the equivalence of *p and i; diagrams show the values of p and i at various points in the computation.

```
p = &i;
```

```
i = 1;
```

```
printf("%d\n", i);    /* prints 1 */
printf("%d\n", *p);   /* prints 1 */
*p = 2;
```

```
printf("%d\n", i);    /* prints 2 */
printf("%d\n", *p);   /* prints 2 */
```

Never apply the indirection operator to an uninitialized pointer variable. If a pointer variable p hasn't been initialized, attempting to use the value of p in any way causes undefined behavior. In the following example, the call of `printf` may print garbage, cause the program to crash, or have some other effect:

```
int *p;
printf("%d", *p);   /*** WRONG ***/
```

Assigning a value to *p is particularly dangerous. If p happens to contain a valid memory address, the following assignment will attempt to modify the data stored at that address:

```
int *p;
*p = 1;   /*** WRONG ***/
```

If the location modified by this assignment belongs to the program, it may behave erratically; if it belongs to the operating system, the program will most likely crash. Your compiler may issue a warning that p is uninitialized, so pay close attention to any warning messages you get.

11.3 Pointer Assignment

C allows the use of the assignment operator to copy pointers, provided that they have the same type. Suppose that i, j, p, and q have been declared as follows:

```
int i, j, *p, *q;
```

The statement

```
p = &i;
```

is an example of pointer assignment; the address of i is copied into p. Here's another example of pointer assignment:

```
q = p;
```

This statement copies the contents of p (the address of i) into q, in effect making q point to the same place as p:

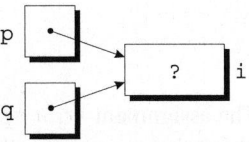

Both p and q now point to i, so we can change i by assigning a new value to either *p or *q:

```
*p = 1;
```

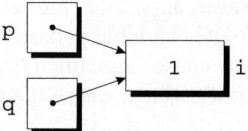

```
*q = 2;
```

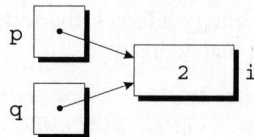

Any number of pointer variables may point to the same object.

Be careful not to confuse

```
q = p;
```

with

```
*q = *p;
```

The first statement is a pointer assignment; the second isn't, as the following example shows:

```
p = &i;
q = &j;
i = 1;
```

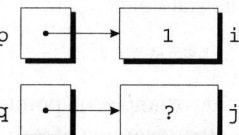

```
*q = *p;
```

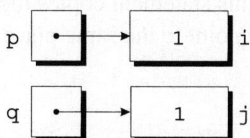

The assignment `*q = *p` copies the value that p points to (the value of i) into the object that q points to (the variable j).

11.4 Pointers as Arguments

So far, we've managed to avoid a rather important question: What are pointers good for? There's no single answer to that question, since pointers have several distinct uses in C. In this section, we'll see how a pointer to a variable can be useful as a function argument. We'll discover other uses for pointers in Section 11.5 and in Chapters 12 and 17.

We saw in Section 9.3 that a variable supplied as an argument in a function call is protected against change, because C passes arguments by value. This property of C can be a nuisance if we want the function to be able to modify the variable. In Section 9.3, we tried—and failed—to write a decompose function that could modify two of its arguments.

Pointers offer a solution to this problem: instead of passing a variable x as the argument to a function, we'll supply &x, a pointer to x. We'll declare the corresponding parameter p to be a pointer. When the function is called, p will have the value &x, hence *p (the object that p points to) will be an alias for x. Each appearance of *p in the body of the function will be an indirect reference to x, allowing the function both to read x and to modify it.

To see this technique in action, let's modify the decompose function by declaring the parameters int_part and frac_part to be pointers. The definition of decompose will now look like this:

```
void decompose(double x, long *int_part, double *frac_part)
{
  *int_part = (long) x;
  *frac_part = x - *int_part;
}
```

The prototype for decompose could be either

```
void decompose(double x, long *int_part, double *frac_part);
```

or

```
void decompose(double, long *, double *);
```

We'll call decompose in the following way:

```
decompose(3.14159, &i, &d);
```

Because of the & operator in front of i and d, the arguments to decompose are *pointers* to i and d, not the *values* of i and d. When decompose is called, the value 3.14159 is copied into x, a pointer to i is stored in int_part, and a pointer to d is stored in frac_part:

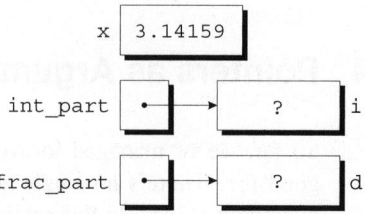

The first assignment in the body of decompose converts the value of x to type long and stores it in the object pointed to by int_part. Since int_part points to i, the assignment puts the value 3 in i:

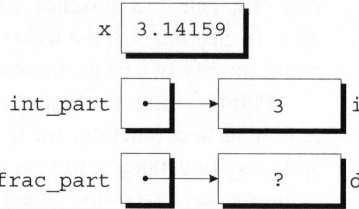

The second assignment fetches the value that int_part points to (the value of i), which is 3. This value is converted to type double and subtracted from x, giving .14159, which is then stored in the object that frac_part points to:

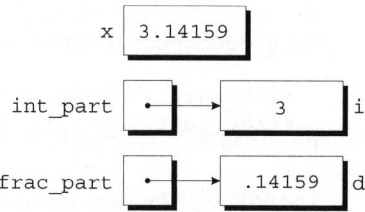

When decompose returns, i and d will have the values 3 and .14159, just as we originally wanted.

Using pointers as arguments to functions is actually nothing new; we've been doing it in calls of scanf since Chapter 2. Consider the following example:

```
int i;
…
scanf("%d", &i);
```

We must put the & operator in front of i so that scanf is given a *pointer* to i; that pointer tells scanf where to put the value that it reads. Without the &, scanf would be supplied with the *value* of i.

Although scanf's arguments must be pointers, it's not always true that every argument needs the & operator. In the following example, scanf is passed a pointer variable:

```
int i, *p;
...
p = &i;
scanf("%d", p);
```

Since p contains the address of i, scanf will read an integer and store it in i. Using the & operator in the call would be wrong:

```
scanf("%d", &p);    /*** WRONG ***/
```

scanf would read an integer and store it in p instead of in i.

Failing to pass a pointer to a function when one is expected can have disastrous results. Suppose that we call decompose without the & operator in front of i and d:

```
decompose(3.14159, i, d);
```

decompose is expecting pointers as its second and third arguments, but it's been given the *values* of i and d instead. decompose has no way to tell the difference, so it will use the values of i and d as though they were pointers. When decompose stores values in *int_part and *frac_part, it will attempt to change unknown memory locations instead of modifying i and d.

If we've provided a prototype for decompose (as we should always do, of course), the compiler will let us know that we're attempting to pass arguments of the wrong type. In the case of scanf, however, failing to pass pointers often goes undetected by the compiler, making scanf an especially error-prone function.

PROGRAM **Finding the Largest and Smallest Elements in an Array**

To illustrate how pointers are passed to functions, let's look at a function named max_min that finds the largest and smallest elements in an array. When we call max_min, we'll pass it pointers to two variables; max_min will then store its answers in these variables. max_min has the following prototype:

```
void max_min(int a[], int n, int *max, int *min);
```

A call of max_min might have the following appearance:

```
max_min(b, N, &big, &small);
```

b is an array of integers; N is the number of elements in b. big and small are ordinary integer variables. When max_min finds the largest element in b, it stores the value in big by assigning it to *max. (Since max points to big, an assignment to *max will modify the value of big.) max_min stores the smallest element of b in small by assigning it to *min.

To test max_min, we'll write a program that reads 10 numbers into an array, passes the array to max_min, and prints the results:

```
Enter 10 numbers: 34 82 49 102 7 94 23 11 50 31
Largest: 102
Smallest: 7
```

Here's the complete program:

maxmin.c

```
/* Finds the largest and smallest elements in an array */

#include <stdio.h>

#define N 10

void max_min(int a[], int n, int *max, int *min);

int main(void)
{
  int b[N], i, big, small;

  printf("Enter %d numbers: ", N);
  for (i = 0; i < N; i++)
    scanf("%d", &b[i]);

  max_min(b, N, &big, &small);

  printf("Largest: %d\n", big);
  printf("Smallest: %d\n", small);

  return 0;
}

void max_min(int a[], int n, int *max, int *min)
{
  int i;

  *max = *min = a[0];
  for (i = 1; i < n; i++) {
    if (a[i] > *max)
      *max = a[i];
    else if (a[i] < *min)
      *min = a[i];
  }
}
```

Using `const` to Protect Arguments

When we call a function and pass it a pointer to a variable, we normally assume
that the function will modify the variable (otherwise, why would the function
require a pointer?). For example, if we see a statement like

```
f(&x);
```

in a program, we'd probably expect f to change the value of x. It's possible, though, that f merely needs to examine the value of x, not change it. The reason for the pointer might be efficiency: passing the value of a variable can waste time and space if the variable requires a large amount of storage. (Section 12.3 covers this point in more detail.)

We can use the word const to document that a function won't change an object whose address is passed to the function. const goes in the parameter's declaration, just before the specification of its type:

Q&A

```
void f(const int *p)
{
  *p = 0;    /*** WRONG ***/
}
```

This use of const indicates that p is a pointer to a "constant integer." Attempting to modify *p is an error that the compiler will detect.

11.5 Pointers as Return Values

We can not only pass pointers to functions but also write functions that *return* pointers. Such functions are relatively common; we'll encounter several in Chapter 13.

The following function, when given pointers to two integers, returns a pointer to whichever integer is larger:

```
int *max(int *a, int *b)
{
  if (*a > *b)
    return a;
  else
    return b;
}
```

When we call max, we'll pass pointers to two int variables and store the result in a pointer variable:

```
int *p, i, j;
...
p = max(&i, &j);
```

During the call of max, *a is an alias for i, while *b is an alias for j. If i has a larger value than j, max returns the address of i; otherwise, it returns the address of j. After the call, p points to either i or j.

Although the max function returns one of the pointers passed to it as an argument, that's not the only possibility. A function could also return a pointer to an external variable or to a local variable that's been declared static.

Never return a pointer to an *automatic* local variable:

```
int *f(void)
{
  int i;
  …
  return &i;
}
```

The variable i doesn't exist once f returns, so the pointer to it will be invalid. Some compilers issue a warning such as "*function returns address of local variable*" in this situation.

Pointers can point to array elements, not just ordinary variables. If a is an array, then &a[i] is a pointer to element i of a. When a function has an array argument, it's sometimes useful for the function to return a pointer to one of the elements in the array. For example, the following function returns a pointer to the middle element of the array a, assuming that a has n elements:

```
int *find_middle(int a[], int n) {
  return &a[n/2];
}
```

Chapter 12 explores the relationship between pointers and arrays in considerable detail.

Q & A

*Q: Is a pointer always the same as an address? [p. 242]

A: Usually, but not always. Consider a computer whose main memory is divided into *words* rather than bytes. A word might contain 36 bits, 60 bits, or some other number of bits. If we assume 36-bit words, memory will have the following appearance:

Address	Contents
0	001010011001010011001010011001010011
1	001110101001110101001110101001110101
2	001110011001110011001110011001110011
3	001100001001100001001100001001100001
4	001101110001101110001101110001101110
⋮	⋮
n-1	001000011001000011001000011001000011

When memory is divided into words, each word has an address. An integer usually occupies one word, so a pointer to an integer can just be an address. However, a word can store more than one character. For example, a 36-bit word might store six 6-bit characters:

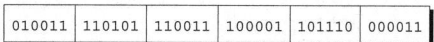

| 010011 | 110101 | 110011 | 100001 | 101110 | 000011 |

or four 9-bit characters:

| 001010011 | 001110101 | 001110011 | 001100001 |

For this reason, a pointer to a character may need to be stored in a different form than other pointers. A pointer to a character might consist of an address (the word in which the character is stored) plus a small integer (the position of the character within the word).

On some computers, pointers may be "offsets" rather than complete addresses. For example, CPUs in the Intel x86 family (used in many personal computers) can execute programs in several modes. The oldest of these, which dates back to the 8086 processor of 1978, is called *real mode*. In this mode, addresses are sometimes represented by a single 16-bit number (an *offset*) and sometimes by two 16-bit numbers (a *segment:offset pair*). An offset isn't a true memory address; the CPU must combine it with a segment value stored in a special register. To support real mode, older C compilers often provide two kinds of pointers: *near pointers* (16-bit offsets) and *far pointers* (32-bit segment:offset pairs). These compilers usually reserve the words `near` and `far` as nonstandard keywords that can be used to declare pointer variables.

*Q: **If a pointer can point to *data* in a program, is it possible to have a pointer to program *code*?**

  A: Yes. We'll cover pointers to functions in Section 17.7.

  Q: **It seems to me that there's an inconsistency between the declaration**

```
int *p = &i;
```

  and the statement

```
p = &i;
```

  Why isn't p preceded by a * symbol in the statement, as it is in the declaration? [p. 244]

  A: The source of the confusion is the fact that the * symbol can have different meanings in C, depending on the context in which it's used. In the declaration

```
int *p = &i;
```

the * symbol is *not* the indirection operator. Instead, it helps specify the type of p, informing the compiler that p is a *pointer* to an `int`. When it appears in a statement, however, the * symbol performs indirection (when used as a unary operator). The statement

```
*p = &i;    /*** WRONG ***/
```

would be wrong, because it assigns the address of i to the object that p points to, not to p itself.

Q: Is there some way to print the address of a variable? [p. 244]

A: Any pointer, including the address of a variable, can be displayed by calling the printf function and using %p as the conversion specification. See Section 22.3 for details.

Q: The following declaration is confusing:

```
void f(const int *p);
```

Does this say that f can't modify p? [p. 251]

A: No. It says that f can't change the integer that p *points to*; it doesn't prevent f from changing p itself.

```
void f(const int *p)
{
  int j;

  *p = 0;    /*** WRONG ***/
  p = &j;    /* legal */
}
```

Since arguments are passed by value, assigning p a new value—by making it point somewhere else—won't have any effect outside the function.

*Q: When declaring a parameter of a pointer type, is it legal to put the word const in front of the parameter's name, as in the following example?

```
void f(int * const p);
```

A: Yes, although the effect isn't the same as if const precedes p's type. We saw in Section 11.4 that putting const *before* p's type protects the object that p points to. Putting const *after* p's type protects p itself:

```
void f(int * const p)
{
  int j;

  *p = 0;    /* legal */
  p = &j;    /*** WRONG ***/
}
```

This feature isn't used very often. Since p is merely a copy of another pointer (the argument when the function is called), there's rarely any reason to protect it.

An even greater rarity is the need to protect both p *and* the object it points to, which can be done by putting const both before and after p's type:

```
void f(const int * const p)
{
  int j;

  *p = 0;    /*** WRONG ***/
  p = &j;    /*** WRONG ***/
}
```

Exercises

Section 11.2

1. If i is a variable and p points to i, which of the following expressions are aliases for i?

   (a) *p   (c) *&p   (e) *i   (g) *&i
   (b) &p   (d) &*p   (f) &i   (h) &*i

Section 11.3   Ⓦ   2. If i is an int variable and p and q are pointers to int, which of the following assignments are legal?

   (a) p = i;   (d) p = &q;   (g) p = *q;
   (b) *p = &i;   (e) p = *&q;   (h) *p = q;
   (c) &p = q;   (f) p = q;   (i) *p = *q;

Section 11.4

3. The following function supposedly computes the sum and average of the numbers in the array a, which has length n. avg and sum point to variables that the function should modify. Unfortunately, the function contains several errors; find and correct them.

```
void avg_sum(double a[], int n, double *avg, double *sum)
{
  int i;

  sum = 0.0;
  for (i = 0; i < n; i++)
    sum += a[i];
  avg = sum / n;
}
```

Ⓦ   4. Write the following function:

```
void swap(int *p, int *q);
```

When passed the addresses of two variables, swap should exchange the values of the variables:

```
swap(&i, &j);   /* exchanges values of i and j */
```

5. Write the following function:

```
void split_time(long total_sec, int *hr, int *min, int *sec);
```

total_sec is a time represented as the number of seconds since midnight. hr, min, and sec are pointers to variables in which the function will store the equivalent time in hours (0–23), minutes (0–59), and seconds (0–59), respectively.

Ⓦ   6. Write the following function:

```
void find_two_largest(int a[], int n, int *largest,
                      int *second_largest);
```

When passed an array a of length n, the function will search a for its largest and second-largest elements, storing them in the variables pointed to by largest and second_largest, respectively.

7. Write the following function:

```
void split_date(int day_of_year, int year,
                int *month, int *day);
```

day_of_year is an integer between 1 and 366, specifying a particular day within the year designated by year. month and day point to variables in which the function will store the equivalent month (1–12) and day within that month (1–31).

Section 11.5

8. Write the following function:

```
int *find_largest(int a[], int n);
```

When passed an array a of length n, the function will return a pointer to the array's largest element.

Programming Projects

1. Modify Programming Project 7 from Chapter 2 so that it includes the following function:

```
void pay_amount(int dollars, int *twenties, int *tens,
                int *fives, int *ones);
```

The function determines the smallest number of $20, $10, $5, and $1 bills necessary to pay the amount represented by the dollars parameter. The twenties parameter points to a variable in which the function will store the number of $20 bills required. The tens, fives, and ones parameters are similar.

2. Modify Programming Project 8 from Chapter 5 so that it includes the following function:

```
void find_closest_flight(int desired_time,
                         int *departure_time,
                         int *arrival_time);
```

This function will find the flight whose departure time is closest to desired_time (expressed in minutes since midnight). It will store the departure and arrival times of this flight (also expressed in minutes since midnight) in the variables pointed to by departure_time and arrival_time, respectively.

3. Modify Programming Project 3 from Chapter 6 so that it includes the following function:

```
void reduce(int numerator, int denominator,
            int *reduced_numerator,
            int *reduced_denominator);
```

numerator and denominator are the numerator and denominator of a fraction. reduced_numerator and reduced_denominator are pointers to variables in which the function will store the numerator and denominator of the fraction once it has been reduced to lowest terms.

4. Modify the poker.c program of Section 10.5 by moving all external variables into main and modifying functions so that they communicate by passing arguments. The analyze_hand function needs to change the straight, flush, four, three, and pairs variables, so it will have to be passed pointers to those variables.

12 Pointers and Arrays

Optimization hinders evolution.

Chapter 11 introduced pointers and showed how they're used as function arguments and as values returned by functions. This chapter covers another application for pointers. When pointers point to array elements, C allows us to perform arithmetic—addition and subtraction—on the pointers, which leads to an alternative way of processing arrays in which pointers take the place of array subscripts.

The relationship between pointers and arrays in C is a close one, as we'll soon see. We'll exploit this relationship in subsequent chapters, including Chapter 13 (Strings) and Chapter 17 (Advanced Uses of Pointers). Understanding the connection between pointers and arrays is critical for mastering C: it will give you insight into how C was designed and help you understand existing programs. Be aware, however, that one of the primary reasons for using pointers to process arrays—efficiency—is no longer as important as it once was, thanks to improved compilers.

Section 12.1 discusses pointer arithmetic and shows how pointers can be compared using the relational and equality operators. Section 12.2 then demonstrates how we can use pointer arithmetic for processing array elements. Section 12.3 reveals a key fact about arrays—an array name can serve as a pointer to the array's first element—and uses it to show how array arguments really work. Section 12.4 shows how the topics of the first three sections apply to multidimensional arrays. Section 12.5 wraps up the chapter by exploring the relationship between pointers and variable-length arrays, a C99 feature.

12.1 Pointer Arithmetic

We saw in Section 11.5 that pointers can point to array elements. For example, suppose that a and p have been declared as follows:

```
int a[10], *p;
```

We can make p point to a[0] by writing

```
p = &a[0];
```

Graphically, here's what we've just done:

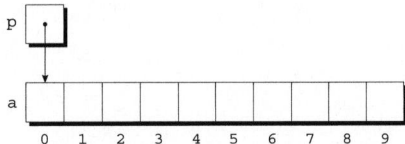

We can now access a[0] through p; for example, we can store the value 5 in a[0] by writing

```
*p = 5;
```

Here's our picture now:

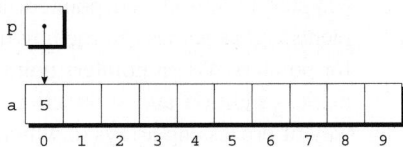

Making a pointer p point to an element of an array a isn't particularly exciting. However, by performing *pointer arithmetic* (or ***address arithmetic***) on p, we can access the other elements of a. C supports three (and only three) forms of pointer arithmetic:

Adding an integer to a pointer
Subtracting an integer from a pointer
Subtracting one pointer from another

Let's take a close look at each of these operations. Our examples assume that the following declarations are in effect:

```
int a[10], *p, *q, i;
```

Adding an Integer to a Pointer

Adding an integer j to a pointer p yields a pointer to the element j places after the one that p points to. More precisely, if p points to the array element a[i], then p + j points to a[i+j] (provided, of course, that a[i+j] exists).

The following example illustrates pointer addition; diagrams show the values of p and q at various points in the computation.

```
p = &a[2];
```

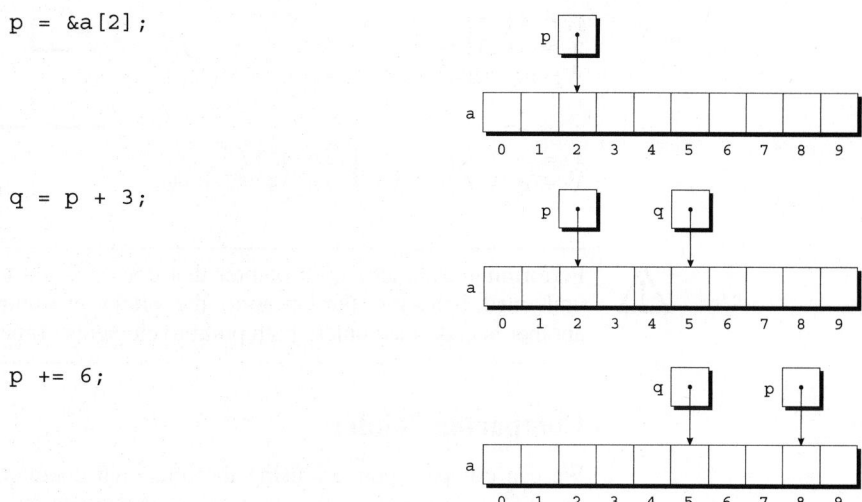

```
q = p + 3;
```

```
p += 6;
```

Subtracting an Integer from a Pointer

If `p` points to the array element `a[i]`, then `p - j` points to `a[i-j]`. For example:

```
p = &a[8];
```

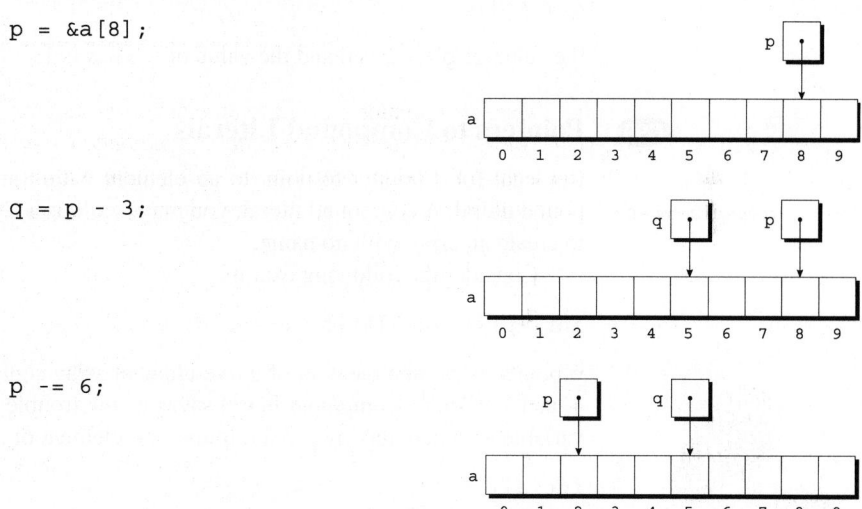

```
q = p - 3;
```

```
p -= 6;
```

Subtracting One Pointer from Another

When one pointer is subtracted from another, the result is the distance (measured in array elements) between the pointers. Thus, if `p` points to `a[i]` and `q` points to `a[j]`, then `p - q` is equal to `i - j`. For example:

```
p = &a[5];
q = &a[1];
```

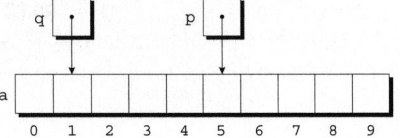

```
i = p - q;    /* i is 4 */
i = q - p;    /* i is -4 */
```

> Performing arithmetic on a pointer that doesn't point to an array element causes undefined behavior. Furthermore, the effect of subtracting one pointer from another is undefined unless both point to elements of the *same* array.

Comparing Pointers

We can compare pointers using the relational operators (`<`, `<=`, `>`, `>=`) and the equality operators (`==` and `!=`). Using the relational operators to compare two pointers is meaningful only when both point to elements of the same array. The outcome of the comparison depends on the relative positions of the two elements in the array. For example, after the assignments

```
p = &a[5];
q = &a[1];
```

the value of `p <= q` is 0 and the value of `p >= q` is 1.

(C99) Pointers to Compound Literals

compound literals ➤9.3

It's legal for a pointer to point to an element within an array created by a compound literal. A compound literal, you may recall, is a C99 feature that can be used to create an array with no name.

Consider the following example:

```
int *p = (int []){3, 0, 3, 4, 1};
```

p points to the first element of a five-element array containing the integers 3, 0, 3, 4, and 1. Using a compound literal saves us the trouble of first declaring an array variable and then making p point to the first element of that array:

```
int a[] = {3, 0, 3, 4, 1};
int *p = &a[0];
```

12.2   Using Pointers for Array Processing

Pointer arithmetic allows us to visit the elements of an array by repeatedly incrementing a pointer variable. The following program fragment, which sums the elements of an array a, illustrates the technique. In this example, the pointer variable p initially points to a[0]. Each time through the loop, p is incremented; as a result, it points to a[1], then a[2], and so forth. The loop terminates when p steps past the last element of a.

```
#define N 10
...
int a[N], sum, *p;
...
sum = 0;
for (p = &a[0]; p < &a[N]; p++)
  sum += *p;
```

The following figures show the contents of a, sum, and p at the end of the first three loop iterations (before p has been incremented).

At the end of the first iteration:

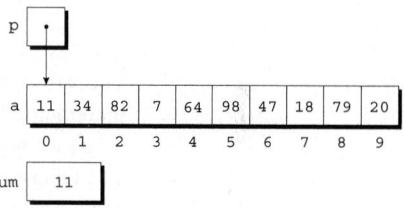

At the end of the second iteration:

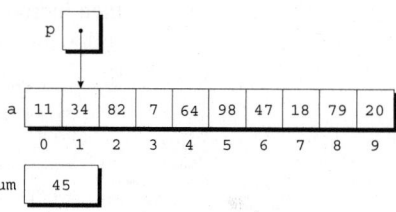

At the end of the third iteration:

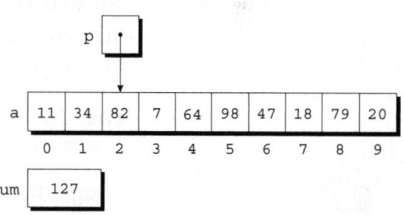

The condition p < &a[N] in the for statement deserves special mention. Strange as it may seem, it's legal to apply the address operator to a[N], even though this element doesn't exist (a is indexed from 0 to N − 1). Using a[N] in this fashion is perfectly safe, since the loop doesn't attempt to examine its value. The body of the loop will be executed with p equal to &a[0], &a[1], ..., &a[N-1], but when p is equal to &a[N], the loop terminates.

We could just as easily have written the loop without pointers, of course, using subscripting instead. The argument most often cited in support of pointer arithmetic is that it can save execution time. However, that depends on the implementation—some C compilers actually produce better code for loops that rely on subscripting.

Combining the * and ++ Operators

C programmers often combine the * (indirection) and ++ operators in statements that process array elements. Consider the simple case of storing a value into an array element and then advancing to the next element. Using array subscripting, we might write

```
a[i++] = j;
```

If p is pointing to an array element, the corresponding statement would be

```
*p++ = j;
```

Because the postfix version of ++ takes precedence over *, the compiler sees this as

```
*(p++) = j;
```

The value of p++ is p. (Since we're using the postfix version of ++, p won't be incremented until after the expression has been evaluated.) Thus, the value of *(p++) will be *p—the object to which p is pointing.

Of course, *p++ isn't the only legal combination of * and ++. We could write (*p)++, for example, which returns the value of the object that p points to, and then increments that object (p itself is unchanged). If you find this confusing, the following table may help:

Expression	Meaning
*p++ or *(p++)	Value of expression is *p before increment; increment p later
(*p)++	Value of expression is *p before increment; increment *p later
*++p or *(++p)	Increment p first; value of expression is *p after increment
++*p or ++(*p)	Increment *p first; value of expression is *p after increment

All four combinations appear in programs, although some are far more common than others. The one we'll see most frequently is *p++, which is handy in loops. Instead of writing

```
for (p = &a[0]; p < &a[N]; p++)
  sum += *p;
```

to sum the elements of the array a, we could write

```
p = &a[0];
while (p < &a[N])
  sum += *p++;
```

The * and -- operators mix in the same way as * and ++. For an application that combines * and --, let's return to the stack example of Section 10.2. The original version of the stack relied on an integer variable named top to keep track of the "top-of-stack" position in the contents array. Let's replace top by a pointer variable that points initially to element 0 of the contents array:

```
int *top_ptr = &contents[0];
```

Here are the new `push` and `pop` functions (updating the other stack functions is left as an exercise):

```
void push(int i)
{
  if (is_full())
    stack_overflow();
  else
    *top_ptr++ = i;
}

int pop(void)
{
  if (is_empty())
    stack_underflow();
  else
    return *--top_ptr;
}
```

Note that I've written `*--top_ptr`, not `*top_ptr--`, since I want pop to decrement `top_ptr` *before* fetching the value to which it points.

12.3 Using an Array Name as a Pointer

Pointer arithmetic is one way in which arrays and pointers are related, but it's not the only connection between the two. Here's another key relationship: *The name of an array can be used as a pointer to the first element in the array.* This relationship simplifies pointer arithmetic and makes both arrays and pointers more versatile.

For example, suppose that `a` is declared as follows:

```
int a[10];
```

Using `a` as a pointer to the first element in the array, we can modify `a[0]`:

```
*a = 7;    /* stores 7 in a[0] */
```

We can modify `a[1]` through the pointer `a + 1`:

```
*(a+1) = 12;    /* stores 12 in a[1] */
```

In general, `a + i` is the same as `&a[i]` (both represent a pointer to element `i` of `a`) and `*(a+i)` is equivalent to `a[i]` (both represent element `i` itself). In other words, array subscripting can be viewed as a form of pointer arithmetic.

The fact that an array name can serve as a pointer makes it easier to write loops that step through an array. Consider the following loop from Section 12.2:

```
for (p = &a[0]; p < &a[N]; p++)
  sum += *p;
```

To simplify the loop, we can replace &a[0] by a and &a[N] by a + N:

idiom
```
for (p = a; p < a + N; p++)
  sum += *p;
```

 Although an array name can be used as a pointer, it's not possible to assign it a new value. Attempting to make it point elsewhere is an error:

```
while (*a != 0)
  a++;              /*** WRONG ***/
```

This is no great loss; we can always copy a into a pointer variable, then change the pointer variable:

```
p = a;
while (*p != 0)
  p++;
```

PROGRAM

Reversing a Series of Numbers (Revisited)

The reverse.c program of Section 8.1 reads 10 numbers, then writes the numbers in reverse order. As the program reads the numbers, it stores them in an array. Once all the numbers are read, the program steps through the array backwards as it prints the numbers.

The original program used subscripting to access elements of the array. Here's a new version in which I've replaced subscripting with pointer arithmetic.

reverse3.c
```
/* Reverses a series of numbers (pointer version) */

#include <stdio.h>

#define N 10

int main(void)
{
  int a[N], *p;

  printf("Enter %d numbers: ", N);
  for (p = a; p < a + N; p++)
    scanf("%d", p);

  printf("In reverse order:");
  for (p = a + N - 1; p >= a; p--)
    printf(" %d", *p);
  printf("\n");

  return 0;
}
```

In the original program, an integer variable i kept track of the current position within the array. The new version replaces i with p, a pointer variable. The numbers are still stored in an array; we're simply using a different technique to keep track of where we are in the array.

Note that the second argument to scanf is p, not &p. Since p points to an array element, it's a satisfactory argument for scanf; &p, on the other hand, would be a pointer to a pointer to an array element.

Array Arguments (Revisited)

When passed to a function, an array name is always treated as a pointer. Consider the following function, which returns the largest element in an array of integers:

```
int find_largest(int a[], int n)
{
  int i, max;

  max = a[0];
  for (i = 1; i < n; i++)
    if (a[i] > max)
      max = a[i];
  return max;
}
```

Suppose that we call find_largest as follows:

```
largest = find_largest(b, N);
```

This call causes a pointer to the first element of b to be assigned to a; the array itself isn't copied.

The fact that an array argument is treated as a pointer has some important consequences:

- When an ordinary variable is passed to a function, its value is copied; any changes to the corresponding parameter don't affect the variable. In contrast, an array used as an argument isn't protected against change, since no copy is made of the array itself. For example, the following function (which we first saw in Section 9.3) modifies an array by storing zero into each of its elements:

  ```
  void store_zeros(int a[], int n)
  {
    int i;

    for (i = 0; i < n; i++)
      a[i] = 0;
  }
  ```

  To indicate that an array parameter won't be changed, we can include the word const in its declaration:

  ```
  int find_largest(const int a[], int n)
  {
    ...
  }
  ```

If `const` is present, the compiler will check that no assignment to an element of a appears in the body of `find_largest`.

- The time required to pass an array to a function doesn't depend on the size of the array. There's no penalty for passing a large array, since no copy of the array is made.

- An array parameter can be declared as a pointer if desired. For example, `find_largest` could be defined as follows:

```
int find_largest(int *a, int n)
{
  ...
}
```

Declaring a to be a pointer is equivalent to declaring it to be an array; the compiler treats the declarations as though they were identical.

Although declaring a *parameter* to be an array is the same as declaring it to be a pointer, the same isn't true for a *variable*. The declaration

```
int a[10];
```

causes the compiler to set aside space for 10 integers. In contrast, the declaration

```
int *a;
```

causes the compiler to allocate space for a pointer variable. In the latter case, a is not an array; attempting to use it as an array can have disastrous results. For example, the assignment

```
*a = 0;   /*** WRONG ***/
```

will store 0 where a is pointing. Since we don't know where a is pointing, the effect on the program is undefined.

- A function with an array parameter can be passed an array "slice"—a sequence of consecutive elements. Suppose that we want `find_largest` to locate the largest element in some portion of an array b, say elements `b[5]`, ..., `b[14]`. When we call `find_largest`, we'll pass it the address of `b[5]` and the number `10`, indicating that we want `find_largest` to examine 10 array elements, starting at `b[5]`:

```
largest = find_largest(&b[5], 10);
```

Using a Pointer as an Array Name

If we can use an array name as a pointer, will C allow us to subscript a pointer as though it were an array name? By now, you'd probably expect the answer to be yes, and you'd be right. Here's an example:

```
#define N 10
...
int a[N], i, sum = 0, *p = a;
...
for (i = 0; i < N; i++)
  sum += p[i];
```

The compiler treats p[i] as *(p+i), which is a perfectly legal use of pointer arithmetic. Although the ability to subscript a pointer may seem to be little more than a curiosity, we'll see in Section 17.3 that it's actually quite useful.

12.4 Pointers and Multidimensional Arrays

Just as pointers can point to elements of one-dimensional arrays, they can also point to elements of multidimensional arrays. In this section, we'll explore common techniques for using pointers to process the elements of multidimensional arrays. For simplicity, I'll stick to two-dimensional arrays, but everything we'll do applies equally to higher-dimensional arrays.

Processing the Elements of a Multidimensional Array

We saw in Section 8.2 that C stores two-dimensional arrays in row-major order; in other words, the elements of row 0 come first, followed by the elements of row 1, and so forth. An array with *r* rows would have the following appearance:

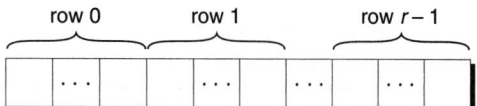

We can take advantage of this layout when working with pointers. If we make a pointer p point to the first element in a two-dimensional array (the element in row 0, column 0), we can visit every element in the array by incrementing p repeatedly.

As an example, let's look at the problem of initializing all elements of a two-dimensional array to zero. Suppose that the array has been declared as follows:

```
int a[NUM_ROWS][NUM_COLS];
```

The obvious technique would be to use nested for loops:

```
int row, col;
...
for (row = 0; row < NUM_ROWS; row++)
  for (col = 0; col < NUM_COLS; col++)
    a[row][col] = 0;
```

But if we view a as a one-dimensional array of integers (which is how it's stored), we can replace the pair of loops by a single loop:

```
int *p;
...
for (p = &a[0][0]; p <= &a[NUM_ROWS-1][NUM_COLS-1]; p++)
  *p = 0;
```

The loop begins with p pointing to a[0][0]. Successive increments of p make it point to a[0][1], a[0][2], a[0][3], and so on. When p reaches a[0][NUM_COLS-1] (the last element in row 0), incrementing it again makes p point to a[1][0], the first element in row 1. The process continues until p goes past a[NUM_ROWS-1][NUM_COLS-1], the last element in the array.

Q&A   Although treating a two-dimensional array as one-dimensional may seem like cheating, it works with most C compilers. Whether it's a good idea to do so is another matter. Techniques like this one definitely hurt program readability, but—at least with some older compilers—produce a compensating increase in efficiency. With many modern compilers, though, there's often little or no speed advantage.

Processing the Rows of a Multidimensional Array

What about processing the elements in just one *row* of a two-dimensional array? Again, we have the option of using a pointer variable p. To visit the elements of row i, we'd initialize p to point to element 0 in row i in the array a:

```
p = &a[i][0];
```

Or we could simply write

```
p = a[i];
```

since, for any two-dimensional array a, the expression a[i] is a pointer to the first element in row i. To see why this works, recall the magic formula that relates array subscripting to pointer arithmetic: for any array a, the expression a[i] is equivalent to *(a + i). Thus, &a[i][0] is the same as &(*(a[i] + 0)), which is equivalent to &*a[i], which is the same as a[i], since the & and * operators cancel. We'll use this simplification in the following loop, which clears row i of the array a:

```
int a[NUM_ROWS][NUM_COLS], *p, i;
...
for (p = a[i]; p < a[i] + NUM_COLS; p++)
  *p = 0;
```

Since a[i] is a pointer to row i of the array a, we can pass a[i] to a function that's expecting a one-dimensional array as its argument. In other words, a function that's designed to work with one-dimensional arrays will also work with a row belonging to a two-dimensional array. As a result, functions such as `find_largest` and `store_zeros` are more versatile than you might expect. Consider `find_largest`, which we originally designed to find the largest element of a one-dimensional array. We can just as easily use `find_largest` to determine the largest element in row i of the two-dimensional array a:

```
largest = find_largest(a[i], NUM_COLS);
```

Processing the Columns of a Multidimensional Array

Processing the elements in a *column* of a two-dimensional array isn't as easy, because arrays are stored by row, not by column. Here's a loop that clears column i of the array a:

```
int a[NUM_ROWS][NUM_COLS], (*p)[NUM_COLS], i;
…
for (p = &a[0]; p < &a[NUM_ROWS]; p++)
  (*p)[i] = 0;
```

I've declared p to be a pointer to an array of length NUM_COLS whose elements are integers. The parentheses around `*p` in `(*p)[NUM_COLS]` are required; without them, the compiler would treat p as an array of pointers instead of a pointer to an array. The expression p++ advances p to the beginning of the next row. In the expression `(*p)[i]`, `*p` represents an entire row of a, so `(*p)[i]` selects the element in column i of that row. The parentheses in `(*p)[i]` are essential, because the compiler would interpret `*p[i]` as `*(p[i])`.

Using the Name of a Multidimensional Array as a Pointer

Just as the name of a one-dimensional array can be used as a pointer, so can the name of *any* array, regardless of how many dimensions it has. Some care is required, though. Consider the following array:

```
int a[NUM_ROWS][NUM_COLS];
```

a is *not* a pointer to `a[0][0]`; instead, it's a pointer to `a[0]`. This makes more sense if we look at it from the standpoint of C, which regards a not as a two-dimensional array but as a one-dimensional array whose elements are one-dimensional arrays. When used as a pointer, a has type `int (*)[NUM_COLS]` (pointer to an integer array of length NUM_COLS).

Knowing that a points to `a[0]` is useful for simplifying loops that process the elements of a two-dimensional array. For example, instead of writing

```
for (p = &a[0]; p < &a[NUM_ROWS]; p++)
  (*p)[i] = 0;
```

to clear column i of the array a, we can write

```
for (p = a; p < a + NUM_ROWS; p++)
  (*p)[i] = 0;
```

Another situation in which this knowledge comes in handy is when we want to "trick" a function into thinking that a multidimensional array is really one-dimensional. For example, consider how we might use `find_largest` to find the largest element in a. As the first argument to `find_largest`, let's try passing a (the address of the array); as the second, we'll pass NUM_ROWS * NUM_COLS (the total number of elements in a):

```
largest = find_largest(a, NUM_ROWS * NUM_COLS);   /* WRONG */
```

Unfortunately, the compiler will object to this statement, because the type of a is `int (*)[NUM_COLS]` but `find_largest` is expecting an argument of type `int *`. The correct call is

```
largest = find_largest(a[0], NUM_ROWS * NUM_COLS);
```

Q&A

a[0] points to element 0 in row 0, and it has type `int *` (after conversion by the compiler), so the latter call will work correctly.

12.5 Pointers and Variable-Length Arrays (C99)

variable-length arrays ➤8.3

Pointers are allowed to point to elements of variable-length arrays (VLAs), a feature of C99. An ordinary pointer variable would be used to point to an element of a one-dimensional VLA:

```
void f(int n)
{
  int a[n], *p;
  p = a;
  …
}
```

When the VLA has more than one dimension, the type of the pointer depends on the length of each dimension except for the first. Let's look at the two-dimensional case:

```
void f(int m, int n)
{
  int a[m][n], (*p)[n];
  p = a;
  …
}
```

Since the type of p depends on n, which isn't constant, p is said to have a *variably modified type*. Note that the validity of an assignment such as p = a can't always be determined by the compiler. For example, the following code will compile but is correct only if m and n are equal:

```
int a[m][n], (*p)[m];
p = a;
```

If m ≠ n, any subsequent use of p will cause undefined behavior.

Variably modified types are subject to certain restrictions, just as variable-length arrays are. The most important restriction is that the declaration of a variably modified type must be inside the body of a function or in a function proto-type.

Pointer arithmetic works with VLAs just as it does for ordinary arrays. Returning to the example of Section 12.4 that clears a single column of a two-dimensional array a, let's declare a as a VLA this time:

```
int a[m][n];
```

A pointer capable of pointing to a row of a would be declared as follows:

```
int (*p)[n];
```

The loop that clears column i is almost identical to the one we used in Section 12.4:

```
for (p = a; p < a + m; p++)
  (*p)[i] = 0;
```

Q & A

Q: **I don't understand pointer arithmetic. If a pointer is an address, does that mean that an expression like p + j adds j to the address stored in p? [p. 258]**

A: No. Integers used in pointer arithmetic are scaled depending on the type of the pointer. If p is of type int *, for example, then p + j typically adds 4 × j to p, assuming that int values are stored using 4 bytes. But if p has type double *, then p + j will probably add 8 × j to p, since double values are usually 8 bytes long.

Q: **When writing a loop to process an array, is it better to use array subscripting or pointer arithmetic? [p. 261]**

A: There's no easy answer to this question, since it depends on the machine you're using and the compiler itself. In the early days of C on the PDP-11, pointer arithmetic yielded a faster program. On today's machines, using today's compilers, array subscripting is often just as good, and sometimes even better. The bottom line: Learn both ways and then use whichever is more natural for the kind of program you're writing.

*Q: **I read somewhere that i[a] is the same as a[i]. Is this true?**

A: Yes, it is, oddly enough. The compiler treats i[a] as *(i + a), which is the same as *(a + i). (Pointer addition, like ordinary addition, is commutative.) But *(a + i) is equivalent to a[i]. Q.E.D. But please don't use i[a] in programs unless you're planning to enter the next Obfuscated C contest.

Q: **Why is `*a` the same as `a[]` in a parameter declaration? [p. 266]**

A: Both indicate that the argument is expected to be a pointer. The same operations on a are possible in both cases (pointer arithmetic and array subscripting, in particular). And, in both cases, a itself can be assigned a new value within the function. (Although C allows us to use the name of an array *variable* only as a "constant pointer," there's no such restriction on the name of an array *parameter*.)

Q: **Is it better style to declare an array parameter as `*a` or `a[]`?**

A: That's a tough one. From one standpoint, a[] is the obvious choice, since *a is ambiguous (does the function want an array of objects or a pointer to a single object?). On the other hand, many programmers argue that declaring the parameter as *a is more accurate, since it reminds us that only a pointer is passed, not a copy of the array. Others switch between *a and a[], depending on whether the function uses pointer arithmetic or subscripting to access the elements of the array. (That's the approach I'll use.) In practice, *a is more common than a[], so you'd better get used to it. For what it's worth, Dennis Ritchie now refers to the a[] notation as "a living fossil" that "serves as much to confuse the learner as to alert the reader."

Q: **We've seen that arrays and pointers are closely related in C. Would it be accurate to say that they're interchangeable?**

A: No. It's true that array *parameters* are interchangeable with pointer parameters, but array *variables* aren't the same as pointer variables. Technically, the name of an array isn't a pointer; rather, the C compiler *converts* it to a pointer when necessary. To see this difference more clearly, consider what happens when we apply the sizeof operator to an array a. The value of sizeof(a) is the total number of bytes in the array—the size of each element multiplied by the number of elements. But if p is a pointer variable, sizeof(p) is the number of bytes required to store a pointer value.

Q: **You said that treating a two-dimensional array as one-dimensional works with "most" C compilers. Doesn't it work with all compilers? [p. 268]**

A: No. Some modern "bounds-checking" compilers track not only the type of a pointer, but—when it points to an array—also the length of the array. For example, suppose that p is assigned a pointer to a[0][0]. Technically, p points to the first element of a[0], a one-dimensional array. If we increment p repeatedly in an effort to visit all the elements of a, we'll go out of bounds once p goes past the last element of a[0]. A compiler that performs bounds-checking may insert code to check that p is used only to access elements in the array pointed to by a[0]; an attempt to increment p past the end of this array would be detected as an error.

Q: **If a is a two-dimensional array, why can we pass `a[0]`—but not a itself—to `find_largest`? Don't both a and `a[0]` point to the same place (the beginning of the array)? [p. 270]**

A: They do, as a matter of fact—both point to element a[0][0]. The problem is that a has the wrong type. When used as an argument, it's a pointer to an array, but find_largest is expecting a pointer to an integer. However, a[0] has type int *, so it's an acceptable argument for find_largest. This concern about types is actually good; if C weren't so picky, we could make all kinds of horrible pointer mistakes without the compiler noticing.

Exercises

Section 12.1

1. Suppose that the following declarations are in effect:

```
int a[] = {5, 15, 34, 54, 14, 2, 52, 72};
int *p = &a[1], *q = &a[5];
```

   (a) What is the value of * (p+3)?
   (b) What is the value of * (q-3)?
   (c) What is the value of q - p?
   (d) Is the condition p < q true or false?
   (e) Is the condition *p < *q true or false?

Ⓦ *2. Suppose that high, low, and middle are all pointer variables of the same type, and that low and high point to elements of an array. Why is the following statement illegal, and how could it be fixed?

```
middle = (low + high) / 2;
```

Section 12.2

3. What will be the contents of the a array after the following statements are executed?

```
#define N 10

int a[N] = {1, 2, 3, 4, 5, 6, 7, 8, 9, 10};
int *p = &a[0], *q = &a[N-1], temp;

while (p < q) {
   temp = *p;
   *p++ = *q;
   *q-- = temp;
}
```

Ⓦ 4. Rewrite the make_empty, is_empty, and is_full functions of Section 10.2 to use the pointer variable top_ptr instead of the integer variable top.

Section 12.3

5. Suppose that a is a one-dimensional array and p is a pointer variable. Assuming that the assignment p = a has just been performed, which of the following expressions are illegal because of mismatched types? Of the remaining expressions, which are true (have a nonzero value)?

   (a) p == a[0]
   (b) p == &a[0]
   (c) *p == a[0]
   (d) p[0] == a[0]

Ⓦ 6. Rewrite the following function to use pointer arithmetic instead of array subscripting. (In other words, eliminate the variable i and all uses of the [] operator.) Make as few changes as possible.

```
int sum_array(const int a[], int n)
{
  int i, sum;

  sum = 0;
  for (i = 0; i < n; i++)
    sum += a[i];
  return sum;
}
```

7. Write the following function:

    ```
    bool search(const int a[], int n, int key);
    ```

    a is an array to be searched, n is the number of elements in the array, and key is the search key. search should return true if key matches some element of a, and false if it doesn't. Use pointer arithmetic—not subscripting—to visit array elements.

8. Rewrite the following function to use pointer arithmetic instead of array subscripting. (In other words, eliminate the variable i and all uses of the [] operator.) Make as few changes as possible.

    ```
    void store_zeros(int a[], int n)
    {
      int i;

      for (i = 0; i < n; i++)
        a[i] = 0;
    }
    ```

9. Write the following function:

    ```
    double inner_product(const double *a, const double *b,
                         int n);
    ```

    a and b both point to arrays of length n. The function should return a[0] * b[0] + a[1] * b[1] + ... + a[n-1] * b[n-1]. Use pointer arithmetic—not subscripting—to visit array elements.

10. Modify the find_middle function of Section 11.5 so that it uses pointer arithmetic to calculate the return value.

11. Modify the find_largest function so that it uses pointer arithmetic—not subscripting—to visit array elements.

12. Write the following function:

    ```
    void find_two_largest(const int *a, int n, int *largest,
                          int *second_largest);
    ```

    a points to an array of length n. The function searches the array for its largest and second-largest elements, storing them in the variables pointed to by largest and second_largest, respectively. Use pointer arithmetic—not subscripting—to visit array elements.

Section 12.4   Ⓦ 13.   Section 8.2 had a program fragment in which two nested for loops initialized the array ident for use as an identity matrix. Rewrite this code, using a single pointer to step through the array one element at a time. *Hint:* Since we won't be using row and col index variables, it won't be easy to tell where to store 1. Instead, we can use the fact that the first element of the array should be 1, the next N elements should be 0, the next element should be 1, and so forth. Use a variable to keep track of how many consecutive 0s have been stored; when the count reaches N, it's time to store 1.

14. Assume that the following array contains a week's worth of hourly temperature readings, with each row containing the readings for one day:

```
int temperatures[7][24];
```

Write a statement that uses the `search` function (see Exercise 7) to search the entire `temperatures` array for the value 32.

15. Write a loop that prints all temperature readings stored in row i of the `temperatures` array (see Exercise 14). Use a pointer to visit each element of the row.

16. Write a loop that prints the highest temperature in the `temperatures` array (see Exercise 14) for each day of the week. The loop body should call the `find_largest` function, passing it one row of the array at a time.

17. Rewrite the following function to use pointer arithmetic instead of array subscripting. (In other words, eliminate the variables i and j and all uses of the [] operator.) Use a single loop instead of nested loops.

```
int sum_two_dimensional_array(const int a[][LEN], int n)
{
  int i, j, sum = 0;

  for (i = 0; i < n; i++)
    for (j = 0; j < LEN; j++)
      sum += a[i][j];

  return sum;
}
```

18. Write the `evaluate_position` function described in Exercise 13 of Chapter 9. Use pointer arithmetic—not subscripting—to visit array elements. Use a single loop instead of nested loops.

Programming Projects

1. (a) Write a program that reads a message, then prints the reversal of the message:

```
Enter a message: Don't get mad, get even.
Reversal is: .neve teg ,dam teg t'noD
```

Hint: Read the message one character at a time (using `getchar`) and store the characters in an array. Stop reading when the array is full or the character read is `'\n'`.

(b) Revise the program to use a pointer instead of an integer to keep track of the current position in the array.

2. (a) Write a program that reads a message, then checks whether it's a palindrome (the letters in the message are the same from left to right as from right to left):

```
Enter a message: He lived as a devil, eh?
Palindrome
```

```
Enter a message: Madam, I am Adam.
Not a palindrome
```

Ignore all characters that aren't letters. Use integer variables to keep track of positions in the array.

(b) Revise the program to use pointers instead of integers to keep track of positions in the array.

W 3. Simplify Programming Project 1(b) by taking advantage of the fact that an array name can be used as a pointer.

4. Simplify Programming Project 2(b) by taking advantage of the fact that an array name can be used as a pointer.

5. Modify Programming Project 14 from Chapter 8 so that it uses a pointer instead of an integer to keep track of the current position in the array that contains the sentence.

6. Modify the qsort.c program of Section 9.6 so that low, high, and middle are pointers to array elements rather than integers. The split function will need to return a pointer, not an integer.

7. Modify the maxmin.c program of Section 11.4 so that the max_min function uses a pointer instead of an integer to keep track of the current position in the array.

13 Strings

*It's difficult to extract sense from strings, but
they're the only communication coin we can count on.*

Although we've used `char` variables and arrays of `char` values in previous chapters, we still lack any convenient way to process a series of characters (a *string,* in C terminology). We'll remedy that defect in this chapter, which covers both string *constants* (or *literals,* as they're called in the C standard) and string *variables,* which can change during the execution of a program.

Section 13.1 explains the rules that govern string literals, including the rules for embedding escape sequences in string literals and for breaking long string literals. Section 13.2 then shows how to declare string variables, which are simply arrays of characters in which a special character—the null character—marks the end of a string. Section 13.3 describes ways to read and write strings. Section 13.4 shows how to write functions that process strings, and Section 13.5 covers some of the string-handling functions in the C library. Section 13.6 presents idioms that are often used when working with strings. Finally, Section 13.7 describes how to set up arrays whose elements are pointers to strings of different lengths. This section also explains how C uses such an array to supply command-line information to programs.

13.1 String Literals

A *string literal* is a sequence of characters enclosed within double quotes:

```
"When you come to a fork in the road, take it."
```

We first encountered string literals in Chapter 2; they often appear as format strings in calls of `printf` and `scanf`.

Escape Sequences in String Literals

escape sequences ►7.3

String literals may contain the same escape sequences as character constants. We've used character escapes in `printf` and `scanf` format strings for some time. For example, we've seen that each `\n` character in the string

```
"Candy\nIs dandy\nBut liquor\nIs quicker.\n  --Ogden Nash\n"
```

causes the cursor to advance to the next line:

```
Candy
Is dandy
But liquor
Is quicker.
  --Ogden Nash
```

Although octal and hexadecimal escapes are also legal in string literals, they're not as common as character escapes.

Be careful when using octal and hexadecimal escape sequences in string literals. An octal escape ends after three digits or with the first non-octal character. For example, the string `"\1234"` contains two characters (`\123` and `4`), and the string `"\189"` contains three characters (`\1`, `8`, and `9`). A hexadecimal escape, on the other hand, isn't limited to three digits; it doesn't end until the first non-hex character. Consider what happens if a string contains the escape `\xfc`, which represents the character *ü* in the Latin1 character set, a common extension of ASCII. The string `"Z\xfcrich"` ("Zürich") has six characters (Z, `\xfc`, r, i, c, and h), but the string `"\xfcber"` (a failed attempt at "über") has only two (`\xfcbe` and `r`). Most compilers will object to the latter string, since hex escapes are usually limited to the range `\x0`–`\xff`.

Q&A

Continuing a String Literal

If we find that a string literal is too long to fit conveniently on a single line, C allows us to continue it on the next line, provided that we end the first line with a backslash character (`\`). No other characters may follow `\` on the same line, other than the (invisible) new-line character at the end:

```
printf("When you come to a fork in the road, take it. \
--Yogi Berra");
```

In general, the `\` character can be used to join two or more lines of a program into a single line (a process that the C standard refers to as "splicing"). We'll see more examples of splicing in Section 14.3.

The `\` technique has one drawback: the string must continue at the beginning of the next line, thereby wrecking the program's indented structure. There's a better way to deal with long string literals, thanks to the following rule: when two or more string literals are adjacent (separated only by white space), the compiler will join them into a single string. This rule allows us to split a string literal over two or more lines:

```
printf("When you come to a fork in the road, take it.  "
       "--Yogi Berra");
```

How String Literals Are Stored

We've used string literals often in calls of printf and scanf. But when we call printf and supply a string literal as an argument, what are we actually passing? To answer this question, we need to know how string literals are stored.

In essence, C treats string literals as character arrays. When a C compiler encounters a string literal of length n in a program, it sets aside $n + 1$ bytes of memory for the string. This area of memory will contain the characters in the string, plus one extra character—the **null character**—to mark the end of the string. The null character is a byte whose bits are all zero, so it's represented by the \0 escape sequence.

 Don't confuse the null character ('\0') with the zero character ('0'). The null character has the code 0; the zero character has a different code (48 in ASCII).

For example, the string literal "abc" is stored as an array of four characters (a, b, c, and \0):

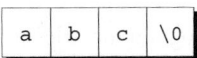

String literals may be empty; the string "" is stored as a single null character:

Since a string literal is stored as an array, the compiler treats it as a pointer of type char *. Both printf and scanf, for example, expect a value of type char * as their first argument. Consider the following example:

```
printf("abc");
```

When printf is called, it's passed the address of "abc" (a pointer to where the letter a is stored in memory).

Operations on String Literals

In general, we can use a string literal wherever C allows a char * pointer. For example, a string literal can appear on the right side of an assignment:

```
char *p;

p = "abc";
```

This assignment doesn't copy the characters in `"abc"`; it merely makes p point to the first character of the string.

C allows pointers to be subscripted, so we can subscript string literals:

```
char ch;

ch = "abc"[1];
```

The new value of ch will be the letter b. The other possible subscripts are 0 (which would select the letter a), 2 (the letter c), and 3 (the null character). This property of string literals isn't used that much, but occasionally it's handy. Consider the following function, which converts a number between 0 and 15 into a character that represents the equivalent hex digit:

```
char digit_to_hex_char(int digit)
{
  return "0123456789ABCDEF"[digit];
}
```

Attempting to modify a string literal causes undefined behavior:

```
char *p = "abc";

*p = 'd';   /*** WRONG ***/
```

A program that tries to change a string literal may crash or behave erratically.

String Literals versus Character Constants

A string literal containing a single character isn't the same as a character constant. The string literal `"a"` is represented by a *pointer* to a memory location that contains the character a (followed by a null character). The character constant `'a'` is represented by an *integer* (the numerical code for the character).

Don't ever use a character when a string is required (or vice versa). The call

```
printf("\n");
```

is legal, because `printf` expects a pointer as its first argument. The following call isn't legal, however:

```
printf('\n');   /*** WRONG ***/
```

13.2 String Variables

Some programming languages provide a special `string` type for declaring string variables. C takes a different tack: any one-dimensional array of characters can be used to store a string, with the understanding that the string is terminated by a null character. This approach is simple, but has significant difficulties. It's sometimes hard to tell whether an array of characters is being used as a string. If we write our own string-handling functions, we've got to be careful that they deal properly with the null character. Also, there's no faster way to determine the length of a string than a character-by-character search for the null character.

Let's say that we need a variable capable of storing a string of up to 80 characters. Since the string will need a null character at the end, we'll declare the variable to be an array of 81 characters:

idiom
```
#define STR_LEN 80
…
char str[STR_LEN+1];
```

We defined `STR_LEN` to be `80` rather than `81`, thus emphasizing the fact that `str` can store strings of no more than 80 characters, and then added 1 to `STR_LEN` in the declaration of `str`. This a common practice among C programmers.

 When declaring an array of characters that will be used to hold a string, always make the array one character longer than the string, because of the C convention that every string is terminated by a null character. Failing to leave room for the null character may cause unpredictable results when the program is executed, since functions in the C library assume that strings are null-terminated.

Declaring a character array to have length `STR_LEN` + 1 doesn't mean that it will always contain a string of `STR_LEN` characters. The length of a string depends on the position of the terminating null character, not on the length of the array in which the string is stored. An array of `STR_LEN` + 1 characters can hold strings of various lengths, ranging from the empty string to strings of length `STR_LEN`.

Initializing a String Variable

A string variable can be initialized at the same time it's declared:

```
char date1[8] = "June 14";
```

The compiler will put the characters from `"June 14"` in the `date1` array, then add a null character so that `date1` can be used as a string. Here's what `date1` will look like:

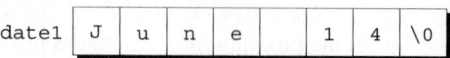

Although `"June 14"` appears to be a string literal, it's not. Instead, C views it as an abbreviation for an array initializer. In fact, we could have written

```
char date1[8] = {'J', 'u', 'n', 'e', ' ', '1', '4', '\0'};
```

I think you'll agree that the original version is easier to read.

What if the initializer is too short to fill the string variable? In that case, the compiler adds extra null characters. Thus, after the declaration

```
char date2[9] = "June 14";
```

`date2` will have the following appearance:

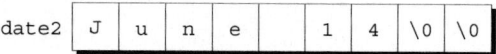

array initializers ➤8.1 This behavior is consistent with C's treatment of array initializers in general. When an array initializer is shorter than the array itself, the remaining elements are initialized to zero. By initializing the leftover elements of a character array to `\0`, the compiler is following the same rule.

What if the initializer is longer than the string variable? That's illegal for strings, just as it's illegal for other arrays. However, C does allow the initializer (not counting the null character) to have exactly the same length as the variable:

```
char date3[7] = "June 14";
```

There's no room for the null character, so the compiler makes no attempt to store one:

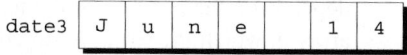

 If you're planning to initialize a character array to contain a string, be sure that the length of the array is longer than the length of the initializer. Otherwise, the compiler will quietly omit the null character, making the array unusable as a string.

The declaration of a string variable may omit its length, in which case the compiler computes it:

```
char date4[] = "June 14";
```

The compiler sets aside eight characters for `date4`, enough to store the characters in `"June 14"` plus a null character. (The fact that the length of `date4` isn't specified doesn't mean that the array's length can be changed later. Once the program is compiled, the length of `date4` is fixed at eight.) Omitting the length of a string variable is especially useful if the initializer is long, since computing the length by hand is error-prone.

Character Arrays versus Character Pointers

Let's compare the declaration

```
char date[] = "June 14";
```

which declares `date` to be an *array*, with the similar-looking

```
char *date = "June 14";
```

which declares `date` to be a *pointer*. Thanks to the close relationship between arrays and pointers, we can use either version of `date` as a string. In particular, any function expecting to be passed a character array or character pointer will accept either version of `date` as an argument.

However, we must be careful not to make the mistake of thinking that the two versions of `date` are interchangeable. There are significant differences between the two:

- In the array version, the characters stored in `date` can be modified, like the elements of any array. In the pointer version, `date` points to a string literal, and we saw in Section 13.1 that string literals shouldn't be modified.
- In the array version, `date` is an array name. In the pointer version, `date` is a variable that can be made to point to other strings during program execution.

If we need a string that can be modified, it's our responsibility to set up an array of characters in which to store the string; declaring a pointer variable isn't enough. The declaration

```
char *p;
```

causes the compiler to set aside enough memory for a pointer variable; unfortunately, it doesn't allocate space for a string. (And how could it? We haven't indicated how long the string would be.) Before we can use `p` as a string, it must point to an array of characters. One possibility is to make `p` point to a string variable:

```
char str[STR_LEN+1], *p;

p = str;
```

`p` now points to the first character of `str`, so we can use `p` as a string. Another
dynamically allocated strings ➤ 17.2 possibility is to make `p` point to a dynamically allocated string.

Using an uninitialized pointer variable as a string is a serious error. Consider the following example, which attempts to build the string `"abc"`:

```
char *p;

p[0] = 'a';    /*** WRONG ***/
p[1] = 'b';    /*** WRONG ***/
p[2] = 'c';    /*** WRONG ***/
p[3] = '\0';   /*** WRONG ***/
```

Since p hasn't been initialized, we don't know where it's pointing. Using the pointer to write the characters a, b, c, and \0 into memory causes undefined behavior.

13.3　Reading and Writing Strings

Writing a string is easy using either the `printf` or `puts` functions. Reading a string is a bit harder, primarily because of the possibility that the input string may be longer than the string variable into which it's being stored. To read a string in a single step, we can use either `scanf` or `gets`. As an alternative, we can read strings one character at a time.

Writing Strings Using `printf` and `puts`

The `%s` conversion specification allows `printf` to write a string. Consider the following example:

```
char str[] = "Are we having fun yet?";

printf("%s\n", str);
```

The output will be

```
Are we having fun yet?
```

`printf` writes the characters in a string one by one until it encounters a null character. (If the null character is missing, `printf` continues past the end of the string until—eventually—it finds a null character somewhere in memory.)

To print just part of a string, we can use the conversion specification `%.ps`, where p is the number of characters to be displayed. The statement

```
printf("%.6s\n", str);
```

will print

```
Are we
```

A string, like a number, can be printed within a field. The %*m*s conversion will display a string in a field of size *m*. (A string with more than *m* characters will be printed in full, not truncated.) If the string has fewer than *m* characters, it will be right-justified within the field. To force left justification instead, we can put a minus sign in front of *m*. The *m* and *p* values can be used in combination: a conversion specification of the form %*m.p*s causes the first *p* characters of a string to be displayed in a field of size *m*.

printf isn't the only function that can write strings. The C library also provides puts, which is used in the following way:

```
puts(str);
```

puts has only one argument (the string to be printed). After writing the string, puts always writes an additional new-line character, thus advancing to the beginning of the next output line.

Reading Strings Using scanf and gets

The %s conversion specification allows scanf to read a string into a character array:

```
scanf("%s", str);
```

There's no need to put the & operator in front of str in the call of scanf; like any array name, str is treated as a pointer when passed to a function.

white-space characters ➤ 3.2 When scanf is called, it skips white space, then reads characters and stores them in str until it encounters a white-space character. scanf always stores a null character at the end of the string.

A string read using scanf will never contain white space. Consequently, scanf won't usually read a full line of input; a new-line character will cause scanf to stop reading, but so will a space or tab character. To read an entire line of input at a time, we can use gets. Like scanf, the gets function reads input characters into an array, then stores a null character. In other respects, however, gets is somewhat different from scanf:

- gets doesn't skip white space before starting to read the string (scanf does).

- gets reads until it finds a new-line character (scanf stops at any white-space character). Incidentally, gets discards the new-line character instead of storing it in the array; the null character takes its place.

To see the difference between scanf and gets, consider the following program fragment:

```
char sentence[SENT_LEN+1];

printf("Enter a sentence:\n");
scanf("%s", sentence);
```

Suppose that after the prompt

```
Enter a sentence:
```

the user enters the line

```
To C, or not to C: that is the question.
```

scanf will store the string "To" in sentence. The next call of scanf will resume reading the line at the space after the word To.

Now suppose that we replace scanf by gets:

```
gets(sentence);
```

When the user enters the same input as before, gets will store the string

```
"   To C, or not to C: that is the question."
```

in sentence.

As they read characters into an array, scanf and gets have no way to detect when it's full. Consequently, they may store characters past the end of the array, causing undefined behavior. scanf can be made safer by using the conversion specification %*ns* instead of %s, where *n* is an integer indicating the maximum number of characters to be stored. gets, unfortunately, is inherently unsafe; fgets is a much better alternative.

fgets function ►22.5

Reading Strings Character by Character

Since both scanf and gets are risky and insufficiently flexible for many applications, C programmers often write their own input functions. By reading strings one character at a time, these functions provide a greater degree of control than the standard input functions.

If we decide to design our own input function, we'll need to consider the following issues:

- Should the function skip white space before beginning to store the string?
- What character causes the function to stop reading: a new-line character, any white-space character, or some other character? Is this character stored in the string or discarded?
- What should the function do if the input string is too long to store: discard the extra characters or leave them for the next input operation?

Suppose we need a function that doesn't skip white-space characters, stops reading at the first new-line character (which isn't stored in the string), and discards extra characters. The function might have the following prototype:

```
int read_line(char str[], int n);
```

str represents the array into which we'll store the input, and n is the maximum number of characters to be read. If the input line contains more than n characters, read_line will discard the additional characters. We'll have read_line return the number of characters it actually stores in str (a number anywhere from 0 to n). We may not always need read_line's return value, but it doesn't hurt to have it available.

getchar function ►7.3

read_line consists primarily of a loop that calls getchar to read a character and then stores the character in str, provided that there's room left. The loop terminates when the new-line character is read. (Strictly speaking, we should also have the loop terminate if getchar should fail to read a character, but we'll ignore that complication for now.) Here's the complete definition of read_line:

Q&A

```c
int read_line(char str[], int n)
{
  int ch, i = 0;

  while ((ch = getchar()) != '\n')
    if (i < n)
      str[i++] = ch;
  str[i] = '\0';          /* terminates string */
  return i;               /* number of characters stored */
}
```

Note that ch has int type rather than char type, because getchar returns the character that it reads as an int value.

Before returning, read_line puts a null character at the end of the string. Standard functions such as scanf and gets automatically put a null character at the end of an input string; if we're writing our own input function, however, we must take on that responsibility.

13.4 Accessing the Characters in a String

Since strings are stored as arrays, we can use subscripting to access the characters in a string. To process every character in a string s, for example, we can set up a loop that increments a counter i and selects characters via the expression s[i].

Suppose that we need a function that counts the number of spaces in a string. Using array subscripting, we might write the function in the following way:

```c
int count_spaces(const char s[])
{
  int count = 0, i;

  for (i = 0; s[i] != '\0'; i++)
    if (s[i] == ' ')
      count++;
  return count;
}
```

I've included `const` in the declaration of s to indicate that `count_spaces` doesn't change the array that s represents. If s were not a string, the function would need a second argument specifying the length of the array. Since s is a string, however, `count_spaces` can determine where it ends by testing for the null character.

Many C programmers wouldn't write `count_spaces` as we have. Instead, they'd use a pointer to keep track of the current position within the string. As we saw in Section 12.2, this technique is always available for processing arrays, but it proves to be especially convenient for working with strings.

Let's rewrite the `count_spaces` function using pointer arithmetic instead of array subscripting. We'll eliminate the variable i and use s itself to keep track of our position in the string. By incrementing s repeatedly, `count_spaces` can step through each character in the string. Here's our new version of the function:

```
int count_spaces(const char *s)
{
  int count = 0;

  for (; *s != '\0'; s++)
    if (*s == ' ')
      count++;
  return count;
}
```

Note that `const` doesn't prevent `count_spaces` from modifying s; it's there to prevent the function from modifying what s points to. And since s is a copy of the pointer that's passed to `count_spaces`, incrementing s doesn't affect the original pointer.

The `count_spaces` example raises some questions about how to write string functions:

■ ***Is it better to use array operations or pointer operations to access the characters in a string?*** We're free to use whichever is more convenient; we can even mix the two. In the second version of `count_spaces`, treating s as a pointer simplifies the function slightly by removing the need for the variable i. Traditionally, C programmers lean toward using pointer operations for processing strings.

■ ***Should a string parameter be declared as an array or as a pointer?*** The two versions of `count_spaces` illustrate the options: the first version declares s to be an array; the second declares s to be a pointer. Actually, there's no difference between the two declarations—recall from Section 12.3 that the compiler treats an array parameter as though it had been declared as a pointer.

■ ***Does the form of the parameter (`s[]` or `*s`) affect what can be supplied as an argument?*** No. When `count_spaces` is called, the argument could be an array name, a pointer variable, or a string literal—`count_spaces` can't tell the difference.

13.5 Using the C String Library

Some programming languages provide operators that can copy strings, compare strings, concatenate strings, select substrings, and the like. C's operators, in contrast, are essentially useless for working with strings. Strings are treated as arrays in C, so they're restricted in the same ways as arrays—in particular, they can't be copied or compared using operators.

 Direct attempts to copy or compare strings will fail. For example, suppose that `str1` and `str2` have been declared as follows:

```
char str1[10], str2[10];
```

Copying a string into a character array using the = operator is not possible:

```
str1 = "abc";    /*** WRONG ***/
str2 = str1;     /*** WRONG ***/
```

We saw in Section 12.3 that using an array name as the left operand of = is illegal. *Initializing* a character array using = is legal, though:

```
char str1[10] = "abc";
```

In the context of a declaration, = is not the assignment operator.

Attempting to compare strings using a relational or equality operator is legal but won't produce the desired result:

```
if (str1 == str2) …    /*** WRONG ***/
```

This statement compares `str1` and `str2` as *pointers*; it doesn't compare the contents of the two arrays. Since `str1` and `str2` have different addresses, the expression `str1 == str2` must have the value 0.

Fortunately, all is not lost: the C library provides a rich set of functions for performing operations on strings. Prototypes for these functions reside in the <string.h> header, so programs that need string operations should contain the following line:

<string.h> header ➤23.6

```
#include <string.h>
```

Most of the functions declared in <string.h> require at least one string as an argument. String parameters are declared to have type `char *`, allowing the argument to be a character array, a variable of type `char *`, or a string literal—all are suitable as strings. Watch out for string parameters that aren't declared `const`, however. Such a parameter may be modified when the function is called, so the corresponding argument shouldn't be a string literal.

There are many functions in `<string.h>`; I'll cover a few of the most basic. In subsequent examples, assume that `str1` and `str2` are character arrays used as strings.

The `strcpy` (String Copy) Function

The `strcpy` function has the following prototype in `<string.h>`:

```
char *strcpy(char *s1, const char *s2);
```

`strcpy` copies the string `s2` into the string `s1`. (To be precise, we should say "`strcpy` copies the string pointed to by `s2` into the array pointed to by `s1`.") That is, `strcpy` copies characters from `s2` to `s1` up to (and including) the first null character in `s2`. `strcpy` returns `s1` (a pointer to the destination string). The string pointed to by `s2` isn't modified, so it's declared `const`.

The existence of `strcpy` compensates for the fact that we can't use the assignment operator to copy strings. For example, suppose that we want to store the string `"abcd"` in `str2`. We can't use the assignment

```
str2 = "abcd";              /*** WRONG ***/
```

because `str2` is an array name and can't appear on the left side of an assignment. Instead, we can call `strcpy`:

```
strcpy(str2, "abcd");   /* str2 now contains "abcd" */
```

Similarly, we can't assign `str2` to `str1` directly, but we can call `strcpy`:

```
strcpy(str1, str2);     /* str1 now contains "abcd" */
```

Most of the time, we'll discard the value that `strcpy` returns. On occasion, though, it can be useful to call `strcpy` as part of a larger expression in order to use its return value. For example, we could chain together a series of `strcpy` calls:

```
strcpy(str1, strcpy(str2, "abcd"));
   /* both str1 and str2 now contain "abcd" */
```

In the call `strcpy(str1, str2)`, `strcpy` has no way to check that the string pointed to by `str2` will actually fit in the array pointed to by `str1`. Suppose that `str1` points to an array of length n. If the string that `str2` points to has no more than $n - 1$ characters, then the copy will succeed. But if `str2` points to a longer string, undefined behavior occurs. (Since `strcpy` always copies up to the first null character, it will continue copying past the end of the array that `str1` points to.)

strncpy function ▸23.6   Calling the `strncpy` function is a safer, albeit slower, way to copy a string. `strncpy` is similar to `strcpy` but has a third argument that limits the number of characters that will be copied. To copy `str2` into `str1`, we could use the following call of `strncpy`:

```
strncpy(str1, str2, sizeof(str1));
```

As long as `str1` is large enough to hold the string stored in `str2` (including the null character), the copy will be done correctly. `strncpy` itself isn't without danger, though. For one thing, it will leave the string in `str1` without a terminating null character if the length of the string stored in `str2` is greater than or equal to the size of the `str1` array. Here's a safer way to use `strncpy`:

```
strncpy(str1, str2, sizeof(str1) - 1);
str1[sizeof(str1)-1] = '\0';
```

The second statement guarantees that `str1` is always null-terminated, even if `strncpy` fails to copy a null character from `str2`.

The `strlen` (String Length) Function

The `strlen` function has the following prototype:

```
size_t strlen(const char *s);
```

size_t type ►7.6 `size_t`, which is defined in the C library, is a `typedef` name that represents one of C's unsigned integer types. Unless we're dealing with extremely long strings, this technicality need not concern us—we can simply treat the return value of `strlen` as an integer.

`strlen` returns the length of a string `s`: the number of characters in `s` up to, but not including, the first null character. Here are a few examples:

```
int len;

len = strlen("abc");    /* len is now 3 */
len = strlen("");       /* len is now 0 */
strcpy(str1, "abc");
len = strlen(str1);     /* len is now 3 */
```

The last example illustrates an important point. When given an array as its argument, `strlen` doesn't measure the length of the array itself; instead, it returns the length of the string stored in the array.

The `strcat` (String Concatenation) Function

The `strcat` function has the following prototype:

```
char *strcat(char *s1, const char *s2);
```

`strcat` appends the contents of the string `s2` to the end of the string `s1`; it returns `s1` (a pointer to the resulting string).

Here are some examples of `strcat` in action:

```
strcpy(str1, "abc");
strcat(str1, "def");   /* str1 now contains "abcdef" */
```

```
strcpy(str1, "abc");
strcpy(str2, "def");
strcat(str1, str2);    /* str1 now contains "abcdef" */
```

As with `strcpy`, the value returned by `strcat` is normally discarded. The following example shows how the return value might be used:

```
strcpy(str1, "abc");
strcpy(str2, "def");
strcat(str1, strcat(str2, "ghi"));
    /* str1 now contains "abcdefghi"; str2 contains "defghi" */
```

 The effect of the call `strcat(str1, str2)` is undefined if the array pointed to by `str1` isn't long enough to accommodate the additional characters from `str2`. Consider the following example:

```
char str1[6] = "abc";

strcat(str1, "def");    /*** WRONG ***/
```

`strcat` will attempt to add the characters d, e, f, and \0 to the end of the string already stored in `str1`. Unfortunately, `str1` is limited to six characters, causing `strcat` to write past the end of the array.

strncat function ▶*23.6*   The `strncat` function is a safer but slower version of `strcat`. Like `strncpy`, it has a third argument that limits the number of characters it will copy. Here's what a call might look like:

```
strncat(str1, str2, sizeof(str1) - strlen(str1) - 1);
```

`strncat` will terminate `str1` with a null character, which isn't included in the third argument (the number of characters to be copied). In the example, the third argument calculates the amount of space remaining in `str1` (given by the expression `sizeof(str1) - strlen(str1)`) and then subtracts 1 to ensure that there will be room for the null character.

The `strcmp` (String Comparison) Function

The `strcmp` function has the following prototype:

```
int strcmp(const char *s1, const char *s2);
```

Q&A   `strcmp` compares the strings `s1` and `s2`, returning a value less than, equal to, or greater than 0, depending on whether `s1` is less than, equal to, or greater than `s2`. For example, to see if `str1` is less than `str2`, we'd write

```
if (strcmp(str1, str2) < 0)    /* is str1 < str2? */
    ...
```

To test whether `str1` is less than or equal to `str2`, we'd write

```
if (strcmp(str1, str2) <= 0)    /* is str1 <= str2? */
  …
```

By choosing the proper relational operator (`<`, `<=`, `>`, `>=`) or equality operator (`==`, `!=`), we can test any possible relationship between `str1` and `str2`.

    `strcmp` compares strings based on their lexicographic ordering, which resembles the way words are arranged in a dictionary. More precisely, `strcmp` considers `s1` to be less than `s2` if either one of the following conditions is satisfied:

- The first *i* characters of `s1` and `s2` match, but the (*i*+1)st character of `s1` is less than the (*i*+1)st character of `s2`. For example, `"abc"` is less than `"bcd"`, and `"abd"` is less than `"abe"`.

- All characters of `s1` match `s2`, but `s1` is shorter than `s2`. For example, `"abc"` is less than `"abcd"`.

As it compares characters from two strings, `strcmp` looks at the numerical codes that represent the characters. Some knowledge of the underlying character set is helpful in order to predict what `strcmp` will do. For example, here are a few important properties of the ASCII character set:

ASCII character set ➤ *Appendix E*

- The characters in each of the sequences A–Z, a–z, and 0–9 have consecutive codes.

- All upper-case letters are less than all lower-case letters. (In ASCII, codes between 65 and 90 represent upper-case letters; codes between 97 and 122 represent lower-case letters.)

- Digits are less than letters. (Codes between 48 and 57 represent digits.)

- Spaces are less than all printing characters. (The space character has the value 32 in ASCII.)

PROGRAM   ## Printing a One-Month Reminder List

To illustrate the use of the C string library, we'll now develop a program that prints a one-month list of daily reminders. The user will enter a series of reminders, with each prefixed by a day of the month. When the user enters 0 instead of a valid day, the program will print a list of all reminders entered, sorted by day. Here's what a session with the program will look like:

```
Enter day and reminder: 24 Susan's birthday
Enter day and reminder: 5 6:00 - Dinner with Marge and Russ
Enter day and reminder: 26 Movie - "Chinatown"
Enter day and reminder: 7 10:30 - Dental appointment
Enter day and reminder: 12 Movie - "Dazed and Confused"
Enter day and reminder: 5 Saturday class
Enter day and reminder: 12 Saturday class
Enter day and reminder: 0
```

```
Day Reminder
  5 Saturday class
  5 6:00 - Dinner with Marge and Russ
  7 10:30 - Dental appointment
 12 Saturday class
 12 Movie - "Dazed and Confused"
 24 Susan's birthday
 26 Movie - "Chinatown"
```

The overall strategy isn't very complicated: we'll have the program read a series of day-and-reminder combinations, storing them in order (sorted by day), and then display them. To read the days, we'll use scanf; to read the reminders, we'll use the read_line function of Section 13.3.

We'll store the strings in a two-dimensional array of characters, with each row of the array containing one string. After the program reads a day and its associated reminder, it will search the array to determine where the day belongs, using strcmp to do comparisons. It will then use strcpy to move all strings *below* that point down one position. Finally, the program will copy the day into the array and call strcat to append the reminder to the day. (The day and the reminder have been kept separate up to this point.).

Of course, there are always a few minor complications. For example, we want the days to be right-justified in a two-character field, so that their ones digits will line up. There are many ways to handle the problem. I've chosen to have the program use scanf to read the day into an integer variable, then call sprintf to convert the day back into string form. sprintf is a library function that's similar to printf, except that it writes output into a string. The call

sprintf function ▸ 22.8

```
sprintf(day_str, "%2d", day);
```

writes the value of day into day_str. Since sprintf automatically adds a null character when it's through writing, day_str will contain a properly null-terminated string.

Another complication is making sure that the user doesn't enter more than two digits. We'll use the following call of scanf for this purpose:

```
scanf("%2d", &day);
```

The number 2 between % and d tells scanf to stop reading after two digits, even if the input has more digits.

With those details out of the way, here's the program:

remind.c   /* Prints a one-month reminder list */

```
#include <stdio.h>
#include <string.h>

#define MAX_REMIND 50    /* maximum number of reminders */
#define MSG_LEN 60       /* max length of reminder message */
```

```
int read_line(char str[], int n);

int main(void)
{
  char reminders[MAX_REMIND][MSG_LEN+3];
  char day_str[3], msg_str[MSG_LEN+1];
  int day, i, j, num_remind = 0;

  for (;;) {
    if (num_remind == MAX_REMIND) {
      printf("-- No space left --\n");
      break;
    }

    printf("Enter day and reminder: ");
    scanf("%2d", &day);
    if (day == 0)
      break;
    sprintf(day_str, "%2d", day);
    read_line(msg_str, MSG_LEN);

    for (i = 0; i < num_remind; i++)
      if (strcmp(day_str, reminders[i]) < 0)
        break;
    for (j = num_remind; j > i; j--)
      strcpy(reminders[j], reminders[j-1]);

    strcpy(reminders[i], day_str);
    strcat(reminders[i], msg_str);

    num_remind++;
  }

  printf("\nDay Reminder\n");
  for (i = 0; i < num_remind; i++)
    printf(" %s\n", reminders[i]);

  return 0;
}

int read_line(char str[], int n)
{
  int ch, i = 0;

  while ((ch = getchar()) != '\n')
    if (i < n)
      str[i++] = ch;
  str[i] = '\0';
  return i;
}
```

Although remind.c is useful for demonstrating the strcpy, strcat, and strcmp functions, it lacks something as a practical reminder program. There are obviously a number of improvements needed, ranging from minor tweaks to major enhancements (such as saving the reminders in a file when the program terminates). We'll discuss several improvements in the programming projects at the end of this chapter and in later chapters.

13.6 String Idioms

Functions that manipulate strings are a particularly rich source of idioms. In this section, we'll explore some of the most famous idioms by using them to write the `strlen` and `strcat` functions. You'll never have to write these functions, of course, since they're part of the standard library, but you may have to write functions that are similar.

The concise style I'll use in this section is popular with many C programmers. You should master this style even if you don't plan to use it in your own programs, since you're likely to encounter it in code written by others.

One last note before we get started. If you want to try out any of the versions of `strlen` and `strcat` in this section, be sure to alter the name of the function (changing `strlen` to `my_strlen`, for example). As Section 21.1 explains, we're not allowed to write a function that has the same name as a standard library function, even when we don't include the header to which the function belongs. In fact, all names that begin with `str` and a lower-case letter are reserved (to allow functions to be added to the `<string.h>` header in future versions of the C standard).

Searching for the End of a String

Many string operations require searching for the end of a string. The `strlen` function is a prime example. The following version of `strlen` searches its string argument to find the end, using a variable to keep track of the string's length:

```
size_t strlen(const char *s)
{
  size_t n;

  for (n = 0; *s != '\0'; s++)
    n++;
  return n;
}
```

As the pointer s moves across the string from left to right, the variable n keeps track of how many characters have been seen so far. When s finally points to a null character, n contains the length of the string.

Let's see if we can condense the function. First, we'll move the initialization of n to its declaration:

```
size_t strlen(const char *s)
{
  size_t n = 0;

  for (; *s != '\0'; s++)
    n++;
  return n;
}
```

Next, we notice that the condition *s != '\0' is the same as *s != 0, because the integer value of the null character is 0. But testing *s != 0 is the same as testing *s; both are true if *s isn't equal to 0. These observations lead to our next version of strlen:

```
size_t strlen(const char *s)
{
  size_t n = 0;

  for (; *s; s++)
    n++;
  return n;
}
```

But, as we saw in Section 12.2, it's possible to increment s and test *s in the same expression:

```
size_t strlen(const char *s)
{
  size_t n = 0;

  for (; *s++;)
    n++;
  return n;
}
```

Replacing the for statement with a while statement, we arrive at the following version of strlen:

```
size_t strlen(const char *s)
{
  size_t n = 0;

  while (*s++)
    n++;
  return n;
}
```

Although we've condensed strlen quite a bit, it's likely that we haven't increased its speed. Here's a version that *does* run faster, at least with some compilers:

```
size_t strlen(const char *s)
{
  const char *p = s;
```

```
    while (*s)
      s++;
    return s - p;
}
```

This version of `strlen` computes the length of the string by locating the position of the null character, then subtracting from it the position of the first character in the string. The improvement in speed comes from not having to increment n inside the `while` loop. Note the appearance of the word `const` in the declaration of p, by the way; without it, the compiler would notice that assigning s to p places the string that s points to at risk.

The statement

idiom
```
    while (*s)
      s++;
```

and the related

idiom
```
    while (*s++)
      ;
```

are idioms meaning "search for the null character at the end of a string." The first version leaves s pointing to the null character. The second version is more concise, but leaves s pointing just past the null character.

Copying a String

Copying a string is another common operation. To introduce C's "string copy" idiom, we'll develop two versions of the `strcat` function. Let's start with a straightforward but somewhat lengthy version:

```
char *strcat(char *s1, const char *s2)
{
  char *p = s1;

  while (*p != '\0')
    p++;
  while (*s2 != '\0') {
    *p = *s2;
    p++;
    s2++;
  }
  *p = '\0';
  return s1;
}
```

This version of `strcat` uses a two-step algorithm: (1) Locate the null character at the end of the string s1 and make p point to it. (2) Copy characters one by one from s2 to where p is pointing.

The first `while` statement in the function implements step (1). p is set to point to the first character in the s1 string. Assuming that s1 points to the string `"abc"`, we have the following picture:

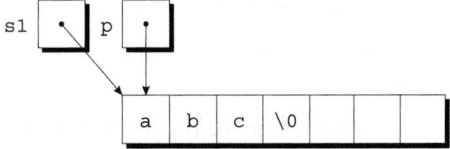

p is then incremented as long as it doesn't point to a null character. When the loop terminates, p must be pointing to the null character:

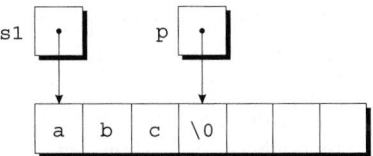

The second `while` statement implements step (2). The loop body copies one character from where s2 points to where p points, then increments both p and s2. If s2 originally points to the string `"def"`, here's what the strings will look like after the first loop iteration:

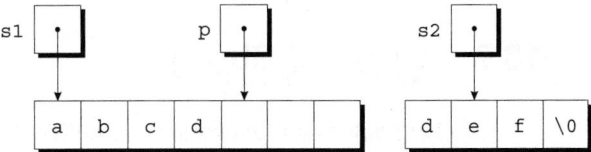

The loop terminates when s2 points to the null character:

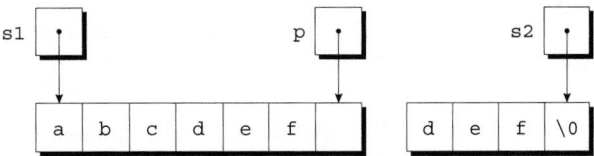

After putting a null character where p is pointing, `strcat` returns.

By a process similar to the one we used for `strlen`, we can condense the definition of `strcat`, arriving at the following version:

```
char *strcat(char *s1, const char *s2)
{
  char *p = s1;

  while (*p)
    p++;
  while (*p++ = *s2++)
    ;
  return s1;
}
```

The heart of our streamlined `strcat` function is the "string copy" idiom:

idiom
```
while (*p++ = *s2++)
    ;
```

If we ignore the two `++` operators, the expression inside the parentheses simplifies to an ordinary assignment:

```
*p = *s2
```

This expression copies a character from where `s2` points to where `p` points. After the assignment, both `p` and `s2` are incremented, thanks to the `++` operators. Repeatedly executing this expression has the effect of copying a series of characters from where `s2` points to where `p` points.

But what causes the loop to terminate? Since the primary operator inside the parentheses is assignment, the `while` statement tests the value of the assignment—the character that was copied. All characters except the null character test true, so the loop won't terminate until the null character has been copied. And since the loop terminates *after* the assignment, we don't need a separate statement to put a null character at the end of the new string.

13.7   Arrays of Strings

Let's now turn to a question that we'll often encounter: what's the best way to store an array of strings? The obvious solution is to create a two-dimensional array of characters, then store the strings in the array, one per row. Consider the following example:

```
char planets[][8] = {"Mercury", "Venus", "Earth",
                     "Mars", "Jupiter", "Saturn",
                     "Uranus", "Neptune", "Pluto"};
```

(In 2006, the International Astronomical Union demoted Pluto from "planet" to "dwarf planet," but I've left it in the `planets` array for old times' sake.) Note that we're allowed to omit the number of rows in the `planets` array—since that's obvious from the number of elements in the initializer—but C requires that we specify the number of columns.

The figure at the top of the next page shows what the `planets` array will look like. Not all our strings were long enough to fill an entire row of the array, so C padded them with null characters. There's a bit of wasted space in this array, since only three planets have names long enough to require eight characters (including the terminating null character). The `remind.c` program (Section 13.5) is a glaring example of this kind of waste. It stores reminders in rows of a two-dimensional character array, with 60 characters set aside for each reminder. In our example, the reminders ranged from 18 to 37 characters in length, so the amount of wasted space was considerable.

	0	1	2	3	4	5	6	7
0	M	e	r	c	u	r	y	\0
1	V	e	n	u	s	\0	\0	\0
2	E	a	r	t	h	\0	\0	\0
3	M	a	r	s	\0	\0	\0	\0
4	J	u	p	i	t	e	r	\0
5	S	a	t	u	r	n	\0	\0
6	U	r	a	n	u	s	\0	\0
7	N	e	p	t	u	n	e	\0
8	P	l	u	t	o	\0	\0	\0

The inefficiency that's apparent in these examples is common when working with strings, since most collections of strings will have a mixture of long strings and short strings. What we need is a ***ragged array:*** a two-dimensional array whose rows can have different lengths. C doesn't provide a "ragged array type," but it does give us the tools to simulate one. The secret is to create an array whose elements are *pointers* to strings.

Here's the `planets` array again, this time as an array of pointers to strings:

```
char *planets[] = {"Mercury", "Venus", "Earth",
                   "Mars", "Jupiter", "Saturn",
                   "Uranus", "Neptune", "Pluto"};
```

Not much of a change, eh? We simply removed one pair of brackets and put an asterisk in front of `planets`. The effect on how `planets` is stored is dramatic, though:

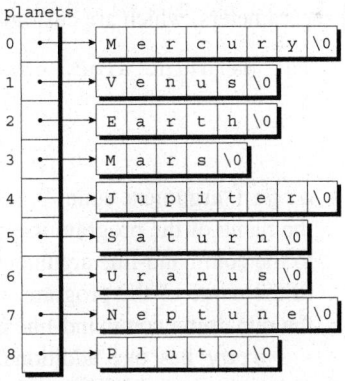

Each element of `planets` is a pointer to a null-terminated string. There are no longer any wasted characters in the strings, although we've had to allocate space for the pointers in the `planets` array.

To access one of the planet names, all we need do is subscript the `planets` array. Because of the relationship between pointers and arrays, accessing a character in a planet name is done in the same way as accessing an element of a two-dimensional array. To search the `planets` array for strings beginning with the letter M, for example, we could use the following loop:

```
for (i = 0; i < 9; i++)
  if (planets[i][0] == 'M')
    printf("%s begins with M\n", planets[i]);
```

Command-Line Arguments

When we run a program, we'll often need to supply it with information—a file name, perhaps, or a switch that modifies the program's behavior. Consider the UNIX `ls` command. If we run `ls` by typing

```
ls
```

at the command line, it will display the names of the files in the current directory. But if we instead type

```
ls -l
```

then `ls` will display a "long" (detailed) listing of files, showing the size of each file, the file's owner, the date and time the file was last modified, and so forth. To modify the behavior of `ls` further, we can specify that it show details for just one file:

```
ls -l remind.c
```

`ls` will display detailed information about the file named `remind.c`.

Command-line information is available to all programs, not just operating system commands. To obtain access to these ***command-line arguments*** (called ***program parameters*** in the C standard), we must define `main` as a function with two parameters, which are customarily named `argc` and `argv`:

```
int main(int argc, char *argv[])
{
    ...
}
```

`argc` ("argument count") is the number of command-line arguments (including the name of the program itself). `argv` ("argument vector") is an array of pointers to the command-line arguments, which are stored in string form. `argv[0]` points to the name of the program, while `argv[1]` through `argv[argc-1]` point to the remaining command-line arguments.

`argv` has one additional element, `argv[argc]`, which is always a ***null pointer***—a special pointer that points to nothing. We'll discuss null pointers in a later chapter; for now, all we need to know is that the macro `NULL` represents a null pointer.

If the user enters the command line

```
ls -l remind.c
```

then `argc` will be 3, `argv[0]` will point to a string containing the program

null pointers ➤ 17.1

name, `argv[1]` will point to the string `"-l"`, `argv[2]` will point to the string `"remind.c"`, and `argv[3]` will be a null pointer:

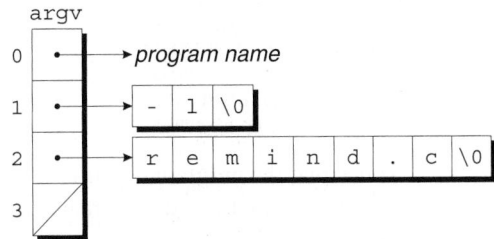

This figure doesn't show the program name in detail, since it may include a path or other information that depends on the operating system. If the program name isn't available, `argv[0]` points to an empty string.

Since `argv` is an array of pointers, accessing command-line arguments is easy. Typically, a program that expects command-line arguments will set up a loop that examines each argument in turn. One way to write such a loop is to use an integer variable as an index into the `argv` array. For example, the following loop prints the command-line arguments, one per line:

```
int i;

for (i = 1; i < argc; i++)
  printf("%s\n", argv[i]);
```

Another technique is to set up a pointer to `argv[1]`, then increment the pointer repeatedly to step through the rest of the array. Since the last element of `argv` is always a null pointer, the loop can terminate when it finds a null pointer in the array:

```
char **p;

for (p = &argv[1]; *p != NULL; p++)
  printf("%s\n", *p);
```

Since p is a *pointer* to a *pointer* to a character, we've got to use it carefully. Setting p equal to `&argv[1]` makes sense; `argv[1]` is a pointer to a character, so `&argv[1]` will be a pointer to a pointer. The test `*p != NULL` is OK, since `*p` and NULL are both pointers. Incrementing p looks good; p points to an array element, so incrementing it will advance it to the next element. Printing `*p` is fine, since `*p` points to the first character in a string.

PROGRAM   **Checking Planet Names**

Our next program, `planet.c`, illustrates how to access command-line arguments. The program is designed to check a series of strings to see which ones are names of planets. When the program is run, the user will put the strings to be tested on the command line:

```
planet Jupiter venus Earth fred
```

The program will indicate whether or not each string is a planet name; if it is, the program will also display the planet's number (with planet 1 being the one closest to the Sun):

```
Jupiter is planet 5
venus is not a planet
Earth is planet 3
fred is not a planet
```

Notice that the program doesn't recognize a string as a planet name unless its first letter is upper-case and its remaining letters are lower-case.

planet.c

```c
/* Checks planet names */

#include <stdio.h>
#include <string.h>

#define NUM_PLANETS 9

int main(int argc, char *argv[])
{
  char *planets[] = {"Mercury", "Venus", "Earth",
                     "Mars", "Jupiter", "Saturn",
                     "Uranus", "Neptune", "Pluto"};
  int i, j;

  for (i = 1; i < argc; i++) {
    for (j = 0; j < NUM_PLANETS; j++)
      if (strcmp(argv[i], planets[j]) == 0) {
        printf("%s is planet %d\n", argv[i], j + 1);
        break;
      }
    if (j == NUM_PLANETS)
      printf("%s is not a planet\n", argv[i]);
  }

  return 0;
}
```

The program visits each command-line argument in turn, comparing it with the strings in the `planets` array until it finds a match or reaches the end of the array. The most interesting part of the program is the call of `strcmp`, in which the arguments are `argv[i]` (a pointer to a command-line argument) and `planets[j]` (a pointer to a planet name).

Q & A

Q: How long can a string literal be?

A: According to the C89 standard, compilers must allow string literals to be at least

509 characters long. (Yes, you read that right—509. Don't ask.) C99 increases the
minimum to 4095 characters.

Q: **Why aren't string literals called "string constants"?**

A: Because they're not necessarily constant. Since string literals are accessed through
pointers, there's nothing to prevent a program from attempting to modify the characters in a string literal.

Q: **How do we write a string literal that represents "über" if `"\xfcber"` doesn't
work? [p. 278]**

A: The secret is to write two adjacent string literals and let the compiler join them into
one. In this example, writing `"\xfc"` `"ber"` will give us a string literal that represents the word "über."

Q: **Modifying a string literal seems harmless enough. Why does it cause undefined behavior? [p. 280]**

A: Some compilers try to reduce memory requirements by storing single copies of
identical string literals. Consider the following example:

```
char *p = "abc", *q = "abc";
```

A compiler might choose to store `"abc"` just once, making both p and q point to
it. If we were to change `"abc"` through the pointer p, the string that q points to
would also be affected. Needless to say, this could lead to some annoying bugs.
Another potential problem is that string literals might be stored in a "read-only"
area of memory; a program that attempts to modify such a literal will simply crash.

Q: **Should every array of characters include room for a null character?**

A: Not necessarily, since not every array of characters is used as a string. Including
room for the null character (and actually putting one into the array) is necessary
only if you're planning to pass it to a function that requires a null-terminated
string.
    You do *not* need a null character if you'll only be performing operations on
individual characters. For example, a program might have an array of characters
that it will use to translate from one character set to another:

```
char translation_table[128];
```

The only operation that the program will perform on this array is subscripting.
(The value of `translation_table[ch]` will be the translated version of the
character ch.) We would not consider `translation_table` to be a string: it
need not contain a null character, and no string operations will be performed on it.

Q: **If `printf` and `scanf` expect their first argument to have type `char *`, does
that mean that the argument can be a string *variable* instead of a string *literal*?**

A: Yes, as the following example shows:

```
char fmt[] = "%d\n";
int i;
...
printf(fmt, i);
```

This ability opens the door to some intriguing possibilities—reading a format string as input, for example.

Q: **If I want `printf` to write a string `str`, can't I just supply `str` as the format string, as in the following example?**

```
printf(str);
```

A: Yes, but it's risky. If `str` contains the % character, you won't get the desired result, since `printf` will assume it's the beginning of a conversion specification.

*Q: **How can `read_line` detect whether `getchar` has failed to read a character? [p. 287]**

A: If it can't read a character, either because of an error or because of end-of-file,

EOF macro ➤ 22.4   `getchar` returns the value EOF, which has type `int`. Here's a revised version of `read_line` that tests whether the return value of `getchar` is EOF. Changes are marked in **bold**:

```
int read_line(char str[], int n)
{
  int ch, i = 0;

  while ((ch = getchar()) != '\n' && ch != EOF)
    if (i < n)
      str[i++] = ch;
  str[i] = '\0';
  return i;
}
```

Q: **Why does `strcmp` return a number that's less than, equal to, or greater than zero? Also, does the exact return value have any significance? [p. 292]**

A: `strcmp`'s return value probably stems from the way the function is traditionally written. Consider the version in Kernighan and Ritchie's *The C Programming Language:*

```
int strcmp(char *s, char *t)
{
  int i;

  for (i = 0; s[i] == t[i]; i++)
    if (s[i] == '\0')
      return 0;
  return s[i] - t[i];
}
```

The return value is the difference between the first "mismatched" characters in the s and t strings, which will be negative if s points to a "smaller" string than t and positive if s points to a "larger" string. There's no guarantee that strcmp is actually written this way, though, so it's best not to assume that the magnitude of its return value has any particular meaning.

Q: **My compiler issues a warning when I try to compile the while statement in the strcat function:**

```
while (*p++ = *s2++)
    ;
```

What am I doing wrong?

A: Nothing. Many compilers—but not all, by any means—issue a warning if you use = where == is normally expected. This warning is valid at least 95% of the time, and it will save you a lot of debugging if you heed it. Unfortunately, the warning isn't relevant in this particular example; we actually *do* mean to use =, not ==. To get rid of the warning, rewrite the while loop as follows:

```
while ((*p++ = *s2++) != 0)
    ;
```

Since the while statement normally tests whether *p++ = *s2++ is not 0, we haven't changed the meaning of the statement. The warning goes away, however, because the statement now tests a condition, not an assignment. With the GCC compiler, putting a pair of parentheses around the assignment is another way to avoid a warning:

```
while ((*p++ = *s2++))
    ;
```

Q: **Are the strlen and strcat functions actually written as shown in Section 13.6?**

A: Possibly, although it's common practice for compiler vendors to write these functions—and many other string functions—in assembly language instead of C. The string functions need to be as fast as possible, since they're used often and have to deal with strings of arbitrary length. Writing these functions in assembly language makes it possible to achieve great efficiency by taking advantage of any special string-handling instructions that the CPU may provide.

Q: **Why does the C standard use the term "program parameters" instead of "command-line arguments"? [p. 302]**

A: Programs aren't always run from a command line. In a typical graphical user interface, for example, programs are launched with a mouse click. In such an environment, there's no traditional command line, although there may be other ways of passing information to a program; the term "program parameters" leaves the door open for these alternatives.

Q: **Do I have to use the names `argc` and `argv` for `main`'s parameters? [p. 302]**

A: No. Using the names `argc` and `argv` is merely a convention, not a language requirement.

Q: **I've seen `argv` declared as `**argv` instead of `*argv[]`. Is this legal?**

A: Certainly. When declaring a parameter, writing `*a` is always the same as writing `a[]`, regardless of the type of a's elements.

Q: **We've seen how to set up an array whose elements are pointers to string literals. Are there any other applications for arrays of pointers?**

A: Yes. Although we've focused on arrays of pointers to character strings, that's not the only application of arrays of pointers. We could just as easily have an array whose elements point to any type of data, whether in array form or not. Arrays of
dynamic storage allocation ➤ 17.1   pointers are particularly useful in conjunction with dynamic storage allocation.

Exercises

Section 13.3

1.   The following function calls supposedly write a single new-line character, but some are incorrect. Identify which calls don't work and explain why.

   (a) `printf("%c", '\n');`   (g) `putchar('\n');`
   (b) `printf("%c", "\n");`   (h) `putchar("\n");`
   (c) `printf("%s", '\n');`   (i) `puts('\n');`
   (d) `printf("%s", "\n");`   (j) `puts("\n");`
   (e) `printf('\n');`   (k) `puts("");`
   (f) `printf("\n");`

Ⓦ 2.   Suppose that p has been declared as follows:

   `char *p = "abc";`

   Which of the following function calls are legal? Show the output produced by each legal call, and explain why the others are illegal.

   (a) `putchar(p);`
   (b) `putchar(*p);`
   (c) `puts(p);`
   (d) `puts(*p);`

*3.   Suppose that we call scanf as follows:

   `scanf("%d%s%d", &i, s, &j);`

   If the user enters `12abc34 56def78`, what will be the values of i, s, and j after the call? (Assume that i and j are `int` variables and s is an array of characters.)

Ⓦ 4.   Modify the `read_line` function in each of the following ways:

   (a) Have it skip white space before beginning to store input characters.
   (b) Have it stop reading at the first white-space character. *Hint:* To determine whether or
isspace function ➤ 23.5   not a character is white space, call the `isspace` function.

(c) Have it stop reading at the first new-line character, then store the new-line character in the string.

(d) Have it leave behind characters that it doesn't have room to store.

Section 13.4

5.   (a) Write a function named `capitalize` that capitalizes all letters in its argument. The argument will be a null-terminated string containing arbitrary characters, not just letters. Use array subscripting to access the characters in the string. *Hint:* Use the `toupper` function to convert each character to upper-case.

toupper function ▶ *23.5*

(b) Rewrite the `capitalize` function, this time using pointer arithmetic to access the characters in the string.

Ⓦ 6.   Write a function named `censor` that modifies a string by replacing every occurrence of `foo` by `xxx`. For example, the string `"food fool"` would become `"xxxd xxxl"`. Make the function as short as possible without sacrificing clarity.

Section 13.5

7.   Suppose that `str` is an array of characters. Which one of the following statements is not equivalent to the other three?

(a) `*str = 0;`
(b) `str[0] = '\0';`
(c) `strcpy(str, "");`
(d) `strcat(str, "");`

Ⓦ *8.   What will be the value of the string `str` after the following statements have been executed?

```
strcpy(str, "tire-bouchon");
strcpy(&str[4], "d-or-wi");
strcat(str, "red?");
```

9.   What will be the value of the string `s1` after the following statements have been executed?

```
strcpy(s1, "computer");
strcpy(s2, "science");
if (strcmp(s1, s2) < 0)
  strcat(s1, s2);
else
  strcat(s2, s1);
s1[strlen(s1)-6] = '\0';
```

Ⓦ 10.   The following function supposedly creates an identical copy of a string. What's wrong with the function?

```
char *duplicate(const char *p)
{
  char *q;

  strcpy(q, p);
  return q;
}
```

11.   The Q&A section at the end of this chapter shows how the `strcmp` function might be written using array subscripting. Modify the function to use pointer arithmetic instead.

12.   Write the following function:

```
void get_extension(const char *file_name, char *extension);
```

`file_name` points to a string containing a file name. The function should store the extension on the file name in the string pointed to by `extension`. For example, if the file name is `"memo.txt"`, the function will store `"txt"` in the string pointed to by `extension`. If the file name doesn't have an extension, the function should store an empty string (a single null character) in the string pointed to by `extension`. Keep the function as simple as possible by having it use the `strlen` and `strcpy` functions.

13.   Write the following function:

```
void build_index_url(const char *domain, char *index_url);
```

`domain` points to a string containing an Internet domain, such as `"knking.com"`. The function should add `"http://www."` to the beginning of this string and `"/index.html"` to the end of the string, storing the result in the string pointed to by `index_url`. (In this example, the result will be `"http://www.knking.com/index.html"`.) You may assume that `index_url` points to a variable that is long enought to hold the resulting string. Keep the function as simple as possible by having it use the `strcat` and `strcpy` functions.

Section 13.6   *14.   What does the following program print?

```
#include <stdio.h>

int main(void)
{
  char s[] = "Hsjodi", *p;

  for (p = s; *p; p++)
    --*p;
  puts(s);
  return 0;
}
```

Ⓦ*15.   Let `f` be the following function:

```
int f(char *s, char *t)
{
  char *p1, *p2;

  for (p1 = s; *p1; p1++) {
    for (p2 = t; *p2; p2++)
      if (*p1 == *p2) break;
    if (*p2 == '\0') break;
  }
  return p1 - s;
}
```

(a) What is the value of `f("abcd", "babc")`?
(b) What is the value of `f("abcd", "bcd")`?
(c) In general, what value does `f` return when passed two strings `s` and `t`?

Ⓦ 16.   Use the techniques of Section 13.6 to condense the `count_spaces` function of Section 13.4. In particular, replace the `for` statement by a `while` loop.

17.   Write the following function:

```
bool test_extension(const char *file_name,
                    const char *extension);
```

toupper function ►*23.5*

file_name points to a string containing a file name. The function should return `true` if the file's extension matches the string pointed to by `extension`, ignoring the case of letters. For example, the call `test_extension("memo.txt", "TXT")` would return `true`. Incorporate the "search for the end of a string" idiom into your function. *Hint:* Use the `toupper` function to convert characters to upper-case before comparing them.

18. Write the following function:

```
void remove_filename(char *url);
```

url points to a string containing a URL (Uniform Resource Locator) that ends with a file name (such as `"http://www.knking.com/index.html"`). The function should modify the string by removing the file name and the preceding slash. (In this example, the result will be `"http://www.knking.com"`.) Incorporate the "search for the end of a string" idiom into your function. *Hint:* Have the function replace the last slash in the string by a null character.

Programming Projects

Ⓦ 1. Write a program that finds the "smallest" and "largest" in a series of words. After the user enters the words, the program will determine which words would come first and last if the words were listed in dictionary order. The program must stop accepting input when the user enters a four-letter word. Assume that no word is more than 20 letters long. An interactive session with the program might look like this:

```
Enter word: dog
Enter word: zebra
Enter word: rabbit
Enter word: catfish
Enter word: walrus
Enter word: cat
Enter word: fish

Smallest word: cat
Largest word: zebra
```

Hint: Use two strings named `smallest_word` and `largest_word` to keep track of the "smallest" and "largest" words entered so far. Each time the user enters a new word, use `strcmp` to compare it with `smallest_word`; if the new word is "smaller," use `strcpy` to save it in `smallest_word`. Do a similar comparison with `largest_word`. Use `strlen` to determine when the user has entered a four-letter word.

2. Improve the `remind.c` program of Section 13.5 in the following ways:
   (a) Have the program print an error message and ignore a reminder if the corresponding day is negative or larger than 31. *Hint:* Use the `continue` statement.
   (b) Allow the user to enter a day, a 24-hour time, and a reminder. The printed reminder list should be sorted first by day, then by time. (The original program allows the user to enter a time, but it's treated as part of the reminder.)
   (c) Have the program print a one-*year* reminder list. Require the user to enter days in the form *month/day*.

3. Modify the `deal.c` program of Section 8.2 so that it prints the full names of the cards it deals:

```
Enter number of cards in hand: 5
Your hand:
Seven of clubs
Two of spades
Five of diamonds
Ace of spades
Two of hearts
```

Hint: Replace rank_code and suit_code by arrays containing pointers to strings.

Ⓦ 4.   Write a program named reverse.c that echoes its command-line arguments in reverse order. Running the program by typing

reverse void and null

should produce the following output:

null and void

5.   Write a program named sum.c that adds up its command-line arguments, which are assumed to be integers. Running the program by typing

sum 8 24 62

should produce the following output:

Total: 94

atoi function ➤26.2   *Hint:* Use the atoi function to convert each command-line argument from string form to integer form.

Ⓦ 6.   Improve the planet.c program of Section 13.7 by having it ignore case when comparing command-line arguments with strings in the planets array.

7.   Modify Programming Project 11 from Chapter 5 so that it uses arrays containing pointers to strings instead of switch statements. For example, instead of using a switch statement to print the word for the first digit, use the digit as an index into an array that contains the strings "twenty", "thirty", and so forth.

8.   Modify Programming Project 5 from Chapter 7 so that it includes the following function:

int compute_scrabble_value(const char *word);

The function returns the SCRABBLE value of the string pointed to by word.

9.   Modify Programming Project 10 from Chapter 7 so that it includes the following function:

int compute_vowel_count(const char *sentence);

The function returns the number of vowels in the string pointed to by the sentence parameter.

10.   Modify Programming Project 11 from Chapter 7 so that it includes the following function:

void reverse_name(char *name);

The function expects name to point to a string containing a first name followed by a last name. It modifies the string so that the last name comes first, followed by a comma, a space, the first initial, and a period. The original string may contain extra spaces before the first name, between the first and last names, and after the last name.

11.   Modify Programming Project 13 from Chapter 7 so that it includes the following function:

double compute_average_word_length(const char *sentence);

The function returns the average length of the words in the string pointed to by sentence.

12. Modify Programming Project 14 from Chapter 8 so that it stores the words in a two-dimensional `char` array as it reads the sentence, with each row of the array storing a single word. Assume that the sentence contains no more than 30 words and no word is more than 20 characters long. Be sure to store a null character at the end of each word so that it can be treated as a string.

13. Modify Programming Project 15 from Chapter 8 so that it includes the following function:

    ```
    void encrypt(char *message, int shift);
    ```

    The function expects `message` to point to a string containing the message to be encrypted; `shift` represents the amount by which each letter in the message is to be shifted.

14. Modify Programming Project 16 from Chapter 8 so that it includes the following function:

    ```
    bool are_anagrams(const char *word1, const char *word2);
    ```

    The function returns `true` if the strings pointed to by `word1` and `word2` are anagrams.

15. Modify Programming Project 6 from Chapter 10 so that it includes the following function:

    ```
    int evaluate_RPN_expression(const char *expression);
    ```

    The function returns the value of the RPN expression pointed to by `expression`.

16. Modify Programming Project 1 from Chapter 12 so that it includes the following function:

    ```
    void reverse(char *message);
    ```

    The function reverses the string pointed to by `message`. *Hint:* Use two pointers, one initially pointing to the first character of the string and the other initially pointing to the last character. Have the function reverse these characters and then move the pointers toward each other, repeating the process until the pointers meet.

17. Modify Programming Project 2 from Chapter 12 so that it includes the following function:

    ```
    bool is_palindrome(const char *message);
    ```

    The function returns `true` if the string pointed to by `message` is a palindrome.

18. Write a program that accepts a date from the user in the form *mm/dd/yyyy* and then displays it in the form *month dd, yyyy*, where *month* is the name of the month:

    ```
    Enter a date (mm/dd/yyyy): 2/17/2011
    You entered the date February 17, 2011
    ```

    Store the month names in an array that contains pointers to strings.

14 The Preprocessor

There will always be things we wish to say in our programs
that in all known languages can only be said poorly.

In previous chapters, I've used the #define and #include directives without going into detail about what they do. These directives—and others that we haven't yet covered—are handled by the **preprocessor**, a piece of software that edits C programs just prior to compilation. Its reliance on a preprocessor makes C (along with C++) unique among major programming languages.

The preprocessor is a powerful tool, but it also can be a source of hard-to-find bugs. Moreover, the preprocessor can easily be misused to create programs that are almost impossible to understand. Although some C programmers depend heavily on the preprocessor, I recommend that it—like so many other things in life—be used in moderation.

This chapter begins by describing how the preprocessor works (Section 14.1) and giving some general rules that affect all preprocessing directives (Section 14.2). Sections 14.3 and 14.4 cover two of the preprocessor's major capabilities: macro definition and conditional compilation. (I'll defer detailed coverage of file inclusion, the other major capability, until Chapter 15.) Section 14.5 discusses the preprocessor's lesser-used directives: #error, #line, and #pragma.

14.1 How the Preprocessor Works

The behavior of the preprocessor is controlled by **preprocessing directives:** commands that begin with a # character. We've encountered two of these directives, #define and #include, in previous chapters.

The #define directive defines a **macro**—a name that represents something else, such as a constant or frequently used expression. The preprocessor responds to a #define directive by storing the name of the macro together with its definition.

When the macro is used later in the program, the preprocessor "expands" the macro, replacing it by its defined value.

The #include directive tells the preprocessor to open a particular file and "include" its contents as part of the file being compiled. For example, the line

```
#include <stdio.h>
```

instructs the preprocessor to open the file named stdio.h and bring its contents into the program. (Among other things, stdio.h contains prototypes for C's standard input/output functions.)

The following diagram shows the preprocessor's role in the compilation process:

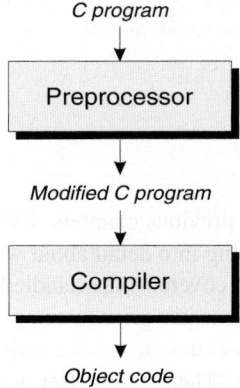

The input to the preprocessor is a C program, possibly containing directives. The preprocessor executes these directives, removing them in the process. The output of the preprocessor is another C program: an edited version of the original program, containing no directives. The preprocessor's output goes directly into the compiler, which checks the program for errors and translates it to object code (machine instructions).

To see what the preprocessor does, let's apply it to the celsius.c program of Section 2.6. Here's the original program:

```
/* Converts a Fahrenheit temperature to Celsius */

#include <stdio.h>

#define FREEZING_PT 32.0f
#define SCALE_FACTOR (5.0f / 9.0f)

int main(void)
{
  float fahrenheit, celsius;

  printf("Enter Fahrenheit temperature: ");
  scanf("%f", &fahrenheit);

  celsius = (fahrenheit - FREEZING_PT) * SCALE_FACTOR;
```

```
    printf("Celsius equivalent is: %.1f\n", celsius);

    return 0;
}
```

After preprocessing, the program will have the following appearance:

Blank line
Blank line
Lines brought in from stdio.h
Blank line
Blank line
Blank line
Blank line
```
int main(void)
{
    float fahrenheit, celsius;

    printf("Enter Fahrenheit temperature: ");
    scanf("%f", &fahrenheit);

    celsius = (fahrenheit - 32.0f) * (5.0f / 9.0f);

    printf("Celsius equivalent is: %.1f\n", celsius);

    return 0;
}
```

The preprocessor responded to the #include directive by bringing in the contents of stdio.h. The preprocessor also removed the #define directives and replaced FREEZING_PT and SCALE_FACTOR wherever they appeared later in the file. Notice that the preprocessor doesn't remove lines containing directives; instead, it simply makes them empty.

As this example shows, the preprocessor does a bit more than just execute directives. In particular, it replaces each comment with a single space character. Some preprocessors go further and remove unnecessary white-space characters, including spaces and tabs at the beginning of indented lines.

In the early days of C, the preprocessor was a separate program that fed its output into the compiler. Nowadays, the preprocessor is often part of the compiler, and some of its output may not necessarily be C code. (For example, including a standard header such as <stdio.h> may have the effect of making its functions available to the program without necessarily copying the contents of the header into the program's source code.) Still, it's useful to think of the preprocessor as separate from the compiler. In fact, most C compilers provide a way to view the output of the preprocessor. Some compilers generate preprocessor output when a certain option is specified (GCC will do so when the -E option is used). Others come with a separate program that behaves like the integrated preprocessor. Check your compiler's documentation for more information.

A word of caution: The preprocessor has only a limited knowledge of C. As a result, it's quite capable of creating illegal programs as it executes directives. Often the original program looks fine, making errors harder to find. In complicated programs, examining the output of the preprocessor may prove useful for locating this kind of error.

14.2   Preprocessing Directives

Most preprocessing directives fall into one of three categories:

- *Macro definition.* The #define directive defines a macro; the #undef directive removes a macro definition.
- *File inclusion.* The #include directive causes the contents of a specified file to be included in a program.
- *Conditional compilation.* The #if, #ifdef, #ifndef, #elif, #else, and #endif directives allow blocks of text to be either included in or excluded from a program, depending on conditions that can be tested by the preprocessor.

The remaining directives—#error, #line, and #pragma—are more specialized and therefore used less often. We'll devote the rest of this chapter to an indepth examination of preprocessing directives. The only directive we won't discuss in detail is #include, since it's covered in Section 15.2.

Before we go further, let's look at a few rules that apply to all directives:

- *Directives always begin with the # symbol.* The # symbol need not be at the beginning of a line, as long as only white space precedes it. After the # comes the name of the directive, followed by any other information the directive requires.
- *Any number of spaces and horizontal tab characters may separate the tokens in a directive.* For example, the following directive is legal:

```
#    define    N    100
```

- *Directives always end at the first new-line character, unless explicitly continued.* To continue a directive to the next line, we must end the current line with a \ character. For example, the following directive defines a macro that represents the capacity of a hard disk, measured in bytes:

```
#define DISK_CAPACITY (SIDES *            \
                       TRACKS_PER_SIDE *   \
                       SECTORS_PER_TRACK * \
                       BYTES_PER_SECTOR)
```

- *Directives can appear anywhere in a program.* Although we usually put #define and #include directives at the beginning of a file, other directives are more likely to show up later, even in the middle of function definitions.
- *Comments may appear on the same line as a directive.* In fact, it's good practice to put a comment at the end of a macro definition to explain the meaning of the macro:

```
#define FREEZING_PT 32.0f    /* freezing point of water */
```

14.3 Macro Definitions

The macros that we've been using since Chapter 2 are known as *simple* macros, because they have no parameters. The preprocessor also supports *parameterized* macros. We'll look first at simple macros, then at parameterized macros. After covering them separately, we'll examine properties shared by both.

Simple Macros

The definition of a *simple macro* (or *object-like macro,* as it's called in the C standard) has the form

**#define directive
(simple macro)**

> #define *identifier replacement-list*

replacement-list is any sequence of ***preprocessing tokens,*** which are similar to the tokens discussed in Section 2.8. Whenever we use the term "token" in this chapter, it means "preprocessing token."

A macro's replacement list may include identifiers, keywords, numeric constants, character constants, string literals, operators, and punctuation. When it encounters a macro definition, the preprocessor makes a note that *identifier* represents *replacement-list*; wherever *identifier* appears later in the file, the preprocessor substitutes *replacement-list*.

⚠️ Don't put any extra symbols in a macro definition—they'll become part of the replacement list. Putting the = symbol in a macro definition is a common error:

```
#define N = 100    /*** WRONG ***/
...
int a[N];          /* becomes int a[= 100]; */
```

In this example, we've (incorrectly) defined N to be a pair of tokens (= and 100). Ending a macro definition with a semicolon is another popular mistake:

```
#define N 100;     /*** WRONG ***/
...
int a[N];          /* becomes int a[100;]; */
```

Here N is defined to be the tokens 100 and ;.

The compiler will detect most errors caused by extra symbols in a macro definition. Unfortunately, the compiler will flag each use of the macro as incorrect, rather than identifying the actual culprit—the macro's definition—which will have been removed by the preprocessor.

Simple macros are primarily used for defining what Kernighan and Ritchie call "manifest constants." Using macros, we can give names to numeric, character, and string values:

```
#define STR_LEN  80
#define TRUE     1
#define FALSE    0
#define PI       3.14159
#define CR       '\r'
#define EOS      '\0'
#define MEM_ERR  "Error: not enough memory"
```

Using #define to create names for constants has several significant advantages:

- *It makes programs easier to read.* The name of the macro—if well-chosen—helps the reader understand the meaning of the constant. The alternative is a program full of "magic numbers" that can easily mystify the reader.

- *It makes programs easier to modify.* We can change the value of a constant throughout a program by modifying a single macro definition. "Hard-coded" constants are more difficult to change, especially since they sometimes appear in a slightly altered form. (For example, a program with an array of length 100 may have a loop that goes from 0 to 99. If we merely try to locate occurrences of 100 in the program, we'll miss the 99.)

- *It helps avoid inconsistencies and typographical errors.* If a numerical constant like 3.14159 appears many times in a program, chances are it will occasionally be written 3.1416 or 3.14195 by accident.

Although simple macros are most often used to define names for constants, they do have other applications:

- *Making minor changes to the syntax of C.* We can—in effect—alter the syntax of C by defining macros that serve as alternate names for C symbols. For example, programmers who prefer Pascal's begin and end to C's { and } can define the following macros:

```
#define BEGIN {
#define END   }
```

We could go so far as to invent our own language. For example, we might create a LOOP "statement" that establishes an infinite loop:

```
#define LOOP for (;;)
```

Changing the syntax of C usually isn't a good idea, though, since it can make programs harder for others to understand.

- *Renaming types.* In Section 5.2, we created a Boolean type by renaming int:

```
#define BOOL int
```

type definitions ➤ 7.5

Although some programmers use macros for this purpose, type definitions are a superior way to define type names.

- *Controlling conditional compilation.* Macros play an important role in controlling conditional compilation, as we'll see in Section 14.4. For example, the presence of the following line in a program might indicate that it's to be compiled in "debugging mode," with extra statements included to produce debugging output:

```
#define DEBUG
```

Incidentally, it's legal for a macro's replacement list to be empty, as this example shows.

When macros are used as constants, C programmers customarily capitalize all letters in their names. However, there's no consensus as to how to capitalize macros used for other purposes. Since macros (especially parameterized macros) can be a source of bugs, some programmers like to draw attention to them by using all upper-case letters in their names. Others prefer lower-case names, following the style of Kernighan and Ritchie's *The C Programming Language*.

Parameterized Macros

The definition of a *parameterized macro* (also known as a *function-like macro*) has the form

#define directive
(parameterized macro)

> #define *identifier* (x_1 , x_2 , ... , x_n) *replacement-list*

where x_1, x_2, ..., x_n are identifiers (the macro's *parameters*). The parameters may appear as many times as desired in the replacement list.

There must be *no space* between the macro name and the left parenthesis. If space is left, the preprocessor will assume that we're defining a simple macro; it will treat $(x_1, x_2, ..., x_n)$ as part of the replacement list.

When the preprocessor encounters the definition of a parameterized macro, it stores the definition away for later use. Wherever a macro *invocation* of the form *identifier* $(y_1, y_2, ..., y_n)$ appears later in the program (where $y_1, y_2, ..., y_n$ are sequences of tokens), the preprocessor replaces it with *replacement-list*, substituting y_1 for x_1, y_2 for x_2, and so forth.

For example, suppose that we've defined the following macros:

```
#define MAX(x,y)    ((x)>(y)?(x):(y))
#define IS_EVEN(n)  ((n)%2==0)
```

(The number of parentheses in these macros may seem excessive, but there's a reason, as we'll see later in this section.) Now suppose that we invoke the two macros in the following way:

```
i = MAX(j+k, m-n);
if (IS_EVEN(i)) i++;
```

The preprocessor will replace these lines by

```
i = ((j+k)>(m-n)?(j+k):(m-n));
if (((i)%2==0)) i++;
```

As this example shows, parameterized macros often serve as simple functions. `MAX` behaves like a function that computes the larger of two values. `IS_EVEN` behaves like a function that returns 1 if its argument is an even number and 0 otherwise.

Here's a more complicated macro that behaves like a function:

```
#define TOUPPER(c) ('a'<=(c)&&(c)<='z'?(c)-'a'+'A':(c))
```

<ctype.h> header ➤23.5

This macro tests whether the character `c` is between `'a'` and `'z'`. If so, it produces the upper-case version of `c` by subtracting `'a'` and adding `'A'`. If not, it leaves `c` unchanged. (The `<ctype.h>` header provides a similar function named `toupper` that's more portable.)

A parameterized macro may have an empty parameter list. Here's an example:

```
#define getchar() getc(stdin)
```

The empty parameter list isn't really needed, but it makes `getchar` resemble a function. (Yes, this is the same `getchar` that belongs to `<stdio.h>`. We'll see in Section 22.4 that `getchar` is usually implemented as a macro as well as a function.)

Using a parameterized macro instead of a true function has a couple of advantages:

- **The program may be slightly faster.** A function call usually requires some overhead during program execution—context information must be saved, arguments copied, and so forth. A macro invocation, on the other hand, requires no run-time overhead. (Note, however, that C99's inline functions provide a way to avoid this overhead without the use of macros.)

inline functions ➤18.6

- **Macros are "generic."** Macro parameters, unlike function parameters, have no particular type. As a result, a macro can accept arguments of any type, provided that the resulting program—after preprocessing—is valid. For example, we could use the `MAX` macro to find the larger of two values of type `int`, `long`, `float`, `double`, and so forth.

But parameterized macros also have disadvantages:

- **The compiled code will often be larger.** Each macro invocation causes the insertion of the macro's replacement list, thereby increasing the size of the source program (and hence the compiled code). The more often the macro is used, the more pronounced this effect is. The problem is compounded when macro invocations are nested. Consider what happens when we use `MAX` to find the largest of three numbers:

```
n = MAX(i, MAX(j, k));
```

Here's the same statement after preprocessing:

```
n = ((i)>(((j)>(k)?(j):(k)))?(i):(((j)>(k)?(j):(k))));
```

- **Arguments aren't type-checked.** When a function is called, the compiler checks each argument to see if it has the appropriate type. If not, either the argument is converted to the proper type or the compiler produces an error message. Macro arguments aren't checked by the preprocessor, nor are they converted.

- **It's not possible to have a pointer to a macro.** As we'll see in Section 17.7, C allows pointers to functions, a concept that's quite useful in certain programming situations. Macros are removed during preprocessing, so there's no corresponding notion of "pointer to a macro"; as a result, macros can't be used in these situations.

- **A macro may evaluate its arguments more than once.** A function evaluates its arguments only once; a macro may evaluate its arguments two or more times. Evaluating an argument more than once can cause unexpected behavior if the argument has side effects. Consider what happens if one of MAX's arguments has a side effect:

```
n = MAX(i++, j);
```

Here's the same line after preprocessing:

```
n = ((i++)>(j)?(i++):(j));
```

If i is larger than j, then i will be (incorrectly) incremented twice and n will be assigned an unexpected value.

Errors caused by evaluating a macro argument more than once can be difficult to find, because a macro invocation looks the same as a function call. To make matters worse, a macro may work properly most of the time, failing only for certain arguments that have side effects. For self-protection, it's a good idea to avoid side effects in arguments.

Parameterized macros are good for more than just simulating functions. In particular, they're often used as patterns for segments of code that we find ourselves repeating. Suppose that we grow tired of writing

```
printf("%d\n", i);
```

every time we need to print an integer i. We might define the following macro, which makes it easier to display integers:

```
#define PRINT_INT(n) printf("%d\n", n)
```

Once PRINT_INT has been defined, the preprocessor will turn the line

```
PRINT_INT(i/j);
```

into

```
printf("%d\n", i/j);
```

The # Operator

Macro definitions may contain two special operators, # and ##. Neither operator is recognized by the compiler; instead, they're executed during preprocessing.

Q&A   The # operator converts a macro argument into a string literal; it can appear only in the replacement list of a parameterized macro. (The operation performed by # is known as "stringization," a term that I'm sure you won't find in the dictionary.)

There are a number of uses for #; let's consider just one. Suppose that we decide to use the PRINT_INT macro during debugging as a convenient way to print the values of integer variables and expressions. The # operator makes it possible for PRINT_INT to label each value that it prints. Here's our new version of PRINT_INT:

```
#define PRINT_INT(n) printf(#n " = %d\n", n)
```

The # operator in front of n instructs the preprocessor to create a string literal from PRINT_INT's argument. Thus, the invocation

```
PRINT_INT(i/j);
```

will become

```
printf("i/j" " = %d\n", i/j);
```

We saw in Section 13.1 that the compiler automatically joins adjacent string literals, so this statement is equivalent to

```
printf("i/j = %d\n", i/j);
```

When the program is executed, printf will display both the expression i/j and its value. If i is 11 and j is 2, for example, the output will be

```
i/j = 5
```

The ## Operator

The ## operator can "paste" two tokens (identifiers, for example) together to form a single token. (Not surprisingly, the ## operation is known as "token-pasting.") If one of the operands is a macro parameter, pasting occurs after the parameter has been replaced by the corresponding argument. Consider the following macro:

```
#define MK_ID(n) i##n
```

When MK_ID is invoked (as MK_ID(1), say), the preprocessor first replaces the parameter n by the argument (1 in this case). Next, the preprocessor joins i and 1 to make a single token (i1). The following declaration uses MK_ID to create three identifiers:

```
int MK_ID(1), MK_ID(2), MK_ID(3);
```

After preprocessing, this declaration becomes

```
int i1, i2, i3;
```

The `##` operator isn't one of the most frequently used features of the preprocessor; in fact, it's hard to think of many situations that require it. To find a realistic application of `##`, let's reconsider the `MAX` macro described earlier in this section. As we observed then, `MAX` doesn't behave properly if its arguments have side effects. The alternative to using the `MAX` macro is to write a `max` function. Unfortunately, one `max` function usually isn't enough; we may need a `max` function whose arguments are `int` values, one whose arguments are `float` values, and so on. All these versions of `max` would be identical except for the types of the arguments and the return type, so it seems a shame to define each one from scratch.

The solution is to write a macro that expands into the definition of a `max` function. The macro will have a single parameter, `type`, which represents the type of the arguments and the return value. There's just one snag: if we use the macro to create more than one `max` function, the program won't compile. (C doesn't allow two functions to have the same name if both are defined in the same file.) To solve this problem, we'll use the `##` operator to create a different name for each version of `max`. Here's what the macro will look like:

```
#define GENERIC_MAX(type)              \
type type##_max(type x, type y)  \
{                                      \
  return x > y ? x : y;                \
}
```

Notice how `type` is joined with `_max` to form the name of the function.

Suppose that we happen to need a `max` function that works with `float` values. Here's how we'd use `GENERIC_MAX` to define the function:

```
GENERIC_MAX(float)
```

The preprocessor expands this line into the following code:

```
float float_max(float x, float y) { return x > y ? x : y; }
```

General Properties of Macros

Now that we've discussed both simple and parameterized macros, let's look at some rules that apply to both:

■ *A macro's replacement list may contain invocations of other macros.* For example, we could define the macro `TWO_PI` in terms of the macro `PI`:

```
#define PI     3.14159
#define TWO_PI (2*PI)
```

When it encounters `TWO_PI` later in the program, the preprocessor replaces it by `(2*PI)`. The preprocessor then *rescans* the replacement list to see if it contains invocations of other macros (PI, in this case). The preprocessor will rescan the replacement list as many times as necessary to eliminate all macro names.

■ **The preprocessor replaces only entire tokens, not portions of tokens.** As a result, the preprocessor ignores macro names that are embedded in identifiers, character constants, and string literals. For example, suppose that a program contains the following lines:

```
#define SIZE 256

int BUFFER_SIZE;

if (BUFFER_SIZE > SIZE)
  puts("Error: SIZE exceeded");
```

After preprocessing, these lines will have the following appearance:

```
int BUFFER_SIZE;

if (BUFFER_SIZE > 256)
  puts("Error: SIZE exceeded");
```

The identifier BUFFER_SIZE and the string "Error: SIZE exceeded" weren't affected by preprocessing, even though both contain the word SIZE.

■ **A macro definition normally remains in effect until the end of the file in which it appears.** Since macros are handled by the preprocessor, they don't obey normal scope rules. A macro defined inside the body of a function isn't local to that function; it remains defined until the end of the file.

■ **A macro may not be defined twice unless the new definition is identical to the old one.** Differences in spacing are allowed, but the tokens in the macro's replacement list (and the parameters, if any) must be the same.

■ **Macros may be "undefined" by the #undef directive.** The #undef directive has the form

#undef directive

> #undef *identifier*

where *identifier* is a macro name. For example, the directive

```
#undef N
```

removes the current definition of the macro N. (If N hasn't been defined as a macro, the #undef directive has no effect.) One use of #undef is to remove the existing definition of a macro so that it can be given a new definition.

Parentheses in Macro Definitions

The replacement lists in our macro definitions have been full of parentheses. Is it really necessary to have so many? The answer is an emphatic yes; if we use fewer parentheses, the macros will sometimes give unexpected—and undesirable—results.

There are two rules to follow when deciding where to put parentheses in a macro definition. First, if the macro's replacement list contains an operator, always enclose the replacement list in parentheses:

```
#define TWO_PI (2*3.14159)
```

Second, if the macro has parameters, put parentheses around each parameter every time it appears in the replacement list:

```
#define SCALE(x) ((x)*10)
```

Without the parentheses, we can't guarantee that the compiler will treat replacement lists and arguments as whole expressions. The compiler may apply the rules of operator precedence and associativity in ways that we didn't anticipate.

To illustrate the importance of putting parentheses around a macro's replacement list, consider the following macro definition, in which the parentheses are missing:

```
#define TWO_PI 2*3.14159
  /* needs parentheses around replacement list */
```

During preprocessing, the statement

```
conversion_factor = 360/TWO_PI;
```

becomes

```
conversion_factor = 360/2*3.14159;
```

The division will be performed before the multiplication, yielding a result different from the one intended.

Putting parentheses around the replacement list isn't enough if the macro has parameters—each occurrence of a parameter needs parentheses as well. For example, suppose that SCALE is defined as follows:

```
#define SCALE(x) (x*10)    /* needs parentheses around x */
```

During preprocessing, the statement

```
j = SCALE(i+1);
```

becomes

```
j = (i+1*10);
```

Since multiplication takes precedence over addition, this statement is equivalent to

```
j = i+10;
```

Of course, what we wanted was

```
j = (i+1)*10;
```

A shortage of parentheses in a macro definition can cause some of C's most frustrating errors. The program will usually compile and the macro will appear to work, failing only at the least convenient times.

Creating Longer Macros

The comma operator can be useful for creating more sophisticated macros by allowing us to make the replacement list a series of expressions. For example, the following macro will read a string and then print it:

```
#define ECHO(s) (gets(s), puts(s))
```

Calls of `gets` and `puts` are expressions, so it's perfectly legal to combine them using the comma operator. We can invoke ECHO as though it were a function:

```
ECHO(str);    /* becomes (gets(str), puts(str)); */
```

Instead of using the comma operator in the definition of ECHO, we could have enclosed the calls of `gets` and `puts` in braces to form a compound statement:

```
#define ECHO(s) { gets(s); puts(s); }
```

Unfortunately, this method doesn't work as well. Suppose that we use ECHO in an `if` statement:

```
if (echo_flag)
  ECHO(str);
else
  gets(str);
```

Replacing ECHO gives the following result:

```
if (echo_flag)
  { gets(str); puts(str); };
else
  gets(str);
```

The compiler treats the first two lines as a complete `if` statement:

```
if (echo_flag)
  { gets(str); puts(str); }
```

It treats the semicolon that follows as a null statement and produces an error message for the `else` clause, since it doesn't belong to any `if`. We could solve the problem by remembering not to put a semicolon after each invocation of ECHO, but then the program would look odd.

The comma operator solves this problem for ECHO, but not for all macros. Suppose that a macro needs to contain a series of *statements*, not just a series of *expressions*. The comma operator is of no help; it can glue together expressions, but not statements. The solution is to wrap the statements in a do loop whose condition is false (and which therefore will be executed just once):

```
do { … } while (0)
```

Notice that the do statement isn't complete—it needs a semicolon at the end. To see this trick (ahem, technique) in action, let's incorporate it into our ECHO macro:

```
#define ECHO(s)        \
          do {         \
            gets(s);   \
            puts(s);   \
          } while (0)
```

When ECHO is used, it must be followed by a semicolon, which completes the do statement:

```
ECHO(str);
  /* becomes do { gets(str); puts(str); } while (0); */
```

Predefined Macros

C has several predefined macros. Each macro represents an integer constant or string literal. As Table 14.1 shows, these macros provide information about the current compilation or about the compiler itself.

Table 14.1
Predefined Macros

Name	Description
__LINE__	Line number of file being compiled
__FILE__	Name of file being compiled
__DATE__	Date of compilation (in the form "Mmm dd yyyy")
__TIME__	Time of compilation (in the form "hh:mm:ss")
__STDC__	1 if the compiler conforms to the C standard (C89 or C99)

The __DATE__ and __TIME__ macros identify when a program was compiled. For example, suppose that a program begins with the following statements:

```
printf("Wacky Windows (c) 2010 Wacky Software, Inc.\n");
printf("Compiled on %s at %s\n", __DATE__, __TIME__);
```

Each time it begins to execute, the program will print two lines of the form

```
Wacky Windows (c) 2010 Wacky Software, Inc.
Compiled on Dec 23 2010 at 22:18:48
```

This information can be helpful for distinguishing among different versions of the same program.

We can use the __LINE__ and __FILE__ macros to help locate errors. Consider the problem of detecting the location of a division by zero. When a C program terminates prematurely because it divided by zero, there's usually no indication of which division caused the problem. The following macro can help us pinpoint the source of the error:

```
#define CHECK_ZERO(divisor) \
  if (divisor == 0) \
    printf("*** Attempt to divide by zero on line %d " \
           "of file %s ***\n", __LINE__, __FILE__)
```

The CHECK_ZERO macro would be invoked prior to a division:

```
CHECK_ZERO(j);
k = i / j;
```

If j happens to be zero, a message of the following form will be printed:

```
*** Attempt to divide by zero on line 9 of file foo.c ***
```

assert macro ▸24.1

Error-detecting macros like this one are quite useful. In fact, the C library has a general-purpose error-detecting macro named assert.

The __STDC__ macro exists and has the value 1 if the compiler conforms to the C standard (either C89 or C99). By having the preprocessor test this macro, a program can adapt to a compiler that predates the C89 standard (see Section 14.4 for an example).

C99   **Additional Predefined Macros in C99**

C99 provides a few additional predefined macros (Table 14.2).

Table 14.2
Additional Predefined
Macros in C99

Name	Description
__STDC__HOSTED__	1 if this is a hosted implementation; 0 if it is freestanding
__STDC__VERSION__	Version of C standard supported
__STDC_IEC_559__ †	1 if IEC 60559 floating-point arithmetic is supported
__STDC_IEC_559_COMPLEX__ †	1 if IEC 60559 complex arithmetic is supported
__STDC_ISO_10646__ †	yyyymmL if wchar_t values match the ISO 10646 standard of the specified year and month

†Conditionally defined

To understand the meaning of __STDC__HOSTED__, we need some new vocabulary. An *implementation* of C consists of the compiler plus other software necessary to execute C programs. C99 divides implementations into two categories: hosted and freestanding. A *hosted implementation* must accept any program that conforms to the C99 standard, whereas a *freestanding implementation*

complex types ▸27.3

doesn't have to compile programs that use complex types or standard headers beyond a few of the most basic. (In particular, a freestanding implementation

doesn't have to support the <stdio.h> header.) The __STDC__HOSTED__ macro represents the constant 1 if the compiler is a hosted implementation; otherwise, the macro has the value 0.

The __STDC__VERSION__ macro provides a way to check which version of the C standard is recognized by the compiler. This macro first appeared in Amendment 1 to the C89 standard, where its value was specified to be the long integer constant `199409L` (representing the year and month of the amendment). If a compiler conforms to the C99 standard, the value is `199901L`. For each subsequent version of the standard (and each amendment to the standard), this macro will have a different value.

A C99 compiler may (or may not) define three additional macros. Each macro is defined only if the compiler meets a certain requirement:

- `__STDC_IEC_559__` is defined (and has the value 1) if the compiler performs floating-point arithmetic according to the IEC 60559 standard (another name for the IEEE 754 standard).

IEEE floating-point standard ➤ *7.2*

- `__STDC_IEC_559_COMPLEX__` is defined (and has the value 1) if the compiler performs complex arithmetic according to the IEC 60559 standard.

wchar_t type ➤ *25.2*

ISO/IEC 10646 standard ➤ *25.2*

- `__STDC_ISO_10646__` is defined as an integer constant of the form *yyyymmL* (for example, `199712L`) if values of type `wchar_t` are represented by the codes in the ISO/IEC 10646 standard (with revisions as of the specified year and month).

C99 Empty Macro Arguments

C99 allows any or all of the arguments in a macro call to be empty. Such a call will contain the same number of commas as a normal call, however. (That way, it's easy to see which arguments have been omitted.)

In most cases, the effect of an empty argument is clear. Wherever the corresponding parameter name appears in the replacement list, it's replaced by nothing—it simply disappears from the replacement list. Here's an example:

```
#define ADD(x,y) (x+y)
```

After preprocessing, the statement

```
i = ADD(j,k);
```

becomes

```
i = (j+k);
```

whereas the statement

```
i = ADD(,k);
```

becomes

```
i = (+k);
```

When an empty argument is an operand of the # or ## operators, special rules apply. If an empty argument is "stringized" by the # operator, the result is `""` (the empty string):

```
#define MK_STR(x) #x
...
char empty_string[] = MK_STR();
```

After preprocessing, the declaration will have the following appearance:

```
char empty_string[] = "";
```

If one of the arguments of the ## operator is empty, it's replaced by an invisible "placemarker" token. Concatenating an ordinary token with a placemarker token yields the original token (the placemarker disappears). If two placemarker tokens are concatenated, the result is a single placemarker. Once macro expansion has been completed, placemarker tokens disappear from the program. Consider the following example:

```
#define JOIN(x,y,z) x##y##z
...
int JOIN(a,b,c), JOIN(a,b,), JOIN(a,,c), JOIN(,,c);
```

After preprocessing, the declaration will have the following appearance:

```
int abc, ab, ac, c;
```

The missing arguments were replaced by placemarker tokens, which then disappeared when concatenated with any nonempty arguments. All three arguments to the JOIN macro could even be missing, which would yield an empty result.

Macros with a Variable Number of Arguments

In C89, a macro must have a fixed number of arguments, if it has any at all. C99 loosens things up a bit, allowing macros that take an unlimited number of arguments. This feature has long been available for functions, so it's not surprising that macros were finally put on an equal footing.

variable-length argument lists
➤26.1

The primary reason for having a macro with a variable number of arguments is that it can pass these arguments to a function that accepts a variable number of arguments, such as printf or scanf. Here's an example:

```
#define TEST(condition, ...) ((condition)? \
  printf("Passed test: %s\n", #condition): \
  printf(__VA_ARGS__))
```

The . . . token, known as *ellipsis,* goes at the end of a macro's parameter list, preceded by ordinary parameters, if there are any. __VA_ARGS__ is a special identifier that can appear only in the replacement list of a macro with a variable number of arguments; it represents all the arguments that correspond to the ellipsis. (There must be at least one argument that corresponds to the ellipsis, although that argument may be empty.) The TEST macro requires at least two arguments. The first argument matches the condition parameter; the remaining arguments match the ellipsis.

Here's an example that shows how the TEST macro might be used:

```
TEST(voltage <= max_voltage,
     "Voltage %d exceeds %d\n", voltage, max_voltage);
```

The preprocessor will produce the following output (reformatted for readability):

```
((voltage <= max_voltage)?
  printf("Passed test: %s\n", "voltage <= max_voltage"):
  printf("Voltage %d exceeds %d\n", voltage, max_voltage));
```

When the program is executed, the program will display the message

```
Passed test: voltage <= max_voltage
```

if voltage is no more than max_voltage. Otherwise, it will display the values of voltage and max_voltage:

```
Voltage 125 exceeds 120
```

C99 ## The __func__ Identifier

Another new feature of C99 is the __func__ identifier. __func__ has nothing to do with the preprocessor, so it actually doesn't belong in this chapter. However, like many preprocessor features, it's useful for debugging, so I've chosen to discuss it here.

Every function has access to the __func__ identifier, which behaves like a string variable that stores the name of the currently executing function. The effect is the same as if each function contains the following declaration at the beginning of its body:

```
static const char __func__[] = "function-name";
```

where *function-name* is the name of the function. The existence of this identifier makes it possible to write debugging macros such as the following:

```
#define FUNCTION_CALLED() printf("%s called\n", __func__);
#define FUNCTION_RETURNS() printf("%s returns\n", __func__);
```

Calls of these macros can then be placed inside functions to trace their calls:

```
void f(void)
{
  FUNCTION_CALLED();   /* displays "f called" */
  ...
  FUNCTION_RETURNS();  /* displays "f returns" */
}
```

Another use of __func__: it can be passed to a function to let it know the name of the function that called it.

14.4 Conditional Compilation

The C preprocessor recognizes a number of directives that support ***conditional compilation***—the inclusion or exclusion of a section of program text depending on the outcome of a test performed by the preprocessor.

The #if and #endif Directives

Suppose we're in the process of debugging a program. We'd like the program to print the values of certain variables, so we put calls of printf in critical parts of the program. Once we've located the bugs, it's often a good idea to let the printf calls remain, just in case we need them later. Conditional compilation allows us to leave the calls in place, but have the compiler ignore them.

Here's how we'll proceed. We'll first define a macro and give it a nonzero value:

```
#define DEBUG 1
```

The name of the macro doesn't matter. Next, we'll surround each group of printf calls by an #if-#endif pair:

```
#if DEBUG
printf("Value of i: %d\n", i);
printf("Value of j: %d\n", j);
#endif
```

During preprocessing, the #if directive will test the value of DEBUG. Since its value isn't zero, the preprocessor will leave the two calls of printf in the program (the #if and #endif lines will disappear, though). If we change the value of DEBUG to zero and recompile the program, the preprocessor will remove all four lines from the program. The compiler won't see the calls of printf, so they won't occupy any space in the object code and won't cost any time when the program is run. We can leave the #if-#endif blocks in the final program, allowing diagnostic information to be produced later (by recompiling with DEBUG set to 1) if any problems turn up.

In general, the #if directive has the form

#if directive

> #if *constant-expression*

The #endif directive is even simpler:

#endif directive

> #endif

 When the preprocessor encounters the #if directive, it evaluates the constant expression. If the value of the expression is zero, the lines between #if and #endif will be removed from the program during preprocessing. Otherwise, the lines between #if and #endif will remain in the program to be processed by the compiler—the #if and #endif will have had no effect on the program.

It's worth noting that the #if directive treats undefined identifiers as macros that have the value 0. Thus, if we neglect to define DEBUG, the test

```
#if DEBUG
```

will fail (but not generate an error message), while the test

```
#if !DEBUG
```

will succeed.

The `defined` Operator

We encountered the # and ## operators in Section 14.3. There's just one other operator, `defined`, that's specific to the preprocessor. When applied to an identifier, `defined` produces the value 1 if the identifier is a currently defined macro; it produces 0 otherwise. The `defined` operator is normally used in conjunction with the #if directive; it allows us to write

```
#if defined(DEBUG)
...
#endif
```

The lines between the #if and #endif directives will be included in the program only if DEBUG is defined as a macro. The parentheses around DEBUG aren't required; we could simply write

```
#if defined DEBUG
```

Since `defined` tests only whether DEBUG is defined or not, it's not necessary to give DEBUG a value:

```
#define DEBUG
```

The `#ifdef` and `#ifndef` Directives

The #ifdef directive tests whether an identifier is currently defined as a macro:

`#ifdef` directive

> `#ifdef` *identifier*

Using #ifdef is similar to using #if:

```
#ifdef identifier
Lines to be included if identifier is defined as a macro
#endif
```

Strictly speaking, there's no need for #ifdef, since we can combine the #if directive with the `defined` operator to get the same effect. In other words, the directive

```
#ifdef identifier
```

is equivalent to

```
#if defined(identifier)
```

The `#ifndef` directive is similar to `#ifdef`, but tests whether an identifier is *not* defined as a macro:

`#ifndef` directive

> `#ifndef` *identifier*

Writing

`#ifndef` *identifier*

is the same as writing

`#if !defined(`*identifier*`)`

The `#elif` and `#else` Directives

`#if`, `#ifdef`, and `#ifndef` blocks can be nested just like ordinary `if` statements. When nesting occurs, it's a good idea to use an increasing amount of indentation as the level of nesting grows. Some programmers put a comment on each closing `#endif` to indicate what condition the matching `#if` tests:

```
#if DEBUG
...
#endif /* DEBUG */
```

This technique makes it easier for the reader to find the beginning of the `#if` block.

For additional convenience, the preprocessor supports the `#elif` and `#else` directives:

`#elif` directive

> `#elif` *constant-expression*

`#else` directive

> `#else`

`#elif` and `#else` can be used in conjunction with `#if`, `#ifdef`, or `#ifndef` to test a series of conditions:

```
#if expr1
Lines to be included if expr1 is nonzero
#elif expr2
Lines to be included if expr1 is zero but expr2 is nonzero
#else
Lines to be included otherwise
#endif
```

Although the `#if` directive is shown above, an `#ifdef` or `#ifndef` directive can be used instead. Any number of `#elif` directives—but at most one `#else`—may appear between `#if` and `#endif`.

Uses of Conditional Compilation

Conditional compilation is certainly handy for debugging, but its uses don't stop there. Here are a few other common applications:

- **Writing programs that are portable to several machines or operating systems.** The following example includes one of three groups of lines depending on whether WIN32, MAC_OS, or LINUX is defined as a macro:

```
#if defined(WIN32)
...
#elif defined(MAC_OS)
...
#elif defined(LINUX)
...
#endif
```

A program might contain many of these #if blocks. At the beginning of the program, one (and only one) of the macros will be defined, thereby selecting a particular operating system. For example, defining the LINUX macro might indicate that the program is to run under the Linux operating system.

- **Writing programs that can be compiled with different compilers.** Different compilers often recognize somewhat different versions of C. Some accept a standard version of C, some don't. Some provide machine-specific language extensions; some don't, or provide a different set of extensions. Conditional compilation can allow a program to adjust to different compilers. Consider the problem of writing a program that might have to be compiled using an older, nonstandard compiler. The __STDC__ macro allows the preprocessor to detect whether a compiler conforms to the standard (either C89 or C99); if it doesn't, we may need to change certain aspects of the program. In particular, we may have to use old-style function declarations (discussed in the Q&A at the end of Chapter 9) instead of function prototypes. At each point where functions are declared, we can put the following lines:

```
#if __STDC__
Function prototypes
#else
Old-style function declarations
#endif
```

- **Providing a default definition for a macro.** Conditional compilation allows us to check whether a macro is currently defined and, if not, give it a default definition. For example, the following lines will define the macro BUFFER_SIZE if it wasn't previously defined:

```
#ifndef BUFFER_SIZE
#define BUFFER_SIZE 256
#endif
```

■ ***Temporarily disabling code that contains comments.*** We can't use a / *...* / comment to "comment out" code that already contains / *...* / comments. Instead, we can use an #if directive:

```
#if 0
Lines containing comments
#endif
```

Q&A

Disabling code in this way is often called "conditioning out."

Section 15.2 discusses another common use of conditional compilation: protecting header files against multiple inclusion.

14.5   Miscellaneous Directives

To end the chapter, we'll take a brief look at the #error, #line, and #pragma directives. These directives are more specialized than the ones we've already examined, and they're used much less frequently.

The #error Directive

The #error directive has the form

#error directive

#error *message*

where *message* is any sequence of tokens. If the preprocessor encounters an #error directive, it prints an error message which must include *message*. The exact form of the error message can vary from one compiler to another; it might be something like

Error directive: *message*

or perhaps just

#error *message*

Encountering an #error directive indicates a serious flaw in the program; some compilers immediately terminate compilation without attempting to find other errors.

#error directives are frequently used in conjunction with conditional compilation to check for situations that shouldn't arise during a normal compilation. For example, suppose that we want to ensure that a program can't be compiled on a machine whose int type isn't capable of storing numbers up to 100,000. The largest possible int value is represented by the INT_MAX macro, so all we need do is invoke an #error directive if INT_MAX isn't at least 100,000:

INT_MAX macro ➤23.2

```
#if INT_MAX < 100000
#error int type is too small
#endif
```

Attempting to compile the program on a machine whose integers are stored in 16 bits will produce a message such as

```
Error directive: int type is too small
```

The `#error` directive is often found in the `#else` part of an `#if`-`#elif`-`#else` series:

```
#if defined(WIN32)
…
#elif defined(MAC_OS)
…
#elif defined(LINUX)
…
#else
#error No operating system specified
#endif
```

The `#line` Directive

The `#line` directive is used to alter the way program lines are numbered. (Lines are usually numbered 1, 2, 3, as you'd expect.) We can also use this directive to make the compiler think that it's reading the program from a file with a different name.

The `#line` directive has two forms. In one form, we specify a line number:

`#line` directive (form 1)

$$\texttt{\#line } n$$

 n must be a sequence of digits representing an integer between 1 and 32767 (2147483647 in C99). This directive causes subsequent lines in the program to be numbered *n*, *n* + 1, *n* + 2, and so forth.

In the second form of the `#line` directive, both a line number and a file name are specified:

`#line` directive (form 2)

$$\texttt{\#line } n \texttt{ "}file\texttt{"}$$

The lines that follow this directive are assumed to come from *file*, with line numbers starting at *n*. The values of *n* and/or the *file* string can be specified using macros.

One effect of the `#line` directive is to change the value of the `__LINE__` macro (and possibly the `__FILE__` macro). More importantly, most compilers will use the information from the `#line` directive when generating error messages.

For example, suppose that the following directive appears at the beginning of the file `foo.c`:

```
#line 10 "bar.c"
```

Let's say that the compiler detects an error on line 5 of `foo.c`. The error message will refer to line 13 of file `bar.c`, not line 5 of file `foo.c`. (Why line 13? The directive occupies line 1 of `foo.c`, so the renumbering of `foo.c` begins at line 2, which is treated as line 10 of `bar.c`.)

At first glance, the `#line` directive is mystifying. Why would we want error messages to refer to a different line and possibly a different file? Wouldn't this make programs harder to debug?

In fact, the `#line` directive isn't used very often by programmers. Instead, it's used primarily by programs that generate C code as output. The most famous example of such a program is `yacc` (Yet Another Compiler-Compiler), a UNIX utility that automatically generates part of a compiler. (The GNU version of `yacc` is named `bison`.) Before using `yacc`, the programmer prepares a file that contains information for `yacc` as well as fragments of C code. From this file, `yacc` generates a C program, `y.tab.c`, that incorporates the code supplied by the programmer. The programmer then compiles `y.tab.c` in the usual way. By inserting `#line` directives in `y.tab.c`, `yacc` tricks the compiler into believing that the code comes from the original file—the one written by the programmer. As a result, any error messages produced during the compilation of `y.tab.c` will refer to lines in the original file, not lines in `y.tab.c`. This makes debugging easier, because error messages refer to the file written by the programmer, not the (more complicated) file generated by `yacc`.

The #pragma Directive

The `#pragma` directive provides a way to request special behavior from the compiler. This directive is most useful for programs that are unusually large or that need to take advantage of the capabilities of a particular compiler.

The `#pragma` directive has the form

#pragma directive

> #pragma *tokens*

where *tokens* are arbitrary tokens. `#pragma` directives can be very simple (a single token) or they can be much more elaborate:

```
#pragma data(heap_size => 1000, stack_size => 2000)
```

Not surprisingly, the set of commands that can appear in `#pragma` directives is different for each compiler; you'll have to consult the documentation for your compiler to see which commands it allows and what those commands do. Incidentally, the preprocessor must ignore any `#pragma` directive that contains an unrecognized command; it's not permitted to give an error message.

In C89, there are no standard pragmas—they're all implementation-defined. C99 has three standard pragmas, all of which use STDC as the first token following #pragma. These pragmas are FP_CONTRACT (covered in Section 23.4), CX_LIMITED_RANGE (Section 27.4), and FENV_ACCESS (Section 27.6).

The _Pragma Operator

C99 introduces the _Pragma operator, which is used in conjunction with the #pragma directive. A _Pragma expression has the form

_Pragma expression

> _Pragma (*string-literal*)

When it encounters such an expression, the preprocessor "destringizes" the string literal (yes, that's the term used in the C99 standard!) by removing the double quotes around the string and replacing the escape sequences \" and \\ by the characters " and \, respectively. The result is a series of tokens, which are then treated as though they appear in a #pragma directive. For example, writing

```
_Pragma("data(heap_size => 1000, stack_size => 2000)")
```

is the same as writing

```
#pragma data(heap_size => 1000, stack_size => 2000)
```

The _Pragma operator lets us work around a limitation of the preprocessor: the fact that a preprocessing directive can't generate another directive. _Pragma, however, is an operator, not a directive, and can therefore appear in a macro definition. This makes it possible for a macro expansion to leave behind a #pragma directive.

Let's look at an example from the GCC manual. The following macro uses the _Pragma operator:

```
#define DO_PRAGMA(x) _Pragma(#x)
```

The macro would be invoked as follows:

```
DO_PRAGMA(GCC dependency "parse.y")
```

After expansion, the result will be

```
#pragma GCC dependency "parse.y"
```

which is one of the pragmas supported by GCC. (It issues a warning if the date of the specified file—parse.y in this example—is more recent than the date of the current file—the one being compiled.) Note that the argument to the call of DO_PRAGMA is a series of tokens. The # operator in the definition of DO_PRAGMA causes the tokens to be stringized into "GCC dependency \"parse.y\""; this string is then passed to the _Pragma operator, which destringizes it, producing a #pragma directive containing the original tokens.

Q & A

Q: **I've seen programs that contain a # on a line by itself. Is this legal?**

A: Yes. This is the ***null directive;*** it has no effect. Some programmers use null directives for spacing within conditional compilation blocks:

```
#if INT_MAX < 100000
#
#error int type is too small
#
#endif
```

Blank lines would also work, of course, but the # helps the reader see the extent of the block.

Q: **I'm not sure which constants in a program need to be defined as macros. Are there any guidelines to follow? [p. 319]**

A: One rule of thumb says that every numeric constant, other than 0 or 1, should be a macro. Character and string constants are problematic, since replacing a character or string constant by a macro doesn't always improve readability. I recommend using a macro instead of a character constant or string literal provided that (1) the constant is used more than once and (2) the possibility exists that the constant might someday be modified. Because of rule (2), I don't use macros such as

```
#define NUL '\0'
```

although some programmers do.

Q: **What does the # operator do if the argument that it's supposed to "stringize" contains a " or \ character? [p. 324]**

A: It converts " to \" and \ to \\. Consider the following macro:

```
#define STRINGIZE(x) #x
```

The preprocessor will replace `STRINGIZE("foo")` by `"\"foo\""`.

*Q: **I can't get the following macro to work properly:**

```
#define CONCAT(x,y) x##y
```

`CONCAT(a,b)` gives ab, as expected, but `CONCAT(a,CONCAT(b,c))` gives an odd result. What's going on?

A: Thanks to rules that Kernighan and Ritchie call "bizarre," macros whose replacement lists depend on ## usually can't be called in a nested fashion. The problem is that `CONCAT(a,CONCAT(b,c))` isn't expanded in a "normal" fashion, with `CONCAT(b,c)` yielding bc, then `CONCAT(a,bc)` giving abc. Macro parameters that are preceded or followed by ## in a replacement list aren't expanded at the time of substitution. As a result, CONCAT(a,CONCAT(b,c)) expands to aCONCAT(b,c), which can't be expanded further, since there's no macro named aCONCAT.

There's a way to solve the problem, but it's not pretty. The trick is to define a second macro that simply calls the first one:

```
#define CONCAT2(x,y) CONCAT(x,y)
```

Writing CONCAT2(a,CONCAT2(b,c)) now yields the desired result. As the preprocessor expands the outer call of CONCAT2, it will expand CONCAT2(b,c) as well; the difference is that CONCAT2's replacement list doesn't contain ##. If none of this makes any sense, don't worry; it's not a problem that arises often.

The # operator has a similar difficulty, by the way. If #x appears in a replacement list, where x is a macro parameter, the corresponding argument is not expanded. Thus, if N is a macro representing 10, and STR(x) has the replacement list #x, expanding STR(N) yields "N", not "10". The solution is similar to the one we used with CONCAT: defining a second macro whose job is to call STR.

*Q: **Suppose that the preprocessor encounters the original macro name during rescanning, as in the following example:**

```
#define N (2*M)
#define M (N+1)

i = N;    /* infinite loop? */
```

The preprocessor will replace N by (2*M), then replace M by (N+1). Will the preprocessor replace N again, thus going into an infinite loop? [p. 326]

A: Some old preprocessors will indeed go into an infinite loop, but newer ones shouldn't. According to the C standard, if the original macro name reappears during the expansion of a macro, the name is not replaced again. Here's how the assignment to i will look after preprocessing:

```
i = (2*(N+1));
```

Some enterprising programmers take advantage of this behavior by writing macros whose names match reserved words or functions in the standard library.

sqrt function ➤*23.3*   Consider the sqrt library function. sqrt computes the square root of its argument, returning an implementation-defined value if the argument is negative. Perhaps we would prefer that sqrt return 0 if its argument is negative. Since sqrt is part of the standard library, we can't easily change it. We can, however, define a sqrt *macro* that evaluates to 0 when given a negative argument:

```
#undef sqrt
#define sqrt(x) ((x)>=0?sqrt(x):0)
```

A later call of sqrt will be intercepted by the preprocessor, which expands it into the conditional expression shown here. The call of sqrt inside the conditional expression won't be replaced during rescanning, so it will remain for the compiler to handle. (Note the use of #undef to undefine sqrt before defining the sqrt macro. As we'll see in Section 21.1, the standard library is allowed to have both a macro and a function with the same name. Undefining sqrt before defining our own sqrt macro is a defensive measure, in case the library has already defined sqrt as a macro.)

Q: **I get an error when I try to use predefined macros such as __LINE__ and __FILE__. Is there a special header that I need to include?**

A: No. These macros are recognized automatically by the preprocessor. Make sure that you have *two* underscores at the beginning and end of each macro name, not one.

Q: **What's the purpose of distinguishing between a "hosted implementation" and a "freestanding implementation"? If a freestanding implementation doesn't even support the <stdio.h> header, what use is it? [p. 330]**

A: A hosted implementation is needed for most programs (including the ones in this book), which rely on the underlying operating system for input/output and other essential services. A freestanding implementation of C would be used for programs that require no operating system (or only a minimal operating system). For example, a freestanding implementation would be needed for writing the kernel of an operating system (which requires no traditional input/output and therefore doesn't need <stdio.h> anyway). Freestanding implementations are also useful for writing software for embedded systems.

Q: **I thought the preprocessor was just an editor. How can it evaluate constant expressions? [p. 334]**

A: The preprocessor is more sophisticated than you might expect; it knows enough about C to be able to evaluate constant expressions, although it doesn't do so in quite the same way as the compiler. (For one thing, the preprocessor treats any undefined name as having the value 0. The other differences are too esoteric to go into here.) In practice, the operands in a preprocessor constant expression are usually constants, macros that represent constants, and applications of the defined operator.

Q: **Why does C provide the #ifdef and #ifndef directives, since we can get the same effect using the #if directive and the defined operator? [p. 335]**

A: The #ifdef and #ifndef directives have been a part of C since the 1970s. The defined operator, on the other hand, was added to C in the 1980s during standardization. So the real question is: Why was defined added to the language? The answer is that defined adds flexibility. Instead of just being able to test the existence of a single macro using #ifdef or #ifndef, we can now test any number of macros using #if together with defined. For example, the following directive checks whether FOO and BAR are defined but BAZ is not defined:

```
#if defined(FOO) && defined(BAR) && !defined(BAZ)
```

Q: **I wanted to compile a program that I hadn't finished writing, so I "conditioned out" the unfinished part:**

```
#if 0
...
#endif
```

When I compiled the program, I got an error message referring to one of the lines between #if and #endif. Doesn't the preprocessor just ignore these lines? [p. 338]

A: No, the lines aren't completely ignored. Comments are processed before preprocessing directives are executed, and the source code is divided into preprocessing tokens. Thus, an unterminated comment between #if and #endif may cause an error message. Also, an unpaired single quote or double quote character may cause undefined behavior.

Exercises

Section 14.3

1. Write parameterized macros that compute the following values.
   (a) The cube of x.
   (b) The remainder when n is divided by 4.
   (c) 1 if the product of x and y is less than 100, 0 otherwise.

   Do your macros always work? If not, describe what arguments would make them fail.

Ⓦ 2. Write a macro NELEMS(a) that computes the number of elements in a one-dimensional array a. *Hint:* See the discussion of the sizeof operator in Section 8.1.

3. Let DOUBLE be the following macro:

   ```
   #define DOUBLE(x) 2*x
   ```

   (a) What is the value of DOUBLE(1+2)?
   (b) What is the value of 4/DOUBLE(2)?
   (c) Fix the definition of DOUBLE.

Ⓦ 4. For each of the following macros, give an example that illustrates a problem with the macro and show how to fix it.
   (a) `#define AVG(x,y)   (x+y)/2`
   (b) `#define AREA(x,y)  (x)*(y)`

Ⓦ *5. Let TOUPPER be the following macro:

   ```
   #define TOUPPER(c)  ('a'<=(c)&&(c)<='z'?(c)-'a'+'A':(c))
   ```

   Let s be a string and let i be an int variable. Show the output produced by each of the following program fragments.

   (a) ```
   strcpy(s, "abcd");
      i = 0;
      putchar(TOUPPER(s[++i]));
   ```
   ```

   (b) `strcpy(s, "0123");`
       `i = 0;`
       `putchar(TOUPPER(s[++i]));`

6. (a) Write a macro `DISP(f,x)` that expands into a call of `printf` that displays the value of the function `f` when called with argument `x`. For example,

   `DISP(sqrt, 3.0);`

   should expand into

   `printf("sqrt(%g) = %g\n", 3.0, sqrt(3.0));`

   (b) Write a macro `DISP2(f,x,y)` that's similar to `DISP` but works for functions with two arguments.

Ⓦ *7. Let `GENERIC_MAX` be the following macro:

```
#define GENERIC_MAX(type)          \
type type##_max(type x, type y)  \
{                                \
  return x > y ? x : y;          \
}
```

   (a) Show the preprocessor's expansion of `GENERIC_MAX(long)`.
   (b) Explain why `GENERIC_MAX` doesn't work for basic types such as `unsigned long`.
   (c) Describe a technique that would allow us to use `GENERIC_MAX` with basic types such as `unsigned long`. *Hint:* Don't change the definition of `GENERIC_MAX`.

*8. Suppose we want a macro that expands into a string containing the current line number and file name. In other words, we'd like to write

   `const char *str = LINE_FILE;`

   and have it expand into

   `const char *str = "Line 10 of file foo.c";`

   where `foo.c` is the file containing the program and 10 is the line on which the invocation of `LINE_FILE` appears. *Warning:* This exercise is for experts only. Be sure to read the Q&A section carefully before attempting!

9. Write the following parameterized macros.
   (a) `CHECK(x,y,n)` – Has the value 1 if both `x` and `y` fall between 0 and $n-1$, inclusive.
   (b) `MEDIAN(x,y,z)` – Finds the median of `x`, `y`, and `z`.
   (c) `POLYNOMIAL(x)` – Computes the polynomial $3x^5 + 2x^4 - 5x^3 - x^2 + 7x - 6$.

10. Functions can often—but not always—be written as parameterized macros. Discuss what characteristics of a function would make it unsuitable as a macro.

11. (C99) C programmers often use the `fprintf` function to write error messages:

   `fprintf` function ►22.3   `fprintf(stderr, "Range error: index = %d\n", index);`

   `stderr` stream ►22.1   `stderr` is C's "standard error" stream; the remaining arguments are the same as those for `printf`, starting with the format string. Write a macro named `ERROR` that generates the call of `fprintf` shown above when given a format string and the items to be displayed:

   `ERROR("Range error: index = %d\n", index);`

Section 14.4   Ⓦ 12. Suppose that the macro `M` has been defined as follows:

   `#define M 10`

Which of the following tests will fail?

(a) `#if M`
(b) `#ifdef M`
(c) `#ifndef M`
(d) `#if defined(M)`
(e) `#if !defined(M)`

13. (a) Show what the following program will look like after preprocessing. You may ignore any lines added to the program as a result of including the `<stdio.h>` header.

```
#include <stdio.h>

#define N 100

void f(void);

int main(void)
{
  f();
#ifdef N
#undef N
#endif
  return 0;
}

void f(void)
{
#if defined(N)
  printf("N is %d\n", N);
#else
  printf("N is undefined\n");
#endif
}
```

(b) What will be the output of this program?

W*14. Show what the following program will look like after preprocessing. Some lines of the program may cause compilation errors; find all such errors.

```
#define N = 10
#define INC(x) x+1
#define SUB (x,y) x-y
#define SQR(x) ((x)*(x))
#define CUBE(x) (SQR(x)*(x))
#define M1(x,y) x##y
#define M2(x,y) #x #y

int main(void)
{
  int a[N], i, j, k, m;

#ifdef N
  i = j;
#else
  j = i;
#endif

  i = 10 * INC(j);
```

```
        i = SUB(j, k);
        i = SQR(SQR(j));
        i = CUBE(j);
        i = M1(j, k);
        puts(M2(i, j));

#undef SQR
        i = SQR(j);
#define SQR
        i = SQR(j);

        return 0;
}
```

15. Suppose that a program needs to display messages in either English, French, or Spanish. Using conditional compilation, write a program fragment that displays one of the following three messages, depending on whether or not the specified macro is defined:

```
Insert Disk 1        (if ENGLISH is defined)
Inserez Le Disque 1  (if FRENCH is defined)
Inserte El Disco 1   (if SPANISH is defined)
```

Section 14.5   *16.   (C99) Assume that the following macro definitions are in effect:

```
#define IDENT(x)  PRAGMA(ident #x)
#define PRAGMA(x) _Pragma(#x)
```

What will the following line look like after macro expansion?

```
IDENT(foo)
```

15 Writing Large Programs

Around computers it is difficult to find the correct unit of time to measure progress. Some cathedrals took a century to complete. Can you imagine the grandeur and scope of a program that would take as long?

Although some C programs are small enough to be put in a single file, most aren't. Programs that consist of more than one file are the rule rather than the exception. In this chapter, we'll see that a typical program consists of several source files and usually some header files as well. Source files contain definitions of functions and external variables; header files contain information to be shared among source files. Section 15.1 discusses source files, while Section 15.2 covers header files. Section 15.3 describes how to divide a program into source files and header files. Section 15.4 then shows how to "build" (compile and link) a program that consists of more than one file, and how to "rebuild" a program after part of it has been changed.

15.1 Source Files

Up to this point, we've assumed that a C program consists of a single file. In fact, a program may be divided among any number of *source files*. By convention, source files have the extension .c. Each source file contains part of the program, primarily definitions of functions and variables. One source file must contain a function named main, which serves as the starting point for the program.

For example, suppose that we want to write a simple calculator program that evaluates integer expressions entered in Reverse Polish notation (RPN), in which operators follow operands. If the user enters an expression such as

```
30 5 - 7 *
```

we want the program to print its value (175, in this case). Evaluating an RPN expression is easy if we have the program read the operands and operators, one by one, using a stack to keep track of intermediate results. If the program reads a

stacks ➤10.2

349

number, we'll have it push the number onto the stack. If it reads an operator, we'll have it pop two numbers from the stack, perform the operation, and then push the result back onto the stack. When the program reaches the end of the user's input, the value of the expression will be on the stack. For example, the program will evaluate the expression 30 5 - 7 * in the following way:

1. Push 30 onto the stack.
2. Push 5 onto the stack.
3. Pop the top two numbers from the stack, subtract 5 from 30, giving 25, and then push the result back onto the stack.
4. Push 7 onto the stack.
5. Pop the top two numbers from the stack, multiply them, and then push the result back onto the stack.

After these steps, the stack will contain the value of the expression (175).

Turning this strategy into a program isn't hard. The program's main function will contain a loop that performs the following actions:

Read a "token" (a number or an operator).

If the token is a number, push it onto the stack.

If the token is an operator, pop its operands from the stack, perform the operation, and then push the result back onto the stack.

When dividing a program like this one into files, it makes sense to put related functions and variables into the same file. The function that reads tokens could go into one source file (token.c, say), together with any functions that have to do with tokens. Stack-related functions such as push, pop, make_empty, is_empty, and is_full could go into a different file, stack.c. The variables that represent the stack would also go into stack.c. The main function would go into yet another file, calc.c.

Splitting a program into multiple source files has significant advantages:

- Grouping related functions and variables into a single file helps clarify the structure of the program.

- Each source file can be compiled separately—a great time-saver if the program is large and must be changed frequently (which is common during program development).

- Functions are more easily reused in other programs when grouped in separate source files. In our example, splitting off stack.c and token.c from the main function makes it simpler to reuse the stack functions and token functions in the future.

15.2 Header Files

When we divide a program into several source files, problems arise: How can a function in one file call a function that's defined in another file? How can a function access an external variable in another file? How can two files share the same macro definition or type definition? The answer lies with the #include directive, which makes it possible to share information—function prototypes, macro definitions, type definitions, and more—among any number of source files.

The #include directive tells the preprocessor to open a specified file and insert its contents into the current file. Thus, if we want several source files to have access to the same information, we'll put that information in a file and then use #include to bring the file's contents into each of the source files. Files that are included in this fashion are called *header files* (or sometimes *include files*); I'll discuss them in more detail later in this section. By convention, header files have the extension .h.

Note: The C standard uses the term "source file" to refer to all files written by the programmer, including both .c and .h files. I'll use "source file" to refer to .c files only.

The #include Directive

The #include directive has two primary forms. The first form is used for header files that belong to C's own library:

**#include directive
(form 1)**

> #include <*filename*>

The second form is used for all other header files, including any that we write:

**#include directive
(form 2)**

> #include "*filename*"

 The difference between the two is a subtle one having to do with how the compiler locates the header file. Here are the rules that most compilers follow:

- #include <*filename*>: Search the directory (or directories) in which system header files reside. (On UNIX systems, for example, system header files are usually kept in the directory /usr/include.)
- #include "*filename*": Search the current directory, then search the directory (or directories) in which system header files reside.

The places to be searched for header files can usually be altered, often by a command-line option such as -I*path*.

 Don't use brackets when including header files that you have written:

#include <myheader.h>   /*** WRONG ***/

The preprocessor will probably look for myheader.h where the system header files are kept (and, of course, won't find it).

The file name in an #include directive may include information that helps locate the file, such as a directory path or drive specifier:

```
#include "c:\cprogs\utils.h"   /* Windows path */

#include "/cprogs/utils.h"     /* UNIX path */
```

Although the quotation marks in the #include directive make file names look like string literals, the preprocessor doesn't treat them that way. (That's fortunate, since \c and \u—which appear in the Windows example—would be treated as escape sequences in a string literal.)

portability tip   *It's usually best not to include path or drive information in #include directives. Such information makes it difficult to compile a program when it's transported to another machine or, worse, another operating system.*

For example, the following Windows #include directives specify drive and/or path information that may not always be valid:

```
#include "d:utils.h"
#include "\cprogs\include\utils.h"
#include "d:\cprogs\include\utils.h"
```

The following directives are better; they don't mention specific drives, and paths are relative rather than absolute:

```
#include "utils.h"
#include "..\include\utils.h"
```

The #include directive has a third form that's used less often than the other two:

#include directive (form 3)

> #include *tokens*

preprocessing tokens ➤ 14.3

where *tokens* is any sequence of preprocessing tokens. The preprocessor will scan the tokens and replace any macros that it finds. After macro replacement, the resulting directive must match one of the other forms of #include. The advantage of the third kind of #include is that the file name can be defined by a macro rather than being "hard-coded" into the directive itself, as the following example shows:

```
#if defined(IA32)
  #define CPU_FILE "ia32.h"
#elif defined(IA64)
  #define CPU_FILE "ia64.h"
#elif defined(AMD64)
  #define CPU_FILE "amd64.h"
#endif

#include CPU_FILE
```

Sharing Macro Definitions and Type Definitions

Most large programs contain macro definitions and type definitions that need to be shared by several source files (or, in the most extreme case, by *all* source files). These definitions should go into header files.

For example, suppose that we're writing a program that uses macros named BOOL, TRUE, and FALSE. (There's no need for these in C99, of course, because the `<stdbool.h>` header defines similar macros.) Instead of repeating the definitions of these macros in each source file that needs them, it makes more sense to put the definitions in a header file with a name like `boolean.h`:

```
#define BOOL int
#define TRUE 1
#define FALSE 0
```

Any source file that requires these macros will simply contain the line

```
#include "boolean.h"
```

In the following figure, two files include `boolean.h`:

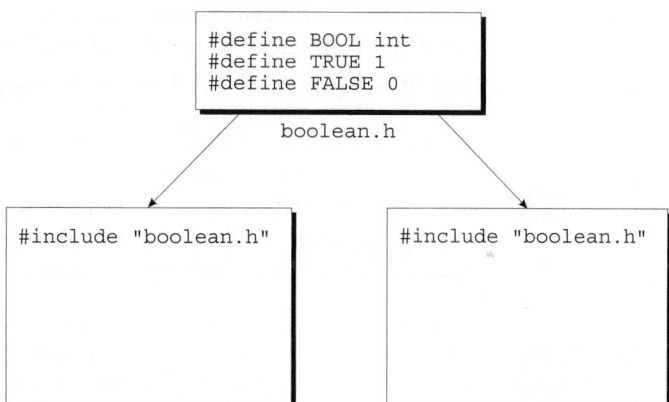

Type definitions are also common in header files. For example, instead of defining a BOOL macro, we might use `typedef` to create a `Bool` type. If we do, the `boolean.h` file will have the following appearance:

```
#define TRUE 1
#define FALSE 0
typedef int Bool;
```

Putting definitions of macros and types in header files has some clear advantages. First, we save time by not having to copy the definitions into the source files where they're needed. Second, the program becomes easier to modify. Changing the definition of a macro or type requires only that we edit a single header file; we don't have to modify the many source files in which the macro or type is used. Third, we don't have to worry about inconsistencies caused by source files containing different definitions of the same macro or type.

Sharing Function Prototypes

Suppose that a source file contains a call of a function f that's defined in another file, foo.c. Calling f without declaring it first is risky. Without a prototype to rely on, the compiler is forced to assume that f's return type is int and that the number of parameters matches the number of arguments in the call of f. The arguments themselves are converted automatically to a kind of "standard form" by the default argument promotions. The compiler's assumptions may well be wrong, but it has no way to check them, since it compiles only one file at a time. If the assumptions are incorrect, the program probably won't work, and there won't be any clues as to why it doesn't. (For this reason, C99 prohibits calling a function for which the compiler has not yet seen a declaration or definition.)

default argument promotions ➤ 9.3

When calling a function f that's defined in another file, always make sure that the compiler has seen a prototype for f prior to the call.

Our first impulse is to declare f in the file where it's called. That solves the problem but can create a maintenance nightmare. Suppose that the function is called in fifty different source files. How can we ensure that f's prototypes are the same in all the files? How can we guarantee that they match the definition of f in foo.c? If f should change later, how can we find all the files where it's used?

The solution is obvious: put f's prototype in a header file, then include the header file in all the places where f is called. Since f is defined in foo.c, let's name the header file foo.h. In addition to including foo.h in the source files where f is called, we'll need to include it in foo.c, enabling the compiler to check that f's prototype in foo.h matches its definition in foo.c.

Always include the header file declaring a function f in the source file that contains f's definition. Failure to do so can cause hard-to-find bugs, since calls of f elsewhere in the program may not match f's definition.

If foo.c contains other functions, most of them should be declared in the same header file as f. After all, the other functions in foo.c are presumably related to f; any file that contains a call of f probably needs some of the other functions in foo.c. Functions that are intended for use only within foo.c shouldn't be declared in a header file, however; to do so would be misleading.

To illustrate the use of function prototypes in header files, let's return to the RPN calculator of Section 15.1. The stack.c file will contain definitions of the make_empty, is_empty, is_full, push, and pop functions. The following prototypes for these functions should go in the stack.h header file:

```
void make_empty(void);
int is_empty(void);
```

```
int is_full(void);
void push(int i);
int pop(void);
```

(To avoid complicating the example, is_empty and is_full will return int values instead of Boolean values.) We'll include stack.h in calc.c to allow the compiler to check any calls of stack functions that appear in the latter file. We'll also include stack.h in stack.c so the compiler can verify that the prototypes in stack.h match the definitions in stack.c. The following figure shows stack.h, stack.c, and calc.c:

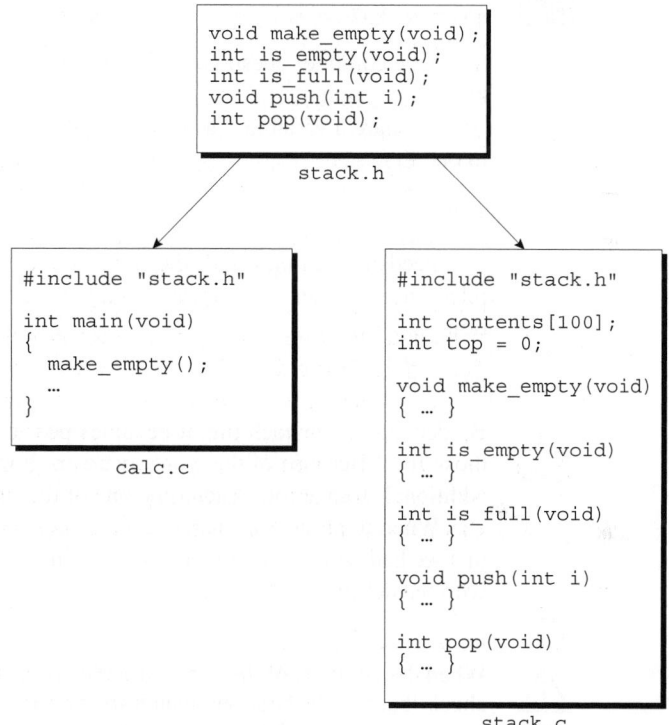

```
void make_empty(void);
int is_empty(void);
int is_full(void);
void push(int i);
int pop(void);
```
stack.h

```
#include "stack.h"

int main(void)
{
  make_empty();
  …
}
```
calc.c

```
#include "stack.h"

int contents[100];
int top = 0;

void make_empty(void)
{ … }

int is_empty(void)
{ … }

int is_full(void)
{ … }

void push(int i)
{ … }

int pop(void)
{ … }
```
stack.c

Sharing Variable Declarations

external variables ➤ 10.2

External variables can be shared among files in much the same way functions are. To share a function, we put its *definition* in one source file, then put *declarations* in other files that need to call the function. Sharing an external variable is done in much the same way.

Up to this point, we haven't needed to distinguish between a variable's declaration and its definition. To declare a variable i, we've written

```
int i;                /* declares i and defines it as well */
```

which not only declares i to be a variable of type int, but defines i as well, by causing the compiler to set aside space for i. To declare i without defining it, we must put the keyword extern at the beginning of its declaration:

extern keyword ➤ 18.2

```
extern int i;    /* declares i without defining it */
```

extern informs the compiler that i is defined elsewhere in the program (most likely in a different source file), so there's no need to allocate space for it.

extern works with variables of all types. When we use it in the declaration of an array, we can omit the length of the array:

```
extern int a[];
```

Since the compiler doesn't allocate space for a at this time, there's no need for it to know a's length.

To share a variable i among several source files, we first put a definition of i in one file:

```
int i;
```

If i needs to be initialized, the initializer would go here. When this file is compiled, the compiler will allocate storage for i. The other files will contain declarations of i:

```
extern int i;
```

By declaring i in each file, it becomes possible to access and/or modify i within those files. Because of the word extern, however, the compiler doesn't allocate additional storage for i each time one of the files is compiled.

When a variable is shared among files, we'll face a challenge similar to one that we had with shared functions: ensuring that all declarations of a variable agree with the definition of the variable.

When declarations of the same variable appear in different files, the compiler can't check that the declarations match the variable's definition. For example, one file may contain the definition

```
int i;
```

while another file contains the declaration

```
extern long i;
```

An error of this kind can cause the program to behave unpredictably.

To avoid inconsistency, declarations of shared variables are usually put in header files. A source file that needs access to a particular variable can then include the appropriate header file. In addition, each header file that contains a variable declaration is included in the source file that contains the variable's definition, enabling the compiler to check that the two match.

Although sharing variables among files is a long-standing practice in the C world, it has significant disadvantages. In Section 19.2, we'll see what the problems are and learn how to design programs that don't need shared variables.

Nested Includes

A header file may itself contain #include directives. Although this practice may seem a bit odd, it can be quite useful in practice. Consider the stack.h file, which contains the following prototypes:

```
int is_empty(void);
int is_full(void);
```

Since these functions return only 0 or 1, it's a good idea to declare their return type to be Bool instead of int, where Bool is the type that we defined earlier in this section:

```
Bool is_empty(void);
Bool is_full(void);
```

Of course, we'll need to include the boolean.h file in stack.h so that the definition of Bool is available when stack.h is compiled. (In C99, we'd include <stdbool.h> instead of boolean.h and declare the return types of the two functions to be bool rather than Bool.)

Traditionally, C programmers shun nested includes. (Early versions of C didn't allow them at all.) However, the bias against nested includes has largely faded away, in part because nested includes are common practice in C++.

Protecting Header Files

If a source file includes the same header file twice, compilation errors may result. This problem is common when header files include other header files. For example, suppose that file1.h includes file3.h, file2.h includes file3.h, and prog.c includes both file1.h and file2.h (see the figure at the top of the next page). When prog.c is compiled, file3.h will be compiled twice.

Including the same header file twice doesn't always cause a compilation error. If the file contains only macro definitions, function prototypes, and/or variable declarations, there won't be any difficulty. If the file contains a type definition, however, we'll get a compilation error.

Just to be safe, it's probably a good idea to protect all header files against multiple inclusion; that way, we can add type definitions to a file later without the risk that we might forget to protect the file. In addition, we might save some time during program development by avoiding unnecessary recompilation of the same header file.

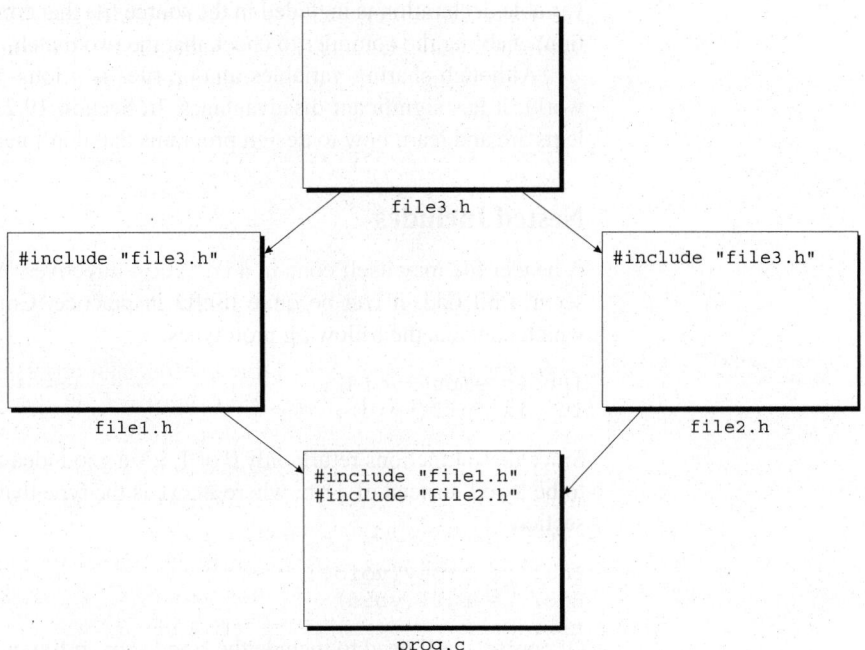

To protect a header file, we'll enclose the contents of the file in an `#ifndef`-`#endif` pair. For example, the `boolean.h` file could be protected in the following way:

```
#ifndef BOOLEAN_H
#define BOOLEAN_H

#define TRUE 1
#define FALSE 0
typedef int Bool;

#endif
```

When this file is included the first time, the BOOLEAN_H macro won't be defined, so the preprocessor will allow the lines between `#ifndef` and `#endif` to stay. But if the file should be included a second time, the preprocessor will remove the lines between `#ifndef` and `#endif`.

The name of the macro (BOOLEAN_H) doesn't really matter. However, making it resemble the name of the header file is a good way to avoid conflicts with other macros. Since we can't name the macro BOOLEAN.H (identifiers can't contain periods), a name such as BOOLEAN_H is a good alternative.

`#error` Directives in Header Files

#error directives ➤14.5   `#error` directives are often put in header files to check for conditions under which the header file shouldn't be included. For example, suppose that a header file uses a feature that didn't exist prior to the original C89 standard. To prevent the header file from being used with older, nonstandard compilers, it could contain an `#ifndef` directive that tests for the existence of the `__STDC__` macro:

__STDC__ macro ➤ 14.3

```
#ifndef __STDC__
#error This header requires a Standard C compiler
#endif
```

15.3 Dividing a Program into Files

Let's now use what we know about header files and source files to develop a simple technique for dividing a program into files. We'll concentrate on functions, but the same principles apply to external variables as well. We'll assume that the program has already been designed; that is, we've decided what functions the program will need and how to arrange the functions into logically related groups. (We'll discuss program design in Chapter 19.)

Here's how we'll proceed. Each set of functions will go into a separate source file (let's use the name `foo.c` for one such file). In addition, we'll create a header file with the same name as the source file, but with the extension `.h` (`foo.h`, in our case). Into `foo.h`, we'll put prototypes for the functions defined in `foo.c`. (Functions that are designed for use only within `foo.c` need not—and should not—be declared in `foo.h`. The `read_char` function in our next program is an example.) We'll include `foo.h` in each source file that needs to call a function defined in `foo.c`. Moreover, we'll include `foo.h` in `foo.c` so that the compiler can check that the function prototypes in `foo.h` are consistent with the definitions in `foo.c`.

The `main` function will go in a file whose name matches the name of the program—if we want the program to be known as `bar`, then `main` should be in the file `bar.c`. It's possible that there are other functions in the same file as `main`, so long as they're not called from other files in the program.

PROGRAM   **Text Formatting**

To illustrate the technique that we've just discussed, let's apply it to a small text-formatting program named `justify`. As sample input to `justify`, we'll use a file named `quote` that contains the following (poorly formatted) quotation from "The development of the C programming language" by Dennis M. Ritchie (in *History of Programming Languages II,* edited by T. J. Bergin, Jr., and R. G. Gibson, Jr., Addison-Wesley, Reading, Mass., 1996, pages 671–687):

```
    C     is quirky,  flawed,    and  an
enormous   success.      Although accidents of   history
 surely  helped,   it evidently   satisfied  a   need

   for  a   system  implementation   language    efficient
```

```
enough   to  displace            assembly    language,
  yet sufficiently   abstract   and fluent    to describe
algorithms    and        interactions    in a    wide    variety
of    environments.
                        --         Dennis    M.        Ritchie
```

To run the program from a UNIX or Windows prompt, we'd enter the command

```
justify <quote
```

input redirection ➤ 22.1 The < symbol informs the operating system that `justify` will read from the file `quote` instead of accepting input from the keyboard. This feature, supported by UNIX, Windows, and other operating systems, is called ***input redirection***. When given the `quote` file as input, the `justify` program will produce the following output:

```
C is quirky,  flawed,  and  an  enormous  success.  Although
accidents of history surely helped, it evidently satisfied a
need for a system implementation language  efficient  enough
to displace assembly language, yet sufficiently abstract and
fluent to describe algorithms and  interactions  in  a  wide
variety of environments. -- Dennis M. Ritchie
```

The output of `justify` will normally appear on the screen, but we can save it in a
output redirection ➤ 22.1 file by using ***output redirection***:

```
justify <quote >newquote
```

The output of `justify` will go into the file `newquote`.

In general, `justify`'s output should be identical to its input, except that extra spaces and blank lines are deleted, and lines are filled and justified. "Filling" a line means adding words until one more word would cause the line to overflow. "Justifying" a line means adding extra spaces between words so that each line has exactly the same length (60 characters). Justification must be done so that the space between words in a line is equal (or as nearly equal as possible). The last line of the output won't be justified.

We'll assume that no word is longer than 20 characters. (A punctuation mark is considered part of the word to which it is adjacent.) That's a bit restrictive, of course, but once the program is written and debugged we can easily increase this limit to the point that it would virtually never be exceeded. If the program encounters a longer word, it must ignore all characters after the first 20, replacing them with a single asterisk. For example, the word

```
antidisestablishmentarianism
```

would be printed as

```
antidisestablishment*
```

Now that we understand what the program should do, it's time to think about a design. We'll start by observing that the program can't write the words one by one as they're read. Instead, it will have to store them in a "line buffer" until there are enough to fill a line. After further reflection, we decide that the heart of the program will be a loop that goes something like this:

```
for (;;) {
    read word;
    if (can't read word) {
        write contents of line buffer without justification;
        terminate program;
    }

    if (word doesn't fit in line buffer) {
        write contents of line buffer with justification;
        clear line buffer;
    }
    add word to line buffer;
}
```

Since we'll need functions that deal with words and functions that deal with the line buffer, let's split the program into three source files, putting all functions related to words in one file (`word.c`) and all functions related to the line buffer in another file (`line.c`). A third file (`justify.c`) will contain the `main` function. In addition to these files, we'll need two header files, `word.h` and `line.h`. The `word.h` file will contain prototypes for the functions in `word.c`; `line.h` will play a similar role for `line.c`.

By examining the main loop, we see that the only word-related function that we'll need is a `read_word` function. (If `read_word` can't read a word because it's reached the end of the input file, we'll have it signal the main loop by pretending to read an "empty" word.) Consequently, the `word.h` file is a small one:

word.h
```
#ifndef WORD_H
#define WORD_H

/************************************************************
 * read_word: Reads the next word from the input and       *
 *            stores it in word. Makes word empty if no     *
 *            word could be read because of end-of-file.    *
 *            Truncates the word if its length exceeds      *
 *            len.                                          *
 ************************************************************/
void read_word(char *word, int len);

#endif
```

Notice how the `WORD_H` macro protects `word.h` from being included more than once. Although `word.h` doesn't really need it, it's good practice to protect all header files in this way.

The line.h file won't be as short as word.h. Our outline of the main loop reveals the need for functions that perform the following operations:

Write contents of line buffer without justification
Determine how many characters are left in line buffer
Write contents of line buffer with justification
Clear line buffer
Add word to line buffer

We'll call these functions flush_line, space_remaining, write_line, clear_line, and add_word. Here's what the line.h header file will look like:

line.h

```
#ifndef LINE_H
#define LINE_H

/**********************************************************
 * clear_line: Clears the current line.                   *
 **********************************************************/
void clear_line(void);

/**********************************************************
 * add_word: Adds word to the end of the current line.    *
 *           If this is not the first word on the line,   *
 *           puts one space before word.                  *
 **********************************************************/
void add_word(const char *word);

/**********************************************************
 * space_remaining: Returns the number of characters left *
 *                  in the current line.                  *
 **********************************************************/
int space_remaining(void);

/**********************************************************
 * write_line: Writes the current line with               *
 *             justification.                             *
 **********************************************************/
void write_line(void);

/**********************************************************
 * flush_line: Writes the current line without            *
 *             justification. If the line is empty, does  *
 *             nothing.                                   *
 **********************************************************/
void flush_line(void);

#endif
```

Before we write the word.c and line.c files, we can use the functions declared in word.h and line.h to write justify.c, the main program. Writing this file is mostly a matter of translating our original loop design into C.

justify.c   `/* Formats a file of text */`

```
#include <string.h>
#include "line.h"
#include "word.h"

#define MAX_WORD_LEN 20

int main(void)
{
  char word[MAX_WORD_LEN+2];
  int word_len;

  clear_line();
  for (;;) {
    read_word(word, MAX_WORD_LEN+1);
    word_len = strlen(word);
    if (word_len == 0) {
      flush_line();
      return 0;
    }
    if (word_len > MAX_WORD_LEN)
      word[MAX_WORD_LEN] = '*';
    if (word_len + 1 > space_remaining()) {
      write_line();
      clear_line();
    }
    add_word(word);
  }
}
```

Including both `line.h` and `word.h` gives the compiler access to the function prototypes in both files as it compiles `justify.c`.

    `main` uses a trick to handle words that exceed 20 characters. When it calls `read_word`, `main` tells it to truncate any word that exceeds 21 characters. After `read_word` returns, `main` checks whether `word` contains a string that's longer than 20 characters. If so, the word that was read must have been at least 21 characters long (before truncation), so `main` replaces the word's 21st character by an asterisk.

    Now it's time to write `word.c`. Although the `word.h` header file has a prototype for only one function, `read_word`, we can put additional functions in `word.c` if we need to. As it turns out, `read_word` is easier to write if we add a small "helper" function, `read_char`. We'll assign `read_char` the task of reading a single character and, if it's a new-line character or tab, converting it to a space. Having `read_word` call `read_char` instead of `getchar` solves the problem of treating new-line characters and tabs as spaces.

    Here's the `word.c` file:

word.c   `#include <stdio.h>`
           `#include "word.h"`

```
int read_char(void)
{
  int ch = getchar();

  if (ch == '\n' || ch == '\t')
    return ' ';
  return ch;
}

void read_word(char *word, int len)
{
  int ch, pos = 0;

  while ((ch = read_char()) == ' ')
    ;
  while (ch != ' ' && ch != EOF) {
    if (pos < len)
      word[pos++] = ch;
    ch = read_char();
  }
  word[pos] = '\0';
}
```

Before we discuss read_word, a couple of comments are in order concerning the use of getchar in the read_char function. First, getchar returns an int value instead of a char value; that's why the variable ch in read_char is declared to have type int and why the return type of read_char is int. Also,

EOF macro ➤22.4   getchar returns the value EOF when it's unable to continue reading (usually because it has reached the end of the input file).

read_word consists of two loops. The first loop skips over spaces, stopping at the first nonblank character. (EOF isn't a blank, so the loop stops if it reaches the end of the input file.) The second loop reads characters until encountering a space or EOF. The body of the loop stores the characters in word until reaching the len limit. After that, the loop continues reading characters but doesn't store them. The final statement in read_word ends the word with a null character, thereby making it a string. If read_word encounters EOF before finding a nonblank character, pos will be 0 at the end, making word an empty string.

The only file left is line.c, which supplies definitions of the functions declared in the line.h file. line.c will also need variables to keep track of the state of the line buffer. One variable, line, will store the characters in the current line. Strictly speaking, line is the only variable we need. For speed and convenience, however, we'll use two other variables: line_len (the number of characters in the current line) and num_words (the number of words in the current line).

Here's the line.c file:

line.c
```
#include <stdio.h>
#include <string.h>
#include "line.h"
```

```c
#define MAX_LINE_LEN 60

char line[MAX_LINE_LEN+1];
int line_len = 0;
int num_words = 0;

void clear_line(void)
{
  line[0] = '\0';
  line_len = 0;
  num_words = 0;
}

void add_word(const char *word)
{
  if (num_words > 0) {
    line[line_len] = ' ';
    line[line_len+1] = '\0';
    line_len++;
  }
  strcat(line, word);
  line_len += strlen(word);
  num_words++;
}

int space_remaining(void)
{
  return MAX_LINE_LEN - line_len;
}

void write_line(void)
{
  int extra_spaces, spaces_to_insert, i, j;

  extra_spaces = MAX_LINE_LEN - line_len;
  for (i = 0; i < line_len; i++) {
    if (line[i] != ' ')
      putchar(line[i]);
    else {
      spaces_to_insert = extra_spaces / (num_words - 1);
      for (j = 1; j <= spaces_to_insert + 1; j++)
        putchar(' ');
      extra_spaces -= spaces_to_insert;
      num_words--;
    }
  }
  putchar('\n');
}

void flush_line(void)
{
  if (line_len > 0)
    puts(line);
}
```

Most of the functions in `line.c` are easy to write. The only tricky one is `write_line`, which writes a line with justification. `write_line` writes the characters in `line` one by one, pausing at the space between each pair of words to write additional spaces if needed. The number of additional spaces is stored in `spaces_to_insert`, which has the value `extra_spaces / (num_words - 1)`, where `extra_spaces` is initially the difference between the maximum line length and the actual line length. Since `extra_spaces` and `num_words` change after each word is printed, `spaces_to_insert` will change as well. If `extra_spaces` is 10 initially and `num_words` is 5, then the first word will be followed by 2 extra spaces, the second by 2, the third by 3, and the fourth by 3.

15.4   Building a Multiple-File Program

In Section 2.1, we examined the process of compiling and linking a program that fits into a single file. Let's expand that discussion to cover multiple-file programs. Building a large program requires the same basic steps as building a small one:

- *Compiling.* Each source file in the program must be compiled separately. (Header files don't need to be compiled; the contents of a header file are automatically compiled whenever a source file that includes it is compiled.) For each source file, the compiler generates a file containing object code. These files—known as *object files*—have the extension `.o` in UNIX and `.obj` in Windows.

- *Linking.* The linker combines the object files created in the previous step—along with code for library functions—to produce an executable file. Among other duties, the linker is responsible for resolving external references left behind by the compiler. (An external reference occurs when a function in one file calls a function defined in another file or accesses a variable defined in another file.)

Most compilers allow us to build a program in a single step. With the GCC compiler, for example, we'd use the following command to build the `justify` program of Section 15.3:

```
gcc -o justify justify.c line.c word.c
```

The three source files are first compiled into object code. The object files are then automatically passed to the linker, which combines them into a single file. The `-o` option specifies that we want the executable file to be named `justify`.

Makefiles

Putting the names of all the source files on the command line quickly gets tedious. Worse still, we could waste a lot of time when rebuilding a program if we recompile all source files, not just the ones that were affected by our most recent changes.

To make it easier to build large programs, UNIX originated the concept of the *makefile,* a file containing the information necessary to build a program. A makefile not only lists the files that are part of the program, but also describes *dependencies* among the files. Suppose that the file foo.c includes the file bar.h. We say that foo.c "depends" on bar.h, because a change to bar.h will require us to recompile foo.c.

Here's a UNIX makefile for the justify program. The makefile uses GCC for compilation and linking:

```
justify: justify.o word.o line.o
        gcc -o justify justify.o word.o line.o

justify.o: justify.c word.h line.h
        gcc -c justify.c

word.o:  word.c word.h
        gcc -c word.c

line.o:  line.c line.h
        gcc -c line.c
```

There are four groups of lines; each group is known as a *rule.* The first line in each rule gives a *target* file, followed by the files on which it depends. The second line is a *command* to be executed if the target should need to be rebuilt because of a change to one of its dependent files. Let's look at the first two rules; the last two are similar.

In the first rule, justify (the executable file) is the target:

```
justify: justify.o word.o line.o
        gcc -o justify justify.o word.o line.o
```

The first line states that justify depends on the files justify.o, word.o, and line.o; if any one of these three files has changed since the program was last built, then justify needs to be rebuilt. The command on the following line shows how the rebuilding is to be done (by using the gcc command to link the three object files).

In the second rule, justify.o is the target:

```
justify.o: justify.c word.h line.h
        gcc -c justify.c
```

The first line indicates that justify.o needs to be rebuilt if there's been a change to justify.c, word.h, or line.h. (The reason for mentioning word.h and line.h is that justify.c includes both these files, so it's potentially affected by a change to either one.) The next line shows how to update justify.o (by recompiling justify.c). The -c option tells the compiler to compile justify.c into an object file but not attempt to link it.

Q&A   Once we've created a makefile for a program, we can use the make utility to build (or rebuild) the program. By checking the time and date associated with each file in the program, `make` can determine which files are out of date. It then invokes the commands necessary to rebuild the program.

If you want to give `make` a try, here are a few details you'll need to know:

- Each command in a makefile must be preceded by a tab character, not a series of spaces. (In our example, the commands appear to be indented eight spaces, but it's actually a single tab character.)

- A makefile is normally stored in a file named `Makefile` (or `makefile`). When the `make` utility is used, it automatically checks the current directory for a file with one of these names.

- To invoke `make`, use the command

  `make` *target*

  where *target* is one of the targets listed in the makefile. To build the `justify` executable using our makefile, we would use the command

  `make justify`

- If no target is specified when `make` is invoked, it will build the target of the first rule. For example, the command

  `make`

  will build the `justify` executable, since `justify` is the first target in our makefile. Except for this special property of the first rule, the order of rules in a makefile is arbitrary.

`make` is complicated enough that entire books have been written about it, so we won't attempt to delve further into its intricacies. Let's just say that real makefiles aren't usually as easy to understand as our example. There are numerous techniques that reduce the amount of redundancy in makefiles and make them easier to modify; at the same time, though, these techniques greatly reduce their readability.

Not everyone uses makefiles, by the way. Other program maintenance tools are also popular, including the "project files" supported by some integrated development environments.

Errors During Linking

Some errors that can't be detected during compilation will be found during linking. In particular, if the definition of a function or variable is missing from a program, the linker will be unable to resolve external references to it, causing a message such as *"undefined symbol"* or *"undefined reference."*

Errors detected by the linker are usually easy to fix. Here are some of the most common causes:

- ***Misspellings.*** If the name of a variable or function is misspelled, the linker will report it as missing. For example, if the function `read_char` is defined in the program but called as `read_cahr`, the linker will report that `read_cahr` is missing.

- *Missing files.* If the linker can't find the functions that are in file `foo.c`, it may not know about the file. Check the makefile or project file to make sure that `foo.c` is listed there.

- *Missing libraries.* The linker may not be able to find all library functions used in the program. A classic example occurs in UNIX programs that use the `<math.h>` header. Simply including the header in a program may not be enough; many versions of UNIX require that the `-lm` option be specified when the program is linked, causing the linker to search a system file that contains compiled versions of the `<math.h>` functions. Failing to use this option may cause "undefined reference" messages during linking.

Rebuilding a Program

During the development of a program, it's rare that we'll need to compile all its files. Most of the time, we'll test the program, make a change, then build the program again. To save time, the rebuilding process should recompile only those files that might be affected by the latest change.

Let's assume that we've designed our program in the way outlined in Section 15.3, with a header file for each source file. To see how many files will need to be recompiled after a change, we need to consider two possibilities.

The first possibility is that the change affects a single source file. In that case, only that file must be recompiled. (After that, the entire program will need to be relinked, of course.) Consider the `justify` program. Suppose that we decide to condense the `read_char` function in `word.c` (changes are marked in **bold**):

```
int read_char(void)
{
  int ch = getchar();

  return (ch == '\n' || ch == '\t') ? ' ' : ch;
}
```

This modification doesn't affect `word.h`, so we need only recompile `word.c` and relink the program.

The second possibility is that the change affects a header file. In that case, we should recompile all files that include the header file, since they could potentially be affected by the change. (Some of them might not be, but it pays to be conservative.)

As an example, consider the `read_word` function in the `justify` program. Notice that `main` calls `strlen` immediately after calling `read_word`, in order to determine the length of the word that was just read. Since `read_word` already knows the length of the word (`read_word`'s `pos` variable keeps track of the length), it seems silly to use `strlen`. Modifying `read_word` to return the word's length is easy. First, we change the prototype of `read_word` in `word.h`:

```
/****************************************************************
 * read_word: Reads the next word from the input and           *
 *            stores it in word. Makes word empty if no         *
 *            word could be read because of end-of-file.        *
 *            Truncates the word if its length exceeds          *
 *            len. Returns the number of characters             *
 *            stored.                                           *
 ****************************************************************/
int read_word(char *word, int len);
```

Of course, we're careful to change the comment that accompanies read_word. Next, we change the definition of read_word in word.c:

```
int read_word(char *word, int len)
{
  int ch, pos = 0;

  while ((ch = read_char()) == ' ')
    ;
  while (ch != ' ' && ch != EOF) {
    if (pos < len)
      word[pos++] = ch;
    ch = read_char();
  }
  word[pos] = '\0';
  return pos;
}
```

Finally, we modify justify.c by removing the include of <string.h> and changing main as follows:

```
int main(void)
{
  char word[MAX_WORD_LEN+2];
  int word_len;

  clear_line();
  for (;;) {
    word_len = read_word(word, MAX_WORD_LEN+1);
    if (word_len == 0) {
      flush_line();
      return 0;
    }
    if (word_len > MAX_WORD_LEN)
      word[MAX_WORD_LEN] = '*';
    if (word_len + 1 > space_remaining()) {
      write_line();
      clear_line();
    }
    add_word(word);
  }
}
```

Once we've made these changes, we'll rebuild the `justify` program by recompiling `word.c` and `justify.c` and then relinking. There's no need to recompile `line.c`, which doesn't include `word.h` and therefore won't be affected by changes to it. With the GCC compiler, we could use the following command to rebuild the program:

```
gcc -o justify justify.c word.c line.o
```

Note the mention of `line.o` instead of `line.c`.

One of the advantages of using makefiles is that rebuilding is handled automatically. By examining the date of each file, the `make` utility can determine which files have changed since the program was last built. It then recompiles these files, together with all files that depend on them, either directly or indirectly. For example, if we make the indicated changes to `word.h`, `word.c`, and `justify.c` and then rebuild the `justify` program, `make` will perform the following actions:

1. Build `justify.o` by compiling `justify.c` (because `justify.c` and `word.h` were changed).

2. Build `word.o` by compiling `word.c` (because `word.c` and `word.h` were changed).

3. Build `justify` by linking `justify.o`, `word.o`, and `line.o` (because `justify.o` and `word.o` were changed).

Defining Macros Outside a Program

C compilers usually provide some method of specifying the value of a macro at the time a program is compiled. This ability makes it easy to change the value of a macro without editing any of the program's files. It's especially valuable when programs are built automatically using makefiles.

Most compilers (including GCC) support the `-D` option, which allows the value of a macro to be specified on the command line:

```
gcc -DDEBUG=1 foo.c
```

In this example, the `DEBUG` macro is defined to have the value `1` in the program `foo.c`, just as if the line

```
#define DEBUG 1
```

appeared at the beginning of `foo.c`. If the `-D` option names a macro without specifying its value, the value is taken to be `1`.

predefined macros ➤ 14.3   Many compilers also support the `-U` option, which "undefines" a macro as if by using `#undef`. We can use `-U` to undefine a predefined macro or one that was defined earlier in the command line using `-D`.

Q & A

Q: **You don't have any examples that use the #include directive to include a source file. What would happen if we were to do this?**

A: That's not a good practice, although it's not illegal. Here's an example of the kind of trouble you can get into. Suppose that foo.c defines a function f that we'll need in bar.c and baz.c, so we put the directive

```
#include "foo.c"
```

in both bar.c and baz.c. Each of these files will compile nicely. The problem comes later, when the linker discovers two copies of the object code for f. Of course, we would have gotten away with including foo.c if only bar.c had included it, not baz.c as well. To avoid problems, it's best to use #include only with header files, not source files.

Q: **What are the exact search rules for the #include directive? [p. 351]**

A: That depends on your compiler. The C standard is deliberately vague in its description of #include. If the file name is enclosed in *brackets*, the preprocessor looks in a "sequence of implementation-defined places," as the standard obliquely puts it. If the file name is enclosed in *quotation marks*, the file "is searched for in an implementation-defined manner" and, if not found, then searched as if its name had been enclosed in brackets. The reason for this waffling is simple: not all operating systems have hierarchical (tree-like) file systems.

To make matters even more interesting, the standard doesn't require that names enclosed in brackets be file names at all, leaving open the possibility that #include directives using < > are handled entirely within the compiler.

Q: **I don't understand why each source file needs its own header file. Why not have one big header file containing macro definitions, type definitions, and function prototypes? By including this file, each source file would have access to all the shared information it needs. [p. 354]**

A: The "one big header file" approach certainly works; a number of programmers use it. And it does have an advantage: with only one header file, there are fewer files to manage. For large programs, however, the disadvantages of this approach tend to outweigh its advantages.

Using a single header file provides no useful information to someone reading the program later. With multiple header files, the reader can quickly see what other parts of the program are used by a particular source file.

But that's not all. Since each source file depends on the big header file, changing it will cause all source files to be recompiled—a significant drawback in a large program. To make matters worse, the header file will probably change frequently because of the large amount of information it contains.

Q: **The chapter says that a shared array should be declared as follows:**

```
extern int a[];
```

Since arrays and pointers are closely related, would it be legal to write

```
extern int *a;
```

instead? [p. 356]

A: No. When used in expressions, arrays "decay" into pointers. (We've noticed this behavior when an array name is used as an argument in a function call.) In variable declarations, however, arrays and pointers are distinct types.

Q: **Does it hurt if a source file includes headers that it doesn't really need?**

A: Not unless the header has a declaration or definition that conflicts with one in the source file. Otherwise, the worst that can happen is a minor increase in the time it takes to compile the source file.

Q: **I needed to call a function in the file foo.c, so I included the matching header file, foo.h. My program compiled, but it won't link. Why?**

A: Compilation and linking are completely separate in C. Header files exist to provide information to the compiler, not the linker. If you want to call a function in foo.c, then you have to make sure that foo.c is compiled and that the linker is aware that it must search the object file for foo.c to find the function. Usually this means naming foo.c in the program's makefile or project file.

Q: **If my program calls a function in <stdio.h>, does that mean that all functions in <stdio.h> will be linked with the program?**

A: No. Including <stdio.h> (or any other header) has no effect on linking. In any event, most linkers will link only functions that your program actually needs.

Q: **Where can I get the make utility? [p. 367]**

A: make is a standard UNIX utility. The GNU version, known as GNU Make, is included in most Linux distributions. It's also available directly from the Free Software Foundation (*www.gnu.org/software/make/*).

Exercises

Section 15.1

1. Section 15.1 listed several advantages of dividing a program into multiple source files.

(a) Describe several other advantages.

(b) Describe some disadvantages.

Section 15.2 Ⓦ 2. Which of the following should *not* be put in a header file? Why not?

(a) Function prototypes

(b) Function definitions

    (c) Macro definitions

    (d) Type definitions

3.   We saw that writing #include <*file*> instead of #include "*file*" may not work if *file* is one that we've written. Would there be any problem with writing #include "*file*" instead of #include <*file*> if *file* is a system header?

4.   Assume that debug.h is a header file with the following contents:

```
#ifdef DEBUG
#define PRINT_DEBUG(n) printf("Value of " #n ": %d\n", n)
#else
#define PRINT_DEBUG(n)
#endif
```

Let testdebug.c be the following source file:

```
#include <stdio.h>

#define DEBUG
#include "debug.h"

int main(void)
{
   int i = 1, j = 2, k = 3;

#ifdef DEBUG
   printf("Output if DEBUG is defined:\n");
#else
   printf("Output if DEBUG is not defined:\n");
#endif

   PRINT_DEBUG(i);
   PRINT_DEBUG(j);
   PRINT_DEBUG(k);
   PRINT_DEBUG(i + j);
   PRINT_DEBUG(2 * i + j - k);

   return 0;
}
```

    (a) What is the output when the program is executed?

    (b) What is the output if the #define directive is removed from testdebug.c?

    (c) Explain why the output is different in parts (a) and (b).

    (d) Is it necessary for the DEBUG macro to be defined *before* debug.h is included in order for PRINT_DEBUG to have the desired effect? Justify your answer.

Section 15.4   5.   Suppose that a program consists of three source files—main.c, f1.c, and f2.c—plus two header files, f1.h and f2.h. All three source files include f1.h, but only f1.c and f2.c include f2.h. Write a makefile for this program, assuming that the compiler is gcc and that the executable file is to be named demo.

   Ⓦ 6.   The following questions refer to the program described in Exercise 5.

    (a) Which files need to be compiled when the program is built for the first time?

    (b) If f1.c is changed after the program has been built, which files need to be recompiled?

    (c) If f1.h is changed after the program has been built, which files need to be recompiled?

    (d) If f2.h is changed after the program has been built, which files need to be recompiled?

Programming Projects

1. The `justify` program of Section 15.3 justifies lines by inserting extra spaces between words. The way the `write_line` function currently works, the words closer to the end of a line tend to have slightly wider gaps between them than the words at the beginning. (For example, the words closer to the end might have three spaces between them, while the words closer to the beginning might be separated by only two spaces.) Improve the program by having `write_line` alternate between putting the larger gaps at the end of the line and putting them at the beginning of the line.

2. Modify the `justify` program of Section 15.3 by having the `read_word` function (instead of `main`) store the `*` character at the end of a word that's been truncated.

3. Modify the `qsort.c` program of Section 9.6 so that the `quicksort` and `split` functions are in a separate file named `quicksort.c`. Create a header file named `quicksort.h` that contains prototypes for the two functions and have both `qsort.c` and `quicksort.c` include this file.

4. Modify the `remind.c` program of Section 13.5 so that the `read_line` function is in a separate file named `readline.c`. Create a header file named `readline.h` that contains a prototype for the function and have both `remind.c` and `readline.c` include this file.

5. Modify Programming Project 6 from Chapter 10 so that it has separate `stack.h` and `stack.c` files, as described in Section 15.2.

16 Structures, Unions, and Enumerations

Functions delay binding: data structures induce binding.
Moral: Structure data late in the programming process.

This chapter introduces three new types: structures, unions, and enumerations. A structure is a collection of values (members), possibly of different types. A union is similar to a structure, except that its members share the same storage; as a result, a union can store one member at a time, but not all members simultaneously. An enumeration is an integer type whose values are named by the programmer.

Of these three types, structures are by far the most important, so I'll devote most of the chapter to them. Section 16.1 shows how to declare structure variables and perform basic operations on them. Section 16.2 then explains how to define structure types, which—among other things—allow us to write functions that accept structure arguments or return structures. Section 16.3 explores how arrays and structures can be nested. The last two sections are devoted to unions (Section 16.4) and enumerations (Section 16.5).

16.1 Structure Variables

The only data structure we've covered so far is the array. Arrays have two important properties. First, all elements of an array have the same type. Second, to select an array element, we specify its position (as an integer subscript).

The properties of a *structure* are quite different from those of an array. The elements of a structure (its *members*, in C parlance) aren't required to have the same type. Furthermore, the members of a structure have names; to select a particular member, we specify its name, not its position.

Structures may sound familiar, since most programming languages provide a similar feature. In some languages, structures are called *records,* and members are known as *fields*.

Declaring Structure Variables

When we need to store a collection of related data items, a structure is a logical choice. For example, suppose that we need to keep track of parts in a warehouse. The information that we'll need to store for each part might include a part number (an integer), a part name (a string of characters), and the number of parts on hand (an integer). To create variables that can store all three items of data, we might use a declaration such as the following:

```
struct {
  int number;
  char name[NAME_LEN+1];
  int on_hand;
} part1, part2;
```

Each structure variable has three members: `number` (the part number), `name` (the name of the part), and `on_hand` (the quantity on hand). Notice that this declaration has the same form as other variable declarations in C: `struct { ... }` specifies a type, while `part1` and `part2` are variables of that type.

The members of a structure are stored in memory in the order in which they're declared. In order to show what the `part1` variable looks like in memory, let's assume that (1) `part1` is located at address 2000, (2) integers occupy four bytes, (3) `NAME_LEN` has the value 25, and (4) there are no gaps between the members. With these assumptions, `part1` will have the following appearance:

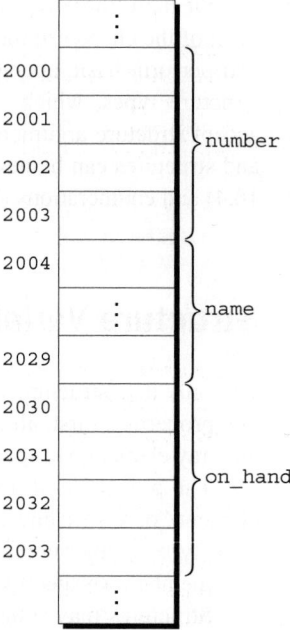

Usually it's not necessary to draw structures in such detail. I'll normally show them more abstractly, as a series of boxes:

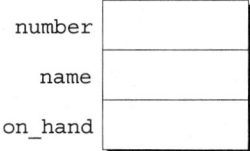

I may sometimes draw the boxes horizontally instead of vertically:

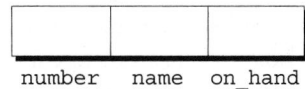

Member values will go in the boxes later; for now, I've left them empty.

Each structure represents a new scope; any names declared in that scope won't conflict with other names in a program. (In C terminology, we say that each structure has a separate *name space* for its members.) For example, the following declarations can appear in the same program:

```
struct {
  int number;
  char name[NAME_LEN+1];
  int on_hand;
} part1, part2;

struct {
  char name[NAME_LEN+1];
  int number;
  char sex;
} employee1, employee2;
```

The `number` and `name` members in the `part1` and `part2` structures don't conflict with the `number` and `name` members in `employee1` and `employee2`.

Initializing Structure Variables

Like an array, a structure variable may be initialized at the time it's declared. To initialize a structure, we prepare a list of values to be stored in the structure and enclose it in braces:

```
struct {
  int number;
  char name[NAME_LEN+1];
  int on_hand;
} part1 = {528, "Disk drive", 10},
  part2 = {914, "Printer cable", 5};
```

The values in the initializer must appear in the same order as the members of the structure. In our example, the `number` member of `part1` will be 528, the `name` member will be `"Disk drive"`, and so on. Here's how `part1` will look after initialization:

number	528
name	Disk drive
on_hand	10

Structure initializers follow rules similar to those for array initializers. Expressions used in a structure initializer must be constant; for example, we couldn't have used a variable to initialize `part1`'s `on_hand` member. (This restriction is relaxed in C99, as we'll see in Section 18.5.) An initializer can have fewer members than the structure it's initializing; as with arrays, any "leftover" members are given 0 as their initial value. In particular, the bytes in a leftover character array will be zero, making it represent the empty string.

C99

Designated Initializers

C99's designated initializers, which were discussed in Section 8.1 in the context of arrays, can also be used with structures. Consider the initializer for `part1` shown in the previous example:

```
{528, "Disk drive", 10}
```

A designated initializer would look similar, but with each value labeled by the name of the member that it initializes:

```
{.number = 528, .name = "Disk drive", .on_hand = 10}
```

The combination of the period and the member name is called a ***designator***. (Designators for array elements have a different form.)

Designated initializers have several advantages. For one, they're easier to read and check for correctness, because the reader can clearly see the correspondence between the members of the structure and the values listed in the initializer. Another is that the values in the initializer don't have to be placed in the same order that the members are listed in the structure. Our example initializer could be written as follows:

```
{.on_hand = 10, .name = "Disk drive", .number = 528}
```

Since the order doesn't matter, the programmer doesn't have to remember the order in which the members were originally declared. Moreover, the order of the members can be changed in the future without affecting designated initializers.

Not all values listed in a designated initializer need be prefixed by a designator. (This is true for arrays as well, as we saw in Section 8.1.) Consider the following example:

```
{.number = 528, "Disk drive", .on_hand = 10}
```

The value `"Disk drive"` doesn't have a designator, so the compiler assumes that it initializes the member that follows `number` in the structure. Any members that the initializer fails to account for are set to zero.

Operations on Structures

Since the most common array operation is subscripting—selecting an element by position—it's not surprising that the most common operation on a structure is selecting one of its members. Structure members are accessed by name, though, not by position.

To access a member within a structure, we write the name of the structure first, then a period, then the name of the member. For example, the following statements will display the values of `part1`'s members:

```
printf("Part number: %d\n", part1.number);
printf("Part name: %s\n", part1.name);
printf("Quantity on hand: %d\n", part1.on_hand);
```

lvalues ►4.2   The members of a structure are lvalues, so they can appear on the left side of an assignment or as the operand in an increment or decrement expression:

```
part1.number = 258;        /* changes part1's part number */
part1.on_hand++;   /* increments part1's quantity on hand */
```

table of operators ►Appendix A   The period that we use to access a structure member is actually a C operator. It has the same precedence as the postfix `++` and `--` operators, so it takes precedence over nearly all other operators. Consider the following example:

```
scanf("%d", &part1.on_hand);
```

The expression `&part1.on_hand` contains two operators (`&` and `.`). The `.` operator takes precedence over the `&` operator, so `&` computes the address of `part1.on_hand`, as we wished.

The other major structure operation is assignment:

```
part2 = part1;
```

The effect of this statement is to copy `part1.number` into `part2.number`, `part1.name` into `part2.name`, and so on.

Since arrays can't be copied using the `=` operator, it comes as something of a surprise to discover that structures can. It's even more surprising when you consider that an array embedded within a structure is copied when the enclosing structure is copied. Some programmers exploit this property by creating "dummy" structures to enclose arrays that will be copied later:

```
struct { int a[10]; } a1, a2;

a1 = a2;    /* legal, since a1 and a2 are structures */
```

The = operator can be used only with structures of ***compatible*** types. Two structures declared at the same time (as part1 and part2 were) are compatible. As we'll see in the next section, structures declared using the same "structure tag" or the same type name are also compatible.

Other than assignment, C provides no operations on entire structures. In particular, we can't use the == and != operators to test whether two structures are equal or not equal.

Q&A

16.2 Structure Types

Although the previous section showed how to declare structure *variables,* it failed to discuss an important issue: naming structure *types.* Suppose that a program needs to declare several structure variables with identical members. If all the variables can be declared at one time, there's no problem. But if we need to declare the variables at different points in the program, then life becomes more difficult. If we write

```
struct {
  int number;
  char name[NAME_LEN+1];
  int on_hand;
} part1;
```

in one place and

```
struct {
  int number;
  char name[NAME_LEN+1];
  int on_hand;
} part2;
```

in another, we'll quickly run into problems. Repeating the structure information will bloat the program. Changing the program later will be risky, since we can't easily guarantee that the declarations will remain consistent.

But those aren't the biggest problems. According to the rules of C, part1 and part2 don't have compatible types. As a result, part1 can't be assigned to part2, and vice versa. Also, since we don't have a name for the type of part1 or part2, we can't use them as arguments in function calls.

To avoid these difficulties, we need to be able to define a name that represents a *type* of structure, not a particular structure *variable.* As it turns out, C provides two ways to name structures: we can either declare a "structure tag" or use typedef to define a type name.

Q&A

type definitions ➤ *7.5*

Declaring a Structure Tag

A *structure tag* is a name used to identify a particular kind of structure. The following example declares a structure tag named `part`:

```
struct part {
  int number;
  char name[NAME_LEN+1];
  int on_hand;
};
```

Notice the semicolon that follows the right brace—it must be present to terminate the declaration.

Accidentally omitting the semicolon at the end of a structure declaration can cause surprising errors. Consider the following example:

```
struct part {
  int number;
  char name[NAME_LEN+1];
  int on_hand;
}                  /*** WRONG: semicolon missing ***/

f(void)
{
  ...
  return 0;    /* error detected at this line */
}
```

The programmer failed to specify the return type of the function `f` (a bit of sloppy programming). Since the preceding structure declaration wasn't terminated properly, the compiler assumes that `f` returns a value of type `struct part`. The error won't be detected until the compiler reaches the first `return` statement in the function. The result: a cryptic error message.

Once we've created the `part` tag, we can use it to declare variables:

```
struct part part1, part2;
```

Unfortunately, we can't abbreviate this declaration by dropping the word `struct`:

```
part part1, part2;    /*** WRONG ***/
```

`part` isn't a type name; without the word `struct`, it is meaningless.

Since structure tags aren't recognized unless preceded by the word `struct`, they don't conflict with other names used in a program. It would be perfectly legal (although more than a little confusing) to have a variable named `part`.

Incidentally, the declaration of a structure *tag* can be combined with the declaration of structure *variables*:

```
struct part {
  int number;
  char name[NAME_LEN+1];
  int on_hand;
} part1, part2;
```

Here, we've declared a structure tag named `part` (making it possible to use `part` later to declare more variables) as well as variables named `part1` and `part2`.

All structures declared to have type `struct part` are compatible with one another:

```
struct part part1 = {528, "Disk drive", 10};
struct part part2;

part2 = part1;    /* legal; both parts have the same type */
```

Defining a Structure Type

As an alternative to declaring a structure tag, we can use `typedef` to define a genuine type name. For example, we could define a type named `Part` in the following way:

```
typedef struct {
  int number;
  char name[NAME_LEN+1];
  int on_hand;
} Part;
```

Note that the name of the type, `Part`, must come at the end, not after the word `struct`.

We can use `Part` in the same way as the built-in types. For example, we might use it to declare variables:

```
Part part1, part2;
```

Since `Part` is a `typedef` name, we're not allowed to write `struct Part`. All `Part` variables, regardless of where they're declared, are compatible.

Q&A

linked lists ➤ 17.5When it comes time to name a structure, we can usually choose either to declare a structure tag or to use `typedef`. However, as we'll see later, declaring a structure tag is mandatory when the structure is to be used in a linked list. I'll use structure tags rather than `typedef` names in most of my examples.

Structures as Arguments and Return Values

Functions may have structures as arguments and return values. Let's look at two examples. Our first function, when given a `part` structure as its argument, prints the structure's members:

```
void print_part(struct part p)
{
  printf("Part number: %d\n", p.number);
```

```
    printf("Part name: %s\n", p.name);
    printf("Quantity on hand: %d\n", p.on_hand);
}
```

Here's how `print_part` might be called:

```
print_part(part1);
```

Our second function returns a `part` structure that it constructs from its arguments:

```
struct part build_part(int number, const char *name,
                       int on_hand)
{
    struct part p;

    p.number = number;
    strcpy(p.name, name);
    p.on_hand = on_hand;
    return p;
}
```

Notice that it's legal for `build_part`'s parameters to have names that match the members of the `part` structure, since the structure has its own name space. Here's how `build_part` might be called:

```
part1 = build_part(528, "Disk drive", 10);
```

Passing a structure to a function and returning a structure from a function both require making a copy of all members in the structure. As a result, these operations impose a fair amount of overhead on a program, especially if the structure is large. To avoid this overhead, it's sometimes advisable to pass a *pointer* to a structure instead of passing the structure itself. Similarly, we might have a function return a pointer to a structure instead of returning an actual structure. Section 17.5 gives examples of functions that have a pointer to a structure as an argument and/or return a pointer to a structure.

There are other reasons to avoid copying structures besides efficiency. For example, the `<stdio.h>` header defines a type named FILE, which is typically a structure. Each FILE structure stores information about the state of an open file and therefore must be unique in a program. Every function in `<stdio.h>` that opens a file returns a pointer to a FILE structure, and every function that performs an operation on an open file requires a FILE pointer as an argument.

FILE type ▶22.1

On occasion, we may want to initialize a structure variable inside a function to match another structure, possibly supplied as a parameter to the function. In the following example, the initializer for `part2` is the parameter passed to the `f` function:

```
void f(struct part part1)
{
    struct part part2 = part1;
    ...
}
```

automatic storage duration ➤ 10.1

C permits initializers of this kind, provided that the structure we're initializing (part2, in this case) has automatic storage duration (it's local to a function and hasn't been declared `static`). The initializer can be any expression of the proper type, including a function call that returns a structure.

C99 **Compound Literals**

Section 9.3 introduced the C99 feature known as the ***compound literal.*** In that section, compound literals were used to create unnamed arrays, usually for the purpose of passing the array to a function. A compound literal can also be used to create a structure "on the fly," without first storing it in a variable. The resulting structure can be passed as a parameter, returned by a function, or assigned to a variable. Let's look at a couple of examples.

First, we can use a compound literal to create a structure that will be passed to a function. For example, we could call the `print_part` function as follows:

```
print_part((struct part) {528, "Disk drive", 10});
```

The compound literal (shown in **bold**) creates a `part` structure containing the members 528, `"Disk drive"`, and 10, in that order. This structure is then passed to `print_part`, which displays it.

Here's how a compound literal might be assigned to a variable:

```
part1 = (struct part) {528, "Disk drive", 10};
```

This statement resembles a declaration containing an initializer, but it's not the same—initializers can appear only in declarations, not in statements such as this one.

In general, a compound literal consists of a type name within parentheses, followed by a set of values enclosed by braces. In the case of a compound literal that represents a structure, the type name can be a structure tag preceded by the word `struct`—as in our examples—or a `typedef` name. A compound literal may contain designators, just like a designated initializer:

```
print_part((struct part) {.on_hand = 10,
                          .name = "Disk drive",
                          .number = 528});
```

A compound literal may fail to provide full initialization, in which case any uninitialized members default to zero.

16.3   Nested Arrays and Structures

Structures and arrays can be combined without restriction. Arrays may have structures as their elements, and structures may contain arrays and structures as members. We've already seen an example of an array nested inside a structure (the name member of the part structure). Let's explore the other possibilities: structures whose members are structures and arrays whose elements are structures.

Nested Structures

Nesting one kind of structure inside another is often useful. For example, suppose that we've declared the following structure, which can store a person's first name, middle initial, and last name:

```
struct person_name {
  char first[FIRST_NAME_LEN+1];
  char middle_initial;
  char last[LAST_NAME_LEN+1];
};
```

We can use the person_name structure as part of a larger structure:

```
struct student {
  struct person_name name;
  int id, age;
  char sex;
} student1, student2;
```

Accessing student1's first name, middle initial, or last name requires two applications of the . operator:

```
strcpy(student1.name.first, "Fred");
```

One advantage of making name a structure (instead of having first, middle_initial, and last be members of the student structure) is that we can more easily treat names as units of data. For example, if we were to write a function that displays a name, we could pass it just one argument—a person_name structure—instead of three arguments:

```
display_name(student1.name);
```

Likewise, copying the information from a person_name structure to the name member of a student structure would take one assignment instead of three:

```
struct person_name new_name;
...
student1.name = new_name;
```

Arrays of Structures

One of the most common combinations of arrays and structures is an array whose elements are structures. An array of this kind can serve as a simple database. For example, the following array of part structures is capable of storing information about 100 parts:

```
struct part inventory[100];
```

To access one of the parts in the array, we'd use subscripting. To print the part stored in position i, for example, we could write

```
print_part(inventory[i]);
```

Accessing a member within a part structure requires a combination of subscripting and member selection. To assign 883 to the number member of inventory[i], we could write

```
inventory[i].number = 883;
```

Accessing a single character in a part name requires subscripting (to select a particular part), followed by selection (to select the name member), followed by subscripting (to select a character within the part name). To change the name stored in inventory[i] to an empty string, we could write

```
inventory[i].name[0] = '\0';
```

Initializing an Array of Structures

Initializing an array of structures is done in much the same way as initializing a multidimensional array. Each structure has its own brace-enclosed initializer; the initializer for the array simply wraps another set of braces around the structure initializers.

One reason for initializing an array of structures is that we're planning to treat it as a database of information that won't change during program execution. For example, suppose that we're working on a program that will need access to the country codes used when making international telephone calls. First, we'll set up a structure that can store the name of a country along with its code:

```
struct dialing_code {
  char *country;
  int code;
};
```

Note that country is a pointer, not an array of characters. That could be a problem if we were planning to use dialing_code structures as variables, but we're not. When we initialize a dialing_code structure, country will end up pointing to a string literal.

Next, we'll declare an array of these structures and initialize it to contain the codes for some of the world's most populous nations:

```
const struct dialing_code country_codes[] =
  {{"Argentina",            54}, {"Bangladesh",       880},
   {"Brazil",               55}, {"Burma (Myanmar)",   95},
   {"China",                86}, {"Colombia",          57},
   {"Congo, Dem. Rep. of", 243}, {"Egypt",             20},
   {"Ethiopia",            251}, {"France",            33},
   {"Germany",              49}, {"India",             91},
```

```
{"Indonesia",              62}, {"Iran",               98},
{"Italy",                  39}, {"Japan",              81},
{"Mexico",                 52}, {"Nigeria",           234},
{"Pakistan",               92}, {"Philippines",        63},
{"Poland",                 48}, {"Russia",              7},
{"South Africa",           27}, {"South Korea",        82},
{"Spain",                  34}, {"Sudan",             249},
{"Thailand",               66}, {"Turkey",             90},
{"Ukraine",               380}, {"United Kingdom",     44},
{"United States",           1}, {"Vietnam",            84}};
```

The inner braces around each structure value are optional. As a matter of style, however, I prefer not to omit them.

 Because arrays of structures (and structures containing arrays) are so common, C99's designated initializers allow an item to have more than one designator. Suppose that we want to initialize the `inventory` array to contain a single part. The part number is 528 and the quantity on hand is 10, but the name is to be left empty for now:

```
struct part inventory[100] =
  {[0].number = 528, [0].on_hand = 10, [0].name[0] = '\0'};
```

The first two items in the list use two designators (one to select array element 0—a `part` structure—and one to select a member within the structure). The last item uses three designators: one to select an array element, one to select the `name` member within that element, and one to select element 0 of `name`.

PROGRAM **Maintaining a Parts Database**

To illustrate how nested arrays and structures are used in practice, we'll now develop a fairly long program that maintains a database of information about parts stored in a warehouse. The program is built around an array of structures, with each structure containing information—part number, name, and quantity—about one part. Our program will support the following operations:

- *Add a new part number, part name, and initial quantity on hand.* The program must print an error message if the part is already in the database or if the database is full.

- *Given a part number, print the name of the part and the current quantity on hand.* The program must print an error message if the part number isn't in the database.

- *Given a part number, change the quantity on hand.* The program must print an error message if the part number isn't in the database.

- *Print a table showing all information in the database.* Parts must be displayed in the order in which they were entered.

- *Terminate program execution.*

We'll use the codes i (insert), s (search), u (update), p (print), and q (quit) to represent these operations. A session with the program might look like this:

```
Enter operation code: i
Enter part number: 528
Enter part name: Disk drive
Enter quantity on hand: 10

Enter operation code: s
Enter part number: 528
Part name: Disk drive
Quantity on hand: 10

Enter operation code: s
Enter part number: 914
Part not found.

Enter operation code: i
Enter part number: 914
Enter part name: Printer cable
Enter quantity on hand: 5

Enter operation code: u
Enter part number: 528
Enter change in quantity on hand: -2

Enter operation code: s
Enter part number: 528
Part name: Disk drive
Quantity on hand: 8

Enter operation code: p
Part Number    Part Name                        Quantity on Hand
    528        Disk drive                              8
    914        Printer cable                           5

Enter operation code: q
```

The program will store information about each part in a structure. We'll limit the size of the database to 100 parts, making it possible to store the structures in an array, which I'll call inventory. (If this limit proves to be too small, we can always change it later.) To keep track of the number of parts currently stored in the array, we'll use a variable named num_parts.

Since this program is menu-driven, it's fairly easy to sketch the main loop:

```
for (;;) {
  prompt user to enter operation code;
  read code;
  switch (code) {
    case 'i': perform insert operation; break;
    case 's': perform search operation; break;
    case 'u': perform update operation; break;
    case 'p': perform print operation; break;
```

```
      case 'q': terminate program;
      default:  print error message;
  }
}
```

It will be convenient to have separate functions perform the insert, search, update, and print operations. Since these functions will all need access to `inventory` and `num_parts`, we might want to make these variables external. As an alternative, we could declare the variables inside `main`, and then pass them to the functions as arguments. From a design standpoint, it's usually better to make variables local to a function rather than making them external (see Section 10.2 if you've forgotten why). In this program, however, putting `inventory` and `num_parts` inside `main` would merely complicate matters.

For reasons that I'll explain later, I've decided to split the program into three files: `inventory.c`, which contains the bulk of the program; `readline.h`, which contains the prototype for the `read_line` function; and `readline.c`, which contains the definition of `read_line`. We'll discuss the latter two files later in this section. For now, let's concentrate on `inventory.c`.

inventory.c

```
/* Maintains a parts database (array version) */

#include <stdio.h>
#include "readline.h"

#define NAME_LEN 25
#define MAX_PARTS 100

struct part {
  int number;
  char name[NAME_LEN+1];
  int on_hand;
} inventory[MAX_PARTS];

int num_parts = 0;   /* number of parts currently stored */

int find_part(int number);
void insert(void);
void search(void);
void update(void);
void print(void);

/************************************************************
 * main: Prompts the user to enter an operation code,      *
 *       then calls a function to perform the requested    *
 *       action. Repeats until the user enters the         *
 *       command 'q'. Prints an error message if the user  *
 *       enters an illegal code.                            *
 ************************************************************/
int main(void)
{
  char code;
```

```
    for (;;) {
      printf("Enter operation code: ");
      scanf(" %c", &code);
      while (getchar() != '\n')    /* skips to end of line */
        ;
      switch (code) {
        case 'i': insert();
                  break;
        case 's': search();
                  break;
        case 'u': update();
                  break;
        case 'p': print();
                  break;
        case 'q': return 0;
        default:  printf("Illegal code\n");
      }
      printf("\n");
    }
}

/**********************************************************
 * find_part: Looks up a part number in the inventory     *
 *            array. Returns the array index if the part   *
 *            number is found; otherwise, returns -1.     *
 **********************************************************/
int find_part(int number)
{
  int i;

  for (i = 0; i < num_parts; i++)
    if (inventory[i].number == number)
      return i;
  return -1;
}

/**********************************************************
 * insert: Prompts the user for information about a new   *
 *         part and then inserts the part into the        *
 *         database. Prints an error message and returns  *
 *         prematurely if the part already exists or the  *
 *         database is full.                              *
 **********************************************************/
void insert(void)
{
  int part_number;

  if (num_parts == MAX_PARTS) {
    printf("Database is full; can't add more parts.\n");
    return;
  }

  printf("Enter part number: ");
  scanf("%d", &part_number);
```

```
  if (find_part(part_number) >= 0) {
    printf("Part already exists.\n");
    return;
  }

  inventory[num_parts].number = part_number;
  printf("Enter part name: ");
  read_line(inventory[num_parts].name, NAME_LEN);
  printf("Enter quantity on hand: ");
  scanf("%d", &inventory[num_parts].on_hand);
  num_parts++;
}

/**********************************************************
 * search: Prompts the user to enter a part number, then  *
 *         looks up the part in the database. If the part  *
 *         exists, prints the name and quantity on hand;   *
 *         if not, prints an error message.                *
 **********************************************************/
void search(void)
{
  int i, number;

  printf("Enter part number: ");
  scanf("%d", &number);
  i = find_part(number);
  if (i >= 0) {
    printf("Part name: %s\n", inventory[i].name);
    printf("Quantity on hand: %d\n", inventory[i].on_hand);
  } else
    printf("Part not found.\n");
}

/**********************************************************
 * update: Prompts the user to enter a part number.       *
 *         Prints an error message if the part doesn't     *
 *         exist; otherwise, prompts the user to enter     *
 *         change in quantity on hand and updates the      *
 *         database.                                       *
 **********************************************************/
void update(void)
{
  int i, number, change;

  printf("Enter part number: ");
  scanf("%d", &number);
  i = find_part(number);
  if (i >= 0) {
    printf("Enter change in quantity on hand: ");
    scanf("%d", &change);
    inventory[i].on_hand += change;
  } else
    printf("Part not found.\n");
}
```

```
/*************************************************************
 * print: Prints a listing of all parts in the database,  *
 *        showing the part number, part name, and         *
 *        quantity on hand. Parts are printed in the      *
 *        order in which they were entered into the       *
 *        database.                                       *
 *************************************************************/
void print(void)
{
  int i;

  printf("Part Number    Part Name                    "
         "Quantity on Hand\n");
  for (i = 0; i < num_parts; i++)
    printf("%7d         %-25s%11d\n", inventory[i].number,
           inventory[i].name, inventory[i].on_hand);
}
```

In the main function, the format string " %c" allows scanf to skip over white space before reading the operation code. The space in the format string is crucial; without it, scanf would sometimes read the new-line character that terminated a previous line of input.

The program contains one function, find_part, that isn't called from main. This "helper" function helps us avoid redundant code and simplify the more important functions. By calling find_part, the insert, search, and update functions can locate a part in the database (or simply determine if the part exists).

There's just one detail left: the read_line function, which the program uses to read the part name. Section 13.3 discussed the issues that are involved in writing such a function. Unfortunately, the version of read_line in that section won't work properly in the current program. Consider what happens when the user inserts a part:

```
Enter part number: 528
Enter part name: Disk drive
```

The user presses the Enter key after entering the part number and again after entering the part name, each time leaving an invisible new-line character that the program must read. For the sake of discussion, let's pretend that these characters are visible:

```
Enter part number: 528¤
Enter part name: Disk drive¤
```

When we call scanf to read the part number, it consumes the 5, 2, and 8, but leaves the ¤ character unread. If we try to read the part name using our original read_line function, it will encounter the ¤ character immediately and stop reading. This problem is common when numerical input is followed by character input. Our solution will be to write a version of read_line that skips white-space characters before it begins storing characters. Not only will this solve the new-line problem, but it also allows us to avoid storing any blanks that precede the part name.

Since `read_line` is unrelated to the other functions in `inventory.c`, and since it's potentially reusable in other programs, I've decided to separate it from `inventory.c`. The prototype for `read_line` will go in the `readline.h` header file:

readline.h

```
#ifndef READLINE_H
#define READLINE_H

/**************************************************************
 * read_line: Skips leading white-space characters, then     *
 *            reads the remainder of the input line and       *
 *            stores it in str. Truncates the line if its    *
 *            length exceeds n. Returns the number of         *
 *            characters stored.                              *
 **************************************************************/
int read_line(char str[], int n);

#endif
```

We'll put the definition of `read_line` in the `readline.c` file:

readline.c

```
#include <ctype.h>
#include <stdio.h>
#include "readline.h"

int read_line(char str[], int n)
{
  int ch, i = 0;

  while (isspace(ch = getchar()))
    ;
  while (ch != '\n' && ch != EOF) {
    if (i < n)
      str[i++] = ch;
    ch = getchar();
  }
  str[i] = '\0';
  return i;
}
```

The expression

```
isspace(ch = getchar())
```

isspace function ➤ 23.5

controls the first `while` statement. This expression calls `getchar` to read a character, stores the character into `ch`, and then uses the `isspace` function to test whether `ch` is a white-space character. If not, the loop terminates with `ch` containing a character that's not white space. Section 15.3 explains why `ch` has type `int` instead of `char` and why it's good to test for EOF.

16.4 Unions

A *union*, like a structure, consists of one or more members, possibly of different types. However, the compiler allocates only enough space for the largest of the members, which overlay each other within this space. As a result, assigning a new value to one member alters the values of the other members as well.

To illustrate the basic properties of unions, let's declare a union variable, u, with two members:

```
union {
  int i;
  double d;
} u;
```

Notice how the declaration of a union closely resembles a structure declaration:

```
struct {
  int i;
  double d;
} s;
```

In fact, the structure s and the union u differ in just one way: the members of s are stored at *different* addresses in memory, while the members of u are stored at the *same* address. Here's what s and u will look like in memory (assuming that int values require four bytes and double values take eight bytes):

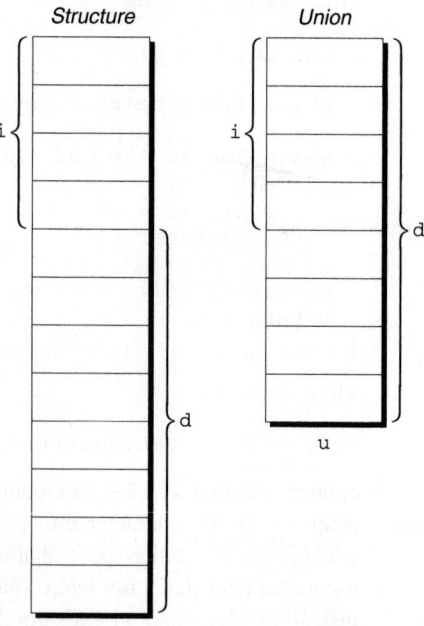

In the s structure, i and d occupy different memory locations; the total size of s is 12 bytes. In the u union, i and d overlap (i is really the first four bytes of d), so u occupies only eight bytes. Also, i and d have the same address.

Members of a union are accessed in the same way as members of a structure. To store the number 82 in the i member of u, we would write

```
u.i = 82;
```

To store the value 74.8 in the d member, we would write

```
u.d = 74.8;
```

Since the compiler overlays storage for the members of a union, changing one member alters any value previously stored in any of the other members. Thus, if we store a value in u.d, any value previously stored in u.i will be lost. (If we examine the value of u.i, it will appear to be meaningless.) Similarly, changing u.i corrupts u.d. Because of this property, we can think of u as a place to store either i *or* d, not both. (The structure s allows us to store i *and* d.)

The properties of unions are almost identical to the properties of structures. We can declare union tags and union types in the same way we declare structure tags and types. Like structures, unions can be copied using the = operator, passed to functions, and returned by functions.

Unions can even be initialized in a manner similar to structures. However, only the first member of a union can be given an initial value. For example, we can initialize the i member of u to 0 in the following way:

```
union {
  int i;
  double d;
} u = {0};
```

Notice the presence of the braces, which are required. The expression inside the braces must be constant. (The rules are slightly different in C99, as we'll see in Section 18.5.)

C99 Designated initializers, a C99 feature that we've previously discussed in the context of arrays and structures, can also be used with unions. A designated initializer allows us to specify which member of a union should be initialized. For example, we can initialize the d member of u as follows:

```
union {
  int i;
  double d;
} u = {.d = 10.0};
```

Only one member can be initialized, but it doesn't have to be the first one.

There are several applications for unions. We'll discuss two of these now. Another application—viewing storage in different ways—is highly machine-dependent, so I'll postpone it until Section 20.3.

Using Unions to Save Space

We'll often use unions as a way to save space in structures. Suppose that we're designing a structure that will contain information about an item that's sold through a gift catalog. The catalog carries only three kinds of merchandise: books, mugs, and shirts. Each item has a stock number and a price, as well as other information that depends on the type of the item:

> *Books:* Title, author, number of pages
>
> *Mugs:* Design
>
> *Shirts:* Design, colors available, sizes available

Our first design attempt might result in the following structure:

```
struct catalog_item {
  int stock_number;
  double price;
  int item_type;
  char title[TITLE_LEN+1];
  char author[AUTHOR_LEN+1];
  int num_pages;
  char design[DESIGN_LEN+1];
  int colors;
  int sizes;
};
```

The `item_type` member would have one of the values BOOK, MUG, or SHIRT. The `colors` and `sizes` members would store encoded combinations of colors and sizes.

Although this structure is perfectly usable, it wastes space, since only part of the information in the structure is common to all items in the catalog. If an item is a book, for example, there's no need to store `design`, `colors`, and `sizes`. By putting a union inside the `catalog_item` structure, we can reduce the space required by the structure. The members of the union will be structures, each containing the data that's needed for a particular kind of catalog item:

```
struct catalog_item {
  int stock_number;
  double price;
  int item_type;
  union {
    struct {
      char title[TITLE_LEN+1];
      char author[AUTHOR_LEN+1];
      int num_pages;
    } book;
    struct {
      char design[DESIGN_LEN+1];
    } mug;
```

```
    struct {
      char design[DESIGN_LEN+1];
      int colors;
      int sizes;
    } shirt;
  } item;
};
```

Notice that the union (named `item`) is a member of the `catalog_item` structure, and the `book`, `mug`, and `shirt` structures are members of `item`. If c is a `catalog_item` structure that represents a book, we can print the book's title in the following way:

```
printf("%s", c.item.book.title);
```

As this example shows, accessing a union that's nested inside a structure can be awkward: to locate a book title, we had to specify the name of a structure (`c`), the name of the union member of the structure (`item`), the name of a structure member of the union (`book`), and then the name of a member of that structure (`title`).

We can use the `catalog_item` structure to illustrate an interesting aspect of unions. Normally, it's not a good idea to store a value into one member of a union and then access the data through a different member, because assigning to one member of a union causes the values of the other members to be undefined. However, the C standard mentions a special case: two or more of the members of the union are structures, and the structures begin with one or more matching members. (These members need to be in the same order and have compatible types, but need not have the same name.) If one of the structures is currently valid, then the matching members in the other structures will also be valid.

Consider the union embedded in the `catalog_item` structure. It contains three structures as members, two of which (`mug` and `shirt`) begin with a matching member (`design`). Now, suppose that we assign a value to one of the `design` members:

```
strcpy(c.item.mug.design, "Cats");
```

The `design` member in the other structure will be defined and have the same value:

```
printf("%s", c.item.shirt.design);    /* prints "Cats" */
```

Using Unions to Build Mixed Data Structures

Unions have another important application: creating data structures that contain a mixture of data of different types. Let's say that we need an array whose elements are a mixture of `int` and `double` values. Since the elements of an array must be of the same type, it seems impossible to create such an array. Using unions, though, it's relatively easy. First, we define a union type whose members represent the different kinds of data to be stored in the array:

```
typedef union {
  int i;
  double d;
} Number;
```

Next, we create an array whose elements are Number values:

```
Number number_array[1000];
```

Each element of `number_array` is a `Number` union. A `Number` union can store either an `int` value or a `double` value, making it possible to store a mixture of `int` and `double` values in `number_array`. For example, suppose that we want element 0 of `number_array` to store 5, while element 1 stores 8.395. The following assignments will have the desired effect:

```
number_array[0].i = 5;
number_array[1].d = 8.395;
```

Adding a "Tag Field" to a Union

Unions suffer from a major problem: there's no easy way to tell which member of a union was last changed and therefore contains a meaningful value. Consider the problem of writing a function that displays the value currently stored in a `Number` union. This function might have the following outline:

```
void print_number(Number n)
{
  if (n contains an integer)
    printf("%d", n.i);
  else
    printf("%g", n.d);
}
```

Unfortunately, there's no way for `print_number` to determine whether n contains an integer or a floating-point number.

In order to keep track of this information, we can embed the union within a structure that has one other member: a "tag field" or "discriminant," whose purpose is to remind us what's currently stored in the union. In the `catalog_item` structure discussed earlier in this section, `item_type` served this purpose.

Let's convert the `Number` type into a structure with an embedded union:

```
#define INT_KIND 0
#define DOUBLE_KIND 1

typedef struct {
  int kind;   /* tag field */
  union {
    int i;
    double d;
  } u;
} Number;
```

Number has two members, kind and u. The value of kind will be either INT_KIND or DOUBLE_KIND.

Each time we assign a value to a member of u, we'll also change kind to remind us which member of u we modified. For example, if n is a Number variable, an assignment to the i member of u would have the following appearance:

```
n.kind = INT_KIND;
n.u.i = 82;
```

Notice that assigning to i requires that we first select the u member of n, then the i member of u.

When we need to retrieve the number stored in a Number variable, kind will tell us which member of the union was the last to be assigned a value. The print_number function can take advantage of this capability:

```
void print_number(Number n)
{
  if (n.kind == INT_KIND)
    printf("%d", n.u.i);
  else
    printf("%g", n.u.d);
}
```

 It's the program's responsibility to change the tag field each time an assignment is made to a member of the union.

16.5 Enumerations

In many programs, we'll need variables that have only a small set of meaningful values. A Boolean variable, for example, should have only two possible values: "true" and "false." A variable that stores the suit of a playing card should have only four potential values: "clubs," "diamonds," "hearts," and "spades." The obvious way to deal with such a variable is to declare it as an integer and have a set of codes that represent the possible values of the variable:

```
int s;    /* s will store a suit */
...
s = 2;    /* 2 represents "hearts" */
```

Although this technique works, it leaves much to be desired. Someone reading the program can't tell that s has only four possible values, and the significance of 2 isn't immediately apparent.

Using macros to define a suit "type" and names for the various suits is a step in the right direction:

```
#define SUIT       int
#define CLUBS      0
#define DIAMONDS   1
#define HEARTS     2
#define SPADES     3
```

Our previous example now becomes easier to read:

```
SUIT s;
…
s = HEARTS;
```

This technique is an improvement, but it's still not the best solution. There's no indication to someone reading the program that the macros represent values of the same "type." If the number of possible values is more than a few, defining a separate macro for each will be tedious. Moreover, the names we've defined—CLUBS, DIAMONDS, HEARTS, and SPADES—will be removed by the preprocessor, so they won't be available during debugging.

C provides a special kind of type designed specifically for variables that have a small number of possible values. An ***enumerated type*** is a type whose values are listed ("enumerated") by the programmer, who must create a name (an ***enumeration constant***) for each of the values. The following example enumerates the values (CLUBS, DIAMONDS, HEARTS, and SPADES) that can be assigned to the variables s1 and s2:

```
enum {CLUBS, DIAMONDS, HEARTS, SPADES} s1, s2;
```

Although enumerations have little in common with structures and unions, they're declared in a similar way. Unlike the members of a structure or union, however, the names of enumeration constants must be different from other identifiers declared in the enclosing scope.

Enumeration constants are similar to constants created with the #define directive, but they're not equivalent. For one thing, enumeration constants are subject to C's scope rules: if an enumeration is declared inside a function, its constants won't be visible outside the function.

Enumeration Tags and Type Names

We'll often need to create names for enumerations, for the same reasons that we name structures and unions. As with structures and unions, there are two ways to name an enumeration: by declaring a tag or by using typedef to create a genuine type name.

Enumeration tags resemble structure and union tags. To define the tag suit, for example, we could write

```
enum suit {CLUBS, DIAMONDS, HEARTS, SPADES};
```

suit variables would be declared in the following way:

```
enum suit s1, s2;
```

As an alternative, we could use `typedef` to make `Suit` a type name:

```
typedef enum {CLUBS, DIAMONDS, HEARTS, SPADES} Suit;
Suit s1, s2;
```

In C89, using `typedef` to name an enumeration is an excellent way to create a Boolean type:

```
typedef enum {FALSE, TRUE} Bool;
```

C99 has a built-in Boolean type, of course, so there's no need for a C99 programmer to define a `Bool` type in this way.

Enumerations as Integers

Behind the scenes, C treats enumeration variables and constants as integers. By default, the compiler assigns the integers 0, 1, 2, … to the constants in a particular enumeration. In our `suit` enumeration, for example, CLUBS, DIAMONDS, HEARTS, and SPADES represent 0, 1, 2, and 3, respectively.

We're free to choose different values for enumeration constants if we like. Let's say that we want CLUBS, DIAMONDS, HEARTS, and SPADES to stand for 1, 2, 3, and 4. We can specify these numbers when declaring the enumeration:

```
enum suit {CLUBS = 1, DIAMONDS = 2, HEARTS = 3, SPADES = 4};
```

The values of enumeration constants may be arbitrary integers, listed in no particular order:

```
enum dept {RESEARCH = 20, PRODUCTION = 10, SALES = 25};
```

It's even legal for two or more enumeration constants to have the same value.

When no value is specified for an enumeration constant, its value is one greater than the value of the previous constant. (The first enumeration constant has the value 0 by default.) In the following enumeration, BLACK has the value 0, LT_GRAY is 7, DK_GRAY is 8, and WHITE is 15:

```
enum EGA_colors {BLACK, LT_GRAY = 7, DK_GRAY, WHITE = 15};
```

Since enumeration values are nothing but thinly disguised integers, C allows us to mix them with ordinary integers:

```
int i;
enum {CLUBS, DIAMONDS, HEARTS, SPADES} s;

i = DIAMONDS;    /* i is now 1               */
s = 0;           /* s is now 0 (CLUBS)       */
s++;             /* s is now 1 (DIAMONDS)    */
i = s + 2;       /* i is now 3               */
```

The compiler treats `s` as a variable of some integer type; CLUBS, DIAMONDS, HEARTS, and SPADES are just names for the integers 0, 1, 2, and 3.

> Although it's convenient to be able to use an enumeration value as an integer, it's dangerous to use an integer as an enumeration value. For example, we might accidentally store the number 4—which doesn't correspond to any suit—into s.

Using Enumerations to Declare "Tag Fields"

Enumerations are perfect for solving a problem that we encountered in Section 16.4: determining which member of a union was the last to be assigned a value. In the Number structure, for example, we can make the kind member an enumeration instead of an int:

```
typedef struct {
  enum {INT_KIND, DOUBLE_KIND} kind;
  union {
    int i;
    double d;
  } u;
} Number;
```

The new structure is used in exactly the same way as the old one. The advantages are that we've done away with the INT_KIND and DOUBLE_KIND macros (they're now enumeration constants), and we've clarified the meaning of kind— it's now obvious that kind has only two possible values: INT_KIND and DOUBLE_KIND.

Q & A

Q: **When I tried using the sizeof operator to determine the number of bytes in a structure, I got a number that was larger than the sizes of the members added together. How can this be?**

A: Let's look at an example:

```
struct {
  char a;
  int b;
} s;
```

If char values occupy one byte and int values occupy four bytes, how large is s? The obvious answer—five bytes—may not be the correct one. Some computers require that the address of certain data items be a multiple of some number of bytes (typically two, four, or eight, depending on the item's type). To satisfy this requirement, a compiler will "align" the members of a structure by leaving "holes" (unused bytes) between adjacent members. If we assume that data items must begin on a multiple of four bytes, the a member of the s structure will be followed by a three-byte hole. As a result, `sizeof(s)` will be 8.

By the way, a structure can have a hole at the end, as well as holes between members. For example, the structure

```
struct {
  int a;
  char b;
} s;
```

might have a three-byte hole after the b member.

Q: **Can there be a "hole" at the beginning of a structure?**

A: No. The C standard specifies that holes are allowed only *between* members or *after* the last member. One consequence is that a pointer to the first member of a structure is guaranteed to be the same as a pointer to the entire structure. (Note, however, that the two pointers won't have the same type.)

Q: **Why isn't it legal to use the == operator to test whether two structures are equal? [p. 382]**

A: This operation was left out of C because there's no way to implement it that would be consistent with the language's philosophy. Comparing structure members one by one would be too inefficient. Comparing all bytes in the structures would be better (many computers have special instructions that can perform such a comparison rapidly). If the structures contain holes, however, comparing bytes could yield an incorrect answer; even if corresponding members have identical values, leftover data stored in the holes might be different. The problem could be solved by having the compiler ensure that holes always contain the same value (zero, say). Initializing holes would impose a performance penalty on all programs that use structures, however, so it's not feasible.

Q: **Why does C provide two ways to name structure types (tags and `typedef` names)? [p. 382]**

A: C originally lacked `typedef`, so tags were the only technique available for naming structure types. When `typedef` was added, it was too late to remove tags. Besides, a tag is still necessary when a member of a structure points to a structure of the same type (see the `node` structure of Section 17.5).

Q: **Can a structure have both a tag *and* a `typedef` name? [p. 384]**

A: Yes. In fact, the tag and the `typedef` name can even be the same, although that's not required:

```
typedef struct part {
  int number;
  char name[NAME_LEN+1];
  int on_hand;
} part;
```

Q: **How can I share a structure type among several files in a program?**

A: Put a declaration of the structure tag (or a `typedef`, if you prefer) in a header file, then include the header file where the structure is needed. To share the `part` structure, for example, we'd put the following lines in a header file:

```
struct part {
  int number;
  char name[NAME_LEN+1];
  int on_hand;
};
```

Notice that we're declaring only the structure *tag*, not variables of this type.

protecting header files ▶ 15.2   Incidentally, a header file that contains a declaration of a structure tag or structure type may need protection against multiple inclusion. Declaring a tag or `typedef` name twice in the same file is an error. Similar remarks apply to unions and enumerations.

Q: **If I include the declaration of the `part` structure into two different files, will `part` variables in one file be of the same type as `part` variables in the other file?**

A: Technically, no. However, the C standard says that the `part` variables in one file have a type that's compatible with the type of the `part` variables in the other file. Variables with compatible types can be assigned to each other, so there's little practical difference between types being "compatible" and being "the same."

C99   The rules for structure compatibility in C89 and C99 are slightly different. In C89, structures defined in different files are compatible if their members have the same names and appear in the same order, with corresponding members having compatible types. C99 goes one step further: it requires that either both structures have the same tag or neither has a tag.

Similar compatibility rules apply to unions and enumerations (with the same difference between C89 and C99).

Q: **Is it legal to have a pointer to a compound literal?**

A: Yes. Consider the `print_part` function of Section 16.2. Currently, the parameter to this function is a `part` structure. The function would be more efficient if it were modified to accept a *pointer* to a `part` structure instead. Using the function to print a compound literal would then be done by prefixing the argument with the & (address) operator:

```
print_part(&(struct part) {528, "Disk drive", 10});
```

Q: **Allowing a pointer to a compound literal would seem to make it possible to**
C99 **modify the literal. Is that the case?**

A: Yes. Compound literals are lvalues that can be modified, although doing so is rare.

Q: **I saw a program in which the last constant in an enumeration was followed by a comma, like this:**

```
enum gray_values {
  BLACK = 0,
  DARK_GRAY = 64,
  GRAY = 128,
  LIGHT_GRAY = 192,
};
```

Is this practice legal?

A: This practice is indeed legal in C99 (and is supported by some pre-C99 compilers as

well). Allowing a "trailing comma" makes enumerations easier to modify, because we can add a constant to the end of an enumeration without changing existing lines of code. For example, we might want to add WHITE to our enumeration:

```
enum gray_values {
  BLACK = 0,
  DARK_GRAY = 64,
  GRAY = 128,
  LIGHT_GRAY = 192,
  WHITE = 255,
};
```

The comma after the definition of LIGHT_GRAY makes it easy to add WHITE to the end of the list.

One reason for this change is that C89 allows trailing commas in initializers, so it seemed inconsistent not to allow the same flexibility in enumerations. Inci-

dentally, C99 also allows trailing commas in compound literals.

Q: **Can the values of an enumerated type be used as subscripts?**

A: Yes, indeed. They are integers and have—by default—values that start at 0 and

count upward, so they make great subscripts. In C99, moreover, enumeration constants can be used as subscripts in designated initializers. Here's an example:

```
enum weekdays {MONDAY, TUESDAY, WEDNESDAY, THURSDAY, FRIDAY};
const char *daily_specials[] = {
  [MONDAY] = "Beef ravioli",
  [TUESDAY] = "BLTs",
  [WEDNESDAY] = "Pizza",
  [THURSDAY] = "Chicken fajitas",
  [FRIDAY] = "Macaroni and cheese"
};
```

Exercises

Section 16.1

1. In the following declarations, the x and y structures have members named x and y:

```
struct { int x, y; } x;
struct { int x, y; } y;
```

Are these declarations legal on an individual basis? Could both declarations appear as shown in a program? Justify your answer.

Ⓦ 2.   (a) Declare structure variables named c1, c2, and c3, each having members real and imaginary of type double.

(b) Modify the declaration in part (a) so that c1's members initially have the values 0.0 and 1.0, while c2's members are 1.0 and 0.0 initially. (c3 is not initialized.)

(c) Write statements that copy the members of c2 into c1. Can this be done in one statement, or does it require two?

(d) Write statements that add the corresponding members of c1 and c2, storing the result in c3.

Section 16.2   3.   (a) Show how to declare a tag named complex for a structure with two members, real and imaginary, of type double.

(b) Use the complex tag to declare variables named c1, c2, and c3.

(c) Write a function named make_complex that stores its two arguments (both of type double) in a complex structure, then returns the structure.

(d) Write a function named add_complex that adds the corresponding members of its arguments (both complex structures), then returns the result (another complex structure).

Ⓦ 4.   Repeat Exercise 3, but this time using a *type* named Complex.

5.   Write the following functions, assuming that the date structure contains three members: month, day, and year (all of type int).

(a) int day_of_year(struct date d);

Returns the day of the year (an integer between 1 and 366) that corresponds to the date d.

(b) int compare_dates(struct date d1, struct date d2);

Returns –1 if d1 is an earlier date than d2, +1 if d1 is a later date than d2, and 0 if d1 and d2 are the same.

6.   Write the following function, assuming that the time structure contains three members: hours, minutes, and seconds (all of type int).

struct time split_time(long total_seconds);

total_seconds is a time represented as the number of seconds since midnight. The function returns a structure containing the equivalent time in hours (0–23), minutes (0–59), and seconds (0–59).

7.   Assume that the fraction structure contains two members: numerator and denominator (both of type int). Write functions that perform the following operations on fractions:

(a) Reduce the fraction f to lowest terms. *Hint:* To reduce a fraction to lowest terms, first compute the greatest common divisor (GCD) of the numerator and denominator. Then divide both the numerator and denominator by the GCD.

(b) Add the fractions f1 and f2.

(c) Subtract the fraction f2 from the fraction f1.

(d) Multiply the fractions f1 and f2.

(e) Divide the fraction f1 by the fraction f2.

The fractions f, f1, and f2 will be arguments of type struct fraction; each function will return a value of type struct fraction. The fractions returned by the functions in parts (b)–(e) should be reduced to lowest terms. *Hint:* You may use the function from part (a) to help write the functions in parts (b)–(e).

8. Let `color` be the following structure:

```
struct color {
   int red;
   int green;
   int blue;
};
```

   (a) Write a declaration for a `const` variable named `MAGENTA` of type `struct color` whose members have the values 255, 0, and 255, respectively.

   (b) (C99) Repeat part (a), but use a designated initializer that doesn't specify the value of `green`, allowing it to default to 0.

9. Write the following functions. (The `color` structure is defined in Exercise 8.)

   (a) `struct color make_color(int red, int green, int blue);`
   Returns a `color` structure containing the specified red, green, and blue values. If any argument is less than zero, the corresponding member of the structure will contain zero instead. If any argument is greater than 255, the corresponding member of the structure will contain 255.

   (b) `int getRed(struct color c);`
   Returns the value of c's red member.

   (c) `bool equal_color(struct color color1, struct color color2);`
   Returns `true` if the corresponding members of `color1` and `color2` are equal.

   (d) `struct color brighter(struct color c);`
   Returns a `color` structure that represents a brighter version of the color c. The structure is identical to c, except that each member has been divided by 0.7 (with the result truncated to an integer). However, there are three special cases: (1) If all members of c are zero, the function returns a color whose members all have the value 3. (2) If any member of c is greater than 0 but less than 3, it is replaced by 3 before the division by 0.7. (3) If dividing by 0.7 causes a member to exceed 255, it is reduced to 255.

   (e) `struct color darker(struct color c);`
   Returns a `color` structure that represents a darker version of the color c. The structure is identical to c, except that each member has been multiplied by 0.7 (with the result truncated to an integer).

Section 16.3   10. The following structures are designed to store information about objects on a graphics screen:

```
struct point { int x, y; };
struct rectangle { struct point upper_left, lower_right; };
```

   A `point` structure stores the x and y coordinates of a point on the screen. A `rectangle` structure stores the coordinates of the upper left and lower right corners of a rectangle. Write functions that perform the following operations on a `rectangle` structure r passed as an argument:

   (a) Compute the area of r.
   (b) Compute the center of r, returning it as a `point` value. If either the x or y coordinate of the center isn't an integer, store its truncated value in the `point` structure.
   (c) Move r by x units in the x direction and y units in the y direction, returning the modified version of r. (x and y are additional arguments to the function.)
   (d) Determine whether a point p lies within r, returning `true` or `false`. (p is an additional argument of type `struct point`.)

Ⓦ 11.   Suppose that s is the following structure:

```
struct {
  double a;
  union {
    char b[4];
    double c;
    int d;
  } e;
  char f[4];
} s;
```

If char values occupy one byte, int values occupy four bytes, and double values occupy eight bytes, how much space will a C compiler allocate for s? (Assume that the compiler leaves no "holes" between members.)

12.   Suppose that u is the following union:

```
union {
  double a;
  struct {
    char b[4];
    double c;
    int d;
  } e;
  char f[4];
} u;
```

If char values occupy one byte, int values occupy four bytes, and double values occupy eight bytes, how much space will a C compiler allocate for u? (Assume that the compiler leaves no "holes" between members.)

13.   Suppose that s is the following structure (point is a structure tag declared in Exercise 10):

```
struct shape {
  int shape_kind;          /* RECTANGLE or CIRCLE */
  struct point center;     /* coordinates of center */
  union {
    struct {
      int height, width;
    } rectangle;
    struct {
      int radius;
    } circle;
  } u;
} s;
```

If the value of shape_kind is RECTANGLE, the height and width members store the dimensions of a rectangle. If the value of shape_kind is CIRCLE, the radius member stores the radius of a circle. Indicate which of the following statements are legal, and show how to repair the ones that aren't:

(a) s.shape_kind = RECTANGLE;

(b) s.center.x = 10;

(c) s.height = 25;

(d) s.u.rectangle.width = 8;

(e) s.u.circle = 5;

(f) s.u.radius = 5;

Ⓦ 14. Let shape be the structure tag declared in Exercise 13. Write functions that perform the following operations on a shape structure s passed as an argument:

(a) Compute the area of s.

(b) Move s by x units in the *x* direction and y units in the *y* direction, returning the modified version of s. (x and y are additional arguments to the function.)

(c) Scale s by a factor of c (a double value), returning the modified version of s. (c is an additional argument to the function.)

Section 16.5   Ⓦ 15. (a) Declare a tag for an enumeration whose values represent the seven days of the week.

(b) Use typedef to define a name for the enumeration of part (a).

16. Which of the following statements about enumeration constants are true?

(a) An enumeration constant may represent any integer specified by the programmer.

(b) Enumeration constants have exactly the same properties as constants created using #define.

(c) Enumeration constants have the values 0, 1, 2, ... by default.

(d) All constants in an enumeration must have different values.

(e) Enumeration constants may be used as integers in expressions.

Ⓦ 17. Suppose that b and i are declared as follows:

```
enum {FALSE, TRUE} b;
int i;
```

Which of the following statements are legal? Which ones are "safe" (always yield a meaningful result)?

(a) b = FALSE;

(b) b = i;

(c) b++;

(d) i = b;

(e) i = 2 * b + 1;

18. (a) Each square of a chessboard can hold one piece—a pawn, knight, bishop, rook, queen, or king—or it may be empty. Each piece is either black or white. Define two enumerated types: Piece, which has seven possible values (one of which is "empty"), and Color, which has two.

(b) Using the types from part (a), define a structure type named Square that can store both the type of a piece and its color.

(c) Using the Square type from part (b), declare an 8 × 8 array named board that can store the entire contents of a chessboard.

(d) Add an initializer to the declaration in part (c) so that board's initial value corresponds to the usual arrangement of pieces at the start of a chess game. A square that's not occupied by a piece should have an "empty" piece value and the color black.

19. Declare a structure with the following members whose tag is pinball_machine:

name – a string of up to 40 characters

year – an integer (representing the year of manufacture)

type – an enumeration with the values EM (electromechanical) and SS (solid state)

players – an integer (representing the maximum number of players)

20. Suppose that the direction variable is declared in the following way:

```
enum {NORTH, SOUTH, EAST, WEST} direction;
```

Let x and y be int variables. Write a switch statement that tests the value of direction, incrementing x if direction is EAST, decrementing x if direction is WEST, incrementing y if direction is SOUTH, and decrementing y if direction is NORTH.

21. What are the integer values of the enumeration constants in each of the following declarations?

    (a) enum {NUL, SOH, STX, ETX};
    (b) enum {VT = 11, FF, CR};
    (c) enum {SO = 14, SI, DLE, CAN = 24, EM};
    (d) enum {ENQ = 45, ACK, BEL, LF = 37, ETB, ESC};

22. Let chess_pieces be the following enumeration:

    enum chess_pieces {KING, QUEEN, ROOK, BISHOP, KNIGHT, PAWN};

    (a) Write a declaration (including an initializer) for a constant array of integers named piece_value that stores the numbers 200, 9, 5, 3, 3, and 1, representing the value of each chess piece, from king to pawn. (The king's value is actually infinite, since "capturing" the king (checkmate) ends the game, but some chess-playing software assigns the king a large value such as 200.)

    (b) (C99) Repeat part (a), but use a designated initializer to initialize the array. Use the enumeration constants in chess_pieces as subscripts in the designators. (*Hint:* See the last question in Q&A for an example.)

Programming Projects

Ⓦ 1. Write a program that asks the user to enter an international dialing code and then looks it up in the country_codes array (see Section 16.3). If it finds the code, the program should display the name of the corresponding country; if not, the program should print an error message.

2. Modify the inventory.c program of Section 16.3 so that the p (print) operation displays the parts sorted by part number.

Ⓦ 3. Modify the inventory.c program of Section 16.3 by making inventory and num_parts local to the main function.

4. Modify the inventory.c program of Section 16.3 by adding a price member to the part structure. The insert function should ask the user for the price of a new item. The search and print functions should display the price. Add a new command that allows the user to change the price of a part.

5. Modify Programming Project 8 from Chapter 5 so that the times are stored in a single array. The elements of the array will be structures, each containing a departure time and the corresponding arrival time. (Each time will be an integer, representing the number of minutes since midnight.) The program will use a loop to search the array for the departure time closest to the time entered by the user.

6. Modify Programming Project 9 from Chapter 5 so that each date entered by the user is stored in a date structure (see Exercise 5). Incorporate the compare_dates function of Exercise 5 into your program.

17 Advanced Uses of Pointers

*One can only display complex information in the mind.
Like seeing, movement or flow or alteration of view is more
important than the static picture, no matter how lovely.*

In previous chapters, we've seen two important uses of pointers. Chapter 11 showed how using a pointer to a variable as a function argument allows the function to modify the variable. Chapter 12 showed how to process arrays by performing arithmetic on pointers to array elements. This chapter completes our coverage of pointers by examining two additional applications: dynamic storage allocation and pointers to functions.

Using dynamic storage allocation, a program can obtain blocks of memory as needed during execution. Section 17.1 explains the basics of dynamic storage allocation. Section 17.2 discusses dynamically allocated strings, which provide more flexibility than ordinary character arrays. Section 17.3 covers dynamic storage allocation for arrays in general. Section 17.4 deals with the issue of storage deallocation—releasing blocks of dynamically allocated memory when they're no longer needed.

Dynamically allocated structures play a big role in C programming, since they can be linked together to form lists, trees, and other highly flexible data structures. Section 17.5 focuses on linked lists, the most fundamental linked data structure. One of the issues that arises in this section—the concept of a "pointer to a pointer"—is important enough to warrant a section of its own (Section 17.6).

Section 17.7 introduces pointers to functions, a surprisingly useful concept. Some of C's most powerful library functions expect function pointers as arguments. We'll examine one of these functions, qsort, which is capable of sorting any array.

The last two sections discuss pointer-related features that first appeared in C99: restricted pointers (Section 17.8) and flexible array members (Section 17.9). These features are primarily of interest to advanced C programmers, so both sections can be safely be skipped by the beginner.

17.1   Dynamic Storage Allocation

C's data structures are normally fixed in size. For example, the number of elements in an array is fixed once the program has been compiled. (In C99, the length of a variable-length array is determined at run time, but it remains fixed for the rest of the array's lifetime.) Fixed-size data structures can be a problem, since we're forced to choose their sizes when writing a program; we can't change the sizes without modifying the program and compiling it again.

variable-length arrays ➤ 8.3

Consider the `inventory` program of Section 16.3, which allows the user to add parts to a database. The database is stored in an array of length 100. To enlarge the capacity of the database, we can increase the size of the array and recompile the program. But no matter how large we make the array, there's always the possibility that it will fill up. Fortunately, all is not lost. C supports *dynamic storage allocation:* the ability to allocate storage during program execution. Using dynamic storage allocation, we can design data structures that grow (and shrink) as needed.

Although it's available for all types of data, dynamic storage allocation is used most often for strings, arrays, and structures. Dynamically allocated structures are of particular interest, since we can link them together to form lists, trees, and other data structures.

Memory Allocation Functions

To allocate storage dynamically, we'll need to call one of the three memory allocation functions declared in the `<stdlib.h>` header:

`<stdlib.h>` header ➤ 26.2

- `malloc`—Allocates a block of memory but doesn't initialize it.
- `calloc`—Allocates a block of memory and clears it.
- `realloc`—Resizes a previously allocated block of memory.

Of the three, `malloc` is the most used. It's more efficient than `calloc`, since it doesn't have to clear the memory block that it allocates.

When we call a memory allocation function to request a block of memory, the function has no idea what type of data we're planning to store in the block, so it can't return a pointer to an ordinary type such as `int` or `char`. Instead, the function returns a value of type `void *`. A `void *` value is a "generic" pointer—essentially, just a memory address.

Null Pointers

When a memory allocation function is called, there's always a possibility that it won't be able to locate a block of memory large enough to satisfy our request. If that should happen, the function will return a ***null pointer.*** A null pointer is a "pointer to nothing"—a special value that can be distinguished from all valid pointers. After we've stored the function's return value in a pointer variable, we must test to see if it's a null pointer.

It's the programmer's responsibility to test the return value of any memory allocation function and take appropriate action if it's a null pointer. The effect of attempting to access memory through a null pointer is undefined; the program may crash or behave unpredictably.

The null pointer is represented by a macro named `NULL`, so we can test `malloc`'s return value in the following way:

```
p = malloc(10000);
if (p == NULL) {
  /* allocation failed; take appropriate action */
}
```

Some programmers combine the call of `malloc` with the `NULL` test:

```
if ((p = malloc(10000)) == NULL) {
  /* allocation failed; take appropriate action */
}
```

The `NULL` macro is defined in six headers: `<locale.h>`, `<stddef.h>`, `<stdio.h>`, `<stdlib.h>`, `<string.h>`, and `<time.h>`. (The C99 header `<wchar.h>` also defines `NULL`.) As long as one of these headers is included in a program, the compiler will recognize `NULL`. A program that uses any of the memory allocation functions will include `<stdlib.h>`, of course, making `NULL` available.

In C, pointers test true or false in the same way as numbers. All non-null pointers test true; only null pointers are false. Thus, instead of writing

```
if (p == NULL) ...
```

we could write

```
if (!p) ...
```

and instead of writing

```
if (p != NULL) ...
```

we could write

```
if (p) ...
```

As a matter of style, I prefer the explicit comparison with `NULL`.

17.2   Dynamically Allocated Strings

Dynamic storage allocation is often useful for working with strings. Strings are stored in character arrays, and it can be hard to anticipate how long these arrays need to be. By allocating strings dynamically, we can postpone the decision until the program is running.

Using `malloc` to Allocate Memory for a String

The `malloc` function has the following prototype:

```
void *malloc(size_t size);
```

size_t type ►7.6

`malloc` allocates a block of `size` bytes and returns a pointer to it. Note that `size` has type `size_t`, an unsigned integer type defined in the C library. Unless we're allocating a very large block of memory, we can just think of `size` as an ordinary integer.

Using `malloc` to allocate memory for a string is easy, because C guarantees that a `char` value requires exactly one byte of storage (`sizeof(char)` is 1, in other words). To allocate space for a string of n characters, we'd write

```
p = malloc(n + 1);
```

where p is a `char *` variable. (The argument is n + 1 rather than n to allow room for the null character.) The generic pointer that `malloc` returns will be converted to `char *` when the assignment is performed; no cast is necessary. (In general, we can assign a `void *` value to a variable of any pointer type and vice versa.) Nevertheless, some programmers prefer to cast `malloc`'s return value:

Q&A

```
p = (char *) malloc(n + 1);
```

 When using `malloc` to allocate space for a string, don't forget to include room for the null character.

Memory allocated using `malloc` isn't cleared or initialized in any way, so p will point to an uninitialized array of n + 1 characters:

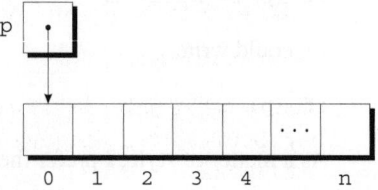

Calling `strcpy` is one way to initialize this array:

```
strcpy(p, "abc");
```

The first four characters in the array will now be a, b, c, and \0:

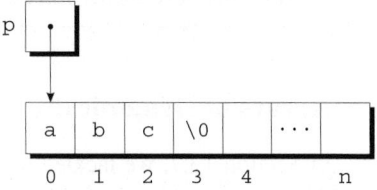

Using Dynamic Storage Allocation in String Functions

Dynamic storage allocation makes it possible to write functions that return a pointer to a "new" string—a string that didn't exist before the function was called. Consider the problem of writing a function that concatenates two strings without changing either one. C's standard library doesn't include such a function (`strcat` isn't quite what we want, since it modifies one of the strings passed to it), but we can easily write our own.

Our function will measure the lengths of the two strings to be concatenated, then call `malloc` to allocate just the right amount of space for the result. The function next copies the first string into the new space and then calls `strcat` to concatenate the second string.

```
char *concat(const char *s1, const char *s2)
{
  char *result;

  result = malloc(strlen(s1) + strlen(s2) + 1);
  if (result == NULL) {
    printf("Error: malloc failed in concat\n");
    exit(EXIT_FAILURE);
  }
  strcpy(result, s1);
  strcat(result, s2);
  return result;
}
```

If `malloc` returns a null pointer, `concat` prints an error message and terminates the program. That's not always the right action to take; some programs need to recover from memory allocation failures and continue running.

Here's how the `concat` function might be called:

```
p = concat("abc", "def");
```

After the call, p will point to the string `"abcdef"`, which is stored in a dynamically allocated array. The array is seven characters long, including the null character at the end.

free function ▶17.4

Functions such as `concat` that dynamically allocate storage must be used with care. When the string that `concat` returns is no longer needed, we'll want to call the `free` function to release the space that the string occupies. If we don't, the program may eventually run out of memory.

Arrays of Dynamically Allocated Strings

In Section 13.7, we tackled the problem of storing strings in an array. We found that storing strings as rows in a two-dimensional array of characters can waste space, so we tried setting up an array of pointers to string literals. The techniques of Section 13.7 work just as well if the elements of an array are pointers to dynamically allocated strings. To illustrate this point, let's rewrite the `remind.c` program of Section 13.5, which prints a one-month list of daily reminders.

PROGRAM ## Printing a One-Month Reminder List (Revisited)

The original `remind.c` program stores the reminder strings in a two-dimensional array of characters, with each row of the array containing one string. After the program reads a day and its associated reminder, it searches the array to determine where the day belongs, using `strcmp` to do comparisons. It then uses `strcpy` to move all strings below that point down one position. Finally, the program copies the day into the array and calls `strcat` to append the reminder to the day.

In the new program (`remind2.c`), the array will be one-dimensional; its elements will be pointers to dynamically allocated strings. Switching to dynamically allocated strings in this program will have two primary advantages. First, we can use space more efficiently by allocating the exact number of characters needed to store a reminder, rather than storing the reminder in a fixed number of characters as the original program does. Second, we won't need to call `strcpy` to move existing reminder strings in order to make room for a new reminder. Instead, we'll merely move *pointers* to strings.

Here's the new program, with changes in **bold.** Switching from a two-dimensional array to an array of pointers turns out to be remarkably easy: we'll only need to change eight lines of the program.

remind2.c
```
/* Prints a one-month reminder list (dynamic string version) */

#include <stdio.h>
#include <stdlib.h>
#include <string.h>

#define MAX_REMIND 50    /* maximum number of reminders */
#define MSG_LEN 60       /* max length of reminder message */

int read_line(char str[], int n);
```

```c
int main(void)
{
  char *reminders[MAX_REMIND];
  char day_str[3], msg_str[MSG_LEN+1];
  int day, i, j, num_remind = 0;

  for (;;) {
    if (num_remind == MAX_REMIND) {
      printf("-- No space left --\n");
      break;
    }

    printf("Enter day and reminder: ");
    scanf("%2d", &day);
    if (day == 0)
      break;
    sprintf(day_str, "%2d", day);
    read_line(msg_str, MSG_LEN);

    for (i = 0; i < num_remind; i++)
      if (strcmp(day_str, reminders[i]) < 0)
        break;
    for (j = num_remind; j > i; j--)
      reminders[j] = reminders[j-1];

    reminders[i] = malloc(2 + strlen(msg_str) + 1);
    if (reminders[i] == NULL) {
      printf("-- No space left --\n");
      break;
    }

    strcpy(reminders[i], day_str);
    strcat(reminders[i], msg_str);

    num_remind++;
  }

  printf("\nDay Reminder\n");
  for (i = 0; i < num_remind; i++)
    printf(" %s\n", reminders[i]);

  return 0;
}

int read_line(char str[], int n)
{
  int ch, i = 0;

  while ((ch = getchar()) != '\n')
    if (i < n)
      str[i++] = ch;
  str[i] = '\0';
  return i;
}
```

17.3 Dynamically Allocated Arrays

Dynamically allocated arrays have the same advantages as dynamically allocated strings (not surprisingly, since strings *are* arrays). When we're writing a program, it's often difficult to estimate the proper size for an array; it would be more convenient to wait until the program is run to decide how large the array should be. C solves this problem by allowing a program to allocate space for an array during execution, then access the array through a pointer to its first element. The close relationship between arrays and pointers, which we explored in Chapter 12, makes a dynamically allocated array just as easy to use as an ordinary array.

Although `malloc` can allocate space for an array, the `calloc` function is sometimes used instead, since it initializes the memory that it allocates. The `realloc` function allows us to make an array "grow" or "shrink" as needed.

Using `malloc` to Allocate Storage for an Array

We can use `malloc` to allocate space for an array in much the same way we used it to allocate space for a string. The primary difference is that the elements of an arbitrary array won't necessarily be one byte long, as they are in a string. As a result, we'll need to use the `sizeof` operator to calculate the amount of space required for each element.

sizeof operator ➤ 7.6

Suppose we're writing a program that needs an array of n integers, where n is to be computed during the execution of the program. We'll first declare a pointer variable:

```
int *a;
```

Once the value of n is known, we'll have the program call `malloc` to allocate space for the array:

```
a = malloc(n * sizeof(int));
```

Always use `sizeof` when calculating how much space is needed for an array. Failing to allocate enough memory can have severe consequences. Consider the following attempt to allocate space for an array of n integers:

```
a = malloc(n * 2);
```

If `int` values are larger than two bytes (as they are on most computers), `malloc` won't allocate a large enough block of memory. When we later try to access elements of the array, the program may crash or behave erratically.

Once it points to a dynamically allocated block of memory, we can ignore the fact that a is a pointer and use it instead as an array name, thanks to the relationship between arrays and pointers in C. For example, we could use the following loop to initialize the array that a points to:

```
for (i = 0; i < n; i++)
  a[i] = 0;
```

We also have the option of using pointer arithmetic instead of subscripting to access the elements of the array.

The `calloc` Function

Although the `malloc` function can be used to allocate memory for an array, C provides an alternative—the `calloc` function—that's sometimes better. `calloc` has the following prototype in `<stdlib.h>`:

```
void *calloc(size_t nmemb, size_t size);
```

`calloc` allocates space for an array with nmemb elements, each of which is size bytes long; it returns a null pointer if the requested space isn't available. After allocating the memory, `calloc` initializes it by setting all bits to 0. For example, the following call of `calloc` allocates space for an array of n integers, which are all guaranteed to be zero initially:

Q&A

```
a = calloc(n, sizeof(int));
```

Since `calloc` clears the memory that it allocates but `malloc` doesn't, we may occasionally want to use `calloc` to allocate space for an object other than an array. By calling `calloc` with 1 as its first argument, we can allocate space for a data item of any type:

```
struct point { int x, y; } *p;

p = calloc(1, sizeof(struct point));
```

After this statement has been executed, p will point to a structure whose x and y members have been set to zero.

The `realloc` Function

Once we've allocated memory for an array, we may later find that it's too large or too small. The `realloc` function can resize the array to better suit our needs. The following prototype for `realloc` appears in `<stdlib.h>`:

```
void *realloc(void *ptr, size_t size);
```

When `realloc` is called, ptr must point to a memory block obtained by a previous call of `malloc`, `calloc`, or `realloc`. The size parameter represents the new size of the block, which may be larger or smaller than the original size. Although `realloc` doesn't require that ptr point to memory that's being used as an array, in practice it usually does.

Be sure that a pointer passed to realloc came from a previous call of malloc, calloc, or realloc. If it didn't, calling realloc causes undefined behavior.

The C standard spells out a number of rules concerning the behavior of realloc:

- When it expands a memory block, realloc doesn't initialize the bytes that are added to the block.

- If realloc can't enlarge the memory block as requested, it returns a null pointer; the data in the old memory block is unchanged.

- If realloc is called with a null pointer as its first argument, it behaves like malloc.

- If realloc is called with 0 as its second argument, it frees the memory block.

The C standard stops short of specifying exactly how realloc works. Still, we expect it to be reasonably efficient. When asked to reduce the size of a memory block, realloc should shrink the block "in place," without moving the data stored in the block. By the same token, realloc should always attempt to expand a memory block without moving it. If it's unable to enlarge the block (because the bytes following the block are already in use for some other purpose), realloc will allocate a new block elsewhere, then copy the contents of the old block into the new one.

 Once realloc has returned, be sure to update all pointers to the memory block, since it's possible that realloc has moved the block elsewhere.

17.4 Deallocating Storage

malloc and the other memory allocation functions obtain memory blocks from a storage pool known as the *heap.* Calling these functions too often—or asking them for large blocks of memory—can exhaust the heap, causing the functions to return a null pointer.

To make matters worse, a program may allocate blocks of memory and then lose track of them, thereby wasting space. Consider the following example:

```
p = malloc(…);
q = malloc(…);
p = q;
```

After the first two statements have been executed, p points to one memory block, while q points to another:

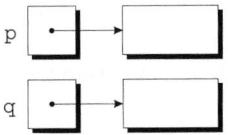

After q is assigned to p, both variables now point to the second memory block:

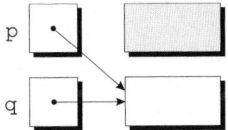

There are no pointers to the first block (shaded), so we'll never be able to use it again.

A block of memory that's no longer accessible to a program is said to be ***garbage***. A program that leaves garbage behind has a ***memory leak***. Some languages provide a ***garbage collector*** that automatically locates and recycles garbage, but C doesn't. Instead, each C program is responsible for recycling its own garbage by calling the free function to release unneeded memory.

The **free** Function

The free function has the following prototype in <stdlib.h>:

```
void free(void *ptr);
```

Using free is easy; we simply pass it a pointer to a memory block that we no longer need:

```
p = malloc(…);
q = malloc(…);
free(p);
p = q;
```

Calling free releases the block of memory that p points to. This block is now available for reuse in subsequent calls of malloc or other memory allocation functions.

The argument to free must be a pointer that was previously returned by a memory allocation function. (The argument may also be a null pointer, in which case the call of free has no effect.) Passing free a pointer to any other object (such as a variable or array element) causes undefined behavior.

The "Dangling Pointer" Problem

Although the `free` function allows us to reclaim memory that's no longer needed, using it leads to a new problem: ***dangling pointers.*** The call `free(p)` deallocates the memory block that `p` points to, but doesn't change `p` itself. If we forget that `p` no longer points to a valid memory block, chaos may ensue:

```
char *p = malloc(4);
...
free(p);
...
strcpy(p, "abc");    /*** WRONG ***/
```

Modifying the memory that `p` points to is a serious error, since our program no longer has control of that memory.

Attempting to access or modify a deallocated memory block causes undefined behavior. Trying to modify a deallocated memory block is likely to have disastrous consequences that may include a program crash.

Dangling pointers can be hard to spot, since several pointers may point to the same block of memory. When the block is freed, all the pointers are left dangling.

17.5   Linked Lists

Dynamic storage allocation is especially useful for building lists, trees, graphs, and other linked data structures. We'll look at linked lists in this section; a discussion of other linked data structures is beyond the scope of this book. For more information, consult a book such as Robert Sedgewick's *Algorithms in C, Parts 1–4: Fundamentals, Data Structures, Sorting, Searching,* Third Edition (Reading, Mass.: Addison-Wesley, 1998).

A ***linked list*** consists of a chain of structures (called ***nodes***), with each node containing a pointer to the next node in the chain:

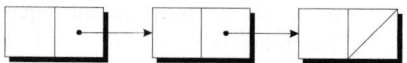

The last node in the list contains a null pointer, shown here as a diagonal line.

In previous chapters, we've used an array whenever we've needed to store a collection of data items; linked lists give us an alternative. A linked list is more flexible than an array: we can easily insert and delete nodes in a linked list, allowing the list to grow and shrink as needed. On the other hand, we lose the "random access" capability of an array. Any element of an array can be accessed in the same amount of time; accessing a node in a linked list is fast if the node is close to the beginning of the list, slow if it's near the end.

This section describes how to set up a linked list in C. It also shows how to perform several common operations on linked lists: inserting a node at the beginning of a list, searching for a node, and deleting a node.

Declaring a Node Type

To set up a linked list, the first thing we'll need is a structure that represents a single node in the list. For simplicity, let's assume that a node contains nothing but an integer (the node's data) plus a pointer to the next node in the list. Here's what our node structure will look like:

```
struct node {
  int value;              /* data stored in the node  */
  struct node *next;      /* pointer to the next node */
};
```

Notice that the `next` member has type `struct node *`, which means that it can store a pointer to a `node` structure. There's nothing special about the name `node`, by the way; it's just an ordinary structure tag.

One aspect of the `node` structure deserves special mention. As Section 16.2 explained, we normally have the option of using either a tag or a `typedef` name to define a name for a particular kind of structure. However, when a structure has a member that points to the same kind of structure, as `node` does, we're required to use a structure tag. Without the `node` tag, we'd have no way to declare the type of **Q&A** `next`.

Now that we have the `node` structure declared, we'll need a way to keep track of where the list begins. In other words, we'll need a variable that always points to the first node in the list. Let's name the variable `first`:

```
struct node *first = NULL;
```

Setting `first` to `NULL` indicates that the list is initially empty.

Creating a Node

As we construct a linked list, we'll want to create nodes one by one, adding each to the list. Creating a node requires three steps:

1. Allocate memory for the node.
2. Store data in the node.
3. Insert the node into the list.

We'll concentrate on the first two steps for now.

When we create a node, we'll need a variable that can point to the node temporarily, until it's been inserted into the list. Let's call this variable `new_node`:

```
struct node *new_node;
```

We'll use `malloc` to allocate memory for the new node, saving the return value in `new_node`:

```
new_node = malloc(sizeof(struct node));
```

`new_node` now points to a block of memory just large enough to hold a `node` structure:

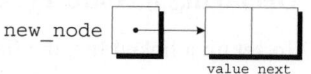

Be careful to give `sizeof` the name of the *type* to be allocated, not the name of a *pointer* to that type:

```
new_node = malloc(sizeof(new_node));    /*** WRONG ***/
```

The program will still compile, but `malloc` will allocate only enough memory for a *pointer* to a node structure. The likely result is a crash later, when the program attempts to store data in the node that `new_node` is presumably pointing to.

Next, we'll store data in the `value` member of the new node:

```
(*new_node).value = 10;
```

Here's how the picture will look after this assignment:

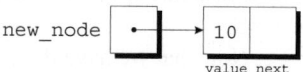

To access the `value` member of the node, we've applied the indirection operator `*` (to reference the structure to which `new_node` points), then the selection operator `.` (to select a member of the structure). The parentheses around `*new_node` are mandatory because the `.` operator would otherwise take precedence over the `*` operator.

table of operators ➤ *Appendix A*

The -> Operator

Before we go on to the next step, inserting a new node into a list, let's take a moment to discuss a useful shortcut. Accessing a member of a structure using a pointer is so common that C provides a special operator just for this purpose. This operator, known as ***right arrow selection,*** is a minus sign followed by `>`. Using the `->` operator, we can write

```
new_node->value = 10;
```

instead of

```
(*new_node).value = 10;
```

The `->` operator is a combination of the `*` and `.` operators; it performs indirection on `new_node` to locate the structure that it points to, then selects the `value` member of the structure.

lvalues ➤4.2   The `->` operator produces an lvalue, so we can use it wherever an ordinary variable would be allowed. We've just seen an example in which `new_node->value` appears on the left side of an assignment. It could just as easily appear in a call of `scanf`:

```
scanf("%d", &new_node->value);
```

Notice that the `&` operator is still required, even though `new_node` is a pointer. Without the `&`, we'd be passing `scanf` the *value* of `new_node->value`, which has type `int`.

Inserting a Node at the Beginning of a Linked List

One of the advantages of a linked list is that nodes can be added at any point in the list: at the beginning, at the end, or anywhere in the middle. The beginning of a list is the easiest place to insert a node, however, so let's focus on that case.

If `new_node` is pointing to the node to be inserted, and `first` is pointing to the first node in the linked list, then we'll need two statements to insert the node into the list. First, we'll modify the new node's `next` member to point to the node that was previously at the beginning of the list:

```
new_node->next = first;
```

Second, we'll make `first` point to the new node:

```
first = new_node;
```

Will these statements work if the list is empty when we insert a node? Yes, fortunately. To make sure this is true, let's trace the process of inserting two nodes into an empty list. We'll insert a node containing the number 10 first, followed by a node containing 20. In the figures that follow, null pointers are shown as diagonal lines.

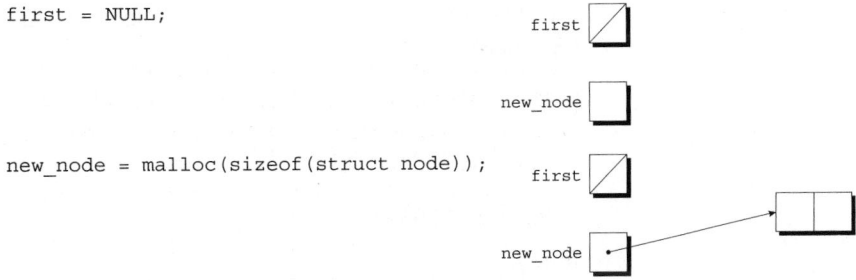

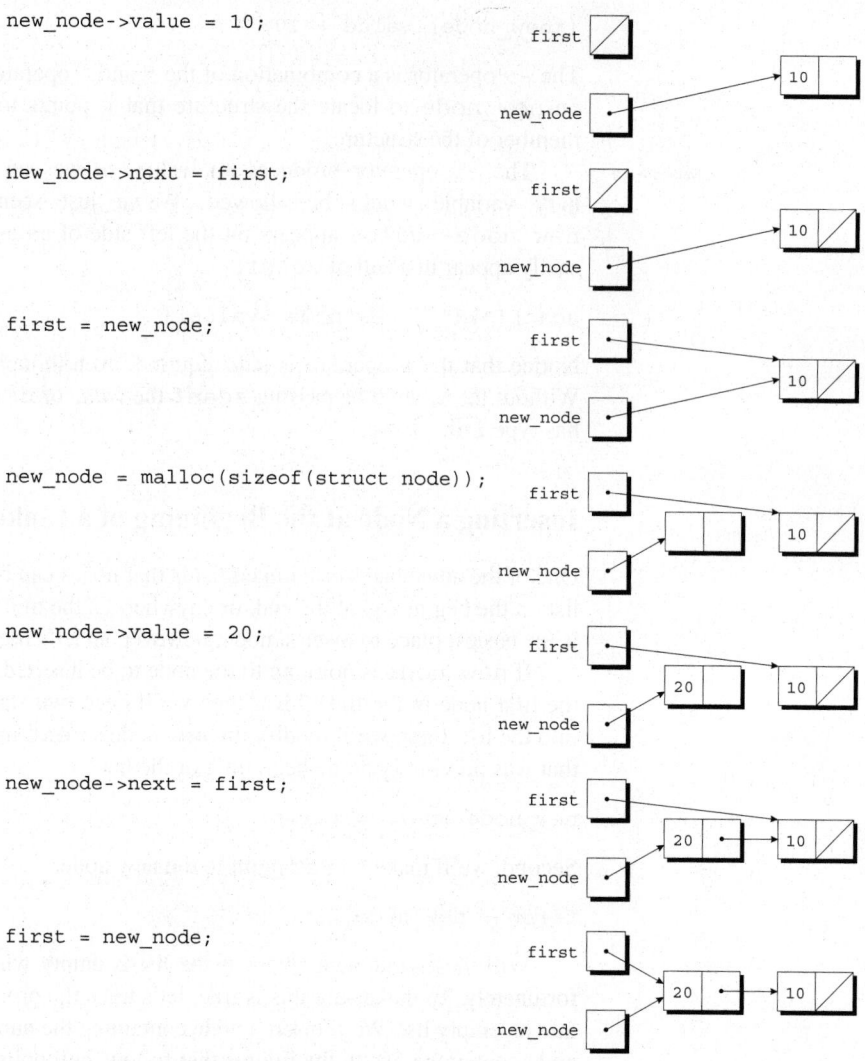

```
new_node->value = 10;

new_node->next = first;

first = new_node;

new_node = malloc(sizeof(struct node));

new_node->value = 20;

new_node->next = first;

first = new_node;
```

Inserting a node into a linked list is such a common operation that we'll probably want to write a function for that purpose. Let's name the function add_to_list. It will have two parameters: list (a pointer to the first node in the old list) and n (the integer to be stored in the new node).

```
struct node *add_to_list(struct node *list, int n)
{
  struct node *new_node;

  new_node = malloc(sizeof(struct node));
  if (new_node == NULL) {
    printf("Error: malloc failed in add_to_list\n");
    exit(EXIT_FAILURE);
  }
```

```
    new_node->value = n;
    new_node->next = list;
    return new_node;
}
```

Note that `add_to_list` doesn't modify the `list` pointer. Instead, it returns a pointer to the newly created node (now at the beginning of the list). When we call `add_to_list`, we'll need to store its return value into `first`:

```
first = add_to_list(first, 10);
first = add_to_list(first, 20);
```

These statements add nodes containing 10 and 20 to the list pointed to by `first`. Getting `add_to_list` to update `first` directly, rather than return a new value for `first`, turns out to be tricky. We'll return to this issue in Section 17.6.

The following function uses `add_to_list` to create a linked list containing numbers entered by the user:

```
struct node *read_numbers(void)
{
    struct node *first = NULL;
    int n;

    printf("Enter a series of integers (0 to terminate): ");
    for (;;) {
        scanf("%d", &n);
        if (n == 0)
            return first;
        first = add_to_list(first, n);
    }
}
```

The numbers will be in reverse order within the list, since `first` always points to the node containing the last number entered.

Searching a Linked List

Once we've created a linked list, we may need to search it for a particular piece of data. Although a `while` loop can be used to search a list, the `for` statement is often superior. We're accustomed to using the `for` statement when writing loops that involve counting, but its flexibility makes the `for` statement suitable for other tasks as well, including operations on linked lists. Here's the customary way to visit the nodes in a linked list, using a pointer variable `p` to keep track of the "current" node:

idiom
```
for (p = first; p != NULL; p = p->next)
    …
```

The assignment

```
p = p->next
```

advances the p pointer from one node to the next. An assignment of this form is invariably used in C when writing a loop that traverses a linked list.

Let's write a function named `search_list` that searches a list (pointed to by the parameter `list`) for an integer n. If it finds n, `search_list` will return a pointer to the node containing n; otherwise, it will return a null pointer. Our first version of `search_list` relies on the "list-traversal" idiom:

```
struct node *search_list(struct node *list, int n)
{
  struct node *p;

  for (p = list; p != NULL; p = p->next)
    if (p->value == n)
      return p;
  return NULL;
}
```

Of course, there are many other ways to write `search_list`. One alternative would be to eliminate the p variable, instead using `list` itself to keep track of the current node:

```
struct node *search_list(struct node *list, int n)
{
  for (; list != NULL; list = list->next)
    if (list->value == n)
      return list;
  return NULL;
}
```

Since `list` is a copy of the original list pointer, there's no harm in changing it within the function.

Another alternative is to combine the `list->value == n` test with the `list != NULL` test:

```
struct node *search_list(struct node *list, int n)
{
  for (; list != NULL && list->value != n; list = list->next)
    ;
  return list;
}
```

Since `list` is NULL if we reach the end of the list, returning `list` is correct even if we don't find n. This version of `search_list` might be a bit clearer if we used a `while` statement:

```
struct node *search_list(struct node *list, int n)
{
  while (list != NULL && list->value != n)
    list = list->next;
  return list;
}
```

Deleting a Node from a Linked List

A big advantage of storing data in a linked list is that we can easily delete nodes that we no longer need. Deleting a node, like creating a node, involves three steps:

1. Locate the node to be deleted.
2. Alter the previous node so that it "bypasses" the deleted node.
3. Call `free` to reclaim the space occupied by the deleted node.

Step 1 is harder than it looks. If we search the list in the obvious way, we'll end up with a pointer to the node to be deleted. Unfortunately, we won't be able to perform step 2, which requires changing the *previous* node.

There are various solutions to this problem. We'll use the "trailing pointer" technique: as we search the list in step 1, we'll keep a pointer to the previous node (`prev`) as well as a pointer to the current node (`cur`). If `list` points to the list to be searched and `n` is the integer to be deleted, the following loop implements step 1:

```
for (cur = list, prev = NULL;
     cur != NULL && cur->value != n;
     prev = cur, cur = cur->next)
  ;
```

Here we see the power of C's `for` statement. This rather exotic example, with its empty body and liberal use of the comma operator, performs all the actions needed to search for n. When the loop terminates, `cur` points to the node to be deleted, while `prev` points to the previous node (if there is one).

To see how this loop works, let's assume that `list` points to a list containing 30, 40, 20, and 10, in that order:

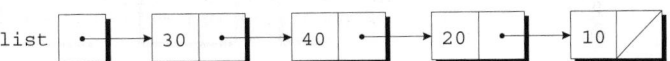

Let's say that n is 20, so our goal is to delete the third node in the list. After `cur = list, prev = NULL` has been executed, `cur` points to the first node in the list:

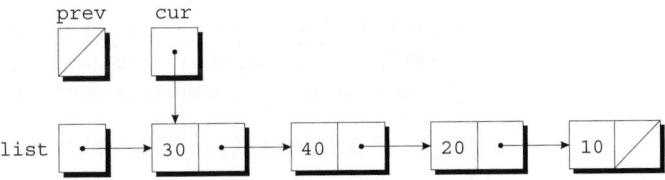

The test `cur != NULL && cur->value != n` is true, since `cur` is pointing to a node and the node doesn't contain 20. After `prev = cur, cur = cur->next` has been executed, we begin to see how the `prev` pointer will trail behind `cur`:

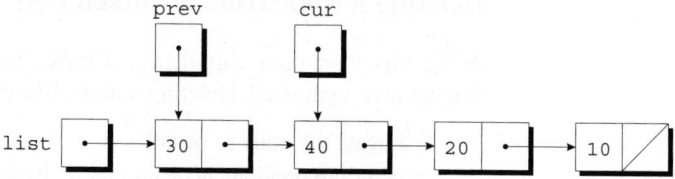

Again, the test cur != NULL && cur->value != n is true, so prev = cur, cur = cur->next is executed once more:

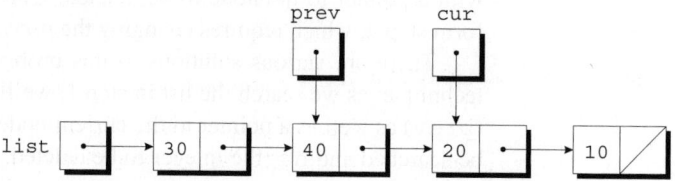

Since cur now points to the node containing 20, the condition cur->value != n is false and the loop terminates.

Next, we'll perform the bypass required by step 2. The statement

```
prev->next = cur->next;
```

makes the pointer in the previous node point to the node *after* the current node:

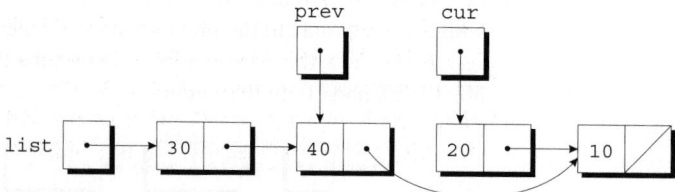

We're now ready for step 3, releasing the memory occupied by the current node:

```
free(cur);
```

The following function, delete_from_list, uses the strategy that we've just outlined. When given a list and an integer n, the function deletes the first node containing n. If no node contains n, delete_from_list does nothing. In either case, the function returns a pointer to the list.

```
struct node *delete_from_list(struct node *list, int n)
{
  struct node *cur, *prev;

  for (cur = list, prev = NULL;
       cur != NULL && cur->value != n;
       prev = cur, cur = cur->next)
    ;
```

```
    if (cur == NULL)
      return list;                  /* n was not found */
    if (prev == NULL)
      list = list->next;            /* n is in the first node */
    else
      prev->next = cur->next;       /* n is in some other node */
    free(cur);
    return list;
}
```

Deleting the first node in the list is a special case. The `prev == NULL` test checks for this case, which requires a different bypass step.

Ordered Lists

When the nodes of a list are kept in order—sorted by the data stored inside the nodes—we say that the list is *ordered.* Inserting a node into an ordered list is more difficult (the node won't always be put at the beginning of the list), but searching is faster (we can stop looking after reaching the point at which the desired node would have been located). The following program illustrates both the increased difficulty of inserting a node and the faster search.

PROGRAM **Maintaining a Parts Database (Revisited)**

Let's redo the parts database program of Section 16.3, this time storing the database in a linked list. Using a linked list instead of an array has two major advantages: (1) We don't need to put a preset limit on the size of the database; it can grow until there's no more memory to store parts. (2) We can easily keep the database sorted by part number—when a new part is added to the database, we simply insert it in its proper place in the list. In the original program, the database wasn't sorted.

In the new program, the `part` structure will contain an additional member (a pointer to the next node in the linked list), and the variable `inventory` will be a pointer to the first node in the list:

```
struct part {
  int number;
  char name[NAME_LEN+1];
  int on_hand;
  struct part *next;
};

struct part *inventory = NULL;   /* points to first part */
```

Most of the functions in the new program will closely resemble their counterparts in the original program. The `find_part` and `insert` functions will be more complex, however, since we'll keep the nodes in the `inventory` list sorted by part number.

In the original program, `find_part` returns an index into the `inventory` array. In the new program, `find_part` will return a pointer to the node that contains the desired part number. If it doesn't find the part number, `find_part` will return a null pointer. Since the `inventory` list is sorted by part number, the new version of `find_part` can save time by stopping its search when it finds a node containing a part number that's greater than or equal to the desired part number. `find_part`'s search loop will have the form

```
for (p = inventory;
     p != NULL && number > p->number;
     p = p->next)
  ;
```

The loop will terminate when p becomes `NULL` (indicating that the part number wasn't found) or when `number > p->number` is false (indicating that the part number we're looking for is less than or equal to a number already stored in a node). In the latter case, we still don't know whether or not the desired number is actually in the list, so we'll need another test:

```
if (p != NULL && number == p->number)
  return p;
```

The original version of `insert` stores a new part in the next available array element. The new version must determine where the new part belongs in the list and insert it there. We'll also have `insert` check whether the part number is already present in the list. `insert` can accomplish both tasks by using a loop similar to the one in `find_part`:

```
for (cur = inventory, prev = NULL;
     cur != NULL && new_node->number > cur->number;
     prev = cur, cur = cur->next)
  ;
```

This loop relies on two pointers: `cur`, which points to the current node, and `prev`, which points to the previous node. Once the loop terminates, `insert` will check whether `cur` isn't `NULL` and `new_node->number` equals `cur->number`; if so, the part number is already in the list. Otherwise `insert` will insert a new node between the nodes pointed to by `prev` and `cur`, using a strategy similar to the one we employed for deleting a node. (This strategy works even if the new part number is larger than any in the list; in that case, `cur` will be `NULL` but `prev` will point to the last node in the list.)

Here's the new program. Like the original program, this version requires the `read_line` function described in Section 16.3; I assume that `readline.h` contains a prototype for this function.

inventory2.c   `/* Maintains a parts database (linked list version) */`

```
#include <stdio.h>
#include <stdlib.h>
#include "readline.h"
```

```
#define NAME_LEN 25

struct part {
  int number;
  char name[NAME_LEN+1];
  int on_hand;
  struct part *next;
};

struct part *inventory = NULL;    /* points to first part */

struct part *find_part(int number);
void insert(void);
void search(void);
void update(void);
void print(void);

/************************************************************
 * main: Prompts the user to enter an operation code,      *
 *       then calls a function to perform the requested    *
 *       action. Repeats until the user enters the         *
 *       command 'q'. Prints an error message if the user  *
 *       enters an illegal code.                           *
 ************************************************************/
int main(void)
{
  char code;

  for (;;) {
    printf("Enter operation code: ");
    scanf(" %c", &code);
    while (getchar() != '\n')    /* skips to end of line */
      ;
    switch (code) {
      case 'i': insert();
                break;
      case 's': search();
                break;
      case 'u': update();
                break;
      case 'p': print();
                break;
      case 'q': return 0;
      default:  printf("Illegal code\n");
    }
    printf("\n");
  }
}

/************************************************************
 * find_part: Looks up a part number in the inventory      *
 *            list. Returns a pointer to the node          *
 *            containing the part number; if the part      *
 *            number is not found, returns NULL.           *
 ************************************************************/
```

```c
struct part *find_part(int number)
{
  struct part *p;

  for (p = inventory;
       p != NULL && number > p->number;
       p = p->next)
    ;
  if (p != NULL && number == p->number)
    return p;
  return NULL;
}

/**************************************************************
 * insert: Prompts the user for information about a new      *
 *         part and then inserts the part into the           *
 *         inventory list; the list remains sorted by        *
 *         part number. Prints an error message and          *
 *         returns prematurely if the part already exists    *
 *         or space could not be allocated for the part.     *
 **************************************************************/
void insert(void)
{
  struct part *cur, *prev, *new_node;

  new_node = malloc(sizeof(struct part));
  if (new_node == NULL) {
    printf("Database is full; can't add more parts.\n");
    return;
  }

  printf("Enter part number: ");
  scanf("%d", &new_node->number);

  for (cur = inventory, prev = NULL;
       cur != NULL && new_node->number > cur->number;
       prev = cur, cur = cur->next)
    ;
  if (cur != NULL && new_node->number == cur->number) {
    printf("Part already exists.\n");
    free(new_node);
    return;
  }

  printf("Enter part name: ");
  read_line(new_node->name, NAME_LEN);
  printf("Enter quantity on hand: ");
  scanf("%d", &new_node->on_hand);

  new_node->next = cur;
  if (prev == NULL)
    inventory = new_node;
  else
    prev->next = new_node;
}
```

```c
/**************************************************************
 * search: Prompts the user to enter a part number, then     *
 *         looks up the part in the database. If the part     *
 *         exists, prints the name and quantity on hand;      *
 *         if not, prints an error message.                   *
 **************************************************************/
void search(void)
{
  int number;
  struct part *p;

  printf("Enter part number: ");
  scanf("%d", &number);
  p = find_part(number);
  if (p != NULL) {
    printf("Part name: %s\n", p->name);
    printf("Quantity on hand: %d\n", p->on_hand);
  } else
    printf("Part not found.\n");
}

/**************************************************************
 * update: Prompts the user to enter a part number.          *
 *         Prints an error message if the part doesn't        *
 *         exist; otherwise, prompts the user to enter         *
 *         change in quantity on hand and updates the         *
 *         database.                                          *
 **************************************************************/
void update(void)
{
  int number, change;
  struct part *p;

  printf("Enter part number: ");
  scanf("%d", &number);
  p = find_part(number);
  if (p != NULL) {
    printf("Enter change in quantity on hand: ");
    scanf("%d", &change);
    p->on_hand += change;
  } else
    printf("Part not found.\n");
}

/**************************************************************
 * print: Prints a listing of all parts in the database,     *
 *        showing the part number, part name, and            *
 *        quantity on hand. Part numbers will appear in       *
 *        ascending order.                                    *
 **************************************************************/
void print(void)
{
  struct part *p;
```

```
     printf("Part Number    Part Name                    "
            "Quantity on Hand\n");
  for (p = inventory; p != NULL; p = p->next)
    printf("%7d          %-25s%11d\n", p->number, p->name,
           p->on_hand);
}
```

Notice the use of free in the insert function. insert allocates memory for a part before checking to see if the part already exists. If it does, insert releases the space to avoid a memory leak.

17.6   Pointers to Pointers

In Section 13.7, we came across the notion of a *pointer* to a *pointer*. In that section, we used an array whose elements were of type char *; a pointer to one of the array elements itself had type char **. The concept of "pointers to pointers" also pops up frequently in the context of linked data structures. In particular, when an argument to a function is a pointer variable, we'll sometimes want the function to be able to modify the variable by making it point somewhere else. Doing so requires the use of a pointer to a pointer.

Consider the add_to_list function of Section 17.5, which inserts a node at the beginning of a linked list. When we call add_to_list, we pass it a pointer to the first node in the original list; it then returns a pointer to the first node in the updated list:

```
struct node *add_to_list(struct node *list, int n)
{
  struct node *new_node;

  new_node = malloc(sizeof(struct node));
  if (new_node == NULL) {
    printf("Error: malloc failed in add_to_list\n");
    exit(EXIT_FAILURE);
  }
  new_node->value = n;
  new_node->next = list;
  return new_node;
}
```

Suppose that we modify the function so that it assigns new_node to list instead of returning new_node. In other words, let's remove the return statement from add_to_list and replace it by

```
list = new_node;
```

Unfortunately, this idea doesn't work. Suppose that we call add_to_list in the following way:

```
add_to_list(first, 10);
```

At the point of the call, `first` is copied into `list`. (Pointers, like all arguments, are passed by value.) The last line in the function changes the value of `list`, making it point to the new node. This assignment doesn't affect `first`, however.

Getting `add_to_list` to modify `first` is possible, but it requires passing `add_to_list` a *pointer* to `first`. Here's the correct version of the function:

```
void add_to_list(struct node **list, int n)
{
  struct node *new_node;

  new_node = malloc(sizeof(struct node));
  if (new_node == NULL) {
    printf("Error: malloc failed in add_to_list\n");
    exit(EXIT_FAILURE);
  }
  new_node->value = n;
  new_node->next = *list;
  *list = new_node;
}
```

When we call the new version of `add_to_list`, the first argument will be the address of `first`:

```
add_to_list(&first, 10);
```

Since `list` is assigned the address of `first`, we can use `*list` as an alias for `first`. In particular, assigning `new_node` to `*list` will modify `first`.

17.7 Pointers to Functions

We've seen that pointers may point to various kinds of data, including variables, array elements, and dynamically allocated blocks of memory. But C doesn't require that pointers point only to *data;* it's also possible to have pointers to *functions*. Pointers to functions aren't as odd as you might think. After all, functions occupy memory locations, so every function has an address, just as each variable has an address.

Function Pointers as Arguments

We can use function pointers in much the same way we use pointers to data. In particular, passing a function pointer as an argument is fairly common in C. Suppose that we're writing a function named `integrate` that integrates a mathematical function `f` between points `a` and `b`. We'd like to make `integrate` as general as possible by passing it `f` as an argument. To achieve this effect in C, we'll declare `f` to be a pointer to a function. Assuming that we want to integrate functions that have a `double` parameter and return a `double` result, the prototype for `integrate` will look like this:

```
double integrate(double (*f)(double), double a, double b);
```

The parentheses around `*f` indicate that `f` is a pointer to a function, not a function that returns a pointer. It's also legal to declare `f` as though it were a function:

```
double integrate(double f(double), double a, double b);
```

From the compiler's standpoint, this prototype is identical to the previous one.

sin function ➤ 23.3

When we call `integrate`, we'll supply a function name as the first argument. For example, the following call will integrate the `sin` (sine) function from 0 to π/2:

```
result = integrate(sin, 0.0, PI / 2);
```

Notice that there are no parentheses after `sin`. When a function name isn't followed by parentheses, the C compiler produces a pointer to the function instead of generating code for a function call. In our example, we're not calling `sin`; instead, we're passing `integrate` a pointer to `sin`. If this seems confusing, think of how C handles arrays. If `a` is the name of an array, then `a[i]` represents one element of the array, while `a` by itself serves as a pointer to the array. In a similar way, if `f` is a function, C treats `f(x)` as a *call* of the function but `f` by itself as a *pointer* to the function.

Within the body of `integrate`, we can call the function that `f` points to:

```
y = (*f)(x);
```

`*f` represents the function that `f` points to; `x` is the argument to the call. Thus, during the execution of `integrate(sin, 0.0, PI / 2)`, each call of `*f` is actually a call of `sin`. As an alternative to `(*f)(x)`, C allows us to write `f(x)` to call the function that `f` points to. Although `f(x)` looks more natural, I'll stick with `(*f)(x)` as a reminder that `f` is a pointer to a function, not a function name.

The `qsort` Function

Although it might seem that pointers to functions aren't relevant to the average programmer, that couldn't be further from the truth. In fact, some of the most useful functions in the C library require a function pointer as an argument. One of these is `qsort`, which belongs to the `<stdlib.h>` header. `qsort` is a general-purpose sorting function that's capable of sorting any array, based on any criteria that we choose.

Since the elements of the array that it sorts may be of any type—even a structure or union type—`qsort` must be told how to determine which of two array elements is "smaller." We'll provide this information to `qsort` by writing a *comparison function.* When given two pointers p and q to array elements, the comparison function must return an integer that is *negative* if *p is "less than" *q, *zero* if *p is "equal to" *q, and *positive* if *p is "greater than" *q. The terms "less than," "equal to," and "greater than" are in quotes because it's our responsibility to determine how *p and *q are compared.

qsort has the following prototype:

```
void qsort(void *base, size_t nmemb, size_t size,
           int (*compar)(const void *, const void *));
```

base must point to the first element in the array. (If only a portion of the array is to be sorted, we'll make base point to the first element in this portion.) In the simplest case, base is just the name of the array. nmemb is the number of elements to be sorted (not necessarily the number of elements in the array). size is the size of each array element, measured in bytes. compar is a pointer to the comparison function. When qsort is called, it sorts the array into ascending order, calling the comparison function whenever it needs to compare array elements.

To sort the inventory array of Section 16.3, we'd use the following call of qsort:

Q&A

```
qsort(inventory, num_parts, sizeof(struct part), compare_parts);
```

Notice that the second argument is num_parts, not MAX_PARTS; we don't want to sort the entire inventory array, just the portion in which parts are currently stored. The last argument, compare_parts, is a function that compares two part structures.

Writing the compare_parts function isn't as easy as you might expect. qsort requires that its parameters have type void *, but we can't access the members of a part structure through a void * pointer; we need a pointer of type struct part * instead. To solve the problem, we'll have compare_parts assign its parameters, p and q, to variables of type struct part *, thereby converting them to the desired type. compare_parts can now use these variables to access the members of the structures that p and q point to. Assuming that we want to sort the inventory array into ascending order by part number, here's how the compare_parts function might look:

```
int compare_parts(const void *p, const void *q)
{
  const struct part *p1 = p;
  const struct part *q1 = q;

  if (p1->number < q1->number)
    return -1;
  else if (p1->number == q1->number)
    return 0;
  else
    return 1;
}
```

The declarations of p1 and q1 include the word const to avoid getting a warning from the compiler. Since p and q are const pointers (indicating that the objects to which they point should not be modified), they should be assigned only to pointer variables that are also declared to be `const`.

Although this version of `compare_parts` works, most C programmers would write the function more concisely. First, notice that we can replace `p1` and `q1` by cast expressions:

```
int compare_parts(const void *p, const void *q)
{
  if (((struct part *) p)->number <
       ((struct part *) q)->number)
    return -1;
  else if (((struct part *) p)->number ==
              ((struct part *) q)->number)
    return 0;
  else
    return 1;
}
```

The parentheses around `((struct part *) p)` are necessary; without them, the compiler would try to cast `p->number` to type `struct part *`.

We can make `compare_parts` even shorter by removing the `if` statements:

```
int compare_parts(const void *p, const void *q)
{
  return ((struct part *) p)->number -
          ((struct part *) q)->number;
}
```

Subtracting q's part number from p's part number produces a negative result if p has a smaller part number, zero if the part numbers are equal, and a positive result if p has a larger part number. (Note that subtracting two integers is potentially risky because of the danger of overflow. I'm assuming that part numbers are positive integers, so that shouldn't happen here.)

To sort the `inventory` array by part name instead of part number, we'd use the following version of `compare_parts`:

```
int compare_parts(const void *p, const void *q)
{
  return strcmp(((struct part *) p)->name,
                 ((struct part *) q)->name);
}
```

All `compare_parts` has to do is call `strcmp`, which conveniently returns a negative, zero, or positive result.

Other Uses of Function Pointers

Although I've emphasized the usefulness of function pointers as arguments to other functions, that's not all they're good for. C treats pointers to functions just like pointers to data; we can store function pointers in variables or use them as elements of an array or as members of a structure or union. We can even write functions that return function pointers.

Here's an example of a variable that can store a pointer to a function:

```
void (*pf)(int);
```

pf can point to any function with an int parameter and a return type of void. If f is such a function, we can make pf point to f in the following way:

```
pf = f;
```

Notice that there's no ampersand preceding f. Once pf points to f, we can call f by writing either

```
(*pf)(i);
```

or

```
pf(i);
```

Arrays whose elements are function pointers have a surprising number of applications. For example, suppose that we're writing a program that displays a menu of commands for the user to choose from. We can write functions that implement these commands, then store pointers to the functions in an array:

```
void (*file_cmd[])(void) = {new_cmd,
                            open_cmd,
                            close_cmd,
                            close_all_cmd,
                            save_cmd,
                            save_as_cmd,
                            save_all_cmd,
                            print_cmd,
                            exit_cmd
                            };
```

If the user selects command n, where n falls between 0 and 8, we can subscript the file_cmd array and call the corresponding function:

```
(*file_cmd[n])();   /* or file_cmd[n](); */
```

Of course, we could get a similar effect with a switch statement. Using an array of function pointers gives us more flexibility, however, since the elements of the array can be changed as the program is running.

PROGRAM   **Tabulating the Trigonometric Functions**

<math.h> header ▶23.3

The following program prints tables showing the values of the cos, sin, and tan functions (all three belong to <math.h>). The program is built around a function named tabulate that, when passed a function pointer f, prints a table showing the values of f.

tabulate.c   `/* Tabulates values of trigonometric functions */`

```
#include <math.h>
#include <stdio.h>

void tabulate(double (*f)(double), double first,
              double last, double incr);

int main(void)
{
  double final, increment, initial;

  printf("Enter initial value: ");
  scanf("%lf", &initial);

  printf("Enter final value: ");
  scanf("%lf", &final);

  printf("Enter increment: ");
  scanf("%lf", &increment);

  printf("\n      x          cos(x)"
         "\n   -------      -------\n");
  tabulate(cos, initial, final, increment);

  printf("\n      x          sin(x)"
         "\n   -------      -------\n");
  tabulate(sin, initial, final, increment);

  printf("\n      x          tan(x)"
         "\n   -------      -------\n");
  tabulate(tan, initial, final, increment);

  return 0;
}

void tabulate(double (*f)(double), double first,
              double last, double incr)
{
  double x;
  int i, num_intervals;

  num_intervals = ceil((last - first) / incr);
  for (i = 0; i <= num_intervals; i++) {
    x = first + i * incr;
    printf("%10.5f %10.5f\n", x, (*f)(x));
  }
}
```

tabulate uses the ceil function, which also in <math.h>. When given an argument x of double type, ceil returns the smallest integer that's greater than or equal to x.

Here's what a session with tabulate.c might look like:

```
Enter initial value: 0
Enter final value: .5
Enter increment: .1

        x          cos(x)
     -------      -------
     0.00000      1.00000
     0.10000      0.99500
     0.20000      0.98007
     0.30000      0.95534
     0.40000      0.92106
     0.50000      0.87758

        x          sin(x)
     -------      -------
     0.00000      0.00000
     0.10000      0.09983
     0.20000      0.19867
     0.30000      0.29552
     0.40000      0.38942
     0.50000      0.47943

        x          tan(x)
     -------      -------
     0.00000      0.00000
     0.10000      0.10033
     0.20000      0.20271
     0.30000      0.30934
     0.40000      0.42279
     0.50000      0.54630
```

17.8   Restricted Pointers (C99)

This section and the next discuss two of C99's pointer-related features. Both are primarily of interest to advanced C programmers; most readers will want to skip these sections.

In C99, the keyword `restrict` may appear in the declaration of a pointer:

```
int * restrict p;
```

A pointer that's been declared using `restrict` is called a ***restricted pointer.*** The intent is that if p points to an object that is later modified, then that object is not accessed in any way other than through p. (Alternative ways to access the object include having another pointer to the same object or having p point to a named variable.) Having more than one way to access an object is often called ***aliasing.***

Let's look at an example of the kind of behavior that restricted pointers are supposed to discourage. Suppose that p and q have been declared as follows:

```
int * restrict p;
int * restrict q;
```

Now suppose that p is made to point to a dynamically allocated block of memory:

```
p = malloc(sizeof(int));
```

(A similar situation would arise if p were assigned the address of a variable or an array element.) Normally it would be legal to copy p into q and then modify the integer through q:

```
q = p;
*q = 0;    /* causes undefined behavior */
```

Because p is a restricted pointer, however, the effect of executing the statement *q = 0; is undefined. By making p and q point to the same object, we caused *p and *q to be aliases.

extern storage class ➤ 18.2
blocks ➤ 10.3

If a restricted pointer p is declared as a local variable without the extern storage class, restrict applies only to p when the block in which p is declared is being executed. (Note that the body of a function is a block.) restrict can be used with function parameters of pointer type, in which case it applies only when the function is executing. When restrict is applied to a pointer variable with file scope, however, the restriction lasts for the entire execution of the program.

file scope ➤ 10.2

The exact rules for using restrict are rather complex; see the C99 standard for details. There are even situations in which an alias created from a restricted pointer is legal. For example, a restricted pointer p can be legally copied into another restricted pointer variable q, provided that p is local to a function and q is defined inside a block nested within the function's body.

To illustrate the use of restrict, let's look at the memcpy and memmove functions, which belong to the <string.h> header. memcpy has the following prototype in C99:

<string.h> header ➤ 23.6

```
void *memcpy(void * restrict s1, const void * restrict s2,
             size_t n);
```

memcpy is similar to strcpy, except that it copies bytes from one object to another (strcpy copies characters from one string into another). s2 points to the data to be copied, s1 points to the destination of the copy, and n is the number of bytes to be copied. The use of restrict with both s1 and s2 indicates that the source of the copy and the destination shouldn't overlap. (It doesn't *guarantee* that they don't overlap, however.)

In contrast, restrict doesn't appear in the prototype for memmove:

```
void *memmove(void *s1, const void *s2, size_t n);
```

memmove does the same thing as memcpy: it copies bytes from one place to another. The difference is that memmove is guaranteed to work even if the source and destination overlap. For example, we could use memmove to shift the elements of an array by one position:

```
int a[100];
...
```

```
memmove(&a[0], &a[1], 99 * sizeof(int));
```

Prior to C99, there was no way to document the difference between `memcpy` and `memmove`. The prototypes for the two functions were nearly identical:

```
void *memcpy(void *s1, const void *s2, size_t n);
void *memmove(void *s1, const void *s2, size_t n);
```

The use of `restrict` in the C99 version of `memcpy`'s prototype lets the programmer know that `s1` and `s2` should point to objects that don't overlap, or else the function isn't guaranteed to work.

Although using `restrict` in function prototypes is useful documentation, that's not the primary reason for its existence. `restrict` provides information to the compiler that may enable it to produce more efficient code—a process known as ***optimization.*** (The `register` storage class serves the same purpose.) Not every compiler attempts to optimize programs, however, and the ones that do normally allow the programmer to disable optimization. As a result, the C99 standard guarantees that `restrict` has no effect on the behavior of a program that conforms to the standard: if all uses of `restrict` are removed from such a program, it should behave the same.

`register` storage class ➤ *18.2*

Most programmers won't use `restrict` unless they're fine-tuning a program to achieve the best possible performance. Still, it's worth knowing about `restrict` because it appears in the C99 prototypes for a number of standard library functions.

17.9   Flexible Array Members (C99)

Every once in a while, we'll need to define a structure that contains an array of an unknown size. For example, we might want to store strings in a form that's different from the usual one. Normally, a string is an array of characters, with a null character marking the end. However, there are advantages to storing strings in other ways. One alternative is to store the length of the string along with the string's characters (but with no null character). The length and the characters could be stored in a structure such as this one:

```
struct vstring {
  int len;
  char chars[N];
};
```

Here `N` is a macro that represents the maximum length of a string. Using a fixed-length array such as this is undesirable, however, because it forces us to limit the length of the string, plus it wastes memory (since most strings won't need all `N` characters in the array).

C programmers have traditionally solved this problem by declaring the length of `chars` to be 1 (a dummy value) and then dynamically allocating each string:

```
struct vstring {
  int len;
  char chars[1];
};
...
struct vstring *str = malloc(sizeof(struct vstring) + n - 1);
str->len = n;
```

We're "cheating" by allocating more memory than the structure is declared to have (in this case, an extra $n - 1$ characters), and then using the memory to store additional elements of the chars array. This technique has become so common over the years that it has a name: the "struct hack."

The struct hack isn't limited to character arrays; it has a variety of uses. Over time, it has become popular enough to be supported by many compilers. Some (including GCC) even allow the chars array to have zero length, which makes this trick a little more explicit. Unfortunately, the C89 standard doesn't guarantee that the struct hack will work, nor does it allow zero-length arrays.

In recognition of the struct hack's usefulness, C99 has a feature known as the *flexible array member* that serves the same purpose. When the last member of a structure is an array, its length may be omitted:

```
struct vstring {
  int len;
  char chars[];    /* flexible array member - C99 only */
};
```

The length of the chars array isn't determined until memory is allocated for a vstring structure, normally using a call of malloc:

```
struct vstring *str = malloc(sizeof(struct vstring) + n);
str->len = n;
```

In this example, str points to a vstring structure in which the chars array occupies n characters. The sizeof operator ignores the chars member when computing the size of the structure. (A flexible array member is unusual in that it takes up no space within a structure.)

A few special rules apply to a structure that contains a flexible array member. The flexible array member must appear last in the structure, and the structure must have at least one other member. Copying a structure that contains a flexible array member will copy the other members but not the flexible array itself.

A structure that contains a flexible array member is an **incomplete type.** An incomplete type is missing part of the information needed to determine how much memory it requires. Incomplete types, which are discussed further in one of the Q&A questions at the end of this chapter and in Section 19.3, are subject to various restrictions. In particular, an incomplete type (and hence a structure that contains a flexible array member) can't be a member of another structure or an element of an array. However, an array may contain pointers to structures that have a flexible array member; Programming Project 7 at the end of this chapter is built around such an array.

Q & A

Q: **What does the `NULL` macro represent? [p. 415]**

A: `NULL` actually stands for 0. When we use 0 in a context where a pointer would be required, C compilers treat it as a null pointer instead of the integer 0. The `NULL` macro is provided merely to help avoid confusion. The assignment

```
p = 0;
```

could be assigning the value 0 to a numeric variable or assigning a null pointer to a pointer variable; we can't easily tell which. In contrast, the assignment

```
p = NULL;
```

makes it clear that `p` is a pointer.

*Q: **In the header files that come with my compiler, `NULL` is defined as follows:**

```
#define NULL (void *) 0
```

What's the advantage of casting 0 to `void *`?

A: This trick, which is allowed by the C standard, enables compilers to spot incorrect uses of the null pointer. For example, suppose that we try to assign `NULL` to an integer variable:

```
i = NULL;
```

If `NULL` is defined as 0, this assignment is perfectly legal. But if `NULL` is defined as `(void *) 0`, the compiler can warn us that we're assigning a pointer to an integer variable.

Defining `NULL` as `(void *) 0` has a second, more important, advantage. Suppose that we call a function with a variable-length argument list and pass `NULL` as one of the arguments. If `NULL` is defined as 0, the compiler will incorrectly pass a zero integer value. (In an ordinary function call, `NULL` works fine because the compiler knows from the function's prototype that it expects a pointer. When a function has a variable-length argument list, however, the compiler lacks this knowledge.) If `NULL` is defined as `(void *) 0`, the compiler will pass a null pointer.

To make matters even more confusing, some header files define `NULL` to be `0L` (the `long` version of 0). This definition, like the definition of `NULL` as 0, is a holdover from C's earlier years, when pointers and integers were compatible. For most purposes, though, it really doesn't matter how `NULL` is defined; just think of it as a name for the null pointer.

variable-length argument lists
➤26.1

Q: **Since 0 is used to represent the null pointer, I guess a null pointer is just an address with all zero bits, right?**

A: Not necessarily. Each C compiler is allowed to represent null pointers in a different way, and not all compilers use a zero address. For example, some compilers use a nonexistent memory address for the null pointer; that way, attempting to access memory through a null pointer can be detected by the hardware.

How the null pointer is stored inside the computer shouldn't concern us; that's a detail for compiler experts to worry about. The important thing is that, when used in a pointer context, 0 is converted to the proper internal form by the compiler.

Q: Is it acceptable to use NULL as a null character?

A: Definitely not. NULL is a macro that represents the null *pointer*, not the null *character*. Using NULL as a null character will work with some compilers, but not with all (since some define NULL as (void *) 0). In any event, using NULL as anything other than a pointer can lead to a great deal of confusion. If you want a name for the null character, define the following macro:

```
#define NUL '\0'
```

*Q: When my program terminates, I get the message *"Null pointer assignment."* What does this mean?

A: This message, which is produced by programs compiled with some older DOS-based C compilers, indicates that the program has stored data in memory using a bad pointer (but not necessarily a null pointer). Unfortunately, the message isn't displayed until the program terminates, so there's no clue as to which statement caused the error. The *"Null pointer assignment"* message can be caused by a missing & in scanf:

```
scanf("%d", i);    /* should have been scanf("%d", &i); */
```

Another possibility is an assignment involving a pointer that's uninitialized or null:

```
*p = i;    /* p is uninitialized or null */
```

*Q: How does a program know that a "null pointer assignment" has occurred?

A: The message depends on the fact that, in the small and medium memory models, data is stored in a single segment, with addresses beginning at 0. The compiler leaves a "hole" at the beginning of the data segment—a small block of memory that's initialized to 0 but otherwise isn't used by the program. When the program terminates, it checks to see if any data in the "hole" area is nonzero. If so, it must have been altered through a bad pointer.

Q: Is there any advantage to casting the return value of malloc or the other memory allocation functions? [p. 416]

A: Not usually. Casting the void * pointer that these functions return is unnecessary, since pointers of type void * are automatically converted to any pointer type upon assignment. The habit of casting the return value is a holdover from older versions of C, in which the memory allocation functions returned a char * value, making the cast necessary. Programs that are designed to be compiled as C++ code may benefit from the cast, but that's about the only reason to do it.

In C89, there's actually a small advantage to *not* performing the cast. Suppose that we've forgotten to include the `<stdlib.h>` header in our program. When we call `malloc`, the compiler will assume that its return type is `int` (the default return value for any C function). If we don't cast the return value of `malloc`, a C89 compiler will produce an error (or at least a warning), since we're trying to assign an integer value to a pointer variable. On the other hand, if we cast the return value to a pointer, the program may compile, but likely won't run properly. With C99, this advantage disappears. Forgetting to include the `<stdlib.h>` header will cause an error when `malloc` is called, because C99 requires that a function be declared before it's called.

Q: **The `calloc` function initializes a memory block by setting its bits to zero. Does this mean that all data items in the block become zero? [p. 421]**

A: Usually, but not always. Setting an integer to zero bits always makes the integer zero. Setting a floating-point number to zero bits usually makes the number zero, but this isn't guaranteed—it depends on how floating-point numbers are stored. The story is the same for pointers; a pointer whose bits are zero isn't necessary a null pointer.

*Q: **I see how the structure tag mechanism allows a structure to contain a pointer to itself. But what if two structures each have a member that points to the other? [p. 425]**

A: Here's how we'd handle that situation:

```
struct s1;    /* incomplete declaration of s1 */

struct s2 {
  ...
  struct s1 *p;
  ...
};

struct s1 {
  ...
  struct s2 *q;
  ...
};
```

incomplete types ➤ *19.3* The first declaration of `s1` creates an incomplete structure type, since we haven't specified the members of `s1`. The second declaration of `s1` "completes" the type by describing the members of the structure. Incomplete declarations of a structure type are permitted in C, although their uses are limited. Creating a pointer to such a type (as we did when declaring `p`) is one of these uses.

Q: **Calling `malloc` with the wrong argument—causing it to allocate too much memory or too little memory—seems to be a common error. Is there a safer way to use `malloc`? [p. 426]**

A: Yes, there is. Some programmers use the following idiom when calling `malloc` to allocate memory for a single object:

```
p = malloc(sizeof(*p));
```

Since `sizeof(*p)` is the size of the object to which p will point, this statement guarantees that the correct amount of memory will be allocated. At first glance, this idiom looks fishy: it's likely that p is uninitialized, making the value of `*p` undefined. However, `sizeof` doesn't evaluate `*p`, it merely computes its size, so the idiom works even if p is uninitialized or contains a null pointer.

To allocate memory for an array with n elements, we can use a slightly modified version of the idiom:

```
p = malloc(n * sizeof(*p));
```

Q: **Why isn't the `qsort` function simply named `sort`? [p. 440]**

A: The name `qsort` comes from the Quicksort algorithm published by C. A. R. Hoare in 1962 (and discussed in Section 9.6). Ironically, the C standard doesn't require that `qsort` use the Quicksort algorithm, although many versions of `qsort` do.

Q: **Isn't it necessary to cast `qsort`'s first argument to type `void *`, as in the following example? [p. 441]**

```
qsort((void *) inventory, num_parts, sizeof(struct part),
      compare_parts);
```

A: No. A pointer of any type can be converted to `void *` automatically.

*Q: **I want to use `qsort` to sort an array of integers, but I'm having trouble writing a comparison function. What's the secret?**

A: Here's a version that works:

```
int compare_ints(const void *p, const void *q)
{
  return *(int *)p - *(int *)q;
}
```

Bizarre, eh? The expression `(int *)p` casts p to type `int *`, so `*(int *)p` would be the integer that p points to. A word of warning, though: Subtracting two integers may cause overflow. If the integers being sorted are completely arbitrary, it's safer to use `if` statements to compare `*(int *)p` with `*(int *)q`.

*Q: **I needed to sort an array of strings, so I figured I'd just use `strcmp` as the comparison function. When I passed it to `qsort`, however, the compiler gave me a warning. I tried to fix the problem by embedding `strcmp` in a comparison function:**

```
int compare_strings(const void *p, const void *q)
{
  return strcmp(p, q);
}
```

Now my program compiles, but qsort doesn't seem to sort the array. What am I doing wrong?

A: First, you can't pass strcmp itself to qsort, since qsort requires a comparison function with two const void * parameters. Your compare_strings function doesn't work because it incorrectly assumes that p and q are strings (char * pointers). In fact, p and q point to array elements containing char * pointers. To fix compare_strings, we'll cast p and q to type char **, then use the * operator to remove one level of indirection:

```
int compare_strings(const void *p, const void *q)
{
  return strcmp(*(char **)p, *(char **)q);
}
```

Exercises

Section 17.1

1. Having to check the return value of malloc (or any other memory allocation function) each time we call it can be an annoyance. Write a function named my_malloc that serves as a "wrapper" for malloc. When we call my_malloc and ask it to allocate n bytes, it in turn calls malloc, tests to make sure that malloc doesn't return a null pointer, and then returns the pointer from malloc. Have my_malloc print an error message and terminate the program if malloc returns a null pointer.

Section 17.2 Ⓦ 2. Write a function named duplicate that uses dynamic storage allocation to create a copy of a string. For example, the call

```
p = duplicate(str);
```

would allocate space for a string of the same length as str, copy the contents of str into the new string, and return a pointer to it. Have duplicate return a null pointer if the memory allocation fails.

Section 17.3

3. Write the following function:

```
int *create_array(int n, int initial_value);
```

The function should return a pointer to a dynamically allocated int array with n members, each of which is initialized to initial_value. The return value should be NULL if the array can't be allocated.

Section 17.5

4. Suppose that the following declarations are in effect:

```
struct point { int x, y; };
struct rectangle { struct point upper_left, lower_right; };
struct rectangle *p;
```

Assume that we want p to point to a `rectangle` structure whose upper left corner is at (10, 25) and whose lower right corner is at (20, 15). Write a series of statements that allocate such a structure and initialize it as indicated.

5. Suppose that f and p are declared as follows:

```
struct {
    union {
        char a, b;
        int c;
    } d;
    int e[5];
} f, *p = &f;
```

Which of the following statements are legal?

(a) `p->b = ' ';`
(b) `p->e[3] = 10;`
(c) `(*p).d.a = '*';`
(d) `p->d->c = 20;`

6. Modify the `delete_from_list` function so that it uses only one pointer variable instead of two (`cur` and `prev`).

7. The following loop is supposed to delete all nodes from a linked list and release the memory that they occupy. Unfortunately, the loop is incorrect. Explain what's wrong with it and show how to fix the bug.

```
for (p = first; p != NULL; p = p->next)
    free(p);
```

8. Section 15.2 describes a file, `stack.c`, that provides functions for storing integers in a stack. In that section, the stack was implemented as an array. Modify `stack.c` so that a stack is now stored as a linked list. Replace the `contents` and `top` variables by a single variable that points to the first node in the list (the "top" of the stack). Write the functions in `stack.c` so that they use this pointer. Remove the `is_full` function, instead having `push` return either `true` (if memory was available to create a node) or `false` (if not).

9. True or false: If x is a structure and a is a member of that structure, then `(&x)->a` is the same as `x.a`. Justify your answer.

10. Modify the `print_part` function of Section 16.2 so that its parameter is a *pointer* to a part structure. Use the `->` operator in your answer.

11. Write the following function:

```
int count_occurrences(struct node *list, int n);
```

The `list` parameter points to a linked list; the function should return the number of times that n appears in this list. Assume that the `node` structure is the one defined in Section 17.5.

12. Write the following function:

```
struct node *find_last(struct node *list, int n);
```

The `list` parameter points to a linked list. The function should return a pointer to the *last* node that contains n; it should return NULL if n doesn't appear in the list. Assume that the node structure is the one defined in Section 17.5.

13. The following function is supposed to insert a new node into its proper place in an ordered list, returning a pointer to the first node in the modified list. Unfortunately, the function

doesn't work correctly in all cases. Explain what's wrong with it and show how to fix it. Assume that the node structure is the one defined in Section 17.5.

```
struct node *insert_into_ordered_list(struct node *list,
                                      struct node *new_node)
{
  struct node *cur = list, *prev = NULL;
  while (cur->value <= new_node->value) {
    prev = cur;
    cur = cur->next;
  }
  prev->next = new_node;
  new_node->next = cur;
  return list;
}
```

Section 17.6   14. Modify the delete_from_list function (Section 17.5) so that its first parameter has type struct node ** (a pointer to a pointer to the first node in a list) and its return type is void. delete_from_list must modify its first argument to point to the list after the desired node has been deleted.

Section 17.7   Ⓦ 15. Show the output of the following program and explain what it does.

```
#include <stdio.h>

int f1(int (*f)(int));
int f2(int i);

int main(void)
{
  printf("Answer: %d\n", f1(f2));
  return 0;
}

int f1(int (*f)(int))
{
  int n = 0;

  while ((*f)(n)) n++;
  return n;
}

int f2(int i)
{
  return i * i + i - 12;
}
```

16. Write the following function. The call sum(g, i, j) should return g(i) + ... + g(j).

```
int sum(int (*f)(int), int start, int end);
```

Ⓦ 17. Let a be an array of 100 integers. Write a call of qsort that sorts only the *last* 50 elements in a. (You don't need to write the comparison function).

18. Modify the compare_parts function so that parts are sorted with their numbers in *descending* order.

19. Write a function that, when given a string as its argument, searches the following array of structures for a matching command name, then calls the function associated with that name.

```
struct {
  char *cmd_name;
  void (*cmd_pointer)(void);
} file_cmd[] =
  {{"new",        new_cmd},
   {"open",       open_cmd},
   {"close",      close_cmd},
   {"close all",  close_all_cmd},
   {"save",       save_cmd},
   {"save as",    save_as_cmd},
   {"save all",   save_all_cmd},
   {"print",      print_cmd},
   {"exit",       exit_cmd}
  };
```

Programming Projects

1. Modify the `inventory.c` program of Section 16.3 so that the `inventory` array is allocated dynamically and later reallocated when it fills up. Use `malloc` initially to allocate enough space for an array of 10 `part` structures. When the array has no more room for new parts, use `realloc` to double its size. Repeat the doubling step each time the array becomes full.

2. Modify the `inventory.c` program of Section 16.3 so that the p (print) command calls `qsort` to sort the `inventory` array before it prints the parts.

3. Modify the `inventory2.c` program of Section 17.5 by adding an e (erase) command that allows the user to remove a part from the database.

4. Modify the `justify` program of Section 15.3 by rewriting the `line.c` file so that it stores the current line in a linked list. Each node in the list will store a single word. The `line` array will be replaced by a variable that points to the node containing the first word. This variable will store a null pointer whenever the line is empty.

5. Write a program that sorts a series of words entered by the user:

    ```
    Enter word: foo
    Enter word: bar
    Enter word: baz
    Enter word: quux
    Enter word:

    In sorted order: bar baz foo quux
    ```

    Assume that each word is no more than 20 characters long. Stop reading when the user enters an empty word (i.e., presses Enter without entering a word). Store each word in a dynamically allocated string, using an array of pointers to keep track of the strings, as in the `remind2.c` program (Section 17.2). After all words have been read, sort the array (using any sorting technique) and then use a loop to print the words in sorted order. *Hint:* Use the `read_line` function to read each word, as in `remind2.c`.

6. Modify Programming Project 5 so that it uses `qsort` to sort the array of pointers.

7. (C99) Modify the `remind2.c` program of Section 17.2 so that each element of the `reminders` array is a pointer to a `vstring` structure (see Section 17.9) rather than a pointer to an ordinary string.

18 Declarations

Making something variable is easy.
Controlling duration of constancy is the trick.

Declarations play a central role in C programming. By declaring variables and functions, we furnish vital information that the compiler will need in order to check a program for potential errors and translate it into object code.

Previous chapters have provided examples of declarations without going into full details; this chapter fills in the gaps. It explores the sophisticated options that can be used in declarations and reveals that variable declarations and function declarations have quite a bit in common. It also provides a firm grounding in the important concepts of storage duration, scope, and linkage.

Section 18.1 examines the syntax of declarations in their most general form, a topic that we've avoided up to this point. The next four sections focus on the items that appear in declarations: storage classes (Section 18.2), type qualifiers (Section 18.3), declarators (Section 18.4), and initializers (Section 18.5). Section 18.6 discusses the `inline` keyword, which can appear in C99 function declarations.

18.1 Declaration Syntax

Declarations furnish information to the compiler about the meaning of identifiers. When we write

```
int i;
```

we're informing the compiler that, in the current scope, the name `i` represents a variable of type `int`. The declaration

```
float f(float);
```

tells the compiler that f is a function that returns a float value and has one argument, also of type float.

In general, a declaration has the following appearance:

declaration

declaration-specifiers declarators ;

Declaration specifiers describe the properties of the variables or functions being declared. *Declarators* give their names and may provide additional information about their properties.

Declaration specifiers fall into three categories:

- *Storage classes.* There are four storage classes: auto, static, extern, and register. At most one storage class may appear in a declaration; if present, it should come first.

- *Type qualifiers.* In C89, there are only two type qualifiers: const and volatile. C99 has a third type qualifier, restrict. A declaration may contain zero or more type qualifiers.

- *Type specifiers.* The keywords void, char, short, int, long, float, double, signed, and unsigned are all type specifiers. These words may be combined as described in Chapter 7; the order in which they appear doesn't matter (int unsigned long is the same as long unsigned int). Type specifiers also include specifications of structures, unions, and enumerations (for example, struct point { int x, y; }, struct { int x, y; }, or struct point). Type names created using typedef are type specifiers as well.

C99 (C99 has a fourth kind of declaration specifier, the *function specifier,* which is used only in function declarations. This category has just one member, the keyword inline.) Type qualifiers and type specifiers should follow the storage class, but there are no other restrictions on their order. As a matter of style, I'll put type qualifiers before type specifiers.

Declarators include identifiers (names of simple variables), identifiers followed by [] (array names), identifiers preceded by * (pointer names), and identifiers followed by () (function names). Declarators are separated by commas. A declarator that represents a variable may be followed by an initializer.

Let's look at a few examples that illustrate these rules. Here's a declaration with a storage class and three declarators:

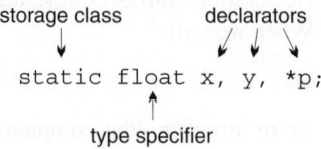

The following declaration has a type qualifier but no storage class. It also has an initializer:

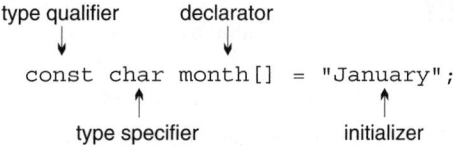

The following declaration has both a storage class and a type qualifier. It also has three type specifiers; their order isn't important:

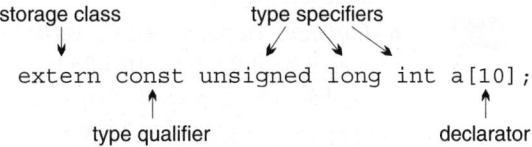

Function declarations, like variable declarations, may have a storage class, type qualifiers, and type specifiers. The following declaration has a storage class and a type specifier:

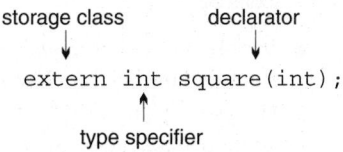

The next four sections cover storage classes, type qualifiers, declarators, and initializers in detail.

18.2 Storage Classes

Storage classes can be specified for variables and—to a lesser extent—functions and parameters. We'll concentrate on variables for now.

Recall from Section 10.3 that the term *block* refers to the body of a function (the part enclosed in braces) or a compound statement, possibly containing declarations. In C99, selection statements (`if` and `switch`) and iteration statements (`while`, `do`, and `for`)—along with the "inner" statements that they control—are considered to be blocks as well, although this is primarily a technicality.

Properties of Variables

Every variable in a C program has three properties:

■ *Storage duration.* The storage duration of a variable determines when memory is set aside for the variable and when that memory is released. Storage for a variable with ***automatic storage duration*** is allocated when the surrounding

Q&A

block is executed; storage is deallocated when the block terminates, causing the variable to lose its value. A variable with ***static storage duration*** stays at the same storage location as long as the program is running, allowing it to retain its value indefinitely.

- *Scope.* The scope of a variable is the portion of the program text in which the variable can be referenced. A variable can have either ***block scope*** (the variable is visible from its point of declaration to the end of the enclosing block) or ***file scope*** (the variable is visible from its point of declaration to the end of the enclosing file).

Q&A

- *Linkage.* The linkage of a variable determines the extent to which it can be shared by different parts of a program. A variable with ***external linkage*** may be shared by several (perhaps all) files in a program. A variable with ***internal linkage*** is restricted to a single file, but may be shared by the functions in that file. (If a variable with the same name appears in another file, it's treated as a different variable.) A variable with ***no linkage*** belongs to a single function and can't be shared at all.

The default storage duration, scope, and linkage of a variable depend on where it's declared:

- Variables declared *inside* a block (including a function body) have *automatic* storage duration, *block* scope, and *no* linkage.
- Variables declared *outside* any block, at the outermost level of a program, have *static* storage duration, *file* scope, and *external* linkage.

The following example shows the default properties of the variables i and j:

```
          ⌐ static storage duration
int i;⸗─── file scope
          ⌐ external linkage

void f(void)
{
              ⌐ automatic storage duration
    int j;⸗─── block scope
              ⌐ no linkage
}
```

For many variables, the default storage duration, scope, and linkage are satisfactory. When they aren't, we can alter these properties by specifying an explicit storage class: auto, static, extern, or register.

The auto Storage Class

The auto storage class is legal only for variables that belong to a block. An auto variable has automatic storage duration (not surprisingly), block scope, and no linkage. The auto storage class is almost never specified explicitly, since it's the default for variables declared inside a block.

The `static` Storage Class

The `static` storage class can be used with all variables, regardless of where they're declared, but it has a different effect on a variable declared outside a block than it does on a variable declared inside a block. When used *outside* a block, the word `static` specifies that a variable has internal linkage. When used *inside* a block, `static` changes the variable's storage duration from automatic to static. The following figure shows the effect of declaring i and j to be `static`:

```
                      ┌─ static storage duration
static int i;├─── file scope
                      └─ internal linkage

void f(void)
{
                      ┌─ static storage duration
    static int j;├─── block scope
                      └─ no linkage
}
```

When used in a declaration outside a block, `static` essentially hides a variable within the file in which it's declared; only functions that appear in the same file can see the variable. In the following example, the functions f1 and f2 both have access to i, but functions in other files don't:

```
static int i;

void f1(void)
{
   /* has access to i */
}

void f2(void)
{
   /* has access to i */
}
```

This use of `static` can help implement a technique known as information hiding.

information hiding ➤ *19.2*

A `static` variable declared within a block resides at the same storage location throughout program execution. Unlike automatic variables, which lose their values each time the program leaves the enclosing block, a `static` variable will retain its value indefinitely. `static` variables have some interesting properties:

- A `static` variable in a block is initialized only once, prior to program execution. An `auto` variable is initialized every time it comes into existence (provided, of course, that it has an initializer).
- Each time a function is called recursively, it gets a new set of `auto` variables. If it has a `static` variable, on the other hand, that variable is shared by all calls of the function.

- Although a function shouldn't return a pointer to an `auto` variable, there's nothing wrong with it returning a pointer to a `static` variable.

Declaring one of its variables to be `static` allows a function to retain information between calls in a "hidden" area that the rest of the program can't access. More often, however, we'll use `static` to make programs more efficient. Consider the following function:

```c
char digit_to_hex_char(int digit)
{
  const char hex_chars[16] = "0123456789ABCDEF";

  return hex_chars[digit];
}
```

Each time the `digit_to_hex_char` function is called, the characters `0123456789ABCDEF` will be copied into the `hex_chars` array to initialize it. Now, let's make the array `static`:

```c
char digit_to_hex_char(int digit)
{
  static const char hex_chars[16] = "0123456789ABCDEF";

  return hex_chars[digit];
}
```

Since `static` variables are initialized only once, we've improved the speed of `digit_to_hex_char`.

The `extern` Storage Class

The `extern` storage class enables several source files to share the same variable. Section 15.2 covered the essentials of using `extern`, so I won't devote much space to it here. Recall that the declaration

```c
extern int i;
```

informs the compiler that `i` is an `int` variable, but doesn't cause it to allocate memory for `i`. In C terminology, this declaration is not a *definition* of `i`; it merely informs the compiler that we need access to a variable that's defined elsewhere (perhaps later in the same file, or—more often—in another file). A variable can have many *declarations* in a program but should have only one *definition*.

There's one exception to the rule that an `extern` declaration of a variable isn't a definition. An `extern` declaration that initializes a variable serves as a definition of the variable. For example, the declaration

```c
extern int i = 0;
```

is effectively the same as

```c
int i = 0;
```

This rule prevents multiple `extern` declarations from initializing a variable in different ways.

A variable in an `extern` declaration always has static storage duration. The scope of the variable depends on the declaration's placement. If the declaration is inside a block, the variable has block scope; otherwise, it has file scope:

Q&A

```
                         static storage duration
extern int i;            file scope
                         ? linkage

void f(void)
{
                             static storage duration
    extern int j;            block scope
                             ? linkage
}
```

Determining the linkage of an `extern` variable is a bit harder. If the variable was declared `static` earlier in the file (outside of any function definition), then it has internal linkage. Otherwise (the normal case), the variable has external linkage.

The `register` Storage Class

Using the `register` storage class in the declaration of a variable asks the compiler to store the variable in a register instead of keeping it in main memory like other variables. (A *register* is a storage area located in a computer's CPU. Data stored in a register can be accessed and updated faster than data stored in ordinary memory.) Specifying the storage class of a variable to be `register` is a request, not a command. The compiler is free to store a `register` variable in memory if it chooses.

The `register` storage class is legal only for variables declared in a block. A `register` variable has the same storage duration, scope, and linkage as an `auto` variable. However, a `register` variable lacks one property that an `auto` variable has: since registers don't have addresses, it's illegal to use the & operator to take the address of a `register` variable. This restriction applies even if the compiler has elected to store the variable in memory.

`register` is best used for variables that are accessed and/or updated frequently. For example, the loop control variable in a `for` statement is a good candidate for `register` treatment:

```
int sum_array(int a[], int n)
{
    register int i;
    int sum = 0;

    for (i = 0; i < n; i++)
        sum += a[i];
    return sum;
}
```

register isn't nearly as popular among C programmers as it once was. Today's compilers are much more sophisticated than early C compilers; many can determine automatically which variables would benefit the most from being kept in registers. Still, using register provides useful information that can help the compiler optimize the performance of a program. In particular, the compiler knows that a register variable can't have its address taken, and therefore can't be modified through a pointer. In this respect, the register keyword is related to C99's restrict keyword.

The Storage Class of a Function

Function declarations (and definitions), like variable declarations, may include a storage class, but the only options are extern and static. The word extern at the beginning of a function declaration specifies that the function has external linkage, allowing it to be called from other files. static indicates internal linkage, limiting use of the function's name to the file in which it's defined. If no storage class is specified, the function is assumed to have external linkage.

Consider the following function declarations:

```
extern int f(int i);
static int g(int i);
int h(int i);
```

f has external linkage, g has internal linkage, and h (by default) has external linkage. Because it has internal linkage, g can't be called directly from outside the file in which it's defined. (Declaring g to be static doesn't completely prevent it from being called in another file; an indirect call via a function pointer is still possible.)

Declaring functions to be extern is like declaring variables to be auto—it serves no purpose. For that reason, I don't use extern in function declarations. Be aware, however, that some programmers use extern extensively, which certainly does no harm.

Declaring functions to be static, on the other hand, is quite useful. In fact, I recommend using static when declaring any function that isn't intended to be called from other files. The benefits of doing so include:

- *Easier maintenance.* Declaring a function f to be static guarantees that f isn't visible outside the file in which its definition appears. As a result, someone modifying the program later knows that changes to f won't affect functions in other files. (One exception: a function in another file that's passed a pointer to f might be affected by changes to f. Fortunately, that situation is easy to spot by examining the file in which f is defined, since the function that passes f must also be defined there.)

- *Reduced "name space pollution."* Since functions declared static have internal linkage, their names can be reused in other files. Although we probably wouldn't deliberately reuse a function name for some other purpose, it can be hard to avoid in large programs. An excessive number of names with external linkage can result in what C programmers call "name space pollution": names in different files accidentally conflicting with each other. Using `static` helps prevent this problem.

Function parameters have the same properties as `auto` variables: automatic storage duration, block scope, and no linkage. The only storage class that can be specified for parameters is `register`.

Summary

Now that we've covered the various storage classes, let's summarize what we know. The following program fragment shows all possible ways to include—or omit—storage classes in declarations of variables and parameters.

```
int a;
extern int b;
static int c;

void f(int d, register int e)
{
  auto int g;
  int h;
  static int i;
  extern int j;
  register int k;
}
```

Table 18.1 shows the properties of each variable and parameter in this example.

Table 18.1

Properties of Variables and Parameters

Name	Storage Duration	Scope	Linkage
a	static	file	external
b	static	file	†
c	static	file	internal
d	automatic	block	none
e	automatic	block	none
g	automatic	block	none
h	automatic	block	none
i	static	block	none
j	static	block	†
k	automatic	block	none

†The definitions of b and j aren't shown, so it's not possible to determine the linkage of these variables. In most cases, the variables will be defined in another file and will have external linkage.

Of the four storage classes, the most important are `static` and `extern`. `auto` has no effect, and modern compilers have made `register` less important.

18.3   Type Qualifiers

restricted pointers ➤ *17.8*

There are two type qualifiers: `const` and `volatile`. (C99 has a third type qualifier, `restrict`, which is used only with pointers.) Since the use of `volatile` is limited to low-level programming, I'll postpone discussing it until Section 20.3. `const` is used to declare objects that resemble variables but are "read-only": a program may access the value of a `const` object, but can't change it. For example, the declaration

```
const int n = 10;
```

creates a `const` object named n whose value is 10. The declaration

```
const int tax_brackets[] = {750, 2250, 3750, 5250, 7000};
```

creates a `const` array named `tax_brackets`.

Declaring an object to be `const` has several advantages:

- It's a form of documentation: it alerts anyone reading the program to the read-only nature of the object.

- The compiler can check that the program doesn't inadvertently attempt to change the value of the object.

- When programs are written for certain types of applications (embedded systems, in particular), the compiler can use the word `const` to identify data to be stored in ROM (read-only memory).

At first glance, it might appear that `const` serves the same role as the `#define` directive, which we've used in previous chapters to create names for constants. There are significant differences between `#define` and `const`, however:

- We can use `#define` to create a name for a numerical, character, or string constant. `const` can be used to create read-only objects of *any* type, including arrays, pointers, structures, and unions.

- `const` objects are subject to the same scope rules as variables; constants created using `#define` aren't. In particular, we can't use `#define` to create a constant with block scope.

- The value of a `const` object, unlike the value of a macro, can be viewed in a debugger.

- Unlike macros, `const` objects can't be used in constant expressions. For example, we can't write

```
const int n = 10;
int a[n];              /*** WRONG ***/
```

since array bounds must be constant expressions. (In C99, this example would be legal if a has automatic storage duration—it would be treated as a variable-length array—but not if it has static storage duration.)

■ It's legal to apply the address operator (&) to a const object, since it has an address. A macro doesn't have an address.

There are no absolute rules that dictate when to use #define and when to use const. I recommend using #define for constants that represent numbers or characters. That way, you'll be able to use the constants as array dimensions, in switch statements, and in other places where constant expressions are required.

18.4 Declarators

A declarator consists of an identifier (the name of the variable or function being declared), possibly preceded by the * symbol or followed by [] or (). By combining *, [], and (), we can create declarators of mind-numbing complexity.

Before we look at the more complicated declarators, let's review the declarators that we've seen in previous chapters. In the simplest case, a declarator is just an identifier, like i in the following example:

```
int i;
```

Declarators may also contain the symbols *, [], and ():

■ A declarator that begins with * represents a pointer:

```
int *p;
```

■ A declarator that ends with [] represents an array:

```
int a[10];
```

The brackets may be left empty if the array is a parameter, if it has an initializer, or if its storage class is extern:

```
extern int a[];
```

Since a is defined elsewhere in the program, the compiler doesn't need to know its length here. (In the case of a multidimensional array, only the first set of brackets can be empty.) C99 provides two additional options for what goes between the brackets in the declaration of an array parameter. One option is the keyword static, followed by an expression that specifies the array's minimum length. The other is the * symbol, which can be used in a function prototype to indicate a variable-length array argument. Section 9.3 discusses both C99 features.

■ A declarator that ends with () represents a function:

```
int abs(int i);
void swap(int *a, int *b);
int find_largest(int a[], int n);
```

C allows parameter names to be omitted in a function declaration:

```
int abs(int);
void swap(int *, int *);
int find_largest(int [], int);
```

The parentheses can even be left empty:

```
int abs();
void swap();
int find_largest();
```

The declarations in the last group specify the return types of the abs, swap, and find_largest functions, but provide no information about their arguments. Leaving the parentheses empty isn't the same as putting the word void between them, which indicates that there are no arguments. The empty-parentheses style of function declaration has largely disappeared. It's inferior to the prototype style introduced in C89, since it doesn't allow the compiler to check whether function calls have the right arguments.

If all declarators were as simple as these, C programming would be a snap. Unfortunately, declarators in actual programs often combine the *, [], and () notations. We've seen examples of such combinations already. We know that

```
int *ap[10];
```

declares an array of 10 pointers to integers. We know that

```
float *fp(float);
```

declares a function that has a float argument and returns a pointer to a float. And, in Section 17.7, we learned that

```
void (*pf)(int);
```

declares a pointer to a function with an int argument and a void return type.

Deciphering Complex Declarations

So far, we haven't had too much trouble understanding declarators. But what about declarators like the one in the following declaration?

```
int *(*x[10])(void);
```

This declarator combines *, [], and (), so it's not obvious whether x is a pointer, an array, or a function.

Fortunately, there are two simple rules that will allow us to understand any declaration, no matter how convoluted:

- **Always read declarators from the inside out.** In other words, locate the identifier that's being declared, and start deciphering the declaration from there.

■ *When there's a choice, always favor* [] *and* () *over* *. If * precedes the identifier and [] follows it, the identifier represents an array, not a pointer. Likewise, if * precedes the identifier and () follows it, the identifier represents a function, not a pointer. (Of course, we can always use parentheses to override the normal priority of [] and () over *.)

Let's apply these rules to our simple examples first. In the declaration

```
int *ap[10];
```

the identifier is ap. Since * precedes ap and [] follows it, we give preference to [], so ap is an *array* of *pointers*. In the declaration

```
float *fp(float);
```

the identifier is fp. Since * precedes fp and () follows it, we give preference to (), so fp is a *function* that returns a *pointer*.

The declaration

```
void (*pf)(int);
```

is a little trickier. Since *pf is enclosed in parentheses, pf must be a pointer. But (*pf) is followed by (int), so pf must point to a function with an int argument. The word void represents the return type of this function.

As the last example shows, understanding a complex declarator often involves zigzagging from one side of the identifier to the other:

```
void (*pf)(int);
```

1. pointer to
2. function with int argument
3. returning void

Type of pf:

Let's use this zigzagging technique to decipher the declaration given earlier:

```
int *(*x[10])(void);
```

First, we locate the identifier being declared (x). We see that x is preceded by * and followed by []; since [] have priority over *, we go right (x is an array). Next, we go left to find out the type of the elements in the array (pointers). Next, we go right to find out what kind of data the pointers point to (functions with no arguments). Finally, we go left to see what each function returns (a pointer to an int). Graphically, here's what the process looks like:

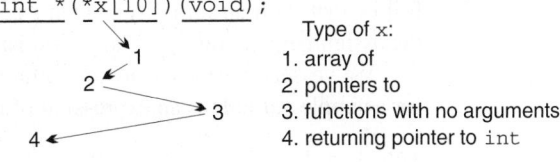

Type of x:
1. array of
2. pointers to
3. functions with no arguments
4. returning pointer to int

Mastering C declarations takes time and practice. The only good news is that there are certain things that can't be declared in C. Functions can't return arrays:

```
int f(int)[];        /*** WRONG ***/
```

Functions can't return functions:

```
int g(int)(int);     /*** WRONG ***/
```

Arrays of functions aren't possible, either:

```
int a[10](int);      /*** WRONG ***/
```

In each case, we can use pointers to get the desired effect. A function can't return an array, but it can return a *pointer* to an array. A function can't return a function, but it can return a *pointer* to a function. Arrays of functions aren't allowed, but an array may contain *pointers* to functions. (Section 17.7 has an example of such an array.)

Using Type Definitions to Simplify Declarations

Some programmers use type definitions to help simplify complex declarations. Consider the declaration of x that we examined earlier in this section:

```
int *(*x[10])(void);
```

To make x's type easier to understand, we could use the following series of type definitions:

```
typedef int *Fcn(void);
typedef Fcn *Fcn_ptr;
typedef Fcn_ptr Fcn_ptr_array[10];
Fcn_ptr_array x;
```

If we read these lines in reverse order, we see that x has type `Fcn_ptr_array`, a `Fcn_ptr_array` is an array of `Fcn_ptr` values, a `Fcn_ptr` is a pointer to type `Fcn`, and a `Fcn` is a function that has no arguments and returns a pointer to an `int` value.

18.5 Initializers

For convenience, C allows us to specify initial values for variables as we're declaring them. To initialize a variable, we write the = symbol after its declarator, then follow that with an initializer. (Don't confuse the = symbol in a declaration with the assignment operator; initialization isn't the same as assignment.)

We've seen various kinds of initializers in previous chapters. The initializer for a simple variable is an expression of the same type as the variable:

```
int i = 5 / 2;    /* i is initially 2 */
```

If the types don't match, C converts the initializer using the same rules as for

conversion during assignment ➤ 7.4 assignment:

```
int j = 5.5;      /* converted to 5 */
```

The initializer for a pointer variable must be a pointer expression of the same type as the variable or of type `void *`:

```
int *p = &i;
```

The initializer for an array, structure, or union is usually a series of values enclosed in braces:

```
int a[5] = {1, 2, 3, 4, 5};
```

 In C99, brace-enclosed initializers can have other forms, thanks to designated ini-

designated initializers ➤ 8.1, 16.1 tializers.

To complete our coverage of declarations, let's take a look at some additional rules that govern initializers:

- An initializer for a variable with static storage duration must be constant:

```
#define FIRST 1
#define LAST 100

static int i = LAST - FIRST + 1;
```

Since `LAST` and `FIRST` are macros, the compiler can compute the initial value of `i` (100 − 1 + 1 = 100). If `LAST` and `FIRST` had been variables, the initializer would be illegal.

- If a variable has automatic storage duration, its initializer need not be constant:

```
int f(int n)
{
  int last = n - 1;
  ...
}
```

- A brace-enclosed initializer for an array, structure, or union must contain only constant expressions, never variables or function calls:

```
#define N 2

int powers[5] = {1, N, N * N, N * N * N, N * N * N * N};
```

 Since `N` is a constant, the initializer for `powers` is legal; if `N` were a variable, the program wouldn't compile. In C99, this restriction applies only if the variable has static storage duration.

- The initializer for an automatic structure or union can be another structure or union:

```
void g(struct part part1)
{
  struct part part2 = part1;
  ...
}
```

The initializer doesn't have to be a variable or parameter name, although it does need to be an expression of the proper type. For example, `part2`'s initializer could be `*p`, where `p` is of type `struct part *`, or `f(part1)`, where `f` is a function that returns a `part` structure.

Uninitialized Variables

In previous chapters, we've implied that uninitialized variables have undefined values. That's not always true; the initial value of a variable depends on its storage duration:

- Variables with *automatic* storage duration have no default initial value. The initial value of an automatic variable can't be predicted and may be different each time the variable comes into existence.

calloc function ➤17.3

- Variables with *static* storage duration have the value zero by default. Unlike memory allocated by `calloc`, which is simply set to zero bits, a static variable is correctly initialized based on its type: integer variables are initialized to 0, floating variables are initialized to 0.0, and pointer variables contain a null pointer.

As a matter of style, it's better to provide initializers for static variables rather than rely on the fact that they're guaranteed to be zero. If a program accesses a variable that hasn't been initialized explicitly, someone reading the program later can't easily determine whether the variable is assumed to be zero or whether it's initialized by an assignment somewhere in the program.

18.6   Inline Functions (C99)

C99 function declarations have an additional option that doesn't exist in C89: they may contain the keyword `inline`. This keyword is a new breed of declaration specifier, distinct from storage classes, type qualifiers, and type specifiers. To understand the effect of `inline`, we'll need to visualize the machine instructions that are generated by a C compiler to handle the process of calling a function and returning from a function.

At the machine level, several instructions may need to be executed to prepare for the call, the call itself requires jumping to the first instruction in the function, and there may be additional instructions executed by the function itself as it begins to execute. If the function has arguments, they'll need to be copied (because C passes its arguments by value). Returning from a function requires a similar amount of effort on both the part of the function that was called and the one that called it. The cumulative work required to call a function and later return from it is often referred to as "overhead," since it's extra work above and beyond what the function is really supposed to accomplish. Although the overhead of a function call slows the program by only a tiny amount, it may add up in certain situations, such as when a function is called millions or billions of times, when an older, slower processor is in use (as might be the case in an embedded system), or when a program has to meet very strict deadlines (as in a real-time system).

parameterized macros ➤ 14.3

In C89, the only way to avoid the overhead of a function call is to use a parameterized macro. Parameterized macros have certain drawbacks, though. C99 offers a better solution to this problem: create an ***inline function.*** The word "inline" suggests an implementation strategy in which the compiler replaces each call of the function by the machine instructions for the function. This technique avoids the usual overhead of a function call, although it may cause a minor increase in the size of the compiled program.

Declaring a function to be `inline` doesn't actually force the compiler to "inline" the function, however. It merely suggests that the compiler should try to make calls of the function as fast as possible, perhaps by performing an inline expansion when the function is called. The compiler is free to ignore this suggestion. In this respect, `inline` is similar to the `register` and `restrict` keywords, which the compiler may use to improve the performance of a program but may also choose to ignore.

Inline Definitions

An inline function has the keyword `inline` as one of its declaration specifiers:

```
inline double average(double a, double b)
{
  return (a + b) / 2;
}
```

Here's where things get a bit complicated. `average` has external linkage, so other source files may contain calls of `average`. However, the definition of `average` isn't considered to be an external definition by the compiler (it's an ***inline definition*** instead), so attempting to call `average` from another file will be considered an error.

There are two ways to avoid this error. One option is to add the word `static` to the function definition:

```
static inline double average(double a, double b)
{
  return (a + b) / 2;
}
```

`average` now has internal linkage, so it can't be called from other files. Other files may contain their own definitions of `average`, which might be the same as this definition or might be different.

The other option is to provide an external definition for `average` so that calls are permitted from other files. One way to do this is to write the `average` function a second time (without using `inline`) and put the second definition in a different source file. Doing so is legal, but it's not a good idea to have two versions of the same function, because we can't guarantee that they'll remain consistent when the program is modified.

Here's a better approach. First, we'll put the inline definition of `average` in a header file (let's name it `average.h`):

```
#ifndef AVERAGE_H
#define AVERAGE_H

inline double average(double a, double b)
{
  return (a + b) / 2;
}

#endif
```

Next, we'll create a matching source file, `average.c`:

```
#include "average.h"

extern double average(double a, double b);
```

Now, any file that needs to call the `average` function may simply include `average.h`, which contains the inline definition of `average`. The `average.c` file contains a prototype for `average` that uses the `extern` keyword, which causes the definition of `average` included from `average.h` to be treated as an external definition in `average.c`.

The general rule in C99 is that if all top-level declarations of a function in a particular file include `inline` but not `extern`, then the definition of the function in that file is inline. If the function is used anywhere in the program (including the file that contains its inline definition), then an external definition of the function will need to be provided by some other file. When the function is called, the compiler may choose to perform an ordinary call (using the function's external definition) or perform inline expansion (using the function's inline definition). There's no way to tell which choice the compiler will make, so it's crucial that the two definitions be consistent. The technique that we just discussed (using the `average.h` and `average.c` files) guarantees that the definitions are the same.

Restrictions on Inline Functions

Since inline functions are implemented in a way that's quite different from ordinary functions, they're subject to different rules and restrictions. Variables with static storage duration are a particular problem for inline functions with external linkage. Consequently, C99 imposes the following restrictions on an inline function with external linkage (but not on one with internal linkage):

- The function may not define a modifiable `static` variable.
- The function may not contain references to variables with internal linkage.

Such a function is allowed to define a variable that is both `static` and `const`, but each inline definition of the function may create its own copy of the variable.

Using Inline Functions with GCC

Some compilers, including GCC, supported inline functions prior to the C99 standard. As a result, their rules for using inline functions may vary from the standard. In particular, the scheme described earlier (using the `average.h` and `average.c` files) may not work with these compilers. Version 4.3 of GCC (not available at the time this book was written) is expected to support inline functions in the way described in the C99 standard.

Functions that are specified to be both `static` and `inline` should work fine, regardless of the version of GCC. This strategy is legal in C99 as well, so it's the safest bet. A `static inline` function can be used within a single file or placed in a header file and included into any source file that needs to call the function.

There's another way to share an inline function among multiple files that works with older versions of GCC but conflicts with C99. This technique involves putting a definition of the function in a header file, specifying that the function is both `extern` and `inline`, then including the header file into any source file that contains a call of the function. A second copy of the definition—without the words `extern` and `inline`—is placed in one of the source files. (That way, if the compiler is unable to "inline" the function for any reason, it will still have a definition.)

A final note about GCC: Functions are "inlined" only when optimization is requested via the `-O` command-line option.

Q & A

*Q: **Why are selection statements and iteration statements (and their "inner" statements) considered to be blocks in C99? [p. 459]**

A: This rather surprising rule stems from a problem that can occur when compound literals are used in selection statements and iteration statements. The problem has to do with the storage duration of compound literals, so let's take a moment to discuss that issue first.

compound literals ➤ 9.3, 16.2

The C99 standard states that the object represented by a compound literal has static storage duration if the compound literal occurs outside the body of a function. Otherwise, it has automatic storage duration; as a result, the memory occupied by the object is deallocated at the end of the block in which the compound literal appears. Consider the following function, which returns a `point` structure created using a compound literal:

```
struct point create_point(int x, int y)
{
  return (struct point) {x, y};
}
```

This function works correctly, because the object created by the compound literal will be copied when the function returns. The original object will no longer exist, but the copy will remain. Now suppose that we change the function slightly:

```
struct point *create_point(int x, int y)
{
  return &(struct point) {x, y};
}
```

This version of create_point suffers from undefined behavior, because it returns a pointer to an object that has automatic storage duration and won't exist after the function returns.

Now let's return to the question we started with: Why are selection statements and iteration statements considered to be blocks? Consider the following example:

```
/* Example 1 - if statement without braces */

double *coefficients, value;

if (polynomial_selected == 1)
  coefficients = (double[3]) {1.5, -3.0, 6.0};
else
  coefficients = (double[3]) {4.5, 1.0, -3.5};
value = evaluate_polynomial(coefficients);
```

This program fragment apparently behaves in the desired fashion (but read on). coefficients will point to one of two objects created by compound literals, and this object will still exist at the time evaluate_polynomial is called. Now consider what happens if we put braces around the "inner" statements—the ones controlled by the if statement:

```
/* Example 2 - if statement with braces */

double *coefficients, value;

if (polynomial_selected == 1) {
  coefficients = (double[3]) {1.5, -3.0, 6.0};
} else {
  coefficients = (double[3]) {4.5, 1.0, -3.5};
}
value = evaluate_polynomial(coefficients);
```

Now we're in trouble. Each compound literal causes an object to be created, but that object exists only within the block formed by the braces that enclose the statement in which the literal appears. By the time evaluate_polynomial is called, coefficients points to an object that no longer exists. The result: undefined behavior.

The creators of C99 were unhappy with this state of affairs, because programmers were unlikely to expect that simply adding braces within an if statement would cause undefined behavior. To avoid the problem, they decided that the inner statements would always be considered blocks. As a result, Example 1 and Example 2 are equivalent, with both exhibiting undefined behavior.

A similar problem can arise when a compound literal is part of the controlling expression of a selection statement or iteration statement. For this reason, each entire selection statement and iteration statement is considered to be a block as well (as though an invisible set of braces surrounds the entire statement). So, for example, an if statement with an else clause consists of three blocks: each of the two inner statements is a block, as is the entire if statement.

Q: **You said that storage for a variable with automatic storage duration is allocated when the surrounding block is executed. Is this true for C99's variable-length arrays? [p. 460]**

A: No. Storage for a variable-length array isn't allocated at the beginning of the surrounding block, because the length of the array isn't yet known. Instead, it's allocated when the declaration of the array is reached during the execution of the block. In this respect, variable-length arrays are different from all other automatic variables.

Q: **What exactly is the difference between "scope" and "linkage"? [p. 460]**

A: Scope is for the benefit of the compiler, while linkage is for the benefit of the linker. The compiler uses the scope of an identifier to determine whether or not it's legal to refer to the identifier at a given point in a file. When the compiler translates a source file into object code, it notes which names have external linkage, eventually storing these names in a table inside the object file. Thus, the linker has access to names with external linkage; names with internal linkage or no linkage are invisible to the linker.

Q: **I don't understand how a name could have block scope but external linkage. Could you elaborate? [p. 463]**

A: Certainly. Suppose that one source file defines a variable i:

```
int i;
```

Let's assume that the definition of i lies outside any function, so i has external linkage by default. In another file, there's a function f that needs to access i, so the body of f declares i as extern:

```
void f(void)
{
  extern int i;
  ...
}
```

In the first file, i has file scope. Within f, however, i has block scope. If other functions besides f need access to i, they'll need to declare it separately. (Or we can simply move the declaration of i outside f so that i has file scope.) What's confusing about this entire business is that each declaration or definition of i establishes a different scope; sometimes it's file scope, and sometimes it's block scope.

*Q: **Why can't `const` objects be used in constant expressions? `const` means "constant," right? [p. 466]**

  A: In C, `const` means "read-only," not "constant." Let's look at a few examples that illustrate why `const` objects can't be used in constant expressions.

To start with, a `const` object might only be constant during its *lifetime*, not throughout the execution of the program. Suppose that a `const` object is declared inside a function:

```
void f(int n)
{
  const int m = n / 2;
  ...
}
```

When f is called, m will be initialized to the value of n / 2. The value of m will then remain constant until f returns. When f is called the next time, m will likely be given a different value. That's where the problem arises. Suppose that m appears in a `switch` statement:

```
void f(int n)
{
  const int m = n / 2;
  ...
  switch (...) {
    ...
    case m: ...    /*** WRONG ***/
    ...
  }
  ...
}
```

The value of m won't be known until f is called, which violates C's rule that the values of case labels must be constant expressions.

Next, let's look at `const` objects declared outside blocks. These objects have external linkage and can be shared among files. If C allowed the use of `const` objects in constant expressions, we could easily find ourselves in the following situation:

```
extern const int n;
int a[n];    /*** WRONG ***/
```

n is probably defined in another file, making it impossible for the compiler to determine a's length. (I'm assuming that a is an external variable, so it can't be a variable-length array.)

volatile type qualifier ►20.3
If that's not enough to convince you, consider this: If a const object is also declared to be volatile, its value may change at any time during execution. Here's an example from the C standard:

```
extern const volatile int real_time_clock;
```

The real_time_clock variable may not be changed by the program (because it's declared const), yet its value may change via some other mechanism (because it's declared volatile).

Q: **Why is the syntax of declarators so odd?**

A: Declarations are intended to mimic use. A pointer declarator has the form *p, which matches the way the indirection operator will later be applied to p. An array declarator has the form a[...], which matches the way the array will later be subscripted. A function declarator has the form f(...), which matches the syntax of a function call. This reasoning extends to even the most complicated declarators. Consider the file_cmd array of Section 17.7, whose elements are pointers to functions. The declarator for file_cmd has the form

```
(*file_cmd[])(void)
```

and a call of one of the functions has the form

```
(*file_cmd[n])();
```

The parentheses, brackets, and * are in identical positions.

Exercises

Section 18.1

1. For each of the following declarations, identify the storage class, type qualifiers, type specifiers, declarators, and initializers.

   (a) `static char **lookup(int level);`
   (b) `volatile unsigned long io_flags;`
   (c) `extern char *file_name[MAX_FILES], path[];`
   (d) `static const char token_buf[] = "";`

Section 18.2 Ⓦ 2. Answer each of the following questions with auto, extern, register, and/or static.

   (a) Which storage class is used primarily to indicate that a variable or function can be shared by several files?
   (b) Suppose that a variable x is to be shared by several functions in one file but hidden from functions in other files. Which storage class should x be declared to have?
   (c) Which storage classes can affect the storage duration of a variable?

3. List the storage duration (static or automatic), scope (block or file), and linkage (internal, external, or none) of each variable and parameter in the following file:

```
extern float a;

void f(register double b)
{
  static int c;
  auto char d;
}
```

Ⓦ 4. Let f be the following function. What will be the value of f(10) if f has never been called before? What will be the value of f(10) if f has been called five times previously?

```
int f(int i)
{
  static int j = 0;
  return i * j++;
}
```

5. State whether each of the following statements is true or false. Justify each answer.

(a) Every variable with static storage duration has file scope.
(b) Every variable declared inside a function has no linkage.
(c) Every variable with internal linkage has static storage duration.
(d) Every parameter has block scope.

6. The following function is supposed to print an error message. Each message is preceded by an integer, indicating the number of times the function has been called. Unfortunately, the function always displays 1 as the number of the error message. Locate the error and show how to fix it without making any changes outside the function.

```
void print_error(const char *message)
{
  int n = 1;
  printf("Error %d: %s\n", n++, message);
}
```

Section 18.3   7. Suppose that we declare x to be a const object. Which one of the following statements about x is *false*?

(a) If x is of type int, it can be used as the value of a case label in a switch statement.
(b) The compiler will check that no assignment is made to x.
(c) x is subject to the same scope rules as variables.
(d) x can be of any type.

Section 18.4   Ⓦ 8. Write a complete description of the type of x as specified by each of the following declarations.

(a) `char (*x[10])(int);`
(b) `int (*x(int))[5];`
(c) `float *(*x(void))(int);`
(d) `void (*x(int, void (*y)(int)))(int);`

9. Use a series of type definitions to simplify each of the declarations in Exercise 8.

Ⓦ 10. Write declarations for the following variables and functions:

(a) p is a pointer to a function with a character pointer argument that returns a character pointer.

(b) f is a function with two arguments: p, a pointer to a structure with tag t, and n, a long integer. f returns a pointer to a function that has no arguments and returns nothing.

(c) a is an array of four pointers to functions that have no arguments and return nothing. The elements of a initially point to functions named insert, search, update, and print.

(d) b is an array of 10 pointers to functions with two int arguments that return structures with tag t.

11. In Section 18.4, we saw that the following declarations are illegal:

```
int f(int)[];      /* functions can't return arrays     */
int g(int)(int);   /* functions can't return functions  */
int a[10](int);    /* array elements can't be functions */
```

We can, however, achieve similar effects by using pointers: a function can return a *pointer* to the first element in an array, a function can return a *pointer* to a function, and the elements of an array can be *pointers* to functions. Revise each of these declarations accordingly.

*12. (a) Write a complete description of the type of the function f, assuming that it's declared as follows:

```
int (*f(float (*)(long), char *))(double);
```

(b) Give an example showing how f would be called.

Section 18.5   Ⓦ 13. Which of the following declarations are legal? (Assume that PI is a macro that represents 3.14159.)

(a) char c = 65;

(b) static int i = 5, j = i * i;

(c) double d = 2 * PI;

(d) double angles[] = {0, PI / 2, PI, 3 * PI / 2};

14. Which kind of variables cannot be initialized?

(a) Array variables

(b) Enumeration variables

(c) Structure variables

(d) Union variables

(e) None of the above

Ⓦ 15. Which property of a variable determines whether or not it has a default initial value?

(a) Storage duration

(b) Scope

(c) Linkage

(d) Type

19 Program Design

*Wherever there is modularity there is the potential for misunderstanding:
Hiding information implies a need to check communication.*

It's obvious that real-world programs are larger than the examples in this book, but you may not realize just how much larger. Faster CPUs and larger main memories have made it possible to write programs that would have been impractical just a few years ago. The popularity of graphical user interfaces has added greatly to the average length of a program. Most full-featured programs today are at least 100,000 lines long. Million-line programs are commonplace, and it's not unheard-of for a program to have 10 million lines or more.

Q&A   Although C wasn't designed for writing large programs, many large programs have in fact been written in C. It's tricky, and it requires a great deal of care, but it can be done. In this chapter, I'll discuss techniques that have proved to be helpful for writing large programs and show which C features (the `static` storage class, for example) are especially useful.

Writing large programs (often called "programming-in-the-large") is quite different from writing small ones—it's like the difference between writing a term paper (10 pages double-spaced, of course) and a 1000-page book. A large program requires more attention to style, since many people will be working on it. It requires careful documentation. It requires planning for maintenance, since it will likely be modified many times.

Above all, a large program requires careful design and much more planning than a small program. As Alan Kay, the designer of the Smalltalk programming language, puts it, "You can build a doghouse out of anything." A doghouse can be built without any particular design, using whatever materials are at hand. A house for humans, on the other hand, is too complex to just throw together.

Chapter 15 discussed writing large programs in C, but it concentrated on language details. In this chapter, we'll revisit the topic, this time focusing on techniques for good program design. A complete discussion of program design issues is obviously beyond the scope of this book. However, I'll try to cover—briefly—

some important concepts in program design and show how to use them to create C programs that are readable and maintainable.

Section 19.1 discusses how to view a C program as a collection of modules that provide services to each other. We'll then see how the concepts of information hiding (Section 19.2) and abstract data types (Section 19.3) can improve modules. By focusing on a single example (a stack data type), Section 19.4 illustrates how an abstract data type can be defined and implemented in C. Section 19.5 describes some limitations of C for defining abstract data types and shows how to work around them.

19.1   Modules

When designing a C program (or a program in any other language, for that matter), it's often useful to view it as a number of independent ***modules.*** A module is a collection of services, some of which are made available to other parts of the program (the ***clients***). Each module has an ***interface*** that describes the available services. The details of the module—including the source code for the services themselves—are stored in the module's ***implementation***.

In the context of C, "services" are functions. The interface of a module is a header file containing prototypes for the functions that will be made available to clients (source files). The implementation of a module is a source file that contains definitions of the module's functions.

To illustrate this terminology, let's look at the calculator program that was sketched in Sections 15.1 and 15.2. This program consists of the file `calc.c`, which contains the `main` function, and a stack module, which is stored in the files `stack.h` and `stack.c` (see the figure at the top of the next page). `calc.c` is a *client* of the stack module. `stack.h` is the *interface* of the stack module; it supplies everything the client needs to know about the module. `stack.c` is the *implementation* of the module; it contains definitions of the stack functions as well as declarations of the variables that make up the stack.

The C library is itself a collection of modules. Each header in the library serves as the interface to a module. `<stdio.h>`, for example, is the interface to a module containing I/O functions, while `<string.h>` is the interface to a module containing string-handling functions.

Dividing a program into modules has several advantages:

- ***Abstraction.*** If modules are properly designed, we can treat them as ***abstractions***; we know what they do, but we don't worry about the details of how they do it. Thanks to abstraction, it's not necessary to understand how the entire program works in order to make changes to one part of it. What's more, abstraction makes it easier for several members of a team to work on the same program. Once the interfaces for the modules have been agreed upon, the responsibility for implementing each module can be delegated to a partic-

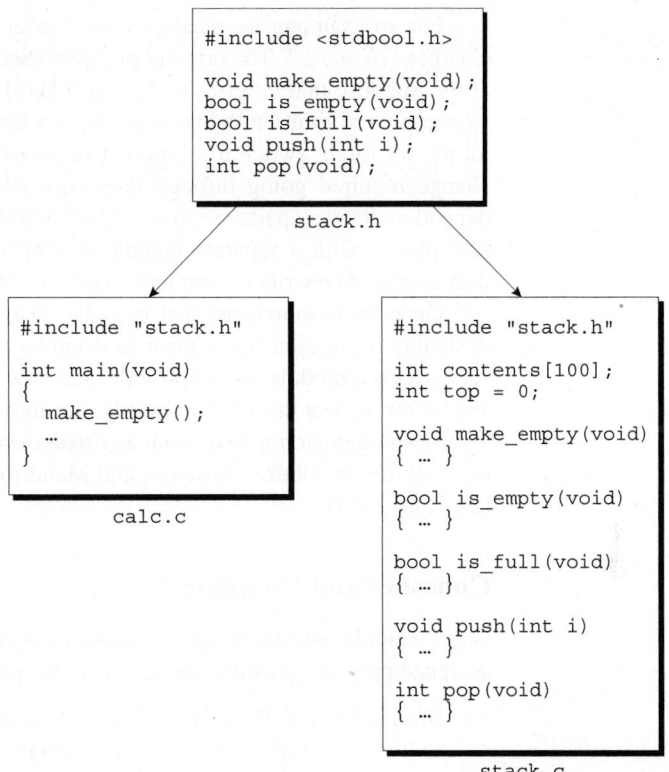

ular person. Team members can then work largely independently of one another.

- **Reusability.** Any module that provides services is potentially reusable in other programs. Our stack module, for example, is reusable. Since it's often hard to anticipate the future uses of a module, it's a good idea to design modules for reusability.

- **Maintainability.** A small bug will usually affect only a single module implementation, making the bug easier to locate and fix. Once the bug has been fixed, rebuilding the program requires only a recompilation of the module implementation (followed by linking the entire program). On a larger scale, we could replace an entire module implementation, perhaps to improve performance or when transporting the program to a different platform.

Although all these advantages are important, maintainability is the most critical. Most real-world programs are in service over a period of years, during which bugs are discovered, enhancements are made, and modifications are made to meet changing requirements. Designing a program in a modular fashion makes maintenance much easier. Maintaining a program should be like maintaining a car—fixing a flat tire shouldn't require overhauling the engine.

For an example, we need look no further than the `inventory` program of Chapters 16 and 17. The original program (Section 16.3) stored part records in an array. Suppose that, after using this program for a while, the customer objects to having a fixed limit on the number of parts that can be stored. To satisfy the customer, we might switch to a linked list (as we did in Section 17.5). Making this change required going through the entire program, looking for all places that depend on the way parts are stored. If we'd designed the program differently in the first place—with a separate module dealing with part storage—we would have only needed to rewrite the implementation of that module, not the entire program.

Once we're convinced that modular design is the way to go, the process of designing a program boils down to deciding what modules it should have, what services each module should provide, and how the modules should be interrelated. We'll now look at these issues briefly. For more information about design, consult a software engineering text, such as *Fundamentals of Software Engineering,* Second Edition, by Ghezzi, Jazayeri, and Mandrioli (Upper Saddle River, N.J.: Prentice-Hall, 2003).

Cohesion and Coupling

Good module interfaces aren't random collections of declarations. In a well-designed program, modules should have two properties:

- *High cohesion.* The elements of each module should be closely related to one another; we might think of them as cooperating toward a common goal. High cohesion makes modules easier to use and makes the entire program easier to understand.

- *Low coupling.* Modules should be as independent of each other as possible. Low coupling makes it easier to modify the program and reuse modules.

Does the calculator program have these properties? The stack module is clearly cohesive: its functions represent operations on a stack. There's little coupling in the program. The `calc.c` file depends on `stack.h` (and `stack.c` depends on `stack.h`, of course), but there are no other apparent dependencies.

Types of Modules

Because of the need for high cohesion and low coupling, modules tend to fall into certain typical categories:

- A *data pool* is a collection of related variables and/or constants. In C, a module of this type is often just a header file. From a design standpoint, putting variables in header files isn't usually a good idea, but collecting related constants in a header file can often be useful. In the C library, `<float.h>` and `<limits.h>` are both data pools.

  `<float.h>` header ➤*23.1*
  `<limits.h>` header ➤*23.2*

- A *library* is a collection of related functions. The `<string.h>` header, for example, is the interface to a library of string-handling functions.

- An *abstract object* is a collection of functions that operate on a hidden data structure. (In this chapter, the term "object" has a different meaning than in the rest of the book. In C terminology, an object is simply a block of memory that can store a value. In this chapter, however, an object is a collection of data bundled with operations on the data. If the data is hidden, the object is "abstract.") The stack module we've been discussing belongs to this category.

- An *abstract data type (ADT)* is a type whose representation is hidden. Client modules can use the type to declare variables, but have no knowledge of the structure of those variables. For a client module to perform an operation on such a variable, it must call a function provided by the abstract data type module. Abstract data types play a significant role in modern programming; we'll return to them in Sections 19.3–19.5.

19.2 Information Hiding

A well-designed module often keeps some information secret from its clients. Clients of our stack module, for example, have no need to know whether the stack is stored in an array, in a linked list, or in some other form. Deliberately concealing information from the clients of a module is known as *information hiding*. Information hiding has two primary advantages:

- *Security.* If clients don't know how the stack is stored, they won't be able to corrupt it by tampering with its internal workings. To perform operations on the stack, they'll have to call functions that are provided by the module itself—functions that we've written and tested.

- *Flexibility.* Making changes—no matter how large—to a module's internal workings won't be difficult. For example, we could implement the stack as an array at first, then later switch to a linked list or other representation. We'll have to rewrite the implementation of the module, of course, but—if the module was designed properly—we won't have to alter the module's interface.

In C, the major tool for enforcing information hiding is the `static` storage class. Declaring a variable with file scope to be `static` gives it internal linkage, thus preventing it from being accessed from other files, including clients of the module. (Declaring a function to be `static` is also useful—the function can be directly called only by other functions in the same file.)

`static` storage class ➤ *18.2*

A Stack Module

To see the benefits of information hiding, let's look at two implementations of a stack module, one using an array and the other a linked list. The module's header file will have the following appearance:

stack.h
```
#ifndef STACK_H
#define STACK_H

#include <stdbool.h>   /* C99 only */

void make_empty(void);
bool is_empty(void);
bool is_full(void);
void push(int i);
int pop(void);

#endif
```

I've included C99's `<stdbool.h>` header so that the is_empty and is_full functions can return a bool result rather than an int value.

Let's first use an array to implement the stack:

stack1.c
```
#include <stdio.h>
#include <stdlib.h>
#include "stack.h"

#define STACK_SIZE 100

static int contents[STACK_SIZE];
static int top = 0;

static void terminate(const char *message)
{
  printf("%s\n", message);
  exit(EXIT_FAILURE);
}

void make_empty(void)
{
  top = 0;
}

bool is_empty(void)
{
  return top == 0;
}

bool is_full(void)
{
  return top == STACK_SIZE;
}

void push(int i)
{
  if (is_full())
    terminate("Error in push: stack is full.");
  contents[top++] = i;
}
```

```
int pop(void)
{
  if (is_empty())
    terminate("Error in pop: stack is empty.");
  return contents[--top];
}
```

The variables that make up the stack (`contents` and `top`) are both declared `static`, since there's no reason for the rest of the program to access them directly. The `terminate` function is also declared `static`. This function isn't part of the module's interface; instead, it's designed for use solely within the implementation of the module.

As a matter of style, some programmers use macros to indicate which functions and variables are "public" (accessible elsewhere in the program) and which are "private" (limited to a single file):

```
#define PUBLIC    /* empty */
#define PRIVATE static
```

The reason for writing `PRIVATE` instead of `static` is that the latter has more than one use in C; `PRIVATE` makes it clear that we're using it to enforce information hiding. Here's what the stack implementation would look like if we were to use `PUBLIC` and `PRIVATE`:

```
PRIVATE int contents[STACK_SIZE];
PRIVATE int top = 0;

PRIVATE void terminate(const char *message) { … }

PUBLIC void make_empty(void) { … }

PUBLIC bool is_empty(void) { … }

PUBLIC bool is_full(void) { … }

PUBLIC void push(int i) { … }

PUBLIC int pop(void) { … }
```

Now we'll switch to a linked-list implementation of the stack module:

stack2.c
```
#include <stdio.h>
#include <stdlib.h>
#include "stack.h"

struct node {
  int data;
  struct node *next;
};

static struct node *top = NULL;
```

```
static void terminate(const char *message)
{
  printf("%s\n", message);
  exit(EXIT_FAILURE);
}

void make_empty(void)
{
  while (!is_empty())
    pop();
}

bool is_empty(void)
{
  return top == NULL;
}

bool is_full(void)
{
  return false;
}

void push(int i)
{
  struct node *new_node = malloc(sizeof(struct node));
  if (new_node == NULL)
    terminate("Error in push: stack is full.");

  new_node->data = i;
  new_node->next = top;
  top = new_node;
}

int pop(void)
{
  struct node *old_top;
  int i;

  if (is_empty())
    terminate("Error in pop: stack is empty.");

  old_top = top;
  i = top->data;
  top = top->next;
  free(old_top);
  return i;
}
```

Note that the is_full function returns false every time it's called. A linked
list has no limit on its size, so the stack will never be full. It's possible (but not
likely) that the program might run out of memory, which will cause the push
function to fail, but there's no easy way to test for that condition in advance.

Our stack example shows clearly the advantage of information hiding: it doesn't matter whether we use `stack1.c` or `stack2.c` to implement the stack module. Both versions match the module's interface, so we can switch from one to the other without having to make changes elsewhere in the program.

19.3   Abstract Data Types

A module that serves as an abstract object, like the stack module in the previous section, has a serious disadvantage: there's no way to have multiple instances of the object (more than one stack, in this case). To accomplish this, we'll need to go a step further and create a new *type*.

Once we've defined a `Stack` type, we'll be able to have as many stacks as we want. The following fragment illustrates how we could have two stacks in the same program:

```
Stack s1, s2;

make_empty(&s1);
make_empty(&s2);
push(&s1, 1);
push(&s2, 2);
if (!is_empty(&s1))
  printf("%d\n", pop(&s1));   /* prints "1" */
```

We're not really sure what `s1` and `s2` are (structures? pointers?), but it doesn't matter. To clients, `s1` and `s2` are *abstractions* that respond to certain operations (`make_empty`, `is_empty`, `is_full`, `push`, and `pop`).

Let's convert our `stack.h` header so that it provides a `Stack` type, where `Stack` is a structure. Doing so will require adding a `Stack` (or `Stack *`) parameter to each function. The header will now look like this (changes to `stack.h` are in **bold;** unchanged portions of the header aren't shown):

```
#define STACK_SIZE 100

typedef struct {
  int contents[STACK_SIZE];
  int top;
} Stack;

void make_empty(Stack *s);
bool is_empty(const Stack *s);
bool is_full(const Stack *s);
void push(Stack *s, int i);
int pop(Stack *s);
```

The stack parameters to `make_empty`, `push`, and `pop` need to be pointers, since these functions modify the stack. The parameter to `is_empty` and `is_full` doesn't need to be a pointer, but I've made it one anyway. Passing these functions a `Stack` *pointer* instead of a `Stack` *value* is more efficient, since the latter would result in a structure being copied.

Encapsulation

Unfortunately, `Stack` isn't an *abstract* data type, since `stack.h` reveals what the `Stack` type really is. Nothing prevents clients from using a `Stack` variable as a structure:

```
Stack s1;

s1.top = 0;
s1.contents[top++] = 1;
```

Providing access to the `top` and `contents` members allows clients to corrupt the stack. Worse still, we won't be able to change the way stacks are stored without having to assess the effect of the change on clients.

What we need is a way to prevent clients from knowing how the `Stack` type is represented. C has only limited support for *encapsulating* types in this way. Newer C-based languages, including C++, Java, and C#, are better equipped for this purpose.

Incomplete Types

The only tool that C gives us for encapsulation is the *incomplete type*. (Incomplete types were mentioned briefly in Section 17.9 and in the Q&A section at the end of Chapter 17.) The C standard describes incomplete types as "types that describe objects but lack information needed to determine their sizes." For example, the declaration

```
struct t;   /* incomplete declaration of t */
```

tells the compiler that `t` is a structure tag but doesn't describe the members of the structure. As a result, the compiler doesn't have enough information to determine the size of such a structure. The intent is that an incomplete type will be completed elsewhere in the program.

As long as a type remains incomplete, its uses are limited. Since the compiler doesn't know the size of an incomplete type, it can't be used to declare a variable:

```
struct t s;   /*** WRONG ***/
```

However, it's perfectly legal to define a pointer type that references an incomplete type:

```
typedef struct t *T;
```

This type definition states that a variable of type `T` is a pointer to a structure with tag `t`. We can now declare variables of type `T`, pass them as arguments to functions, and perform other operations that are legal for pointers. (The size of a pointer doesn't depend on what it points to, which explains why C allows this behavior.) What we can't do, though, is apply the `->` operator to one of these variables, since the compiler knows nothing about the members of a `t` structure.

19.4 A Stack Abstract Data Type

To illustrate how abstract data types can be encapsulated using incomplete types, we'll develop a stack ADT based on the stack module described in Section 19.2. In the process, we'll explore three different ways to implement the stack.

Defining the Interface for the Stack ADT

First, we'll need a header file that defines our stack ADT type and gives prototypes for the functions that represent stack operations. Let's name this file stack-ADT.h. The Stack type will be a pointer to a stack_type structure that stores the actual contents of the stack. This structure is an incomplete type that will be completed in the file that implements the stack. The members of this structure will depend on how the stack is implemented. Here's what the stackADT.h file will look like:

stackADT.h
(version 1)

```
#ifndef STACKADT_H
#define STACKADT_H

#include <stdbool.h>    /* C99 only */

typedef struct stack_type *Stack;

Stack create(void);
void destroy(Stack s);
void make_empty(Stack s);
bool is_empty(Stack s);
bool is_full(Stack s);
void push(Stack s, int i);
int pop(Stack s);

#endif
```

Clients that include stackADT.h will be able to declare variables of type Stack, each of which is capable of pointing to a stack_type structure. Clients can then call the functions declared in stackADT.h to perform operations on stack variables. However, clients can't access the members of the stack_type structure, since that structure will be defined in a separate file.

Note that each function has a Stack parameter or returns a Stack value. The stack functions in Section 19.3 had parameters of type Stack *. The reason for the difference is that a Stack variable is now a pointer; it points to a stack_type structure that stores the contents of the stack. If a function needs to modify the stack, it changes the structure itself, not the pointer to the structure.

Also note the presence of the create and destroy functions. A module generally doesn't need these functions, but an ADT does. `create` will dynamically allocate memory for a stack (including the memory required for a `stack_type` structure), as well as initializing the stack to its "empty" state. `destroy` will release the stack's dynamically allocated memory.

The following client file can be used to test the stack ADT. It creates two stacks and performs a variety of operations on them.

stackclient.c

```c
#include <stdio.h>
#include "stackADT.h"

int main(void)
{
  Stack s1, s2;
  int n;

  s1 = create();
  s2 = create();

  push(s1, 1);
  push(s1, 2);

  n = pop(s1);
  printf("Popped %d from s1\n", n);
  push(s2, n);
  n = pop(s1);
  printf("Popped %d from s1\n", n);
  push(s2, n);

  destroy(s1);

  while (!is_empty(s2))
    printf("Popped %d from s2\n", pop(s2));

  push(s2, 3);
  make_empty(s2);
  if (is_empty(s2))
    printf("s2 is empty\n");
  else
    printf("s2 is not empty\n");

  destroy(s2);

  return 0;
}
```

If the stack ADT is implemented correctly, the program should produce the following output:

```
Popped 2 from s1
Popped 1 from s1
Popped 1 from s2
Popped 2 from s2
s2 is empty
```

Implementing the Stack ADT Using a Fixed-Length Array

There are several ways to implement the stack ADT. Our first approach is the simplest. We'll have the `stackADT.c` file define the `stack_type` structure so that it contains a fixed-length array (to hold the contents of the stack) along with an integer that keeps track of the top of the stack:

```
struct stack_type {
  int contents[STACK_SIZE];
  int top;
};
```

Here's what `stackADT.c` will look like:

stackADT.c

```
#include <stdio.h>
#include <stdlib.h>
#include "stackADT.h"

#define STACK_SIZE 100

struct stack_type {
  int contents[STACK_SIZE];
  int top;
};

static void terminate(const char *message)
{
  printf("%s\n", message);
  exit(EXIT_FAILURE);
}

Stack create(void)
{
  Stack s = malloc(sizeof(struct stack_type));
  if (s == NULL)
    terminate("Error in create: stack could not be created.");
  s->top = 0;
  return s;
}

void destroy(Stack s)
{
  free(s);
}

void make_empty(Stack s)
{
  s->top = 0;
}

bool is_empty(Stack s)
{
  return s->top == 0;
}
```

```
bool is_full(Stack s)
{
  return s->top == STACK_SIZE;
}

void push(Stack s, int i)
{
  if (is_full(s))
    terminate("Error in push: stack is full.");
  s->contents[s->top++] = i;
}

int pop(Stack s)
{
  if (is_empty(s))
    terminate("Error in pop: stack is empty.");
  return s->contents[--s->top];
}
```

The most striking thing about the functions in this file is that they use the `->` operator, not the `.` operator, to access the `contents` and `top` members of the
`stack_type` structure. The `s` parameter is a pointer to a `stack_type` structure, not a structure itself, so using the `.` operator would be illegal.

Changing the Item Type in the Stack ADT

Now that we have a working version of the stack ADT, let's try to improve it. First,
note that items in the stack must be integers. That's too restrictive; in fact, the item
type doesn't really matter. The stack items could just as easily be other basic types
(`float`, `double`, `long`, etc.) or even structures, unions, or pointers, for that
matter.

To make the stack ADT easier to modify for different item types, let's add a
type definition to the `stackADT.h` header. It will define a type named `Item`,
representing the type of data to be stored on the stack.

stackADT.h
(version 2)

```
#ifndef STACKADT_H
#define STACKADT_H

#include <stdbool.h>    /* C99 only */

typedef int Item;

typedef struct stack_type *Stack;

Stack create(void);
void destroy(Stack s);
void make_empty(Stack s);
bool is_empty(Stack s);
bool is_full(Stack s);
```

```
void push(Stack s, Item i);
Item pop(Stack s);

#endif
```

The changes to the file are shown in **bold.** Besides the addition of the `Item` type, the `push` and `pop` functions have been modified. `push` now has a parameter of type `Item`, and `pop` returns a value of type `Item`. We'll use this version of `stackADT.h` from now on; it replaces the earlier version.

The `stackADT.c` file will need to be modified to match the new `stack-ADT.h`. The changes are minimal, however. The `stack_type` structure will now contain an array whose elements have type `Item` instead of `int`:

```
struct stack_type {
  Item contents[STACK_SIZE];
  int top;
};
```

The only other changes are to `push` (the second parameter now has type `Item`) and `pop` (which returns a value of type `Item`). The bodies of `push` and `pop` are unchanged.

The `stackclient.c` file can be used to test the new `stackADT.h` and `stackADT.c` to verify that the `Stack` type still works (it does!). Now we can change the item type any time we want by simply modifying the definition of the `Item` type in `stackADT.h`. (Although we won't have to change the `stack-ADT.c` file, we'll still need to recompile it.)

Implementing the Stack ADT Using a Dynamic Array

Another problem with the stack ADT as it currently stands is that each stack has a fixed maximum size, which is currently set at 100 items. This limit can be increased to any number we wish, of course, but all stacks created using the `Stack` type will have the same limit. There's no way to have stacks with different capacities or to set the stack size as the program is running.

There are two solutions to this problem. One is to implement the stack as a linked list, in which case there's no fixed limit on its size. We'll investigate this solution in a moment. First, though, let's try the other approach, which involves

dynamically allocated arrays ➤ 17.3 storing stack items in a dynamically allocated array.

The crux of the latter approach is to modify the `stack_type` structure so that the `contents` member is a *pointer* to the array in which the items are stored, not the array itself:

```
struct stack_type {
  Item *contents;
  int top;
  int size;
};
```

I've also added a new member, size, that stores the stack's maximum size (the length of the array that contents points to). We'll use this member to check for the "stack full" condition.

The create function will now have a parameter that specifies the desired maximum stack size:

```
Stack create(int size);
```

When create is called, it will create a stack_type structure plus an array of length size. The contents member of the structure will point to this array.

The stackADT.h file will be the same as before, except that we'll need to add a size parameter to the create function. (Let's name the new version stackADT2.h.) The stackADT.c file will need more extensive modification, however. The new version appears below, with changes shown in **bold**.

stackADT2.c
```c
#include <stdio.h>
#include <stdlib.h>
#include "stackADT2.h"

struct stack_type {
  Item *contents;
  int top;
  int size;
};

static void terminate(const char *message)
{
  printf("%s\n", message);
  exit(EXIT_FAILURE);
}

Stack create(int size)
{
  Stack s = malloc(sizeof(struct stack_type));
  if (s == NULL)
    terminate("Error in create: stack could not be created.");
  s->contents = malloc(size * sizeof(Item));
  if (s->contents == NULL) {
    free(s);
    terminate("Error in create: stack could not be created.");
  }
  s->top = 0;
  s->size = size;
  return s;
}

void destroy(Stack s)
{
  free(s->contents);
  free(s);
}
```

```
void make_empty(Stack s)
{
  s->top = 0;
}

bool is_empty(Stack s)
{
  return s->top == 0;
}

bool is_full(Stack s)
{
  return s->top == s->size;
}

void push(Stack s, Item i)
{
  if (is_full(s))
    terminate("Error in push: stack is full.");
  s->contents[s->top++] = i;
}

Item pop(Stack s)
{
  if (is_empty(s))
    terminate("Error in pop: stack is empty.");
  return s->contents[--s->top];
}
```

The create function now calls malloc twice: once to allocate a stack_type structure and once to allocate the array that will contain the stack items. Either call of malloc could fail, causing terminate to be called. The destroy function must call free twice to release all the memory allocated by create.

The stackclient.c file can again be used to test the stack ADT. The calls of create will need to be changed, however, since create now requires an argument. For example, we could replace the statements

```
s1 = create();
s2 = create();
```

with the following statements:

```
s1 = create(100);
s2 = create(200);
```

Implementing the Stack ADT Using a Linked List

Implementing the stack ADT using a dynamically allocated array gives us more flexibility than using a fixed-size array. However, the client is still required to specify a maximum size for a stack at the time it's created. If we use a linked-list implementation instead, there won't be any preset limit on the size of a stack.

Our implementation will be similar to the one in the `stack2.c` file of Section 19.2. The linked list will consist of nodes, represented by the following structure:

```
struct node {
  Item data;
  struct node *next;
};
```

The type of the `data` member is now `Item` rather than `int`, but the structure is otherwise the same as before.

The `stack_type` structure will contain a pointer to the first node in the list:

```
struct stack_type {
  struct node *top;
};
```

At first glance, the `stack_type` structure seems superfluous; we could just define `Stack` to be `struct node *` and let a `Stack` value be a pointer to the first node in the list. However, we still need the `stack_type` structure so that the interface to the stack remains unchanged. (If we did away with it, any function that modified the stack would need a `Stack *` parameter instead of a `Stack` parameter.) Moreover, having the `stack_type` structure will make it easier to change the implementation in the future, should we decide to store additional information. For example, if we later decide that the `stack_type` structure should contain a count of how many items are currently stored in the stack, we can easily add a member to the `stack_type` structure to store this information.

We won't need to make any changes to the `stackADT.h` header. (We'll use this header file, not `stackADT2.h`.) We can also use the original `stack-client.c` file for testing. All the changes will be in the `stackADT.c` file. Here's the new version:

stackADT3.c

```
#include <stdio.h>
#include <stdlib.h>
#include "stackADT.h"

struct node {
  Item data;
  struct node *next;
};

struct stack_type {
  struct node *top;
};

static void terminate(const char *message)
{
  printf("%s\n", message);
  exit(EXIT_FAILURE);
}
```

```c
Stack create(void)
{
  Stack s = malloc(sizeof(struct stack_type));
  if (s == NULL)
    terminate("Error in create: stack could not be created.");
  s->top = NULL;
  return s;
}

void destroy(Stack s)
{
  make_empty(s);
  free(s);
}

void make_empty(Stack s)
{
  while (!is_empty(s))
    pop(s);
}

bool is_empty(Stack s)
{
  return s->top == NULL;
}

bool is_full(Stack s)
{
  return false;
}

void push(Stack s, Item i)
{
  struct node *new_node = malloc(sizeof(struct node));
  if (new_node == NULL)
    terminate("Error in push: stack is full.");

  new_node->data = i;
  new_node->next = s->top;
  s->top = new_node;
}

Item pop(Stack s)
{
  struct node *old_top;
  Item i;

  if (is_empty(s))
    terminate("Error in pop: stack is empty.");

  old_top = s->top;
  i = old_top->data;
  s->top = old_top->next;
  free(old_top);
  return i;
}
```

Note that the `destroy` function calls `make_empty` (to release the memory occupied by the nodes in the linked list) before it calls `free` (to release the memory for the `stack_type` structure).

19.5 Design Issues for Abstract Data Types

Section 19.4 described a stack ADT and showed several ways to implement it. Unfortunately, this ADT suffers from several problems that prevent it from being industrial-strength. Let's look at each of these problems and discuss possible solutions.

Naming Conventions

The stack ADT functions currently have short, easy-to-understand names: `create`, `destroy`, `make_empty`, `is_empty`, `is_full`, `push`, and `pop`. If we have more than one ADT in a program, name clashes are likely, with functions in two modules having the same name. (Each ADT will need its own `create` function, for example.) Therefore, we'll probably need to use function names that incorporate the name of the ADT itself, such as `stack_create` instead of `create`.

Error Handling

The stack ADT deals with errors by displaying an error message and terminating the program. That's not a bad thing to do. The programmer can avoid popping an empty stack or pushing data onto a full stack by being careful to call `is_empty` prior to each call of `pop` and `is_full` prior to each call of `push`, so in theory there's no reason for a call of `push` or `pop` to fail. (In the linked-list implementation, however, calling `is_full` isn't foolproof; a subsequent call of `push` can still fail.) Nevertheless, we might want to provide a way for a program to recover from these errors rather than terminating.

An alternative is to have the `push` and `pop` functions return a `bool` value to indicate whether or not they succeeded. `push` currently has a `void` return type, so it would be easy to modify it to return `true` if the `push` operation succeeds and `false` if the stack is full. Modifying the `pop` function would be more difficult, since `pop` currently returns the value that was popped. However, if `pop` were to return a *pointer* to this value, instead of the value itself, then `pop` could return `NULL` to indicate that the stack is empty.

assert macro ➤24.1 A final comment about error handling: The C standard library contains a parameterized macro named `assert` that can terminate a program if a specified condition isn't satisfied. We could use calls of this macro as replacements for the `if` statements and calls of `terminate` that currently appear in the stack ADT.

Generic ADTs

Midway through Section 19.4, we improved the stack ADT by making it easier to change the type of items stored in a stack—all we had to do was modify the definition of the `Item` type. It's still somewhat of a nuisance to do so; it would be nicer if a stack could accommodate items of any type, without the need to modify the `stack.h` file. Also note that our stack ADT suffers from a serious flaw: a program can't create two stacks whose items have different types. It's easy to create multiple stacks, but those stacks must have items with identical types. To allow stacks with different item types, we'd have to make copies of the stack ADT's header file and source file and modify one set of files so that the `Stack` type and its associated functions have different names.

What we'd like to have is a single "generic" stack type from which we could create a stack of integers, a stack of strings, or any other stack that we might need. There are various ways to create such a type in C, but none are completely satisfactory. The most common approach uses `void *` as the item type, which allows arbitrary pointers to be pushed and popped. With this technique, the `stack-ADT.h` file would be similar to our original version; however, the prototypes of the `push` and `pop` functions would have the following appearance:

```
void push(Stack s, void *p);
void *pop(Stack s);
```

`pop` returns a pointer to the item popped from the stack; if the stack is empty, it returns a null pointer.

There are two disadvantages to using `void *` as the item type. One is that this approach doesn't work for data that can't be represented in pointer form. Items could be strings (which are represented by a pointer to the first character in the string) or dynamically allocated structures but not basic types such as `int` and `double`. The other disadvantage is that error checking is no longer possible. A stack that stores `void *` items will happily allow a mixture of pointers of different types; there's no way to detect an error caused by pushing a pointer of the wrong type.

ADTs in Newer Languages

The problems that we've just discussed are dealt with much more cleanly in newer C-based languages, such as C++, Java, and C#. Name clashes are prevented by defining function names within a ***class.*** A stack ADT would be represented by a `Stack` class; the stack functions would belong to this class, and would only be recognized by the compiler when applied to a `Stack` object. These languages have a feature known as ***exception handling*** that allows functions such as `push` and `pop` to "throw" an exception when they detect an error condition. Code in the client can then deal with the error by "catching" the exception. C++, Java, and C# also provide special features for defining generic ADTs. In C++, for example, we would define a stack ***template,*** leaving the item type unspecified.

Q & A

Q: You said that C wasn't designed for writing large programs. Isn't UNIX a large program? [p. 483]

A: Not at the time C was designed. In a 1978 paper, Ken Thompson estimated that the UNIX kernel was about 10,000 lines of C code (plus a small amount of assembler). Other components of UNIX were of comparable size; in another 1978 paper, Dennis Ritchie and colleagues put the size of the PDP-11 C compiler at 9660 lines. By today's standards, these are indeed small programs.

Q: Are there any abstract data types in the C library?

A: Technically there aren't, but a few come close, including the `FILE` type (defined in `<stdio.h>`). Before performing an operation on a file, we must declare a variable of type `FILE *`:

FILE type ►22.1

```
FILE *fp;
```

The `fp` variable will then be passed to various file-handling functions.

   Programmers are expected to treat `FILE` as an abstraction. It's not necessary to know what a `FILE` is in order to use the `FILE` type. Presumably `FILE` is a structure type, but the C standard doesn't even guarantee that. In fact, it's better not to know too much about how `FILE` values are stored, since the definition of the `FILE` type can (and often does) vary from one C compiler to another.

   Of course, we can always look in the `stdio.h` file and see what a `FILE` is. Having done so, there's nothing to prevent us from writing code to access the internals of a `FILE`. For example, we might discover that `FILE` is a structure with a member named `bsize` (the file's buffer size):

```
typedef struct {
  ...
  int bsize;    /* buffer size */
  ...
} FILE;
```

Once we know about the `bsize` member, there's nothing to prevent us from accessing the buffer size for a particular file:

```
printf("Buffer size: %d\n", fp->bsize);
```

Doing so isn't a good idea, however, because other C compilers might store the buffer size under a different name, or keep track of it in some entirely different way. Changing the `bsize` member is an even worse idea:

```
fp->bsize = 1024;
```

Unless we know all the details about how files are stored, this is a dangerous thing to do. Even if we *do* know the details, they may change with a different compiler or the next release of the same compiler.

Q: **What other incomplete types are there besides incomplete structure types? [p. 492]**

A: One of the most common incomplete types occurs when an array is declared with no specified size:

```
extern int a[];
```

After this declaration (which we first encountered in Section 15.2), a has an incomplete type, because the compiler doesn't know a's length. Presumably a is defined in another file within the program; that definition will supply the missing length. Another incomplete type occurs in declarations that specify no length for an array but provide an initializer:

```
int a[] = {1, 2, 3};
```

In this example, the array a initially has an incomplete type, but the type is completed by the initializer.

flexible array members ➤17.9

Declaring a union tag without specifying the members of the union also creates an incomplete type. Flexible array members (a C99 feature) have an incomplete type. Finally, void is an incomplete type. The void type has the unusual property that it can never be completed, thus making it impossible to declare a variable of this type.

Q: **What other restrictions are there on the use of incomplete types? [p. 492]**

A: The sizeof operator can't be applied to an incomplete type (not surprisingly, since the size of an incomplete type is unknown). A member of a structure or union (other than a flexible array member) can't have an incomplete type. Similarly, the elements of an array can't have an incomplete type. Finally, a parameter in a function definition can't have an incomplete type (although this is allowed in a function *declaration*). The compiler "adjusts" each array parameter in a function definition so that it has a pointer type, thus preventing it from having an incomplete type.

Exercises

Section 19.1

1. A *queue* is similar to a stack, except that items are added at one end but removed from the other in a *FIFO* (first-in, first-out) fashion. Operations on a queue might include:

   > Inserting an item at the end of the queue
   > Removing an item from the beginning of the queue
   > Returning the first item in the queue (without changing the queue)
   > Returning the last item in the queue (without changing the queue)
   > Testing whether the queue is empty

   Write an interface for a queue module in the form of a header file named queue.h.

Section 19.2

ⓦ 2. Modify the stack2.c file to use the PUBLIC and PRIVATE macros.

3. (a) Write an array-based implementation of the queue module described in Exercise 1. Use three integers to keep track of the queue's status, with one integer storing the position of the first empty slot in the array (used when an item is inserted), the second storing the position of the next item to be removed, and the third storing the number of items in the queue. An insertion or removal that would cause either of the first two integers to be incremented past the end of the array should instead reset the variable to zero, thus causing it to "wrap around" to the beginning of the array.

    (b) Write a linked-list implementation of the queue module described in Exercise 1. Use two pointers, one pointing to the first node in the list and the other pointing to the last node. When an item is inserted into the queue, add it to the end of the list. When an item is removed from the queue, delete the first node in the list.

Section 19.3 Ⓦ 4. (a) Write an implementation of the Stack type, assuming that Stack is a structure containing a fixed-length array.

    (b) Redo the Stack type, this time using a linked-list representation instead of an array. (Show both stack.h and stack.c.)

5. Modify the queue.h header of Exercise 1 so that it defines a Queue type, where Queue is a structure containing a fixed-length array (see Exercise 3(a)). Modify the functions in queue.h to take a Queue * parameter.

Section 19.4 6. (a) Add a peek function to stackADT.c. This function will have a parameter of type Stack. When called, it returns the top item on the stack but doesn't modify the stack.

    (b) Repeat part (a), modifying stackADT2.c this time.

    (c) Repeat part (a), modifying stackADT3.c this time.

7. Modify stackADT2.c so that a stack automatically doubles in size when it becomes full. Have the push function dynamically allocate a new array that's twice as large as the old one and then copy the stack contents from the old array to the new one. Be sure to have push deallocate the old array once the data has been copied.

Programming Projects

1. Modify Programming Project 1 from Chapter 10 so that it uses the stack ADT described in Section 19.4. You may use any of the implementations of the ADT described in that section.

2. Modify Programming Project 6 from Chapter 10 so that it uses the stack ADT described in Section 19.4. You may use any of the implementations of the ADT described in that section.

3. Modify the stackADT3.c file of Section 19.4 by adding an int member named len to the stack_type structure. This member will keep track of how many items are currently stored in a stack. Add a new function named length that has a Stack parameter and returns the value of the len member. (Some of the existing functions in stackADT3.c will need to be modified as well.) Modify stackclient.c so that it calls the length function (and displays the value that it returns) after each operation that modifies a stack.

4. Modify the stackADT.h and stackADT3.c files of Section 19.4 so that a stack stores values of type void *, as described in Section 19.5; the Item type will no longer be used. Modify stackclient.c so that it stores pointers to strings in the s1 and s2 stacks.

5. Starting from the `queue.h` header of Exercise 1, create a file named `queueADT.h` that defines the following `Queue` type:

    ```
    typedef struct queue_type *Queue;
    ```

    `queue_type` is an incomplete structure type. Create a file named `queueADT.c` that contains the full definition of `queue_type` as well as definitions for all the functions in `queue.h`. Use a fixed-length array to store the items in a queue (see Exercise 3(a)). Create a file named `queueclient.c` (similar to the `stackclient.c` file of Section 19.4) that creates two queues and performs operations on them. Be sure to provide `create` and `destroy` functions for your ADT.

6. Modify Programming Project 5 so that the items in a queue are stored in a dynamically allocated array whose length is passed to the `create` function.

7. Modify Programming Project 5 so that the items in a queue are stored in a linked list (see Exercise 3(b)).

20 Low-Level Programming

*A programming language is low level when its
programs require attention to the irrelevant.*

Previous chapters have described C's high-level, machine-independent features. Although these features are adequate for many applications, some programs need to perform operations at the bit level. Bit manipulation and other low-level operations are especially useful for writing systems programs (including compilers and operating systems), encryption programs, graphics programs, and programs for which fast execution and/or efficient use of space is critical.

Section 20.1 covers C's bitwise operators, which provide easy access to both individual bits and bit-fields. Section 20.2 then shows how to declare structures that contain bit-fields. Finally, Section 20.3 describes how certain ordinary C features (type definitions, unions, and pointers) can help in writing low-level programs.

Some of the techniques described in this chapter depend on knowledge of how data is stored in memory, which can vary depending on the machine and the compiler. Relying on these techniques will most likely make a program nonportable, so it's best to avoid them unless absolutely necessary. If you do need them, try to limit their use to certain modules in your program; don't spread them around. And, above all, be sure to document what you're doing!

20.1 Bitwise Operators

C provides six *bitwise operators*, which operate on integer data at the bit level. We'll discuss the two bitwise shift operators first, followed by the four other bitwise operators (bitwise complement, bitwise *and*, bitwise exclusive *or*, and bitwise inclusive *or*).

Bitwise Shift Operators

The bitwise shift operators can transform the binary representation of an integer by shifting its bits to the left or right. C provides two shift operators, which are shown in Table 20.1.

Table 20.1
Bitwise Shift Operators

Symbol	Meaning
<<	left shift
>>	right shift

The operands for `<<` and `>>` may be of any integer type (including `char`). The integer promotions are performed on both operands; the result has the type of the left operand after promotion.

The value of `i << j` is the result when the bits in `i` are shifted left by `j` places. For each bit that is "shifted off" the left end of `i`, a zero bit enters at the right. The value of `i >> j` is the result when `i` is shifted right by `j` places. If `i` is of an unsigned type or if the value of `i` is nonnegative, zeros are added at the left as needed. If `i` is a negative number, the result is implementation-defined; some implementations add zeros at the left end, while others preserve the sign bit by adding ones.

portability tip   *For portability, it's best to perform shifts only on unsigned numbers.*

The following examples illustrate the effect of applying the shift operators to the number 13. (For simplicity, these examples—and others in this section—use short integers, which are typically 16 bits.)

```
unsigned short i, j;

i = 13;       /* i is now 13 (binary 0000000000001101) */
j = i << 2;   /* j is now 52 (binary 0000000000110100) */
j = i >> 2;   /* j is now  3 (binary 0000000000000011) */
```

As these examples show, neither operator modifies its operands. To modify a variable by shifting its bits, we'd use the compound assignment operators `<<=` and `>>=`:

```
i = 13;       /* i is now 13 (binary 0000000000001101) */
i <<= 2;      /* i is now 52 (binary 0000000000110100) */
i >>= 2;      /* i is now 13 (binary 0000000000001101) */
```

The bitwise shift operators have lower precedence than the arithmetic operators, which can cause surprises. For example, `i << 2 + 1` means `i << (2 + 1)`, not `(i << 2) + 1`.

Bitwise Complement, *And,* Exclusive *Or,* and Inclusive *Or*

Table 20.2 lists the remaining bitwise operators.

Table 20.2
Other Bitwise Operators

Symbol	Meaning
~	bitwise complement
&	bitwise *and*
^	bitwise exclusive *or*
|	bitwise inclusive *or*

The ~ operator is unary; the integer promotions are performed on its operand. The other operators are binary; the usual arithmetic conversions are performed on their operands.

The ~, &, ^, and | operators perform Boolean operations on all bits in their operands. The ~ operator produces the complement of its operand, with zeros replaced by ones and ones replaced by zeros. The & operator performs a Boolean *and* operation on all corresponding bits in its two operands. The ^ and | operators are similar (both perform a Boolean *or* operation on the bits in their operands); however, ^ produces 0 whenever both operands have a 1 bit, whereas | produces 1.

Don't confuse the *bitwise* operators & and | with the *logical* operators && and ||. The bitwise operators sometimes produce the same results as the logical operators, but they're not equivalent.

The following examples illustrate the effect of the ~, &, ^, and | operators:

```
unsigned short i, j, k;

i = 21;         /* i is now     21 (binary 0000000000010101) */
j = 56;         /* j is now     56 (binary 0000000000111000) */
k = ~i;         /* k is now  65514 (binary 1111111111101010) */
k = i & j;      /* k is now     16 (binary 0000000000010000) */
k = i ^ j;      /* k is now     45 (binary 0000000000101101) */
k = i | j;      /* k is now     61 (binary 0000000000111101) */
```

The value shown for ~i is based on the assumption that an unsigned short value occupies 16 bits.

The ~ operator deserves special mention, since we can use it to help make even low-level programs more portable. Suppose that we need an integer whose bits are all 1. The preferred technique is to write ~0, which doesn't depend on the number of bits in an integer. Similarly, if we need an integer whose bits are all 1 except for the last five, we could write ~0x1f.

Each of the ~, &, ^, and | operators has a different precedence:

Highest: ~

&

^

Lowest: |

As a result, we can combine these operators in expressions without having to use parentheses. For example, we could write i & ~j | k instead of (i & (~j)) | k and i ^ j & ~k instead of i ^ (j & (~k)). Of course, it doesn't hurt to use parentheses to avoid confusion.

table of operators ➤ *Appendix A*

The precedence of &, ^, and | is lower than the precedence of the relational and equality operators. Consequently, statements like the following one won't have the desired effect:

```
if (status & 0x4000 != 0) …
```

Instead of testing whether status & 0x4000 isn't zero, this statement will evaluate 0x4000 != 0 (which has the value 1), then test whether the value of status & 1 isn't zero.

The compound assignment operators &=, ^=, and |= correspond to the bit-wise operators &, ^, and |:

```
i = 21;     /* i is now 21 (binary 0000000000010101) */
j = 56;     /* j is now 56 (binary 0000000000111000) */
i &= j;     /* i is now 16 (binary 0000000000010000) */
i ^= j;     /* i is now 40 (binary 0000000000101000) */
i |= j;     /* i is now 56 (binary 0000000000111000) */
```

Using the Bitwise Operators to Access Bits

When we do low-level programming, we'll often need to store information as single bits or collections of bits. In graphics programming, for example, we may want to squeeze two or more pixels into a single byte. Using the bitwise operators, we can extract or modify data that's stored in a small number of bits.

Let's assume that i is a 16-bit unsigned short variable. Let's see how to perform the most common single-bit operations on i:

■ ***Setting a bit.*** Suppose that we want to set bit 4 of i. (We'll assume that the leftmost—or ***most significant***—bit is numbered 15 and the least significant is numbered 0.) The easiest way to set bit 4 is to *or* the value of i with the constant 0x0010 (a "mask" that contains a 1 bit in position 4):

```
i = 0x0000;         /* i is now 0000000000000000 */
i |= 0x0010;        /* i is now 0000000000010000 */
```

More generally, if the position of the bit is stored in the variable j, we can use a shift operator to create the mask:

idiom
```
i |= 1 << j;          /* sets bit j */
```

For example, if j has the value 3, then 1 << j is 0x0008.

■ *Clearing a bit.* To clear bit 4 of i, we'd use a mask with a 0 bit in position 4 and 1 bits everywhere else:

```
i = 0x00ff;           /* i is now 0000000011111111 */
i &= ~0x0010;         /* i is now 0000000011101111 */
```

Using the same idea, we can easily write a statement that clears a bit whose position is stored in a variable:

idiom
```
i &= ~(1 << j);       /* clears bit j */
```

■ *Testing a bit.* The following if statement tests whether bit 4 of i is set:

```
if (i & 0x0010) …     /* tests bit 4 */
```

To test whether bit j is set, we'd use the following statement:

idiom
```
if (i & 1 << j) …     /* tests bit j */
```

To make working with bits easier, we'll often give them names. For example, suppose that we want bits 0, 1, and 2 of a number to correspond to the colors blue, green, and red, respectively. First, we define names that represent the three bit positions:

```
#define BLUE   1
#define GREEN  2
#define RED    4
```

Setting, clearing, and testing the BLUE bit would be done as follows:

```
i |= BLUE;            /* sets BLUE bit   */
i &= ~BLUE;           /* clears BLUE bit */
if (i & BLUE) …       /* tests BLUE bit  */
```

It's also easy to set, clear, or test several bits at time:

```
i |= BLUE | GREEN;              /* sets BLUE and GREEN bits   */
i &= ~(BLUE | GREEN);           /* clears BLUE and GREEN bits */
if (i & (BLUE | GREEN)) …       /* tests BLUE and GREEN bits  */
```

The if statement tests whether either the BLUE bit *or* the GREEN bit is set.

Using the Bitwise Operators to Access Bit-Fields

Dealing with a group of several consecutive bits (a *bit-field*) is slightly more complicated than working with single bits. Here are examples of the two most common bit-field operations:

■ *Modifying a bit-field.* Modifying a bit-field requires a bitwise *and* (to clear the bit-field), followed by a bitwise *or* (to store new bits in the bit-field). The following statement shows how we might store the binary value 101 in bits 4–6 of the variable i:

```
i = i & ~0x0070 | 0x0050;    /* stores 101 in bits 4-6 */
```

The & operator clears bits 4–6 of i; the | operator then sets bits 6 and 4. Notice that i |= 0x0050 by itself wouldn't always work: it would set bits 6 and 4 but not change bit 5. To generalize the example a little, let's assume that the variable j contains the value to be stored in bits 4–6 of i. We'll need to shift j into position before performing the bitwise *or*:

```
i = (i & ~0x0070) | (j << 4);    /* stores j in bits 4-6 */
```

The | operator has lower precedence than & and <<, so we can drop the parentheses if we wish:

```
i = i & ~0x0070 | j << 4;
```

- **Retrieving a bit-field.** When the bit-field is at the right end of a number (in the least significant bits), fetching its value is easy. For example, the following statement retrieves bits 0–2 in the variable i:

```
j = i & 0x0007;              /* retrieves bits 0-2 */
```

If the bit-field isn't at the right end of of i, then we can first shift the bit-field to the end before extracting the field using the & operator. To extract bits 4–6 of i, for example, we could use the following statement:

```
j = (i >> 4) & 0x0007;    /* retrieves bits 4-6 */
```

PROGRAM   **XOR Encryption**

One of the simplest ways to encrypt data is to exclusive-*or* (XOR) each character with a secret key. Suppose that the key is the & character. If we XOR this key with the character z, we'll get the \ character (assuming that we're using the ASCII character set):

ASCII character set ➤*Appendix E*

```
     00100110  (ASCII code for &)
XOR  01111010  (ASCII code for z)
     01011100  (ASCII code for \)
```

To decrypt a message, we just apply the same algorithm. In other words, by encrypting an already-encrypted message, we'll recover the original message. If we XOR the & character with the \ character, for example, we'll get the original character, z:

```
     00100110  (ASCII code for &)
XOR  01011100  (ASCII code for \)
     01111010  (ASCII code for z)
```

The following program, xor.c, encrypts a message by XORing each character with the & character. The original message can be entered by the user or read from a file using input redirection; the encrypted message can be viewed on the screen or saved in a file using output redirection. For example, suppose that the file

input and output redirection ➤*22.1*

`msg` contains the following lines:

```
Trust not him with your secrets, who, when left
alone in your room, turns over your papers.
                --Johann Kaspar Lavater (1741-1801)
```

To encrypt the `msg` file, saving the encrypted message in `newmsg`, we'd use the following command:

```
xor <msg >newmsg
```

`newmsg` will now contain these lines:

```
rTSUR HIR NOK QORN _IST UCETCRU, QNI, QNCH JC@R
GJIHC OH _IST TIIK, RSTHU IPCT _IST VGVCTU.
                --lINGHH mGUVGT jGPGRCT (1741-1801)
```

To recover the original message, we'd use the command

```
xor <newmsg
```

which will display it on the screen.

As the example shows, our program won't change some characters, including digits. XORing these characters with & would produce invisible control characters, which could cause problems with some operating systems. In Chapter 22, we'll see how to avoid problems when reading and writing files that contain control charac-

isprint function ►23.5 ters. Until then, we'll play it safe by using the `isprint` function to make sure that both the original character and the new (encrypted) character are printing characters (i.e., not control characters). If either character fails this test, we'll have the program write the original character instead of the new character.

Here's the finished program, which is remarkably short:

xor.c
```c
/* Performs XOR encryption */

#include <ctype.h>
#include <stdio.h>

#define KEY '&'

int main(void)
{
  int orig_char, new_char;

  while ((orig_char = getchar()) != EOF) {
    new_char = orig_char ^ KEY;
    if (isprint(orig_char) && isprint(new_char))
      putchar(new_char);
    else
      putchar(orig_char);
  }

  return 0;
}
```

20.2 Bit-Fields in Structures

Although the techniques of Section 20.1 allow us to work with bit-fields, these techniques can be tricky to use and potentially confusing. Fortunately, C provides an alternative: declaring structures whose members represent bit-fields.

As an example, let's look at how the MS-DOS operating system (often just called DOS) stores the date at which a file was created or last modified. Since days, months, and years are small numbers, storing them as normal integers would waste space. Instead, DOS allocates only 16 bits for a date, with 5 bits for the day, 4 bits for the month, and 7 bits for the year:

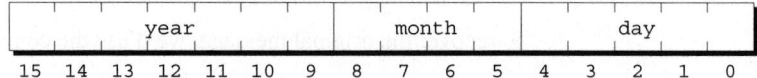

Using bit-fields, we can define a C structure with an identical layout:

```
struct file_date {
  unsigned int day: 5;
  unsigned int month: 4;
  unsigned int year: 7;
};
```

The number after each member indicates its length in bits. Since the members all have the same type, we can condense the declaration if we want:

```
struct file_date {
  unsigned int day: 5, month: 4, year: 7;
};
```

The type of a bit-field must be either `int`, `unsigned int`, or `signed int`. Using `int` is ambiguous; some compilers treat the field's high-order bit as a sign bit, but others don't.

portability tip   *Declare all bit-fields to be either `unsigned int` or `signed int`.*

C99   In C99, bit-fields may also have type `_Bool`. C99 compilers may allow additional bit-field types.

We can use a bit-field just like any other member of a structure, as the following example shows:

```
struct file_date fd;

fd.day = 28;
fd.month = 12;
fd.year = 8;     /* represents 1988 */
```

Note that the `year` member is stored relative to 1980 (the year the world began, according to Microsoft). After these assignments, the `fd` variable will have the following appearance:

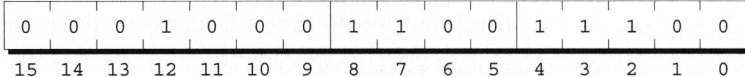

We could have used the bitwise operators to accomplish the same effect; using these operators might even make the program a little faster. However, having a readable program is usually more important than gaining a few microseconds.

Bit-fields do have one restriction that doesn't apply to other members of a structure. Since bit-fields don't have addresses in the usual sense, C doesn't allow us to apply the address operator (`&`) to a bit-field. Because of this rule, functions such as `scanf` can't store data directly in a bit-field:

```
scanf("%d", &fd.day);    /*** WRONG ***/
```

Of course, we can always use `scanf` to read input into an ordinary variable and then assign it to `fd.day`.

How Bit-Fields Are Stored

Let's take a close look at how a compiler processes the declaration of a structure that has bit-field members. As we'll see, the C standard allows the compiler considerable latitude in choosing how it stores bit-fields.

The rules concerning how the compiler handles bit-fields depend on the notion of "storage units." The size of a storage unit is implementation-defined; typical values are 8 bits, 16 bits, and 32 bits. As it processes a structure declaration, the compiler packs bit-fields one by one into a storage unit, with no gaps between the fields, until there's not enough room for the next field. At that point, some compilers skip to the beginning of the next storage unit, while others split the bit-field across the storage units. (Which one occurs is implementation-defined.) The order in which bit-fields are allocated (left to right or right to left) is also implementation-defined.

Our `file_date` example assumes that storage units are 16 bits long. (An 8-bit storage unit would also be acceptable, provided that the compiler splits the `month` field across two storage units.) We also assume that bit-fields are allocated from right to left (with the first bit-field occupying the low-order bits).

C allows us to omit the name of any bit-field. Unnamed bit-fields are useful as "padding" to ensure that other bit fields are properly positioned. Consider the time associated with a DOS file, which is stored in the following way:

```
struct file_time {
  unsigned int seconds: 5;
  unsigned int minutes: 6;
  unsigned int hours: 5;
};
```

(You may be wondering how it's possible to store the seconds—a number between 0 and 59—in a field with only 5 bits. Well, DOS cheats: it divides the number of seconds by 2, so the seconds member is actually between 0 and 29.) If we're not interested in the seconds field, we can leave out its name:

```
struct file_time {
  unsigned int : 5;          /* not used */
  unsigned int minutes: 6;
  unsigned int hours: 5;
};
```

The remaining bit-fields will be aligned as if the seconds field were still present.

Another trick that we can use to control the storage of bit-fields is to specify 0 as the length of an unnamed bit-field:

```
struct s {
  unsigned int a: 4;
  unsigned int : 0;    /* 0-length bit-field */
  unsigned int b: 8;
};
```

A 0-length bit-field is a signal to the compiler to align the following bit-field at the beginning of a storage unit. If storage units are 8 bits long, the compiler will allocate 4 bits for the a member, skip 4 bits to the next storage unit, and then allocate 8 bits for b. If storage units are 16 bits long, the compiler will allocate 4 bits for a, skip 12 bits, and then allocate 8 bits for b.

20.3 Other Low-Level Techniques

Some of the language features that we've covered in previous chapters are used often in low-level programming. To wrap up this chapter, we'll take a look at several important examples: defining types that represent units of storage, using unions to bypass normal type-checking, and using pointers as addresses. We'll also cover the volatile type qualifier, which we avoided discussing in Section 18.3 because of its low-level nature.

Defining Machine-Dependent Types

Since the char type—by definition—occupies one byte, we'll sometimes treat characters as bytes, using them to store data that's not necessarily in character form. When we do so, it's a good idea to define a BYTE type:

```
typedef unsigned char BYTE;
```

Depending on the machine, we may want to define additional types. The x86 architecture makes extensive use of 16-bit words, so the following definition would be useful for that platform:

```
typedef unsigned short WORD;
```

We'll use the BYTE and WORD types in later examples.

Using Unions to Provide Multiple Views of Data

Although unions can be used in a portable way—see Section 16.4 for examples—they're often used in C for an entirely different purpose: viewing a block of memory in two or more different ways.

Here's a simple example based on the file_date structure described in Section 20.2. Since a file_date structure fits into two bytes, we can think of any two-byte value as a file_date structure. In particular, we could view an unsigned short value as a file_date structure (assuming that short integers are 16 bits long). The following union allows us to easily convert a short integer to a file date or vice versa:

```
union int_date {
  unsigned short i;
  struct file_date fd;
};
```

With the help of this union, we could fetch a file date from disk as two bytes, then extract its month, day, and year fields. Conversely, we could construct a date as a file_date structure, then write it to disk as a pair of bytes.

As an example of how we might use the int_date union, here's a function that, when passed an unsigned short argument, prints it as a file date:

```
void print_date(unsigned short n)
{
  union int_date u;

  u.i = n;
  printf("%d/%d/%d\n", u.fd.month, u.fd.day, u.fd.year + 1980);
}
```

Using unions to allow multiple views of data is especially useful when working with registers, which are often divided into smaller units. x86 processors, for example, have 16-bit registers named AX, BX, CX, and DX. Each of these registers can be treated as two 8-bit registers. AX, for example, is divided into registers named AH and AL. (The H and L stand for "high" and "low.")

When writing low-level applications for x86-based computers, we may need variables that represent the contents of the AX, BX, CX, and DX registers. We want access to both the 16- and 8-bit registers; at the same time, we need to take their relationships into account (a change to AX affects both AH and AL; changing AH or AL modifies AX). The solution is to set up two structures, one containing members that correspond to the 16-bit registers, and the other containing members that match the 8-bit registers. We then create a union that encloses the two structures:

```
union {
  struct {
    WORD ax, bx, cx, dx;
  } word;
  struct {
    BYTE al, ah, bl, bh, cl, ch, dl, dh;
  } byte;
} regs;
```

The members of the `word` structure will be overlaid with the members of the `byte` structure; for example, `ax` will occupy the same memory as `al` and `ah`. And that, of course, is exactly what we wanted. Here's an example showing how the `regs` union might be used:

```
regs.byte.ah = 0x12;
regs.byte.al = 0x34;
printf("AX: %hx\n", regs.word.ax);
```

Changing `ah` and `al` affects `ax`, so the output will be

```
AX: 1234
```

Note that the `byte` structure lists `al` before `ah`, even though the AL register is the "low" half of AX and AH is the "high" half. Here's the reason. When a data item consists of more than one byte, there are two logical ways to store it in memory: with the bytes in the "natural" order (with the leftmost byte stored first) or with the bytes in reverse order (the leftmost byte is stored last). The first alternative is called **big-endian;** the second is known as **little-endian.** C doesn't require a specific byte ordering, since that depends on the CPU on which a program will be executed. Some CPUs use the big-endian approach and some use the little-endian approach. What does this have to do with the `byte` structure? It turns out that x86 processors assume that data is stored in little-endian order, so the first byte of `regs.word.ax` is the low byte.

We don't normally need to worry about byte ordering. However, programs that deal with memory at a low level must be aware of the order in which bytes are stored (as the `regs` example illustrates). It's also relevant when working with files that contain non-character data.

⚠️ Be careful when using unions to provide multiple views of data. Data that is valid in its original format may be invalid when viewed as a different type, causing unexpected problems.

Using Pointers as Addresses

We saw in Section 11.1 that a pointer is really some kind of memory address, although we usually don't need to know the details. When we do low-level programming, however, the details matter.

An address often has the same number of bits as an integer (or long integer). Creating a pointer that represents a specific address is easy: we just cast an integer into a pointer. For example, here's how we might store the address 1000 (hex) in a pointer variable:

```
BYTE *p;

p = (BYTE *) 0x1000;   /* p contains address 0x1000 */
```

PROGRAM   **Viewing Memory Locations**

Our next program allows the user to view segments of computer memory; it relies on C's willingness to allow an integer to be used as a pointer. Most CPUs execute programs in "protected mode," however, which means that a program can access only those portions of memory that belong to the program. This prevents a program from accessing (or changing) memory that belongs to another application or to the operating system itself. As a result, we'll only be able to use our program to view areas of memory that have been allocated for use by the program itself. Going outside these regions will cause the program to crash.

The `viewmemory.c` program begins by displaying the address of its own `main` function as well as the address of one of its variables. This will give the user a clue as to which areas of memory can be probed. The program next prompts the user to enter an address (in the form of a hexadecimal integer) plus the number of bytes to view. The program then displays a block of bytes of the chosen length, starting at the specified address.

Bytes are displayed in groups of 10 (except for the last group, which may have fewer than 10 bytes). The address of a group of bytes is displayed at the beginning of a line, followed by the bytes in the group (displayed as hexadecimal numbers), followed by the same bytes displayed as characters (just in case the bytes happen to represent characters, as some of them may). Only printing characters (as determined by the `isprint` function) will be displayed; other characters will be shown as periods.

We'll assume that `int` values are stored using 32 bits and that addresses are also 32 bits long. Addresses are displayed in hexadecimal, as is customary.

viewmemory.c

```
/* Allows the user to view regions of computer memory */

#include <ctype.h>
#include <stdio.h>

typedef unsigned char BYTE;

int main(void)
{
  unsigned int addr;
  int i, n;
  BYTE *ptr;

  printf("Address of main function: %x\n", (unsigned int) main);
  printf("Address of addr variable: %x\n", (unsigned int) &addr);
```

```
        printf("\nEnter a (hex) address: ");
        scanf("%x", &addr);
        printf("Enter number of bytes to view: ");
        scanf("%d", &n);

        printf("\n");
        printf(" Address                      Bytes                     Characters\n");
        printf(" -------   -------------------------------   ----------\n");

        ptr = (BYTE *) addr;
        for (; n > 0; n -= 10) {
          printf("%8X  ", (unsigned int) ptr);
          for (i = 0; i < 10 && i < n; i++)
            printf("%.2X ", *(ptr + i));
          for (; i < 10; i++)
            printf("   ");
          printf(" ");
          for (i = 0;  i < 10 && i < n; i++) {
            BYTE ch = *(ptr + i);
            if (!isprint(ch))
              ch = '.';
            printf("%c", ch);
          }
          printf("\n");
          ptr += 10;
        }

        return 0;
}
```

The program is complicated somewhat by the possibility that the value of n isn't a multiple of 10, so there may be fewer than 10 bytes in the last group. Two of the `for` statements are controlled by the condition `i < 10 && i < n`. This condition causes the loops to execute 10 times or n times, whichever is smaller. There's also a `for` statement that compensates for any missing bytes in the last group by displaying three spaces for each missing byte. That way, the characters that follow the last group of bytes will align properly with the character groups on previous lines.

The %X conversion specifier used in this program is similar to %x, which was discussed in Section 7.1. The difference is that %X displays the hexadecimal digits A, B, C, D, E, and F as upper-case letters; %x displays them in lower case.

Here's what happened when I compiled the program using GCC and tested it on an x86 system running Linux:

```
Address of main function: 804847c
Address of addr variable: bff41154

Enter a (hex) address: 8048000
Enter number of bytes to view: 40

 Address                      Bytes                     Characters
 -------   -------------------------------   ----------
 8048000   7F 45 4C 46 01 01 01 00 00 00   .ELF......
 804800A   00 00 00 00 00 00 02 00 03 00   ..........
 8048014   01 00 00 00 C0 83 04 08 34 00   ........4.
 804801E   00 00 C0 0A 00 00 00 00 00 00   ..........
```

I asked the program to display 40 bytes starting at address 8048000, which precedes the address of the `main` function. Note the 7F byte followed by bytes representing the letters E, L, and F. These four bytes identify the format (ELF) in which the executable file was stored. ELF (Executable and Linking Format) is widely used by UNIX systems, including Linux. 8048000 is the default address at which ELF executables are loaded on x86 platforms.

Let's run the program again, this time displaying a block of bytes that starts at the address of the `addr` variable:

```
Address of main function: 804847c
Address of addr variable: bfec5484

Enter a (hex) address: bfec5484
Enter number of bytes to view: 64

   Address                     Bytes                    Characters
   -------   --------------------------------------     ----------
   BFEC5484  84 54 EC BF B0 54 EC BF F4 6F             .T...T...o
   BFEC548E  68 00 34 55 EC BF C0 54 EC BF             h.4U...T..
   BFEC5498  08 55 EC BF E3 3D 57 00 00 00             .U...=W...
   BFEC54A2  00 00 A0 BC 55 00 08 55 EC BF             ....U..U..
   BFEC54AC  E3 3D 57 00 01 00 00 00 34 55             .=W.....4U
   BFEC54B6  EC BF 3C 55 EC BF 56 11 55 00             ..<U..V.U.
   BFEC54C0  F4 6F 68 00                               .oh.
```

None of the data stored in this region of memory is in character form, so it's a bit hard to follow. However, we do know one thing: the `addr` variable occupies the first four bytes of this region. When reversed, these bytes form the number BFEC5484, the address entered by the user. Why the reversal? Because x86 processors store data in little-endian order, as we saw earlier in this section.

The `volatile` Type Qualifier

On some computers, certain memory locations are "volatile"; the value stored at such a location can change as a program is running, even though the program itself isn't storing new values there. For example, some memory locations might hold data coming directly from input devices.

The `volatile` type qualifier allows us to inform the compiler if any of the data used in a program is volatile. `volatile` typically appears in the declaration of a pointer variable that will point to a volatile memory location:

```
volatile BYTE *p;   /* p will point to a volatile byte */
```

To see why `volatile` is needed, suppose that p points to a memory location that contains the most recent character typed at the user's keyboard. This location is volatile: its value changes each time the user enters a character. We might use the following loop to obtain characters from the keyboard and store them in a buffer array:

```
while (buffer not full) {
  wait for input;
  buffer[i] = *p;
  if (buffer[i++] == '\n')
    break;
}
```

A sophisticated compiler might notice that this loop changes neither p nor *p, so it could optimize the program by altering it so that *p is fetched just once:

```
store *p in a register;
while (buffer not full) {
  wait for input;
  buffer[i] = value stored in register;
  if (buffer[i++] == '\n')
    break;
}
```

The optimized program will fill the buffer with many copies of the same character—not exactly what we had in mind. Declaring that p points to volatile data avoids this problem by telling the compiler that *p must be fetched from memory each time it's needed.

Q & A

Q: What do you mean by saying that the & and | operators sometimes produce the same results as the && and || operators, but not always? [p. 511]

A: Let's compare i & j with i && j (similar remarks apply to | and ||). As long as i and j have the value 0 or 1 (in any combination), the two expressions will have the same value. However, if i and j should have other values, the expressions may not always match. If i is 1 and j is 2, for example, then i & j has the value 0 (i and j have no corresponding 1 bits), while i && j has the value 1. If i is 3 and j is 2, then i & j has the value 2, while i && j has the value 1.

   Side effects are another difference. Evaluating i & j++ *always* increments j as a side effect, whereas evaluating i && j++ *sometimes* increments j.

Q: Who cares how DOS stores file dates? Isn't DOS dead? [p. 516]

A: For the most part, yes. However, there are still plenty of files created years ago whose dates are stored in the DOS format. In any event, DOS file dates are a good example of how bit-fields are used.

Q: Where do the terms "big-endian" and "little-endian" come from? [p. 520]

A: In Jonathan Swift's novel *Gulliver's Travels,* the fictional islands of Lilliput and Blefuscu are perpetually at odds over whether to open boiled eggs on the big end or the little end. The choice is arbitrary, of course, just like the order of bytes in a data item.

Exercises

*1. Show the output produced by each of the following program fragments. Assume that i, j, and k are `unsigned short` variables.

    (a) `i = 8; j = 9;`
        `printf("%d", i >> 1 + j >> 1);`
    (b) `i = 1;`
        `printf("%d", i & ~i);`
    (c) `i = 2; j = 1; k = 0;`
        `printf("%d", ~i & j ^ k);`
    (d) `i = 7; j = 8; k = 9;`
        `printf("%d", i ^ j & k);`

W 2. Describe a simple way to "toggle" a bit (change it from 0 to 1 or from 1 to 0). Illustrate the technique by writing a statement that toggles bit 4 of the variable i.

*3. Explain what effect the following macro has on its arguments. You may assume that the arguments have the same type.

```
#define M(x,y)  ((x)^=(y),(y)^=(x),(x)^=(y))
```

W 4. In computer graphics, colors are often stored as three numbers, representing red, green, and blue intensities. Suppose that each number requires eight bits, and we'd like to store all three values in a single long integer. Write a macro named `MK_COLOR` with three parameters (the red, green, and blue intensities). `MK_COLOR` should return a `long` in which the last three bytes contain the red, green, and blue intensities, with the red value as the last byte and the green value as the next-to-last byte.

5. Write macros named `GET_RED`, `GET_GREEN`, and `GET_BLUE` that, when given a color as an argument (see Exercise 4), return its 8-bit red, green, and blue intensities.

W 6. (a) Use the bitwise operators to write the following function:

```
unsigned short swap_bytes(unsigned short i);
```

`swap_bytes` should return the number that results from swapping the two bytes in i. (Short integers occupy two bytes on most computers.) For example, if i has the value 0x1234 (00010010 00110100 in binary), then `swap_bytes` should return 0x3412 (00110100 00010010 in binary). Test your function by writing a program that reads a number in hexadecimal, then writes the number with its bytes swapped:

```
Enter a hexadecimal number (up to four digits): 1234
Number with bytes swapped: 3412
```

Hint: Use the `%hx` conversion to read and write the hex numbers.

(b) Condense the `swap_bytes` function so that its body is a single statement.

7. Write the following functions:

```
unsigned int rotate_left(unsigned int i, int n);
unsigned int rotate_right(unsigned int i, int n);
```

`rotate_left` should return the result of shifting the bits in i to the left by n places, with the bits that were "shifted off" moved to the right end of i. (For example, the call rotate_left(0x12345678, 4) should return 0x23456781 if integers are 32 bits long.) rotate_right is similar, but it should "rotate" bits to the right instead of the left.

Ⓦ 8. Let f be the following function:

```
unsigned int f(unsigned int i, int m, int n)
{
    return (i >> (m + 1 - n)) & ~(~0 << n);
}
```

   (a) What is the value of ~(~0 << n)?

   (b) What does this function do?

9. (a) Write the following function:

   int count_ones(unsigned char ch);

   count_ones should return the number of 1 bits in ch.

   (b) Write the function in part (a) without using a loop.

10. Write the following function:

   unsigned int reverse_bits(unsigned int n);

   reverse_bits should return an unsigned integer whose bits are the same as those in n but in reverse order.

11. Each of the following macros defines the position of a single bit within an integer:

```
#define SHIFT_BIT 1
#define CTRL_BIT  2
#define ALT_BIT   4
```

   The following statement is supposed to test whether any of the three bits have been set, but it never displays the specified message. Explain why the statement doesn't work and show how to fix it. Assume that key_code is an int variable.

```
if (key_code & (SHIFT_BIT | CTRL_BIT | ALT_BIT) == 0)
    printf("No modifier keys pressed\n");
```

12. The following function supposedly combines two bytes to form an unsigned short integer. Explain why the function doesn't work and show how to fix it.

```
unsigned short create_short(unsigned char high_byte,
                            unsigned char low_byte)
{
    return high_byte << 8 + low_byte;
}
```

*13. If n is an unsigned int variable, what effect does the following statement have on the bits in n?

   n &= n - 1;

   Hint: Consider the effect on n if this statement is executed more than once.

Section 20.2 Ⓦ 14. When stored according to the IEEE floating-point standard, a float value consists of a 1-bit sign (the leftmost—or most significant—bit), an 8-bit exponent, and a 23-bit fraction, in that order. Design a structure type that occupies 32 bits, with bit-field members corresponding to the sign, exponent, and fraction. Declare the bit-fields to have type unsigned int. Check the manual for your compiler to determine the order of the bit-fields.

*15. (a) Assume that the variable s has been declared as follows:

```
struct {
  int flag: 1;
} s;
```

With some compilers, executing the following statements causes 1 to be displayed, but with other compilers, the output is –1. Explain the reason for this behavior.

```
s.flag = 1;
printf("%d\n", s.flag);
```

(b) How can this problem be avoided?

Section 20.3 16. Starting with the 386 processor, x86 CPUs have 32-bit registers named EAX, EBX, ECX, and EDX. The second half (the least significant bits) of these registers is the same as AX, BX, CX, and DX, respectively. Modify the `regs` union so that it includes these registers as well as the older ones. Your union should be set up so that modifying EAX changes AX and modifying AX changes the second half of EAX. (The other new registers will work in a similar fashion.) You'll need to add some "dummy" members to the `word` and `byte` structures, corresponding to the other half of EAX, EBX, ECX, and EDX. Declare the type of the new registers to be DWORD (double word), which should be defined as `unsigned long`. Don't forget that the x86 architecture is little-endian.

Programming Projects

1. Design a union that makes it possible to view a 32-bit value as either a `float` or the structure described in Exercise 14. Write a program that stores 1 in the structure's sign field, 128 in the exponent field, and 0 in the fraction field, then prints the `float` value stored in the union. (The answer should be –2.0 if you've set up the bit-fields correctly.)

21 The Standard Library

Every program is a part of some other program and rarely fits.

In previous chapters we've looked at the C library piecemeal; this chapter focuses on the library as a whole. Section 21.1 lists general guidelines for using the library. It also describes a trick found in some library headers: using a macro to "hide" a function. Section 21.2 gives an overview of each header in the C89 library; Section 21.3 does the same for the new headers in the C99 library.

Later chapters cover the library's headers in depth, with related headers grouped together into chapters. The <stddef.h> and <stdbool.h> headers are very brief, so I've chosen to discuss them in this chapter (in Sections 21.4 and 21.5, respectively).

21.1 Using the Library

The C89 standard library is divided into 15 parts, with each part described by a header. C99 has an additional nine headers, for a total of 24 (see Table 21.1).

Table 21.1
Standard Library Headers

<assert.h>	<inttypes.h>[†]	<signal.h>	<stdlib.h>
<complex.h>[†]	<iso646.h>[†]	<stdarg.h>	<string.h>
<ctype.h>	<limits.h>	<stdbool.h>[†]	<tgmath.h>[†]
<errno.h>	<locale.h>	<stddef.h>	<time.h>
<fenv.h>[†]	<math.h>	<stdint.h>[†]	<wchar.h>[†]
<float.h>	<setjmp.h>	<stdio.h>	<wctype.h>[†]

[†]C99 only

Most compilers come with a more extensive library that invariably has many headers that don't appear in Table 21.1. The extra headers aren't standard, of

529

course, so we can't count on them to be available with other compilers. These headers often provide functions that are specific on a particular computer or operating system (which explains why they're not standard). They may provide functions that allow more control over the screen and keyboard. Headers that support graphics or a window-based user interface are also common.

The standard headers consist primarily of function prototypes, type definitions, and macro definitions. If one of our files contains a call of a function declared in a header or uses one of the types or macros defined there, we'll need to include the header at the beginning of the file. When a file includes several standard headers, the order of `#include` directives doesn't matter. It's also legal to include a standard header more than once.

Restrictions on Names Used in the Library

Any file that includes a standard header must obey a couple of rules. First, it can't use the names of macros defined in that header for any other purpose. If a file includes `<stdio.h>`, for example, it can't reuse NULL, since a macro by that name is already defined in `<stdio.h>`. Second, library names with file scope (`typedef` names, in particular) can't be redefined at the file level. Thus, if a file includes `<stdio.h>`, it can't define `size_t` as a identifier with file scope, since `<stdio.h>` defines `size_t` to be a `typedef` name.

Although these restrictions are pretty obvious, C has other restrictions that you might not expect:

- ***Identifiers that begin with an underscore followed by an upper-case letter or a second underscore*** are reserved for use within the library; programs should never use names of this form for any purpose.

- ***Identifiers that begin with an underscore*** are reserved for use as identifiers and tags with file scope. You should never use such a name for your own purposes unless it's declared inside a function.

- ***Every identifier with external linkage in the standard library*** is reserved for use as an identifier with external linkage. In particular, the names of all standard library functions are reserved. Thus, even if a file *doesn't* include `<stdio.h>`, it shouldn't define an external function named `printf`, since there's already a function with this name in the library.

These rules apply to *every* file in a program, regardless of which headers the file includes. Although these rules aren't always enforced, failing to obey them can lead to a program that's not portable.

The rules listed above apply not just to names that are currently used in the library, but also to names that are set aside for future use. The complete description of which names are reserved is rather lengthy; you'll find it in the C standard under "future library directions." As an example, C reserves identifiers that begin with `str` followed by a lower-case letter, so that functions with such names can be added to the `<string.h>` header.

Functions Hidden by Macros

It's common for C programmers to replace small functions by parameterized macros. This practice occurs even in the standard library. The C standard allows headers to define macros that have the same names as library functions, but protects the programmer by requiring that a true function be available as well. As a result, it's not unusual for a library header to declare a function *and* define a macro with the same name.

We've already seen an example of a macro duplicating a library function. `getchar` is a library function declared in the `<stdio.h>` header. It has the following prototype:

```
int getchar(void);
```

`<stdio.h>` usually defines `getchar` as a macro as well:

```
#define getchar() getc(stdin)
```

By default, a call of `getchar` will be treated as a macro invocation (since macro names are replaced during preprocessing).

Most of the time, we're happy using a macro instead of a true function, because it will probably make our program run faster. Occasionally, though, we want a genuine function, perhaps to minimize the size of the executable code.

If the need arises, we can remove a macro definition (thus gaining access to the true function) by using the `#undef` directive. For example, we could undefine the `getchar` macro after including `<stdio.h>`:

`#undef` directive ➤ *14.3*

```
#include <stdio.h>
#undef getchar
```

If `getchar` *isn't* a macro, no harm has been done; `#undef` has no effect when given a name that's not defined as a macro.

As an alternative, we can disable individual uses of a macro by putting parentheses around its name:

```
ch = (getchar)();    /* instead of ch = getchar(); */
```

The preprocessor can't spot a parameterized macro unless its name is followed by a left parenthesis. The compiler isn't so easily fooled, however; it can still recognize `getchar` as a function.

21.2　C89 Library Overview

We'll now take a quick look at the headers in the C89 standard library. This section can serve as a "road map" to help you determine which part of the library you need. Each header is described in detail later in this chapter or in a subsequent chapter.

`<assert.h>`   *Diagnostics*

`<assert.h>` header ➤*24.1*   Contains only the `assert` macro, which allows us to insert self-checks into a program. If any check fails, the program terminates.

`<ctype.h>`   *Character Handling*

`<ctype.h>` header ➤*23.5*   Provides functions for classifying characters and for converting letters from lower to upper case or vice versa.

`<errno.h>`   *Errors*

`<errno.h>` header ➤*24.2*   Provides `errno` ("error number"), an lvalue that can be tested after a call of certain library functions to see if an error occurred during the call.

`<float.h>`   *Characteristics of Floating Types*

`<float.h>` header ➤*23.1*   Provides macros that describe the characteristics of floating types, including their range and accuracy.

`<limits.h>`   *Sizes of Integer Types*

`<limits.h>` header ➤*23.2*   Provides macros that describe the characteristics of integer types (including character types), including their maximum and minimum values.

`<locale.h>`   *Localization*

`<locale.h>` header ➤*25.1*   Provides functions to help a program adapt its behavior to a country or other geographic region. Locale-specific behavior includes the way numbers are printed (such as the character used as the decimal point), the format of monetary values (the currency symbol, for example), the character set, and the appearance of the date and time.

`<math.h>`   *Mathematics*

`<math.h>` header ➤*23.3*   Provides common mathematical functions, including trigonometric, hyperbolic, exponential, logarithmic, power, nearest integer, absolute value, and remainder functions.

`<setjmp.h>`   *Nonlocal Jumps*

`<setjmp.h>` header ➤*24.4*   Provides the `setjmp` and `longjmp` functions. `setjmp` "marks" a place in a program; `longjmp` can then be used to return to that place later. These functions make it possible to jump from one function into another, still-active function, bypassing the normal function-return mechanism. `setjmp` and `longjmp` are used primarily for handling serious problems that arise during program execution.

`<signal.h>` *Signal Handling*

`<signal.h>` header ➤*24.3*

Provides functions that deal with exceptional conditions (signals), including interrupts and run-time errors. The `signal` function installs a function to be called if a given signal should occur later. The `raise` function causes a signal to occur.

`<stdarg.h>` *Variable Arguments*

`<stdarg.h>` header ➤*26.1*

Provides tools for writing functions that, like `printf` and `scanf`, can have a variable number of arguments.

`<stddef.h>` *Common Definitions*

`<stddef.h>` header ➤*21.4*

Provides definitions of frequently used types and macros.

`<stdio.h>` *Input/Output*

`<stdio.h>` header ➤*22.1–22.8*

Provides a large assortment of input/output functions, including operations on both sequential and random-access files.

`<stdlib.h>` *General Utilities*

`<stdlib.h>` header ➤*26.2*

A "catchall" header for functions that don't fit into any of the other headers. The functions in this header can convert strings to numbers, generate pseudo-random numbers, perform memory management tasks, communicate with the operating system, do searching and sorting, and perform conversions between multibyte characters and wide characters.

`<string.h>` *String Handling*

`<string.h>` header ➤*23.6*

Provides functions that perform string operations, including copying, concatenation, comparison, and searching, as well as functions that operate on arbitrary blocks of memory.

`<time.h>` *Date and Time*

`<time.h>` header ➤*26.3*

Provides functions for determining the time (and date), manipulating times, and formatting times for display.

21.3 C99 Library Changes

Some of the biggest changes in C99 affect the standard library. These changes fall into three groups:

- *Additional headers.* The C99 standard library has nine headers that don't exist in C89. Three of these (`<iso646.h>`, `<wchar.h>`, and `<wctype.h>`) were actually added to C in 1995 when the C89 standard was amended. The other six (`<complex.h>`, `<fenv.h>`, `<inttypes.h>`, `<stdbool.h>`, `<stdint.h>`, and `<tgmath.h>`) are new in C99.
- *Additional macros and functions.* The C99 standard adds macros and functions to several existing headers, primarily `<float.h>`, `<math.h>`, and `<stdio.h>`. The additions to the `<math.h>` header are so extensive that they're covered in a separate section (Section 23.4).
- *Enhanced versions of existing functions.* Some existing functions, including `printf` and `scanf`, have additional capabilities in C99.

We'll now take a quick look at the nine additional headers in the C99 standard library, just as we did in Section 21.2 for the headers in the C89 library.

`<complex.h>`   *Complex Arithmetic*

`<complex.h>` header ➤27.4

Defines the `complex` and `I` macros, which are useful when working with complex numbers. Also provides functions for performing mathematical operations on complex numbers.

`<fenv.h>`   *Floating-Point Environment*

`<fenv.h>` header ➤27.6

Provides access to floating-point status flags and control modes. For example, a program might test a flag to see if overflow occurred during a floating-point operation or set a control mode to specify how rounding should be done.

`<inttypes.h>`   *Format Conversion of Integer Types*

`<inttypes.h>` header ➤27.2

Defines macros that can be used in format strings for input/output of the integer types declared in `<stdint.h>`. Also provides functions for working with greatest-width integers.

`<iso646.h>`   *Alternative Spellings*

`<iso646.h>` header ➤25.3

Defines macros that represent certain operators (the ones containing the characters `&`, `|`, `~`, `!`, and `^`). These macros are useful for writing programs in an environment where these characters might not be part of the local character set.

<table>
<tr><td>

`<stdbool.h>`

</td><td>

Boolean Type and Values

</td></tr>
</table>

<stdbool.h> header ➤*21.5*   Defines the `bool`, `true`, and `false` macros, as well as a macro that can be used to test whether these macros have been defined.

`<stdint.h>` *Integer Types*

<stdint.h> header ➤*27.1*   Declares integer types with specified widths and defines related macros (such as macros that specify the maximum and minimum values of each type). Also defines parameterized macros that construct integer constants with specific types.

`<tgmath.h>` *Type-Generic Math*

<tgmath.h> header ➤*27.5*   In C99, there are multiple versions of many math functions in the `<math.h>` and `<complex.h>` headers. The "type-generic" macros in `<tgmath.h>` can detect the types of the arguments passed to them and substitute a call of the appropriate `<math.h>` or `<complex.h>` function.

`<wchar.h>` *Extended Multibyte and Wide-Character Utilities*

<wchar.h> header ➤*25.5*   Provides functions for wide-character input/output and wide string manipulation.

`<wctype.h>` *Wide-Character Classification and Mapping Utilities*

<wctype.h> header ➤*25.6*   The wide-character version of `<ctype.h>`. Provides functions for classifying and changing the case of wide characters.

21.4   The `<stddef.h>` Header: Common Definitions

The `<stddef.h>` header provides definitions of frequently used types and macros; it doesn't declare any functions. The types are:

- `ptrdiff_t`. The type of the result when two pointers are subtracted.
- `size_t`. The type returned by the `sizeof` operator.
- `wchar_t`. A type large enough to represent all possible characters in all supported locales.

All three are names for integer types; `ptrdiff_t` must be a signed type, while `size_t` must be an unsigned type. For more information about `wchar_t`, see Section 25.2.

The `<stddef.h>` header also defines two macros. One of them is NULL, which represents the null pointer. The other macro, `offsetof`, requires two arguments: *type* (a structure type) and *member-designator* (a member of the structure).

`offsetof` computes the number of bytes between the beginning of the structure and the specified member.

Consider the following structure:

```
struct s {
  char a;
  int b[2];
  float c;
};
```

The value of `offsetof(struct s, a)` must be 0; C guarantees that the first member of a structure has the same address as the structure itself. We can't say for sure what the offsets of `b` and `c` are. One possibility is that `offsetof(struct s, b)` is 1 (since `a` is one byte long), and `offsetof(struct s, c)` is 9 (assuming 32-bit integers). However, some compilers leave "holes"—unused bytes—in structures (see the Q&A section at the end of Chapter 16), which can affect the value produced by `offsetof`. If a compiler should leave a three-byte hole after `a`, for example, then the offsets of `b` and `c` would be 4 and 12, respectively. But that's the beauty of `offsetof`: it produces the correct offsets for any compiler, enabling us to write portable programs.

There are various uses for `offsetof`. For example, suppose that we want to save the first two members of an `s` structure in a file, ignoring the `c` member.

fwrite function ►22.6 Instead of having the `fwrite` function write `sizeof(struct s)` bytes, which would save the entire structure, we'll tell it to write only `offsetof(struct s, c)` bytes.

A final remark: Some of the types and macros defined in `<stddef.h>` appear in other headers as well. (The `NULL` macro, for example, is also defined in `<locale.h>`, `<stdio.h>`, `<stdlib.h>`, `<string.h>`, and `<time.h>`, as well as in the C99 header `<wchar.h>`.) As a result, few programs need to include `<stddef.h>`.

21.5   The `<stdbool.h>` Header (C99): Boolean Type and Values

The `<stdbool.h>` header defines four macros:

- `bool` (defined to be `_Bool`)
- `true` (defined to be 1)
- `false` (defined to be 0)
- `__bool_true_false_are_defined` (defined to be 1)

We've seen many examples of how `bool`, `true`, and `false` are used. Potential uses of the `__bool_true_false_are_defined` macro are more limited. A program could use a preprocessing directive (such as `#if` or `#ifdef`) to test this macro before attempting to define its own version of `bool`, `true`, or `false`.

Q & A

Q: I notice that you use the term "standard header" rather than "standard header file." Is there any reason for not using the word "file"?

A: Yes. According to the C standard, a "standard header" need not be a file. Although most compilers do indeed store standard headers as files, the headers could in fact be built into the compiler itself.

Q: Section 14.3 described some disadvantages of using parameterized macros in place of functions. In light of these problems, isn't it dangerous to provide a macro substitute for a standard library function? [p. 531]

A: According to the C standard, a parameterized macro that substitutes for a library function must be "fully protected" by parentheses and must evaluate its arguments exactly once. These rules avoid most of the problems mentioned in Section 14.3.

Exercises

Section 21.1

1. Locate where header files are kept on your system. Find the nonstandard headers and determine the purpose of each.

2. Having located the header files on your system (see Exercise 1), find a standard header in which a macro hides a function.

3. When a macro hides a function, which must come first in the header file: the macro definition or the function prototype? Justify your answer.

4. Make a list of all reserved identifiers in the "future library directions" section of the C99 standard. Distinguish between identifiers that are reserved for use only when a specific header is included versus identifiers that are reserved for use as external names.

*5. The `islower` function, which belongs to `<ctype.h>`, tests whether a character is a lower-case letter. Why would the following macro version of `islower` not be legal, according to the C standard? (You may assume that the character set is ASCII.)

```
#define islower(c) ((c) >= 'a' && (c) <= 'z')
```

6. The `<ctype.h>` header usually defines most of its functions as macros as well. These macros rely on a static array that's declared in `<ctype.h>` but defined in a separate file. A portion of a typical `<ctype.h>` header appears below. Use this sample to answer the following questions.

(a) Why do the names of the "bit" macros (such as `_UPPER`) and the `_ctype` array begin with an underscore?

(b) Explain what the `_ctype` array will contain. Assuming that the character set is ASCII, show the values of the array elements at positions 9 (the horizontal tab character), 32 (the space character), 65 (the letter A), and 94 (the ^ character). See Section 23.5 for a description of what each macro should return.

(c) What's the advantage of using an array to implement these macros?

```
#define _UPPER   0x01    /* upper-case letter */
#define _LOWER   0x02    /* lower-case letter */
#define _DIGIT   0x04    /* decimal digit */
#define _CONTROL 0x08    /* control character */
#define _PUNCT   0x10    /* punctuation character */
#define _SPACE   0x20    /* white-space character */
#define _HEX     0x40    /* hexadecimal digit */
#define _BLANK   0x80    /* space character */

#define isalnum(c)  (_ctype[c] & (_UPPER|_LOWER|_DIGIT))
#define isalpha(c)  (_ctype[c] & (_UPPER|_LOWER))
#define iscntrl(c)  (_ctype[c] & _CONTROL)
#define isdigit(c)  (_ctype[c] & _DIGIT)
#define isgraph(c)  (_ctype[c] &
                     (_PUNCT|_UPPER|_LOWER|_DIGIT))
#define islower(c)  (_ctype[c] & _LOWER)
#define isprint(c)  (_ctype[c] &
                     (_BLANK|_PUNCT|_UPPER|_LOWER|_DIGIT))
#define ispunct(c)  (_ctype[c] & _PUNCT)
#define isspace(c)  (_ctype[c] & _SPACE)
#define isupper(c)  (_ctype[c] & _UPPER)
#define isxdigit(c) (_ctype[c] & (_DIGIT|_HEX))
```

Section 21.2   Ⓦ   7.   In which standard header would you expect to find each of the following?

(a) A function that determines the current day of the week

(b) A function that tests whether a character is a digit

(c) A macro that gives the largest `unsigned int` value

(d) A function that rounds a floating-point number to the next higher integer

(e) A macro that specifies the number of bits in a character

(f) A macro that specifies the number of significant digits in a `double` value

(g) A function that searches a string for a particular character

(h) A function that opens a file for reading

Programming Projects

1.   Write a program that declares the `s` structure (see Section 21.4) and prints the sizes and off-sets of the `a`, `b`, and `c` members. (Use `sizeof` to find sizes; use `offsetof` to find off-sets.) Have the program print the size of the entire structure as well. From this information, determine whether or not the structure has any holes. If it does, describe the location and size of each.

22 Input/Output

In man-machine symbiosis, it is man
who must adjust: The machines can't.

C's input/output library is the biggest and most important part of the standard library. As befits its lofty status, we'll devote an entire chapter (the longest in the book) to the <stdio.h> header, the primary repository of input/output functions.

We've been using <stdio.h> since Chapter 2, and we have experience with the printf, scanf, putchar, getchar, puts, and gets functions. This chapter provides more information about these six functions, as well as introducing a host of new functions, most of which deal with files. Fortunately, many of the new functions are closely related to functions with which we're already acquainted. fprintf, for instance, is the "file version" of the printf function.

We'll start the chapter with a discussion of some basic issues: the stream concept, the FILE type, input and output redirection, and the difference between text files and binary files (Section 22.1). We'll then turn to functions that are designed specifically for use with files, including functions that open and close files (Section 22.2). After covering printf, scanf, and related functions for "formatted" input/output (Section 22.3), we'll look at functions that read and write unformatted data:

- getc, putc, and related functions, which read and write one *character* at a time (Section 22.4).
- gets, puts, and related functions, which read and write one *line* at a time (Section 22.5).
- fread and fwrite, which read and write *blocks* of data (Section 22.6).

Section 22.7 then shows how to perform random access operations on files. Finally, Section 22.8 describes the sprintf, snprintf, and sscanf functions, variants of printf and scanf that write to a string or read from a string.

This chapter covers all but eight of the functions in <stdio.h>. One of these eight, the perror function, is closely related to the <errno.h> header, so

I'll postpone it until Section 24.2, which discusses that header. Section 26.1 covers the remaining functions (vfprintf, vprintf, vsprintf, vsnprintf, vfscanf, vscanf, and vsscanf). These functions rely on the va_list type, which is introduced in that section.

<wchar.h> header ►25.5

In C89, all standard input/output functions belong to <stdio.h>, but such is not the case in C99, where some I/O functions are declared in the <wchar.h> header. The <wchar.h> functions deal with wide characters rather than ordinary characters; the good news is that most of these functions closely resemble those of <stdio.h>. Functions in <stdio.h> that read or write data are known as ***byte input/output functions;*** similar functions in <wchar.h> are called ***wide-character input/output functions.***

22.1 Streams

In C, the term ***stream*** means any source of input or any destination for output. Many small programs, like the ones in previous chapters, obtain all their input from one stream (usually associated with the keyboard) and write all their output to another stream (usually associated with the screen).

Larger programs may need additional streams. These streams often represent files stored on various media (such as hard drives, CDs, DVDs, and flash memory), but they could just as easily be associated with devices that don't store files: network ports, printers, and the like. We'll concentrate on files, since they're common and easy to understand. (I may even occasionally use the term *file* when I should say *stream.*) Keep in mind, however, that many of the functions in <stdio.h> work equally well with all streams, not just the ones that represent files.

File Pointers

Accessing a stream in a C program is done through a ***file pointer***, which has type FILE * (the FILE type is declared in <stdio.h>). Certain streams are represented by file pointers with standard names; we can declare additional file pointers as needed. For example, if a program needs two streams in addition to the standard ones, it might contain the following declaration:

```
FILE *fp1, *fp2;
```

A program may declare any number of FILE * variables, although operating systems usually limit the number of streams that can be open at one time.

Standard Streams and Redirection

<stdio.h> provides three standard streams (Table 22.1). These streams are ready to use—we don't declare them, and we don't open or close them.

Table 22.1
Standard Streams

File Pointer	Stream	Default Meaning
stdin	Standard input	Keyboard
stdout	Standard output	Screen
stderr	Standard error	Screen

The functions that we've used in previous chapters—printf, scanf, putchar, getchar, puts, and gets—obtain input from stdin and send output to stdout. By default, stdin represents the keyboard; stdout and stderr represent the screen. However, many operating systems allow these default meanings to be changed via a mechanism known as *redirection*.

Typically, we can force a program to obtain its input from a file instead of from the keyboard by putting the name of the file on the command line, preceded by the < character:

```
demo <in.dat
```

This technique, known as *input redirection*, essentially makes the stdin stream represent a file (in.dat, in this case) instead of the keyboard. The beauty of redirection is that the demo program doesn't realize that it's reading from in.dat; as far as it knows, any data it obtains from stdin is being entered at the keyboard.

Output redirection is similar. Redirecting the stdout stream is usually done by putting a file name on the command line, preceded by the > character:

```
demo >out.dat
```

All data written to stdout will now go into the out.dat file instead of appearing on the screen. Incidentally, we can combine output redirection with input redirection:

```
demo <in.dat >out.dat
```

The < and > characters don't have to be adjacent to file names, and the order in which the redirected files are listed doesn't matter, so the following examples would work just as well:

```
demo < in.dat > out.dat
demo >out.dat <in.dat
```

One problem with output redirection is that *everything* written to stdout is put into a file. If the program goes off the rails and begins writing error messages, we won't see them until we look at the file. This is where stderr comes in. By writing error messages to stderr instead of stdout, we can guarantee that those messages will appear on the screen even when stdout has been redirected. (Operating systems often allow stderr itself to be redirected, though.)

Text Files versus Binary Files

<stdio.h> supports two kinds of files: text and binary. The bytes in a *text file* represent characters, making it possible for a human to examine the file or edit it.

The source code for a C program is stored in a text file, for example. In a ***binary file***, on the other hand, bytes don't necessarily represent characters; groups of bytes might represent other types of data, such as integers and floating-point numbers. An executable C program is stored in a binary file, as you'll quickly realize if you try to look at the contents of one.

Text files have two characteristics that binary files don't possess:

■ ***Text files are divided into lines.*** Each line in a text file normally ends with one or two special characters; the choice of characters depends on the operating system. In Windows, the end-of-line marker is a carriage-return character (`'\x0d'`) followed immediately by a line-feed character (`'\x0a'`). In UNIX and newer versions of the Macintosh operating system (Mac OS), the end-of-line marker is a single line-feed character. Older versions of Mac OS use a single carriage-return character.

■ ***Text files may contain a special "end-of-file" marker.*** Some operating systems allow a special byte to be used as a marker at the end of a text file. In Windows, the marker is `'\x1a'` (Ctrl-Z). There's no requirement that Ctrl-Z be present, but if it is, it marks the end of the file; any bytes after Ctrl-Z are to be ignored. The Ctrl-Z convention is a holdover from DOS, which in turn inherited it from CP/M, an early operating system for personal computers. Most other operating systems, including UNIX, have no special end-of-file character.

Binary files aren't divided into lines. In a binary file, there are no end-of-line or end-of-file markers; all bytes are treated equally.

When we write data to a file, we'll need to consider whether to store it in text form or in binary form. To see the difference, consider how we might store the number 32767 in a file. One option would be to write the number in text form as the characters 3, 2, 7, 6, and 7. If the character set is ASCII, we'd have the following five bytes:

00110011	00110010	00110111	00110110	00110111
'3'	'2'	'7'	'6'	'7'

The other option is to store the number in binary, which would take as few as two bytes:

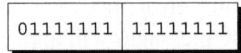

01111111 | 11111111

little-endian order ▶20.3   (The bytes will be reversed on systems that store data in little-endian order.) As this example shows, storing numbers in binary can often save quite a bit of space.

When we're writing a program that reads from a file or writes to a file, we need to take into account whether it's a text file or a binary file. A program that displays the contents of a file on the screen will probably assume it's a text file. A file-copying program, on the other hand, can't assume that the file to be copied is a text file. If it does, binary files containing an end-of-file character won't be copied completely. When we can't say for sure whether a file is text or binary, it's safer to assume that it's binary.

22.2   File Operations

Simplicity is one of the attractions of input and output redirection; there's no need to open a file, close a file, or perform any other explicit file operations. Unfortunately, redirection is too limited for many applications. When a program relies on redirection, it has no control over its files; it doesn't even know their names. Worse still, redirection doesn't help if the program needs to read from two files or write to two files at the same time.

When redirection isn't enough, we'll end up using the file operations that `<stdio.h>` provides. In this section, we'll explore these operations, which include opening a file, closing a file, changing the way a file is buffered, deleting a file, and renaming a file.

Opening a File

```
FILE *fopen(const char * restrict filename,
            const char * restrict mode);
```

fopen   Opening a file for use as a stream requires a call of the `fopen` function. `fopen`'s first argument is a string containing the name of the file to be opened. (A "file name" may include information about the file's location, such as a drive specifier or path.) The second argument is a "mode string" that specifies what operations we intend to perform on the file. The string `"r"`, for instance, indicates that data will be read from the file, but none will be written to it.

`restrict` keyword ➤ *17.8*   Note that `restrict` appears twice in the prototype for the `fopen` function. `restrict`, which is a C99 keyword, indicates that `filename` and `mode` should point to strings that don't share memory locations. The C89 prototype for `fopen` doesn't contain `restrict` but is otherwise identical. `restrict` has no effect on the behavior of `fopen`, so it can usually just be ignored. In this and subsequent chapters, I'll italicize `restrict` as a reminder that it's a C99 feature.

escape sequences ➤ *7.3*   Windows programmers: Be careful when the file name in a call of `fopen` includes the \ character, since C treats \ as the beginning of an escape sequence. The call

```
fopen("c:\project\test1.dat", "r")
```

will fail, because the compiler treats \t as a character escape. (\p isn't a valid character escape, but it looks like one. The C standard states that its meaning is undefined.) There are two ways to avoid the problem. One is to use \\ instead of \:

```
fopen("c:\\project\\test1.dat", "r")
```

The other technique is even easier—just use the / character instead of \:

```
fopen("c:/project/test1.dat", "r")
```

Windows will happily accept / instead of \ as the directory separator.

fopen returns a file pointer that the program can (and usually will) save in a variable and use later whenever it needs to perform an operation on the file. Here's a typical call of fopen, where fp is a variable of type FILE *:

```
fp = fopen("in.dat", "r");    /* opens in.dat for reading */
```

When the program calls an input function to read from in.dat later, it will supply fp as an argument.

When it can't open a file, fopen returns a null pointer. Perhaps the file doesn't exist, or it's in the wrong place, or we don't have permission to open it.

⚠ Never assume that a file can be opened; always test the return value of fopen to make sure it's not a null pointer.

Modes

Which mode string we'll pass to fopen depends not only on what operations we plan to perform on the file later but also on whether the file contains text or binary data. To open a text file, we'd use one of the mode strings in Table 22.2.

Table 22.2
Mode Strings
for Text Files

String	Meaning
"r"	Open for reading
"w"	Open for writing (file need not exist)
"a"	Open for appending (file need not exist)
"r+"	Open for reading and writing, starting at beginning
"w+"	Open for reading and writing (truncate if file exists)
"a+"	Open for reading and writing (append if file exists)

 When we use fopen to open a binary file, we'll need to include the letter b in the mode string. Table 22.3 lists mode strings for binary files.

From Tables 22.2 and 22.3, we see that <stdio.h> distinguishes between *writing* data and *appending* data. When data is written to a file, it normally over-writes what was previously there. When a file is opened for appending, however, data written to the file is added at the end, thus preserving the file's original contents.

By the way, special rules apply when a file is opened for both reading and writing (the mode string contains the + character). We can't switch from reading to writ-

file-positioning functions ►22.7

Table 22.3
Mode Strings for
Binary Files

String	*Meaning*
"rb"	Open for reading
"wb"	Open for writing (file need not exist)
"ab"	Open for appending (file need not exist)
"r+b" or "rb+"	Open for reading and writing, starting at beginning
"w+b" or "wb+"	Open for reading and writing (truncate if file exists)
"a+b" or "ab+"	Open for reading and writing (append if file exists)

ing without first calling a file-positioning function unless the reading operation encountered the end of the file. Also, we can't switch from writing to reading without either calling fflush (covered later in this section) or calling a file-positioning function.

Closing a File

```
int fclose(FILE *stream);
```

fclose   The fclose function allows a program to close a file that it's no longer using. The argument to fclose must be a file pointer obtained from a call of fopen or freopen (discussed later in this section). fclose returns zero if the file was closed successfully; otherwise, it returns the error code EOF (a macro defined in
Q&A   <stdio.h>).

To show how fopen and fclose are used in practice, here's the outline of a program that opens the file example.dat for reading, checks that it was opened successfully, then closes it before terminating:

```
#include <stdio.h>
#include <stdlib.h>

#define FILE_NAME "example.dat"

int main(void)
{
  FILE *fp;

  fp = fopen(FILE_NAME, "r");
  if (fp == NULL) {
    printf("Can't open %s\n", FILE_NAME);
    exit(EXIT_FAILURE);
  }
  ...
  fclose(fp);
  return 0;
}
```

Of course, C programmers being the way they are, it's not unusual to see the call of fopen combined with the declaration of fp:

```
FILE *fp = fopen(FILE_NAME, "r");
```

or the test against NULL:

```
if ((fp = fopen(FILE_NAME, "r")) == NULL) ...
```

Attaching a File to an Open Stream

```
FILE *freopen(const char * restrict filename,
              const char * restrict mode,
              FILE * restrict stream);
```

freopen   `freopen` attaches a different file to a stream that's already open. The most common use of `freopen` is to associate a file with one of the standard streams
(`stdin`, `stdout`, or `stderr`). To cause a program to begin writing to the file
`foo`, for instance, we could use the following call of `freopen`:

```
if (freopen("foo", "w", stdout) == NULL) {
  /* error; foo can't be opened */
}
```

After closing any file previously associated with `stdout` (by command-line redirection or a previous call of `freopen`), `freopen` will open `foo` and associate it
with `stdout`.

`freopen`'s normal return value is its third argument (a file pointer). If it can't
open the new file, `freopen` returns a null pointer. (`freopen` ignores the error if
the old file can't be closed.)

C99   C99 adds a new twist. If `filename` is a null pointer, `freopen` attempts to
change the stream's mode to that specified by the `mode` parameter. Implementations aren't required to support this feature, however; if they do, they may place
restrictions on which mode changes are permitted.

Obtaining File Names from the Command Line

When we're writing a program that will need to open a file, one problem soon
becomes apparent: how do we supply the file name to the program? Building file
names into the program itself doesn't provide much flexibility, and prompting the
Q&A   user to enter file names can be awkward. Often, the best solution is to have the program obtain file names from the command line. When we execute a program
named `demo`, for example, we might supply it with file names by putting them on
the command line:

```
demo names.dat dates.dat
```

In Section 13.7, we saw how to access command-line arguments by defining
`main` as a function with two parameters:

```
int main(int argc, char *argv[])
{
  ...
}
```

argc is the number of command-line arguments; argv is an array of pointers to the argument strings. argv[0] points to the program name, argv[1] through argv[argc-1] point to the remaining arguments, and argv[argc] is a null pointer. In the example above, argc is 3, argv[0] points to a string containing the program name, argv[1] points to the string "names.dat", and argv[2] points to the string "dates.dat":

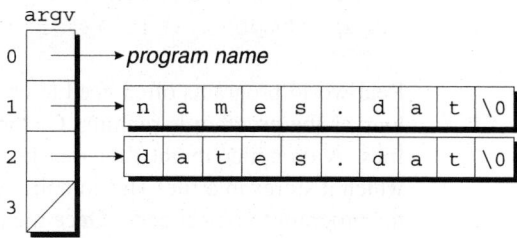

PROGRAM   **Checking Whether a File Can Be Opened**

The following program determines if a file exists and can be opened for reading. When the program is run, the user will give it a file name to check:

canopen *file*

The program will then print either *file* can be opened or *file* can't be opened. If the user enters the wrong number of arguments on the command line, the program will print the message usage: canopen filename to remind the user that canopen requires a single file name.

canopen.c

```
/* Checks whether a file can be opened for reading */

#include <stdio.h>
#include <stdlib.h>

int main(int argc, char *argv[])
{
  FILE *fp;

  if (argc != 2) {
    printf("usage: canopen filename\n");
    exit(EXIT_FAILURE);
  }

  if ((fp = fopen(argv[1], "r")) == NULL) {
    printf("%s can't be opened\n", argv[1]);
    exit(EXIT_FAILURE);
  }

  printf("%s can be opened\n", argv[1]);
  fclose(fp);
  return 0;
}
```

Note that we can use redirection to discard the output of canopen and simply test the status value it returns.

Temporary Files

```
FILE *tmpfile(void);
char *tmpnam(char *s);
```

Real-world programs often need to create temporary files—files that exist only as long as the program is running. C compilers, for instance, often create temporary files. A compiler might first translate a C program to some intermediate form, which it stores in a file. The compiler would then read the file later as it translates the program to object code. Once the program is completely compiled, there's no need to preserve the file containing the program's intermediate form. <stdio.h> provides two functions, tmpfile and tmpnam, for working with temporary files.

tmpfile

tmpfile creates a temporary file (opened in "wb+" mode) that will exist until it's closed or the program ends. A call of tmpfile returns a file pointer that can be used to access the file later:

```
FILE *tempptr;
...
tempptr = tmpfile();    /* creates a temporary file */
```

If it fails to create a file, tmpfile returns a null pointer.

Although tmpfile is easy to use, it has a couple of drawbacks: (1) we don't know the name of the file that tmpfile creates, and (2) we can't decide later to make the file permanent. If these restrictions turn out to be a problem, the alternative is to create a temporary file using fopen. Of course, we don't want this file to have the same name as a previously existing file, so we need some way to generate new file names; that's where the tmpnam function comes in.

tmpnam

tmpnam generates a name for a temporary file. If its argument is a null pointer, tmpnam stores the file name in a static variable and returns a pointer to it:

```
char *filename;
...
filename = tmpnam(NULL);    /* creates a temporary file name */
```

Otherwise, tmpnam copies the file name into a character array provided by the programmer:

```
char filename[L_tmpnam];
...
tmpnam(filename);            /* creates a temporary file name */
```

In the latter case, tmpnam also returns a pointer to the first character of this array. L_tmpnam is a macro in <stdio.h> that specifies how long to make a character array that will hold a temporary file name.

Be sure that tmpnam's argument points to an array of at least L_tmpnam characters. Also, be careful not to call tmpnam too often; the TMP_MAX macro (defined in <stdio.h>) specifies the maximum number of temporary file names that can potentially be generated by tmpnam during the execution of a program. If it fails to generate a file name, tmpnam returns a null pointer.

File Buffering

```
int fflush(FILE *stream);
void setbuf(FILE * restrict stream,
            char * restrict buf);
int setvbuf(FILE * restrict stream,
            char * restrict buf,
            int mode, size_t size);
```

Transferring data to or from a disk drive is a relatively slow operation. As a result, it isn't feasible for a program to access a disk file directly each time it wants to read or write a byte. The secret to achieving acceptable performance is *buffering:* data written to a stream is actually stored in a buffer area in memory; when it's full (or the stream is closed), the buffer is "flushed" (written to the actual output device). Input streams can be buffered in a similar way: the buffer contains data from the input device; input is read from this buffer instead of the device itself. Buffering can result in enormous gains in efficiency, since reading a byte from a buffer or storing a byte in a buffer takes hardly any time at all. Of course, it takes time to transfer the buffer contents to or from disk, but one large "block move" is much faster than many tiny byte moves.

The functions in <stdio.h> perform buffering automatically when it seems advantageous. The buffering takes place behind the scenes, and we usually don't worry about it. On rare occasions, though, we may need to take a more active role. If so, we can use the functions fflush, setbuf, and setvbuf.

fflush   When a program writes output to a file, the data normally goes into a buffer first. The buffer is flushed automatically when it's full or the file is closed. By call-
Q&A ing fflush, however, a program can flush a file's buffer as often as it wishes. The call

```
fflush(fp);     /* flushes buffer for fp */
```

flushes the buffer for the file associated with fp. The call

```
fflush(NULL);   /* flushes all buffers */
```

flushes *all* output streams. fflush returns zero if it's successful and EOF if an error occurs.

setvbuf   `setvbuf` allows us to change the way a stream is buffered and to control the size and location of the buffer. The function's third argument, which specifies the kind of buffering desired, should be one of the following macros:

- `_IOFBF` (full buffering). Data is read from the stream when the buffer is empty or written to the stream when it's full.
- `_IOLBF` (line buffering). Data is read from the stream or written to the stream one line at a time.
- `_IONBF` (no buffering). Data is read from the stream or written to the stream directly, without a buffer.

(All three macros are defined in `<stdio.h>`.) Full buffering is the default for streams that aren't connected to interactive devices.

     `setvbuf`'s second argument (if it's not a null pointer) is the address of the desired buffer. The buffer might have static storage duration, automatic storage duration, or even be allocated dynamically. Making the buffer automatic allows its space to be reclaimed automatically at block exit; allocating it dynamically enables us to free the buffer when it's no longer needed. `setvbuf`'s last argument is the number of bytes in the buffer. A larger buffer may give better performance; a smaller buffer saves space.

     For example, the following call of `setvbuf` changes the buffering of `stream` to full buffering, using the N bytes in the `buffer` array as the buffer:

```
char buffer[N];
…
setvbuf(stream, buffer, _IOFBF, N);
```

 `setvbuf` must be called after `stream` is opened but before any other operations are performed on it.

     It's also legal to call `setvbuf` with a null pointer as the second argument, which requests that `setvbuf` create a buffer with the specified size. `setvbuf` returns zero if it's successful. It returns a nonzero value if the mode argument is invalid or the request can't be honored.

setbuf   `setbuf` is an older function that assumes default values for the buffering mode and buffer size. If `buf` is a null pointer, the call `setbuf(stream, buf)` is equivalent to

```
(void) setvbuf(stream, NULL, _IONBF, 0);
```

Otherwise, it's equivalent to

```
(void) setvbuf(stream, buf, _IOFBF, BUFSIZ);
```

where `BUFSIZ` is a macro defined in `<stdio.h>`. The `setbuf` function is considered obsolete; it's not recommended for use in new programs.

When using `setvbuf` or `setbuf`, be sure to close the stream before its buffer is deallocated. In particular, if the buffer is local to a function and has automatic storage duration, be sure to close the stream before the function returns.

Miscellaneous File Operations

```
int remove(const char *filename);
int rename(const char *old, const char *new);
```

The functions `remove` and `rename` allow a program to perform basic file management operations. Unlike most other functions in this section, `remove` and `rename` work with file *names* instead of file *pointers*. Both functions return zero if they succeed and a nonzero value if they fail.

remove   `remove` deletes a file:

```
remove("foo");          /* deletes the file named "foo" */
```

If a program uses `fopen` (instead of `tmpfile`) to create a temporary file, it can use `remove` to delete the file before the program terminates. Be sure that the file to be removed has been closed; the effect of removing a file that's currently open is implementation-defined.

rename   `rename` changes the name of a file:

```
rename("foo", "bar");   /* renames "foo" to "bar" */
```

`rename` is handy for renaming a temporary file created using `fopen` if a program should decide to make it permanent. If a file with the new name already exists, the effect is implementation-defined.

 If the file to be renamed is open, be sure to close it before calling `rename`; the function may fail if asked to rename an open file.

22.3 Formatted I/O

In this section, we'll examine library functions that use format strings to control reading and writing. These functions, which include our old friends `printf` and `scanf`, have the ability to convert data from character form to numeric form during input and from numeric form to character form during output. None of the other I/O functions can do such conversions.

The ...printf Functions

```
int fprintf(FILE * restrict stream,
            const char * restrict format, ...);
int printf(const char * restrict format, ...);
```

fprintf
printf

ellipsis ➤ 26.1

The fprintf and printf functions write a variable number of data items to an output stream, using a format string to control the appearance of the output. The prototypes for both functions end with the ... symbol (an *ellipsis*), which indicates a variable number of additional arguments. Both functions return the number of characters written; a negative return value indicates that an error occurred.

The only difference between printf and fprintf is that printf always writes to stdout (the standard output stream), whereas fprintf writes to the stream indicated by its first argument:

```
printf("Total: %d\n", total);        /* writes to stdout */
fprintf(fp, "Total: %d\n", total);   /* writes to fp */
```

A call of printf is equivalent to a call of fprintf with stdout as the first argument.

Don't think of fprintf as merely a function that writes data to disk files, though. Like many functions in <stdio.h>, fprintf works fine with any output stream. In fact, one of the most common uses of fprintf—writing error messages to stderr, the standard error stream—has nothing to do with disk files. Here's what such a call might look like:

```
fprintf(stderr, "Error: data file can't be opened.\n");
```

Writing the message to stderr guarantees that it will appear on the screen even if the user redirects stdout.

v...printf functions ➤ 26.1 There are two other functions in <stdio.h> that can write formatted output to a stream. These functions, named vfprintf and vprintf, are fairly obscure. Both rely on the va_list type, which is declared in <stdarg.h>, so they're discussed along with that header.

...printf Conversion Specifications

Both printf and fprintf require a format string containing ordinary characters and/or conversion specifications. Ordinary characters are printed as is; conversion specifications describe how the remaining arguments are to be converted to character form for display. Section 3.1 described conversion specifications briefly, and we added more details in later chapters. We'll now review what we know about conversion specifications and fill in the remaining gaps.

A ...printf conversion specification consists of the % character, followed by as many as five distinct items:

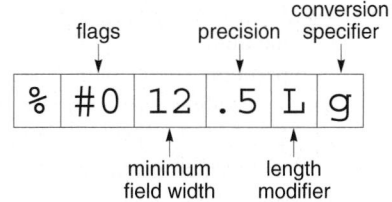

Here's a detailed description of these items, which must appear in the order shown:

■ *Flags* (optional; more than one permitted). The - flag causes left justification within a field; the other flags affect the way numbers are displayed. Table 22.4 gives a complete list of flags.

Table 22.4
Flags for …printf
Functions

Flag	Meaning
-	Left-justify within field. (The default is right justification.)
+	Numbers produced by signed conversions always begin with + or -. (Normally, only negative numbers are preceded by a sign.)
space	Nonnegative numbers produced by signed conversions are preceded by a space. (The + flag overrides the *space* flag.)
#	Octal numbers begin with 0, nonzero hexadecimal numbers with 0x or 0X. Floating-point numbers always have a decimal point. Trailing zeros aren't removed from numbers printed with the g or G conversions.
0 *(zero)*	Numbers are padded with leading zeros up to the field width. The 0 flag is ignored if the conversion is d, i, o, u, x, or X and a precision is specified. (The - flag overrides the 0 flag.)

■ *Minimum field width* (optional). An item that's too small to occupy this number of characters will be padded. (By default, spaces are added to the left of the item, thus right-justifying it within the field.) An item that's too large for the field width will still be displayed in its entirety. The field width is either an integer or the character *. If * is present, the field width is obtained from the next argument. If this argument is negative, it's treated as a positive number preceded by a - flag.

■ *Precision* (optional). The meaning of the precision depends on the conversion:

d, i, o, u, x, X: minimum number of digits
(leading zeros are added if the number has fewer digits)
a, A, e, E, f, F: number of digits after the decimal point
g, G: number of significant digits
s: maximum number of bytes

The precision is a period (.) followed by an integer or the character *. If * is present, the precision is obtained from the next argument. (If this argument is negative, the effect is the same as not specifying a precision.) If only the period is present, the precision is zero.

- **Length modifier** (optional). The presence of a length modifier indicates that the item to be displayed has a type that's longer or shorter than is normal for a particular conversion specification. (For example, %d normally refers to an int value; %hd is used to display a short int and %ld is used to display a long int.) Table 22.5 lists each length modifier, the conversion specifiers with which it may be used, and the type indicated by the combination of the two. (Any combination of length modifier and conversion specifier not shown in the table causes undefined behavior.)

Table 22.5
Length Modifiers for
...printf Functions

Length Modifier	Conversion Specifiers	Meaning
hh[†]	d, i, o, u, x, X	signed char, unsigned char
	n	signed char *
h	d, i, o, u, x, X	short int, unsigned short int
	n	short int *
l (ell)	d, i, o, u, x, X	long int, unsigned long int
	n	long int *
	c	wint_t
	s	wchar_t *
	a, A, e, E, f, F, g, G	no effect
ll[†] (ell-ell)	d, i, o, u, x, X	long long int, unsigned long long int
	n	long long int *
j[†]	d, i, o, u, x, X	intmax_t, uintmax_t
	n	intmax_t *
z[†]	d, i, o, u, x, X	size_t
	n	size_t *
t[†]	d, i, o, u, x, X	ptrdiff_t
	n	ptrdiff_t *
L	a, A, e, E, f, F, g, G	long double

[†]C99 only

- **Conversion specifier.** The conversion specifier must be one of the characters listed in Table 22.6. Notice that f, F, e, E, g, G, a, and A are all designed to write double values. However, they work fine with float values as well; thanks to the default argument promotions, float arguments are converted automatically to double when passed to a function with a variable number of arguments. Similarly, a character passed to ...printf is converted automatically to int, so the c conversion works properly.

default argument promotions ➤9.3

 Be careful to follow the rules described here; the effect of using an invalid conversion specification is undefined.

Table 22.6
Conversion Specifiers for
...printf Functions

Conversion Specifier	Meaning
d, i	Converts an int value to decimal form.
o, u, x, X	Converts an unsigned int value to base 8 (o), base 10 (u), or base 16 (x, X). x displays the hexadecimal digits a–f in lower case; X displays them in upper case.
f, F†	Converts a double value to decimal form, putting the decimal point in the correct position. If no precision is specified, displays six digits after the decimal point.
e, E	Converts a double value to scientific notation. If no precision is specified, displays six digits after the decimal point. If e is chosen, the exponent is preceded by the letter e; if E is chosen, the exponent is preceded by E.
g, G	g converts a double value to either f form or e form. e form is selected if the number's exponent is less than –4 *or* greater than or equal to the precision. Trailing zeros are not displayed (unless the # flag is used); a decimal point appears only when followed by a digit. G chooses between F and E forms.
a†, A†	Converts a double value to hexadecimal scientific notation using the form [-]0xh.$hhhh$p±d, where [-] is an optional minus sign, the h's represent hex digits, ± is either a plus or minus sign, and d is the exponent. d is a decimal number that represents a power of 2. If no precision is specified, enough digits are displayed after the decimal point to represent the exact value of the number (if possible). a displays the hex digits a–f in lower case; A displays them in upper case. The choice of a or A also affects the case of the letters x and p.
c	Displays an int value as an unsigned character.
s	Writes the characters pointed to by the argument. Stops writing when the number of bytes specified by the precision (if present) is reached or a null character is encountered.
p	Converts a void * value to printable form.
n	The corresponding argument must point to an object of type int. Stores in this object the number of characters written so far by this call of ...printf; produces no output.
%	Writes the character %.

†C99 only

greatest-width integers ►*27.1*

C99 Changes to ...printf Conversion Specifications

The conversion specifications for printf and fprintf have undergone a number of changes in C99:

- *Additional length modifiers.* C99 adds the hh, ll, j, z, and t length modifiers. hh and ll provide additional length options, j allows greatest-width integers to be written, and z and t make it easier to write values of type size_t and ptrdiff_t, respectively.

- *Additional conversion specifiers.* C99 adds the F, a, and A conversion specifiers. F is the same as f except for the way in which infinity and NaN (see below) are written. The a and A conversion specifications are rarely used. They're related to hexadecimal floating constants, which are discussed in the Q&A section at the end of Chapter 7.

IEEE floating-point standard ➤ 23.4

- *Ability to write infinity and NaN.* The IEEE 754 floating-point standard allows the result of a floating-point operation to be infinity, negative infinity, or NaN ("not a number"). For example, dividing 1.0 by 0.0 yields positive infinity, dividing −1.0 by 0.0 yields negative infinity, and dividing 0.0 by 0.0 yields NaN (because the result is mathematically undefined). In C99, the a, A, e, E, f, F, g, and G conversion specifiers are capable of converting these special values to a form that can be displayed. a, e, f, and g convert positive infinity to inf or infinity (either one is legal), negative infinity to -inf or -infinity, and NaN to nan or -nan (possibly followed by a series of characters enclosed in parentheses). A, E, F, and G are equivalent to a, e, f, and g, except that upper-case letters are used (INF, INFINITY, NAN).

wide characters ➤ 25.2

- *Support for wide characters.* Another C99 feature is the ability of fprintf to write wide characters. The %lc conversion specification is used to write a single wide character; %ls is used for a string of wide characters.

- *Previously undefined conversion specifications now allowed.* In C89, the effect of using %le, %lE, %lf, %lg, and %lG is undefined. These conversion specifications are legal in C99 (the l length modifier is simply ignored).

Examples of ...printf Conversion Specifications

Whew! It's about time for a few examples. We've seen plenty of everyday conversion specifications in previous chapters, so we'll concentrate here on illustrating some of the more advanced ones. As in previous chapters, I'll use • to represent the space character.

Let's start off by examining the effect of flags on the %d conversion (they have a similar effect on other conversions). The first line of Table 22.7 shows the effect of %8d without any flags. The next four lines show the effect of the -, +, *space*, and 0 flags (the # flag is never used with %d). The remaining lines show the effect of combinations of flags.

Table 22.7
Effect of Flags on
the %d Conversion

Conversion Specification	Result of Applying Conversion to 123	Result of Applying Conversion to −123
%8d	•••••123	••••-123
%-8d	123•••••	-123••••
%+8d	••••+123	••••-123
% 8d	•••••123	••••-123
%08d	00000123	-0000123
%-+8d	+123••••	-123••••
%- 8d	•123••••	-123••••
%+08d	+0000123	-0000123
% 08d	•0000123	-0000123

Table 22.8 shows the effect of the # flag on the o, x, X, g, and G conversions.

Conversion Specification	Result of Applying Conversion to 123	Result of Applying Conversion to 123.0
%8o	•••••173	
%#8o	••••0173	
%8x	••••••7b	
%#8x	••••0x7b	
%8X	••••••7B	
%#8X	••••0X7B	
%8g		•••••123
%#8g		•123.000
%8G		•••••123
%#8G		•123.000

In previous chapters, we've used the minimum field width and precision when displaying numbers, so there's no point in more examples here. Instead, Table 22.9 shows the effect of the minimum field width and precision on the %s conversion.

Conversion Specification	Result of Applying Conversion to "bogus"	Result of Applying Conversion to "buzzword"
%6s	•bogus	buzzword
%-6s	bogus•	buzzword
%.4s	bogu	buzz
%6.4s	••bogu	••buzz
%-6.4s	bogu••	buzz••

Table 22.10 illustrates how the %g conversion displays some numbers in %e form and others in %f form. All numbers in the table were written using the %.4g conversion specification. The first two numbers have exponents of at least 4, so they're displayed in %e form. The next eight numbers are displayed in %f form. The last two numbers have exponents less than –4, so they're displayed in %e form.

Number	Result of Applying %.4g Conversion to Number
123456.	1.235e+05
12345.6	1.235e+04
1234.56	1235
123.456	123.5
12.3456	12.35
1.23456	1.235
.123456	0.1235
.0123456	0.01235
.00123456	0.001235
.000123456	0.0001235
.0000123456	1.235e-05
.00000123456	1.235e-06

In the past, we've assumed that the minimum field width and precision were constants embedded in the format string. Putting the * character where either number would normally go allows us to specify it as an argument *after* the format string. For example, the following calls of `printf` all produce the same output:

```
printf("%6.4d", i);
printf("%*.4d", 6, i);
printf("%6.*d", 4, i);
printf("%*.*d", 6, 4, i);
```

Notice that the values to be filled in for the * come just before the value to be displayed. A major advantage of *, by the way, is that it allows us to use a macro to specify the width or precision:

```
printf("%*d", WIDTH, i);
```

We can even compute the width or precision during program execution:

```
printf("%*d", page_width / num_cols, i);
```

The most unusual specifications are %p and %n. The %p conversion allows us to print the value of a pointer:

```
printf("%p", (void *) ptr);    /* displays value of ptr */
```

Although %p is occasionally useful during debugging, it's not a feature that most programmers use on a daily basis. The C standard doesn't specify what a pointer looks like when printed using %p, but it's likely to be shown as an octal or hexadecimal number.

The %n conversion is used to find out how many characters have been printed so far by a call of ...`printf`. For example, after the call

```
printf("%d%n\n", 123, &len);
```

the value of `len` will be 3, since `printf` had written 3 characters (123) by the time it reached %n. Notice that & must precede `len` (because %n requires a pointer) and that `len` itself isn't printed.

The ...`scanf` Functions

```
int fscanf(FILE * restrict stream,
           const char * restrict format, ...);
int scanf(const char * restrict format, ...);
```

fscanf
scanf

`fscanf` and `scanf` read data items from an input stream, using a format string to indicate the layout of the input. After the format string, any number of pointers—each pointing to an object—follow as additional arguments. Input items are converted (according to conversion specifications in the format string) and stored in these objects.

scanf always reads from stdin (the standard input stream), whereas fscanf reads from the stream indicated by its first argument:

```
scanf("%d%d", &i, &j);        /* reads from stdin */
fscanf(fp, "%d%d", &i, &j);   /* reads from fp */
```

A call of scanf is equivalent to a call of fscanf with stdin as the first argument.

The ...scanf functions return prematurely if an ***input failure*** occurs (no more input characters could be read) or if a ***matching failure*** occurs (the input characters didn't match the format string). (In C99, an input failure can also occur because of an ***encoding error,*** which means that an attempt was made to read a multibyte character, but the input characters didn't correspond to any valid multibyte character.) Both functions return the number of data items that were read and assigned to objects; they return EOF if an input failure occurs before any data items can be read.

Loops that test scanf's return value are common in C programs. The following loop, for example, reads a series of integers one by one, stopping at the first sign of trouble:

idiom
```
while (scanf("%d", &i) == 1) {
  ...
}
```

...scanf Format Strings

Calls of the ...scanf functions resemble those of the ...printf functions. That similarity can be misleading, however; the ...scanf functions work quite differently from the ...printf functions. It pays to think of scanf and fscanf as "pattern-matching" functions. The format string represents a pattern that a ...scanf function attempts to match as it reads input. If the input doesn't match the format string, the function returns as soon as it detects the mismatch; the input character that didn't match is "pushed back" to be read in the future.

A ...scanf format string may contain three things:

- ***Conversion specifications.*** Conversion specifications in a ...scanf format string resemble those in a ...printf format string. Most conversion specifications skip white-space characters at the beginning of an input item (the exceptions are % [, %c, and %n). Conversion specifications never skip *trailing* white-space characters, however. If the input contains •123¤, the %d conversion specification consumes •, 1, 2, and 3, but leaves ¤ unread. (I'm using • to represent the space character and ¤ to represent the new-line character.)

- ***White-space characters.*** One or more consecutive white-space characters in a ...scanf format string match zero or more white-space characters in the input stream.

- ***Non-white-space characters.*** A non-white-space character other than % matches the same character in the input stream.

multibyte characters ➤25.2

white-space characters ➤3.2

For example, the format string `"ISBN %d-%d-%ld-%d"` specifies that the input will consist of:

the letters `ISBN`
possibly some white-space characters
an integer
the - character
an integer (possibly preceded by white-space characters)
the - character
a long integer (possibly preceded by white-space characters)
the - character
an integer (possibly preceded by white-space characters)

...`scanf` Conversion Specifications

Conversion specifications for ...`scanf` functions are actually a little simpler than those for ...`printf` functions. A ...`scanf` conversion specification consists of the character `%` followed by the items listed below (in the order shown).

- ***** (optional). The presence of `*` signifies *assignment suppression:* an input item is read but not assigned to an object. Items matched using `*` aren't included in the count that ...`scanf` returns.

- *Maximum field width* (optional). The maximum field width limits the number of characters in an input item; conversion of the item ends if this number is reached. White-space characters skipped at the beginning of a conversion don't count.

- *Length modifier* (optional). The presence of a length modifier indicates that the object in which the input item will be stored has a type that's longer or shorter than is normal for a particular conversion specification. Table 22.11 lists each length modifier, the conversion specifiers with which it may be used, and the type indicated by the combination of the two. (Any combination of length modifier and conversion specifier not shown in the table causes undefined behavior.)

Table 22.11
Length Modifiers for
...`scanf` Functions

Length Modifier	Conversion Specifiers	Meaning
hh[†]	d, i, o, u, x, X, n	`signed char *`, `unsigned char *`
h	d, i, o, u, x, X, n	`short int *`, `unsigned short int *`
l *(ell)*	d, i, o, u, x, X, n	`long int *`, `unsigned long int *`
	a, A, e, E, f, F, g, G	`double *`
	c, s, or [	`wchar_t *`
ll[†] *(ell-ell)*	d, i, o, u, x, X, n	`long long int *`, `unsigned long long int *`
j[†]	d, i, o, u, x, X, n	`intmax_t *`, `uintmax_t *`
z[†]	d, i, o, u, x, X, n	`size_t *`
t[†]	d, i, o, u, x, X, n	`ptrdiff_t *`
L	a, A, e, E, f, F, g, G	`long double *`

[†]C99 only

- *Conversion specifier.* The conversion specifier must be one of the characters listed in Table 22.12.

Table 22.12

Conversion Specifiers for
...scanf Functions

Conversion Specifier	Meaning
d	Matches a decimal integer; the corresponding argument is assumed to have type int *.
i	Matches an integer; the corresponding argument is assumed to have type int *. The integer is assumed to be in base 10 unless it begins with 0 (indicating octal) or with 0x or 0X (hexadecimal).
o	Matches an octal integer; the corresponding argument is assumed to have type unsigned int *.
u	Matches a decimal integer; the corresponding argument is assumed to have type unsigned int *.
x, X	Matches a hexadecimal integer; the corresponding argument is assumed to have type unsigned int *.
a†, A†, e, E, f, F†, g, G	Matches a floating-point number; the corresponding argument is assumed to have type float *. In C99, the number can be infinity or NaN.
c	Matches *n* characters, where *n* is the maximum field width, or one character if no field width is specified. The corresponding argument is assumed to be a pointer to a character array (or a character object, if no field width is specified). Doesn't add a null character at the end.
s	Matches a sequence of non-white-space characters, then adds a null character at the end. The corresponding argument is assumed to be a pointer to a character array.
[	Matches a nonempty sequence of characters from a scanset, then adds a null character at the end. The corresponding argument is assumed to be a pointer to a character array.
p	Matches a pointer value in the form that ...printf would have written it. The corresponding argument is assumed to be a pointer to a void * object.
n	The corresponding argument must point to an object of type int. Stores in this object the number of characters read so far by this call of ...scanf. No input is consumed and the return value of ...scanf isn't affected.
%	Matches the character %.

†C99 only

Numeric data items can always begin with a sign (+ or -). The o, u, x, and X specifiers convert the item to unsigned form, however, so they're not normally used to read negative numbers.

The [specifier is a more complicated (and more flexible) version of the s specifier. A complete conversion specification using [has the form %[*set*] or %[^*set*], where *set* can be any set of characters. (If] is one of the characters in *set*, however, it must come first.) %[*set*] matches any sequence of characters in *set* (the **scanset**). %[^*set*] matches any sequence of characters *not* in *set* (in other words, the scanset consists of all characters not in *set*). For example, %[abc]

matches any string containing only the letters a, b, and c, while %[^abc] matches any string that doesn't contain a, b, or c.

numeric conversion functions ➤ 26.2

Many of the ...scanf conversion specifiers are closely related to the numeric conversion functions in <stdlib.h>. These functions convert strings (like "-297") to their equivalent numeric values (–297). The d specifier, for example, looks for an optional + or - sign, followed by a series of decimal digits; this is exactly the same form that the strtol function requires when asked to convert a string to a decimal number. Table 22.13 shows the correspondence between conversion specifiers and numeric conversion functions.

Table 22.13
Correspondence between
...scanf Conversion
Specifiers and Numeric
Conversion Functions

Conversion Specifier	Numeric Conversion Function
d	strtol with 10 as the base
i	strtol with 0 as the base
o	strtoul with 8 as the base
u	strtoul with 10 as the base
x, X	strtoul with 16 as the base
a, A, e, E, f, F, g, G	strtod

It pays to be careful when writing calls of scanf. An invalid conversion specification in a scanf format string is just as bad as one in a printf format string; either one causes undefined behavior.

C99 Changes to ...scanf Conversion Specifications

The conversion specifications for scanf and fscanf have undergone some changes in C99, but the list isn't as extensive as it was for the ...printf functions:

- **Additional length modifiers.** C99 adds the hh, ll, j, z, and t length modifiers. These correspond to the length modifiers in ...printf conversion specifications.

- **Additional conversion specifiers.** C99 adds the F, a, and A conversion specifiers. They're provided for symmetry with ...printf; the ...scanf functions treat them the same as e, E, f, g, and G.

- **Ability to read infinity and NaN.** Just as the ...printf functions can write infinity and NaN, the ...scanf functions can read these values. To be read properly, they should have the same appearance as values written by the ...printf functions, with case being ignored. (For example, either INF or inf will be read as infinity.)

- **Support for wide characters.** The ...scanf functions are able to read multibyte characters, which are then converted to wide characters for storage. The %lc conversion specification is used to read a single multibyte character or a sequence of multibyte characters; %ls is used to read a string of multibyte characters (a null character is added at the end). The %l [*set*] and %l [^*set*] conversion specifications can also read a string of multibyte characters.

scanf Examples

The next three tables contain sample calls of scanf. Each call is applied to the input characters shown to its right. Characters printed in ~~strikeout~~ are consumed by the call. The values of the variables after the call appear to the right of the input.

The examples in Table 22.14 show the effect of combining conversion specifications, white-space characters, and non-white-space characters. In three cases no value is assigned to j, so it retains its value from before the call of scanf. The examples in Table 22.15 show the effect of assignment suppression and specifying a field width. The examples in Table 22.16 illustrate the more esoteric conversion specifiers (i, [, and n).

Table 22.14
scanf Examples
(Group 1)

scanf *Call*	*Input*	*Variables*
n = scanf("%d%d", &i, &j);	~~12~~•,•34¤	n: 1 i: 12 j: unchanged
n = scanf("%d,%d", &i, &j);	~~12~~•,•34¤	n: 1 i: 12 j: unchanged
n = scanf("%d ,%d", &i, &j);	~~12~~•,•~~34~~¤	n: 2 i: 12 j: 34
n = scanf("%d, %d", &i, &j);	~~12~~•,•34¤	n: 1 i: 12 j: unchanged

Table 22.15
scanf Examples
(Group 2)

scanf *Call*	*Input*	*Variables*
n = scanf("%*d%d", &i);	~~12~~•~~34~~¤	n: 1 i: 34
n = scanf("%*s%s", str);	~~My~~•~~Fair~~•Lady¤	n: 1 str: "Fair"
n = scanf("%1d%2d%3d", &i, &j, &k);	~~12345~~¤	n: 3 i: 1 j: 23 k: 45
n = scanf("%2d%2s%2d", &i, str, &j);	~~123456~~¤	n: 3 i: 12 str: "34" j: 56

Table 22.16
scanf Examples
(Group 3)

scanf *Call*	*Input*	*Variables*
n = scanf("%i%i%i", &i, &j, &k);	~~12•012•0x12~~¤	n: 3 i: 12 j: 10 k: 18
n = scanf("%[0123456789]", str);	~~123~~abc¤	n: 1 str: "123"
n = scanf("%[0123456789]", str);	abc123¤	n: 0 str: unchanged
n = scanf("%[^0123456789]", str);	~~abc~~123¤	n: 1 str: "abc"
n = scanf("%*d%d%n", &i, &j);	~~10•20•~~30¤	n: 1 i: 20 j: 5

Detecting End-of-File and Error Conditions

```
void clearerr(FILE *stream);
int feof(FILE *stream);
int ferror(FILE *stream);
```

If we ask a ...scanf function to read and store *n* data items, we expect its return value to be *n*. If the return value is less than *n*, something went wrong. There are three possibilities:

- *End-of-file.* The function encountered end-of-file before matching the format string completely.
- *Read error.* The function was unable to read characters from the stream.
- *Matching failure.* A data item was in the wrong format. For example, the function might have encountered a letter while searching for the first digit of an integer.

But how can we tell which kind of failure occurred? In many cases, it doesn't matter; something went wrong, and we've got to abandon the program. There may be times, however, when we'll need to pinpoint the reason for the failure.

Every stream has two indicators associated with it: an *error indicator* and an *end-of-file indicator.* These indicators are cleared when the stream is opened. Not surprisingly, encountering end-of-file sets the end-of-file indicator, and a read error sets the error indicator. (The error indicator is also set when a write error occurs on an output stream.) A matching failure doesn't change either indicator.

clearerr   Once the error or end-of-file indicator is set, it remains in that state until it's explicitly cleared, perhaps by a call of the clearerr function. clearerr clears both the end-of-file and error indicators:

```
clearerr(fp);    /* clears eof and error indicators for fp */
```

Q&A
feof
ferror
Q&A

`clearerr` isn't needed often, since some of the other library functions clear one or both indicators as a side effect.

We can call the `feof` and `ferror` functions to test a stream's indicators to determine why a prior operation on the stream failed. The call `feof(fp)` returns a nonzero value if the end-of-file indicator is set for the stream associated with `fp`. The call `ferror(fp)` returns a nonzero value if the error indicator is set. Both functions return zero otherwise.

When `scanf` returns a smaller-than-expected value, we can use `feof` and `ferror` to determine the reason. If `feof` returns a nonzero value, we've reached the end of the input file. If `ferror` returns a nonzero value, a read error occurred during input. If neither returns a nonzero value, a matching failure must have occurred. Regardless of what the problem was, the return value of `scanf` tells us how many data items were read before the problem occurred.

To see how `feof` and `ferror` might be used, let's write a function that searches a file for a line that begins with an integer. Here's how we intend to call the function:

```
n = find_int("foo");
```

`"foo"` is the name of the file to be searched. The function returns the value of the integer that it finds, which is then assigned to n. If a problem arises—the file can't be opened, a read error occurs, or no line begins with an integer—`find_int` will return an error code (–1, –2, or –3, respectively). I'll assume that no line in the file begins with a negative integer.

```
int find_int(const char *filename)
{
  FILE *fp = fopen(filename, "r");
  int n;

  if (fp == NULL)
    return -1;                    /* can't open file */

  while (fscanf(fp, "%d", &n) != 1) {
    if (ferror(fp)) {
      fclose(fp);
      return -2;                  /* read error */
    }
    if (feof(fp)) {
      fclose(fp);
      return -3;                  /* integer not found */
    }
    fscanf(fp, "%*[^\n] ");       /* skips rest of line */
  }

  fclose(fp);
  return n;
}
```

The `while` loop's controlling expression calls `fscanf` in an attempt to read an integer from the file. If the attempt fails (`fscanf` returns a value other than 1), `find_int` calls `ferror` and `feof` to see if the problem was a read error or end-of-file. If not, `fscanf` must have failed because of a matching error, so `find_int` skips the rest of the characters on the current line and tries again. Note the use of the conversion `%*[^\n]` to skip all characters up to the next new-line. (Now that we know about scansets, it's time to show off!)

22.4   Character I/O

In this section, we'll examine library functions that read and write single characters. These functions work equally well with text streams and binary streams.

You'll notice that the functions in this section treat characters as values of type `int`, not `char`. One reason is that the input functions indicate an end-of-file (or error) condition by returning `EOF`, which is a negative integer constant.

Output Functions

```
int fputc(int c, FILE *stream);
int putc(int c, FILE *stream);
int putchar(int c);
```

putchar

`putchar` writes one character to the `stdout` stream:

```
putchar(ch);      /* writes ch to stdout */
```

fputc
putc

`fputc` and `putc` are more general versions of `putchar` that write a character to an arbitrary stream:

```
fputc(ch, fp);    /* writes ch to fp */
putc(ch, fp);     /* writes ch to fp */
```

Although `putc` and `fputc` do the same thing, `putc` is usually implemented as a macro (as well as a function), while `fputc` is implemented only as a function. `putchar` itself is usually a macro defined in the following way:

```
#define putchar(c) putc((c), stdout)
```

It may seem odd that the library provides both `putc` and `fputc`. But, as we saw in Section 14.3, macros have several potential problems. The C standard allows the `putc` macro to evaluate the `stream` argument more than once, which `fputc` isn't permitted to do. Although programmers usually prefer `putc`, which gives a

Q&A

faster program, `fputc` is available as an alternative.

If a write error occurs, all three functions set the error indicator for the stream and return `EOF`; otherwise, they return the character that was written.

Input Functions

```
int fgetc(FILE *stream);
int getc(FILE *stream);
int getchar(void);
int ungetc(int c, FILE *stream);
```

getchar   `getchar` reads a character from the `stdin` stream:

```
ch = getchar();    /* reads a character from stdin */
```

fgetc   `fgetc` and `getc` read a character from an arbitrary stream:
getc

```
ch = fgetc(fp);    /* reads a character from fp */
ch = getc(fp);     /* reads a character from fp */
```

All three functions treat the character as an `unsigned char` value (which is then converted to `int` type before it's returned). As a result, they never return a negative value other than EOF.

The relationship between `getc` and `fgetc` is similar to that between `putc` and `fputc`. `getc` is usually implemented as a macro (as well as a function), while `fgetc` is implemented only as a function. `getchar` is normally a macro as well:

```
#define getchar() getc(stdin)
```

For reading characters from a file, programmers usually prefer `getc` over `fgetc`. Since `getc` is normally available in macro form, it tends to be faster. `fgetc` can be used as a backup if `getc` isn't appropriate. (The standard allows the `getc` macro to evaluate its argument more than once, which may be a problem.)

The `fgetc`, `getc`, and `getchar` functions behave the same if a problem occurs. At end-of-file, they set the stream's end-of-file indicator and return EOF. If a read error occurs, they set the stream's error indicator and return EOF. To differentiate between the two situations, we can call either `feof` or `ferror`.

One of the most common uses of `fgetc`, `getc`, and `getchar` is to read characters from a file, one by one, until end-of-file occurs. It's customary to use the following `while` loop for that purpose:

idiom

```
while ((ch = getc(fp)) != EOF) {
  ...
}
```

After reading a character from the file associated with `fp` and storing it in the variable `ch` (which must be of type `int`), the `while` test compares `ch` with EOF. If `ch` isn't equal to EOF, we're not at the end of the file yet, so the body of the loop is executed. If `ch` is equal to EOF, the loop terminates.

Always store the return value of `fgetc`, `getc`, or `getchar` in an `int` variable, not a `char` variable. Testing a `char` variable against `EOF` may give the wrong result.

ungetc

There's one other character input function, `ungetc`, which "pushes back" a character read from a stream and clears the stream's end-of-file indicator. This capability can be handy if we need a "lookahead" character during input. For instance, to read a series of digits, stopping at the first nondigit, we could write

isdigit function ➤23.5

```
while (isdigit(ch = getc(fp))) {
  ...
}
ungetc(ch, fp);    /* pushes back last character read */
```

file-positioning functions ➤22.7

The number of characters that can be pushed back by consecutive calls of `ungetc`—with no intervening read operations—depends on the implementation and the type of stream involved; only the first call is guaranteed to succeed. Calling a file-positioning function (`fseek`, `fsetpos`, or `rewind`) causes the pushed-back characters to be lost.

`ungetc` returns the character it was asked to push back. However, it returns `EOF` if an attempt is made to push back `EOF` or to push back more characters than the implementation allows.

PROGRAM ## Copying a File

The following program makes a copy of a file. The names of the original file and the new file will be specified on the command line when the program is executed. For example, to copy the file `f1.c` to `f2.c`, we'd use the command

```
fcopy f1.c f2.c
```

`fcopy` will issue an error message if there aren't exactly two file names on the command line or if either file can't be opened.

fcopy.c

```
/* Copies a file */

#include <stdio.h>
#include <stdlib.h>

int main(int argc, char *argv[])
{
  FILE *source_fp, *dest_fp;
  int ch;
```

```
if (argc != 3) {
  fprintf(stderr, "usage: fcopy source dest\n");
  exit(EXIT_FAILURE);
}

if ((source_fp = fopen(argv[1], "rb")) == NULL) {
  fprintf(stderr, "Can't open %s\n", argv[1]);
  exit(EXIT_FAILURE);
}

if ((dest_fp = fopen(argv[2], "wb")) == NULL) {
  fprintf(stderr, "Can't open %s\n", argv[2]);
  fclose(source_fp);
  exit(EXIT_FAILURE);
}

while ((ch = getc(source_fp)) != EOF)
  putc(ch, dest_fp);

fclose(source_fp);
fclose(dest_fp);
return 0;
}
```

Using `"rb"` and `"wb"` as the file modes enables `fcopy` to copy both text and binary files. If we used `"r"` and `"w"` instead, the program wouldn't necessarily be able to copy binary files.

22.5 Line I/O

We'll now turn to library functions that read and write lines. These functions are used mostly with text streams, although it's legal to use them with binary streams as well.

Output Functions

```
int fputs(const char * restrict s,
          FILE * restrict stream);
int puts(const char *s);
```

puts   We encountered the `puts` function in Section 13.3; it writes a string of characters to `stdout`:

```
puts("Hi, there!");   /* writes to stdout */
```

After it writes the characters in the string, `puts` always adds a new-line character.

fputs   `fputs` is a more general version of `puts`. Its second argument indicates the stream to which the output should be written:

```
fputs("Hi, there!", fp);    /* writes to fp */
```

Unlike `puts`, the `fputs` function doesn't write a new-line character unless one is present in the string.

Both functions return `EOF` if a write error occurs; otherwise, they return a nonnegative number.

Input Functions

```
char *fgets(char * restrict s, int n,
            FILE * restrict stream);
char *gets(char *s);
```

gets   The `gets` function, which we first encountered in Section 13.3, reads a line of input from `stdin`:

```
gets(str);    /* reads a line from stdin */
```

`gets` reads characters one by one, storing them in the array pointed to by `str`, until it reads a new-line character (which it discards).

fgets   `fgets` is a more general version of `gets` that can read from any stream. `fgets` is also safer than `gets`, since it limits the number of characters that it will store. Here's how we might use `fgets`, assuming that `str` is the name of a character array:

```
fgets(str, sizeof(str), fp);    /* reads a line from fp */
```

This call will cause `fgets` to read characters until it reaches the first new-line character or `sizeof(str)` − 1 characters have been read, whichever happens first. If it reads the new-line character, `fgets` stores it along with the other characters. (Thus, `gets` *never* stores the new-line character, but `fgets` *sometimes* does.)

Both `gets` and `fgets` return a null pointer if a read error occurs or they reach the end of the input stream before storing any characters. (As usual, we can call `feof` or `ferror` to determine which situation occurred.) Otherwise, both return their first argument, which points to the array in which the input was stored. As you'd expect, both functions store a null character at the end of the string.

Now that you know about `fgets`, I'd suggest using it instead of `gets` in most situations. With `gets`, there's always the possibility of stepping outside the bounds of the receiving array, so it's safe to use only when the string being read is *guaranteed* to fit into the array. When there's no guarantee (and there usually isn't), it's much safer to use `fgets`. Note that `fgets` will read from the standard input stream if passed `stdin` as its third argument:

```
fgets(str, sizeof(str), stdin);
```

22.6 Block I/O

```
size_t fread(void * restrict ptr,
             size_t size, size_t nmemb,
             FILE * restrict stream);
size_t fwrite(const void * restrict ptr,
              size_t size, size_t nmemb,
              FILE * restrict stream);
```

The `fread` and `fwrite` functions allow a program to read and write large blocks of data in a single step. `fread` and `fwrite` are used primarily with binary streams, although—with care—it's possible to use them with text streams as well.

Q&A
fwrite   `fwrite` is designed to copy an array from memory to a stream. The first argument in a call of `fwrite` is the array's address, the second argument is the size of each array element (in bytes), and the third argument is the number of elements to write. The fourth argument is a file pointer, indicating where the data should be written. To write the entire contents of the array `a`, for instance, we could use the following call of `fwrite`:

```
fwrite(a, sizeof(a[0]), sizeof(a) / sizeof(a[0]), fp);
```

There's no rule that we have to write the entire array; we could just as easily write any portion of it. `fwrite` returns the number of elements (*not* bytes) actually written. This number will be less than the third argument if a write error occurs.

fread   `fread` will read the elements of an array from a stream. `fread`'s arguments are similar to `fwrite`'s: the array's address, the size of each element (in bytes), the number of elements to read, and a file pointer. To read the contents of a file into the array `a`, we might use the following call of `fread`:

```
n = fread(a, sizeof(a[0]), sizeof(a) / sizeof(a[0]), fp);
```

It's important to check `fread`'s return value, which indicates the actual number of elements (*not* bytes) read. This number should equal the third argument unless the end of the input file was reached or a read error occurred. The `feof` and `ferror` functions can be used to determine the reason for any shortage.

Be careful not to confuse `fread`'s second and third arguments. Consider the following call of `fread`:

```
fread(a, 1, 100, fp)
```

We're asking `fread` to read 100 one-byte elements, so it will return a value between 0 and 100. The following call asks `fread` to read one block of 100 bytes:

```
fread(a, 100, 1, fp)
```

`fread`'s return value in this case will be either 0 or 1.

`fwrite` is convenient for a program that needs to store data in a file before terminating. Later, the program (or another program, for that matter) can use `fread` to read the data back into memory. Despite appearances, the data doesn't need to be in array form; `fread` and `fwrite` work just as well with variables of all kinds. Structures, in particular, can be read by `fread` or written by `fwrite`. To write a structure variable s to a file, for instance, we could use the following call of `fwrite`:

```
fwrite(&s, sizeof(s), 1, fp);
```

 Be careful when using `fwrite` to write out structures that contain pointer values; these values aren't guaranteed to be valid when read back in.

22.7   File Positioning

```
int fgetpos(FILE * restrict stream,
            fpos_t * restrict pos);
int fseek(FILE *stream, long int offset, int whence);
int fsetpos(FILE *stream, const fpos_t *pos);
long int ftell(FILE *stream);
void rewind(FILE *stream);
```

Every stream has an associated ***file position.*** When a file is opened, the file position is set at the beginning of the file. (If the file is opened in "append" mode, however, the initial file position may be at the beginning or end of the file, depending on the implementation.) Then, when a read or write operation is performed, the file position advances automatically, allowing us to move through the file in a sequential manner.

Although sequential access is fine for many applications, some programs need the ability to jump around within a file, accessing some data here and other data there. If a file contains a series of records, for example, we might want to jump directly to a particular record and read it or update it. `<stdio.h>` supports this form of access by providing five functions that allow a program to determine the current file position or to change it.

fseek   The `fseek` function changes the file position associated with the first argument (a file pointer). The third argument specifies whether the new position is to be calculated with respect to the beginning of the file, the current position, or the end of the file. <stdio.h> defines three macros for this purpose:

SEEK_SET   Beginning of file
SEEK_CUR   Current file position
SEEK_END   End of file

The second argument is a (possibly negative) byte count. To move to the beginning of a file, for example, the seek direction would be SEEK_SET and the byte count would be zero:

```
fseek(fp, 0L, SEEK_SET);      /* moves to beginning of file */
```

To move to the end of a file, the seek direction would be SEEK_END:

```
fseek(fp, 0L, SEEK_END);      /* moves to end of file */
```

To move back 10 bytes, the seek direction would be SEEK_CUR and the byte count would be –10:

```
fseek(fp, -10L, SEEK_CUR);    /* moves back 10 bytes */
```

Note that the byte count has type long int, so I've used 0L and -10L as arguments. (0 and -10 would also work, of course, since arguments are converted to the proper type automatically.)

Normally, fseek returns zero. If an error occurs (the requested position doesn't exist, for example), fseek returns a nonzero value.

The file-positioning functions are best used with binary streams, by the way. C doesn't prohibit programs from using them with text streams, but care is required because of operating system differences. fseek in particular is sensitive to whether a stream is text or binary. For text streams, either (1) offset (fseek's second argument) must be zero or (2) whence (its third argument) must be SEEK_SET and offset a value obtained by a previous call of ftell. (In other words, we can only use fseek to move to the beginning or end of a text stream or to return to a place that was visited previously.) For binary streams, fseek isn't required to support calls in which whence is SEEK_END.

ftell

errno variable ▶24.2

The ftell function returns the current file position as a long integer. (If an error occurs, ftell returns -1L and stores an error code in errno.) The value returned by ftell may be saved and later supplied to a call of fseek, making it possible to return to a previous file position:

```
long file_pos;
…
file_pos = ftell(fp);             /* saves current position */
…
fseek(fp, file_pos, SEEK_SET);    /* returns to old position */
```

If fp is a binary stream, the call ftell(fp) returns the current file position as a byte count, where zero represents the beginning of the file. If fp is a text stream, however, ftell(fp) isn't necessarily a byte count. As a result, it's best not to perform arithmetic on values returned by ftell. For example, it's not a good idea to subtract values returned by `ftell` to see how far apart two file positions are.

The `rewind` function sets the file position at the beginning. The call `rewind(fp)` is nearly equivalent to `fseek(fp, 0L, SEEK_SET)`. The difference? `rewind` doesn't return a value but does clear the error indicator for `fp`.

`fseek` and `ftell` have one problem: they're limited to files whose positions can be stored in a long integer. For working with very large files, C provides two additional functions: `fgetpos` and `fsetpos`. These functions can handle large files because they use values of type `fpos_t` to represent file positions. An `fpos_t` value isn't necessarily an integer; it could be a structure, for instance.

The call `fgetpos(fp, &file_pos)` stores the file position associated with `fp` in the `file_pos` variable. The call `fsetpos(fp, &file_pos)` sets the file position for `fp` to be the value stored in `file_pos`. (This value must have been obtained by a previous call of `fgetpos`.) If a call of `fgetpos` or `fsetpos` fails, it stores an error code in `errno`. Both functions return zero when they succeed and a nonzero value when they fail.

Here's how we might use `fgetpos` and `fsetpos` to save a file position and return to it later:

```
fpos_t file_pos;
…
fgetpos(fp, &file_pos);    /* saves current position */
…
fsetpos(fp, &file_pos);    /* returns to old position */
```

PROGRAM **Modifying a File of Part Records**

The following program opens a binary file containing `part` structures, reads the structures into an array, sets the `on_hand` member of each structure to 0, and then writes the structures back to the file. Note that the program opens the file in `"rb+"` mode, allowing both reading and writing.

invclear.c

```
/* Modifies a file of part records by setting the quantity
   on hand to zero for all records */

#include <stdio.h>
#include <stdlib.h>

#define NAME_LEN 25
#define MAX_PARTS 100

struct part {
  int number;
  char name[NAME_LEN+1];
  int on_hand;
} inventory[MAX_PARTS];
```

```
int num_parts;

int main(void)
{
  FILE *fp;
  int i;

  if ((fp = fopen("inventory.dat", "rb+")) == NULL) {
    fprintf(stderr, "Can't open inventory file\n");
    exit(EXIT_FAILURE);
  }

  num_parts = fread(inventory, sizeof(struct part),
                    MAX_PARTS, fp);

  for (i = 0; i < num_parts; i++)
    inventory[i].on_hand = 0;

  rewind(fp);
  fwrite(inventory, sizeof(struct part), num_parts, fp);
  fclose(fp);

  return 0;
}
```

Calling `rewind` is critical, by the way. After the `fread` call, the file position is at the end of the file. If we were to call `fwrite` without calling `rewind` first, `fwrite` would add new data to the end of the file instead of overwriting the old data.

22.8 String I/O

The functions described in this section are a bit unusual, since they have nothing to do with streams or files. Instead, they allow us to read and write data using a string as though it were a stream. The `sprintf` and `snprintf` functions write characters into a string in the same way they would be written to a stream; the `sscanf` function reads characters from a string as though it were reading from a stream. These functions, which closely resemble `printf` and `scanf`, are quite useful. `sprintf` and `snprintf` give us access to `printf`'s formatting capabilities without actually having to write data to a stream. Similarly, `sscanf` gives us access to `scanf`'s powerful pattern-matching capabilities. The remainder of this section covers `sprintf`, `snprintf`, and `sscanf` in detail.

Three similar functions (`vsprintf`, `vsnprintf`, and `vsscanf`) also belong to `<stdio.h>`. However, these functions rely on the `va_list` type, which is declared in `<stdarg.h>`. I'll postpone discussing them until Section 26.1, which covers that header.

Output Functions

```
int sprintf(char * restrict s,
            const char * restrict format, ...);
int snprintf(char * restrict s, size_t n,
             const char * restrict format, ...);
```

Note: In this and subsequent chapters, the prototype for a function that is new in C99 will be in italics. Also, the name of the function will be italicized when it appears in the left margin.

sprintf   The `sprintf` function is similar to `printf` and `fprintf`, except that it writes output into a character array (pointed to by its first argument) instead of a stream. `sprintf`'s second argument is a format string identical to that used by `printf` and `fprintf`. For example, the call

```
sprintf(date, "%d/%d/%d", 9, 20, 2010);
```

will write `"9/20/2010"` into `date`. When it's finished writing into a string, `sprintf` adds a null character and returns the number of characters stored (not counting the null character). If an encoding error occurs (a wide character could not be translated into a valid multibyte character), `sprintf` returns a negative value.

   `sprintf` has a variety of uses. For example, we might occasionally want to format data for output without actually writing it. We can use `sprintf` to do the formatting, then save the result in a string until it's time to produce output. `sprintf` is also convenient for converting numbers to character form.

snprintf   The `snprintf` function is the same as `sprintf`, except for the additional parameter n. No more than n − 1 characters will be written to the string, not counting the terminating null character, which is always written unless n is zero. (Equivalently, we could say that `snprintf` writes at most n characters to the string, the last of which is a null character.) For example, the call

```
snprintf(name, 13, "%s, %s", "Einstein", "Albert");
```

will write `"Einstein, Al"` into `name`.

   `snprintf` returns the number of characters that would have been written (not including the null character) had there been no length restriction. If an encoding error occurs, `snprintf` returns a negative number. To see if `snprintf` had room to write all the requested characters, we can test whether its return value was nonnegative and less than n.

Input Functions

```
int sscanf(const char * restrict s,
           const char * restrict format, ...);
```

sscanf The sscanf function is similar to scanf and fscanf, except that it reads from a string (pointed to by its first argument) instead of reading from a stream. sscanf's second argument is a format string identical to that used by scanf and fscanf.

sscanf is handy for extracting data from a string that was read by another input function. For example, we might use fgets to obtain a line of input, then pass the line to sscanf for further processing:

```
fgets(str, sizeof(str), stdin);   /* reads a line of input */
sscanf(str, "%d%d", &i, &j);      /* extracts two integers */
```

One advantage of using sscanf instead of scanf or fscanf is that we can examine an input line as many times as needed, not just once, making it easier to recognize alternate input forms and to recover from errors. Consider the problem of reading a date that's written either in the form *month / day / year* or *month - day - year*. Assuming that str contains a line of input, we can extract the month, day, and year as follows:

```
if (sscanf(str, "%d /%d /%d", &month, &day, &year) == 3)
  printf("Month: %d, day: %d, year: %d\n", month, day, year);
else if (sscanf(str, "%d -%d -%d", &month, &day, &year) == 3)
  printf("Month: %d, day: %d, year: %d\n", month, day, year);
else
  printf("Date not in the proper form\n");
```

Like the scanf and fscanf functions, sscanf returns the number of data items successfully read and stored. sscanf returns EOF if it reaches the end of the string (marked by a null character) before finding the first item.

Q & A

Q: **If I use input or output redirection, will the redirected file names show up as command-line arguments? [p. 541]**

A: No; the operating system removes them from the command line. Let's say that we run a program by entering

```
demo foo <in_file bar >out_file baz
```

The value of argc will be 4, argv[0] will point to the program name, argv[1] will point to "foo", argv[2] will point to "bar", and argv[3] will point to "baz".

Q: **I thought that the end of a line was always marked by a new-line character. Now you're saying that the end-of-line marker varies, depending on the operating system. How you explain this discrepancy? [p. 542]**

A: C library functions make it *appear* as though each line ends with a single new-line character. Regardless of whether an input file contains a carriage-return character, a line-feed character, or both, a library function such as `getc` will return a single new-line character. The output functions perform the reverse translation. If a program calls a library function to write a new-line character to a file, the function will translate the character into the appropriate end-of-line marker. C's approach makes programs more portable and easier to write; we can work with text files without having to worry about how end-of-line is actually represented. Note that input/output performed on a file opened in binary mode isn't subject to any character translation—carriage return and line feed are treated the same as the other characters.

Q: I'm writing a program that needs to save data in a file, to be read later by another program. Is it better to store the data in text form or binary form? [p. 542]

A: That depends. If the data is all text to start with, there's not much difference. If the data contains numbers, however, the decision is tougher.

   Binary form is usually preferable, since it can be read and written quickly. Numbers are already in binary form when stored in memory, so copying them to a file is easy. Writing numbers in text form is much slower, since each number must be converted (usually by `fprintf`) to character form. Reading the file later will also take more time, since numbers will have to be converted from text form back to binary. Moreover, storing data in binary form often saves space, as we saw in Section 22.1.

   Binary files have two disadvantages, however. They're hard for humans to read, which can hamper debugging. Also, binary files generally aren't portable from one system to another, since different kinds of computers store data in different ways. For instance, some machines store `int` values using two bytes but others use four bytes. There's also the issue of byte order (big-endian versus little-endian).

Q: C programs for UNIX never seem to use the letter `b` in the mode string, even when the file being opened is binary. What gives? [p. 544]

A: In UNIX, text files and binary files have exactly the same format, so there's never any need to use `b`. UNIX programmers should still include the `b`, however, so that their programs will be more portable to other operating systems.

Q: I've seen programs that call `fopen` and put the letter `t` in the mode string. What does `t` mean?

A: The C standard allows additional characters to appear in the mode string, provided that they follow `r`, `w`, `a`, `b`, or `+`. Some compilers allow the use of `t` to indicate that a file is to be opened in text mode instead of binary mode. Of course, text mode is the default anyway, so `t` adds nothing. Whenever possible, it's best to avoid using `t` and other nonportable features.

Q: Why bother to call `fclose` to close a file? Isn't it true that all open files are closed automatically when a program terminates? [p. 545]

A: That's usually true, but not if the program calls `abort` to terminate. Even when
abort function ►26.2
`abort` isn't used, though, there are still good reasons to call `fclose`. First, it
reduces the number of open files. Operating systems limit the number of files that
a program may have open at the same time; large programs may bump into this
limit. (The macro `FOPEN_MAX`, defined in `<stdio.h>`, specifies the minimum
number of files that the implementation guarantees can be open simultaneously.)
Second, the program becomes easier to understand and modify; by looking for the
call of `fclose`, it's easier for the reader to determine the point at which a file is
no longer in use. Third, there's the issue of safety. Closing a file ensures that its
contents and directory entry are updated properly; if the program should crash
later, at least the file will be intact.

Q: **I'm writing a program that will prompt the user to enter a file name. How
long should I make the character array that will store the file name? [p. 546]**

A: That depends on your operating system. Fortunately, you can use the macro
`FILENAME_MAX` (defined in `<stdio.h>`) to specify the size of the array.
`FILENAME_MAX` is the length of a string that will hold the longest file name that
the implementation guarantees can be opened.

Q: **Can `fflush` flush a stream that was opened for both reading and writing?
[p. 549]**

A: According to the C standard, the effect of calling `fflush` is defined for a stream
that (a) was opened for output, or (b) was opened for updating and whose last operation was not a read. In all other cases, the effect of calling `fflush` is undefined.
When `fflush` is passed a null pointer, it flushes all streams that satisfy either (a)
or (b).

Q: **Can the format string in a call of ...`printf` or ...`scanf` be a variable?**

A: Sure; it can be any expression of type `char *`. This property makes the ...`printf`
and ...`scanf` functions even more versatile than we've had reason to suspect. Consider the following classic example from Kernighan and Ritchie's *The C Programming Language*, which prints a program's command-line arguments, separated by
spaces:

```
while (--argc > 0)
  printf((argc > 1) ? "%s " : "%s", *++argv);
```

The format string is the expression `(argc > 1) ? "%s " : "%s"`, which evaluates to `"%s "` for all command-line arguments but the last.

Q: **Which library functions other than `clearerr` clear a stream's error and
end-of-file indicators? [p. 565]**

A: Calling `rewind` clears both indicators, as does opening or reopening the stream.
Calling `ungetc`, `fseek`, or `fsetpos` clears just the end-of-file indicator.

Q: **I can't get `feof` to work; it seems to return zero even at end-of-file. What am
I doing wrong? [p. 565]**

A: `feof` will only return a nonzero value when a previous read operation has failed; you can't use `feof` to check for end-of-file *before* attempting to read. Instead, you should first attempt to read, then check the return value from the input function. If the return value indicates that the operation was unsuccessful, you can then use `feof` to determine whether the failure was due to end-of-file. In other words, it's best not to think of calling `feof` as a way to *detect* end-of-file. Instead, think of it as a way to *confirm* that end-of-file was the reason for the failure of a read operation.

Q: **I still don't understand why the I/O library provides macros named `putc` and `getc` in addition to functions named `fputc` and `fgetc`. According to Section 21.1, there are already two versions of `putc` and `getc` (a macro and a function). If we need a genuine function instead of a macro, we can expose the `putc` or `getc` function by undefining the macro. So why do `fputc` and `fgetc` exist? [p. 566]**

A: Historical reasons. Prior to standardization, C had no rule that there be a true function to back up each parameterized macro in the library. `putc` and `getc` were traditionally implemented only as macros; `fputc` and `fgetc` were implemented only as functions.

*Q: **What's wrong with storing the return value of `fgetc`, `getc`, or `getchar` in a `char` variable? I don't see how testing a `char` variable against `EOF` could give the wrong answer. [p. 568]**

A: There are two cases in which this test can give the wrong result. To make the following discussion concrete, I'll assume two's-complement arithmetic.

First, suppose that `char` is an unsigned type. (Recall that some compilers treat `char` as a signed type but others treat it as an unsigned type.) Now suppose that `getc` returns `EOF`, which we store in a `char` variable named `ch`. If `EOF` represents -1 (its typical value), `ch` will end up with the value 255. Comparing `ch` (an unsigned character) with `EOF` (a signed integer) requires converting `ch` to a signed integer (255, in this case). The comparison against `EOF` fails, since 255 is not equal to -1.

Now assume that `char` is a signed type instead. Consider what happens if `getc` reads a byte containing the value 255 from a binary stream. Storing 255 in the `ch` variable gives it the value -1, since `ch` is a signed character. Testing whether `ch` is equal to `EOF` will (erroneously) give a true result.

Q: **The character input functions described in Section 22.4 require that the Enter key be pressed before they can read what the user has typed. How can I write a program that responds to individual keystrokes?**

A: As you've noticed, the `getc`, `fgetc`, and `getchar` functions are buffered; they don't start to read input until the user has pressed the Enter key. In order to read characters as they're entered—which is important for some kinds of programs—you'll need to use a nonstandard library that's tailored to your operating system. In UNIX, for example, the `curses` library often provides this capability.

Q: **When I'm reading user input, how can I skip all characters left on the current input line?**

A: One possibility is to write a small function that reads and ignores all characters up to (and including) the first new-line character:

```
void skip_line(void)
{
  while (getchar() != '\n')
    ;
}
```

Another possibility is to ask `scanf` to skip all characters up to the first new-line character:

```
scanf("%*[^\n]");   /* skips characters up to new-line */
```

`scanf` will read all characters up to the first new-line character, but not store them anywhere (the `*` indicates assignment suppression). The only problem with using `scanf` is that it leaves the new-line character unread, so you may have to discard it separately.

Whatever you do, don't call the `fflush` function:

```
fflush(stdin);   /* effect is undefined */
```

Although some implementations allow the use of `fflush` to "flush" unread input, it's not a good idea to assume that all do. `fflush` is designed to flush *output* streams; the C standard states that its effect on input streams is undefined.

Q: **Why is it not a good idea to use `fread` and `fwrite` with text streams? [p. 571]**

A: One difficulty is that, under some operating systems, the new-line character becomes a pair of characters when written to a text file (see Section 22.1 for details). We must take this expansion into account, or else we're likely to lose track of our data. For example, if we use `fwrite` to write blocks of 80 characters, some of the blocks may end up occupying more than 80 bytes in the file because of new-line characters that were expanded.

Q: **Why are there two sets of file-positioning functions (`fseek`/`ftell` and `fsetpos`/`fgetpos`)? Wouldn't one set be enough? [p. 574]**

A: `fseek` and `ftell` have been part of the C library for eons. They have one drawback, though: they assume that a file position will fit in a `long int` value. Since `long int` is typically a 32-bit type, this means that `fseek` and `ftell` may not work with files containing more than 2,147,483,647 bytes. In recognition of this problem, `fsetpos` and `fgetpos` were added to `<stdio.h>` when C89 was created. These functions aren't required to treat file positions as numbers, so they're not subject to the `long int` restriction. But don't assume that you have to use `fsetpos` and `fgetpos`; if your implementation supports a 64-bit `long int` type, `fseek` and `ftell` are fine even for very large files.

> **Q:** **Why doesn't this chapter discuss screen control: moving the cursor, changing the colors of characters on the screen, and so on?**
>
> **A:** C provides no standard functions for screen control. The C standard addresses only issues that can reasonably be standardized across a wide range of computers and operating systems; screen control is outside this realm. The customary way to solve this problem in UNIX is to use the `curses` library, which supports screen control in a terminal-independent manner.
>
> Similarly, there are no standard functions for building programs with a graphical user interface. However, you can most likely use C function calls to access the windowing API (application programming interface) for your operating system.

Exercises

Section 22.1   1. Indicate whether each of the following files is more likely to contain text data or binary data:

  (a) A file of object code produced by a C compiler
  (b) A program listing produced by a C compiler
  (c) An email message sent from one computer to another
  (d) A file containing a graphics image

Section 22.2   Ⓦ 2. Indicate which mode string is most likely to be passed to `fopen` in each of the following situations:

  (a) A database management system opens a file containing records to be updated.
  (b) A mail program opens a file of saved messages so that it can add additional messages to the end.
  (c) A graphics program opens a file containing a picture to be displayed on the screen.
  (d) An operating system command interpreter opens a "shell script" (or "batch file") containing commands to be executed.

3. Find the error in the following program fragment and show how to fix it.

```
FILE *fp;

if (fp = fopen(filename, "r")) {
  read characters until end-of-file
}
fclose(fp);
```

Section 22.3   Ⓦ 4. Show how each of the following numbers will look if displayed by `printf` with `%#012.5g` as the conversion specification:

  (a) 83.7361
  (b) 29748.6607
  (c) 1054932234.0
  (d) 0.0000235218

5. Is there any difference between the `printf` conversion specifications `%.4d` and `%04d`? If so, explain what it is.

W *6. Write a call of `printf` that prints

1 widget

if the `widget` variable (of type `int`) has the value 1, and

n widgets

otherwise, where *n* is the value of `widget`. You are not allowed to use the `if` statement or any other statement; the answer must be a single call of `printf`.

*7. Suppose that we call `scanf` as follows:

```
n = scanf("%d%f%d", &i, &x, &j);
```

(`i`, `j`, and `n` are `int` variables and `x` is a `float` variable.) Assuming that the input stream contains the characters shown, give the values of `i`, `j`, `n`, and `x` after the call. In addition, indicate which characters were consumed by the call.

(a) 10•20•30¤
(b) 1.0•2.0•3.0¤
(c) 0.1•0.2•0.3¤
(d) .1•.2•.3¤

W 8. In previous chapters, we've used the `scanf` format string `" %c"` when we wanted to skip white-space characters and read a nonblank character. Some programmers use `"%1s"` instead. Are the two techniques equivalent? If not, what are the differences?

Section 22.4 9. Which one of the following calls is *not* a valid way of reading one character from the standard input stream?

(a) `getch()`
(b) `getchar()`
(c) `getc(stdin)`
(d) `fgetc(stdin)`

W 10. The `fcopy.c` program has one minor flaw: it doesn't check for errors as it's writing to the destination file. Errors during writing are rare, but do occasionally occur (the disk might become full, for example). Show how to add the missing error check to the program, assuming that we want it to display a message and terminate immediately if an error occurs.

11. The following loop appears in the `fcopy.c` program:

```
while ((ch = getc(source_fp)) != EOF)
  putc(ch, dest_fp);
```

Suppose that we neglected to put parentheses around `ch = getc(source_fp)`:

```
while (ch = getc(source_fp) != EOF)
  putc(ch, dest_fp);
```

Would the program compile without an error? If so, what would the program do when it's run?

12. Find the error in the following function and show how to fix it.

```
int count_periods(const char *filename)
{
  FILE *fp;
  int n = 0;
```

```
        if ((fp = fopen(filename, "r")) != NULL) {
          while (fgetc(fp) != EOF)
            if (fgetc(fp) == '.')
              n++;
          fclose(fp);
        }

        return n;
      }
```

13.   Write the following function:

```
int line_length(const char *filename, int n);
```

The function should return the length of line n in the text file whose name is `filename` (assuming that the first line in the file is line 1). If the line doesn't exist, the function should return 0.

Section 22.5   Ⓦ 14.   (a) Write your own version of the `fgets` function. Make it behave as much like the real `fgets` function as possible; in particular, make sure that it has the proper return value. To avoid conflicts with the standard library, don't name your function `fgets`.

(b) Write your own version of `fputs`, following the same rules as in part (a).

Section 22.7   Ⓦ 15.   Write calls of `fseek` that perform the following file-positioning operations on a binary file whose data is arranged in 64-byte "records." Use `fp` as the file pointer in each case.

(a) Move to the beginning of record n. (Assume that the first record in the file is record 0.)
(b) Move to the beginning of the last record in the file.
(c) Move forward one record.
(d) Move backward two records.

Section 22.8   16.   Assume that `str` is a string that contains a "sales rank" immediately preceded by the # symbol (other characters may precede the # and/or follow the sales rank). A sales rank is a series of decimal digits possibly containing commas, such as the following examples:

```
989
24,675
1,162,620
```

Write a call of `sscanf` that extracts the sales rank (but not the # symbol) and stores it in a string variable named `sales_rank`.

Programming Projects

1.   Extend the `canopen.c` program of Section 22.2 so that the user may put any number of file names on the command line:

```
canopen foo bar baz
```

The program should print a separate `can be opened` or `can't be opened` message for each file. Have the program terminate with status `EXIT_FAILURE` if one or more of the files can't be opened.

Ⓦ 2.   Write a program that converts all letters in a file to upper case. (Characters other than letters shouldn't be changed.) The program should obtain the file name from the command line and write its output to `stdout`.

3. Write a program named `fcat` that "concatenates" any number of files by writing them to standard output, one after the other, with no break between files. For example, the following command will display the files `f1.c`, `f2.c`, and `f3.c` on the screen:

```
fcat f1.c f2.c f3.c
```

`fcat` should issue an error message if any file can't be opened. *Hint:* Since it has no more than one file open at a time, `fcat` needs only a single file pointer variable. Once it's finished with a file, `fcat` can use the same variable when it opens the next file.

Ⓦ 4. (a) Write a program that counts the number of characters in a text file.

(b) Write a program that counts the number of words in a text file. (A "word" is any sequence of non-white-space characters.)

(c) Write a program that counts the number of lines in a text file.

Have each program obtain the file name from the command line.

5. The `xor.c` program of Section 20.1 refuses to encrypt bytes that—in original or encrypted form—are control characters. We can now remove this restriction. Modify the program so that the names of the input and output files are command-line arguments. Open both files in binary mode, and remove the test that checks whether the original and encrypted characters are printing characters.

Ⓦ 6. Write a program that displays the contents of a file as bytes and as characters. Have the user specify the file name on the command line. Here's what the output will look like when the program is used to display the `pun.c` file of Section 2.1:

```
Offset                  Bytes                   Characters
------  ------------------------------------    ----------
     0  23 69 6E 63 6C 75 64 65 20 3C           #include <
    10  73 74 64 69 6F 2E 68 3E 0D 0A           stdio.h>..
    20  0D 0A 69 6E 74 20 6D 61 69 6E           ..int main
    30  28 76 6F 69 64 29 0D 0A 7B 0D           (void)..{.
    40  0A 20 20 70 72 69 6E 74 66 28           .  printf(
    50  22 54 6F 20 43 2C 20 6F 72 20           "To C, or
    60  6E 6F 74 20 74 6F 20 43 3A 20           not to C:
    70  74 68 61 74 20 69 73 20 74 68           that is th
    80  65 20 71 75 65 73 74 69 6F 6E           e question
    90  2E 5C 6E 22 29 3B 0D 0A 20 20           .\n");..
   100  72 65 74 75 72 6E 20 30 3B 0D           return 0;.
   110  0A 7D                                   .}
```

Each line shows 10 bytes from the file, as hexadecimal numbers and as characters. The number in the `Offset` column indicates the position within the file of the first byte on the line. Only printing characters (as determined by the `isprint` function) are displayed; other characters are shown as periods. Note that the appearance of a text file may vary, depending on the character set and the operating system. The example above assumes that `pun.c` is a Windows file, so 0D and 0A bytes (the ASCII carriage-return and line-feed characters) appear at the end of each line. *Hint:* Be sure to open the file in `"rb"` mode.

7. Of the many techniques for compressing the contents of a file, one of the simplest and fastest is known as ***run-length encoding***. This technique compresses a file by replacing sequences of identical bytes by a pair of bytes: a repetition count followed by a byte to be repeated. For example, suppose that the file to be compressed begins with the following sequence of bytes (shown in hexadecimal):

```
46 6F 6F 20 62 61 72 21 21 21 20 20 20 20 20
```

The compressed file will contain the following bytes:

```
01 46 02 6F 01 20 01 62 01 61 01 72 03 21 05 20
```

Run-length encoding works well if the original file contains many long sequences of identical bytes. In the worst case (a file with no repeated bytes), run-length encoding can actually double the length of the file.

(a) Write a program named `compress_file` that uses run-length encoding to compress a file. To run `compress_file`, we'd use a command of the form

`compress_file` *original-file*

`compress_file` will write the compressed version of *original-file* to *original-file*`.rle`.

For example, the command

`compress_file foo.txt`

will cause `compress_file` to write a compressed version of `foo.txt` to a file named `foo.txt.rle`. *Hint:* The program described in Programming Project 6 could be useful for debugging.

(b) Write a program named `uncompress_file` that reverses the compression performed by the `compress_file` program. The `uncompress_file` command will have the form

`uncompress_file` *compressed-file*

compressed-file should have the extension `.rle`. For example, the command

`uncompress_file foo.txt.rle`

will cause `uncompress_file` to open the file `foo.txt.rle` and write an uncompressed version of its contents to `foo.txt`. `uncompress_file` should display an error message if its command-line argument doesn't end with the `.rle` extension.

8. Modify the `inventory.c` program of Section 16.3 by adding two new operations:

   ■ Save the database in a specified file.
   ■ Load the database from a specified file.

   Use the codes d (dump) and r (restore), respectively, to represent these operations. The interaction with the user should have the following appearance:

   ```
   Enter operation code: d
   Enter name of output file: inventory.dat

   Enter operation code: r
   Enter name of input file: inventory.dat
   ```

   Hint: Use `fwrite` to write the array containing the parts to a binary file. Use `fread` to restore the array by reading it from a file.

Ⓦ 9. Write a program that merges two files containing part records stored by the `inventory.c` program (see Programming Project 8). Assume that the records in each file are sorted by part number, and that we want the resulting file to be sorted as well. If both files have a part with the same number, combine the quantities stored in the records. (As a consistency check, have the program compare the part names and print an error message if they don't match.) Have the program obtain the names of the input files and the merged file from the command line.

*10. Modify the `inventory2.c` program of Section 17.5 by adding the d (dump) and r (restore) operations described in Programming Project 8. Since the part structures aren't stored in an array, the d operation can't save them all by a single call of `fwrite`. Instead, it will need to visit each node in the linked list, writing the part number, part name, and quantity on hand to a file. (Don't save the `next` pointer; it won't be valid once the program terminates.) As it reads parts from a file, the `r` operation will rebuild the list one node at a time.

11. Write a program that reads a date from the command line and displays it in the following form:

    ```
    September 13, 2010
    ```

    Allow the user to enter the date as either `9-13-2010` or `9/13/2010`; you may assume that there are no spaces in the date. Print an error message if the date doesn't have one of the specified forms. *Hint:* Use `sscanf` to extract the month, day, and year from the command-line argument.

12. Modify Programming Project 2 from Chapter 3 so that the program reads a series of items from a file and displays the data in columns. Each line of the file will have the following form:

    item , price , mm / dd / yyyy

    For example, suppose that the file contains the following lines:

    ```
    583,13.5,10/24/2005
    3912,599.99,7/27/2008
    ```

    The output of the program should have the following appearance:

    ```
    Item            Unit           Purchase
                    Price          Date
    583             $   13.50      10/24/2005
    3912            $ 599.99       7/27/2008
    ```

    Have the program obtain the file name from the command line.

13. Modify Programming Project 8 from Chapter 5 so that the program obtains departure and arrival times from a file named `flights.dat`. Each line of the file will contain a departure time followed by an arrival time, with one or more spaces separating the two. Times will be expressed using the 24-hour clock. For example, here's what `flights.dat` might look like if it contained the flight information listed in the original project:

    ```
    8:00 10:16
    9:43 11:52
    11:19 13:31
    12:47 15:00
    14:00 16:08
    15:45 17:55
    19:00 21:20
    21:45 23:58
    ```

14. Modify Programming Project 15 from Chapter 8 so that the program prompts the user to enter the name of a file containing the message to be encrypted:

    ```
    Enter name of file to be encrypted: message.txt
    Enter shift amount (1-25): 3
    ```

    The program then writes the encrypted message to a file with the same name but an added extension of `.enc`. In this example, the original file name is `message.txt`, so the encrypted message will be stored in a file named `message.txt.enc`. There's no limit on the size of the file to be encrypted or on the length of each line in the file.

15. Modify the `justify` program of Section 15.3 so that it reads from one text file and writes to another. Have the program obtain the names of both files from the command line.

16. Modify the `fcopy.c` program of Section 22.4 so that it uses `fread` and `fwrite` to copy the file in blocks of 512 bytes. (The last block may contain fewer than 512 bytes, of course.)

17. Write a program that reads a series of phone numbers from a file and displays them in a standard format. Each line of the file will contain a single phone number, but the numbers may be in a variety of formats. You may assume that each line contains 10 digits, possibly mixed with other characters (which should be ignored). For example, suppose that the file contains the following lines:

```
404.817.6900
(215) 686-1776
312-746-6000
877 275 5273
6173434200
```

The output of the program should have the following appearance:

```
(404)  817-6900
(215)  686-1776
(312)  746-6000
(877)  275-5273
(617)  343-4200
```

Have the program obtain the file name from the command line.

18. Write a program that reads integers from a text file whose name is given as a command-line argument. Each line of the file may contain any number of integers (including none) separated by one or more spaces. Have the program display the largest number in the file, the smallest number, and the median (the number closest to the middle if the integers were sorted). If the file contains an even number of integers, there will be two numbers in the middle; the program should display their average (rounded down). You may assume that the file contains no more than 10,000 integers. *Hint:* Store the integers in an array and then sort the array.

19. (a) Write a program that converts a Windows text file to a UNIX text file. (See Section 22.1 for a discussion of the differences between Windows and UNIX text files.)

    (b) Write a program that converts a UNIX text file to a Windows text file.

    In each case, have the program obtain the names of both files from the command line. *Hint:* Open the input file in `"rb"` mode and the output file in `"wb"` mode.

Library Support for Numbers and Character Data

Prolonged contact with the computer turns mathematicians into clerks and vice versa.

This chapter describes the five most important library headers that provide support for working with numbers, characters, and character strings. Sections 23.1 and 23.2 cover the `<float.h>` and `<limits.h>` headers, which contain macros describing the characteristics of numeric and character types. Sections 23.3 and 23.4 describe the `<math.h>` header, which provides mathematical functions. Section 23.3 discusses the C89 version of `<math.h>`; Section 23.4 covers the C99 additions, which are so extensive that I've chosen to cover them separately. Sections 23.5 and 23.6 are devoted to the `<ctype.h>` and `<string.h>` headers, which provide character functions and string functions, respectively.

C99 adds several headers that also deal with numbers, characters, and strings. The `<wchar.h>` and `<wctype.h>` headers are discussed in Chapter 25. Chapter 27 covers `<complex.h>`, `<fenv.h>`, `<inttypes.h>`, `<stdint.h>`, and `<tgmath.h>`.

23.1 The `<float.h>` Header: Characteristics of Floating Types

The `<float.h>` header provides macros that define the range and accuracy of the `float`, `double`, and `long double` types. There are no types or functions in `<float.h>`.

Two macros apply to all floating types. The `FLT_ROUNDS` macro represents rounding direction ➤23.4 the current rounding direction for floating-point addition. Table 23.1 shows the possible values of `FLT_ROUNDS`. (Values not shown in the table indicate implementation-defined rounding behavior.)

Table 23.1
Rounding Directions

Value	Meaning
-1	Indeterminable
0	Toward zero
1	To nearest
2	Toward positive infinity
3	Toward negative infinity

fesetround function ▸27.6

Unlike the other macros in `<float.h>`, which represent constant expressions, the value of `FLT_ROUNDS` may change during execution. (The `fesetround` function allows a program to change the current rounding direction.) The other macro, `FLT_RADIX`, specifies the radix of exponent representation; it has a minimum value of 2 (indicating binary representation).

The remaining macros, which I'll present in a series of tables, describe the characteristics of specific types. Each macro begins with either FLT, DBL, or LDBL, depending on whether it refers to the `float`, `double`, or `long double` type. The C standard provides extremely detailed definitions of these macros; my descriptions will be less precise but easier to understand. The tables indicate maximum or minimum values for some macros, as specified in the standard.

Table 23.2 lists macros that define the number of significant digits guaranteed by each floating type.

Table 23.2
Significant-Digit Macros
in `<float.h>`

Name	Value	Description
FLT_MANT_DIG DBL_MANT_DIG LDBL_MANT_DIG		Number of significant digits (base FLT_RADIX)
FLT_DIG DBL_DIG LDBL_DIG	≥6 ≥10 ≥10	Number of significant digits (base 10)

Table 23.3 lists macros having to do with exponents.

Table 23.3
Exponent Macros
in `<float.h>`

Name	Value	Description
FLT_MIN_EXP DBL_MIN_EXP LDBL_MIN_EXP		Smallest (most negative) power to which FLT_RADIX can be raised
FLT_MIN_10_EXP DBL_MIN_10_EXP LDBL_MIN_10_EXP	≤−37 ≤−37 ≤−37	Smallest (most negative) power to which 10 can be raised
FLT_MAX_EXP DBL_MAX_EXP LDBL_MAX_EXP		Largest power to which FLT_RADIX can be raised
FLT_MAX_10_EXP DBL_MAX_10_EXP LDBL_MAX_10_EXP	≥+37 ≥+37 ≥+37	Largest power to which 10 can be raised

Table 23.4 lists macros that describe how large numbers can be, how close to zero they can get, and how close two consecutive numbers can be.

Table 23.4
Max, Min, and Epsilon
Macros in `<float.h>`

Name	Value	Description
FLT_MAX	$\geq 10^{+37}$	Largest finite value
DBL_MAX	$\geq 10^{+37}$	
LDBL_MAX	$\geq 10^{+37}$	
FLT_MIN	$\leq 10^{-37}$	Smallest positive value
DBL_MIN	$\leq 10^{-37}$	
LDBL_MIN	$\leq 10^{-37}$	
FLT_EPSILON	$\leq 10^{-5}$	Smallest representable difference between two numbers
DBL_EPSILON	$\leq 10^{-9}$	
LDBL_EPSILON	$\leq 10^{-9}$	

C99 provides two other macros, DECIMAL_DIG and FLT_EVAL_METHOD. DECIMAL_DIG represents the number of significant digits (base 10) in the widest supported floating type; it has a minimum value of 10. The value of FLT_EVAL_METHOD indicates whether an implementation will perform floating-point arithmetic using greater range and precision than is strictly necessary. If this macro has the value 0, for example, then adding two `float` values would be done in the normal way. If it has the value 1, however, then the `float` values would be converted to `double` before the addition is performed. Table 23.5 lists the possible values of FLT_EVAL_METHOD. (Negative values not shown in the table indicate implementation-defined behavior.)

Table 23.5
Evaluation Methods

Value	Meaning
-1	Indeterminable
0	Evaluate all operations and constants just to the range and precision of the type
1	Evaluate operations and constants of type `float` and `double` to the range and precision of the `double` type
2	Evaluate all operations and constants to the range and precision of the `long double` type

Most of the macros in `<float.h>` are of interest only to experts in numerical analysis, making it probably one of the least-used headers in the standard library.

23.2   The `<limits.h>` Header: Sizes of Integer Types

The `<limits.h>` header provides macros that define the range of each integer type (including the character types). `<limits.h>` declares no types or functions.

One set of macros in `<limits.h>` deals with the character types: `char`, `signed char`, and `unsigned char`. Table 23.6 lists these macros and shows the maximum or minimum value of each.

The other macros in `<limits.h>` deal with the remaining integer types: `short int`, `unsigned short int`, `int`, `unsigned int`, `long int`, and

Table 23.6
Character Macros
in <limits.h>

Name	Value	Description
CHAR_BIT	≥8	Number of bits per byte
SCHAR_MIN	≤–127	Minimum signed char value
SCHAR_MAX	≥+127	Maximum signed char value
UCHAR_MAX	≥255	Maximum unsigned char value
CHAR_MIN	†	Minimum char value
CHAR_MAX	††	Maximum char value
MB_LEN_MAX	≥1	Maximum number of bytes per multibyte character in any supported locale (see Section 25.2)

†CHAR_MIN is equal to SCHAR_MIN if char is treated as a signed type; otherwise, CHAR_MIN is 0.
††CHAR_MAX has the same value as either SCHAR_MAX or UCHAR_MAX, depending on whether char is treated as a signed type or an unsigned type.

unsigned long int. Table 23.7 lists these macros and shows the maximum or minimum value of each; the formula used to compute each value is also given. Note that C99 provides three macros that describe the characteristics of the long long int types.

Table 23.7
Integer Macros in
<limits.h>

Name	Value	Formula	Description
SHRT_MIN	≤–32767	$-(2^{15}-1)$	Minimum short int value
SHRT_MAX	≥+32767	$2^{15}-1$	Maximum short int value
USHRT_MAX	≥65535	$2^{16}-1$	Maximum unsigned short int value
INT_MIN	≤–32767	$-(2^{15}-1)$	Minimum int value
INT_MAX	≥+32767	$2^{15}-1$	Maximum int value
UINT_MAX	≥65535	$2^{16}-1$	Maximum unsigned int value
LONG_MIN	≤–2147483647	$-(2^{31}-1)$	Minimum long int value
LONG_MAX	≥+2147483647	$2^{31}-1$	Maximum long int value
ULONG_MAX	≥4294967295	$2^{32}-1$	Maximum unsigned long int value
LLONG_MIN†	≤–9223372036854775807	$-(2^{63}-1)$	Minimum long long int value
LLONG_MAX†	≥+9223372036854775807	$2^{63}-1$	Maximum long long int value
ULLONG_MAX†	≥18446744073709551615	$2^{64}-1$	Maximum unsigned long long int value

†C99 only

The macros in <limits.h> are handy for checking whether a compiler supports integers of a particular size. For example, to determine whether the int type can store numbers as large as 100,000, we might use the following preprocessing directives:

```
#if INT_MAX < 100000
#error int type is too small
#endif
```

#error directive ➤14.5   If the int type isn't adequate, the #error directive will cause the preprocessor to display an error message.

Going a step further, we might use the macros in <limits.h> to help a program *choose* how to represent a type. Let's say that variables of type Quantity must be able to hold integers as large as 100,000. If INT_MAX is at least 100,000, we can define Quantity to be int; otherwise, we'll need to make it long int:

```
#if INT_MAX >= 100000
typedef int Quantity;
#else
typedef long int Quantity;
#endif
```

23.3   The <math.h> Header (C89): Mathematics

The functions in the C89 version of <math.h> fall into five groups:

Trigonometric functions
Hyperbolic functions
Exponential and logarithmic functions
Power functions
Nearest integer, absolute value, and remainder functions

C99 adds a number of functions to these groups as well as introducing other categories of math functions. The C99 changes to <math.h> are so extensive that I've chosen to cover them in a separate section that follows this one. That way, readers who are primarily interested in the C89 version of the header—or who are using a compiler that doesn't support C99—won't be overwhelmed by all the C99 additions.

Before we delve into the functions provided by <math.h>, let's take a brief look at how these functions deal with errors.

Errors

The <math.h> functions handle errors in a way that's different from other library functions. When an error occurs, most <math.h> functions store an error code in a special variable named errno (declared in the <errno.h> header). In addition, when the return value of a function would be larger than the largest double value, the functions in <math.h> return a special value, represented by the macro HUGE_VAL (defined in <math.h>). HUGE_VAL is of type double, but it isn't necessarily an ordinary number. (The IEEE standard for floating-point arithmetic defines a value named "infinity"—a logical choice for HUGE_VAL.)

<errno.h> header ➤24.2

infinity ➤23.4

The functions in <math.h> detect two kinds of errors:

■ ***Domain error:*** An argument is outside a function's domain. If a domain error occurs, the function's return value is implementation-defined and EDOM

NaN ➤*23.4*

("domain error") is stored in `errno`. In some implementations of `<math.h>`, functions return a special value known as NaN ("not a number") when a domain error occurs.

- **Range error:** The return value of a function is outside the range of `double` values. If the return value's magnitude is too large (overflow), the function returns positive or negative HUGE_VAL, depending on the sign of the correct result. In addition, `ERANGE` ("range error") is stored in `errno`. If the return underflow ➤*23.4* value's magnitude is too small to represent (underflow), the function returns zero; some implementations may also store `ERANGE` in `errno`.

We'll ignore the possibility of error for the remainder of this section. However, the function descriptions in Appendix D explain the circumstances that lead to each type of error.

Trigonometric Functions

```
double acos(double x);
double asin(double x);
double atan(double x);
double atan2(double y, double x);
double cos(double x);
double sin(double x);
double tan(double x);
```

cos
sin
tan

The `cos`, `sin`, and `tan` functions compute the cosine, sine, and tangent, respectively. If PI is defined to be 3.14159265, passing PI/4 to `cos`, `sin`, and `tan` produces the following results:

```
cos(PI/4) ⟹ 0.707107
sin(PI/4) ⟹ 0.707107
tan(PI/4) ⟹ 1.0
```

Note that arguments to `cos`, `sin`, and `tan` are expressed in radians, not degrees.

acos
asin
atan

`acos`, `asin`, and `atan` compute the arc cosine, arc sine, and arc tangent:

```
acos(1.0) ⟹ 0.0
asin(1.0) ⟹ 1.5708
atan(1.0) ⟹ 0.785398
```

Applying `acos` to a value returned by `cos` won't necessarily yield the original argument to `cos`, since `acos` always returns a value between 0 and π. `asin` and `atan` return a value between $-\pi/2$ and $\pi/2$.

atan2

`atan2` computes the arc tangent of y/x, where y is the function's first argument and x is its second. The return value of `atan2` is between $-\pi$ and π. The call `atan(x)` is equivalent to `atan2(x, 1.0)`.

Hyperbolic Functions

```
double cosh(double x);
double sinh(double x);
double tanh(double x);
```

cosh
sinh
tanh

The cosh, sinh, and tanh functions compute the hyperbolic cosine, sine, and tangent:

cosh(0.5) $\Rightarrow$ 1.12763
sinh(0.5) $\Rightarrow$ 0.521095
tanh(0.5) $\Rightarrow$ 0.462117

Arguments to cosh, sinh, and tanh must be expressed in radians, not degrees.

Exponential and Logarithmic Functions

```
double exp(double x);
double frexp(double value, int *exp);
double ldexp(double x, int exp);
double log(double x);
double log10(double x);
double modf(double value, double *iptr);
```

exp

The exp function returns *e* raised to a power:

exp(3.0) $\Rightarrow$ 20.0855

log
log10

log is the inverse of exp—it computes the logarithm of a number to the base *e*. log10 computes the "common" (base 10) logarithm:

log(20.0855) $\Rightarrow$ 3.0
log10(1000) $\Rightarrow$ 3.0

Computing the logarithm to a base other than *e* or 10 isn't difficult. The following function, for example, computes the logarithm of x to the base b, for arbitrary x and b:

```
double log_base(double x, double b)
{
  return log(x) / log(b);
}
```

modf

The modf and frexp functions decompose a double value into two parts. modf splits its first argument into integer and fractional parts. It returns the fractional part and stores the integer part in the object pointed to by the second argument:

`modf(3.14159, &int_part)` ⇒ 0.14159 (int_part is assigned 3.0)

Although `int_part` must have type `double`, we can always cast it to `int` or `long int` later.

frexp   The `frexp` function splits a floating-point number into a fractional part f and an exponent n in such a way that the original number equals $f \times 2^n$, where either $0.5 \leq f < 1$ or $f = 0$. `frexp` returns f and stores n in the (integer) object pointed to by the second argument:

`frexp(12.0, &exp)` ⇒ .75 (exp is assigned 4)
`frexp(0.25, &exp)` ⇒ 0.5 (exp is assigned –1)

ldexp   `ldexp` undoes the work of `frexp` by combining a fraction and an exponent into a single number:

`ldexp(.75, 4)` ⇒ 12.0
`ldexp(0.5, -1)` ⇒ 0.25

In general, the call `ldexp(x, exp)` returns $x \times 2^{exp}$.

The `modf`, `frexp`, and `ldexp` functions are primarily used by other functions in `<math.h>`. They are rarely called directly by programs.

Power Functions

```
double pow(double x, double y);
double sqrt(double x);
```

pow   The `pow` function raises its first argument to the power specified by its second argument:

`pow(3.0, 2.0)` ⇒ 9.0
`pow(3.0, 0.5)` ⇒ 1.73205
`pow(3.0, -3.0)` ⇒ 0.037037

sqrt   `sqrt` computes the square root:

`sqrt(3.0)` ⇒ 1.73205

Using `sqrt` to find square roots is preferable to calling `pow`, since `sqrt` is usually a much faster function.

Nearest Integer, Absolute Value, and Remainder Functions

```
double ceil(double x);
double fabs(double x);
double floor(double x);
double fmod(double x, double y);
```

ceil
floor

The `ceil` ("ceiling") function returns—as a `double` value—the smallest integer that's greater than or equal to its argument. `floor` returns the largest integer that's less than or equal to its argument:

```
ceil(7.1)    ⇒  8.0
ceil(7.9)    ⇒  8.0
ceil(-7.1)   ⇒ –7.0
ceil(-7.9)   ⇒ –7.0

floor(7.1)   ⇒  7.0
floor(7.9)   ⇒  7.0
floor(-7.1)  ⇒ –8.0
floor(-7.9)  ⇒ –8.0
```

In other words, `ceil` "rounds up" to the nearest integer, while `floor` "rounds down." C89 lacks a standard function that rounds to the nearest integer, but we can easily use `ceil` and `floor` to write our own:

```
double round_nearest(double x)
{
   return x < 0.0 ? ceil(x - 0.5) : floor(x + 0.5);
}
```

C99

C99 provides several functions that round to the nearest integer, as we'll see in the next section.

fabs

`fabs` computes the absolute value of a number:

```
fabs(7.1)   ⇒ 7.1
fabs(-7.1)  ⇒ 7.1
```

fmod

`fmod` returns the remainder when its first argument is divided by its second argument:

```
fmod(5.5, 2.2)  ⇒ 1.1
```

C doesn't allow the `%` operator to have floating-point operands, but `fmod` is a more-than-adequate substitute.

23.4   The `<math.h>` Header (C99): Mathematics

The C99 version of the `<math.h>` header includes the entire C89 version, plus a host of additional types, macros, and functions. The changes to this header are so numerous that I've chosen to cover them separately. There are several reasons why the standards committee added so many capabilities to `<math.h>`:

- ■ *Provide better support for the IEEE floating-point standard.* C99 doesn't mandate the use of the IEEE standard; other ways of representing floating-point numbers are permitted. However, it's safe to say that the vast majority of C programs are executed on systems that support this standard.

- *Provide more control over floating-point arithmetic.* Better control over floating-point arithmetic may allow programs to achieve greater accuracy and speed.

- *Make C more attractive to Fortran programmers.* The addition of many math functions, along with enhancements elsewhere in C99 (such as support for complex numbers), was intended to increase C's appeal to programmers who might have used other programming languages (primarily Fortran) in the past.

Another reason that I've decided to cover C99's <math.h> header in a separate section is that it's not likely to be of much interest to the average C programmer. Those using C for its traditional applications, which include systems programming and embedded systems, probably won't need the additional functions that C99 provides. However, programmers developing engineering, mathematics, or science applications may find these functions to be quite useful.

IEEE Floating-Point Standard

One motivation for the changes to the <math.h> header is better support for IEEE Standard 754, the most widely used representation for floating-point numbers. The full title of the standard is "IEEE Standard for Binary Floating-Point Arithmetic" (ANSI/IEEE Standard 754-1985). It's also known as IEC 60559, which is how the C99 standard refers to it.

Section 7.2 described some of the basic properties of the IEEE standard. We saw that the standard provides two primary formats for floating-point numbers: single precision (32 bits) and double precision (64 bits). Numbers are stored in a form of scientific notation, with each number having three parts: a sign, an exponent, and a fraction. That limited knowledge of the IEEE standard is enough to use the C89 version of <math.h> effectively. Understanding the C99 version, however, requires knowing more about the standard. Here's some additional information that we'll need:

- *Positive/negative zero.* One of the bits in the IEEE representation of a floating-point number represents the number's sign. As a result, the number zero can be either positive or negative, depending on the value of this bit. The fact that zero has two representations may sometimes require us to treat it differently from other floating-point numbers.

- *Subnormal numbers.* When a floating-point operation is performed, the result may be too small to represent, a condition known as ***underflow***. Think of what happens if you repeatedly divide a number using a hand calculator: eventually the result is zero, because it becomes too small to represent using the calculator's number representation. The IEEE standard has a way to reduce the impact of this phenomenon. Ordinary floating-point numbers are stored in a "normalized" format, in which the number is scaled so that there's exactly one digit to the left of the binary point. When a number gets small enough, however, it's stored in a different format in which it's not normalized. These ***subnormal numbers*** (also known as ***denormalized numbers*** or ***denormals***) can be much smaller than normalized numbers; the trade-off is that they get progressively less accurate as they get smaller.

- ■ ***Special values.*** Each floating-point format allows the representation of three special values: ***positive infinity, negative infinity,*** and ***NaN*** ("not a number"). Dividing a positive number by zero produces positive infinity. Dividing a negative number by zero yields negative infinity. The result of a mathematically undefined operation, such as dividing zero by zero, is NaN. (It's more accurate to say "the result is *a* NaN" rather than "the result is NaN," because the IEEE standard has multiple representations for NaN. The exponent part of a NaN value is all 1 bits, but the fraction can be any nonzero sequence of bits.) Special values can be operands in subsequent operations. Infinity behaves just as it does in ordinary mathematics. For example, dividing a positive number by positive infinity yields zero. (Note that an arithmetic expression could produce infinity as an intermediate result but have a noninfinite value overall.) Performing any operation on NaN gives NaN as the result.

- ■ ***Rounding direction.*** When a number can't be stored exactly using a floating-point representation, the current ***rounding direction*** (or ***rounding mode***) determines which floating-point value will be selected to represent the number. There are four rounding directions: (1) *Round toward nearest.* Rounds to the nearest representable value. If a number falls halfway between two values, it is rounded to the "even" value (the one whose least significant bit is zero). (2) *Round toward zero.* (3) *Round toward positive infinity.* (4) *Round toward negative infinity.* The default rounding direction is round toward nearest.

- ■ ***Exceptions.*** There are five types of floating-point exceptions: *overflow, underflow, division by zero, invalid operation* (the result of an arithmetic operation was NaN), and *inexact* (the result of an arithmetic operation had to be rounded). When one of these conditions is detected, we say that the exception is ***raised.***

Types

C99 adds two types, `float_t` and `double_t`, to `<math.h>`. The `float_t` type is at least as "wide" as the `float` type (meaning that it could be the `float` type or any wider type, such as `double`). Similarly, `double_t` is required to be at least as wide as the `double` type. (It must also be at least as wide as `float_t`.) These types are provided for the programmer who's trying to maximize the performance of floating-point arithmetic. `float_t` should be the most efficient floating-point type that's at least as wide as `float`; `double_t` should be the most efficient floating-point type that's at least as wide as `double`.

FLT_EVAL_METHOD ➤*23.1* The `float_t` and `double_t` types are related to the `FLT_EVAL_METHOD` macro, as shown in Table 23.8.

Table 23.8

Relationship between
FLT_EVAL_METHOD
and the float_t and
double_t Types

Value of FLT_EVAL_METHOD	*Meaning of* float_t	*Meaning of* double_t
0	float	double
1	double	double
2	long double	long double
Other	Implementation-defined	Implementation-defined

Macros

C99 adds a number of macros to <math.h>. I'll mention just two of them at this point. INFINITY represents the float version of positive or unsigned infinity. (If the implementation doesn't support infinity, then INFINITY represents a float value that overflows at compile time.) The NAN macro represents the float version of "not a number." More specifically, it represents a "quiet" NaN (one that doesn't raise an exception if used in an arithmetic expression). If quiet NaNs aren't supported, the NAN macro won't be defined.

I'll cover the function-like macros in <math.h> later in the section, along with ordinary functions. Macros that are relevant only to a specific function will be described with the function itself.

Errors

For the most part, the C99 version of <math.h> deals with errors in the same way as the C89 version. However, there are a few twists that we'll need to discuss.

First, C99 provides several macros that give implementations a choice of how errors are signaled: via a value stored in errno, via a floating-point exception, or both. The macros MATH_ERRNO and MATH_ERREXCEPT represent the integer constants 1 and 2, respectively. A third macro, math_errhandling, represents an int expression whose value is either MATH_ERRNO, MATH_ERREXCEPT, or the bitwise OR of the two values. (It's also possible that math_errhandling isn't really a macro; it might be an identifier with external linkage.) The value of math_errhandling can't be changed within a program.

Now, let's see what happens when a domain error occurs during a call of one of the functions in <math.h>. The C89 standard says that EDOM is stored in errno. The C99 standard, on the other hand, states that if the expression math_errhandling & MATH_ERRNO is nonzero (i.e., the MATH_ERRNO bit is set), then EDOM is stored in errno. If the expression math_errhandling & MATH_ERREXCEPT is nonzero, the *invalid* floating-point exception is raised. Thus, either or both actions are possible, depending on the value of math_errhandling.

Finally, let's turn to the actions that take place when a range error is detected during a function call. There are two cases, based on the magnitude of the function's return value.

Overflow. If the magnitude is too large, the C89 standard requires the function to return positive or negative HUGE_VAL, depending on the sign of the correct result. In addition, ERANGE is stored in `errno`. The C99 standard describes a more complicated set of actions when overflow occurs:

- If default rounding is in effect or if the return value is an "exact infinity" (such as `log(0.0)`), then the function returns either HUGE_VAL, HUGE_VALF, or HUGE_VALL, depending on the function's return type. (HUGE_VALF and HUGE_VALL—the `float` and `long double` versions of HUGE_VAL—are new in C99. Like HUGE_VAL, they may represent positive infinity.) The value returned has the sign of the correct result.
- If the value of `math_errhandling` & MATH_ERRNO is nonzero, ERANGE is stored in `errno`.
- If the value of `math_errhandling` & MATH_ERREXCEPT is nonzero, the *divide-by-zero* floating-point exception is raised if the mathematical result is an exact infinity. Otherwise, the *overflow* exception is raised.

Underflow. If the magnitude is too small to represent, the C89 standard requires the function to return zero; some implementations may also store ERANGE in `errno`. The C99 standard prescribes a somewhat different set of actions:

- The function returns a value whose magnitude is less than or equal to the smallest normalized positive number belonging to the function's return type. (This value might be zero or a subnormal number.)
- If the value of `math_errhandling` & MATH_ERRNO is nonzero, an implementation may store ERANGE in `errno`.
- If the value of `math_errhandling` & MATH_ERREXCEPT is nonzero, an implementation may raise the *underflow* floating-point exception.

Notice the word "may" in the latter two cases. For reasons of efficiency, an implementation is not required to modify `errno` or raise the *underflow* exception.

Functions

We're now ready to tackle the functions that C99 adds to `<math.h>`. I'll present the functions in groups, using the same categories as the C99 standard. These categories differ somewhat from the ones in Section 23.3, which came from the C89 standard.

One of the biggest changes in the C99 version of `<math.h>` is the addition of two more versions of most functions. In C89, there's only a single version of each math function; typically, it takes at least one argument of type `double` and/ or returns a `double` value. In C99, however, there are two additional versions: one for `float` and one for `long double`. The names of these functions are identical to the name of the original function except for the addition of an `f` or `l` suffix. For example, the original `sqrt` function, which takes the square root of a `double` value, is now joined by `sqrtf` (the `float` version) and `sqrtl` (the `long double` version). I'll list the prototypes for the new versions (in italics, as is my custom for functions that are new in C99). I won't describe the functions further, though, since they're virtually identical to their C89 counterparts.

The C99 version of <math.h> also includes a number of completely new functions (and function-like macros). I'll give a brief description of each one. As in Section 23.3, I won't discuss error conditions for these functions, but Appendix D—which lists all standard library functions in alphabetical order—provides this information. I won't list the names of all the new functions in the left margin; instead, I'll show just the name of the primary function. For example, there are three new functions that compute the arc hyperbolic cosine: acosh, acoshf, and acoshl. I'll describe acosh and display only its name in the left margin.

Keep in mind that many of the new functions are highly specialized. As a result, the descriptions of these functions may seem sketchy. A discussion of what these functions are used for is outside the scope of this book.

Classification Macros

```
int fpclassify(real-floating x);
int isfinite(real-floating x);
int isinf(real-floating x);
int isnan(real-floating x);
int isnormal(real-floating x);
int signbit(real-floating x);
```

Our first category consists of function-like macros that are used to determine whether a floating-point value is a "normal" number or a special value such as infinity or NaN. The macros in this group are designed to accept arguments of any real floating type (float, double, or long double).

fpclassify   The fpclassify macro classifies its argument, returning the value of one of the number-classification macros shown in Table 23.9. An implementation may support other classifications by defining additional macros whose names begin with FP_ and an upper-case letter.

Table 23.9
Number-Classification
Macros

Name	Meaning
FP_INFINITE	Infinity (positive or negative)
FP_NAN	Not a number
FP_NORMAL	Normal (not zero, subnormal, infinite, or NaN)
FP_SUBNORMAL	Subnormal
FP_ZERO	Zero (positive or negative)

isfinite   The isfinite macro returns a nonzero value if its argument has a finite
isinf   value (zero, subnormal, or normal, but not infinite or NaN). isinf returns a non-
isnan   zero value if its argument has the value infinity (positive or negative). isnan
isnormal   returns a nonzero value if its argument is a NaN value. isnormal returns a non-zero value if its argument has a normal value (not zero, subnormal, infinite, or NaN).

signbit   The last classification macro is a bit different from the others. signbit returns a nonzero value if the sign of its argument is negative. The argument need not be a finite number; signbit also works for infinity and NaN.

Trigonometric Functions

`float acosf(float x);`	*see* acos
`long double acosl(long double x);`	*see* acos
`float asinf(float x);`	*see* asin
`long double asinl(long double x);`	*see* asin
`float atanf(float x);`	*see* atan
`long double atanl(long double x);`	*see* atan
`float atan2f(float y, float x);`	*see* atan2
`long double atan2l(long double y,`	
`                    long double x);`	*see* atan2
`float cosf(float x);`	*see* cos
`long double cosl(long double x);`	*see* cos
`float sinf(float x);`	*see* sin
`long double sinl(long double x);`	*see* sin
`float tanf(float x);`	*see* tan
`long double tanl(long double x);`	*see* tan

The only new trigonometric functions in C99 are analogs of C89 functions. For descriptions, see the corresponding functions in Section 23.3.

Hyperbolic Functions

`double acosh(double x);`	
`float acoshf(float x);`	
`long double acoshl(long double x);`	
`double asinh(double x);`	
`float asinhf(float x);`	
`long double asinhl(long double x);`	
`double atanh(double x);`	
`float atanhf(float x);`	
`long double atanhl(long double x);`	
`float coshf(float x);`	*see* cosh
`long double coshl(long double x);`	*see* cosh
`float sinhf(float x);`	*see* sinh
`long double sinhl(long double x);`	*see* sinh
`float tanhf(float x);`	*see* tanh
`long double tanhl(long double x);`	*see* tanh

acosh
asinh
atanh
Six functions in this group correspond to the C89 functions `cosh`, `sinh`, and `tanh`. The new functions are `acosh`, which computes the arc hyperbolic cosine; `asinh`, which computes the arc hyperbolic sine; and `atanh`, which computes the arc hyperbolic tangent.

Exponential and Logarithmic Functions

```
float expf(float x);                                see exp
long double expl(long double x);                    see exp

double exp2(double x);
float exp2f(float x);
long double exp2l(long double x);

double expm1(double x);
float expm1f(float x);
long double expm1l(long double x);

float frexpf(float value, int *exp);               see frexp
long double frexpl(long double value,
                   int *exp);                      see frexp

int ilogb(double x);
int ilogbf(float x);
int ilogbl(long double x);

float ldexpf(float x, int exp);                    see ldexp
long double ldexpl(long double x, int exp);        see ldexp

float logf(float x);                                see log
long double logl(long double x);                    see log

float log10f(float x);                              see log10
long double log10l(long double x);                  see log10

double log1p(double x);
float log1pf(float x);
long double log1pl(long double x);

double log2(double x);
float log2f(float x);
long double log2l(long double x);

double logb(double x);
float logbf(float x);
long double logbl(long double x);

float modff(float value, float *iptr);             see modf
long double modfl(long double value,
                  long double *iptr);              see modf
```

```
double scalbn(double x, int n);
float scalbnf(float x, int n);
long double scalbnl(long double x, int n);
double scalbln(double x, long int n);
float scalblnf(float x, long int n);
long double scalblnl(long double x, long int n);
```

exp2
expm1

In additional to new versions of `exp`, `frexp`, `ldexp`, `log`, `log10`, and `modf`, there are several entirely new functions in this category. Two of these, `exp2` and `expm1`, are variations on the `exp` function. When applied to the argument x, the `exp2` function returns 2^x, and `expm1` returns $e^x - 1$.

Q&A
logb
ilogb
log1p
log2

The `logb` function returns the exponent of its argument. More precisely, the call `logb(x)` returns $\log_r(|x|)$, where *r* is the radix of floating-point arithmetic (defined by the macro `FLT_RADIX`, which typically has the value 2). The `ilogb` function returns the value of `logb` after it has been cast to `int` type. The `log1p` function returns $\ln(1 + x)$ when given x as its argument. The `log2` function computes the base-2 logarithm of its argument.

scalbn
scalbln

The `scalbn` function returns $x \times \texttt{FLT\_RADIX}^n$, which it computes in an efficient way (not by explicitly raising `FLT_RADIX` to the nth power). `scalbln` is the same as `scalbn`, except that its second parameter has type `long int` instead of `int`.

Power and Absolute Value Functions

```
double cbrt(double x);
float cbrtf(float x);
long double cbrtl(long double x);

float fabsf(float x);                              see fabs
long double fabsl(long double x);                  see fabs

double hypot(double x, double y);
float hypotf(float x, float y);
long double hypotl(long double x, long double y);

float powf(float x, float y);                      see pow
long double powl(long double x,
                 long double y);                   see pow

float sqrtf(float x);                              see sqrt
long double sqrtl(long double x);                  see sqrt
```

Several functions in this group are new versions of old ones (`fabs`, `pow`, and `sqrt`). Only the functions `cbrt` and `hypot` (and their variants) are entirely new.

cbrt

The `cbrt` function computes the cube root of its argument. The `pow` function can also be used for this purpose, but `pow` is unable to handle negative arguments

hypot

(a domain error occurs). cbrt, on the other hand, is defined for both positive and negative arguments. When its argument is negative, cbrt returns a negative result.

When applied to arguments x and y, the hypot function returns $\sqrt{x^2 + y^2}$. In other words, this function computes the hypotenuse of a right triangle with legs x and y.

Error and Gamma Functions

```
double erf(double x);
float erff(float x);
long double erfl(long double x);

double erfc(double x);
float erfcf(float x);
long double erfcl(long double x);

double lgamma(double x);
float lgammaf(float x);
long double lgammal(long double x);

double tgamma(double x);
float tgammaf(float x);
long double tgammal(long double x);
```

erf
erfc

The erf function computes the **error function** erf (also known as the **Gaussian error function**), which is used in probability, statistics and partial differential equations. The mathematical definition of erf is

$$\text{erf}(x) = \frac{2}{\sqrt{\pi}} \int_0^x e^{-t^2} dt$$

erfc computes the **complementary error function**, erfc(x) = 1 − erf(x).

lgamma
tgamma

The **gamma function** Γ is an extension of the factorial function that can be applied to real numbers as well as to integers. When applied to an integer n, $\Gamma(n) = (n−1)!$; the definition of Γ for nonintegers is more complicated. The tgamma function computes Γ. The lgamma function computes $\ln(|\Gamma(x)|)$, the natural logarithm of the absolute value of the gamma function. lgamma can sometimes be more useful than the gamma function itself, because Γ grows so quickly that using it in calculations may cause overflow.

Nearest Integer Functions

`float ceilf(float x);`	*see* ceil
`long double ceill(long double x);`	*see* ceil
`float floorf(float x);`	*see* floor
`long double floorl(long double x);`	*see* floor

```
double nearbyint(double x);
float nearbyintf(float x);
long double nearbyintl(long double x);

double rint(double x);
float rintf(float x);
long double rintl(long double x);

long int lrint(double x);
long int lrintf(float x);
long int lrintl(long double x);
long long int llrint(double x);
long long int llrintf(float x);
long long int llrintl(long double x);

double round(double x);
float roundf(float x);
long double roundl(long double x);

long int lround(double x);
long int lroundf(float x);
long int lroundl(long double x);
long long int llround(double x);
long long int llroundf(float x);
long long int llroundl(long double x);

double trunc(double x);
float truncf(float x);
long double truncl(long double x);
```

Besides additional versions of `ceil` and `floor`, C99 has a number of new functions that convert a floating-point value to the nearest integer. Be careful when using these functions: although all of them return an integer, some functions return it in floating-point format (as a `float`, `double`, or `long double` value) and some return it in integer format (as a `long int` or `long long int` value).

nearbyint   The `nearbyint` function rounds its argument to an integer, returning it as a
rint   floating-point number. `nearbyint` uses the current rounding direction and does not raise the *inexact* floating-point exception. `rint` is the same as `nearbyint`, except that it may raise the *inexact* floating-point exception if the result has a different value than the argument.

lrint   The `lrint` function rounds its argument to the nearest integer, according to
llrint   the current rounding direction. `lrint` returns a `long int` value. `llrint` is the same as `lrint`, except that it returns a `long long int` value.

round   The `round` function rounds its argument to the nearest integer value, returning it as a floating-point number. `round` always rounds away from zero (so 3.5 is rounded to 4.0, for example).

lround
llround
    The `lround` function rounds its argument to the nearest integer value, returning it as a `long int` value. Like `round`, it rounds away from zero. `llround` is the same as `lround`, except that it returns a `long long int` value.

trunc
    The `trunc` function rounds its argument to the nearest integer not larger in magnitude. (In other words, it truncates the argument toward zero.) `trunc` returns the result as a floating-point number.

Remainder Functions

```
float fmodf(float x, float y);                          see fmod
long double fmodl(long double x,
                        long double y);                 see fmod

double remainder(double x, double y);
float remainderf(float x, float y);
long double remainderl(long double x,
                        long double y);

double remquo(double x, double y, int *quo);
float remquof(float x, float y, int *quo);
long double remquol(long double x, long double y,
                        int *quo);
```

Besides additional versions of `fmod`, this category includes new remainder functions named `remainder` and `remquo`.

remainder
    The `remainder` function returns x REM y, where REM is a function defined in the IEEE standard. For $y \neq 0$, the value of x REM y is $r = x - ny$, where n is the integer nearest the exact value of x/y. (If x/y is halfway between two integers, n is even.) If $r = 0$, it has the same sign as x.

remquo
    The `remquo` function returns the same value as `remainder` when given the same first two arguments. In addition, `remquo` modifies the object pointed to by the `quo` parameter so that it contains n low-order bits of the integer quotient $|x/y|$, where n depends on the implementation but must be at least three. The value stored in this object will be negative if $x/y < 0$.

Manipulation Functions

```
double copysign(double x, double y);
float copysignf(float x, float y);
long double copysignl(long double x, long double y);

double nan(const char *tagp);
float nanf(const char *tagp);
long double nanl(const char *tagp);

double nextafter(double x, double y);
float nextafterf(float x, float y);
```

```
long double nextafterl(long double x, long double y);

double nexttoward(double x, long double y);
float nexttowardf(float x, long double y);
long double nexttowardl(long double x,
                                   long double y);
```

The mysteriously named "manipulation functions" are all new in C99. They provide access to the low-level details of floating-point numbers.

copysign   The copysign function copies the sign of one number to another number. The call copysign(x, y) returns a value with the magnitude of x and the sign of y.

nan   The nan function converts a string to a NaN value. The call nan("*n-char-sequence*") is equivalent to strtod("NAN(*n-char-sequence*)", (char**) NULL). (See the discussion of strtod for a description of the format of *n-char-sequence*.) The call nan("") is equivalent to strtod("NAN()", (char**) NULL). If the argument in a call of nan doesn't have the value "*n-char-sequence*" or "", the call is equivalent to strtod("NAN", (char**) NULL). If quiet NaNs aren't supported, nan returns zero. Calls of nanf and nanl are equivalent to calls of strtof and strtold, respectively. This function is used to construct a NaN value containing a specific binary pattern. (Recall from earlier in this section that the fraction part of a NaN value is arbitrary.)

strtod function ▶26.2

nextafter   The nextafter function determines the next representable value of a number x (if all values of x's type were listed in order, the number that would come just before or just after x). The value of y determines the direction: if y < x, then the function returns the value just before x; if x < y, it returns the value just after x. If x and y are equal, nextafter returns y.

Q&A

nexttoward   The nexttoward function is the same as nextafter, except that the y parameter has type long double instead of double. If x and y are equal, nexttoward returns y converted to the function's return type. The advantage of nexttoward is that a value of any (real) floating type can be passed as the second argument without the danger of it being incorrectly converted to a narrower type.

Maximum, Minimum, and Positive Difference Functions

```
double fdim(double x, double y);
float fdimf(float x, float y);
long double fdiml(long double x, long double y);

double fmax(double x, double y);
float fmaxf(float x, float y);
long double fmaxl(long double x, long double y);

double fmin(double x, double y);
float fminf(float x, float y);
long double fminl(long double x, long double y);
```

fdim   The `fdim` function computes the positive difference of x and y:

$$\begin{cases} x - y & \text{if } x > y \\ +0 & \text{if } x \le y \end{cases}$$

fmax   The `fmax` function returns the larger of its two arguments. `fmin` returns the
fmin   value of the smaller argument.

Floating Multiply-Add

```
double fma(double x, double y, double z);
float fmaf(float x, float y, float z);
long double fmal(long double x, long double y,
                 long double z);
```

fma   The `fma` function multiplies its first two arguments, then adds the third argument.
In other words, we could replace the statement

```
a = b * c + d;
```

with

```
a = fma(b, c, d);
```

This function was added to C99 because some newer CPUs have a "fused multiply-add" instruction that both multiplies and adds. Calling `fma` tells the compiler to use this instruction (if available), which can be faster than performing separate multiply and add instructions. Moreover, the fused multiply-add instruction performs only one rounding operation, not two, so it may produce a more accurate result. It's particularly useful for algorithms that perform a series of multiplications and additions, such as the algorithms for finding the dot product of two vectors or multiplying two matrices.

To determine whether calling the `fma` function is a good idea, a C99 program can test whether the `FP_FAST_FMA` macro is defined. If it is, then calling `fma` should be faster than—or at least as fast as—performing separate multiply and add operations. The `FP_FAST_FMAF` and `FP_FAST_FMAL` macros play the same role for the `fmaf` and `fmal` functions, respectively.

Performing a combined multiply and add is an example of what the C99 standard calls "contraction," where two or more mathematical operations are combined and performed as a single operation. As we saw with the `fma` function, contraction often leads to better speed and greater accuracy. However, programmers may wish to control whether contraction is done automatically (as opposed to calls of `fma`, which are explicit requests for contraction), since contraction can lead to slightly different results. In extreme cases, contraction can avoid a float-point exception that would otherwise be raised.

`#pragma` directive ➤ *14.5*

C99 provides a pragma named `FP_CONTRACT` that gives the programmer control over contraction. Here's how the pragma is used:

`#pragma STDC FP_CONTRACT` *on-off-switch*

The value of *on-off-switch* is either `ON`, `OFF`, or `DEFAULT`. If `ON` is selected, the compiler is allowed to contract expressions; if `OFF` is selected, the compiler is prohibited from contracting expressions. `DEFAULT` is useful for restoring the default setting (which may be either `ON` or `OFF`). If the pragma is used at the outer level of a program (outside any function definitions), it remains in effect until a subsequent `FP_CONTRACT` pragma appears in the same file, or until the file ends. If the pragma is used inside a compound statement (including the body of a function), it must appear first, before any declarations or statements; it remains in effect until the end of the statement, unless overridden by another pragma. A program may still call `fma` to perform an explicit contraction even when `FP_CONTRACT` has been used to prohibit automatic contraction of expressions.

Comparison Macros

```
int isgreater(real-floating x, real-floating y);
int isgreaterequal(real-floating x, real-floating y);
int isless(real-floating x, real-floating y);
int islessequal(real-floating x, real-floating y);
int islessgreater(real-floating x, real-floating y);
int isunordered(real-floating x, real-floating y);
```

Our final category consists of function-like macros that compare two numbers. These macros are designed to accept arguments of any real floating type.

The comparison macros exist because of a problem that can arise when floating-point numbers are compared using the ordinary relational operators such as `<` and `>`. If either operand (or both) is a NaN, such a comparison may cause the *invalid* floating-point exception to be raised, because NaN values—unlike other floating-point values—are considered to be unordered. The comparison macros can be used to avoid this exception. These macros are said to be "quiet" versions of the relational operators because they do their job without raising an exception.

isgreater
isgreaterequal
isless
islessequal

The `isgreater`, `isgreaterequal`, `isless`, and `islessequal` macros perform the same operation as the `>`, `>=`, `<`, and `<=` operators, respectively, except that they don't cause the *invalid* floating-point exception to be raised when the arguments are unordered.

islessgreater

The call `islessgreater(x, y)` is equivalent to `(x) < (y) || (x) > (y)`, except that it guarantees not to evaluate x and y twice, and—like the previous macros—doesn't cause the *invalid* floating-point exception to be raised when x and y are unordered.

isunordered

The `isunordered` macro returns 1 if its arguments are unordered (at least one of them is a NaN) and 0 otherwise.

23.5 The `<ctype.h>` Header: Character Handling

The `<ctype.h>` header provides two kinds of functions: character-classification functions (like `isdigit`, which tests whether a character is a digit) and character case-mapping functions (like `toupper`, which converts a lower-case letter to upper case).

Although C doesn't require that we use the functions in `<ctype.h>` to test characters and perform case conversions, it's a good idea to do so. First, these functions have been optimized for speed (in fact, many are implemented as macros). Second, we'll end up with a more portable program, since these functions work with any character set. Third, the `<ctype.h>` functions adjust their behavior when the locale is changed, which helps us write programs that run properly in different parts of the world.

locales ►25.1

The functions in `<ctype.h>` all take `int` arguments and return `int` values. In many cases, the argument is already stored in an `int` variable (often as a result of having been read by a call of `fgetc`, `getc`, or `getchar`). If the argument has `char` type, however, we need to be careful. C can automatically convert a `char` argument to `int` type; if `char` is an unsigned type or if we're using a seven-bit character set such as ASCII, the conversion will go smoothly. But if `char` is a signed type and if some characters require eight bits, then converting such a character from `char` to `int` will give a negative result. The behavior of the `<ctype.h>` functions is undefined for negative arguments (other than `EOF`), potentially causing serious problems. In such a situation, the argument should be cast to `unsigned char` for safety. (For maximum portability, some programmers always cast a `char` value to `unsigned char` when passing it to a `<ctype.h>` function.)

Character-Classification Functions

```
int isalnum(int c);
int isalpha(int c);
int isblank(int c);
int iscntrl(int c);
int isdigit(int c);
int isgraph(int c);
int islower(int c);
int isprint(int c);
int ispunct(int c);
int isspace(int c);
int isupper(int c);
int isxdigit(int c);
```

Each character-classification function returns a nonzero value if its argument has a particular property. Table 23.10 lists the property that each function tests.

Table 23.10
Character-Classification
Functions

Function	*Test*
`isalnum(c)`	Is c alphanumeric?
`isalpha(c)`	Is c alphabetic?
`isblank(c)`	Is c a blank?[†]
`iscntrl(c)`	Is c a control character?[††]
`isdigit(c)`	Is c a decimal digit?
`isgraph(c)`	Is c a printing character (other than a space)?
`islower(c)`	Is c a lower-case letter?
`isprint(c)`	Is c a printing character (including a space)?
`ispunct(c)`	Is c punctuation?[†††]
`isspace(c)`	Is c a white-space character?[††††]
`isupper(c)`	Is c an upper-case letter?
`isxdigit(c)`	Is c a hexadecimal digit?

[†]The standard blank characters are space and horizontal tab (\t). This function is new in C99.
[††]In ASCII, the control characters are \x00 through \x1f plus \x7f.
[†††]All printing characters except those for which `isspace` or `isalnum` are true are considered punctuation.
[††††]The white-space characters are space, form feed (\f), new-line (\n), carriage return (\r), horizontal tab (\t), and vertical tab (\v).

C99
The C99 definition of `ispunct` is slightly different than the one in C89. In C89, `ispunct(c)` tests whether c is a printing character but not a space or a character for which `isalnum(c)` is true. In C99, `ispunct(c)` tests whether c is a printing character for which neither `isspace(c)` nor `isalnum(c)` is true.

PROGRAM

Testing the Character-Classification Functions

The following program demonstrates the character-classification functions (with the exception of `isblank`, which is new in C99) by applying them to the characters in the string `"azAZ0 !\t"`.

tclassify.c

```
/* Tests the character-classification functions */

#include <ctype.h>
#include <stdio.h>

#define TEST(f) printf(" %c ", f(*p) ? 'x' : ' ')

int main(void)
{
  char *p;

  printf("    alnum    cntrl    graph    print"
         "    space    xdigit\n"
         "      alpha    digit    lower    punct"
         "    upper\n");
```

```
        for (p = "azAZ0 !\t"; *p != '\0'; p++) {
          if (iscntrl(*p))
            printf("\\x%02x:", *p);
          else
            printf("  %c:", *p);
          TEST(isalnum);
          TEST(isalpha);
          TEST(iscntrl);
          TEST(isdigit);
          TEST(isgraph);
          TEST(islower);
          TEST(isprint);
          TEST(ispunct);
          TEST(isspace);
          TEST(isupper);
          TEST(isxdigit);
          printf("\n");
        }

        return 0;
}
```

The program produces the following output:

| | alnum | | cntrl | | graph | | print | | space | xdigit |
		alpha		digit		lower		punct		upper	
a:	x	x			x	x	x				x
z:	x	x			x	x	x				
A:	x	x			x		x			x	x
Z:	x	x			x		x			x	
0:	x			x	x		x				x
:							x		x		
!:					x		x	x			
\x09:			x						x		

Character Case-Mapping Functions

```
int tolower(int c);
int toupper(int c);
```

tolower
toupper

The `tolower` function returns the lower-case version of a letter passed to it as an argument, while `toupper` returns the upper-case version. If the argument to either function is not a letter, it returns the character unchanged.

PROGRAM   ## Testing the Case-Mapping Functions

The following program applies the case-mapping functions to the characters in the string `"aA0!"`.

tcasemap.c   ```
/* Tests the case-mapping functions */
```

```c
#include <ctype.h>
#include <stdio.h>

int main(void)
{
  char *p;

  for (p = "aA0!"; *p != '\0'; p++) {
    printf("tolower('%c') is '%c'; ", *p, tolower(*p));
    printf("toupper('%c') is '%c'\n", *p, toupper(*p));
  }
  return 0;
}
```

The program produces the following output:

```
tolower('a') is 'a'; toupper('a') is 'A'
tolower('A') is 'a'; toupper('A') is 'A'
tolower('0') is '0'; toupper('0') is '0'
tolower('!') is '!'; toupper('!') is '!'
```

23.6 The `<string.h>` Header: String Handling

We first encountered the `<string.h>` header in Section 13.5, which covered the most basic string operations: copying strings, concatenating strings, comparing strings, and finding the length of a string. As we'll see now, there are quite a few string-handling functions in `<string.h>`, as well as functions that operate on character arrays that aren't necessarily null-terminated. Functions in the latter category have names that begin with mem, to suggest that these functions deal with blocks of memory rather than strings. These memory blocks may contain data of any type, hence the arguments to the mem functions have type void * rather than char *.

`<string.h>` provides five kinds of functions:

- *Copying functions.* Functions that copy characters from one place in memory to another place.
- *Concatenation functions.* Functions that add characters to the end of a string.
- *Comparison functions.* Functions that compare character arrays.
- *Search functions.* Functions that search an array for a particular character, a set of characters, or a string.
- *Miscellaneous functions.* Functions that initialize a memory block or compute the length of a string.

We'll now discuss these functions, one group at a time.
```

Copying Functions

```
void *memcpy(void * restrict s1,
             const void * restrict s2, size_t n);
void *memmove(void *s1, const void *s2, size_t n);
char *strcpy(char * restrict s1,
             const char * restrict s2);
char *strncpy(char * restrict s1,
              const char * restrict s2, size_t n);
```

Q&A   The functions in this category copy characters (bytes) from one place in memory (the "source") to another (the "destination"). Each function requires that the first argument point to the destination and the second point to the source. All copying functions return the first argument (a pointer to the destination).

memcpy
memmove   memcpy copies n characters from the source to the destination, where n is the function's third argument. If the source and destination overlap, the behavior of memcpy is undefined. memmove is the same as memcpy, except that it works correctly when the source and destination overlap.

strcpy
strncpy   strcpy copies a null-terminated string from the source to the destination. strncpy is similar to strcpy, but it won't copy more than n characters, where n is the function's third argument. (If n is too small, strncpy won't be able to copy a terminating null character.) If it encounters a null character in the source, strncpy adds null characters to the destination until it has written a total of n characters. strcpy and strncpy, like memcpy, aren't guaranteed to work if the source and destination overlap.

The following examples illustrate the copying functions; the comments show which characters are copied.

```
char source[] = {'h', 'o', 't', '\0', 't', 'e', 'a'};
char dest[7];

memcpy(dest, source, 3);     /* h, o, t                 */
memcpy(dest, source, 4);     /* h, o, t, \0             */
memcpy(dest, source, 7);     /* h, o, t, \0, t, e, a    */

memmove(dest, source, 3);    /* h, o, t                 */
memmove(dest, source, 4);    /* h, o, t, \0             */
memmove(dest, source, 7);    /* h, o, t, \0, t, e, a    */

strcpy(dest, source);        /* h, o, t, \0             */

strncpy(dest, source, 3);    /* h, o, t                 */
strncpy(dest, source, 4);    /* h, o, t, \0             */
strncpy(dest, source, 7);    /* h, o, t, \0, \0, \0, \0 */
```

Note that memcpy, memmove, and strncpy don't require a null-terminated string; they work just as well with any block of memory. The strcpy function, on the other hand, doesn't stop copying until it reaches a null character, so it works only with null-terminated strings.

Section 13.5 gives examples of how `strcpy` and `strncpy` are typically used. Although neither function is completely safe, `strncpy` at least provides a way to limit the number of characters it will copy.

Concatenation Functions

```
char *strcat(char * restrict s1,
             const char * restrict s2);
char *strncat(char * restrict s1,
              const char * restrict s2, size_t n);
```

strcat `strcat` appends its second argument to the end of the first argument. Both arguments must be null-terminated strings; `strcat` puts a null character at the end of the concatenated string. Consider the following example:

```
char str[7] = "tea";

strcat(str, "bag");    /* adds b, a, g, \0 to end of str */
```

The letter b overwrites the null character after the a in `"tea"`, so that `str` now contains the string `"teabag"`. `strcat` returns its first argument (a pointer).

strncat `strncat` is the same as `strcat`, except that its third argument limits the number of characters it will copy:

```
char str[7] = "tea";

strncat(str, "bag", 2);    /* adds b, a, \0 to str    */
strncat(str, "bag", 3);    /* adds b, a, g, \0 to str */
strncat(str, "bag", 4);    /* adds b, a, g, \0 to str */
```

As these examples show, `strncat` always leaves the resulting string properly null-terminated.

In Section 13.5, we saw that a call of `strncat` often has the following appearance:

```
strncat(str1, str2, sizeof(str1) - strlen(str1) - 1);
```

The third argument calculates the amount of space remaining in `str1` (given by the expression `sizeof(str1) - strlen(str1)`) and then subtracts 1 to ensure that there will be room for the null character.

Comparison Functions

```
int memcmp(const void *s1, const void *s2, size_t n);
int strcmp(const char *s1, const char *s2);
int strcoll(const char *s1, const char *s2);
int strncmp(const char *s1, const char *s2,
            size_t n);
size_t strxfrm(char * restrict s1,
               const char * restrict s2, size_t n);
```

The comparison functions fall into two groups. Functions in the first group (mem-cmp, strcmp, and strncmp) compare the contents of two character arrays. Functions in the second group (strcoll and strxfrm) are used if the locale needs to be taken into account.

The memcmp, strcmp, and strncmp functions have much in common. All three expect to be passed pointers to character arrays. The characters in the first array are then compared one by one with the characters in the second array. All three functions return as soon as a mismatch is found. Also, all three return a negative, zero, or positive integer, depending on whether the stopping character in the first array was less than, equal to, or greater than the stopping character in the second.

The differences among the three functions have to do with when to stop comparing characters if no mismatch is found. The memcmp function is passed a third argument, n, that limits the number of comparisons performed; it pays no particular attention to null characters. strcmp doesn't have a preset limit, stopping instead when it reaches a null character in either array. (As a result, strcmp works only with null-terminated strings.) strncmp is a blend of memcmp and strcmp; it stops when n comparisons have been performed or a null character is reached in either array.

The following examples illustrate memcmp, strcmp, and strncmp:

```
char s1[] = {'b', 'i', 'g', '\0', 'c', 'a', 'r'};
char s2[] = {'b', 'i', 'g', '\0', 'c', 'a', 't'};

if (memcmp(s1, s2, 3) == 0) …      /* true  */
if (memcmp(s1, s2, 4) == 0) …      /* true  */
if (memcmp(s1, s2, 7) == 0) …      /* false */

if (strcmp(s1, s2) == 0) …         /* true  */

if (strncmp(s1, s2, 3) == 0) …     /* true  */
if (strncmp(s1, s2, 4) == 0) …     /* true  */
if (strncmp(s1, s2, 7) == 0) …     /* true  */
```

The strcoll function is similar to strcmp, but the outcome of the comparison depends on the current locale.

Most of the time, strcoll is fine for performing a locale-dependent string comparison. Occasionally, however, we might need to perform the comparison more than once (a potential problem, since strcoll isn't especially fast) or change the locale without affecting the outcome of the comparison. In these situations, the strxfrm ("string transform") function is available as an alternative to strcoll.

strxfrm transforms its second argument (a string), placing the result in the array pointed to by the first argument. The third argument limits the number of characters written to the array, including the terminating null character. Calling strcmp with two transformed strings should produce the same outcome (negative, zero, or positive) as calling strcoll with the original strings.

locales ➤25.1
memcmp
strcmp
strncmp

strcoll

strxfrm

`strxfrm` returns the length of the transformed string. As a result, it's typically called twice: once to determine the length of the transformed string and once to perform the transformation. Here's an example:

```
size_t len;
char *transformed;

len = strxfrm(NULL, original, 0);
transformed = malloc(len + 1);
strxfrm(transformed, original, len);
```

Search Functions

```
void *memchr(const void *s, int c, size_t n);
char *strchr(const char *s, int c);
size_t strcspn(const char *s1, const char *s2);
char *strpbrk(const char *s1, const char *s2);
char *strrchr(const char *s, int c);
size_t strspn(const char *s1, const char *s2);
char *strstr(const char *s1, const char *s2);
char *strtok(char * restrict s1,
             const char * restrict s2);
```

strchr
The `strchr` function searches a string for a particular character. The following example shows how we might use `strchr` to search a string for the letter `f`.

```
char *p, str[] = "Form follows function.";

p = strchr(str, 'f');    /* finds first 'f' */
```

`strchr` returns a pointer to the first occurrence of `f` in `str` (the one in the word `follows`). Locating multiple occurrences of a character is easy; for example, the call

```
p = strchr(p + 1, 'f');    /* finds next 'f' */
```

finds the second `f` in `str` (the one in `function`). If it can't locate the desired character, `strchr` returns a null pointer.

memchr
`memchr` is similar to `strchr`, but it stops searching after a set number of characters instead of stopping at the first null character. `memchr`'s third argument limits the number of characters it can examine—a useful capability if we don't want to search an entire string or if we're searching a block of memory that's not terminated by a null character. The following example uses `memchr` to search an array of characters that lacks a null character at the end:

```
char *p, str[22] = "Form follows function.";

p = memchr(str, 'f', sizeof(str));
```

Like the `strchr` function, `memchr` returns a pointer to the first occurrence of the character. If it can't find the desired character, `memchr` returns a null pointer.

strrchr   `strrchr` is similar to `strchr`, but it searches the string in *reverse* order:

```
char *p, str[] = "Form follows function.";

p = strrchr(str, 'f');    /* finds last 'f' */
```

In this example, `strrchr` will first search for the null character at the end of the string, then go backwards to locate the letter f (the one in `function`). Like `strchr` and `memchr`, `strrchr` returns a null pointer if it fails to find the desired character.

strpbrk   `strpbrk` is more general than `strchr`; it returns a pointer to the leftmost character in the first argument that matches *any* character in the second argument:

```
char *p, str[] = "Form follows function.";

p = strpbrk(str, "mn");    /* finds first 'm' or 'n' */
```

In this example, p will point to the letter m in `Form`. `strpbrk` returns a null pointer if no match is found.

strspn   The `strspn` and `strcspn` functions, unlike the other search functions,
strcspn   return an integer (of type `size_t`), representing a position within a string. When
Q&A   given a string to search and a set of characters to look for, `strspn` returns the index of the first character that's *not* in the set. When passed similar arguments, `strcspn` returns the index of the first character that's *in* the set. Here are examples of both functions:

```
size_t n;
char str[] = "Form follows function.";

n = strspn(str, "morF");    /* n = 4 */
n = strspn(str, " \t\n");    /* n = 0 */
n = strcspn(str, "morF");    /* n = 0 */
n = strcspn(str, " \t\n");    /* n = 4 */
```

strstr   `strstr` searches its first argument (a string) for a match with its second argument (also a string). In the following example, `strstr` searches for the word fun:

```
char *p, str[] = "Form follows function.";

p = strstr(str, "fun");    /* locates "fun" in str */
```

`strstr` returns a pointer to the first occurrence of the search string; it returns a null pointer if it can't locate the string. After the call above, p will point to the letter f in `function`.

strtok   `strtok` is the most complicated of the search functions. It's designed to search a string for a "token"—a sequence of characters that doesn't include certain delimiting characters. The call `strtok(s1, s2)` scans the `s1` string for a nonempty sequence of characters that are *not* in the `s2` string. `strtok` marks the end of the token by storing a null character in s1 just after the last character in the token; it then returns a pointer to the first character in the token.

What makes strtok especially useful is that later calls can find additional tokens in the same string. The call strtok(NULL, s2) continues the search begun by the previous strtok call. As before, strtok marks the end of the token with a null character, then returns a pointer to the beginning of the token. The process can be repeated until strtok returns a null pointer, indicating that no token was found.

To see how strtok works, we'll use it to extract a month, day, and year from a date written in the form

month day, year

where spaces and/or tabs separate the month from the day and the day from the year. In addition, spaces and tabs may precede the comma. Let's say that the string str has the following appearance to start with:

After the call

```
p = strtok(str, " \t");
```

str will have the following appearance:

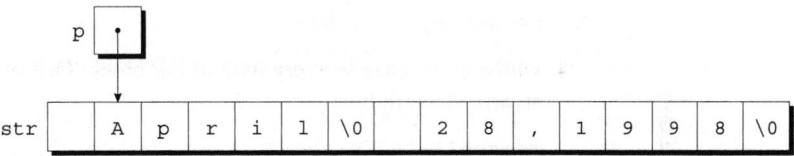

p points to the first character in the month string, which is now terminated by a null character. Calling strtok with a null pointer as its first argument causes it to resume the search from where it left off:

```
p = strtok(NULL, " \t,");
```

After this call, p points to the first character in the day:

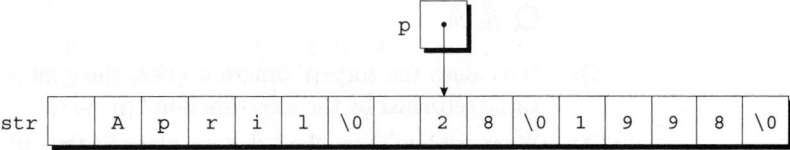

A final call of strtok locates the year:

```
p = strtok(NULL, " \t");
```

After this call, `str` will have the following appearance:

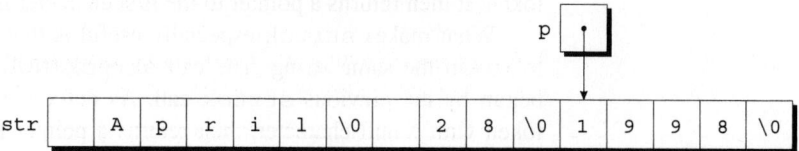

When `strtok` is called repeatedly to break a string into tokens, the second argument isn't required to be the same in each call. In our example, the second call of `strtok` has the argument `" \t, "` instead of `" \t"`.

`strtok` has several well-known problems that limit its usefulness; I'll mention just a couple. First, it works with only one string at a time; it can't conduct simultaneous searches through two different strings. Also, `strtok` treats a sequence of delimiters in the same way as a single delimiter, making it unsuitable for applications in which a string contains a series of fields separated by a delimiter (such as a comma) and some of the fields are empty.

Miscellaneous Functions

```
void *memset(void *s, int c, size_t n);
size_t strlen(const char *s);
```

memset
    `memset` stores multiple copies of a character in a specified area of memory. If `p` points to a block of N bytes, for example, the call

```
memset(p, ' ', N);
```

will store a space in every byte of the block. One of `memset`'s uses is initializing an array to zero bits:

```
memset(a, 0, sizeof(a));
```

`memset` returns its first argument (a pointer).

strlen
    `strlen` returns the length of a string, not counting the null character. See Section 13.5 for examples of `strlen` calls.

strerror function ➤24.2
    There's one other miscellaneous string function, `strerror`, which is covered along with the `<errno.h>` header.

Q & A

Q: **Why does the `expm1` function exist, since all it does is subtract 1 from the value returned by the `exp` function? [p. 605]**

A: When applied to numbers that are close to zero, the `exp` function returns a value that's very close to 1. The result of subtracting 1 from the value returned by `exp` may not be accurate because of round-off error. `expm1` is designed to give a more accurate result in this situation.

The log1p function exists for a similar reason. For values of x that are close to zero, log1p(x) should be more accurate than log(1 + x).

Q: **Why is the function that computes the gamma function named `tgamma` instead of just `gamma`? [p. 606]**

A: At the time the C99 standard was being written, some compilers provided a function named `gamma`, but it computed the log of the gamma function. This function was later renamed `lgamma`. Choosing the name `gamma` for the gamma function would have conflicted with existing practice, so the C99 committee decided on the name `tgamma` ("true gamma") instead.

Q: **Why does the description of the `nextafter` function say that if x and y are equal, `nextafter` returns y? If x and y are equal, what's the difference between returning x or y? [p. 609]**

A: Consider the call `nextafter(-0.0, +0.0)`, in which the arguments are mathematically equal. By returning y instead of x, the function has a return value of +0.0 (rather than –0.0, which would be counterintuitive). Similarly, the call `nextafter(+0.0, -0.0)` returns –0.0.

Q: **Why does `<string.h>` provide so many ways to do the same thing? Do we really need four copying functions (`memcpy`, `memmove`, `strcpy`, and `strncpy`)? [p. 616]**

A: Let's start with `memcpy` and `strcpy`. These functions are used for different purposes. `strcpy` will only copy a character array that's terminated with a null character (a string, in other words); `memcpy` can copy a memory block that lacks such a terminator (an array of integers, for example).

The other functions allow us to choose between safety and performance. `strncpy` is safer than `strcpy`, since it limits the number of characters that can be copied. We pay a price for safety, however, since `strncpy` is likely to be slower than `strcpy`. Using `memmove` involves a similar trade-off. `memmove` will copy bytes from one region of memory into a possibly overlapping region. `memcpy` isn't guaranteed to work properly in this situation; however, if we can guarantee no overlap, `memcpy` is likely to be faster than `memmove`.

Q: **Why does the `strspn` function have such an odd name? [p. 620]**

A: Instead of thinking of `strspn`'s return value as the index of the first character that's *not* in a specified set, we could think of it as the length of the longest "span" of characters that *are* in the set.

Exercises

Section 23.3   **Ⓦ**   1.   Extend the `round_nearest` function so that it rounds a floating-point number x to n digits after the decimal point. For example, the call `round_nearest(3.14159, 3)` would return 3.142. *Hint:* Multiply x by 10^n, round to the nearest integer, then divide by 10^n. Be sure that your function works correctly for both positive and negative values of x.

Section 23.4   2.   (C99) Write the following function:

```
double evaluate_polynomial(double a[], int n, double x);
```

The function should return the value of the polynomial $a_n x^n + a_{n-1} x^{n-1} + \ldots + a_0$, where the a_i's are stored in corresponding elements of the array a, which has length n + 1. Have the function use Horner's Rule to compute the value of the polynomial:

$$((\ldots((a_n x + a_{n-1})x + a_{n-2})x + \ldots)x + a_1)x + a_0$$

Use the fma function to perform the multiplications and additions.

3.   (C99) Check the documentation for your compiler to see if it performs contraction on arithmetic expressions and, if so, under what circumstances.

Section 23.5   4.   Using isalpha and isalnum, write a function that checks whether a string has the syntax of a C identifier (it consists of letters, digits, and underscores, with a letter or underscore at the beginning).

5.   Using isxdigit, write a function that checks whether a string represents a valid hexadecimal number (it consists solely of hexadecimal digits). If so, the function returns the value of the number as a long int. Otherwise, the function returns –1.

Section 23.6   Ⓦ   6.   In each of the following cases, indicate which function would be the best to use: memcpy, memmove, strcpy, or strncpy. Assume that the indicated action is to be performed by a single function call.

(a)   Moving all elements of an array "down" one position in order to leave room for a new element in position 0.

(b)   Deleting the first character in a null-terminated string by moving all other characters back one position.

(c)   Copying a string into a character array that may not be large enough to hold it. If the array is too small, assume that the string is to be truncated; no null character is necessary at the end.

(d)   Copying the contents of one array variable into another.

7.   Section 23.6 explains how to call strchr repeatedly to locate all occurrences of a character within a string. Is it possible to locate all occurrences *in reverse order* by calling strchr repeatedly?

Ⓦ   8.   Use strchr to write the following function:

```
int numchar(const char *s, char ch);
```

numchar returns the number of times the character ch occurs in the string s.

9.   Replace the test condition in the following if statement by a single call of strchr:

```
if (ch == 'a' || ch == 'b' || ch == 'c') ...
```

Ⓦ   10.   Replace the test condition in the following if statement by a single call of strstr:

```
if (strcmp(str, "foo") == 0 || strcmp(str, "bar") == 0 ||
    strcmp(str, "baz") == 0) ...
```

Hint: Combine the string literals into a single string, separating them with a special character. Does your solution assume anything about the contents of str?

Ⓦ 11. Write a call of memset that replaces the last n characters in a null-terminated string s with ! characters.

12. Many versions of <string.h> provide additional (nonstandard) functions, such as those listed below. Write each function using only the features of the C standard.

(a) strdup(s) — Returns a pointer to a copy of s stored in memory obtained by calling malloc. Returns a null pointer if enough memory couldn't be allocated.

(b) stricmp(s1, s2) — Similar to strcmp, but ignores the case of letters.

(c) strlwr(s) — Converts upper-case letters in s to lower case, leaving other characters unchanged; returns s.

(d) strrev(s) — Reverses the characters in s (except the null character); returns s.

(e) strset(s, ch) — Fills s with copies of the character ch; returns s.

If you test any of these functions, you may need to alter its name. Functions whose names begin with str are reserved by the C standard.

13. Use strtok to write the following function:

```
int count_words(char *sentence);
```

count_words returns the number of words in the string sentence, where a "word" is any sequence of non-white-space characters. count_words is allowed to modify the string.

Programming Projects

1. Write a program that finds the roots of the equation $ax^2 + bx + c = 0$ using the formula

$$x = \frac{-b \pm \sqrt{b^2 - 4ac}}{2a}$$

Have the program prompt for the values of *a*, *b*, and *c*, then print both values of *x*. (If $b^2 - 4ac$ is negative, the program should instead print a message to the effect that the roots are complex.)

Ⓦ 2. Write a program that copies a text file from standard input to standard output, removing all white-space characters from the beginning of each line. A line consisting entirely of white-space characters will not be copied.

3. Write a program that copies a text file from standard input to standard output, capitalizing the first letter in each word.

4. Write a program that prompts the user to enter a series of words separated by single spaces, then prints the words in reverse order. Read the input as a string, and then use strtok to break it into words.

5. Suppose that money is deposited into a savings account and left for *t* years. Assume that the annual interest rate is *r* and that interest is compounded continuously. The formula $A(t) = Pe^{rt}$ can be used to calculate the final value of the account, where *P* is the original amount deposited. For example, $1000 left on deposit for 10 years at 6% interest would be worth $1000 \times e^{.06 \times 10} = \$1000 \times e^{.6} = \$1000 \times 1.8221188 = \$1,822.12$. Write a program that displays the result of this calculation after prompting the user to enter the original amount deposited, the interest rate, and the number of years.

6.   Write a program that copies a text file from standard input to standard output, replacing each control character (other than \n) by a question mark.

7.   Write a program that counts the number of sentences in a text file (obtained from standard input). Assume that each sentence ends with a ., ?, or ! followed by a white-space character (including \n).

24 Error Handling

*There are two ways to write error-free
programs; only the third one works.*

Although student programs often fail when subjected to unexpected input, commercial programs need to be "bulletproof"—able to recover gracefully from errors instead of crashing. Making programs bulletproof requires that we anticipate errors that might arise during the execution of the program, include a check for each one, and provide a suitable action for the program to perform if the error should occur.

This chapter describes two ways for programs to check for errors: by using the `assert` macro and by testing the `errno` variable. Section 24.1 covers the `<assert.h>` header, where `assert` is defined. Section 24.2 discusses the `<errno.h>` header, to which the `errno` variable belongs. This section also includes coverage of the `perror` and `strerror` functions. These functions, which come from `<stdio.h>` and `<string.h>`, respectively, are closely related to the `errno` variable.

Section 24.3 explains how programs can detect and handle conditions known as signals, some of which represent errors. The functions that deal with signals are declared in the `<signal.h>` header.

Finally, Section 24.4 explores the `setjmp/longjmp` mechanism, which is often used for responding to errors. Both `setjmp` and `longjmp` belong to the `<setjmp.h>` header.

Error detection and handling aren't among C's strengths. C indicates run-time errors in a variety of ways rather than in a single, uniform way. Furthermore, it's the programmer's responsibility to include code to test for errors. It's easy to overlook potential errors; if one of these should actually occur, the program often continues running, albeit not very well. Newer languages such as C++, Java, and C# have an "exception handling" feature that makes it easier to detect and respond to errors.

24.1 The `<assert.h>` Header: Diagnostics

> `void assert(`*scalar* `expression);`

assert
    `assert`, which is defined in the `<assert.h>` header, allows a program to monitor its own behavior and detect possible problems at an early stage.

    Although `assert` is actually a macro, it's designed to be used like a function. It has one argument, which must be an "assertion"—an expression that we expect to be true under normal circumstances. Each time `assert` is executed, it tests the value of its argument. If the argument has a nonzero value, `assert` does
stderr stream ➤22.1 nothing. If the argument's value is zero, `assert` writes a message to `stderr`
abort function ➤26.2 (the standard error stream) and calls the `abort` function to terminate program execution.

    For example, let's say that the file `demo.c` declares an array `a` of length 10. We're concerned that the statement

```
a[i] = 0;
```

in `demo.c` might cause the program to fail because `i` isn't between 0 and 9. We can use `assert` to check this condition before we perform the assignment to `a[i]`:

```
assert(0 <= i && i < 10);   /* checks subscript first */
a[i] = 0;                   /* now does the assignment */
```

If `i`'s value is less than 0 or greater than or equal to `10`, the program will terminate after displaying a message like the following one:

```
Assertion failed: 0 <= i && i < 10, file demo.c, line 109
```

    C99 changes `assert` in a couple of minor ways. The C89 standard states that the argument to `assert` must have `int` type. The C99 standard relaxes this requirement, allowing the argument to have any scalar type (hence the word *scalar* in the prototype for `assert`). This change allows the argument to be a floating-point number or a pointer, for example. Also, C99 requires that a failed `assert` display the name of the function in which it appears. (C89 requires only that `assert` display the argument—in text form—along with the name of the source file and the source line number). The suggested form of the message is

```
Assertion failed: expression, function abc, file xyz, line nnn.
```

    The exact form of the message produced by `assert` may vary from one compiler to another, although it should always contain the information required by the standard. For example, the GCC compiler produces the following message in the situation described earlier:

```
a.out: demo.c:109: main: Assertion `0 <= i && i < 10' failed.
```

assert has one disadvantage: it slightly increases the running time of a program because of the extra check it performs. Using assert once in a while probably won't have any great effect on a program's speed, but even this small time penalty may be unacceptable in critical applications. As a result, many programmers use assert during testing, then disable it when the program is finished. Disabling assert is easy: we need only define the macro NDEBUG prior to including the <assert.h> header:

```
#define NDEBUG
#include <assert.h>
```

The value of NDEBUG doesn't matter, just the fact that it's defined. If the program should fail later, we can reactivate assert by removing NDEBUG's definition.

 Avoid putting an expression that has a side effect—including a function call—inside an assert; if assert is disabled at a later date, the expression won't be evaluated. Consider the following example:

```
assert((p = malloc(n)) != NULL);
```

If NDEBUG is defined, assert will be ignored and malloc won't be called.

24.2 The <errno.h> Header: Errors

Some functions in the standard library indicate failure by storing an error code (a positive integer) in errno, an int variable declared in <errno.h>. (errno may actually be a macro. If so, the C standard requires that it represent an lvalue, allowing us to use it like a variable.) Most of the functions that rely on errno belong to <math.h>, but there are a few in other parts of the library.

lvalues ➤4.2

Let's say that we need to use a library function that signals an error by storing a value in errno. After calling the function, we can check whether the value of errno is nonzero; if so, an error occurred during the function call. For example, suppose that we want to check whether a call of the sqrt (square root) function has failed. Here's what the code would look like:

sqrt function ➤23.3

```
errno = 0;
y = sqrt(x);
if (errno != 0) {
  fprintf(stderr, "sqrt error; program terminated.\n");
  exit(EXIT_FAILURE);
}
```

Q&A When errno is used to detect an error in a call of a library function, it's important to store zero in errno before calling the function. Although errno is zero at the beginning of program execution, it could have been altered by a later function call. Library functions never clear errno; that's the program's responsibility.

The value stored in errno when an error occurs is often either EDOM or ERANGE. (Both are macros defined in <errno.h>.) These macros represent the two kinds of errors that can occur when a math function is called:

- **Domain errors** (EDOM): An argument passed to a function is outside the function's domain. For example, passing a negative number to sqrt causes a domain error.

exp function ➤ 23.3

- **Range errors** (ERANGE): A function's return value is too large to be represented in the function's return type. For example, passing 1000 to the exp function usually causes a range error, because e^{1000} is too large to represent as a double on most computers.

Some functions can experience both kinds of errors; by comparing errno to EDOM or ERANGE, we can determine which error occurred.

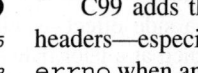

<wchar.h> header ➤ 25.5
encoding error ➤ 22.3

C99 adds the EILSEQ macro to <errno.h>. Library functions in certain headers—especially the <wchar.h> header—store the value of EILSEQ in errno when an encoding error occurs.

The perror and strerror Functions

```
void perror(const char *s);              from <stdio.h>
char *strerror(int errnum);              from <string.h>
```

We'll now look at two functions that are related to the errno variable, although neither function belongs to <errno.h>.

perror

When a library function stores a nonzero value in errno, we may want to display a message that indicates the nature of the error. One way to do this is to call the perror function (declared in <stdio.h>), which prints the following items, in the order shown: (1) its argument, (2) a colon, (3) a space, (4) an error message determined by the value of errno, and (5) a new-line character. perror

stderr stream ➤ 22.1

writes to the stderr stream, not to standard output.

Here's how we might use perror:

```
errno = 0;
y = sqrt(x);
if (errno != 0) {
  perror("sqrt error");
  exit(EXIT_FAILURE);
}
```

If the call of sqrt fails because of a domain error, perror will generate the following output:

```
sqrt error: Numerical argument out of domain
```

The error message that perror displays after sqrt error is implementation-defined. In this example, Numerical argument out of domain is the message that corresponds to the EDOM error. An ERANGE error usually produces a different message, such as Numerical result out of range.

strerror   The strerror function belongs to <string.h>. When passed an error code, strerror returns a pointer to a string describing the error. For example, the call

```
puts(strerror(EDOM));
```

might print

```
Numerical argument out of domain
```

The argument to strerror is usually one of the values of errno, but strerror will return a string for any integer passed to it.

strerror is closely related to the perror function. The error message that perror displays is the same message that strerror would return if passed errno as its argument.

24.3   The `<signal.h>` Header: Signal Handling

The <signal.h> header provides facilities for handling exceptional conditions, known as *signals*. Signals fall into two categories: run-time errors (such as division by zero) and events caused outside the program. Many operating systems, for example, allow users to interrupt or kill running programs; these events are treated as signals in C. When an error or external event occurs, we say that a signal has been *raised*. Many signals are asynchronous: they can happen at any time during program execution, not just at certain points that are known to the programmer. Since signals may occur at unexpected times, they have to be dealt with in a unique way.

This section covers signals as they're described in the C standard. Signals play a more prominent role in UNIX than you might expect from their limited coverage here. For information about UNIX signals, consult one of the UNIX programming books listed in the bibliography.

Signal Macros

 <signal.h> defines a number of macros that represent signals; Table 24.1 lists these macros and their meanings. The value of each macro is a positive integer constant. C implementations are allowed to provide other signal macros, as long as their names begin with SIG followed by an upper-case letter. (UNIX implementations, in particular, provide a large number of additional signal macros.)

The C standard doesn't require that the signals in Table 24.1 be raised automatically, since not all of them may be meaningful for a particular computer and operating system. Most implementations support at least some of these signals.

Table 24.1
Signals

Name	Meaning
SIGABRT	Abnormal termination (possibly caused by a call of abort)
SIGFPE	Error during an arithmetic operation (possibly division by zero or overflow)
SIGILL	Invalid instruction
SIGINT	Interrupt
SIGSEGV	Invalid storage access
SIGTERM	Termination request

The `signal` Function

```
void (*signal(int sig, void (*func)(int)))(int);
```

signal

<signal.h> provides two functions: `raise` and `signal`. We'll start with `signal`, which installs a signal-handling function for use later if a given signal should occur. `signal` is much easier to use than you might expect from its rather intimidating prototype. Its first argument is the code for a particular signal; the second argument is a pointer to a function that will handle the signal if it's raised later in the program. For example, the following call of `signal` installs a handler for the `SIGINT` signal:

```
signal(SIGINT, handler);
```

`handler` is the name of a signal-handling function. If the `SIGINT` signal occurs later during program execution, `handler` will be called automatically.

Every signal-handling function must have an `int` parameter and a return type of `void`. When a particular signal is raised and its handler is called, the handler will be passed the code for the signal. Knowing which signal caused it to be called can be useful for a signal handler; in particular, it allows us to use the same handler for several different signals.

A signal-handling function can do a variety of things. Possibilities include ignoring the signal, performing some sort of error recovery, or terminating the program. Unless it's invoked by `abort` or `raise`, however, a signal handler shouldn't call a library function or attempt to use a variable with static storage duration. (There are a few exceptions to these rules, however.)

abort function ►*26.2*
static storage duration ►*18.2*

Q&A

If a signal-handling function returns, the program resumes executing from the point at which the signal occurred, except in two cases: (1) If the signal was `SIGABRT`, the program will terminate (abnormally) when the handler returns. (2) The effect of returning from a function that has handled `SIGFPE` is undefined. (In other words, don't do it.)

Although `signal` has a return value, it's often discarded. The return value, a pointer to the previous handler for the specified signal, can be saved in a variable if desired. In particular, if we plan to restore the original signal handler later, we need to save `signal`'s return value:

```
void (*orig_handler)(int);    /* function pointer variable */
...
```

```
orig_handler = signal(SIGINT, handler);
```

This statement installs `handler` as the handler for `SIGINT` and then saves a pointer to the original handler in the `orig_handler` variable. To restore the original handler later, we'd write

```
signal(SIGINT, orig_handler); /* restores original handler */
```

Predefined Signal Handlers

Instead of writing our own signal handlers, we have the option of using one of the predefined handlers that `<signal.h>` provides. There are two of these, each represented by a macro:

- **SIG_DFL.** `SIG_DFL` handles signals in a "default" way. To install `SIG_DFL`, we'd use a call such as

  ```
  signal(SIGINT, SIG_DFL);   /* use default handler */
  ```

  The effect of calling `SIG_DFL` is implementation-defined, but in most cases it causes program termination.

- **SIG_IGN.** The call

  ```
  signal(SIGINT, SIG_IGN);   /* ignore SIGINT signal */
  ```

  specifies that `SIGINT` is to be ignored if it should be raised later.

In addition to `SIG_DFL` and `SIG_IGN`, the `<signal.h>` header may provide other signal handlers; their names must begin with `SIG_` followed by an upper-case letter. At the beginning of program execution, the handler for each signal is initialized to either `SIG_DFL` or `SIG_IGN`, depending on the implementation.

`<signal.h>` defines another macro, `SIG_ERR`, that looks like it should be a signal handler. `SIG_ERR` is actually used to test for an error when installing a signal handler. If a call of `signal` is unsuccessful—it can't install a handler for the specified signal—it returns `SIG_ERR` and stores a positive value in `errno`. Thus, to test whether `signal` has failed, we could write

```
if (signal(SIGINT, handler) == SIG_ERR) {
  perror("signal(SIGINT, handler) failed");
  ...
}
```

There's one tricky aspect to the entire signal-handling mechanism: what happens if a signal is raised by the function that handles that signal? To prevent infinite recursion, the C89 standard prescribes a two-step process when a signal is raised for which a signal-handling function has been installed by the programmer. First, either the handler for that signal is reset to `SIG_DFL` (the default handler) or else the signal is blocked from occurring while the handler is executing. (`SIGILL` is a special case; neither action is required when `SIGILL` is raised.) Only then is the handler provided by the programmer called.

After a signal has been handled, whether or not the handler needs to be reinstalled is implementation-defined. UNIX implementations typically leave the signal handler installed after it's been used, but other implementations may reset the handler to `SIG_DFL`. In the latter case, the handler can reinstall itself by calling `signal` before it returns.

 C99 changes the signal-handling process in a few minor ways. When a signal is raised, an implementation may choose to disable not just that signal but others as well. If a signal-handling function returns from handling a `SIGILL` or `SIGSEGV` signal (as well as a `SIGFPE` signal), the effect is undefined. C99 also adds the restriction that if a signal occurs as a result of calling the `abort` function or the `raise` function, the signal handler itself must not call `raise`.

The `raise` Function

```
int raise(int sig);
```

raise   Although signals usually arise from run-time errors or external events, it's occasionally handy for a program to cause a signal to occur. The `raise` function does just that. The argument to `raise` specifies the code for the desired signal:

```
raise(SIGABRT);    /* raises the SIGABRT signal */
```

The return value of `raise` can be used to test whether the call was successful: zero indicates success, while a nonzero value indicates failure.

PROGRAM   **Testing Signals**

The following program illustrates the use of signals. First, it installs a custom handler for the `SIGINT` signal (carefully saving the original handler), then calls `raise_sig` to raise that signal. Next, it installs `SIG_IGN` as the handler for the `SIGINT` signal and calls `raise_sig` again. Finally, it reinstalls the original handler for `SIGINT`, then calls `raise_sig` one last time.

tsignal.c
```
/* Tests signals */

#include <signal.h>
#include <stdio.h>

void handler(int sig);
void raise_sig(void);

int main(void)
{
  void (*orig_handler)(int);
```

```
    printf("Installing handler for signal %d\n", SIGINT);
    orig_handler = signal(SIGINT, handler);
    raise_sig();

    printf("Changing handler to SIG_IGN\n");
    signal(SIGINT, SIG_IGN);
    raise_sig();

    printf("Restoring original handler\n");
    signal(SIGINT, orig_handler);
    raise_sig();

    printf("Program terminates normally\n");
    return 0;
}

void handler(int sig)
{
    printf("Handler called for signal %d\n", sig);
}

void raise_sig(void)
{
    raise(SIGINT);
}
```

Incidentally, the call of raise doesn't need to be in a separate function. I defined raise_sig simply to make a point: regardless of where a signal is raised—whether it's in main or in some other function—it will be caught by the most recently installed handler for that signal.

The output of this program can vary somewhat. Here's one possibility:

```
Installing handler for signal 2
Handler called for signal 2
Changing handler to SIG_IGN
Restoring original handler
```

From this output, we see that our implementation defines SIGINT to be 2 and that the original handler for SIGINT must have been SIG_DFL. (If it had been SIG_IGN, we'd also see the message Program terminates normally.) Finally, we observe that SIG_DFL caused the program to terminate without displaying an error message.

24.4 The `<setjmp.h>` Header: Nonlocal Jumps

```
int setjmp(jmp_buf env);
void longjmp(jmp_buf env, int val);
```

Normally, a function returns to the point at which it was called. We can't use a

goto statement ➤ 6.4

`goto` statement to make it go elsewhere, because a `goto` can jump only to a label within the same function. The `<setjmp.h>` header, however, makes it possible for one function to jump directly to another function without returning.

The most important items in `<setjmp.h>` are the `setjmp` macro and the `longjmp` function. `setjmp` "marks" a place in a program; `longjmp` can then be used to return to that place later. Although this powerful mechanism has a variety of potential applications, it's used primarily for error handling.

setjmp

To mark the target of a future jump, we call `setjmp`, passing it a variable of type `jmp_buf` (declared in `<setjmp.h>`). `setjmp` stores the current "environment" (including a pointer to the location of the `setjmp` itself) in the variable for later use in a call of `longjmp`; it then returns zero.

longjmp

Returning to the point of the `setjmp` is done by calling `longjmp`, passing it the same `jmp_buf` variable that we passed to `setjmp`. After restoring the environment represented by the `jmp_buf` variable, `longjmp` will—here's where it gets tricky—*return from the* `setjmp` *call*. `setjmp`'s return value this time is `val`, the second argument to `longjmp`. (If `val` is 0, `setjmp` returns 1.)

Be sure that the argument to `longjmp` was previously initialized by a call of `setjmp`. It's also important that the function containing the original call of `setjmp` must not have returned prior to the call of `longjmp`. If either restriction is violated, calling `longjmp` results in undefined behavior. (The program will probably crash.)

To summarize, `setjmp` returns zero the first time it's called; later, `longjmp` transfers control back to the original call of `setjmp`, which this time returns a nonzero value. Got it? Perhaps we need an example…

PROGRAM   **Testing `setjmp/longjmp`**

The following program uses `setjmp` to mark a place in `main`; the function `f2` later returns to that place by calling `longjmp`.

tsetjmp.c

```
/* Tests setjmp/longjmp */

#include <setjmp.h>
#include <stdio.h>

jmp_buf env;

void f1(void);
void f2(void);

int main(void)
{
  if (setjmp(env) == 0)
    printf("setjmp returned 0\n");
```

```
  else {
    printf("Program terminates: longjmp called\n");
    return 0;
  }

  f1();
  printf("Program terminates normally\n");
  return 0;
}

void f1(void)
{
  printf("f1 begins\n");
  f2();
  printf("f1 returns\n");
}

void f2(void)
{
  printf("f2 begins\n");
  longjmp(env, 1);
  printf("f2 returns\n");
}
```

The output of this program will be

```
setjmp returned 0
f1 begins
f2 begins
Program terminates: longjmp called
```

The original call of setjmp returns 0, so main calls f1. Next, f1 calls f2, which uses longjmp to transfer control back to main instead of returning to f1. When longjmp is executed, control goes back to the setjmp call. This time, setjmp returns 1 (the value specified in the longjmp call).

Q & A

Q: **You said that it's important to store zero in errno before calling a library function that may change it, but I've seen UNIX programs that test errno without ever setting it to zero. What's the story? [p. 629]**

A: UNIX programs often contain calls of functions that belong to the operating system. These *system calls* rely on errno, but they use it in a slightly different way than described in this chapter. When such a call fails, it returns a special value (such as –1 or a null pointer) in addition to storing a value in errno. Programs don't need to store zero in errno before such a call, because the function's return value alone indicates that an error occurred. Some functions in the C standard library work this way as well, using errno not so much to signal an error as to specify which error it was.

Q: My version of `<errno.h>` defines other macros besides `EDOM` and `ERANGE`. Is this practice legal? [p. 630]

A: Yes. The C standard allows macros that represent other error conditions, provided that their names begin with the letter E followed by a digit or an upper-case letter. UNIX implementations typically define a huge number of such macros.

Q: Some of the macros that represent signals have cryptic names, like `SIGFPE` and `SIGSEGV`. Where do these names come from? [p. 631]

A: The names of these signals date back to the early C compilers, which ran on a DEC PDP-11. The PDP-11 hardware could detect errors with names like "Floating Point Exception" and "Segmentation Violation."

Q: OK, I'm curious. Unless it's invoked by `abort` or `raise`, a signal handler shouldn't call a standard library function, but you said there were exceptions to this rule. What are they? [p. 632]

A: A signal handler is allowed to call the `signal` function, provided that the first argument is the signal that it's handling at the moment. This proviso is important, because it allows a signal handler to reinstall itself. In C99, a signal handler may also call the `abort` function or the `_Exit` function.

(C99)

_Exit function ➤26.2

*Q: Following up on the previous question, a signal handler normally isn't supposed to access variables with static storage duration. What's the exception to this rule?

A: That one's a bit harder. The answer involves a type named `sig_atomic_t` that's declared in the `<signal.h>` header. `sig_atomic_t` is an integer type that can be accessed "as an atomic entity," according to the C standard. In other words, the CPU can fetch a `sig_atomic_t` value from memory or store one in memory with a single machine instruction, rather than using two or more machine instructions. `sig_atomic_t` is often defined to be `int`, since most CPUs can load or store an `int` value in one instruction.

That brings us to the exception to the rule that a signal-handling function isn't supposed to access static variables. The C standard allows a signal handler to store a value in a `sig_atomic_t` variable—even one with static storage duration—provided that it's declared `volatile`. To see the reason for this arcane rule, consider what might happen if a signal handler were to modify a static variable that's of a type that's wider than `sig_atomic_t`. If the program had fetched part of the variable from memory just before the signal occurred, then completed the fetch after the signal is handled, it could end up with a garbage value. `sig_atomic_t` variables can be fetched in a single step, so this problem doesn't occur. Declaring the variable to be `volatile` warns the compiler that the variable's value may change at any time. (A signal could suddenly be raised, invoking a signal handler that modifies the variable.)

volatile type qualifier ➤20.3

Q: The `tsignal.c` program calls `printf` from inside a signal handler. Isn't that illegal?

A: A signal-handling function invoked as a result of `raise` or `abort` may call library functions. `tsignal.c` uses `raise` to invoke the signal handler.

Q: **How can `setjmp` modify the argument that's passed to it? I thought that C always passed arguments by value. [p. 636]**

A: The C standard says that `jmp_buf` must be an array type, so `setjmp` is actually being passed a pointer.

Q: **I'm having trouble with `setjmp`. Are there any restrictions on how it can be used?**

A: According to the C standard, there are only two legal ways to use `setjmp`:

- As the expression in an expression statement (possibly cast to `void`).

- As part of the controlling expression in an `if`, `switch`, `while`, `do`, or `for` statement. The entire controlling expression must have one of the following forms, where *constexpr* is an integer constant expression and *op* is a relational or equality operator:

```
setjmp (...)
!setjmp (...)
constexpr op setjmp (...)
setjmp (...) op constexpr
```

Using `setjmp` in any other way causes undefined behavior.

Q: **After a program has executed a call of `longjmp`, what are the values of the variables in the program?**

A: Most variables retain the values they had at the time of the `longjmp`. However, an automatic variable inside the function that contains the `setjmp` has an indeterminate value unless it was declared `volatile` or it hasn't been modified since the `setjmp` was performed.

Q: **Is it legal to call `longjmp` inside a signal handler?**

A: Yes, provided that the signal handler wasn't invoked because of a signal raised during the execution of a signal handler. (C99 removes this restriction.)

(C99)

Exercises

Section 24.1

1. (a) Assertions can be used to test for two kinds of problems: (1) problems that should never occur if the program is correct, and (2) problems that are beyond the control of the program. Explain why `assert` is best suited for problems in the first category.

   (b) Give three examples of problems that are beyond the control of the program.

2. Write a call of `assert` that causes a program to terminate if a variable named `top` has the value NULL.

3. Modify the stackADT2.c file of Section 19.4 so that it uses assert to test for errors instead of using if statements. (Note that the terminate function is no longer necessary and can be removed.)

Section 24.2   Ⓦ   4. (a) Write a "wrapper" function named try_math_fcn that calls a math function (assumed to have a double argument and return a double value) and then checks whether the call succeeded. Here's how we might use try_math_fcn:

```
y = try_math_fcn(sqrt, x, "Error in call of sqrt");
```

If the call sqrt(x) is successful, try_math_fcn returns the value computed by sqrt. If the call fails, try_math_fcn calls perror to print the message Error in call of sqrt, then calls exit to terminate the program.

(b) Write a macro that has the same effect as try_math_fcn but builds the error message from the function's name:

```
y = TRY_MATH_FCN(sqrt, x);
```

If the call of sqrt fails, the message will be Error in call of sqrt. *Hint:* Have TRY_MATH_FCN call try_math_fcn.

Section 24.4   Ⓦ   5. In the inventory.c program (see Section 16.3), the main function has a for loop that prompts the user to enter an operation code, reads the code, and then calls either insert, search, update, or print. Add a call of setjmp to main in such a way that a subsequent call of longjmp will return to the for loop. (After the longjmp, the user will be prompted for an operation code, and the program will continue normally.) setjmp will need a jmp_buf variable; where should it be declared?

25 International Features

If your computer speaks English
it was probably made in Japan.

For many years, C wasn't especially suitable for use in non-English-speaking countries. C originally assumed that characters were always single bytes and that all computers recognized the characters #, [, \,], ^, {, |, }, and ~, which are needed to write programs. Unfortunately, these assumptions aren't valid in all parts of the world. As a result, the experts who created C89 added language features and libraries in an effort to make C a more international language.

In 1994, Amendment 1 to the ISO C standard was approved, creating an enhanced version of C89 that's sometimes known as C94 or C95. This amendment provides additional library support for international programming via the digraph language feature and the `<iso646.h>`, `<wchar.h>`, and `<wctype.h>` headers. C99 adds even more support for internationalization in the form of universal character names. This chapter covers all of C's international features, whether they come from C89, Amendment 1, or C99. I'll flag the Amendment 1 changes as C99 changes, although they actually predate C99.

The `<locale.h>` header (Section 25.1) provides functions that allow a program to tailor its behavior to a particular "locale"—often a country or other geographical area in which a particular language is spoken. Multibyte characters and wide characters (Section 25.2) enable programs to work with large character sets such as those found in Asian countries. Digraphs, trigraphs, and the `<iso646.h>` header (Section 25.3) make it possible to write programs on computers that lack some of the characters normally used in C programming. Universal character names (Section 25.4) allow programmers to embed characters from the Universal Character Set into the source code of a program. The `<wchar.h>` header (Section 25.5) supplies functions for wide-character input/output and wide-string manipulation. Finally, the `<wctype.h>` header (Section 25.6) provides wide-character classification and case-mapping functions.

25.1   The `<locale.h>` Header: Localization

The `<locale.h>` header provides functions to control portions of the C library whose behavior varies from one locale to another. (A **locale** is typically a country or a region in which a particular language is spoken.)

Locale-dependent aspects of the library include:

- **Formatting of numerical quantities.** In some locales, for example, the decimal point is a period (297.48), while in others it's a comma (297,48).

- **Formatting of monetary quantities.** For example, the currency symbol varies from country to country.

- **Character set.** The character set often depends on the language in a particular locale. Asian countries usually require a much larger character set than Western countries.

- **Appearance of date and time.** In some locales, it's customary to put the month first when writing a date (8/24/2012); in others, the day goes first (24/8/2012).

Categories

By changing locale, a program can adapt its behavior to a different area of the world. But a locale change can affect many parts of the library, some of which we might prefer not to alter. Fortunately, we're not required to change all aspects of a locale at the same time. Instead, we can use one of the following macros to specify a **category:**

- `LC_COLLATE`. Affects the behavior of two string-comparison functions, `strcoll` and `strxfrm`. (Both functions are declared in `<string.h>`.)

> `<string.h>` header ➤23.6

- `LC_CTYPE`. Affects the behavior of the functions in `<ctype.h>` (except `isdigit` and `isxdigit`). Also affects the multibyte and wide-character functions discussed in this chapter.

> `<ctype.h>` header ➤23.5

- `LC_MONETARY`. Affects the monetary formatting information returned by the `localeconv` function.

- `LC_NUMERIC`. Affects the decimal-point character used by formatted I/O functions (like `printf` and `scanf`) and the numeric conversion functions (such as `strtod`) in `<stdlib.h>`. Also affects the nonmonetary formatting information returned by `localeconv`.

> numeric conversion functions ➤26.2

- `LC_TIME`. Affects the behavior of the `strftime` function (declared in `<time.h>`), which converts a time into a character string. In C99, also affects the behavior of the `wcsftime` function.

> strftime function ➤26.3
> **C99**
> wcsftime function ➤25.5

Implementations are free to provide additional categories and define `LC_` macros not listed above. For example, most UNIX systems provide an `LC_MESSAGES` category, which affects the format of affirmative and negative system responses.

The `setlocale` Function

```
char *setlocale(int category, const char *locale);
```

setlocale

The `setlocale` function changes the current locale, either for a single category or for all categories. If the first argument is one of the macros LC_COLLATE, LC_CTYPE, LC_MONETARY, LC_NUMERIC, or LC_TIME, a call of `setlocale` affects only a single category. If the first argument is LC_ALL, the call affects all categories. The C standard defines only two values for the second argument: `"C"` and `" "`. Other locales, if any, depend on the implementation.

At the beginning of program execution, the call

```
setlocale(LC_ALL, "C");
```

occurs behind the scenes. In the `"C"` locale, library functions behave in the "normal" way, and the decimal point is a period.

Changing locale after the program has begun execution requires an explicit call of `setlocale`. Calling `setlocale` with `" "` as the second argument switches to the ***native locale,*** allowing the program to adapt its behavior to the local environment. The C standard doesn't define the exact effect of switching to the native locale. Some implementations of `setlocale` check the execution environment (in the same way as `getenv`) for an environment variable with a particular name (perhaps the same as the category macro). Other implementations don't do anything at all. (The standard doesn't require `setlocale` to have any effect. Of course, a library whose version of `setlocale` does nothing isn't likely to sell too well in some parts of the world.)

getenv function ➤26.2

Locales

Locales other than `"C"` and `" "` vary from one compiler to another. The GNU C library, known as `glibc`, provides a `"POSIX"` locale, which is the same as the `"C"` locale. `glibc`, which is used by Linux, allows additional locales to be installed if desired. These locales have the form

language [*_territory*] [*.codeset*] [*@modifier*]

where each bracketed item is optional. Possible values for *language* are listed in a standard known as ISO 639, *territory* comes from another standard (ISO 3166), and *codeset* specifies a character set or an encoding of a character set. Here are a few examples:

```
"swedish"
"en_GB" (English – United Kingdom)
"en_IE" (English – Ireland)
"fr_CH" (French – Switzerland)
```

There are several variations on the `"en_IE"` locale, including `"en_IE@euro"` (using the euro currency), `"en_IE.iso88591"` (using the ISO/IEC 8859-1 character set),

UTF-8 ▸*25.2*

"en_IE.iso885915@euro" (using the ISO/IEC 8859-15 character set and the euro currency), and "en_IE.utf8" (using the UTF-8 encoding of the Unicode character set).

Linux and other versions of UNIX support the `locale` command, which can be used to get locale information. One use of the `locale` command is to get a list of all available locales, which can be done by entering

```
locale -a
```

at the command line.

Because locale information is becoming increasingly important, the Unicode Consortium created the Common Locale Data Repository (CLDR) project to establish a standard set of locales. More information about the CLDR project can be found at *www.unicode.org/cldr/*.

When a call of `setlocale` succeeds, it returns a pointer to a string associated with the category in the new locale. (The string might be the locale name itself, for example.) On failure, `setlocale` returns a null pointer.

`setlocale` can also be used as a query function. If its second argument is a null pointer, `setlocale` returns a pointer to a string associated with the category in the *current* locale. This feature is especially useful if the first argument is `LC_ALL`, since it allows us to fetch the current settings for all categories. A string returned by `setlocale` can be saved (by copying it into a variable) and then **Q&A** used in a later call of `setlocale`.

The `localeconv` Function

```
struct lconv *localeconv(void);
```

localeconv   Although we can ask `setlocale` about the current locale, the information that it returns isn't necessarily in the most useful form. To find out highly specific information about the current locale (What's the decimal-point character? What's the currency symbol?), we need `localeconv`, the only other function declared in `<locale.h>`.

`localeconv` returns a pointer to a structure of type `struct lconv`. The members of this structure contain detailed information about the current locale. The structure has static storage duration and may be modified by a later call of `localeconv` or `setlocale`. Be sure to extract the desired information from the `lconv` structure before it's wiped out by one of these functions.

Some members of the `lconv` structure have `char *` type; other members have `char` type. Table 25.1 lists the `char *` members. The first three members describe the formatting of nonmonetary quantities, while the others deal with monetary quantities. The table also shows the value of each member in the `"C"` locale (the default); a value of `" "` means "not available."

The `grouping` and `mon_grouping` members deserve special mention.

Table 25.1
char * Members of
lconv Structure

	Name	Value in "C" Locale	Description
Nonmonetary	decimal_point	"."	Decimal-point character
	thousands_sep	""	Character used to separate groups of digits before decimal point
	grouping	""	Sizes of digit groups
Monetary	mon_decimal_point	""	Decimal-point character
	mon_thousands_sep	""	Character used to separate groups of digits before decimal point
	mon_grouping	""	Sizes of digit groups
	positive_sign	""	String indicating nonnegative quantity
	negative_sign	""	String indicating negative quantity
	currency_symbol	""	Local currency symbol
	int_curr_symbol	""	International currency symbol[†]

[†]A three-letter abbreviation followed by a separator (often a space or a period). For example, the international currency symbols for Switzerland, the United Kingdom, and the United States are "CHF ", "GBP ", and "USD ", respectively.

Each character in these strings specifies the size of one group of digits. (Grouping takes place from right to left, starting at the decimal point.) A value of CHAR_MAX indicates that no further grouping is to be performed; 0 indicates that the previous element should be used for the remaining digits. For example, the string "\3" (\3 followed by \0) indicates that the first group should have 3 digits, then all other digits should be grouped in 3's as well.

The char members of the lconv structure are divided into two groups. The members of the first group (Table 25.2) affect the *local* formatting of monetary quantities. The members of the second group (Table 25.3) affect the *international* formatting of monetary quantities. All but one of the members in Table 25.3 were added in C99. As Tables 25.2 and 25.3 show, the value of each char member in the "C" locale is CHAR_MAX, which means "not available."

Table 25.2
char Members of
lconv Structure
(Local Formatting)

Name	Value in "C" Locale	Description
frac_digits	CHAR_MAX	Number of digits after decimal point
p_cs_precedes	CHAR_MAX	1 if currency_symbol precedes nonnegative quantity; 0 if it succeeds quantity
n_cs_precedes	CHAR_MAX	1 if currency_symbol precedes negative quantity; 0 if it succeeds quantity
p_sep_by_space	CHAR_MAX	Separation of currency_symbol and sign string from nonnegative quantity (see Table 25.4)
n_sep_by_space	CHAR_MAX	Separation of currency_symbol and sign string from negative quantity (see Table 25.4)
p_sign_posn	CHAR_MAX	Position of positive_sign for nonnegative quantity (see Table 25.5)
n_sign_posn	CHAR_MAX	Position of negative_sign for negative quantity (see Table 25.5)

Table 25.3
char Members of
lconv Structure
(International Formatting)

Name	Value in "C" Locale	Description
int_frac_digits	CHAR_MAX	Number of digits after decimal point
int_p_cs_precedes[†]	CHAR_MAX	1 if int_curr_symbol precedes nonnegative quantity; 0 if it succeeds quantity
int_n_cs_precedes[†]	CHAR_MAX	1 if int_curr_symbol precedes negative quantity; 0 if it succeeds quantity
int_p_sep_by_space[†]	CHAR_MAX	Separation of int_curr_symbol and sign string from nonnegative quantity (see Table 25.4)
int_n_sep_by_space[†]	CHAR_MAX	Separation of int_curr_symbol and sign string from negative quantity (see Table 25.4)
int_p_sign_posn[†]	CHAR_MAX	Position of positive_sign for nonnegative quantity (see Table 25.5)
int_n_sign_posn[†]	CHAR_MAX	Position of negative_sign for negative quantity (see Table 25.5)

[†]C99 only

Table 25.4 explains the meaning of the values of the p_sep_by_space, n_sep_by_space, int_p_sep_by_space, and int_n_sep_by_space members. The meaning of p_sep_by_space and n_sep_by_space has changed in C99. In C89, there are only two possible values for these members: 1 (if there's a space between currency_symbol and a monetary quantity) or 0 (if there's not).

Table 25.4
Values of
...sep_by_space
Members

Value	Meaning
0	No space separates currency symbol and quantity.
1	If currency symbol and sign are adjacent, a space separates them from quantity; otherwise, a space separates currency symbol from quantity.
2	If currency symbol and sign are adjacent, a space separates them; otherwise, a space separates sign from quantity.

Table 25.5 explains the meaning of the values of the p_sign_posn, n_sign_posn, int_p_sign_posn and int_n_sign_posn members.

Table 25.5
Values of
...sign_posn
Members

Value	Meaning
0	Parentheses surround quantity and currency symbol
1	Sign precedes quantity and currency symbol
2	Sign succeeds quantity and currency symbol
3	Sign immediately precedes currency symbol
4	Sign immediately succeeds currency symbol

To see how the members of the lconv structure might vary from one locale to another, let's look at two examples. Table 25.6 shows typical values of the monetary lconv members for the U.S.A. and Finland (which uses the euro as its currency).

Member	U.S.A.	Finland
mon_decimal_point	"."	","
mon_thousands_sep	","	" "
mon_grouping	"\3"	"\3"
positive_sign	""	""
negative_sign	"-"	"-"
currency_symbol	"$"	"EUR"
frac_digits	2	2
p_cs_precedes	1	0
n_cs_precedes	1	0
p_sep_by_space	0	2
n_sep_by_space	0	2
p_sign_posn	1	1
n_sign_posn	1	1
int_curr_symbol	"USD "	"EUR "
int_frac_digits	2	2
int_p_cs_precedes	1	0
int_n_cs_precedes	1	0
int_p_sep_by_space	1	2
int_n_sep_by_space	1	2
int_p_sign_posn	1	1
int_n_sign_posn	1	1

Here's how the monetary quantity 7593.86 would be formatted in the two locales, depending on the sign of the quantity and whether the formatting is local or international:

	U.S.A.	Finland
Local format (positive)	$7,593.86	7 593,86 EUR
Local format (negative)	-$7,593.86	- 7 593,86 EUR
International format (positive)	USD 7,593.86	7 593,86 EUR
International format (negative)	-USD 7,593.86	- 7 593,86 EUR

Keep in mind that none of C's library functions are able to format monetary quantities automatically. It's up to the programmer to use the information in the lconv structure to accomplish the formatting.

25.2   Multibyte Characters and Wide Characters

Latin-1 ►*7.3*

One of the biggest problems in adapting programs to different locales is the character-set issue. ASCII and its extensions, which include Latin-1, are the most popular character sets in North America. Elsewhere, the situation is more complicated. In many countries, computers employ character sets that are similar to ASCII, but lack certain characters; we'll discuss this issue further in Section 25.3. Other countries, especially those in Asia, face a different problem: written languages that require a very large character set, usually numbering in the thousands.

Changing the meaning of type char to handle larger character sets isn't possible, since char values are—by definition—limited to single bytes. Instead, C allows compilers to provide an ***extended character set.*** This character set may be used for writing C programs (in comments and strings, for example), in the environment in which the program is run, or in both places. C provides two techniques **Q&A** for encoding an extended character set: multibyte characters and wide characters. It also supplies functions that convert from one kind of encoding to the other.

Multibyte Characters

In a ***multibyte character*** encoding, each extended character is represented by a sequence of one or more bytes. The number of bytes may vary, depending on the character. C requires that any extended character set include certain essential characters (letters, digits, operators, punctuation, and white-space characters); these characters must be single bytes. Other bytes can be interpreted as the beginning of a multibyte character.

Japanese Character Sets

The Japanese employ several different writing systems. The most complex, *kanji*, consists of thousands of symbols—far too many to represent in a one-byte encoding. (*Kanji* symbols actually come from Chinese, which has a similar problem with large character sets.) There's no single way to encode *kanji*; common encodings include JIS (Japanese Industrial Standard), Shift-JIS (the most popular encoding), and EUC (Extended UNIX Code).

Some multibyte character sets rely on a ***state-dependent encoding.*** In this kind of encoding, each sequence of multibyte characters begins in an ***initial shift state.*** Certain bytes encountered later (known as a ***shift sequence***) may change the shift state, affecting the meaning of subsequent bytes. Japan's JIS encoding, for example, mixes one-byte codes with two-byte codes; "escape sequences" embedded in strings indicate when to switch between one-byte and two-byte modes. (In contrast, the Shift-JIS encoding is not state-dependent. Each character requires either one or two bytes, but the first byte of a two-byte character can always be distinguished from a one-byte character.)

In any encoding, the C standard requires that a zero byte always represent a null character, regardless of shift state. Also, a zero byte can't be the second (or later) byte of a multibyte character.

The C library provides two macros, MB_LEN_MAX and MB_CUR_MAX, that are related to multibyte characters. Both macros specify the maximum number of bytes in a multibyte character. MB_LEN_MAX (defined in <limits.h>) gives the maximum for any supported locale; MB_CUR_MAX (defined in <stdlib.h>) gives the maximum for the current locale. (Changing locales may affect the interpretation of multibyte characters.) Obviously, MB_CUR_MAX can't be larger than MB_LEN_MAX.

Any string may contain multibyte characters, although the length of such a string (as determined by the `strlen` function) is the number of bytes in the string, not the number of characters. In particular, the format strings in calls of the ...`printf` and ...`scanf` functions may contain multibyte characters. As a result, the C99 standard defines the term **multibyte string** to be a synonym for *string*.

Wide Characters

The other way to encode an extended character set is to use wide characters. A **wide character** is an integer whose value represents a character. Unlike multibyte characters, which may vary in length, all wide characters supported by a particular implementation require the same number of bytes. A **wide string** is a string consisting of wide characters, with a null wide character at the end. (A **null wide character** is a wide character whose numerical value is zero.)

Wide characters have the type `wchar_t` (declared in `<stddef.h>` and certain other headers), which must be an integer type able to represent the largest extended character set for any supported locale. For example, if two bytes are enough to represent any extended character set, then `wchar_t` could be defined as `unsigned short int`.

C supports both wide character constants and wide string literals. Wide character constants resemble ordinary character constants but are prefixed by the letter `L`:

```
L'a'
```

Wide string literals are also prefixed by `L`:

```
L"abc"
```

This string represents an array containing the wide characters `L'a'`, `L'b'`, and `L'c'`, followed by a null wide character.

Unicode and the Universal Character Set

The differences between multibyte characters and wide characters become apparent when discussing **Unicode.** Unicode is an enormous character set developed by the Unicode Consortium, an organization established by a group of computer manufacturers to create an international character set for computer use. The first 256 characters of Unicode are identical to Latin-1 (and therefore the first 128 characters of Unicode match the ASCII character set). However, Unicode goes far beyond Latin-1, providing the characters needed for nearly all modern and ancient languages. Unicode also includes a number of specialized symbols, such as those used in mathematics and music. The Unicode standard was first published in 1991.

Unicode is closely related to international standard ISO/IEC 10646, which defines a character encoding known as the **Universal Character Set (UCS)**. UCS was developed by the International Organization for Standardization (ISO), starting at about the same time that Unicode was initially defined. Although UCS originally differed from Unicode, the two character sets were later unified. ISO now works closely with the Unicode Consortium to ensure that ISO/IEC 10646 remains consistent with Unicode. Because Unicode and UCS are so similar, I'll use the two terms interchangeably.

Unicode was originally limited to 65,536 characters (the number of characters that can be represented using 16 bits). That limit was later found to be insufficient; Unicode currently has over 100,000 characters. (For the most recent version, visit *www.unicode.org*.) The first 65,536 characters of Unicode—which include the most frequently used characters—are known as the **Basic Multilingual Plane (BMP)**.

Encodings of Unicode

Unicode assigns a unique number (known as a **code point**) to each character. There are a number of ways to represent these code points using bytes; I'll mention two of the simpler techniques. One of these encodings uses wide characters; the other uses multibyte characters.

UCS-2 is a wide-character encoding in which each Unicode code point is stored as two bytes. UCS-2 can represent all the characters in the Basic Multilingual Plane (those with code points between 0000 and FFFF in hexadecimal), but it is unable to represent Unicode characters that don't belong to the BMP.

A popular alternative is the **8-bit UCS Transformation Format (UTF-8)**, which uses multibyte characters. UTF-8 was devised by Ken Thompson and his Bell Labs colleague Rob Pike in 1992. (Yes, that's the same Ken Thompson who designed the B language, the predecessor of C.) UTF-8 has the useful property that ASCII characters look identical in UTF-8: each character is one byte and has the same binary encoding. Thus, software designed to read UTF-8 data can also handle ASCII data with no change. For these reasons, UTF-8 is widely used on the Internet for text-based applications such as web pages and email.

In UTF-8, each code point requires between one and four bytes. UTF-8 is organized so that the most commonly used characters require fewer bytes, as shown in Table 25.7.

Table 25.7
UTF-8 Encoding

Code Point Range (Hexadecimal)	UTF-8 Byte Sequence (Binary)
000000-00007F	0xxxxxxx
000080-0007FF	110xxxxx 10xxxxxx
000800-00FFFF	1110xxxx 10xxxxxx 10xxxxxx
010000-10FFFF	11110xxx 10xxxxxx 10xxxxxx 10xxxxxx

UTF-8 takes the bits in the code point value, divides them into groups (represented by the x's in Table 25.7), and assigns each group to a different byte. The simplest case is a code point in the range 0–7F (an ASCII character), which is represented by a 0 followed by the seven bits in the original number.

A code point in the range 80–7FF (which includes all the Latin-1 characters) would have its bits split into groups of five bits and six bits. The five-bit group is prefixed by 110 and the six-bit group is prefixed by 10. For example, the code point for the character *ä* is E4 (hexadecimal) or 11100100 (binary). In UTF-8, it would be represented by the two-byte sequence 110<u>00011</u> 10<u>100100</u>. Note how the underlined portions, when joined together, spell out 00011100100.

Characters whose code points fall in the range 800–FFFF, which includes the remaining characters in the Basic Multilingual Plane, require three bytes. All other Unicode characters (most of them rarely used) are assigned four bytes.

UTF-8 has a number of useful properties:

- Each of the 128 ASCII characters is represented by one byte. A string consisting solely of ASCII characters looks exactly the same in UTF-8.

- Any byte in a UTF-8 string whose leftmost bit is 0 must be an ASCII character, because all other bytes begin with a 1 bit.

- The first byte of a multibyte character indicates how long the character will be. If the number of 1 bits at the beginning of the byte is two, the character is two bytes long. If the number of 1 bits is three or four, the character is three or four bytes long, respectively.

- Every other byte in a multibyte sequence has 10 as its leftmost bits.

The last three properties are especially important, because they guarantee that no sequence of bytes within a multibyte character can possibly represent another valid multibyte character. This makes it possible to search a multibyte string for a particular character or sequence of characters by simply doing byte comparisons.

So how does UTF-8 stack up against UCS-2? UCS-2 has the advantage that characters are stored in their most natural form. On the other hand, UTF-8 can handle all Unicode characters (not just those in the BMP), often requires less space than UCS-2, and retains compatibility with ASCII. UCS-2 isn't nearly as popular as UTF-8, although it was used in the Windows NT operating system. A newer version that uses four bytes (*UCS-4*) is gradually taking its place. Some systems extend UCS-2 into a multibyte encoding by allowing a variable number of byte pairs to represent a character (unlike UCS-2, which uses a single byte pair per character). This encoding, known as *UTF-16,* has the advantage that it's compatible with UCS-2.

Multibyte/Wide-Character Conversion Functions

```
int mblen(const char *s, size_t n);        from <stdlib.h>
int mbtowc(wchar_t * restrict pwc,
           const char * restrict s,
           size_t n);                       from <stdlib.h>
int wctomb(char *s, wchar_t wc);            from <stdlib.h>
```

Although the C89 standard introduced the concepts of multibyte characters and wide characters, it provides only five functions for working with these kinds of characters. We'll now describe these functions, which belong to the `<stdlib.h>` header. C99's `<wchar.h>` and `<wctype.h>` headers, which are discussed in Sections 25.5 and 25.6, supply a number of additional multibyte and wide-character functions.

C89's multibyte/wide-character functions are divided into two groups. The first group converts single characters from multibyte form to wide form and vice versa. The behavior of these functions depends on the `LC_CTYPE` category of the current locale. If the multibyte encoding is state-dependent, the behavior also depends on the current ***conversion state.*** The conversion state consists of the current shift state as well as the current position within a multibyte character. Calling any of these functions with a null pointer as the value of its `char *` parameter sets the function's internal conversion state to the ***initial conversion state,*** signifying that no multibyte character is yet in progress and that the initial shift state is in effect. Later calls of the function cause its internal conversion state to be updated.

mblen

The `mblen` function checks whether its first argument points to a series of bytes that form a valid multibyte character. If so, the function returns the number of bytes in the character; if not, it returns –1. As a special case, `mblen` returns 0 if the first argument points to a null character. The second argument limits the number of bytes that `mblen` will examine; typically, we'll pass `MB_CUR_MAX`.

The following function, which comes from P. J. Plauger's *The Standard C Library*, uses `mblen` to determine whether a string consists of valid multibyte characters. The function returns zero if s points to a valid string.

```
int mbcheck(const char *s)
{
  int n;

  for (mblen(NULL, 0); ; s += n)
    if ((n = mblen(s, MB_CUR_MAX)) <= 0)
      return n;
}
```

Two aspects of the `mbcheck` function deserve special mention. First, there's the mysterious call `mblen(NULL, 0)`, which sets `mblen`'s internal conversion state to the initial conversion state (in case the multibyte encoding is state-dependent). Second, there's the matter of termination. Keep in mind that s points to an ordinary character string, which is assumed to end with a null character. `mblen` will return zero when it reaches this null character, causing `mbcheck` to return. `mbcheck` will return sooner if `mblen` returns –1 because of an invalid multibyte character.

mbtowc

The `mbtowc` function converts a multibyte character (pointed to by the second argument) into a wide character. The first argument points to a `wchar_t` variable into which the function will store the result. The third argument limits the number of bytes that `mbtowc` will examine. `mbtowc` returns the same value as `mblen`: the number of bytes in the multibyte character if it's valid, –1 if it's not, and zero if the second argument points to a null character.

wctomb   The wctomb function converts a wide character (the second argument) into a multibyte character, which it stores into the array pointed to by the first argument. wctomb may store as many as MB_LEN_MAX characters in the array, but doesn't append a null character. wctomb returns the number of bytes in the multibyte character or −1 if the wide character doesn't correspond to any valid multibyte character. (Note that wctomb returns 1 if asked to convert a null wide character.)

The following function (also from Plauger's *The Standard C Library*) uses wctomb to determine whether a string of wide characters can be converted to valid multibyte characters:

```
int wccheck(wchar_t *wcs)
{
  char buf[MB_LEN_MAX];
  int n;

  for (wctomb(NULL, 0); ; ++wcs)
    if ((n = wctomb(buf, *wcs)) <= 0)
      return -1;                    /* invalid character */
    else if (buf[n-1] == '\0')
      return 0;                     /* all characters are valid */
}
```

Incidentally, all three functions—mblen, mbtowc, and wctomb—can be used to test whether a multibyte encoding is state-dependent. When passed a null pointer as its char * argument, each function returns a nonzero value if multibyte characters have state-dependent encodings or zero if they don't.

Multibyte/Wide-String Conversion Functions

```
size_t mbstowcs(wchar_t * restrict pwcs,
                const char * restrict s,
                size_t n);                  from <stdlib.h>
size_t wcstombs(char * restrict s,
                const wchar_t * restrict pwcs,
                size_t n);                  from <stdlib.h>
```

The remaining C89 multibyte/wide-character functions convert a string containing multibyte characters to a wide-character string and vice versa. How the conversion is performed depends on the LC_CTYPE category of the current locale.

mbstowcs   The mbstowcs function converts a sequence of multibyte characters into wide characters. The second argument points to an array containing the multibyte characters to be converted. The first argument points to a wide-character array; the third argument limits the number of wide characters that can be stored in the array. mbstowcs stops when it reaches the limit or encounters a null character (which it stores in the wide-character array). It returns the number of array elements modified, not including the terminating null wide character, if any. mbstowcs returns −1 (cast to type size_t) if it encounters an invalid multibyte character.

wcstombs   The wcstombs function is the opposite of mbstowcs: it converts a sequence of wide characters into multibyte characters. The second argument points to the wide-character string. The first argument points to the array in which the multibyte characters are to be stored. The third argument limits the number of bytes that can be stored in the array. wcstombs stops when it reaches the limit or encounters a null character (which it stores). It returns the number of bytes stored, not including the terminating null character, if any. wcstombs returns –1 (cast to type size_t) if it encounters a wide character that doesn't correspond to any multibyte character.

The mbstowcs function assumes that the string to be converted begins in the initial shift state. The string created by wcstombs always begins in the initial shift state.

25.3 Digraphs and Trigraphs

Programmers in certain countries have traditionally had trouble entering C programs because their keyboards lacked some of the characters that are required by C. This has been especially true in Europe, where older keyboards provided the accented characters used in European languages in place of the characters that C needs, such as #, [, \,], ^, {, |, }, and ~. C89 introduced trigraphs—three-character codes that represent problematic characters—as a solution to this problem. Trigraphs proved to be unpopular, however, so Amendment 1 to the standard added two improvements: digraphs, which are more readable than trigraphs, and the <iso646.h> header, which defines macros that represent certain C operators.

Trigraphs

A **trigraph sequence** (or simply, a **trigraph**) is a three-character code that can be used as an alternative to an ASCII character. Table 25.8 gives a complete list of trigraphs. All trigraphs begin with ??, which makes them, if not exactly attractive, at least easy to spot.

Table 25.8
Trigraph Sequences

Trigraph Sequence	ASCII Equivalent
??=	#
??(	[
??/	\
??)	]
??'	^
??<	{
??!	|
??>	}
??-	~

Trigraphs can be freely substituted for their ASCII equivalents. For example, the program

```
#include <stdio.h>

int main(void)
{
  printf("hello, world\n");
  return 0;
}
```

could be written

```
??=include <stdio.h>

int main(void)
??<
  printf("hello, world??/n");
  return 0;
??>
```

Compilers that conform to the C89 or C99 standards are required to accept trigraphs, even though they're rarely used. Occasionally, this feature can cause problems.

> Be careful about putting ?? in a string literal—it's possible that the compiler will treat it as the beginning of a trigraph. If this should happen, turn the second ? character into an escape sequence by preceding it with a \ character. The resulting ?\? combination can't be mistaken for the beginning of a trigraph.

 Digraphs

Acknowledging that trigraphs are difficult to read, Amendment 1 to the C89 standard added an alternative notation known as **_digraphs._** As the name implies, a digraph requires just two characters instead of three. Digraphs are available as substitutes for the six tokens shown in Table 25.9.

tokens ➤ 2.8

Table 25.9
Digraphs

Digraph	Token
<:	[
:>	]
<%	{
%>	}
%:	#
%:%:	##

Digraphs—unlike trigraphs—are *token* substitutes, not *character* substitutes. Thus, digraphs won't be recognized inside a string literal or character constant. For example, the string `"<::>"` has length four; it contains the characters: <, :, :, and >, not the characters [and]. In contrast, the string "??(??)" has length two, because the compiler replaces the trigraph ??(by the character [and the trigraph ??) by the character].

Digraphs are more limited than trigraphs. First, as we've seen, digraphs are of no use inside a string literal or character constant; trigraphs are still needed in these situations. Second, digraphs don't solve the problem of providing alternate representations for the characters \, ^, |, and ~. The <iso646.h> header, described next, helps with this problem.

C99 **The <iso646.h> Header: Alternative Spellings**

The <iso646.h> header is quite simple. It contains nothing but the definitions of the eleven macros shown in Table 25.10. Each macro represents a C operator that contains one of the characters &, |, ~, !, or ^, making it possible to use the operators listed in the table even when these characters are absent from the keyboard.

Table 25.10
Macros Defined in
<iso646.h>

Macro	Value
and	&&
and_eq	&=
bitand	&
bitor		
compl	~
not	!
not_eq	!=
or	||
or_eq	|=
xor	^
xor_eq	^=

The name of the header comes from ISO/IEC 646, an older standard for an ASCII-like character set. This standard allows for "national variants," in which countries substitute local characters for certain ASCII characters, thereby causing the problem that digraphs and the <iso646.h> header are trying to solve.

25.4 Universal Character Names (C99)

Section 25.2 discussed the Universal Character Set (UCS), which is closely related to Unicode. C99 provides a special feature, ***universal character names,*** that allows us to use UCS characters in the source code of a program.

A universal character name resembles an escape sequence. However, unlike ordinary escape sequences, which can appear only in character constants and string literals, universal character names may also be used in identifiers. This feature allows programmers to use their native languages when defining names for variables, functions, and the like.

There are two ways to write a universal character name (\u*dddd* and \U*dddddddd*), where each *d* is a hexadecimal digit. In the form \U*dddddddd*, the *d*'s form an eight-digit hexadecimal number that identifies the UCS code point of the desired character. The form \u*dddd* can be used for characters whose code points have hexadecimal values of FFFF or less, which includes all characters in the Basic Multilingual Plane.

For example, the UCS code point for the Greek letter β is 000003B2, so the universal character name for this character is \U000003B2 (or \U000003b2, since the case of hexadecimal digits doesn't matter). Because the first four hexadecimal digits of the UCS code point are 0, we can also use the \u notation, writing the character as \u03B2 or \u03b2. The code point values for UCS (which match those for Unicode) can be found at *www.unicode.org/charts/*.

Not all universal character names may be used in identifiers; the C99 standard contains a list of which ones are allowed. Also, an identifier may not begin with a universal character name that represents a digit.

25.5 The `<wchar.h>` Header (C99)
Extended Multibyte and Wide-Character Utilities

The `<wchar.h>` header provides functions for wide-character input/output and wide-string manipulation. The vast majority of functions in `<wchar.h>` are wide-character versions of functions from other headers (primarily `<stdio.h>` and `<string.h>`).

The `<wchar.h>` header declares several types and macros, including the following:

- `mbstate_t` — A value of this type can be used to store the conversion state when a sequence of multibyte characters is converted to a sequence of wide characters or vice versa.

- `wint_t` — An integer type whose values represent extended characters.

EOF macro ➤22.2
- `WEOF` — A macro representing a `wint_t` value that's different from any extended character. `WEOF` is used in much the same way as `EOF`, typically to indicate an error or end-of-file condition.

Note that `<wchar.h>` provides functions for wide characters but not multibyte characters. That's because C's ordinary library functions are capable of dealing with multibyte characters, so no special functions are needed. For example, the `fprintf` function allows its format string to contain multibyte characters.

Most wide-character functions behave the same as a function that belongs to another part of the standard library. Usually, the only changes involve arguments and return values of type `wchar_t` instead of `char` (or `wchar_t *` instead of `char *`). In addition, arguments and return values that represent character counts are measured in wide characters rather than bytes. In the remainder of this section, I'll indicate which other library function (if any) corresponds to each wide-character function. I won't discuss the wide-character function further unless there's a significant difference between it and its "non-wide" counterpart.

Stream Orientation

Before we look at the input/output functions provided by `<wchar.h>`, it's important to understand *stream orientation,* a concept that doesn't exist in C89.

Every stream is either ***byte-oriented*** (the traditional orientation) or ***wide-oriented*** (data is written to the stream as wide characters). When a stream is first

standard streams ➤22.1

opened, it has no orientation. (In particular, the standard streams `stdin`, `stdout`, and `stderr` have no orientation at the beginning of program execution.) Performing an operation on the stream using a byte input/output function causes the stream to become byte-oriented; performing an operation using a wide-character input/output function causes the stream to become wide-oriented. The orientation of a stream can also be selected by calling the `fwide` function (described later in this section). A stream retains its orientation as long as it remains open. Calling the

freopen function ➤22.2

`freopen` function to reopen the stream will remove its orientation.

When wide characters are written to a wide-oriented stream, they are converted to multibyte characters before being stored in the file that is associated with the stream. Conversely, when input is read from a wide-oriented stream, the multibyte characters found in the stream are converted to wide characters. The multibyte encoding used in a file is similar to that used for characters and strings within a program, except that encodings used in files may contain embedded null bytes.

Each wide-oriented stream has an associated `mbstate_t` object, which keeps track of the stream's conversion state. An encoding error occurs when a wide character written to a stream doesn't correspond to any multibyte character, or when a sequence of characters read from a stream doesn't form a valid multibyte character. In either case, the value of the `EILSEQ` macro (defined in the `<errno.h>` header)

errno variable ➤24.2

is stored in the `errno` variable to indicate the nature of the error.

Once a stream is byte-oriented, it's illegal to apply a wide-character input/output function to that stream. Similarly, it's illegal to apply a byte input/output function to a wide-oriented stream. Other stream functions may be applied to streams of either orientation, although there are a few special considerations for wide-oriented streams:

- Binary wide-oriented streams are subject to the file-positioning restrictions of both text and binary streams.

- After a file-positioning operation on a wide-oriented stream, a wide-character output function may end up overwriting part of a multibyte character. Doing so leaves the rest of the file in an indeterminate state.

fgetpos function ➤22.7

fsetpos function ➤22.7

- Calling `fgetpos` for a wide-oriented stream retrieves the stream's `mbstate_t` object as part of the `fpos_t` object associated with the stream. A later call of `fsetpos` using this `fpos_t` object will restore the `mbstate_t` object to its previous value.

Formatted Wide-Character Input/Output Functions

```
int fwprintf(FILE * restrict stream,
             const wchar_t * restrict format, ...);
int fwscanf(FILE * restrict stream,
            const wchar_t * restrict format, ...);
int swprintf(wchar_t * restrict s, size_t n,
             const wchar_t * restrict format, ...);
int swscanf(const wchar_t * restrict s,
            const wchar_t * restrict format, ...);
int vfwprintf(FILE * restrict stream,
              const wchar_t * restrict format,
              va_list arg);
int vfwscanf(FILE * restrict stream,
             const wchar_t * restrict format,
             va_list arg);
int vswprintf(wchar_t * restrict s, size_t n,
              const wchar_t * restrict format,
              va_list arg);
int vswscanf(const wchar_t * restrict s,
             const wchar_t * restrict format,
             va_list arg);
int vwprintf(const wchar_t * restrict format,
             va_list arg);
int vwscanf(const wchar_t * restrict format,
            va_list arg);
int wprintf(const wchar_t * restrict format, ...);
int wscanf(const wchar_t * restrict format, ...);
```

The functions in this group are wide-character versions of the formatted input/output functions found in `<stdio.h>` and described in Section 22.3. The `<wchar.h>` functions have arguments of type `wchar_t *` instead of `char *`, but their behavior is mostly the same as the `<stdio.h>` functions. Table 25.11 shows the correspondence between the `<stdio.h>` functions and their wide-character counterparts. Unless mentioned otherwise, each function in the left column behaves the same as the function(s) to its right.

All functions in this group share several characteristics:

- All have a format string, which consists of *wide* characters.
- ...`printf` functions, which return the number of characters written, now return the count in *wide* characters.
- The `%n` conversion specifier refers to the number of *wide* characters written so far (in the case of a ...`printf` function) or read so far (in the case of a ...`scanf` function).

Table 25.11
Formatted Wide-Character
Input/Output Functions
and Their `<stdio.h>`
Equivalents

`<wchar.h>` *Function*	`<stdio.h>` *Equivalent*
fwprintf	fprintf
fwscanf	fscanf
swprintf	snprintf, sprintf
swscanf	sscanf
vfwprintf	vfprintf
vfwscanf	vfscanf
vswprintf	vsnprintf, vsprintf
vswscanf	vsscanf
vwprintf	vprintf
vwscanf	vscanf
wprintf	printf
wscanf	scanf

fwprintf

Additional differences between `fwprintf` and `fprintf` include the following:

■ The `%c` conversion specifier is used when the corresponding argument has type `int`. If the `l` length modifier is present (making the conversion `%lc`), the argument is assumed to have type `wint_t`. In either case, the corresponding argument is written as a wide character.

■ The `%s` conversion specifier is used with a pointer to a character array, which may contain multibyte characters. (`fprintf` has no special provision for multibyte characters.) If the `l` length modifier is present, as in `%ls`, the corresponding argument should be an array containing wide characters. In either case, the characters in the array are written as wide characters. (With `fprintf`, the `%ls` specification also indicates an array of wide characters, but they're converted to multibyte characters before being written.)

fwscanf

Unlike `fscanf`, the `fwscanf` function reads wide characters. The `%c`, `%s`, and `%[` conversions require special mention. Each of these causes wide characters to be read and then converted to multibyte characters before being stored in a character array. `fwscanf` uses an `mbstate_t` object to keep track of the state of the conversion during this process; the object is set to zero at the beginning of each conversion. If the `l` length modifier is present (making the conversion `%lc`, `%ls`, or `%l[`), then the input characters are not converted but instead are stored directly in an array of `wchar_t` elements. Thus, it's necessary to use `%ls` when reading a string of wide characters if the intent is to store them as wide characters. If `%s` is used instead, wide characters will be read from the input stream but converted to multibyte characters before being stored.

swprintf

`swprintf` writes wide characters into an array of `wchar_t` elements. It's similar to `sprintf` and `snprintf` but not identical to either one. Like `snprintf`, it uses the parameter `n` to limit the number of (wide) characters that it will write. However, `swprintf` returns the number of wide characters actually written, not including the null character. In this respect, it resembles `sprintf` rather than `snprintf`, which returns the number of characters that would have been written (not including the null character) had there been no length restriction.

swprintf returns a negative value if the number of wide characters to be written is n or more, which differs from the behavior of both sprintf and snprintf.

vswprintf   vswprintf is equivalent to swprintf, with arg replacing the variable argument list of swprintf. Like swprintf, which is similar—but not identical—to sprintf and snprintf, the vswprintf function is a combination of vsprintf and vsnprintf. If an attempt is made to write n or more wide characters, vswprintf returns a negative integer, in a manner similar to swprintf.

Wide-Character Input/Output Functions

```
wint_t fgetwc(FILE *stream);
wchar_t *fgetws(wchar_t * restrict s, int n,
                FILE * restrict stream);
wint_t fputwc(wchar_t c, FILE *stream);
int fputws(const wchar_t * restrict s,
                FILE * restrict stream);
int fwide(FILE *stream, int mode);
wint_t getwc(FILE *stream);
wint_t getwchar(void);
wint_t putwc(wchar_t c, FILE *stream);
wint_t putwchar(wchar_t c);
wint_t ungetwc(wint_t c, FILE *stream);
```

The functions in this group are wide-character versions of the character input/output functions found in <stdio.h> and described in Section 22.4. Table 25.12 shows the correspondence between the <stdio.h> functions and their wide-character counterparts. As the table shows, fwide is the only truly new function.

Table 25.12
Wide-Character Input/
Output Functions and
Their <stdio.h>
Equivalents

<wchar.h> Function	*<stdio.h> Equivalent*
fgetwc	fgetc
fgetws	fgets
fputwc	fputc
fputws	fputs
fwide	–
getwc	getc
getwchar	getchar
putwc	putc
putwchar	putchar
ungetwc	ungetc

Unless otherwise indicated, you can assume that each <wchar.h> function listed in Table 25.12 behaves like the corresponding <stdio.h> function. However, one minor difference is common to most of these functions. To indicate an error or end-of-file condition, some <stdio.h> character I/O functions return EOF. The equivalent <wchar.h> functions return WEOF instead.

fgetwc
getwc
getwchar
fgetws

There's another twist that affects the wide-character input functions. A call of a function that reads a single character (fgetwc, getwc, and getwchar) may fail because the bytes found in the input stream don't form a valid wide character or there aren't enough bytes available. The result is an encoding error, which causes the function to store EILSEQ in errno and return WEOF. The fgetws function, which reads a string of wide characters, may also fail because of an encoding error, in which case it returns a null pointer.

fputwc
putwc
putwchar
fputws

Wide-character output functions may also encounter encoding errors. Functions that write a single character (fputwc, putwc, and putwchar) store EILSEQ in errno and return WEOF if an encoding error occurs. However, the fputws function, which writes a wide-character string, is different: it returns EOF (not WEOF) if an encoding error occurs.

fwide

The fwide function doesn't correspond to any C89 function. fwide is used to determine the current orientation of a stream and, if desired, attempt to set its orientation. The mode parameter determines the behavior of the function:

- mode > 0. Attempts to make the stream wide-oriented if it has no orientation.
- mode < 0. Attempts to make the stream byte-oriented if it has no orientation.
- mode = 0. The orientation is not changed.

fwide doesn't change the orientation if the stream already has one.

The value returned by fwide depends on the orientation of the stream *after* the call. The return value is positive if the stream has wide orientation, negative if it has byte orientation, and zero if it has no orientation.

General Wide-String Utilities

The <wchar.h> header provides a number of functions that perform operations on wide strings. These are wide-character versions of functions that belong to the <stdlib.h> and <string.h> headers.

Wide-String Numeric Conversion Functions

```
double wcstod(const wchar_t * restrict nptr,
              wchar_t ** restrict endptr);
float wcstof(const wchar_t * restrict nptr,
             wchar_t ** restrict endptr);
long double wcstold(const wchar_t * restrict nptr,
                    wchar_t ** restrict endptr);
long int wcstol(const wchar_t * restrict nptr,
                wchar_t ** restrict endptr,
                int base);
long long int wcstoll(const wchar_t * restrict nptr,
                      wchar_t ** restrict endptr,
                      int base);
```

```
unsigned long int wcstoul(
                        const wchar_t * restrict nptr,
                        wchar_t ** restrict endptr,
                        int base);
unsigned long long int wcstoull(
                        const wchar_t * restrict nptr,
                        wchar_t ** restrict endptr,
                        int base);
```

The functions in this group are wide-character versions of the numeric conversion functions found in `<stdlib.h>` and described in Section 26.2. The `<wchar.h>` functions have arguments of type wchar_t * and wchar_t ** instead of char * and char **, but their behavior is mostly the same as the `<stdlib.h>` functions. Table 25.13 shows the correspondence between the `<stdlib.h>` functions and their wide-character counterparts.

Table 25.13
Wide-String Numeric
Conversion Functions and
Their `<stdlib.h>`
Equivalents

`<wchar.h>` *Function*	`<stdlib.h>` *Equivalent*
wcstod	strtod
wcstof	strtof
wcstold	strtold
wcstol	strtol
wcstoll	strtoll
wcstoul	strtoul
wcstoull	strtoull

Wide-String Copying Functions

```
wchar_t *wcscpy(wchar_t * restrict s1,
                const wchar_t * restrict s2);
wchar_t *wcsncpy(wchar_t * restrict s1,
                 const wchar_t * restrict s2,
                 size_t n);
wchar_t *wmemcpy(wchar_t * restrict s1,
                 const wchar_t * restrict s2,
                 size_t n);
wchar_t *wmemmove(wchar_t *s1, const wchar_t *s2,
                  size_t n);
```

The functions in this group are wide-character versions of the string copying functions found in `<string.h>` and described in Section 23.6. The `<wchar.h>` functions have arguments of type wchar_t * instead of char *, but their behavior is mostly the same as the `<string.h>` functions. Table 25.14 shows the correspondence between the `<string.h>` functions and their wide-character counterparts.

<wchar.h> Function	*<string.h> Equivalent*
wcscpy	strcpy
wcsncpy	strncpy
wmemcpy	memcpy
wmemmove	memmove

Wide-String Concatenation Functions

```
wchar_t *wcscat(wchar_t * restrict s1,
                const wchar_t * restrict s2);
wchar_t *wcsncat(wchar_t * restrict s1,
                 const wchar_t * restrict s2,
                 size_t n);
```

The functions in this group are wide-character versions of the string concatenation functions found in <string.h> and described in Section 23.6. The <wchar.h> functions have arguments of type wchar_t * instead of char *, but their behavior is mostly the same as the <string.h> functions. Table 25.15 shows the correspondence between the <string.h> functions and their wide-character counterparts.

<wchar.h> Function	*<string.h> Equivalent*
wcscat	strcat
wcsncat	strncat

Wide-String Comparison Functions

```
int wcscmp(const wchar_t *s1, const wchar_t *s2);
int wcscoll(const wchar_t *s1, const wchar_t *s2);
int wcsncmp(const wchar_t *s1, const wchar_t *s2,
            size_t n);
size_t wcsxfrm(wchar_t * restrict s1,
               const wchar_t * restrict s2,
               size_t n);
int wmemcmp(const wchar_t * s1, const wchar_t * s2,
            size_t n);
```

The functions in this group are wide-character versions of the string comparison functions found in <string.h> and described in Section 23.6. The <wchar.h> functions have arguments of type wchar_t * instead of char *, but their behavior is mostly the same as the <string.h> functions. Table 25.16 shows the correspondence between the <string.h> functions and their wide-character counterparts.

Table 25.16	
Wide-String Comparison	
Functions and Their	
<string.h>	
Equivalents	

<wchar.h> Function	*<string.h> Equivalent*
wcscmp	strcmp
wcscoll	strcoll
wcsncmp	strncmp
wcsxfrm	strxfrm
wmemcmp	memcmp

Wide-String Search Functions

```
wchar_t *wcschr(const wchar_t *s, wchar_t c);
size_t wcscspn(const wchar_t *s1, const wchar_t *s2);
wchar_t *wcspbrk(const wchar_t *s1,
                 const wchar_t *s2);
wchar_t *wcsrchr(const wchar_t *s, wchar_t c);
size_t wcsspn(const wchar_t *s1, const wchar_t *s2);
wchar_t *wcsstr(const wchar_t *s1,
                const wchar_t *s2);
wchar_t *wcstok(wchar_t * restrict s1,
                const wchar_t * restrict s2,
                wchar_t ** restrict ptr);
wchar_t *wmemchr(const wchar_t *s, wchar_t c,
                 size_t n);
```

The functions in this group are wide-character versions of the string search functions found in <string.h> and described in Section 23.6. The <wchar.h> functions have arguments of type wchar_t * and wchar_t ** instead of char * and char **, but their behavior is mostly the same as the <string.h> functions. Table 25.17 shows the correspondence between the <string.h> functions and their wide-character counterparts.

Table 25.17	
Wide-String Search	
Functions and Their	
<string.h>	
Equivalents	

<wchar.h> Function	*<string.h> Equivalent*
wcschr	strchr
wcscspn	strcspn
wcspbrk	strpbrk
wcsrchr	strrchr
wcsspn	strspn
wcsstr	strstr
wcstok	strtok
wmemchr	memchr

wcstok The wcstok function serves the same purpose as strtok, but is used somewhat differently, thanks to its third parameter. (strtok has only two parameters.) To understand how wcstok works, we'll first need to review the behavior of strtok.

We saw in Section 23.6 that `strtok` searches a string for a "token"—a sequence of characters that doesn't include certain delimiting characters. The call `strtok(s1, s2)` scans the `s1` string for a nonempty sequence of characters that are *not* in the `s2` string. `strtok` marks the end of the token by storing a null character in `s1` just after the last character in the token; it then returns a pointer to the first character in the token.

Later calls of `strtok` can find additional tokens in the same string. The call `strtok(NULL, s2)` continues the search begun by the previous `strtok` call. As before, `strtok` marks the end of the token with a null character, and then returns a pointer to the beginning of the token. The process can be repeated until `strtok` returns a null pointer, indicating that no token was found.

One problem with `strtok` is that it uses a static variable to keep track of a search, which makes it impossible to use `strtok` to conduct simultaneous searches on two or more strings. Thanks to its extra parameter, `wcstok` doesn't have this problem.

The first two parameters to `wcstok` are the same as for `strtok` (except that they point to wide strings, of course). The third parameter, `ptr`, will point to a variable of type `wchar_t *`. The function will save information in this variable that enables later calls of `wcstok` to continue scanning the same string (when the first argument is a null pointer). When the search is resumed by a subsequent call of `wcstok`, a pointer to the same variable should be supplied as the third argument; the value of this variable must not be changed between calls of `wcstok`.

To see how `wcstok` works, let's redo the example of Section 23.6. Assume that `str`, `p`, and `q` are declared as follows:

```
wchar_t str[] = L" April   28,1998";
wchar_t *p, *q;
```

Our initial call of `wcstok` will pass `str` as the first argument:

```
p = wcstok(str, L" \t", &q);
```

`p` now points to the first character in `April`, which is followed by a null wide character. Calling `wcstok` with a null pointer as its first argument and `&q` as the third argument causes it to resume the search from where it left off:

```
p = wcstok(NULL, L" \t,", &q);
```

After this call, `p` points to the first character in `28`, which is now terminated by a null wide character. A final call of `wcstok` locates the year:

```
p = wcstok(NULL, L" \t", &q);
```

`p` now points to the first character in `1998`.

Miscellaneous Functions

```
size_t wcslen(const wchar_t *s);
wchar_t *wmemset(wchar_t *s, wchar_t c, size_t n);
```

The functions in this group are wide-character versions of the miscellaneous string functions found in `<string.h>` and described in Section 23.6. The `<wchar.h>` functions have arguments of type `wchar_t *` instead of `char *`, but their behavior is mostly the same as the `<string.h>` functions. Table 25.18 shows the correspondence between the `<string.h>` functions and their wide-character counterparts.

Table 25.18
Miscellaneous Wide-String
Functions and Their
`<string.h>` Equivalents

`<wchar.h>` *Function*	`<string.h>` *Equivalent*
`wcslen`	`strlen`
`wmemset`	`memset`

Wide-Character Time-Conversion Functions

```
size_t wcsftime(wchar_t * restrict s, size_t maxsize,
                const wchar_t * restrict format,
                const struct tm * restrict timeptr);
```

wcsftime   The `wcsftime` function is the wide-character version of `strftime`, which belongs to the `<time.h>` header and is described in Section 26.3.

Extended Multibyte/Wide-Character Conversion Utilities

We'll now examine `<wchar.h>` functions that perform conversions between multibyte characters and wide characters. Five of these functions (`mbrlen`, `mbrtowc`, `wcrtomb`, `mbsrtowcs`, and `wcsrtombs`) correspond to the multibyte/wide-character and multibyte/wide-string conversion functions declared in `<stdlib.h>`. The `<wchar.h>` functions have an additional parameter, a pointer to a variable of type `mbstate_t`. This variable keeps track of the state of the conversion of a multibyte character sequence to a wide-character sequence (or vice versa), based on the current locale. As a result, the `<wchar.h>` functions are "restartable"; by passing a pointer to an `mbstate_t` variable modified by a previous function call, we can "restart" the function using the conversion state from that call. One advantage of this arrangement is that it allows two functions to share the same conversion state. For example, calls of `mbrtowc` and `mbsrtowcs` that are used to process a single multibyte character string could share an `mbstate_t` variable.

The conversion state stored in an `mbstate_t` variable consists of the current shift state plus the current position within a multibyte character. Setting the bytes of an `mbstate_t` variable to zero puts it in the initial conversion state, signifying that no multibyte character is yet in progress and that the initial shift state is in effect:

```
mbstate_t state;
...
memset(&state, '\0', sizeof(state));
```

Passing &state to one of the restartable functions causes the conversion to begin in the initial conversion state. Once an mbstate_t variable has been altered by one of these functions, it should not be used to convert a different multibyte character sequence, nor should it be used to perform a conversion in the opposite direction. Attempting to perform either action causes undefined behavior. Using the variable after a change in the LC_CTYPE category of a locale also causes undefined behavior.

Single-Byte/Wide-Character Conversion Functions

```
wint_t btowc(int c);
int wctob(wint_t c);
```

The functions in this group convert single-byte characters to wide characters and vice versa.

btowc   The btowc function returns WEOF if c is equal to EOF or if c (when cast to unsigned char) isn't a valid single-byte character in the initial shift state. Otherwise, btowc returns the wide-character representation of c.

wctob   The wctob function is the opposite of btowc. It returns EOF if c doesn't correspond to one multibyte character in the initial shift state. Otherwise, it returns the single-byte representation of c.

Conversion-State Functions

```
int mbsinit(const mbstate_t *ps);
```

mbsinit   This group consists of a single function, mbsinit, which returns a nonzero value if ps is a null pointer or it points to an mbstate_t variable that describes an initial conversion state.

Restartable Multibyte/Wide-Character Conversion Functions

```
size_t mbrlen(const char * restrict s, size_t n,
              mbstate_t * restrict ps);
size_t mbrtowc(wchar_t * restrict pwc,
               const char * restrict s, size_t n,
               mbstate_t * restrict ps);
size_t wcrtomb(char * restrict s, wchar_t wc,
               mbstate_t * restrict ps);
```

The functions in this group are restartable versions of the mblen, mbtowc, and wctomb functions, which belong to <stdlib.h> and are discussed in Section 25.2. The newer mbrlen, mbrtowc, and wcrtomb functions differ from their <stdlib.h> counterparts in several ways:

- `mbrlen`, `mbrtowc`, and `wcrtomb` have an additional parameter named `ps`. When one of these functions is called, the corresponding argument should point to a variable of type `mbstate_t`; the function will store the state of the conversion in this variable. If the argument corresponding to `ps` is a null pointer, the function will use an internal variable to store the conversion state. (At the beginning of program execution, this variable is set to the initial conversion state.)

- When the `s` parameter is a null pointer, the older `mblen`, `mbtowc`, and `wctomb` functions return a nonzero value if multibyte character encodings have state-dependent encodings (and zero otherwise). The newer functions don't have this behavior.

- `mbrlen`, `mbrtowc`, and `wcrtomb` return a value of type `size_t` instead of `int`, the return type of the older functions.

mbrlen A call of `mbrlen` is equivalent to the call

```
mbrtowc(NULL, s, n, ps)
```

except that if `ps` is a null pointer, then the address of an internal variable is used instead.

mbrtowc If `s` is a null pointer, a call of `mbrtowc` is equivalent to the call

```
mbrtowc(NULL, "", 1, ps)
```

Otherwise, a call of `mbrtowc` examines up to n bytes pointed to by s to see if they complete a valid multibyte character. (Note that a multibyte character may already be in progress prior to the call, as tracked by the `mbstate_t` variable to which `ps` points.) If so, these bytes are converted into a wide character. The wide character is stored in the location pointed to by `pwc` as long as `pwc` isn't null. If this character is the null wide character, the `mbstate_t` variable used during the call is left in the initial conversion state.

`mbrtowc` has a variety of possible return values. It returns 0 if the conversion produces a null wide character. It returns a number between 1 and n if the conversion produces a wide character other than null, where the value returned is the number of bytes used to complete the multibyte character. It returns –2 if the n bytes pointed to by s aren't enough to complete a multibyte character (although the bytes themselves were valid). Finally, it returns –1 if an encoding error occurs (the function encounters bytes that don't form a valid multibyte character). In the last case, `mbrtowc` also stores `EILSEQ` in `errno`.

wcrtomb If `s` is a null pointer, a call of `wcrtomb` is equivalent to

```
wcrtomb(buf, L'\0', ps)
```

where `buf` is an internal buffer. Otherwise, `wcrtomb` converts `wc` from a wide character into a multibyte character, which it stores in the array pointed to by `s`. If `wc` is a null wide character, `wcrtomb` stores a null byte, preceded by a shift sequence if one is necessary to restore the initial shift state. In this case, the mbstate_t variable used during the call is left in the initial conversion state. wcrtomb returns the number of bytes that it stores, including shift sequences. If wc isn't a valid wide character, the function returns −1 and stores EILSEQ in errno.

Restartable Multibyte/Wide-String Conversion Functions

```
size_t mbsrtowcs(wchar_t * restrict dst,
                 const char ** restrict src,
                 size_t len,
                 mbstate_t * restrict ps);
size_t wcsrtombs(char * restrict dst,
                 const wchar_t ** restrict src,
                 size_t len,
                 mbstate_t * restrict ps);
```

mbsrtowcs
wcsrtombs
The mbsrtowcs and wcsrtombs functions are restartable versions of mbstowcs and wcstombs, which belong to <stdlib.h> and are discussed in Section 25.2. mbsrtowcs and wcsrtombs are the same as their <stdlib.h> counterparts, except for the following differences:

- mbsrtowcs and wcsrtombs have an additional parameter named ps. When one of these functions is called, the corresponding argument should point to a variable of type mbstate_t; the function will store the state of the conversion in this variable. If the argument corresponding to ps is a null pointer, the function will use an internal variable to store the conversion state. (At the beginning of program execution, this variable is set to the initial conversion state.) Both functions update the state as the conversion proceeds. If the conversion stops because a null character is reached, the mbstate_t variable will be left in the initial conversion state.

- The src parameter, which represents the array containing characters to be converted (the source array), is a pointer to a pointer for mbsrtowcs and wcsrtombs. (In the older mbstowcs and wcstombs functions, the corresponding parameter was simply a pointer.) This change allows mbsrtowcs and wcsrtombs to keep track of where the conversion stopped. The pointer to which src points is set to null if the conversion stopped because a null character was reached. Otherwise, this pointer is set to point just past the last source character converted.

- The dst parameter may be a null pointer, in which case the converted characters aren't stored and the pointer to which src points isn't modified.

- When either function encounters an invalid character in the source array, it stores EILSEQ in errno (in addition to returning −1, as the older functions do).

25.6 The `<wctype.h>` Header (C99)
Wide-Character Classification and Mapping Utilities

`<ctype.h>` header ➤23.5

The `<wctype.h>` header is the wide-character version of the `<ctype.h>` header. `<ctype.h>` provides two kinds of functions: character-classification functions (like `isdigit`, which tests whether a character is a digit) and character case-mapping functions (like `toupper`, which converts a lower-case letter to upper case). `<wctype.h>` provides similar functions for wide characters, although it differs from `<ctype.h>` in one important way: some of the functions in `<wctype.h>` are "extensible," meaning that they can perform custom character classification or case mapping.

`<wctype.h>` declares three types and a macro. The `wint_t` type and the `WEOF` macro were discussed in Section 25.5. The remaining types are `wctype_t`, whose values represent locale-specific character classifications, and `wctrans_t`, whose values represent locale-specific character mappings.

Most of the functions in `<wctype.h>` require a `wint_t` argument. The value of this argument must be a wide character (a `wchar_t` value) or `WEOF`. Passing any other argument causes undefined behavior.

The behavior of the functions in `<wctype.h>` is affected by the `LC_CTYPE` category of the current locale.

Wide-Character Classification Functions

```
int iswalnum(wint_t wc);
int iswalpha(wint_t wc);
int iswblank(wint_t wc);
int iswcntrl(wint_t wc);
int iswdigit(wint_t wc);
int iswgraph(wint_t wc);
int iswlower(wint_t wc);
int iswprint(wint_t wc);
int iswpunct(wint_t wc);
int iswspace(wint_t wc);
int iswupper(wint_t wc);
int iswxdigit(wint_t wc);
```

Each wide-character classification function returns a nonzero value if its argument has a particular property. Table 25.19 lists the property that each function tests.

The descriptions in Table 25.19 ignore some of the subtleties of wide characters. For example, the definition of `iswgraph` in the C99 standard states that it "tests for any wide character for which `iswprint` is true and `iswspace` is false,"

Table 25.19

Wide-Character
Classification Functions

Function	Test
iswalnum(wc)	Is wc alphanumeric?
iswalpha(wc)	Is wc alphabetic?
iswblank(wc)	Is wc a blank?[†]
iswcntrl(wc)	Is wc a control character?
iswdigit(wc)	Is wc a decimal digit?
iswgraph(wc)	Is wc a printing character (other than a space)?
iswlower(wc)	Is wc a lower-case letter?
iswprint(wc)	Is wc a printing character (including a space)?
iswpunct(wc)	Is wc punctuation?
iswspace(wc)	Is wc a white-space character?
iswupper(wc)	Is wc an upper-case letter?
iswxdigit(wc)	Is wc a hexadecimal digit?

[†]The standard blank wide characters are space (L' ') and horizontal tab
(L'\t').

leaving open the possibility that more than one wide character is considered to be a
"space." See Appendix D for more detailed descriptions of these functions.

In most cases, the wide-character classification functions are consistent with
the corresponding functions in <ctype.h>: if a <ctype.h> function returns a
nonzero value (indicating "true") for a particular character, then the corresponding
<wctype.h> function will return true for the wide version of the same character.
The only exception involves white-space wide characters (other than space) that
are also printing characters, which may be classified differently by iswgraph
and iswpunct than by isgraph and ispunct. For example, a character for
which isgraph returns true may cause iswgraph to return false.

Extensible Wide-Character Classification Functions

```
int iswctype(wint_t wc, wctype_t desc);
wctype_t wctype(const char *property);
```

Each of the wide-character classification functions just discussed is able to test a
single fixed condition. The wctype and iswctype functions—which are designed to be used together—make it possible to test for other conditions as well.

wctype   The wctype function is passed a string describing a class of wide characters;
it returns a wctype_t value that represents this class. For example, the call

```
wctype("upper")
```

returns a wctype_t value representing the class of upper-case letters. The C99
standard requires that the following strings be allowed as arguments to wctype:

```
"alnum"  "alpha"  "blank"  "cntrl"  "digit"  "graph"
"lower"  "print"  "punct"  "space"  "upper"  "xdigit"
```

Additional strings may be provided by an implementation. Which strings are legal
arguments to wctype at a given time depends on the LC_CTYPE category of the

current locale; the 12 strings listed above are legal in all locales. If `wctype` is passed a string that's not supported in the current locale, it returns zero.

iswctype   A call of the `iswctype` function requires two parameters: `wc` (a wide character) and `desc` (a value returned by `wctype`). `iswctype` returns a nonzero value if `wc` belongs to the class of characters corresponding to `desc`. For example, the call

```
iswctype(wc, wctype("alnum"))
```

is equivalent to

```
iswalnum(wc)
```

`wctype` and `iswctype` are most useful when the argument to `wctype` is a string other than the standard ones listed above.

Wide-Character Case-Mapping Functions

```
wint_t towlower(wint_t wc);
wint_t towupper(wint_t wc);
```

towlower   The `towlower` and `towupper` functions are the wide-character counterparts of
towupper   `tolower` and `toupper`. For example, `towlower` returns the lower-case version of its argument, if the argument is an upper-case letter; otherwise, it returns the argument unchanged. As usual, there may be quirks when dealing with wide characters. For example, more than one lower-case version of a letter may exist in the current locale, in which case `towlower` is allowed to return any one of them.

Extensible Wide-Character Case-Mapping Functions

```
wint_t towctrans(wint_t wc, wctrans_t desc);
wctrans_t wctrans(const char *property);
```

The `wctrans` and `towctrans` functions are used together to support generalized wide-character mapping.

wctrans   The `wctrans` function is passed a string describing a character mapping; it returns a `wctrans_t` value that represents the mapping. For example, the call

```
wctrans("tolower")
```

returns a `wctrans_t` value representing the mapping of upper-case letters to lower case. The C99 standard requires that the strings `"tolower"` and `"toupper"` be allowed as arguments to `wctrans`. Additional strings may be provided by an implementation. Which strings are legal arguments to `wctrans` at a given time depends on the `LC_CTYPE` category of the current locale; `"tolower"` and `"toupper"` are legal in all locales. If `wctrans` is passed a string that's not supported in the current locale, it returns zero.

towctrans   A call of the `towctrans` function requires two parameters: `wc` (a wide character) and `desc` (a value returned by `wctrans`). `towctrans` maps `wc` to another wide character based on the mapping specified by `desc`. For example, the call

```
towctrans(wc, wctrans("tolower"))
```

is equivalent to

```
towlower(wc)
```

`towctrans` is most useful in conjunction with implementation-defined mappings.

Q & A

Q: **How long is the locale information string returned by `setlocale`? [p. 644]**

A: There's no maximum length, which raises a question: how can we set aside space for the string if we don't know how long it will be? The answer, of course, is dynamic storage allocation. The following program fragment (based on a similar example in Harbison and Steele's *C: A Reference Manual*) shows how to determine the amount of memory needed, allocate the memory dynamically, and then copy the locale information into that memory:

```
char *temp, *old_locale;

temp = setlocale(LC_ALL, NULL);
if (temp == NULL) {
  /* locale information not available */
}
old_locale = malloc(strlen(temp) + 1);
if (old_locale == NULL) {
  /* memory allocation failed */
}
strcpy(old_locale, temp);
```

We can now switch to a different locale and then later restore the old locale:

```
setlocale(LC_ALL, "");          /* switches to native locale */
...
setlocale(LC_ALL, old_locale); /* restores old locale */
```

Q: **Why does C provide both multibyte characters and wide characters? Wouldn't either one be enough by itself? [p. 648]**

A: The two encodings serve different purposes. Multibyte characters are handy for input/output purposes, since I/O devices are often byte-oriented. Wide characters, on the other hand, are more convenient to work with inside a program, since every wide character occupies the same amount of space. Thus, a program might read multibyte characters, convert them to wide characters for manipulation within the program, and then convert the wide characters back to multibyte form for output.

Q: **Unicode and UCS seem to be pretty much the same. What's the difference between the two? [p. 650]**

A: Both contain the same characters, and characters are represented by the same code points in both. Unicode is more than just a character set, though. For example, Unicode supports "bidirectional display order." Some languages, including Arabic and Hebrew, allow text to be written from right to left instead of left to right. Unicode is capable of specifying the display order of characters, allowing text to contain some characters that are to be displayed from left to right along with others that go from right to left.

Exercises

Section 25.1

1. Determine which locales are supported by your compiler.

Section 25.2

2. The Shift-JIS encoding for *kanji* requires either one or two bytes per character. If the first byte of a character is between `0x81` and `0x9f` or between `0xe0` and `0xef`, a second byte is required. (Any other byte is treated as a whole character.) The second byte must be between `0x40` and `0x7e` or between `0x80` and `0xfc`. (All ranges are inclusive.) For each of the following strings, give the value that the `mbcheck` function of Section 25.2 will return when passed that string as its argument, assuming that multibyte characters are encoded using Shift-JIS in the current locale.

   (a) `"\x05\x87\x80\x36\xed\xaa"`
   (b) `"\x20\xe4\x50\x88\x3f"`
   (c) `"\xde\xad\xbe\xef"`
   (d) `"\x8a\x60\x92\x74\x41"`

3. One of the useful properties of UTF-8 is that no sequence of bytes within a multibyte character can possibly represent another valid multibyte character. Does the Shift-JIS encoding for *kanji* (discussed in Exercise 2) have this property?

4. Give a C string literal that represents each of the following phrases. Assume that the characters à, è, é, ê, î, ô, û, and ü are represented by single-byte Latin-1 characters. (You'll need to look up the Latin-1 code points for these characters.) For example, the phrase *déjà vu* could be represented by the string `"d\xe9j\xe0 vu"`.

   (a) *Côte d'Azur*
   (b) *crème brûlée*
   (c) *crème fraîche*
   (d) *Fahrvergnügen*
   (e) *tête-à-tête*

5. Repeat Exercise 4, this time using the UTF-8 multibyte encoding. For example, the phrase *déjà vu* could be represented by the string `"d\xc3\xa9j\xc3\xa0 vu"`.

Section 25.3   Ⓦ   6.   Modify the following program fragment by replacing as many characters as possible by trigraphs.

```
while ((orig_char = getchar()) != EOF) {
  new_char = orig_char ^ KEY;
  if (isprint(orig_char) && isprint(new_char))
    putchar(new_char);
  else
    putchar(orig_char);
}
```

7.   (C99) Modify the program fragment in Exercise 6 by replacing as many tokens as possible by digraphs and macros defined in `<iso646.h>`.

Programming Projects

Ⓦ   1.   Write a program that tests whether your compiler's `""` (native) locale is the same as its `"C"` locale.

2.   Write a program that obtains the name of a locale from the command line and then displays the values stored in the corresponding `lconv` structure. For example, if the locale is `"fi_FI"` (Finland), the output of the program might look like this:

```
decimal_point = ","
thousands_sep = " "
grouping = 3
mon_decimal_point = ","
mon_thousands_sep = " "
mon_grouping = 3
positive_sign = ""
negative_sign = "-"
currency_symbol = "EUR"
frac_digits = 2
p_cs_precedes = 0
n_cs_precedes = 0
p_sep_by_space = 2
n_sep_by_space = 2
p_sign_posn = 1
n_sign_posn = 1
int_curr_symbol = "EUR "
int_frac_digits = 2
int_p_cs_precedes = 0
int_n_cs_precedes = 0
int_p_sep_by_space = 2
int_n_sep_by_space = 2
int_p_sign_posn = 1
int_n_sign_posn = 1
```

For readability, the characters in `grouping` and `mon_grouping` should be displayed as decimal numbers.

26 Miscellaneous Library Functions

It is the user who should parametrize procedures, not their creators.

<stdarg.h>, <stdlib.h>, and <time.h>—the only C89 headers that weren't covered in previous chapters—are unlike any others in the standard library. The <stdarg.h> header (Section 26.1) makes it possible to write functions with a variable number of arguments. <stdlib.h> (Section 26.2) is an assortment of functions that don't fit into one of the other headers. The <time.h> header (Section 26.3) allows programs to work with dates and times.

26.1 The <stdarg.h> Header: Variable Arguments

```
type va_arg(va_list ap, type);
void va_copy(va_list dest, va_list src);
void va_end(va_list ap);
void va_start(va_list ap, parmN);
```

Functions such as printf and scanf have an unusual property: they allow any number of arguments. The ability to handle a variable number of arguments isn't limited to library functions, as it turns out. The <stdarg.h> header provides the tools we'll need to write our own functions with variable-length argument lists. <stdarg.h> declares one type (va_list) and defines several macros. In C89, there are three macros, named va_start, va_arg, and va_end, which can be thought of as functions with the prototypes shown above. C99 adds a function-like macro named va_copy.

677

To see how these macros work, we'll use them to write a function named `max_int` that finds the maximum of *any* number of integer arguments. Here's how we might call the function:

```
max_int(3, 10, 30, 20)
```

The first argument specifies how many additional arguments will follow. This call of `max_int` will return 30 (the largest of the numbers 10, 30, and 20).

Here's the definition of the `max_int` function:

```
int max_int(int n, ...)    /* n must be at least 1 */
{
  va_list ap;
  int i, current, largest;

  va_start(ap, n);
  largest = va_arg(ap, int);

  for (i = 1; i < n; i++) {
    current = va_arg(ap, int);
    if (current > largest)
      largest = current;
  }

  va_end(ap);
  return largest;
}
```

The `...` symbol in the parameter list (known as an ***ellipsis***) indicates that the parameter n is followed by a variable number of additional parameters.

The body of `max_int` begins with the declaration of a variable of type `va_list`:

```
va_list ap;
```

Declaring such a variable is mandatory for `max_int` to be able to access the arguments that follow n.

va_start   The statement

```
va_start(ap, n);
```

indicates where the variable-length part of the argument list begins (in this case, after n). A function with a variable number of arguments must have at least one "normal" parameter; the ellipsis always goes at the end of the parameter list, after the last normal parameter.

va_arg   The statement

```
largest = va_arg(ap, int);
```

fetches `max_int`'s second argument (the one after n), assigns it to `largest`, and automatically advances to the next argument. The word `int` indicates that we expect `max_int`'s second argument to have `int` type. The statement

```
current = va_arg(ap, int);
```

fetches `max_int`'s remaining arguments, one by one, as it is executed inside a loop.

Don't forget that `va_arg` always advances to the next argument after fetching the current one. Because of this property, we couldn't have written `max_int`'s loop in the following way:

```
for (i = 1; i < n; i++)
  if (va_arg(ap, int) > largest)    /*** WRONG ***/
    largest = va_arg(ap, int);
```

va_end   The statement

```
va_end(ap);
```

is required to "clean up" before the function returns. (Or, instead of returning, the function might call `va_start` and traverse the argument list again.)

va_copy   The `va_copy` macro copies `src` (a `va_list` value) into `dest` (also a `va_list`). The usefulness of `va_copy` lies in the fact that multiple calls of `va_arg` may have been made using `src` before it's copied into `dest`, thus processing some of the arguments. Calling `va_copy` allows a function to remember where it is in the argument list so that it can later return to the same point to reexamine an argument (and possibly the arguments that follow it).

Each call of `va_start` or `va_copy` must be paired with a call of `va_end`, and the calls must appear in the same function. All calls of `va_arg` must appear between the call of `va_start` (or `va_copy`) and the matching call of `va_end`.

default argument promotions ➤9.3
When a function with a variable argument list is called, the compiler performs the default argument promotions on all arguments that match the ellipsis. In particular, `char` and `short` arguments are promoted to `int`, and `float` values are promoted to `double`. Consequently, it doesn't make sense to pass types such as `char`, `short`, or `float` to `va_arg`, since arguments—after promotion—will never have one of those types.

Calling a Function with a Variable Argument List

Calling a function with a variable argument list is an inherently risky proposition. As far back as Chapter 3, we saw how dangerous it can be to pass the wrong arguments to `printf` and `scanf`. Other functions with variable argument lists are equally sensitive. The primary difficulty is that a function with a variable argument list has no way to determine the number of arguments or their types. This information must be passed into the function and/or assumed by the function. `max_int` relies on the first argument to specify how many additional arguments follow; it assumes that the arguments are of type `int`. Functions such as `printf` and `scanf` rely on the format string, which describes the number of additional arguments and the type of each.

Another problem has to do with passing `NULL` as an argument. `NULL` is usually defined to represent `0`. When `0` is passed to a function with a variable argument list, the compiler assumes that it represents an integer—there's no way it can tell that we want it to represent the null pointer. The solution is to add a cast, writing `(void *) NULL` or `(void *) 0` instead of `NULL`. (See the Q&A section at the end of Chapter 17 for more discussion of this point.)

The `v...printf` Functions

```
int vfprintf(FILE * restrict stream,
             const char * restrict format,
             va_list arg);              from <stdio.h>
int vprintf(const char * restrict format,
            va_list arg);               from <stdio.h>
int vsnprintf(char * restrict s, size_t n,
              const char * restrict format,
              va_list arg);             from <stdio.h>
int vsprintf(char * restrict s,
             const char * restrict format,
             va_list arg);              from <stdio.h>
```

vfprintf
vprintf
vsprintf

The `vfprintf`, `vprintf`, and `vsprintf` functions (the "`v...printf` functions") belong to `<stdio.h>`. We're discussing them in this section because they're invariably used in conjunction with the macros in `<stdarg.h>`. C99 adds the `vsnprintf` function.

The `v...printf` functions are closely related to `fprintf`, `printf`, and `sprintf`. Unlike these functions, however, the `v...printf` functions have a fixed number of arguments. Each function's last argument is a `va_list` value, which implies that it will be called by a function with a variable argument list. In practice, the `v...printf` functions are used primarily for writing "wrapper" functions that accept a variable number of arguments, which are then passed to a `v...printf` function.

As an example, let's say that we're working on a program that needs to display error messages from time to time. We'd like each message to begin with a prefix of the form

`** Error` *n*:

where *n* is `1` for the first error message and increases by one for each subsequent error. To make it easier to produce error messages, we'll write a function named `errorf` that's similar to `printf`, but adds `** Error` *n*: to the beginning of its output and always writes to `stderr` instead of `stdout`. We'll have `errorf` call `vfprintf` to do most of the actual output. Here's what `errorf` might look like:

```
int errorf(const char *format, ...)
{
  static int num_errors = 0;
  int n;
  va_list ap;

  num_errors++;
  fprintf(stderr, "** Error %d: ", num_errors);
  va_start(ap, format);
  n = vfprintf(stderr, format, ap);
  va_end(ap);
  fprintf(stderr, "\n");
  return n;
}
```

The wrapper function—`errorf`, in our example—is responsible for calling `va_start` prior to calling the `v...printf` function and for calling `va_end` after the `v...printf` function returns. The wrapper function is allowed to call `va_arg` one or more times before calling the `v...printf` function.

vsnprintf   The `vsnprintf` function was added to the C99 version of `<stdio.h>`. It corresponds to `snprintf` (discussed in Section 22.8), which is also a C99 function.

C99   **The `v...scanf` Functions**

```
int vfscanf(FILE * restrict stream,
            const char * restrict format,
            va_list arg);                      from <stdio.h>
int vscanf(const char * restrict format,
           va_list arg);                       from <stdio.h>
int vsscanf(const char * restrict s,
            const char * restrict format,
            va_list arg);                      from <stdio.h>
```

vfscanf
vscanf
vsscanf   C99 adds a set of "v...scanf functions" to the `<stdio.h>` header. `vfscanf`, `vscanf`, and `vsscanf` are equivalent to `fscanf`, `scanf`, and `sscanf`, respectively, except that they have a `va_list` parameter through which a variable argument list can be passed. Like the `v...printf` functions, each `v...scanf` function is designed to be called by a wrapper function that accepts a variable number of arguments, which it then passes to the `v...scanf` function. The wrapper function is responsible for calling `va_start` prior to calling the `v...scanf` function and for calling `va_end` after the `v...scanf` function returns.

26.2 The `<stdlib.h>` Header: General Utilities

`<stdlib.h>` serves as a catch-all for functions that don't fit into any of the other headers. The functions in `<stdlib.h>` fall into eight groups:

Numeric conversion functions
Pseudo-random sequence generation functions
Memory-management functions
Communication with the environment
Searching and sorting utilities
Integer arithmetic functions
Multibyte/wide-character conversion functions
Multibyte/wide-string conversion functions

We'll look at each group in turn, with three exceptions: the memory management functions, the multibyte/wide-character conversion functions, and the multibyte/wide-string conversion functions.

The memory-management functions (`malloc`, `calloc`, `realloc`, and `free`) permit a program to allocate a block of memory and then later release it or change its size. Chapter 17 describes all four functions in some detail.

The multibyte/wide-character conversion functions are used to convert a multibyte character to a wide character or vice-versa. The multibyte/wide-string conversion functions perform similar conversions between multibyte strings and wide strings. Both groups of functions are discussed in Section 25.2.

Numeric Conversion Functions

```
double atof(const char *nptr);

int atoi(const char *nptr);
long int atol(const char *nptr);
long long int atoll(const char *nptr);

double strtod(const char * restrict nptr,
              char ** restrict endptr);
float strtof(const char * restrict nptr,
             char ** restrict endptr);
long double strtold(const char * restrict nptr,
                    char ** restrict endptr);

long int strtol(const char * restrict nptr,
                char ** restrict endptr, int base);
```

```
long long int strtoll(const char * restrict nptr,
                      char ** restrict endptr,
                      int base);
unsigned long int strtoul(
    const char * restrict nptr,
    char ** restrict endptr, int base);
unsigned long long int strtoull(
    const char * restrict nptr,
    char ** restrict endptr, int base);
```

The numeric conversion functions (or "string conversion functions," as they're known in C89) convert strings containing numbers in character form to their equivalent numeric values. Three of these functions are fairly old, another three were added when the C89 standard was created, and five more were added in **C99** C99.

All the numeric conversion functions—whether new or old—work in much the same way. Each function attempts to convert a string (pointed to by the `nptr` parameter) to a number. Each function skips white-space characters at the beginning of the string, treats subsequent characters as part of a number (possibly beginning with a plus or minus sign), and stops at the first character that can't be part of the number. In addition, each function returns zero if no conversion can be performed (the string is empty or the characters following any initial white space don't have the form the function is looking for).

atof
atoi
atol
The old functions (`atof`, `atoi`, and `atol`) convert a string to a `double`, `int`, or `long int` value, respectively. Unfortunately, these functions lack any way to indicate how much of the string was consumed during a conversion. Moreover, the functions have no way to indicate that a conversion was unsuccessful.

`errno` variable ➤24.2 (Some implementations of these functions may modify the `errno` variable when a conversion fails, but that's not guaranteed.)

strtod
strtol
strtoul
The C89 functions (`strtod`, `strtol`, and `strtoul`) are more sophisticated. For one thing, they indicate where the conversion stopped by modifying the variable that `endptr` points to. (The second argument can be a null pointer if we're not interested in where the conversion ended.) To check whether a function was able to consume the entire string, we can just test whether this variable points to a null character. If no conversion could be performed, the variable that `endptr` points to is given the value of `nptr` (as long as `endptr` isn't a null pointer). What's more, `strtol` and `strtoul` have a `base` argument that specifies the base of the number being converted. All bases between 2 and 36 (inclusive) are supported.

Besides being more versatile than the old functions, `strtod`, `strtol`, and `strtoul` are better at detecting errors. Each function stores ERANGE in `errno` if a conversion produces a value that's outside the range of the function's return
`HUGE_VAL` macro ➤23.3 type. In addition, the `strtod` function returns plus or minus HUGE_VAL; the

strtol and strtoul functions return the smallest or largest values of their respective return types. (strtol returns either LONG_MIN or LONG_MAX, and

<limits.h> macros ▶23.2   strtoul returns ULONG_MAX.)

atoll
strtof
strtold
strtoll
strtoull

C99 adds the atoll, strtof, strtold, strtoll, and strtoull functions. atoll is the same as the atol function, except that it converts a string to a long long int value. strtof and strtold are the same as strtod, except that they convert a string to a float or long double value, respectively. strtoll is the same as strtol, except that it converts a string to a long long int value. strtoull is the same as strtoul, except that it converts a string to an unsigned long long int value. C99 also makes a small change to the floating-point numeric conversion functions: the string passed to strtod (as well as its newer cousins, strtof and strtold) may contain a

Q&A   hexadecimal floating-point number, infinity, or NaN.

PROGRAM   **Testing the Numeric Conversion Functions**

The following program converts a string to numeric form by applying each of the six numeric conversion functions that exist in C89. After calling the strtod, strtol, and strtoul functions, the program also shows whether each conversion produced a valid result and whether it was able to consume the entire string. The program obtains the input string from the command line.

tnumconv.c

```
/* Tests C89 numeric conversion functions */

#include <errno.h>
#include <stdio.h>
#include <stdlib.h>

#define CHK_VALID  printf("     %s              %s\n",         \
                          errno != ERANGE ? "Yes" : "No ",  \
                          *ptr == '\0' ? "Yes" : "No")

int main(int argc, char *argv[])
{
  char *ptr;

  if (argc != 2) {
    printf("usage: tnumconv string\n");
    exit(EXIT_FAILURE);
  }

  printf("Function   Return Value\n");
  printf("--------   ------------\n");
  printf("atof       %g\n", atof(argv[1]));
  printf("atoi       %d\n", atoi(argv[1]));
  printf("atol       %ld\n\n", atol(argv[1]));

  printf("Function   Return Value   Valid?   "
         "String Consumed?\n"
```

```
               "--------     ------------    ------     "
               "----------------\n");

    errno = 0;
    printf("strtod      %-12g", strtod(argv[1], &ptr));
    CHK_VALID;

    errno = 0;
    printf("strtol      %-12ld", strtol(argv[1], &ptr, 10));
    CHK_VALID;

    errno = 0;
    printf("strtoul     %-12lu", strtoul(argv[1], &ptr, 10));
    CHK_VALID;

    return 0;
}
```

If 3000000000 is the command-line argument, the output of the program might have the following appearance:

```
Function   Return Value
--------   ------------
atof       3e+09
atoi       2147483647
atol       2147483647


Function   Return Value   Valid?   String Consumed?
--------   ------------   ------   ----------------
strtod     3e+09          Yes      Yes
strtol     2147483647     No       Yes
strtoul    3000000000     Yes      Yes
```

On many machines, the number 3000000000 is too large to represent as a long integer, although it's valid as an unsigned long integer. The atoi and atol functions had no way to indicate that the number represented by their argument was out of range. In the output shown, they returned 2147483647 (the largest long integer), but the C standard doesn't guarantee this behavior. The strtoul function performed the conversion correctly; strtol returned 2147483647 (the standard requires it to return the largest long integer) and stored ERANGE in errno.

If 123.456 is the command-line argument, the output will be

```
Function   Return Value
--------   ------------
atof       123.456
atoi       123
atol       123


Function   Return Value   Valid?   String Consumed?
--------   ------------   ------   ----------------
strtod     123.456        Yes      Yes
strtol     123            Yes      No
strtoul    123            Yes      No
```

All six functions treated this string as a valid number, although the integer functions stopped at the decimal point. The `strtol` and `strtoul` functions were able to indicate that they didn't completely consume the string.

If `foo` is the command-line argument, the output will be

```
Function    Return Value
--------    ------------
atof        0
atoi        0
atol        0


Function    Return Value    Valid?    String Consumed?
--------    ------------    ------    ----------------
strtod      0               Yes             No
strtol      0               Yes             No
strtoul     0               Yes             No
```

All the functions looked at the letter `f` and immediately returned zero. The `str...` functions didn't change `errno`, but we can tell that something went wrong from the fact that the functions didn't consume the string.

Pseudo-Random Sequence Generation Functions

```
int rand(void);
void srand(unsigned int seed);
```

The `rand` and `srand` functions support the generation of pseudo-random numbers. These functions are useful in simulation programs and game-playing programs (to simulate a dice roll or the deal in a card game, for example).

rand   Each time it's called, `rand` returns a number between 0 and `RAND_MAX` (a macro defined in `<stdlib.h>`). The numbers returned by `rand` aren't actually random; they're generated from a "seed" value. To the casual observer, however, `rand` appears to produce an unrelated sequence of numbers.

srand   Calling `srand` supplies the seed value for `rand`. If `rand` is called prior to `srand`, the seed value is assumed to be 1. Each seed value determines a particular sequence of pseudo-random numbers; `srand` allows us to select which sequence we want.

A program that always uses the same seed value will always get the same sequence of numbers from `rand`. This property can sometimes be useful: the program behaves the same way each time it's run, making testing easier. However, we usually want `rand` to produce a *different* sequence each time the program is run. (A poker-playing program that always deals the same cards isn't likely to be popular.) The easiest way to "randomize" the seed values is to call the `time` function, which returns a number that encodes the current date and time. Passing `time`'s return value to `srand` makes the behavior of `rand` vary from one run to the next. See the `guess.c` and `guess2.c` programs (Section 10.2) for examples of this technique.

time function ➤ 26.3

PROGRAM   **Testing the Pseudo-Random Sequence Generation Functions**

The following program displays the first five values returned by the `rand` function, then allows the user to choose a new seed value. The process repeats until the user enters zero as the seed.

trand.c   `/* Tests the pseudo-random sequence generation functions */`

```
#include <stdio.h>
#include <stdlib.h>

int main(void)
{
  int i, seed;

  printf("This program displays the first five values of "
         "rand.\n");

  for (;;) {
    for (i = 0; i < 5; i++)
      printf("%d ", rand());
    printf("\n\n");
    printf("Enter new seed value (0 to terminate): ");
    scanf("%d", &seed);
    if (seed == 0)
      break;
    srand(seed);
  }

  return 0;
}
```

Here's how a session with the program might look:

```
This program displays the first five values of rand.
1804289383 846930886 1681692777 1714636915 1957747793

Enter new seed value (0 to terminate): 100
677741240 611911301 516687479 1039653884 807009856

Enter new seed value (0 to terminate): 1
1804289383 846930886 1681692777 1714636915 1957747793

Enter new seed value (0 to terminate): 0
```

There are many ways to write the `rand` function, so there's no guarantee that every version of `rand` will generate the numbers shown here. Note that choosing 1 as the seed gives the same sequence of numbers as not specifying the seed at all.

Communication with the Environment

```
void abort(void);
int atexit(void (*func)(void));
```

```
void exit(int status);
void _Exit(int status);
char *getenv(const char *name);
int system(const char *string);
```

The functions in this group provide a simple interface to the operating system, allowing programs to (1) terminate, either normally or abnormally, and return a status code to the operating system, (2) fetch information from the user's environment, and (3) execute operating system commands. One of the functions, `_Exit`, is a C99 addition.

C99

exit   Performing the call `exit(n)` anywhere in a program is normally equivalent to executing the statement `return n;` in `main`: the program terminates, and *n* is

Q&A   returned to the operating system as a status code. `<stdlib.h>` defines the macros `EXIT_FAILURE` and `EXIT_SUCCESS`, which can be used as arguments to `exit`. The only other portable argument to `exit` is 0, which has the same meaning as `EXIT_SUCCESS`. Returning status codes other than these is legal but not necessarily portable to all operating systems.

atexit   When a program terminates, it usually performs a few final actions behind the scenes, including flushing output buffers that contain unwritten data, closing open streams, and deleting temporary files. We may have other "clean-up" actions that we'd like a program to perform at termination. The `atexit` function allows us to "register" a function to be called upon program termination. To register a function named `cleanup`, for example, we could call `atexit` as follows:

```
atexit(cleanup);
```

When we pass a function pointer to `atexit`, it stores the pointer away for future reference. If the program later terminates normally (via a call of `exit` or a `return` statement in the `main` function), any function registered with `atexit` will be called automatically. (If two or more functions have been registered, they're called in the reverse of the order in which they were registered.)

_Exit   The `_Exit` function is similar to `exit`. However, `_Exit` doesn't call functions that have been registered with `atexit`, nor does it call any signal handlers

signal function ►24.3   previously passed to the `signal` function. Also, `_Exit` doesn't necessarily flush output buffers, close open streams, or delete temporary files—whether these actions are performed is implementation-defined.

abort   `abort` is also similar to `exit`, but calling it causes abnormal program termination. Functions registered with `atexit` aren't called. Depending on the implementation, it may be the case that output buffers containing unwritten data aren't flushed, streams aren't closed, and temporary files aren't deleted. `abort` returns

Q&A   an implementation-defined status code indicating unsuccessful termination.

getenv   Many operating systems provide an "environment": a set of strings that describe the user's characteristics. These strings typically include the path to be searched when the user runs a program, the type of the user's terminal (in the case of a multi-user system), and so on. For example, a UNIX search path might look something like this:

```
PATH=/usr/local/bin:/bin:/usr/bin:.
```

getenv provides access to any string in the user's environment. To find the current value of the PATH string, for example, we could write

```
char *p = getenv("PATH");
```

p now points to the string "/usr/local/bin:/bin:/usr/bin:.". Be careful with getenv: it returns a pointer to a statically allocated string that may be changed by a later call of the function.

system   The system function allows a C program to run another program (possibly an operating system command). The argument to system is a string containing a command, similar to one that we'd enter at the operating system prompt. For example, suppose that we're writing a program that needs a listing of the files in the current directory. A UNIX program would call system in the following way:

```
system("ls >myfiles");
```

This call invokes the UNIX command ls and asks it to write a listing of the current directory into the file named myfiles.

The return value of system is implementation-defined. system typically returns the termination status code from the program that we asked it to run; testing this value allows us to check whether the program worked properly. Calling system with a null pointer has a special meaning: the function returns a nonzero value if a command processor is available.

Searching and Sorting Utilities

```
void *bsearch(const void *key, const void *base,
              size_t nmemb, size_t size,
              int (*compar)(const void *,
                            const void *));
void qsort(void *base, size_t nmemb, size_t size,
           int (*compar)(const void *, const void *));
```

bsearch   The bsearch function searches a sorted array for a particular value (the "key"). When bsearch is called, the key parameter points to the key, base points to the array, nmemb is the number of elements in the array, size is the size of each element (in bytes), and compar is a pointer to a comparison function. The comparison function is similar to the one required by qsort: when passed pointers to the key and an array element (in that order), the function must return a negative, zero, or positive integer depending on whether the key is less than, equal to, or greater than the array element. bsearch returns a pointer to an element that matches the key; if it doesn't find a match, bsearch returns a null pointer.

Although the C standard doesn't require it to, `bsearch` normally uses the binary search algorithm to search the array. `bsearch` first compares the key with the element in the middle of the array; if there's a match, the function returns. If the key is smaller than the middle element, `bsearch` limits its search to the first half of the array; if the key is larger, `bsearch` searches only the last half of the array. `bsearch` repeats this strategy until it finds the key or runs out of elements to search. Thanks to this technique, `bsearch` is quite fast—searching an array of 1000 elements requires only 10 comparisons at most; searching an array of 1,000,000 elements requires no more than 20 comparisons.

qsort   Section 17.7 discusses the `qsort` function, which can sort any array. `bsearch` works only for sorted arrays, but we can always use `qsort` to sort an array prior to asking `bsearch` to search it.

PROGRAM   **Determining Air Mileage**

Our next program computes the air mileage from New York City to various international cities. The program first asks the user to enter a city name, then displays the mileage to that city:

```
Enter city name: Shanghai
Shanghai is 7371 miles from New York City.
```

The program will store city/mileage pairs in an array. By using `bsearch` to search the array for a city name, the program can easily find the corresponding mileage. (Mileages are from *Infoplease.com*.)

airmiles.c
```c
/* Determines air mileage from New York to other cities */

#include <stdio.h>
#include <stdlib.h>
#include <string.h>

struct city_info {
  char *city;
  int miles;
};

int compare_cities(const void *key_ptr,
                   const void *element_ptr);

int main(void)
{
  char city_name[81];
  struct city_info *ptr;
  const struct city_info mileage[] =
    {{"Berlin",          3965}, {"Buenos Aires", 5297},
     {"Cairo",           5602}, {"Calcutta",     7918},
     {"Cape Town",       7764}, {"Caracas",      2132},
     {"Chicago",          713}, {"Hong Kong",    8054},
     {"Honolulu",        4964}, {"Istanbul",     4975},
```

```
{"Lisbon",          3364}, {"London",         3458},
{"Los Angeles",     2451}, {"Manila",         8498},
{"Mexico City",     2094}, {"Montreal",        320},
{"Moscow",          4665}, {"Paris",          3624},
{"Rio de Janeiro", 4817}, {"Rome",           4281},
{"San Francisco",   2571}, {"Shanghai",       7371},
{"Stockholm",       3924}, {"Sydney",         9933},
{"Tokyo",           6740}, {"Warsaw",         4344},
{"Washington",       205}};

  printf("Enter city name: ");
  scanf("%80[^\n]", city_name);
  ptr = bsearch(city_name, mileage,
                sizeof(mileage) / sizeof(mileage[0]),
                sizeof(mileage[0]), compare_cities);
  if (ptr != NULL)
    printf("%s is %d miles from New York City.\n",
           city_name, ptr->miles);
  else
    printf("%s wasn't found.\n", city_name);

  return 0;
}

int compare_cities(const void *key_ptr,
                   const void *element_ptr)
{
  return strcmp((char *) key_ptr,
                ((struct city_info *) element_ptr)->city);
}
```

Integer Arithmetic Functions

```
int abs(int j);
long int labs(long int j);
long long int llabs(long long int j);

div_t div(int numer, int denom);
ldiv_t ldiv(long int numer, long int denom);
lldiv_t lldiv(long long int numer,
              long long int denom);
```

abs
labs   The abs function returns the absolute value of an int value; the labs function
returns the absolute value of a long int value.

div   The div function divides its first argument by its second, returning a div_t
value. div_t is a structure that contains both a quotient member (named quot)
and a remainder member (rem). For example, if ans is a div_t variable, we
could write

```
ans = div(5, 2);
printf("Quotient: %d Remainder: %d\n", ans.quot, ans.rem);
```

ldiv

The `ldiv` function is similar but works with long integers; it returns an `ldiv_t` structure, which also has `quot` and `rem` members. (The `div_t` and `ldiv_t` types are declared in `<stdlib.h>`.)

llabs
lldiv

C99 provides two additional functions. The `llabs` function returns the absolute value of a `long long int` value. `lldiv` is similar to `div` and `ldiv`, except that it divides two `long long int` values and returns an `lldiv_t` structure. (The `lldiv_t` type was also added in C99.)

26.3   The `<time.h>` Header: Date and Time

The `<time.h>` header provides functions for determining the time (including the date), performing arithmetic on time values, and formatting times for display. Before we explore these functions, however, we need to discuss how times are stored. `<time.h>` provides three types, each of which represents a different way to store a time:

- `clock_t`: A time value measured in "clock ticks."
- `time_t`: A compact, encoded time and date (a ***calendar time***).
- `struct tm`: A time that has been divided into seconds, minutes, hours, and so on. A value of type `struct tm` is often called a ***broken-down time.*** Table 26.1 shows the members of the `tm` structure. All members are of type `int`.

Table 26.1
Members of the
tm Structure

Name	Description	Minimum Value	Maximum Value
tm_sec	Seconds after the minute	0	61[†]
tm_min	Minutes after the hour	0	59
tm_hour	Hours since midnight	0	23
tm_mday	Day of the month	1	31
tm_mon	Months since January	0	11
tm_year	Years since 1900	0	–
tm_wday	Days since Sunday	0	6
tm_yday	Days since January 1	0	365
tm_isdst	Daylight Saving Time flag	[††]	[††]

[†]Allows for two extra "leap seconds." In C99, the maximum value is 60.
[††]Positive if Daylight Saving Time is in effect, zero if it's not in effect, and negative if this information is unknown.

These types are used for different purposes. A `clock_t` value is good only for representing a time duration; `time_t` and `struct tm` values can store an entire date and time. `time_t` values are tightly encoded, so they occupy little space. `struct tm` values require much more space, but they're often easier to work with. The C standard states that `clock_t` and `time_t` must be "arithmetic types," but leaves it at that. We don't even know if `clock_t` and `time_t` values are stored as integers or floating-point numbers.

We're now ready to look at the functions in `<time.h>`, which fall into two groups: time manipulation functions and time conversion functions.

Time Manipulation Functions

```
clock_t clock(void);
double difftime(time_t time1, time_t time0);
time_t mktime(struct tm *timeptr);
time_t time(time_t *timer);
```

clock   The `clock` function returns a `clock_t` value representing the processor time used by the program since execution began. To convert this value to seconds, we can divide it by `CLOCKS_PER_SEC`, a macro defined in `<time.h>`.

When `clock` is used to determine how long a program has been running, it's customary to call it twice: once at the beginning of `main` and once just before the program terminates:

```
#include <stdio.h>
#include <time.h>

int main(void)
{
  clock_t start_clock = clock();
  …
  printf("Processor time used: %g sec.\n",
          (clock() - start_clock) / (double) CLOCKS_PER_SEC);
  return 0;
}
```

The reason for the initial call of `clock` is that the program will use some processor time before it reaches `main`, thanks to hidden "start-up" code. Calling `clock` at the beginning of `main` determines how much time the start-up code requires so that we can subtract it later.

The C89 standard says only that `clock_t` is an arithmetic type; the type of `CLOCKS_PER_SEC` is unspecified. As a result, the type of the expression

```
(clock() - start_clock) / CLOCKS_PER_SEC
```

may vary from one implementation to another, making it difficult to display using `printf`. To solve the problem, our example converts `CLOCKS_PER_SEC` to **C99**   double, forcing the entire expression to have type `double`. In C99, the type of `CLOCKS_PER_SEC` is specified to be `clock_t`, but `clock_t` is still an implementation-defined type.

time   The `time` function returns the current calendar time. If its argument isn't a null pointer, `time` also stores the calendar time in the object that the argument points to. `time`'s ability to return a time in two different ways is an historical quirk, but it gives us the option of writing either

```
cur_time = time(NULL);
```

or

```
time(&cur_time);
```

where `cur_time` is a variable of type `time_t`.

difftime   The `difftime` function returns the difference between `time0` (the earlier time) and `time1`, measured in seconds. Thus, to compute the actual running time of a program (not the processor time), we could use the following code:

```
#include <stdio.h>
#include <time.h>

int main(void)
{
  time_t start_time = time(NULL);
  ...
  printf("Running time: %g sec.\n",
         difftime(time(NULL), start_time));
  return 0;
}
```

mktime   The `mktime` function converts a broken-down time (stored in the structure that its argument points to) into a calendar time, which it then returns. As a side effect, `mktime` adjusts the members of the structure according to the following rules:

- `mktime` changes any members whose values aren't within their legal ranges (see Table 26.1). Those alterations may in turn require changes to other members. If `tm_sec` is too large, for example, `mktime` reduces it to the proper range (0–59), adding the extra minutes to `tm_min`. If `tm_min` is now too large, `mktime` reduces it and adds the extra hours to `tm_hour`. If necessary, the process will continue to the `tm_mday`, `tm_mon`, and `tm_year` members.

- After adjusting the other members of the structure (if necessary), `mktime` sets `tm_wday` (day of the week) and `tm_yday` (day of the year) to their correct values. There's never any need to initialize the values of `tm_wday` and `tm_yday` before calling `mktime`; it ignores the original values of these members.

`mktime`'s ability to adjust the members of a `tm` structure makes it useful for time-related arithmetic. As a example, let's use `mktime` to answer the following question: If the 2012 Olympics begin on July 27 and end 16 days later, what is the ending date? We'll start by storing July 27, 2012 in a `tm` structure:

```
struct tm t;

t.tm_mday = 27;
t.tm_mon = 6;        /* July */
t.tm_year = 112;     /* 2012 */
```

We'll also initialize the other members of the structure (except `tm_wday` and `tm_yday`) to ensure that they don't contain undefined values that could affect the answer:

```
t.tm_sec = 0;
t.tm_min = 0;
t.tm_hour = 0;
t.tm_isdst = -1;
```

Next, we'll add 16 to the tm_mday member:

```
t.tm_mday += 16;
```

That leaves 43 in tm_mday, which is out of range for that member. Calling mktime will bring the members of the structure back into their proper ranges:

```
mktime(&t);
```

We'll discard mktime's return value, since we're interested only in the function's effect on t. The relevant members of t now have the following values:

Member	Value	Meaning
tm_mday	12	12
tm_mon	7	August
tm_year	112	2012
tm_wday	0	Sunday
tm_yday	224	225th day of the year

Time Conversion Functions

```
char *asctime(const struct tm *timeptr);
char *ctime(const time_t *timer);
struct tm *gmtime(const time_t *timer);
struct tm *localtime(const time_t *timer);
size_t strftime(char * restrict s, size_t maxsize,
                const char * restrict format,
                const struct tm * restrict timeptr);
```

The time conversion functions make it possible to convert calendar times to broken-down times. They can also convert times (calendar or broken-down) to string form. The following figure shows how these functions are related:

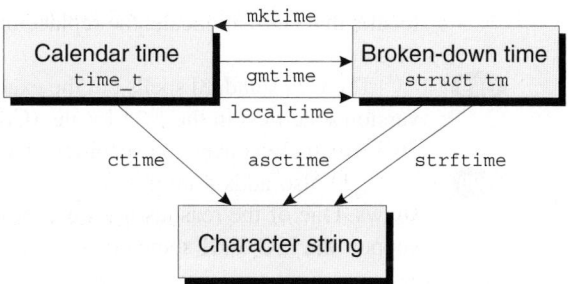

The figure includes the mktime function, which the C standard classifies as a "manipulation" function rather than a "conversion" function.

gmtime
localtime

Q&A

The gmtime and localtime functions are similar. When passed a pointer to a calendar time, both return a pointer to a structure containing the equivalent broken-down time. localtime produces a local time, while gmtime's return value is expressed in UTC (Coordinated Universal Time). The return value of gmtime and localtime points to a statically allocated structure that may be changed by a later call of either function.

asctime

The asctime (ASCII time) function returns a pointer to a null-terminated string of the form

```
Sun Jun  3 17:48:34 2007\n
```

constructed from the broken-down time pointed to by its argument.

ctime

The ctime function returns a pointer to a string describing a local time. If cur_time is a variable of type time_t, the call

```
ctime(&cur_time)
```

is equivalent to

```
asctime(localtime(&cur_time))
```

The return value of asctime and ctime points to a statically allocated string that may be changed by a later call of either function.

strftime

sprintf function ►22.8

The strftime function, like the asctime function, converts a broken-down time to string form. Unlike asctime, however, it gives us a great deal of control over how the time is formatted. In fact, strftime resembles sprintf in that it writes characters into a string s (the first argument) according to a format string (the third argument). The format string may contain ordinary characters (which are copied into s unchanged) along with the conversion specifiers shown in Table 26.2 (which are replaced by the indicated strings). The last argument points to a tm structure, which is used as the source of date and time information. The second argument is a limit on the number of characters that can be stored in s.

locales ►25.1

The strftime function, unlike the other functions in <time.h>, is sensitive to the current locale. Changing the LC_TIME category may affect the behavior of the conversion specifiers. The examples in Table 26.2 are strictly for the "C" locale; in a German locale, the replacement for %A might be Dienstag instead of Tuesday.

C99

The C99 standard spells out the exact replacement strings for some of the conversion specifiers in the "C" locale. (C89 didn't go into this level of detail.) Table 26.3 lists these conversion specifiers and the strings they're replaced by.

C99

C99 also adds a number of strftime conversion specifiers, as Table 26.2 shows. One of the reasons for the additional conversion specifiers is the desire to support the ISO 8601 standard.

Table 26.2
Conversion Specifiers for
the strftime Function

Conversion	Replacement
%a	Abbreviated weekday name (e.g., Sun)
%A	Full weekday name (e.g., Sunday)
%b	Abbreviated month name (e.g., Jun)
%B	Full month name (e.g., June)
%c	Complete day and time (e.g., Sun Jun 3 17:48:34 2007)
%C[†]	Year divided by 100 and truncated to an integer (00–99)
%d	Day of month (01–31)
%D[†]	Equivalent to %m/%d/%y
%e[†]	Day of month (1–31); a single digit is preceded by a space
%F[†]	Equivalent to %Y-%m-%d
%g[†]	Last two digits of ISO 8601 week-based year (00–99)
%G[†]	ISO 8601 week-based year
%h[†]	Equivalent to %b
%H	Hour on 24-hour clock (00–23)
%I	Hour on 12-hour clock (01–12)
%j	Day of year (001–366)
%m	Month (01–12)
%M	Minute (00–59)
%n[†]	New-line character
%p	AM/PM designator (AM or PM)
%r[†]	12-hour clock time (e.g., 05:48:34 PM)
%R[†]	Equivalent to %H:%M
%S	Second (00–61); maximum value in C99 is 60
%t[†]	Horizontal-tab character
%T[†]	Equivalent to %H:%M:%S
%u[†]	ISO 8601 weekday (1–7); Monday is 1
%U	Week number (00–53); first Sunday is beginning of week 1
%V[†]	ISO 8601 week number (01–53)
%w	Weekday (0–6); Sunday is 0
%W	Week number (00–53); first Monday is beginning of week 1
%x	Complete date (e.g., 06/03/07)
%X	Complete time (e.g., 17:48:34)
%y	Last two digits of year (00–99)
%Y	Year
%z[†]	Offset from UTC in ISO 8601 format (e.g., -0530 or +0200)
%Z	Time zone name or abbreviation (e.g., EST)
%%	%

[†]C99 only

Table 26.3
Replacement Strings for
strftime Conversion
Specifiers in the
"C" Locale

Conversion	Replacement
%a	First three characters of %A
%A	One of "Sunday", "Monday", ..., "Saturday"
%b	First three characters of %B
%B	One of "January", "February", ..., "December"
%c	Equivalent to "%a %b %e %T %Y"
%p	One of "AM" or "PM"
%r	Equivalent to "%I:%M:%S %p"
%x	Equivalent to "%m/%d/%y"
%X	Equivalent to %T
%Z	Implementation-defined

ISO 8601

ISO 8601 is an international standard that describes ways of representing dates and times. It was originally published in 1988 and later updated in 2000 and 2004. According to this standard, dates and times are entirely numeric (i.e., months are not represented by names) and hours are expressed using the 24-hour clock.

There are a number of ISO 8601 date and time formats, some of which are directly supported by `strftime` conversion specifiers in C99. The primary ISO 8601 date format (*YYYY–MM–DD*) and the primary time format (*hh:mm:ss*) correspond to the `%F` and `%T` conversion specifiers, respectively.

ISO 8601 has a system of numbering the weeks of a year; this system is supported by the `%g`, `%G`, and `%V` conversion specifiers. Weeks begin on Monday, and week 1 is the week containing the first Thursday of the year. Consequently, the first few days of January (as many as three) may belong to the last week of the previous year. For example, consider the calendar for January 2011:

January 2011

Mo	Tu	We	Th	Fr	Sa	Su	Year	Week
					1	2	2010	52
3	4	5	6	7	8	9	2011	1
10	11	12	13	14	15	16	2011	2
17	18	19	20	21	22	23	2011	3
24	25	26	27	28	29	30	2011	4
31							2011	5

January 6 is the first Thursday of the year, so the week of January 3–9 is week 1. January 1 and January 2 belong to the last week (week 52) of the previous year. For these two dates, `strftime` will replace `%g` by `10`, `%G` by `2010`, and `%V` by `52`. Note that the last few days of December will sometimes belong to week 1 of the following year; this happens whenever December 29, 30, or 31 is a Monday.

The `%z` conversion specifier corresponds to the ISO 8601 time zone specification: *–hhmm* means that a time zone is *hh* hours and *mm* minutes behind UTC; the string *+hhmm* indicates the amount by which a time zone is ahead of UTC.

C99 allows the use of an E or O character to modify the meaning of certain `strftime` conversion specifiers. Conversion specifiers that begin with an E or O modifier cause a replacement to be performed using an alternative format that depends on the current locale. If an alternative representation doesn't exist in the current locale, the modifier has no effect. (In the `"C"` locale, E and O are ignored.) Table 26.4 lists all conversion specifiers that are allowed to have E or O modifiers.

PROGRAM **Displaying the Date and Time**

Let's say we need a program that displays the current date and time. The program's first step, of course, is to call the `time` function to obtain the calendar time. The

Table 26.4

E- and O-Modified
Conversion Specifiers
for the `strftime`
Function (C99 only)

Conversion	Replacement
`%Ec`	Alternative date and time representation
`%EC`	Name of base year (period) in alternative representation
`%Ex`	Alternative date representation
`%EX`	Alternative time representation
`%Ey`	Offset from `%EC` (year only) in alternative representation
`%EY`	Full alternative year representation
`%Od`	Day of month, using alternative numeric symbols (filled with leading zeros or with leading spaces if there is no alternative symbol for zero)
`%Oe`	Day of month, using alternative numeric symbols (filled with leading spaces)
`%OH`	Hour on 24-hour clock, using alternative numeric symbols
`%OI`	Hour on 12-hour clock, using alternative numeric symbols
`%Om`	Month, using alternative numeric symbols
`%OM`	Minute, using alternative numeric symbols
`%OS`	Second, using alternative numeric symbols
`%Ou`	ISO 8601 weekday as a number in alternative representation, where Monday is 1
`%OU`	Week number, using alternative numeric symbols
`%OV`	ISO 8601 week number, using alternative numeric symbols
`%Ow`	Weekday as a number, using alternative numeric symbols
`%OW`	Week number, using alternative numeric symbols
`%Oy`	Last two digits of year, using alternative numeric symbols

second step is to convert the time to string form and print it. The easiest way to do the second step is to call `ctime`, which returns a pointer to a string containing a date and time, then pass this pointer to `puts` or `printf`.

So far, so good. But what if we want the program to display the date and time in a particular way? Let's assume that we need the following format, where `06` is the month and `03` is the day of the month:

```
06-03-2007   5:48p
```

The `ctime` function always uses the same format for the date and time, so it's no help. The `strftime` function is better; using it, we can almost achieve the appearance that we want. Unfortunately, `strftime` won't let us display a one-digit hour without a leading zero. Also, `strftime` uses AM and PM instead of a and p.

When `strftime` isn't good enough, we have another alternative: convert the calendar time to a broken-down time, then extract the relevant information from the `tm` structure and format it ourselves using `printf` or a similar function. We might even use `strftime` to do some of the formatting before having other functions complete the job.

The following program illustrates the options. It displays the current date and time in three formats: the one used by `ctime`, one close to what we want (created using `strftime`), and the desired format (created using `printf`). The `ctime` version is easy to do, the `strftime` version is a little harder, and the `printf` version is the most difficult.

datetime.c   /* Displays the current date and time in three formats */

```c
#include <stdio.h>
#include <time.h>

int main(void)
{
  time_t current = time(NULL);
  struct tm *ptr;
  char date_time[21];
  int hour;
  char am_or_pm;

  /* Print date and time in default format */
  puts(ctime(&current));

  /* Print date and time, using strftime to format */
  strftime(date_time, sizeof(date_time),
           "%m-%d-%Y  %I:%M%p\n", localtime(&current));
  puts(date_time);

  /* Print date and time, using printf to format */
  ptr = localtime(&current);
  hour = ptr->tm_hour;
  if (hour <= 11)
    am_or_pm = 'a';
  else {
    hour -= 12;
    am_or_pm = 'p';
  }
  if (hour == 0)
    hour = 12;
  printf("%.2d-%.2d-%d  %2d:%.2d%c\n", ptr->tm_mon + 1,
         ptr->tm_mday, ptr->tm_year + 1900, hour,
         ptr->tm_min, am_or_pm);

  return 0;
}
```

The output of `datetime.c` will have the following appearance:

```
Sun Jun  3 17:48:34 2007

06-03-2007  05:48PM

06-03-2007   5:48p
```

Q & A

Q: **Although `<stdlib.h>` provides a number of functions that convert strings to numbers, there don't appear to be any functions that convert numbers to strings. What gives?**

A: Some C libraries supply functions with names like itoa that convert numbers to strings. Using these functions isn't a great idea, though: they aren't part of the C standard and won't be portable. The best way to perform this kind of conversion is to call a function such as sprintf that writes formatted output into a string:

sprintf function ➤22.8

```
char str[20];
int i;
…
sprintf(str, "%d", i);    /* writes i into the string str */
```

Not only is sprintf portable, but it also provides a great deal of control over the appearance of the number.

*Q: **The description of the strtod function says that C99 allows the string argument to contain a hexadecimal floating-point number, infinity, or NaN. What is the format of these numbers? [p. 684]**

A: A hexadecimal floating-point number begins with 0x or 0X, followed by one or more hexadecimal digits (possibly including a decimal-point character), and then possibly a binary exponent. (See the Q&A at the end of Chapter 7 for a discussion of hexadecimal floating constants, which have a similar—but not identical—format.) Infinity has the form INF or INFINITY; any or all of the letters may be lower-case. NaN is represented by the string NAN (again ignoring case), possibly followed by a pair of parentheses. The parentheses may be empty or they may contain a series of characters, where each character is a letter, digit, or underscore. The characters may be used to specify some of the bits in the binary representation of the NaN value, but their exact meaning is implementation-defined. The same kind of character sequence—which the C99 standard calls an *n-char-*

nan function ➤23.4

sequence—is also used in calls of the nan function.

*Q: **You said that performing the call exit(*n*) anywhere in a program is *normally* equivalent to executing the statement return *n*; in main. When would it not be equivalent? [p. 688]**

A: There are two issues. First, when the main function returns, the lifetime of its

automatic storage duration ➤18.2

local variables ends (assuming that they have automatic storage duration, as they will unless they're declared to be static), which isn't true if the exit function is called. A problem will occur if any action that takes place at program termination—such as calling a function previously registered using atexit or flushing an output stream buffer—requires access to one of these variables. In particular, a

setvbuf function ➤22.2

program might have called setvbuf and used one of main's variables as a buffer. Thus, in rare cases a program may behave improperly if it attempts to return from main but work if it calls exit instead.

The other issue occurs only in C99, which makes it legal for main to have a return type other than int if an implementation explicitly allows the programmer to do so. In these circumstances, the call exit(*n*) isn't necessarily equivalent to executing return *n*; in main. In fact, the statement return *n*; may be illegal (if main is declared to return void, for example).

*Q: **Is there a relationship between the `abort` function and `SIGABRT` signal? [p. 688]***

A: Yes. A call of `abort` actually raises the `SIGABRT` signal. If there's no handler for `SIGABRT`, the program terminates abnormally as described in Section 26.2. If a

`signal` function ➤24.3   handler has been installed for `SIGABRT` (by a call of the `signal` function), the handler is called. If the handler returns, the program then terminates abnormally.

`longjmp` function ➤24.4   However, if the handler *doesn't* return (it calls `longjmp`, for example), then the program doesn't terminate.

Q: **Why do the `div` and `ldiv` functions exist? Can't we just use the `/` and `%` operators? [p. 692]**

A: `div` and `ldiv` aren't quite the same as `/` and `%`. Recall from Section 4.1 that applying `/` and `%` to negative operands doesn't give a portable result in C89. If `i` or `j` is negative, whether the value of `i / j` is rounded up or down is implementation-defined, as is the sign of `i % j`. The answers computed by `div` and `ldiv`, on the other hand, don't depend on the implementation. The quotient is rounded toward zero; the remainder is computed according to the formula $n = q \times d + r$, where n is the original number, q is the quotient, d is the divisor, and r is the remainder. Here are a few examples:

n	d	q	r
7	3	2	1
−7	3	−2	−1
7	−3	−2	1
−7	−3	2	−1

 In C99, the `/` and `%` operators are guaranteed to produce the same result as `div` and `ldiv`.

Efficiency is the other reason that `div` and `ldiv` exist. Many machines have an instruction that can compute both the quotient and remainder, so calling `div` or `ldiv` may be faster than using the `/` and `%` operators separately.

Q: **Where does the name of the `gmtime` function come from? [p. 696]**

A: The name `gmtime` stands for Greenwich Mean Time (GMT), referring to the local (solar) time at the Royal Observatory in Greenwich, England. In 1884, GMT was adopted as an international reference time, with other time zones expressed as hours "behind GMT" or "ahead of GMT." In 1972, Coordinated Universal Time (UTC)—a system based on atomic clocks rather than solar observations—replaced GMT as the international time reference. By adding a "leap second" once every few years, UTC is kept synchronized with GMT to within 0.9 second, so for all but the most precise time measurements the two systems are identical.

Exercises

Section 26.1   1.   Rewrite the `max_int` function so that, instead of passing the number of integers as the first argument, we must supply 0 as the last argument. *Hint:* `max_int` must have at least one "normal" parameter, so you can't remove the parameter n. Instead, assume that it represents one of the numbers to be compared.

2. Write a simplified version of printf in which the only conversion specification is %d, and all arguments after the first are assumed to have int type. If the function encounters a % character that's not immediately followed by a d character, it should ignore both characters. The function should use calls of putchar to produce all output. You may assume that the format string doesn't contain escape sequences.

3. Extend the function of Exercise 2 so that it allows two conversion specifications: %d and %s. Each %d in the format string indicates an int argument, and each %s indicates a char * (string) argument.

4. Write a function named display that takes any number of arguments. The first argument must be an integer. The remaining arguments will be strings. The first argument specifies how many strings the call contains. The function will print the strings on a single line, with adjacent strings separated by one space. For example, the call

```
display(4, "Special", "Agent", "Dale", "Cooper");
```

will produce the following output:

```
Special Agent Dale Cooper
```

5. Write the following function:

```
char *vstrcat(const char *first, ...);
```

All arguments of vstrcat are assumed to be strings, except for the last argument, which must be a null pointer (cast to char * type). The function returns a pointer to a dynamically allocated string containing the concatenation of the arguments. vstrcat should return a null pointer if not enough memory is available. *Hint:* Have vstrcat go through the arguments twice: once to determine the amount of memory required for the returned string and once to copy the arguments into the string.

6. Write the following function:

```
char *max_pair(int num_pairs, ...);
```

The arguments of max_pair are assumed to be "pairs" of integers and strings; the value of num_pairs indicates how many pairs will follow. (A pair consists of an int argument followed by a char * argument). The function searches the integers to find the largest one; it then returns the string argument that follows it. Consider the following call:

```
max_pair(5, 180, "Seinfeld", 180, "I Love Lucy",
            39, "The Honeymooners", 210, "All in the Family",
            86, "The Sopranos")
```

The largest int argument is 210, so the function returns "All in the Family", which follows it in the argument list.

Section 26.2   7. Explain the meaning of the following statement, assuming that value is a variable of type long int and p is a variable of type char *:

```
value = strtol(p, &p, 10);
```

8. Write a statement that randomly assigns one of the numbers 7, 11, 15, or 19 to the variable n.

9. Write a function that returns a random double value d in the range $0.0 \le d < 1.0$.

10. Convert the following calls of atoi, atol, and atoll into calls of strtol, strtol, and strtoll, respectively.

       (a) `atoi(str)`

       (b) `atol(str)`

       (c) `atoll(str)`

11. Although the `bsearch` function is normally used with a sorted array, it will sometimes work correctly with an array that is only partially sorted. What condition must an array satisfy to guarantee that `bsearch` works properly for a particular key? *Hint:* The answer appears in the C standard.

Section 26.3

12. Write a function that, when passed a year, returns a `time_t` value representing 12:00 a.m. on the first day of that year.

13. Section 26.3 described some of the ISO 8601 date and time formats. Here are a few more:

    (a) Year followed by day of year: *YYYY–DDD*, where *DDD* is a number between 001 and 366

    (b) Year, week, and day of week: *YYYY–Www–D*, where *ww* is a number between 01 and 53, and *D* is a digit between 1 through 7, beginning with Monday and ending with Sunday

    (c) Combined date and time: *YYYY–MM–DDThh:mm:ss*

Give `strftime` strings that correspond to each of these formats.

Programming Projects

1. (a) Write a program that calls the `rand` function 1000 times, printing the low-order bit of each value it returns (0 if the return value is even, 1 if it's odd). Do you see any patterns? (Often, the last few bits of `rand`'s return value aren't especially random.)

    (b) How can we improve the randomness of `rand` for generating numbers within a small range?

2. Write a program that tests the `atexit` function. The program should have two functions (in addition to `main`), one of which prints `That's all`, and the other `folks!`. Use the `atexit` function to register both to be called at program termination. Make sure they're called in the proper order, so that we see the message `That's all, folks!` on the screen.

3. Write a program that uses the `clock` function to measure how long it takes `qsort` to sort an array of 1000 integers that are originally in reverse order. Run the program for arrays of 10000 and 100000 integers as well.

4. Write a program that prompts the user for a date (month, day, and year) and an integer n, then prints the date that's n days later.

5. Write a program that prompts the user to enter two dates, then prints the difference between them, measured in days. *Hint:* Use the `mktime` and `difftime` functions.

6. Write programs that display the current date and time in each of the following formats. Use `strftime` to do all or most of the formatting.

    (a) `Sunday, June 3, 2007   05:48p`

    (b) `Sun, 3 Jun 07   17:48`

    (c) `06/03/07   5:48:34 PM`

27 Additional C99 Support for Mathematics

Simplicity does not precede complexity, but follows it.

This chapter completes our coverage of the standard library by describing five headers that are new in C99. These headers, like some of the older ones, provide support for working with numbers. However, the new headers are more specialized than the old ones. Some of them will appeal primarily to engineers, scientists, and mathematicians, who may need complex numbers as well as greater control over the representation of numbers and the way floating-point arithmetic is performed.

The first two sections discuss headers related to the integer types. The `<stdint.h>` header (Section 27.1) declares integer types that have a specified number of bits. The `<inttypes.h>` header (Section 27.2) provides macros that are useful for reading and writing values of the `<stdint.h>` types.

The next two sections describe C99's support for complex numbers. Section 27.3 includes a review of complex numbers as well as a discussion of C99's complex types. Section 27.4 then covers the `<complex.h>` header, which supplies functions that perform mathematical operations on complex numbers.

The headers discussed in the last two sections are related to the floating types. The `<tgmath.h>` header (Section 27.5) provides type-generic macros that make it easier to call library functions in `<complex.h>` and `<math.h>`. The functions in the `<fenv.h>` header (Section 27.6) give programs access to floating-point status flags and control modes.

27.1 The `<stdint.h>` Header (C99): Integer Types

The `<stdint.h>` header declares integer types containing a specified number of bits. In addition, it defines macros that represent the minimum and maximum values of these types as well as of integer types declared in other headers.

<limits.h> header ➤ *23.2* (These macros augment the ones in the <limits.h> header.) <stdint.h> also defines parameterized macros that construct integer constants with specific types. There are no functions in <stdint.h>.

The primary motivation for the <stdint.h> header lies in an observation made in Section 7.5, which discussed the role of type definitions in making programs portable. For example, if i is an int variable, the assignment

```
i = 100000;
```

is fine if int is a 32-bit type but will fail if int is a 16-bit type. The problem is that the C standard doesn't specify exactly how many bits an int value has. The standard *does* guarantee that the values of the int type must include all numbers between –32767 and +32767 (which requires at least 16 bits), but that's all it has to say on the matter. In the case of the variable i, which needs to be able to store 100000, the traditional solution is to declare i to be of some type T, where T is a type name created using typedef. The declaration of T can then be adjusted based on the sizes of integers in a particular implementation. (On a 16-bit machine, T would need to be long int, but on a 32-bit machine, it can be int.) This is the strategy that Section 7.5 discusses.

If your compiler supports C99, there's a better technique. The <stdint.h> header declares names for types based on the **width** of the type (the number of bits sign bit ➤ *7.1* used to store values of the type, including the sign bit, if any). The typedef names declared in <stdint.h> may refer to basic types (such as int, unsigned int, and long int) or to extended integer types that are supported by a particular implementation.

<stdint.h> Types

The types declared in <stdint.h> fall into five groups:

- **Exact-width integer types.** Each name of the form int$N$_t represents a signed integer type with N bits, stored in two's-complement form. (Two's complement, a technique used to represent signed integers in binary, is nearly universal among modern computers.) For example, a value of type int16_t would be a 16-bit signed integer. A name of the form uint$N$_t represents an unsigned integer type with N bits. An implementation is required to provide both int$N$_t and uint$N$_t for $N = 8$, 16, 32, and 64 if it supports integers with these widths.

- **Minimum-width integer types.** Each name of the form int_least$N$_t represents a signed integer type with at least N bits. A name of the form uint_least$N$_t represents an unsigned integer type with N or more bits. <stdint.h> is required to provide at least the following minimum-width types:

```
int_least8_t      uint_least8_t
int_least16_t     uint_least16_t
```

```
int_least32_t    uint_least32_t
int_least64_t    uint_least64_t
```

- *Fastest minimum-width integer types.* Each name of the form int_fast*N*_t represents the fastest signed integer type with at least *N* bits. (The meaning of "fastest" is up to the implementation. If there's no reason to classify a particular type as the fastest, the implementation may choose any signed integer type with at least *N* bits.) Each name of the form uint_fast*N*_t represents the fastest unsigned integer type with *N* or more bits. <stdint.h> is required to provide at least the following fastest minimum-width types:

```
int_fast8_t      uint_fast8_t
int_fast16_t     uint_fast16_t
int_fast32_t     uint_fast32_t
int_fast64_t     uint_fast64_t
```

- *Integer types capable of holding object pointers.* The intptr_t type represents a signed integer type that can safely store any void * value. More precisely, if a void * pointer is converted to intptr_t type and then back to void *, the resulting pointer and the original pointer will compare equal. The uintptr_t type is an unsigned integer type with the same property as intptr_t. The <stdint.h> header isn't required to provide either type.

- *Greatest-width integer types.* intmax_t is a signed integer type that includes all values that belong to any signed integer type. uintmax_t is an unsigned integer type that includes all values that belong to any unsigned integer type. <stdint.h> is required to provide both types, which might be wider than long long int.

The names in the first three groups are declared using typedef.

An implementation may provide exact-width integer types, minimum-width integer types, and fastest minimum-width integer types for values of *N* in addition to the ones listed above. Also, *N* isn't required to be a power of 2 (although it will normally be a multiple of 8). For example, an implementation might provide types named int24_t and uint24_t.

Limits of Specified-Width Integer Types

For each signed integer type declared in <stdint.h>, the header defines macros that specify the type's minimum and maximum values. For each unsigned integer type, <stdint.h> defines a macro that specifies the type's maximum value. The first three rows of Table 27.1 show the values of these macros for the exact-width integer types. The remaining rows show the constraints imposed by the C99 standard on the minimum and maximum values of the other <stdint.h> types. (The precise values of these macros are implementation-defined.) All macros in the table represent constant expressions.

Name	*Value*	*Description*
INTN_MIN	$-(2^{N-1})$	Minimum int$N$_t value
INTN_MAX	$2^{N-1}-1$	Maximum int$N$_t value
UINTN_MAX	$2^{N}-1$	Maximum uint$N$_t value
INT_LEASTN_MIN	$\leq-(2^{N-1}-1)$	Minimum int_least$N$_t value
INT_LEASTN_MAX	$\geq 2^{N-1}-1$	Maximum int_least$N$_t value
UINT_LEASTN_MAX	$\geq 2^{N}-1$	Maximum uint_least$N$_t value
INT_FASTN_MIN	$\leq-(2^{N-1}-1)$	Minimum int_fast$N$_t value
INT_FASTN_MAX	$\geq 2^{N-1}-1$	Maximum int_fast$N$_t value
UINT_FASTN_MAX	$\geq 2^{N}-1$	Maximum uint_fast$N$_t value
INTPTR_MIN	$\leq-(2^{15}-1)$	Minimum intptr_t value
INTPTR_MAX	$\geq 2^{15}-1$	Maximum intptr_t value
UINTPTR_MAX	$\geq 2^{16}-1$	Maximum uintptr_t value
INTMAX_MIN	$\leq-(2^{63}-1)$	Minimum intmax_t value
INTMAX_MAX	$\geq 2^{63}-1$	Maximum intmax_t value
UINTMAX_MAX	$\geq 2^{64}-1$	Maximum uintmax_t value

Limits of Other Integer Types

When the C99 committee created the `<stdint.h>` header, they decided that it would be a good place to put macros describing the limits of integer types besides the ones declared in `<stdint.h>` itself. These types are `ptrdiff_t`, `size_t`,

`<stddef.h>` header ➤*21.4*
`<signal.h>` header ➤*24.3*
`<wchar.h>` header ➤*25.5*

and `wchar_t` (which belong to `<stddef.h>`), `sig_atomic_t` (declared in `<signal.h>`), and `wint_t` (declared in `<wchar.h>`). Table 27.2 lists these macros and shows the value of each (or any constraints on the value imposed by the C99 standard). In some cases, the constraints on the minimum and maximum values of a type depend on whether the type is signed or unsigned. The macros in Table 27.2, like the ones in Table 27.1, represent constant expressions.

Macros for Integer Constants

The `<stdint.h>` header also provides function-like macros that are able to con-

integer constants ➤*7.1*

vert an integer constant (expressed in decimal, octal, or hexadecimal, but without a `U` and/or `L` suffix) into a constant expression belonging to a minimum-width integer type or greatest-width integer type.

For each `int_least`N`_t` type declared in `<stdint.h>`, the header defines a parameterized macro named INTN_C that converts an integer constant to

integer promotions ➤*7.4*

this type (possibly using the integer promotions). For each `uint_least`N`_t` type, there's a similar parameterized macro named UINTN_C. These macros are useful for initializing variables, among other things. For example, if `i` is a variable of type `int_least32_t`, writing

Name	Value	Description
PTRDIFF_MIN PTRDIFF_MAX	≤–65535 ≥+65535	Minimum ptrdiff_t value Maximum ptrdiff_t value
SIG_ATOMIC_MIN	≤–127 (if signed) 0 (if unsigned)	Minimum sig_atomic_t value
SIG_ATOMIC_MAX	≥+127 (if signed) ≥255 (if unsigned)	Maximum sig_atomic_t value
SIZE_MAX	≥65535	Maximum size_t value
WCHAR_MIN	≤–127 (if signed) 0 (if unsigned)	Minimum wchar_t value
WCHAR_MAX	≥+127 (if signed) ≥255 (if unsigned)	Maximum wchar_t value
WINT_MIN	≤–32767 (if signed) 0 (if unsigned)	Minimum wint_t value
WINT_MAX	≥+32767 (if signed) ≥65535 (if unsigned)	Maximum wint_t value

Table 27.2
<stdint.h> Limit
Macros for Other
Integer Types

```
i = 100000;
```

is problematic, because the constant `100000` might be too large to represent using type `int` (if `int` is a 16-bit type). However, the statement

```
i = INT32_C(100000);
```

is safe. If `int_least32_t` represents the `int` type, then `INT32_C(100000)` has type `int`. But if `int_least32_t` corresponds to `long int`, then `INT32_C(100000)` has type `long int`.

    <stdint.h> has two other parameterized macros. `INTMAX_C` converts an integer constant to type `intmax_t`, and `UINTMAX_C` converts an integer constant to type `uintmax_t`.

27.2 The <inttypes.h> Header (C99)
Format Conversion of Integer Types

Q&A

The <inttypes.h> header is closely related to the <stdint.h> header, the topic of Section 27.1. In fact, <inttypes.h> includes <stdint.h>, so programs that include <inttypes.h> don't need to include <stdint.h> as well. The <inttypes.h> header extends <stdint.h> in two ways. First, it defines macros that can be used in ...printf and ...scanf format strings for input/output of the integer types declared in <stdint.h>. Second, it provides functions for working with greatest-width integers.

Macros for Format Specifiers

The types declared in the `<stdint.h>` header can be used to make programs more portable, but they create new headaches for the programmer. Consider the problem of displaying the value of the variable `i`, where `i` has type `int_least32_t`. The statement

```
printf("i = %d\n", i);
```

may not work, because `i` doesn't necessarily have `int` type. If `int_least32_t` is another name for the `long int` type, then the correct conversion specification is `%ld`, not `%d`. In order to use the ...`printf` and ...`scanf` functions in a portable manner, we need a way to write conversion specifications that correspond to each of the types declared in `<stdint.h>`. That's where the `<inttypes.h>` header comes in. For each `<stdint.h>` type, `<inttypes.h>` provides a macro that expands into a string literal containing the proper conversion specifier for that type.

Each macro name has three parts:

- The name begins with either `PRI` or `SCN`, depending on whether the macro will be used in a call of a ...`printf` function or a ...`scanf` function.
- Next comes a one-letter conversion specifier (`d` or `i` for a signed type; `o`, `u`, `x`, or `X` for an unsigned type).
- The last part of the name indicates which `<stdint.h>` type is involved. For example, the name of a macro that corresponds to the `int_leastN_t` type would end with LEAST*N*.

Let's return to our previous example, which involved displaying an integer of type `int_least32_t`. Instead of using `d` as the conversion specifier, we'll switch to the `PRIdLEAST32` macro. To use the macro, we'll split the `printf` format string into three pieces and replace the `d` in `%d` by `PRIdLEAST32`:

```
printf("i = %" PRIdLEAST32 "\n", i);
```

The value of `PRIdLEAST32` is probably either `"d"` (if `int_least32_t` is the same as the `int` type) or `"ld"` (if `int_least32_t` is the same as `long int`). Let's assume that it's `"ld"` for the sake of discussion. After macro replacement, the statement becomes

```
printf("i = %" "ld" "\n", i);
```

Once the compiler joins the three string literals into one (which it will do automatically), the statement will have the following appearance:

```
printf("i = %ld\n", i);
```

Note that we can still include flags, a field width, and other options in our conversion specification; `PRIdLEAST32` supplies only the conversion specifier and possibly a length modifier, such as the letter `l`.

Table 27.3 lists the `<inttypes.h>` macros.

Table 27.3
Format-Specifier Macros
in `<inttypes.h>`

...**printf** *Macros for Signed Integers*				
PRId*N*	PRIdLEAST*N*	PRIdFAST*N*	PRIdMAX	PRIdPTR
PRIi*N*	PRIiLEAST*N*	PRIiFAST*N*	PRIiMAX	PRIiPTR
...**printf** *Macros for Unsigned Integers*				
PRIo*N*	PRIoLEAST*N*	PRIoFAST*N*	PRIoMAX	PRIoPTR
PRIu*N*	PRIuLEAST*N*	PRIuFAST*N*	PRIuMAX	PRIuPTR
PRIx*N*	PRIxLEAST*N*	PRIxFAST*N*	PRIxMAX	PRIxPTR
PRIX*N*	PRIXLEAST*N*	PRIXFAST*N*	PRIXMAX	PRIXPTR
...**scanf** *Macros for Signed Integers*				
SCNd*N*	SCNdLEAST*N*	SCNdFAST*N*	SCNdMAX	SCNdPTR
SCNi*N*	SCNiLEAST*N*	SCNiFAST*N*	SCNiMAX	SCNiPTR
...**scanf** *Macros for Unsigned Integers*				
SCNo*N*	SCNoLEAST*N*	SCNoFAST*N*	SCNoMAX	SCNoPTR
SCNu*N*	SCNuLEAST*N*	SCNuFAST*N*	SCNuMAX	SCNuPTR
SCNx*N*	SCNxLEAST*N*	SCNxFAST*N*	SCNxMAX	SCNxPTR

Functions for Greatest-Width Integer Types

```
intmax_t imaxabs(intmax_t j);
imaxdiv_t imaxdiv(intmax_t numer, intmax_t denom);
intmax_t strtoimax(const char * restrict nptr,
                   char ** restrict endptr,
                   int base);
uintmax_t strtoumax(const char * restrict nptr,
                    char ** restrict endptr,
                    int base);
intmax_t wcstoimax(const wchar_t * restrict nptr,
                   wchar_t ** restrict endptr,
                   int base);
uintmax_t wcstoumax(const wchar_t * restrict nptr,
                    wchar_t ** restrict endptr,
                    int base);
```

In addition to defining macros, the `<inttypes.h>` header provides functions for working with greatest-width integers, which were introduced in Section 27.1. A greatest-width integer has type `intmax_t` (the widest signed integer type supported by an implementation) or `uintmax_t` (the widest unsigned integer type). These types might be the same width as the `long long int` type, but they could be wider. For example, `long long int` might be 64 bits wide and `intmax_t` and `uintmax_t` might be 128 bits wide.

imaxabs
imaxdiv

`<stdlib.h>` header ➤*26.2*

The `imaxabs` and `imaxdiv` functions are greatest-width versions of the integer arithmetic functions declared in `<stdlib.h>`. The `imaxabs` function returns the absolute value of its argument. Both the argument and the return value have type `intmax_t`. The `imaxdiv` function divides its first argument by its second, returning an `imaxdiv_t` value. `imaxdiv_t` is a structure that contains both a quotient member (named `quot`) and a remainder member (`rem`); both members have type `intmax_t`.

strtoimax
strtoumax

The `strtoimax` and `strtoumax` functions are greatest-width versions of the numeric conversion functions of `<stdlib.h>`. The `strtoimax` function is the same as `strtol` and `strtoll`, except that it returns a value of type `intmax_t`. The `strtoumax` function is equivalent to `strtoul` and `strtoull`, except that it returns a value of type `uintmax_t`. Both `strtoimax` and `strtoumax` return zero if no conversion could be performed. Both functions store `ERANGE` in `errno` if a conversion produces a value that's outside the range of the function's return type. In addition, `strtoimax` returns the smallest or largest `intmax_t` value (`INTMAX_MIN` or `INTMAX_MAX`); `strtoumax` returns the largest `uintmax_t` value, `UINTMAX_MAX`.

wcstoimax
wcstoumax

<wchar.h> header ➤*25.5*

The `wcstoimax` and `wcstoumax` functions are greatest-width versions of the wide-string numeric conversion functions of `<wchar.h>`. The `wcstoimax` function is the same as `wcstol` and `wcstoll`, except that it returns a value of type `intmax_t`. The `wcstoumax` function is equivalent to `wcstoul` and `wcstoull`, except that it returns a value of type `uintmax_t`. Both `wcstoimax` and `wcstoumax` return zero if no conversion could be performed. Both functions store `ERANGE` in `errno` if a conversion produces a value that's outside the range of the function's return type. In addition, `wcstoimax` returns the smallest or largest `intmax_t` value (`INTMAX_MIN` or `INTMAX_MAX`); `wcstoumax` returns the largest `uintmax_t` value, `UINTMAX_MAX`.

27.3 Complex Numbers (C99)

Complex numbers are used in scientific and engineering applications as well as in mathematics. C99 provides several complex types, allows operators to have complex operands, and adds a header named `<complex.h>` to the standard library. There's a catch, though: complex numbers aren't supported by all implementations of C99. Section 14.3 discussed the difference between a *hosted* C99 implementation and a *freestanding* implementation. A hosted implementation must accept any program that conforms to the C99 standard, whereas a freestanding implementation doesn't have to compile programs that use complex types or standard headers other than `<float.h>`, `<iso646.h>`, `<limits.h>`, `<stdarg.h>`, `<stdbool.h>`, `<stddef.h>`, and `<stdint.h>`. Thus, a freestanding implementation may lack both complex types and the `<complex.h>` header.

We'll start with a review of the mathematical definition of complex numbers and complex arithmetic. We'll then look at C99's complex types and the operations that can be performed on values of these types. Coverage of complex numbers continues in Section 27.4, which describes the `<complex.h>` header.

Definition of Complex Numbers

Let i be the square root of -1 (a number such that $i^2 = -1$). i is known as the ***imaginary unit;*** engineers often represent it by the symbol j instead of i. A ***complex number*** has the form $a + bi$, where a and b are real numbers. a is said to be the ***real part*** of the number, and b is the ***imaginary part.*** Note that the complex numbers include the real numbers as a special case (when $b = 0$).

Why are complex numbers useful? For one thing, they allow solutions to problems that are otherwise unsolvable. Consider the equation $x^2 + 1 = 0$, which has no solution if x is restricted to the real numbers. If complex numbers are allowed, there are two solutions: $x = i$ and $x = -i$.

Complex numbers can be thought of as points in a two-dimensional space known as the ***complex plane.*** Each complex number—a point in the complex plane—is represented by Cartesian coordinates, where the real part of the number corresponds to the x-coordinate of the point, and the imaginary part corresponds to the y-coordinate. For example, the complex numbers $2 + 2.5i$, $1 - 3i$, $-3 - 2i$, and $-3.5 + 1.5i$ can be plotted as follows:

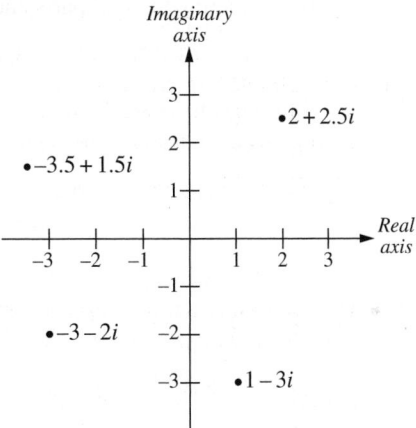

An alternative system known as ***polar coordinates*** can also be used to specify a point on the complex plane. With polar coordinates, a complex number z is represented by the values r and θ, where r is the length of a line segment from the origin to z, and θ is the angle between this segment and the real axis:

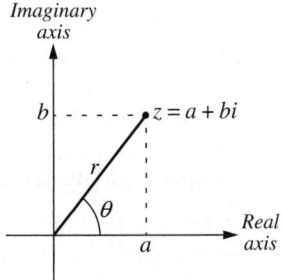

r is called the **absolute value** of *z*. (The absolute value is also known as the *norm, modulus,* or *magnitude.*) θ is said to be the **argument** (or *phase angle*) of *z*. The absolute value of *a* + *bi* is given by the following equation:

$$|a + bi| = \sqrt{a^2 + b^2}$$

For additional information about converting from Cartesian coordinates to polar coordinates and vice versa, see the Programming Projects at the end of the chapter.

Complex Arithmetic

The sum of two complex numbers is found by separately adding the real parts of the two numbers and the imaginary parts. For example,

$$(3 - 2i) + (1.5 + 3i) = (3 + 1.5) + (-2 + 3)i = 4.5 + i$$

The difference of two complex numbers is computed in a similar manner, by separately subtracting the real parts and the imaginary parts. For example,

$$(3 - 2i) - (1.5 + 3i) = (3 - 1.5) + (-2 - 3)i = 1.5 - 5i$$

Multiplying complex numbers is done by multiplying each term of the first number by each term of the second and then summing the products:

$$(3 - 2i) \times (1.5 + 3i) = (3 \times 1.5) + (3 \times 3i) + (-2i \times 1.5) + (-2i \times 3i)$$
$$= 4.5 + 9i - 3i - 6i^2 = 10.5 + 6i$$

Note that the identity $i^2 = -1$ is used to simplify the result.

Dividing complex numbers is a bit harder. First, we need the concept of the **complex conjugate** of a number, which is found by switching the sign of the number's imaginary part. For example, 7 − 4*i* is the conjugate of 7 + 4*i*, and 7 + 4*i* is the conjugate of 7 − 4*i*. We'll use *z** to denote the conjugate of a complex number *z*.

The quotient of two complex numbers *y* and *z* is given by the formula

$$y/z = yz^*/zz^*$$

It turns out that *zz** is always a real number, so dividing *zz** into *yz** is easy (just divide both the real part and the imaginary part of *yz** separately). The following example shows how to divide 10.5 + 6*i* by 3 − 2*i*:

$$\frac{10.5 + 6i}{3 - 2i} = \frac{(10.5 + 6i)(3 + 2i)}{(3 - 2i)(3 + 2i)} = \frac{19.5 + 39i}{13} = 1.5 + 3i$$

Complex Types in C99

C99 has considerable built-in support for complex numbers. Without including any library headers, we can declare variables that represent complex numbers and then perform arithmetic and other operations on these variables.

C99 provides three complex types, which were first introduced in Section 7.2: `float _Complex`, `double _Complex`, and `long double _Complex`. These types can be used in the same way as other types in C: to declare variables, parameters, return types, array elements, members of structures and unions, and so forth. For example, we could declare three variables as follows:

```
float _Complex x;
double _Complex y;
long double _Complex z;
```

Each of these variables is stored just like an array of two ordinary floating-point numbers. Thus, `y` is stored as two adjacent `double` values, with the first value containing the real part of `y` and the second containing the imaginary part.

C99 also allows implementations to provide imaginary types (the keyword `_Imaginary` is reserved for this purpose) but doesn't make this a requirement.

Operations on Complex Numbers

Complex numbers may be used in expressions, although only the following operators allow complex operands:

- Unary + and -
- Logical negation (`!`)
- `sizeof`
- Cast
- Multiplicative (`*` and `/` only)
- Additive (`+` and `-`)
- Equality (`==` and `!=`)
- Logical *and* (`&&`)
- Logical *or* (`||`)
- Conditional (`?:`)
- Simple assignment (`=`)
- Compound assignment (`*=`, `/=`, `+=`, and `-=` only)
- Comma (`,`)

Some notable omissions from the list include the relational operators (`<`, `<=`, `>`, and `>=`), along with the increment (`++`) and decrement (`--`) operators.

Conversion Rules for Complex Types

Section 7.4 described the C99 rules for type conversion, but without covering the complex types. It's now time to rectify that situation. Before we get to the conversion rules, though, we'll need some new terminology. For each floating type there is a ***corresponding real type.*** In the case of the real floating types (`float`, `double`, and `long double`), the corresponding real type is the same as the original type.

For the complex types, the corresponding real type is the original type without the word _Complex. (The corresponding real type for float _Complex is float, for example.)

We're now ready to discuss the general rules that govern type conversions involving complex types. I'll group them into three categories.

- **Complex to complex.** The first rule concerns conversions from one complex type to another, such as converting from float _Complex to double _Complex. In this situation, the real and imaginary parts are converted separately, using the rules for the corresponding real types (see Section 7.4). In our example, the real part of the float _Complex value would be converted to double, yielding the real part of the double _Complex value; the imaginary part would be converted to double in a similar fashion.

- **Real to complex.** When a value of a real type is converted to a complex type, the real part of the number is converted using the rules for converting from one real type to another. The imaginary part of the result is set to positive or unsigned zero.

- **Complex to real.** When a value of a complex type is converted to a real type, the imaginary part of the number is discarded; the real part is converted using the rules for converting from one real type to another.

One particular set of type conversions, known as the usual arithmetic conversions, are automatically applied to the operands of most binary operators. There are special rules for performing the usual arithmetic conversions when at least one of the two operands has a complex type:

1. If the corresponding real type of either operand is long double, convert the other operand so that its corresponding real type is long double.
2. Otherwise, if the corresponding real type of either operand is double, convert the other operand so that its corresponding real type is double.
3. Otherwise, one of the operands must have float as its corresponding real type. Convert the other operand so that its corresponding real type is also float.

A real operand still belongs to a real type after conversion, and a complex operand still belongs to a complex type.

Normally, the goal of the usual arithmetic conversions is to convert both operands to a common type. However, when a real operand is mixed with a complex operand, performing the usual arithmetic conversions causes the operands to have a common real type, but not necessarily the *same* type. For example, adding a float operand and a double _Complex operand causes the float operand to be converted to double rather than double _Complex. The type of the result will be the complex type whose corresponding real type matches the common real type. In our example, the type of the result will be double _Complex.

27.4 The `<complex.h>` Header (C99): Complex Arithmetic

As we saw in Section 27.3, C99 has significant built-in support for complex numbers. The `<complex.h>` header provides additional support in the form of mathematical functions on complex numbers, as well as some very useful macros and a pragma. Let's look at the macros first.

`<complex.h>` Macros

The `<complex.h>` header defines the macros shown in Table 27.4.

Table 27.4
`<complex.h>` Macros

Name	Value
complex	`_Complex`
`_Complex_I`	Imaginary unit; has type `const float _Complex`
I	`_Complex_I`

`complex` serves as an alternative name for the awkward `_Complex` keyword. We've seen a situation like this before with the Boolean type: the C99 committee chose a new keyword (`_Bool`) that shouldn't break existing programs, but provided a better name (`bool`) as a macro defined in the `<stdbool.h>` header. `<stdbool.h>` header ➤21.5 Programs that include `<complex.h>` may use `complex` instead of `_Complex`, just as programs that include `<stdbool.h>` may use `bool` rather than `_Bool`.

The I macro plays an important role in C99. There's no special language feature for creating a complex number from its real part and imaginary part. Instead, a complex number can be constructed by multiplying the imaginary part by I and adding the real part:

```
double complex dc = 2.0 + 3.5 * I;
```

The value of the variable dc is $2 + 3.5i$.

Note that both `_Complex_I` and I represent the imaginary unit i. Presumably most programmers will use I rather than `_Complex_I`. However, since I might already be used in existing code for some other purpose, `_Complex_I` is available as a backup. If the name I causes a conflict, it can always be undefined:

```
#include <complex.h>
#undef I
```

The programmer might then define a different—but still short—name for i, such as J:

```
#define J _Complex_I
```

Also note that the type of `_Complex_I` (and hence the type of `I`) is `float _Complex`, not `double _Complex`. When it's used in expressions, `I` will automatically be widened to `double _Complex` or `long double _Complex` if necessary.

The `CX_LIMITED_RANGE` Pragma

#pragma directive ➤ 14.5

The `<complex.h>` header provides a pragma named `CX_LIMITED_RANGE` that allows the compiler to use the following standard formulas for multiplication, division, and absolute value:

$$(a + bi) \times (c + di) = (ac - bd) + (bc + ad)i$$

$$(a + bi)/(c + di) = [(ac + bd) + (bc - ad)i]/(c^2 + d^2)$$

$$|a + bi| = \sqrt{a^2 + b^2}$$

Using these formulas may cause anomalous results in some cases because of overflow or underflow; moreover, the formulas don't handle infinities properly. Because of these potential problems, C99 doesn't use the formulas without the programmer's permission.

The `CX_LIMITED_RANGE` pragma has the following appearance:

`#pragma STDC CX_LIMITED_RANGE` *on-off-switch*

where *on-off-switch* is either `ON`, `OFF`, or `DEFAULT`. If the pragma is used with the value `ON`, it allows the compiler to use the formulas listed above. The value `OFF` causes the compiler to perform the calculations in a way that's safer but possibly slower. The default setting, indicated by the `DEFAULT` choice, is equivalent to `OFF`.

The duration of the `CX_LIMITED_RANGE` pragma depends on where it's used in a program. When it appears at the top level of a source file, outside any external declarations, it remains in effect until the next `CX_LIMITED_RANGE` pragma or the end of the file. The only other place that a `CX_LIMITED_RANGE` pragma might appear is at the beginning of a compound statement (possibly the body of a function); in that case, the pragma remains in effect until the next `CX_LIMITED_RANGE` pragma (even one inside a nested compound statement) or the end of the compound statement. At the end of a compound statement, the state of the switch returns to its value before the compound statement was entered.

`<complex.h>` Functions

The `<complex.h>` header provides functions similar to those in the C99 version of `<math.h>`. The `<complex.h>` functions are divided into groups, just as they were in `<math.h>`: trigonometric, hyperbolic, exponential and logarithmic, and power and absolute-value. The only functions that are unique to complex numbers are the manipulation functions, the last group discussed in this section.

Each `<complex.h>` function comes in three versions: a `float complex` version, a `double complex` version, and a `long double complex` version. The name of the `float complex` version ends with `f`, and the name of the `long double complex` version ends with `l`.

Before we delve into the `<complex.h>` functions, a few general comments are in order. First, as with the `<math.h>` functions, the `<complex.h>` functions expect angle measurements to be in radians, not degrees. Second, when an error occurs, the `<complex.h>` functions may store a value in the `errno` variable, but aren't required to.

errno variable ►24.2

There's one last thing we'll need before tackling the `<complex.h>` functions. The term **branch cut** often appears in descriptions of functions that might conceivably have more than one possible return value. In the realm of complex numbers, choosing which value to return creates a branch cut: a curve (often just a line) in the complex plane around which a function is discontinuous. Branch cuts are usually not unique, but rather are determined by convention. An exact definition of branch cuts takes us further into complex analysis than I'd like to go, so I'll simply reproduce the restrictions from the C99 standard without further explanation.

Trigonometric Functions

```
double complex cacos(double complex z);
float complex cacosf(float complex z);
long double complex cacosl(long double complex z);

double complex casin(double complex z);
float complex casinf(float complex z);
long double complex casinl(long double complex z);

double complex catan(double complex z);
float complex catanf(float complex z);
long double complex catanl(long double complex z);

double complex ccos(double complex z);
float complex ccosf(float complex z);
long double complex ccosl(long double complex z);

double complex csin(double complex z);
float complex csinf(float complex z);
long double complex csinl(long double complex z);

double complex ctan(double complex z);
float complex ctanf(float complex z);
long double complex ctanl(long double complex z);
```

cacos   The `cacos` function computes the complex arc cosine, with branch cuts outside the interval [−1, +1] along the real axis. The return value lies in a strip mathematically unbounded along the imaginary axis and in the interval [0, π] along the real axis.

casin   The `casin` function computes the complex arc sine, with branch cuts outside the interval [−1, +1] along the real axis. The return value lies in a strip mathematically unbounded along the imaginary axis and in the interval [−π/2, +π/2] along the real axis.

catan   The `catan` function computes the complex arc tangent, with branch cuts outside the interval [−*i*, +*i*] along the imaginary axis. The return value lies in a strip mathematically unbounded along the imaginary axis and in the interval [−π/2, +π/2] along the real axis.

ccos
csin   The `ccos` function computes the complex cosine, the `csin` function computes the complex sine, and the `ctan` function computes the complex tangent.
ctan

Hyperbolic Functions

```
double complex cacosh(double complex z);
float complex cacoshf(float complex z);
long double complex cacoshl(long double complex z);

double complex casinh(double complex z);
float complex casinhf(float complex z);
long double complex casinhl(long double complex z);

double complex catanh(double complex z);
float complex catanhf(float complex z);
long double complex catanhl(long double complex z);

double complex ccosh(double complex z);
float complex ccoshf(float complex z);
long double complex ccoshl(long double complex z);

double complex csinh(double complex z);
float complex csinhf(float complex z);
long double complex csinhl(long double complex z);

double complex ctanh(double complex z);
float complex ctanhf(float complex z);
long double complex ctanhl(long double complex z);
```

cacosh   The `cacosh` function computes the complex arc hyperbolic cosine, with a branch cut at values less than 1 along the real axis. The return value lies in a half-strip of nonnegative values along the real axis and in the interval [−*i*π, +*i*π] along the imaginary axis.

casinh   The `casinh` function computes the complex arc hyperbolic sine, with branch cuts outside the interval [−*i*, +*i*] along the imaginary axis. The return value lies in a strip mathematically unbounded along the real axis and in the interval [−*i*π/2, +*i*π/2] along the imaginary axis.

catanh   The `catanh` function computes the complex arc hyperbolic tangent, with branch cuts outside the interval [−1, +1] along the real axis. The return value lies in a strip mathematically unbounded along the real axis and in the interval [$-i\pi/2$, $+i\pi/2$] along the imaginary axis.

ccosh
csinh
ctanh
    The ccosh function computes the complex hyperbolic cosine, the `csinh` function computes the complex hyperbolic sine, and the `ctanh` function computes the complex hyperbolic tangent.

Exponential and Logarithmic Functions

```
double complex cexp(double complex z);
float complex cexpf(float complex z);
long double complex cexpl(long double complex z);

double complex clog(double complex z);
float complex clogf(float complex z);
long double complex clogl(long double complex z);
```

cexp
clog
The `cexp` function computes the complex base-*e* exponential value.
    The `clog` function computes the complex natural (base-*e*) logarithm, with a branch cut along the negative real axis. The return value lies in a strip mathematically unbounded along the real axis and in the interval [$-i\pi$, $+i\pi$] along the imaginary axis.

Power and Absolute-Value Functions

```
double cabs(double complex z);
float cabsf(float complex z);
long double cabsl(long double complex z);

double complex cpow(double complex x,
                    double complex y);
float complex cpowf(float complex x,
                    float complex y);
long double complex cpowl(long double complex x,
                          long double complex y);

double complex csqrt(double complex z);
float complex csqrtf(float complex z);
long double complex csqrtl(long double complex z);
```

cabs
cpow
The `cabs` function computes the complex absolute value.
    The `cpow` function returns x raised to the power y, with a branch cut for the first parameter along the negative real axis.

csqrt
    The `csqrt` function computes the complex square root, with a branch cut along the negative real axis. The return value lies in the right half-plane (including the imaginary axis).

Manipulation Functions

```
double carg(double complex z);
float cargf(float complex z);
long double cargl(long double complex z);

double cimag(double complex z);
float cimagf(float complex z);
long double cimagl(long double complex z);

double complex conj(double complex z);
float complex conjf(float complex z);
long double complex conjl(long double complex z);

double complex cproj(double complex z);
float complex cprojf(float complex z);
long double complex cprojl(long double complex z);

double creal(double complex z);
float crealf(float complex z);
long double creall(long double complex z);
```

carg   The `carg` function returns the argument (phase angle) of z, with a branch cut along the negative real axis. The return value lies in the interval $[-\pi, +\pi]$.

cimag   The `cimag` function returns the imaginary part of z.

conj   The `conj` function returns the complex conjugate of z.

cproj   The `cproj` function computes a projection of z onto the Riemann sphere. The return value is equal to z unless one of its parts is infinite, in which case `cproj` returns `INFINITY + I * copysign(0.0, cimag(z))`.

creal   The `creal` function returns the real part of z.

PROGRAM   ### Finding the Roots of a Quadratic Equation

The roots of the quadratic equation

$$ax^2 + bx + c = 0$$

are given by the ***quadratic formula:***

$$x = \frac{-b \pm \sqrt{b^2 - 4ac}}{2a}$$

In general, the value of x will be a complex number, because the square root of $b^2 - 4ac$ is imaginary if $b^2 - 4ac$ (known as the ***discriminant***) is less than 0.

For example, suppose that $a = 5$, $b = 2$, and $c = 1$, which gives us the equation

$$5x^2 + 2x + 1 = 0$$

The value of the discriminant is $4 - 20 = -16$, so the roots of the equation will be complex numbers. The following program, which uses several `<complex.h>` functions, computes and displays the roots.

quadratic.c
```
/* Finds the roots of the equation 5x**2 + 2x + 1 = 0 */

#include <complex.h>
#include <stdio.h>

int main(void)
{
  double a = 5, b = 2, c = 1;
  double complex discriminant_sqrt = csqrt(b * b - 4 * a * c);
  double complex root1 = (-b + discriminant_sqrt) / (2 * a);
  double complex root2 = (-b - discriminant_sqrt) / (2 * a);

  printf("root1 = %g + %gi\n", creal(root1), cimag(root1));
  printf("root2 = %g + %gi\n", creal(root2), cimag(root2));

  return 0;
}
```

Here's the output of the program:

```
root1 = -0.2 + 0.4i
root2 = -0.2 + -0.4i
```

The `quadratic.c` program shows how to display a complex number by extracting the real and imaginary parts and then writing each as a floating-point number. `printf` lacks conversion specifiers for complex numbers, so there's no easier technique. There's also no shortcut for reading complex numbers; a program will need to obtain the real and imaginary parts separately and then combine them into a single complex number.

27.5 The `<tgmath.h>` Header (C99): Type-Generic Math

The `<tgmath.h>` header provides parameterized macros with names that match functions in `<math.h>` and `<complex.h>`. These **type-generic macros** can detect the types of the arguments passed to them and substitute a call of the appropriate version of a `<math.h>` or `<complex.h>` function.

In C99, there are multiple versions of many math functions, as we saw in Sections 23.3, 23.4, and 27.4. For example, the `sqrt` function comes in a `double` version (`sqrt`), a `float` version (`sqrtf`), and a `long double` version (`sqrtl`), as well as three versions for complex numbers (`csqrt`, `csqrtf`, and `csqrtl`). By using `<tgmath.h>`, the programmer can simply invoke `sqrt` without having to worry about which version is needed: the call `sqrt(x)` could be a call of any of the six versions of `sqrt`, depending on the type of x.

One advantage of using <tgmath.h> is that calls of math functions become easier to write (and read!). More importantly, a call of a type-generic macro won't have to be modified in the future should the type of its argument(s) change.

The <tgmath.h> header includes both <math.h> and <complex.h>, by the way, so including <tgmath.h> provides access to the functions in both headers.

Type-Generic Macros

The type-generic macros defined in the <tgmath.h> header fall into three groups, depending on whether they correspond to functions in <math.h>, <complex.h>, or both headers.

Table 27.5 lists the type-generic macros that correspond to functions in both <math.h> and <complex.h>. Note that the name of each type-generic macro matches the name of the "unsuffixed" <math.h> function (acos as opposed to acosf or acosl, for example).

Table 27.5

Type-Generic Macros in <tgmath.h> (Group 1)

`<math.h>` Function	`<complex.h>` Function	*Type-Generic Macro*
acos	cacos	acos
asin	casin	asin
atan	catan	atan
acosh	cacosh	acosh
asinh	casinh	asinh
atanh	catanh	atanh
cos	ccos	cos
sin	csin	sin
tan	ctan	tan
cosh	ccosh	cosh
sinh	csinh	sinh
tanh	ctanh	tanh
exp	cexp	exp
log	clog	log
pow	cpow	pow
sqrt	csqrt	sqrt
fabs	cabs	fabs

The macros in the second group (Table 27.6) correspond only to functions in <math.h>. Each macro has the same name as the unsuffixed <math.h> function. Passing a complex argument to any of these macros causes undefined behavior.

Table 27.6

Type-Generic Macros in <tgmath.h> (Group 2)

atan2	fma	llround	remainder
cbrt	fmax	log10	remquo
ceil	fmin	log1p	rint
copysign	fmod	log2	round
erf	frexp	logb	scalbn
erfc	hypot	lrint	scalbln
exp2	ilogb	lround	tgamma
expm1	ldexp	nearbyint	trunc
fdim	lgamma	nextafter	
floor	llrint	nexttoward	

The macros in the final group (Table 27.7) correspond only to functions in `<complex.h>`.

Table 27.7

Type-Generic Macros in
`<tgmath.h>` (Group 3)

carg	conj	creal
cimag	cproj	

Between the three tables, all functions in `<math.h>` and `<complex.h>` that have multiple versions are accounted for, with the exception of `modf`.

Invoking a Type-Generic Macro

To understand what happens when a type-generic macro is invoked, we first need the concept of a ***generic parameter.*** Consider the prototypes for the three versions of the `nextafter` function (from `<math.h>`):

```
double nextafter(double x, double y);
float nextafterf(float x, float y);
long double nextafterl(long double x, long double y);
```

The types of both `x` and `y` change depending on the version of `nextafter`, so both parameters are generic. Now consider the prototypes for the three versions of the `nexttoward` function:

```
double nexttoward(double x, long double y);
float nexttowardf(float x, long double y);
long double nexttowardl(long double x, long double y);
```

The first parameter is generic, but the second is not (it always has type `long double`). Generic parameters always have type `double` (or `double complex`) in the unsuffixed version of a function.

When a type-generic macro is invoked, the first step is to determine whether it should be replaced by a `<math.h>` function or a `<complex.h>` function. (This step doesn't apply to the macros in Table 27.6, which are always replaced by a `<math.h>` function, or the macros in Table 27.7, which are always replaced by a `<complex.h>` function.) The rule is simple: if any argument corresponding to a generic parameter is complex, then a `<complex.h>` function is chosen; otherwise, a `<math.h>` function is selected.

The next step is to deduce which version of the `<math.h>` function or `<complex.h>` function is being called. Let's assume that the function being called belongs to `<math.h>`. (The rules for the `<complex.h>` case are analogous.) The following rules are used, in the order listed:

1. If any argument corresponding to a generic parameter has type `long double`, the `long double` version of the function is called.
2. If any argument corresponding to a generic parameter has type `double` or any integer type, the `double` version of the function is called.
3. Otherwise, the `float` version of the function is called.

Rule 2 is a little unusual: it states that an integer argument causes the `double` version of a function to be called, not the `float` version, which you might expect.

As an example, assume that the following variables have been declared:

```
int i;
float f;
double d;
long double ld;
float complex fc;
double complex dc;
long double complex ldc;
```

For each macro invocation in the left column below, the corresponding function call appears in the right column:

Macro Invocation	*Equivalent Function Call*
sqrt(i)	sqrt(i)
sqrt(f)	sqrtf(f)
sqrt(d)	sqrt(d)
sqrt(ld)	sqrtl(ld)
sqrt(fc)	csqrtf(fc)
sqrt(dc)	csqrt(dc)
sqrt(ldc)	csqrtl(ldc)

Note that writing sqrt(i) causes the double version of sqrt to be called, not the float version.

These rules also cover macros with more than one parameter. For example, the macro invocation pow(ld, f) will be replaced by the call powl(ld, f). Both of pow's parameters are generic; because one of the arguments has type long double, rule 1 states that the long double version of pow will be called.

27.6 The `<fenv.h>` Header (C99): Floating-Point Environment

IEEE Standard 754 is the most widely used representation for floating-point numbers. (This standard is also known as IEC 60559, which is how the C99 standard refers to it.) The purpose of the `<fenv.h>` header is to give programs access to the floating-point status flags and control modes specified in the IEEE standard. Although `<fenv.h>` was designed in a general fashion that allows it to work with other floating-point representations, supporting the IEEE standard was the reason for the header's creation.

A discussion of why programs might need access to status flags and control modes is beyond the scope of this book. For good examples, see "What every computer scientist should know about floating-point arithmetic" by David Goldberg (*ACM Computing Surveys,* vol. 23, no. 1 (March 1991): 5–48), which can be found on the Web.

Floating-Point Status Flags and Control Modes

Section 7.2 discussed some of the basic properties of IEEE Standard 754. Section 23.4, which covered the C99 additions to the `<math.h>` header, gave additional detail. Some of that discussion, particularly concerning exceptions and rounding directions, is directly relevant to the `<fenv.h>` header. Before we continue, let's review some of the material from Section 23.4 as well as define a few new terms.

A ***floating-point status flag*** is a system variable that's set when a floating-point exception is raised. In the IEEE standard, there are five types of floating-point exceptions: *overflow, underflow, division by zero, invalid operation* (the result of an arithmetic operation was NaN), and *inexact* (the result of an arithmetic operation had to be rounded). Each exception has a corresponding status flag.

The `<fenv.h>` header declares a type named `fexcept_t` that's used for working with the floating-point status flags. An `fexcept_t` object represents the collective value of these flags. Although `fexcept_t` can simply be an integer type, with single bits representing individual flags, the C99 standard doesn't make this a requirement. Other alternatives exist, including the possibility that `fexcept_t` is a structure, with one member for each exception. This member could store additional information about the corresponding exception, such as the address of the floating-point instruction that caused the exception to be raised.

A ***floating-point control mode*** is a system variable that may be set by a program to change the future behavior of floating-point arithmetic. The IEEE standard requires a "directed-rounding" mode that controls the rounding direction when a number can't be represented exactly using a floating-point representation. There are four rounding directions: (1) *Round toward nearest.* Rounds to the nearest representable value. If a number falls halfway between two values, it's rounded to the "even" value (the one whose least significant bit is zero). (2) *Round toward zero.* (3) *Round toward positive infinity.* (4) *Round toward negative infinity.* The default rounding direction is round toward nearest. Some implementations of the IEEE standard provide two additional control modes: a mode that controls rounding precision and a "trap enablement" mode that determines whether a floating-point processor will trap (or stop) when an exception is raised.

The term ***floating-point environment*** refers to the combination of floating-point status flags and control modes supported by a particular implementation. A value of type `fenv_t` represents an entire floating-point environment. The `fenv_t` type, like the `fexcept_t` type, is declared in `<fenv.h>`.

`<fenv.h>` Macros

The `<fenv.h>` header potentially defines the macros listed in Table 27.8. Only two of these macros (`FE_ALL_EXCEPT` and `FE_DFL_ENV`) are required, however. An implementation may define additional macros not listed in the table; the names of these macros must begin with `FE_` and an uppercase letter.

Table 27.8

`<fenv.h>` Macros

Name	*Value*	*Description*
FE_DIVBYZERO FE_INEXACT FE_INVALID FE_OVERFLOW FE_UNDERFLOW	Integer constant expressions whose bits do not overlap	Defined only if the corresponding floating-point exception is supported by the implementation. An implementation may define additional macros that represent floating-point exceptions.
FE_ALL_EXCEPT	See description	Bitwise *or* of all floating-point exception macros defined by the implementation. Has the value 0 if no such macros are defined.
FE_DOWNWARD FE_TONEAREST FE_TOWARDZERO FE_UPWARD	Integer constant expressions with distinct nonnegative values	Defined only if the corresponding rounding direction can be retrieved and set via the `fegetround` and `fesetround` functions. An implementation may define additional macros that represent rounding directions.
FE_DFL_ENV	A value of type `const fenv_t *`	Represents the default (program start-up) floating-point environment. An implementation may define additional macros that represent floating-point environments.

The `FENV_ACCESS` Pragma

#pragma directive ➤ 14.5

The `<fenv.h>` header provides a pragma named `FENV_ACCESS` that's used to notify the compiler of a program's intention to use the functions provided by this header. Knowing which portions of a program will use the capabilities of `<fenv.h>` is important for the compiler, because some common optimizations can't be performed if control modes don't have their customary settings or may change during program execution.

The `FENV_ACCESS` pragma has the following appearance:

```
#pragma STDC FENV_ACCESS on-off-switch
```

where *on-off-switch* is either `ON`, `OFF`, or `DEFAULT`. If the pragma is used with the value `ON`, it informs the compiler that the program might test floating-point status flags or alter a floating-point control mode. The value `OFF` indicates that flags won't be tested and default control modes are in effect. The meaning of `DEFAULT` is implementation-defined; it represents either `ON` or `OFF`.

The duration of the `FENV_ACCESS` pragma depends on where it's used in a program. When it appears at the top level of a source file, outside any external declarations, it remains in effect until the next `FENV_ACCESS` pragma or the end of the file. The only other place that an `FENV_ACCESS` pragma might appear is at the beginning of a compound statement (possibly the body of a function); in that case, the pragma remains in effect until the next `FENV_ACCESS` pragma (even one inside a nested compound statement) or the end of the compound statement. At the end of a compound statement, the state of the switch returns to its value before the compound statement was entered.

It's the programmer's responsibility to use the `FENV_ACCESS` pragma to indicate regions of a program in which low-level access to floating-point hardware is needed. Undefined behavior occurs if a program tests floating-point status flags or runs under non-default control modes in a region for which the value of the pragma switch is OFF.

Typically, an FENV_ACCESS pragma that specifies the ON switch would be placed at the beginning of a function body:

```
void f(double x, double y)
{
  #pragma STDC FENV_ACCESS ON
  ...
}
```

The function f may test floating-point status flags or change control modes as needed. At the end of f's body, the pragma switch will return to its previous state.

When a program goes from an FENV_ACCESS "off" region to an "on" region during execution, the floating-point status flags have unspecified values and the control modes have their default settings.

Floating-Point Exception Functions

```
int feclearexcept(int excepts);
int fegetexceptflag(fexcept_t *flagp, int excepts);
int feraiseexcept(int excepts);
int fesetexceptflag(const fexcept_t *flagp,
                    int excepts);
int fetestexcept(int excepts);
```

The `<fenv.h>` functions are divided into three groups. Functions in the first group deal with the floating-point status flags. Each of the five functions has an int parameter named excepts, which is the bitwise *or* of one or more of the floating-point exception macros (the first group of macros listed in Table 27.8). For example, the argument passed to one of these functions might be FE_INVALID | FE_OVERFLOW | FE_UNDERFLOW, to represent the combination of these three status flags. The argument may also be zero, to indicate that no flags are selected.

feclearexcept   The feclearexcept function attempts to clear the floating-point exceptions represented by excepts. It returns zero if excepts is zero or if all specified exceptions were successfully cleared; otherwise, it returns a nonzero value.

fegetexceptflag   The fegetexceptflag function attempts to retrieve the states of the floating-point status flags represented by excepts. This data is stored in the fexcept_t object pointed to by flagp. The fegetexceptflag function returns zero if the states of the status flags were successfully stored; otherwise, it returns a nonzero value.

feraiseexcept   The feraiseexcept function attempts to raise supported floating-point exceptions represented by excepts. It is implementation-defined whether feraiseexcept also raises the *inexact* floating-point exception whenever it raises the *overflow* or *underflow* exception. (Implementations that conform to the IEEE standard will have this property.) `feraiseexcept` returns zero if `excepts` is zero or if all specified exceptions were successfully raised; otherwise, it returns a nonzero value.

fesetexceptflag   The `fesetexceptflag` function attempts to set the floating-point status flags represented by `excepts`. The states of the flags are stored in the `fexcept_t` object pointed to by `flagp`; this object must have been set by a previous call of `fegetexceptflag`. Moreover, the second argument in the prior call of `fegetexceptflag` must have included all floating-point exceptions represented by `excepts`. The `fesetexceptflag` function returns zero if `excepts` is zero or if all specified exceptions were successfully set; otherwise, it returns a nonzero value.

fetestexcept   The `fetestexcept` function tests only those floating-point status flags represented by `excepts`. It returns the bitwise *or* of the floating-point exception macros corresponding to the flags that are currently set. For example, if the value of `excepts` is `FE_INVALID | FE_OVERFLOW | FE_UNDERFLOW`, the `fetestexcept` function might return `FE_INVALID | FE_UNDERFLOW`, indicating that, of the exceptions represented by `FE_INVALID`, `FE_OVERFLOW`, and `FE_UNDERFLOW`, only the flags for `FE_INVALID` and `FE_UNDERFLOW` are currently set.

Rounding Functions

```
int fegetround(void);
int fesetround(int round);
```

The `fegetround` and `fesetround` functions are used to determine the rounding direction and modify it. Both functions rely on the rounding-direction macros (the third group in Table 27.8).

fegetround   The `fegetround` function returns the value of the rounding-direction macro that matches the current rounding direction. If the current rounding direction can't be determined or doesn't match any rounding-direction macro, `fegetround` returns a negative number.

fesetround   When passed the value of a rounding-direction macro, the `fesetround` function attempts to establish the corresponding rounding direction. If the call is successful, `fesetround` returns zero; otherwise, it returns a nonzero value.

Environment Functions

```
int fegetenv(fenv_t *envp);
int feholdexcept(fenv_t *envp);
int fesetenv(const fenv_t *envp);
int feupdateenv(const fenv_t *envp);
```

The last four functions in `<fenv.h>` deal with the entire floating-point environment, not just the status flags or control modes. Each function returns zero if it succeeds at the operation it was asked to perform. Otherwise, it returns a nonzero value.

fegetenv   The `fegetenv` function attempts to retrieve the current floating-point environment from the processor and store it in the object pointed to by `envp`.

feholdexcept   The `feholdexcept` function (1) stores the current floating-point environment in the object pointed to by `envp`, (2) clears the floating-point status flags, and (3) attempts to install a non-stop mode—if available—for all floating-point exceptions (so that future exceptions won't cause a trap or stop).

fesetenv   The `fesetenv` function attempts to establish the floating-point environment represented by `envp`, which either points to a floating-point environment stored by a previous call of `fegetenv` or `feholdexcept`, or is equal to a floating-point environment macro such as `FE_DFL_ENV`. Unlike the `feupdateenv` function, `fesetenv` doesn't raise any exceptions. If a call of `fegetenv` is used to save the current floating-point environment, then a later call of `fesetenv` can restore the environment to its previous state.

feupdateenv   The `feupdateenv` function attempts to (1) save the currently raised floating-point exceptions, (2) install the floating-point environment pointed to by `envp`, and (3) raise the saved exceptions. `envp` either points to a floating-point environment stored by a previous call of `fegetenv` or `feholdexcept`, or is equal to a floating-point environment macro such as `FE_DFL_ENV`.

Q & A

Q: **If the `<inttypes.h>` header includes the `<stdint.h>` header, why do we need the `<stdint.h>` header at all? [p. 709]**

A: The primary reason that `<stdint.h>` exists as a separate header is so that programs in a freestanding implementation may include it. (C99 requires conforming
freestanding implementation ➤ 14.3
implementations—both hosted and freestanding—to provide the `<stdint.h>` header, but `<inttypes.h>` is required only for hosted implementations.) Even in a hosted environment, it may be advantageous to include `<stdint.h>` rather than `<inttypes.h>` to avoid defining all the macros that belong to the latter.

*Q: **There are three versions of the `modf` function in `<math.h>`, so why isn't there a type-generic macro named `modf`? [p. 725]**

A: Let's take a look at the prototypes for the three versions of `modf`:

```
double modf(double value, double *iptr);
float modff(float value, float *iptr);
long double modfl(long double value, long double *iptr);
```

`modf` is unusual in that it has a pointer parameter, and the type of the pointer isn't the same among the three versions of the function. (`frexp` and `remquo` have a pointer parameter, but it always has `int *` type.) Having a type-generic macro for `modf` would pose some difficult problems. For example, the meaning of `modf(d, &f)`, where d has type `double` and f has type `float`, is unclear: are we calling the `modf` function or the `modff` function? Rather than develop a complicated set of rules for a single function (and probably taking into account that `modf` isn't a very popular function), the C99 committee chose not to provide a type-generic `modf` macro.

Q: When a `<tgmath.h>` macro is invoked with an integer argument, the `double` version of the corresponding function is called. Shouldn't the `float` version be

usual arithmetic conversions ▶ 7.4 **called, according to the usual arithmetic conversions? [p. 725]**

A: We're dealing with a macro, not a function, so the usual arithmetic conversions don't come into play. The C99 committee had to create a rule for determining which version of a function would be called when an integer argument is passed to a `<tgmath.h>` macro. Although the committee at one point considered having the `float` version called (for consistency with the usual arithmetic conversions), they eventually decided that choosing the `double` version was better. First, it's safer: converting an integer to `float` may cause a loss of accuracy, especially for integer types whose width is 32 bits or more. Second, it causes fewer surprises for the programmer. Suppose that i is an integer variable. If the `<tgmath.h>` header isn't included, the call `sin(i)` calls the `sin` function. On the other hand, if `<tgmath.h>` *is* included, the call `sin(i)` invokes the `sin` macro; because i is an integer, the preprocessor replaces the `sin` macro with the `sin` function, and the end result is the same.

Q: When a program invokes one of the type-generic macros in `<tgmath.h>`, how does the implementation determine which function to call? Is there a way for a macro to test the types of its arguments?

A: One unusual aspect of `<tgmath.h>` is that its macros need to be able to test the types of the arguments that are passed to them. C has no features for testing types, so it would normally be impossible to write such a macro. The `<tgmath.h>` macros rely on special facilities provided by a particular compiler to make such testing possible. We don't know what these facilities are, and they're not guaranteed to be portable from one compiler to another.

Exercises

Section 27.1   1.   (C99) Locate the declarations of the `int`*N*`_t` and `uint`*N*`_t` types in the `<stdint.h>` header installed on your system. Which values of *N* are supported?

2.   (C99) Write the parameterized macros `INT32_C(n)`, `UINT32_C(n)`, `INT64_C(n)`, and `UINT64_C(n)`, assuming that the `int` type and `long int` types are 32 bits wide and the `long long int` type is 64 bits wide. *Hint:* Use the `##` preprocessor operator to attach

a suffix to n containing a combination of L and/or U characters. (See Section 7.1 for a discussion of how to use the L and U suffixes with integer constants.)

Section 27.2

3. (C99) In each of the following statements, assume that the variable i has the indicated original type. Using macros from the `<inttypes.h>` header, modify each statement so that it will work correctly if the type of i is changed to the indicated new type.

(a) `printf("%d", i);`   Original type: int   New type: int8_t
(b) `printf("%12.4d", i);` Original type: int   New type: int32_t
(c) `printf("%-6o", i);`   Original type: unsigned int New type: uint16_t
(d) `printf("%#x", i);`   Original type: unsigned int New type: uint64_t

Section 27.5

4. (C99) Assume that the following variable declarations are in effect:

```
int i;
float f;
double d;
long double ld;
float complex fc;
double complex dc;
long double complex ldc;
```

Each of the following is an invocation of a macro in `<tgmath.h>`. Show what it will look like after preprocessing, when the macro has been replaced by a function from `<math.h>` or `<complex.h>`.

(a) `tan(i)`
(b) `fabs(f)`
(c) `asin(d)`
(d) `exp(ld)`
(e) `log(fc)`
(f) `acosh(dc)`
(g) `nexttoward(d, ld)`
(h) `remainder(f, i)`
(i) `copysign(d, ld)`
(j) `carg(i)`
(k) `cimag(f)`
(l) `conj(ldc)`

Programming Projects

1. (C99) Make the following modifications to the `quadratic.c` program of Section 27.4:

(a) Have the user enter the coefficients of the polynomial (the values of the variables a, b, and c).

(b) Have the program test the discriminant before displaying the values of the roots. If the discriminant is negative, have the program display the roots in the same way as before. If it's nonnegative, have the program display the roots as real numbers (without an imaginary part). For example, if the quadratic equation is $x^2 + x - 2 = 0$, the output of the program would be

```
root1 = 1
root2 = -2
```

(c) Modify the program so that it displays a complex number with a negative imaginary part as $a - bi$ instead of $a + -bi$. For example, the output of the program with the original coefficients would be

```
root1 = -0.2 + 0.4i
root2 = -0.2 - 0.4i
```

2.   (C99) Write a program that converts a complex number in Cartesian coordinates to polar form. The user will enter a and b (the real and imaginary parts of the number); the program will display the values of r and θ.

3.   (C99) Write a program that converts a complex number in polar coordinates to Cartesian form. After the user enters the values of r and θ, the program will display the number in the form $a + bi$, where

$a = r \cos \theta$
$b = r \sin \theta$

4.   (C99) Write a program that displays the nth roots of unity when given a positive integer n. The nth roots of unity are given by the formula $e^{2\pi i k/n}$, where k is an integer between 0 and $n - 1$.

APPENDIX A
C Operators

Precedence	Name	Symbol(s)	Associativity
1	Array subscripting	[]	Left
1	Function call	()	Left
1	Structure and union member	. ->	Left
1	Increment (postfix)	++	Left
1	Decrement (postfix)	--	Left
2	Increment (prefix)	++	Right
2	Decrement (prefix)	--	Right
2	Address	&	Right
2	Indirection	*	Right
2	Unary plus	+	Right
2	Unary minus	-	Right
2	Bitwise complement	~	Right
2	Logical negation	!	Right
2	Size	sizeof	Right
3	Cast	()	Right
4	Multiplicative	* / %	Left
5	Additive	+ -	Left
6	Bitwise shift	<< >>	Left
7	Relational	< > <= >=	Left
8	Equality	== !=	Left
9	Bitwise *and*	&	Left
10	Bitwise exclusive *or*	^	Left
11	Bitwise inclusive *or*	|	Left
12	Logical *and*	&&	Left
13	Logical *or*	||	Left
14	Conditional	?:	Right
15	Assignment	= *= /= %= += -= <<= >>= &= ^= |=	Right
16	Comma	,	Left

APPENDIX B
C99 versus C89

This appendix lists many of the most significant differences between C89 and C99. (The smaller differences are too numerous to mention here.) The headings indicate which chapter contains the primary discussion of each C99 feature. Some of the changes attributed to C99 actually occurred earlier, in Amendment 1 to the C89 standard; these changes are marked "Amendment 1."

2 C Fundamentals

// comments   C99 adds a second kind of comment, which begins with `//`.

identifiers   C89 requires compilers to remember the first 31 characters of identifiers; in C99, the requirement is 63 characters. Only the first six characters of names with external linkage are significant in C89. Moreover, the case of letters may not matter. In C99, the first 31 characters are significant, and the case of letters is taken into account.

keywords   Five keywords are new in C99: `inline`, `restrict`, `_Bool`, `_Complex`, and `_Imaginary`.

returning from `main`   In C89, if a program reaches the end of the `main` function without executing a `return` statement, the value returned to the operating system is undefined. In C99, if `main` is declared to return an `int`, the program returns 0 to the operating system.

4 Expressions

/ and % operators   The C89 standard states that if either operand is negative, the result of an integer division can be rounded either up or down. Moreover, if `i` or `j` is negative, the sign of `i % j` depends on the implementation. In C99, the result of a division is always truncated toward zero and the value of `i % j` has the same sign as `i`.

5   Selection Statements

_Bool type   C99 provides a Boolean type named _Bool; C89 has no Boolean type.

6   Loops

for statements   In C99, the first expression in a for statement can be replaced by a declaration, allowing the statement to declare its own control variable(s).

7   Basic Types

long long integer types   C99 provides two additional standard integer types, long long int and unsigned long long int.

extended integer types   In addition to the standard integer types, C99 allows implementation-defined extended signed and unsigned integer types.

long long integer constants   C99 provides a way to indicate that an integer constant has type long long int or unsigned long long int.

types of integer constants   C99's rules for determining the type of an integer constant are different from those in C89.

hexadecimal floating constants   C99 provides a way to write floating constants in hexadecimal.

implicit conversions   The rules for implicit conversions in C99 are somewhat different from the rules in C89, primarily because of C99's additional basic types.

8   Arrays

designated initializers   C99 supports designated initializers, which can be used to initialize arrays, structures, and unions.

variable-length arrays   In C99, the length of an array may be specified by an expression that's not constant, provided that the array doesn't have static storage duration and its declaration doesn't contain an initializer.

9   Functions

no default return type   If the return type of a function is omitted in C89, the function is presumed to return a value of type int. In C99, it's illegal to omit the return type of a function.

mixed declarations and statements   In C89, declarations must precede statements within a block (including the body of a function). In C99, declarations and statements can be mixed, as long as each variable is declared prior to the first statement that uses the variable.

declaration or definition required prior to function call	C99 requires that either a declaration or a definition of a function be present prior to any call of the function. C89 doesn't have this requirement; if a function is called without a prior declaration or definition, the compiler assumes that the function returns an `int` value.
variable-length array parameters	C99 allows variable-length array parameters. In a function declaration, the * symbol may appear inside brackets to indicate a variable-length array parameter.
`static` *array parameters*	C99 allows the use of the word `static` in the declaration of an array parameter, indicating a minimum length for the first dimension of the array.
compound literals	C99 supports the use of compound literals, which allow the creation of unnamed array and structure values.
declaration of `main`	C99 allows `main` to be declared in an implementation-defined manner, with a return type other than `int` and/or parameters other than those specified by the standard.
`return` *statement without expression*	In C89, executing a `return` statement without an expression in a non-void function causes undefined behavior (but only if the program attempts to use the value returned by the function). In C99, such a statement is illegal.

14   The Preprocessor

additional predefined macros	C99 provides several new predefined macros.
empty macro arguments	C99 allows any or all of the arguments in a macro call to be empty, provided that the call contains the correct number of commas.
macros with a variable number of arguments	In C89, a macro must have a fixed number of arguments, if it has any at all. C99 allows macros that take an unlimited number of arguments.
`__func__` *identifier*	In C99, the `__func__` identifier behaves like a string variable that stores the name of the currently executing function.
standard pragmas	In C89, there are no standard pragmas. C99 has three: `CX_LIMITED_RANGE`, `FENV_ACCESS`, and `FP_CONTRACT`.
`_Pragma` *operator*	C99 provides the `_Pragma` operator, which is used in conjunction with the `#pragma` directive.

16   Structures, Unions, and Enumerations

structure type compatibility	In C89, structures defined in different files are compatible if their members have the same names and appear in the same order, with corresponding members having

compatible types. C99 also requires that either both structures have the same tag or neither has a tag.

trailing comma in enumerations

In C99, the last constant in an enumeration may be followed by a comma.

17   Advanced Uses of Pointers

restricted pointers

C99 has a new keyword, `restrict`, that can appear in the declaration of a pointer.

flexible array members

C99 allows the last member of a structure to be an array of unspecified length.

18   Declarations

block scopes for selection and iteration statements

In C99, selection statements (`if` and `switch`) and iteration statements (`while`, `do`, and `for`)—along with the "inner" statements that they control—are considered to be blocks.

array, structure, and union initializers

In C89, a brace-enclosed initializer for an array, structure, or union must contain only constant expressions. In C99, this restriction applies only if the variable has static storage duration.

inline functions

C99 allows functions to be declared `inline`.

21   The Standard Library

`<stdbool.h>` header

The `<stdbool.h>` header, which defines the `bool`, `true`, and `false` macros, is new in C99.

22   Input/Output

...`printf` conversion specifications

The conversion specifications for the ...`printf` functions have undergone a number of changes in C99, with new length modifiers, new conversion specifiers, the ability to write infinity and NaN, and support for wide characters. Also, the `%le`, `%lE`, `%lf`, `%lg`, and `%lG` conversions are legal in C99; they caused undefined behavior in C89.

...`scanf` conversion specifications

In C99, the conversion specifications for the ...`scanf` functions have new length modifiers, new conversion specifiers, the ability to read infinity and NaN, and support for wide characters.

`snprintf` function

C99 adds the `snprintf` function to the `<stdio.h>` header.

23   Library Support for Numbers and Character Data

additional macros in `<float.h>` header

C99 adds the `DECIMAL_DIG` and `FLT_EVAL_METHOD` macros to the `<float.h>` header.

additional macros in `<limits.h>` *header*	In C99, the `<limits.h>` header contains three new macros that describe the characteristics of the `long long int` types.
`math_errhandling` *macro*	C99 gives implementations a choice of how to inform a program that an error has occurred in a mathematical function: via a value stored in `errno`, via a floating-point exception, or both. The value of the `math_errhandling` macro (defined in `<math.h>`) indicates how errors are signaled by a particular implementation.
additional functions in `<math.h>` *header*	C99 adds two new versions of most `<math.h>` functions, one for `float` and one for `long double`. C99 also adds a number of completely new functions and function-like macros to `<math.h>`.

24 Error Handling

`EILSEQ` *macro*	C99 adds the `EILSEQ` macro to the `<errno.h>` header.

25 International Features

digraphs	Digraphs, which are two-character symbols that can be used as substitutes for the [,], {, }, #, and ## tokens, are new in C99. (Amendment 1)
`<iso646.h>` *header*	The `<iso646.h>` header, which defines macros that represent operators containing the characters &, |, ~, !, and ^, is new in C99. (Amendment 1)
universal character names	Universal character names, which provide a way to embed UCS characters in the source code of a program, are new in C99.
`<wchar.h>` *header*	The `<wchar.h>` header, which provides functions for wide-character input/output and wide string manipulation, is new in C99. (Amendment 1)
`<wctype.h>` *header*	The `<wctype.h>` header, the wide-character version of `<ctype.h>`, is new in C99. `<wctype.h>` provides functions for classifying and changing the case of wide characters. (Amendment 1)

26 Miscellaneous Library Functions

`va_copy` *macro*	C99 adds a function-like macro named `va_copy` to the `<stdarg.h>` header.
additional functions in `<stdio.h>` *header*	C99 adds the `vsnprintf`, `vfscanf`, `vscanf`, and `vsscanf` functions to the `<stdio.h>` header.
additional functions in `<stdlib.h>` *header*	C99 adds five numeric conversion functions, the `_Exit` function, and `long long` versions of the `abs` and `div` functions to the `<stdlib.h>` header.
additional `strftime` *conversion specifiers*	C99 adds a number of new `strftime` conversion specifiers. It also allows the use of an E or O character to modify the meaning of certain conversion specifiers.

27   Additional C99 Support for Mathematics

<stdint.h> header   The `<stdint.h>` header, which declares integer types with specified widths, is new in C99.

<inttypes.h> header   The `<inttypes.h>` header, which provides macros that are useful for input/output of the integer types in `<stdint.h>`, is new in C99.

complex types   C99 provides three complex types: `float _Complex`, `double _Complex`, and `long double _Complex`.

<complex.h> header   The `<complex.h>` header, which provides functions that perform mathematical operations on complex numbers, is new in C99.

<tgmath.h> header   The `<tgmath.h>` header, which provides type-generic macros that make it easier to call library functions in `<math.h>` and `<complex.h>`, is new in C99.

<fenv.h> header   The `<fenv.h>` header, which gives programs access to floating-point status flags and control modes, is new in C99.

APPENDIX C
C89 versus K&R C

This appendix lists most of the significant differences between C89 and K&R C (the language described in the first edition of Kernighan and Ritchie's *The C Programming Language*). The headings indicate which chapter of this book discusses each C89 feature. This appendix doesn't address the C library, which has changed much over the years. For other (less important) differences between C89 and K&R C, consult Appendices A and C in the second edition of K&R.

Most of today's C compilers can handle all of C89, but this appendix is useful if you to happen to encounter older programs that were originally written for pre-C89 compilers.

2 C Fundamentals

identifiers   In K&R C, only the first eight characters of an identifier are significant.

keywords   K&R C lacks the keywords `const`, `enum`, `signed`, `void`, and `volatile`. In K&R C, the word `entry` is a keyword.

4 Expressions

unary +   K&R C doesn't support the unary + operator.

5 Selection Statements

`switch`   In K&R C, the controlling expression (and case labels) in a `switch` statement must have type `int` after promotion. In C89, the expression and labels may be of any integral type, including `unsigned int` and `long int`.

7 Basic Types

unsigned types   K&R C provides only one unsigned type (`unsigned int`).

signed   K&R C doesn't support the `signed` type specifier.

number suffixes   K&R C doesn't support the `U` (or `u`) suffix to specify that an integer constant is unsigned, nor does it support the `F` (or `f`) suffix to indicate that a floating constant is to be stored as a `float` value instead of a `double` value. In K&R C, the `L` (or `l`) suffix can't be used with floating constants.

long float   K&R C allows the use of `long float` as a synonym for `double`; this usage isn't legal in C89.

long double   K&R C doesn't support the `long double` type.

escape sequences   The escape sequences `\a`, `\v`, and `\?` don't exist in K&R C. Also, K&R C doesn't support hexadecimal escape sequences.

size_t   In K&R C, the `sizeof` operator returns a value of type `int`; in C89, it returns a value of type `size_t`.

usual arithmetic conversions   K&R C requires that `float` operands be converted to `double`. Also, K&R C specifies that combining a shorter unsigned integer with a longer signed integer always produces an unsigned result.

9 Functions

function definitions   In a C89 function definition, the types of the parameters are included in the parameter list:

```
double square(double x)
{
   return x * x;
}
```

K&R C requires that the types of parameters be specified in separate lists:

```
double square(x)
double x;
{
   return x * x;
}
```

function declarations   A C89 function declaration (prototype) specifies the types of the function's parameters (and the names as well, if desired):

```
double square(double x);
double square(double);      /* alternate form */
int rand(void);             /* no parameters  */
```

A K&R C function declaration omits all information about parameters:

```
double square();
int rand();
```

function calls   When a K&R C definition or declaration is used, the compiler doesn't check that the function is called with arguments of the proper number and type. Furthermore, the arguments aren't automatically converted to the types of the corresponding parameters. Instead, the integral promotions are performed, and `float` arguments are converted to `double`.

void   K&R C doesn't support the `void` type.

12   Pointers and Arrays

pointer subtraction   Subtracting two pointers produces an `int` value in K&R C but a `ptrdiff_t` value in C89.

13   Strings

string literals   In K&R C, adjacent string literals aren't concatenated. Also, K&R C doesn't prohibit the modification of string literals.

string initialization   In K&R C, an initializer for a character array of length n is limited to $n - 1$ characters (leaving room for a null character at the end). C89 allows the initializer to have length n.

14   The Preprocessor

#elif, #error, #pragma   K&R C doesn't support the `#elif`, `#error`, and `#pragma` directives.

#, ##, defined   K&R C doesn't support the `#`, `##`, and `defined` operators.

16   Structures, Unions, and Enumerations

structure and union members and tags   In C89, each structure and union has its own name space for members; structure and union tags are kept in a separate name space. K&R C uses a single name space for members and tags, so members can't have the same name (with some exceptions), and members and tags can't overlap.

whole-structure operations   K&R C doesn't allow structures to be assigned, passed as arguments, or returned by functions.

enumerations   K&R C doesn't support enumerations.

17   Advanced Uses of Pointers

*void *   In C89, void * is used as a "generic" pointer type; for example, malloc returns a value of type void *. In K&R C, char * is used for this purpose.

pointer mixing   K&R C allows pointers of different types to be mixed in assignments and comparisons. In C89, pointers of type void * can be mixed with pointers of other types, but any other mixing isn't allowed without casting. Similarly, K&R C allows the mixing of integers and pointers in assignments and comparisons; C89 requires casting.

pointers to functions   If pf is a pointer to a function, C89 permits using either (*pf) (...) or pf (...) to call the function. K&R C allows only (*pf) (...).

18   Declarations

const and volatile   K&R C doesn't support the const and volatile type qualifiers.

initialization of arrays, structures, and unions   K&R C doesn't allow the initialization of automatic arrays and structures, nor does it allow initialization of unions (regardless of storage duration).

25   International Features

wide characters   K&R C doesn't support wide character constants and wide string literals.

trigraph sequences   K&R C doesn't support trigraph sequences.

26   Miscellaneous Library Functions

variable arguments   K&R C doesn't provide a portable way to write functions with a variable number of arguments, and it lacks the . . . (ellipsis) notation.

APPENDIX D
Standard Library Functions

This appendix describes all library functions supported by C89 and C99.* When using this appendix, please keep the following points in mind:

- In the interest of brevity and clarity, I've omitted many details. Some functions (notably `printf` and `scanf` and their variants) are covered in depth elsewhere in the book, so their descriptions here are minimal. For more information about a function (including examples of how it's used), see the section(s) listed in italic at the lower right corner of the function's description.

- As in other parts of the book, italics are used to indicate C99 differences. The names and prototypes of functions that were added in C99 are shown in italics. Changes to C89 prototypes (the addition of the word `restrict` to the declaration of certain parameters) are also italicized.

- Function-like macros are included in this appendix (with the exception of the type-generic macros in `<tgmath.h>`). Each prototype for a macro is followed by the word *macro*.

- In C99, some `<math.h>` functions have three versions (one each for `float`, `double`, and `long double`). All three are grouped into a single entry, under the name of the `double` version. For example, there's only one entry (under `acos`) for the `acos`, `acosf`, and `acosl` functions. The name of each additional version (`acosf` and `acosl`, in this example) appears to the left of its prototype. The `<complex.h>` functions, which also come in three versions, are treated in a similar fashion.

- Most of the `<wchar.h>` functions are wide-character versions of functions found in other headers. Unless there's a significant difference in behavior, the

---

*This material is adapted from international standard ISO/IEC 9899:1999.

description of each wide-character function simply refers the reader to the corresponding function found elsewhere.

- If some aspect of a function's behavior is described as *implementation-defined,* that means that it depends on how the C library is implemented. The function will always behave consistently, but the results may vary from one system to another. (In other words, check the manual to see what happens.) *Undefined* behavior, on the other hand, is bad news: not only may the behavior vary between systems, but the program may act strangely or even crash.

- The descriptions of many `<math.h>` functions refer to the terms *domain error* and *range error.* The way in which these errors are indicated changed between C89 and C99. For the C89 treatment of these errors, see Section 23.3. For the C99 treatment, see Section 23.4.

- The behavior of the following functions is affected by the current locale:

`<ctype.h>`	All functions
`<stdio.h>`	Formatted input/output functions
`<stdlib.h>`	Multibyte/wide-character conversion functions, numeric conversion functions
`<string.h>`	`strcoll`, `strxfrm`
`<time.h>`	`strftime`
`<wchar.h>`	`wcscoll`, `wcsftime`, `wcsxfrm`, formatted input/output functions, numeric conversion functions, extended multibyte/wide-character conversion functions
`<wctype.h>`	All functions

  The `isalpha` function, for example, usually checks whether a character lies between a and z or A and Z. In some locales, other characters are considered alphabetic as well.

---

abort   *Abort Program*   `<stdlib.h>`

`void abort(void);`

Raises the `SIGABRT` signal. If the signal isn't caught (or if the signal handler returns), the program terminates abnormally and returns an implementation-defined code indicating unsuccessful termination. Whether output buffers are flushed, open streams are closed, or temporary files are removed is implementation-defined.

26.2

---

abs   *Integer Absolute Value*   `<stdlib.h>`

`int abs(int j);`

Returns   Absolute value of j. The behavior is undefined if the absolute value of j can't be represented.

26.2

---

acos   *Arc Cosine*   `<math.h>`

`double acos(double x);`
acosf   `float acosf(float x);`
acosl   `long double acosl(long double x);`

Returns	Arc cosine of x; the return value is in the range 0 to π. A domain error occurs if x isn't between −1 and +1.	23.3

---

acosh	*Arc Hyperbolic Cosine (C99)*	`<math.h>`

```
        double acosh(double x);
acoshf  float acoshf(float x);
acoshl  long double acoshl(long double x);
```

Returns	Arc hyperbolic cosine of x; the return value is in the range 0 to +∞. A domain error occurs if x is less than 1.	23.4

---

asctime	*Convert Broken-Down Time to String*	`<time.h>`

```
char *asctime(const struct tm *timeptr);
```

Returns A pointer to a null-terminated string of the form

```
Sun Jun  3 17:48:34 2007\n
```

constructed from the broken-down time in the structure pointed to by `timeptr`.
                                                                        26.3

---

asin	*Arc Sine*	`<math.h>`

```
       double asin(double x);
asinf  float asinf(float x);
asinl  long double asinl(long double x);
```

Returns	Arc sine of x; the return value is in the range −π/2 to +π/2. A domain error occurs if x isn't between −1 and +1.	23.3

---

asinh	*Arc Hyperbolic Sine (C99)*	`<math.h>`

```
        double asinh(double x);
asinhf  float asinhf(float x);
asinhl  long double asinhl(long double x);
```

Returns	Arc hyperbolic sine of x.	23.4

---

assert	*Assert Truth of Expression*	`<assert.h>`

```
void assert(scalar expression);
```
                                                                      macro

If the value of `expression` is nonzero, `assert` does nothing. If the value is zero, `assert` writes a message to `stderr` (specifying the text of `expression`, the name of the source file containing the `assert`, and the line number of the `assert`); it then terminates the program by calling `abort`. To disable `assert`, define the macro `NDEBUG` before including `<assert.h>`. *C99 changes:* The argument is allowed to have any scalar type; C89 specifies that the type is `int`. Also, C99 requires that the message written by `assert` include the name of the function in which the `assert` appears; C89 doesn't have this requirement.   24.1

---

atan	*Arc Tangent*	`<math.h>`

```
       double atan(double x);
atanf  float atanf(float x);
```

atanl	`long double atanl(long double x);`	

Returns   Arc tangent of x; the return value is in the range –π/2 to +π/2.   *23.3*

---

atan2   *Arc Tangent of Quotient*   `<math.h>`

```
double atan2(double y, double x);
```
atan2f   `float atan2f(float y, float x);`
atan2l   `long double atan2l(long double y, long double x);`

Returns   Arc tangent of y/x; the return value is in the range –π to +π. A domain error may occur if x and y are both zero.   *23.3*

---

atanh   *Arc Hyperbolic Tangent (C99)*   `<math.h>`

```
double atanh(double x);
```
atanhf   `float atanhf(float x);`
atanhl   `long double atanhl(long double x);`

Returns   Arc hyperbolic tangent of x. A domain error occurs if x is not between –1 and +1. A range error may occur if x is equal to –1 or +1.   *23.4*

---

atexit   *Register Function to Be Called at Program Exit*   `<stdlib.h>`

```
int atexit(void (*func)(void));
```

Registers the function pointed to by `func` as a termination function. The function will be called if the program terminates normally (via `return` or `exit` but not `abort`).

Returns   Zero if successful, nonzero if unsuccessful (an implementation-dependent limit has been reached).   *26.2*

---

atof   *Convert String to Floating-Point Number*   `<stdlib.h>`

```
double atof(const char *nptr);
```

Returns   A `double` value corresponding to the longest initial part of the string pointed to by `nptr` that has the form of a floating-point number. Returns zero if no conversion could be performed. The function's behavior is undefined if the number can't be represented.   *26.2*

---

atoi   *Convert String to Integer*   `<stdlib.h>`

```
int atoi(const char *nptr);
```

Returns   An `int` value corresponding to the longest initial part of the string pointed to by `nptr` that has the form of an integer. Returns zero if no conversion could be performed. The function's behavior is undefined if the number can't be represented.   *26.2*

---

atol   *Convert String to Long Integer*   `<stdlib.h>`

```
long int atol(const char *nptr);
```

Returns   A `long int` value corresponding to the longest initial part of the string pointed to by `nptr` that has the form of an integer. Returns zero if no conversion could be performed. The function's behavior is undefined if the number can't be represented.   *26.2*

---

atoll   *Convert String to Long Long Integer (C99)*   `<stdlib.h>`

`long long int atoll(const char *nptr);`

Returns   A `long long int` value corresponding to the longest initial part of the string pointed to by `nptr` that has the form of an integer. Returns zero if no conversion could be performed. The function's behavior is undefined if the number can't be represented.   *26.2*

---

bsearch   *Binary Search*   `<stdlib.h>`

```
void *bsearch(const void *key, const void *base,
              size_t memb, size_t size,
              int (*compar)(const void *,
                            const void *));
```

Searches for the value pointed to by `key` in the sorted array pointed to by `base`. The array has nmemb elements, each `size` bytes long. compar is a pointer to a comparison function. When passed pointers to the key and an array element, in that order, the comparison function must return a negative, zero, or positive integer, depending on whether the key is less than, equal to, or greater than the array element.

Returns   A pointer to an array element that tests equal to the key. Returns a null pointer if the key isn't found.   *26.2*

---

btowc   *Convert Byte to Wide Character (C99)*   `<wchar.h>`

`wint_t btowc(int c);`

Returns   Wide-character representation of c. Returns WEOF if c is equal to EOF or if c (when cast to `unsigned char`) isn't a valid single-byte character in the initial shift state.   *25.5*

---

cabs   *Complex Absolute Value (C99)*   `<complex.h>`

`double cabs(double complex z);`
cabsf   `float cabsf(float complex z);`
cabsl   `long double cabsl(long double complex z);`

Returns   Complex absolute value of z.   *27.4*

---

cacos   *Complex Arc Cosine (C99)*   `<complex.h>`

`double complex cacos(double complex z);`
cacosf   `float complex cacosf(float complex z);`
cacosl   `long double complex cacosl(long double complex z);`

Returns   Complex arc cosine of z, with branch cuts outside the interval [−1, +1] along the real axis. The return value lies in a strip mathematically unbounded along the imaginary axis and in the interval [0, π] along the real axis.   *27.4*

cacosh	*Complex Arc Hyperbolic Cosine (C99)*	`<complex.h>`

cacoshf
cacoshl

```
double complex cacosh(double complex z);
float complex cacoshf(float complex z);
long double complex cacoshl(long double complex z);
```

Returns   Complex arc hyperbolic cosine of z, with a branch cut at values less than 1 along the real axis. The return value lies in a half-strip of nonnegative values along the real axis and in the interval $[-i\pi, +i\pi]$ along the imaginary axis.   *27.4*

calloc	*Allocate and Clear Memory Block*	`<stdlib.h>`

```
void *calloc(size_t nmemb, size_t size);
```

Allocates a block of memory for an array with nmemb elements, each with `size` bytes. The block is cleared by setting all bits to zero.

Returns   A pointer to the beginning of the block. Returns a null pointer if a block of the requested size can't be allocated.   *17.3*

carg	*Complex Argument (C99)*	`<complex.h>`

cargf
cargl

```
double carg(double complex z);
float cargf(float complex z);
long double cargl(long double complex z);
```

Returns   Argument (phase angle) of z, with a branch cut along the negative real axis. The return value lies in the interval $[-\pi, +\pi]$.   *27.4*

casin	*Complex Arc Sine (C99)*	`<complex.h>`

casinf
casinl

```
double complex casin(double complex z);
float complex casinf(float complex z);
long double complex casinl(long double complex z);
```

Returns   Complex arc sine of z, with branch cuts outside the interval $[-1, +1]$ along the real axis. The return value lies in a strip mathematically unbounded along the imaginary axis and in the interval $[-\pi/2, +\pi/2]$ along the real axis.   *27.4*

casinh	*Complex Arc Hyperbolic Sine (C99)*	`<complex.h>`

casinhf
casinhl

```
double complex casinh(double complex z);
float complex casinhf(float complex z);
long double complex casinhl(long double complex z);
```

Returns   Complex arc hyperbolic sine of z, with branch cuts outside the interval $[-i, +i]$ along the imaginary axis. The return value lies in a strip mathematically unbounded along the real axis and in the interval $[-i\pi/2, +i\pi/2]$ along the imaginary axis.   *27.4*

catan	*Complex Arc Tangent (C99)*	`<complex.h>`

catanf
catanl

```
double complex catan(double complex z);
float complex catanf(float complex z);
long double complex catanl(long double complex z);
```

Returns	Complex arc tangent of z, with branch cuts outside the interval [–*i*, +*i*] along the imaginary axis. The return value lies in a strip mathematically unbounded along the imaginary axis and in the interval [–π/2, +π/2] along the real axis. *27.4*

---

catanh   *Complex Arc Hyperbolic Tangent (C99)*   `<complex.h>`

```
double complex catanh(double complex z);
```
catanhf   `float complex catanhf(float complex z);`
catanhl   `long double complex catanhl(long double complex z);`

Returns   Complex arc hyperbolic tangent of z, with branch cuts outside the interval [–1, +1] along the real axis. The return value lies in a strip mathematically unbounded along the real axis and in the interval [–*i*π/2, +*i*π/2] along the imaginary axis. *27.4*

---

cbrt   *Cube Root (C99)*   `<math.h>`

```
double cbrt(double x);
```
cbrtf   `float cbrtf(float x);`
cbrtl   `long double cbrtl(long double x);`

Returns   Real cube root of x.   *23.4*

---

ccos   *Complex Cosine (C99)*   `<complex.h>`

```
double complex ccos(double complex z);
```
ccosf   `float complex ccosf(float complex z);`
ccosl   `long double complex ccosl(long double complex z);`

Returns   Complex cosine of z.   *27.4*

---

ccosh   *Complex Hyperbolic Cosine (C99)*   `<complex.h>`

```
double complex ccosh(double complex z);
```
ccoshf   `float complex ccoshf(float complex z);`
ccoshl   `long double complex ccoshl(long double complex z);`

Returns   Complex hyperbolic cosine of z.   *27.4*

---

ceil   *Ceiling*   `<math.h>`

```
double ceil(double x);
```
ceilf   `float ceilf(float x);`
ceill   `long double ceill(long double x);`

Returns   Smallest integer that is greater than or equal to x.   *23.3*

---

cexp   *Complex Base-e Exponential (C99)*   `<complex.h>`

```
double complex cexp(double complex z);
```
cexpf   `float complex cexpf(float complex z);`
cexpl   `long double complex cexpl(long double complex z);`

Returns   Complex base-*e* exponential of z.   *27.4*

---

cimag   *Imaginary Part of Complex Number (C99)*   `<complex.h>`

```
double cimag(double complex z);
```

cimagf	`float cimagf(float complex z);`	
cimagl	`long double cimagl(long double complex z);`	
Returns	Imaginary part of z.	*27.4*

clearerr   *Clear Stream Error*   <stdio.h>

`void clearerr(FILE *stream);`

Clears the end-of-file and error indicators for the stream pointed to by `stream`.

22.3

clock   *Processor Clock*   <time.h>

`clock_t clock(void);`

Returns   Elapsed processor time (measured in "clock ticks") since the beginning of program execution. (To convert into seconds, divide by CLOCKS_PER_SEC.) Returns `(clock_t) (-1)` if the time is unavailable or can't be represented.   *26.3*

clog   *Complex Natural Logarithm (C99)*   <complex.h>

`double complex clog(double complex z);`
clogf   `float complex clogf(float complex z);`
clogl   `long double complex clogl(long double complex z);`

Returns   Complex natural (base-*e*) logarithm of z, with a branch cut along the negative real axis. The return value lies in a strip mathematically unbounded along the real axis and in the interval $[-i\pi, +i\pi]$ along the imaginary axis.   *27.4*

conj   *Complex Conjugate (C99)*   <complex.h>

`double complex conj(double complex z);`
conjf   `float complex conjf(float complex z);`
conjl   `long double complex conjl(long double complex z);`

Returns   Complex conjugate of z.   *27.4*

copysign   *Copy Sign (C99)*   <math.h>

`double copysign(double x, double y);`
copysignf   `float copysignf(float x, float y);`
copysignl   `long double copysignl(long double x, long double y);`

Returns   A value with the magnitude of x and the sign of y.   *23.4*

cos   *Cosine*   <math.h>

`double cos(double x);`
cosf   `float cosf(float x);`
cosl   `long double cosl(long double x);`

Returns   Cosine of x (measured in radians).   *23.3*

cosh   *Hyperbolic Cosine*   <math.h>

`double cosh(double x);`
coshf   `float coshf(float x);`

coshl	`long double coshl(long double x);`
Returns	Hyperbolic cosine of x. A range error occurs if the magnitude of x is too large.

23.3

---

cpow *Complex Power (C99)*   `<complex.h>`

```
double complex cpow(double complex x,
                    double complex y);
```

cpowf `float complex cpowf(float complex x,
                    float complex y);`

cpowl `long double complex cpowl(long double complex x,
                         long double complex y);`

Returns x raised to the power y, with a branch cut for the first parameter along the negative real axis.   27.4

---

cproj *Complex Projection (C99)*   `<complex.h>`

```
double complex cproj(double complex z);
```
cprojf `float complex cprojf(float complex z);`
cprojl `long double complex cprojl(long double complex z);`

Returns Projection of z onto the Riemann sphere. z is returned unless one of its parts is infinite, in which case the return value is INFINITY + I * copysign(0.0, cimag(z)).   27.4

---

creal *Real Part of Complex Number (C99)*   `<complex.h>`

```
double creal(double complex z);
```
crealf `float crealf(float complex z);`
creall `long double creall(long double complex z);`

Returns Real part of z.   27.4

---

csin *Complex Sine (C99)*   `<complex.h>`

```
double complex csin(double complex z);
```
csinf `float complex csinf(float complex z);`
csinl `long double complex csinl(long double complex z);`

Returns Complex sine of z.   27.4

---

csinh *Complex Hyperbolic Sine (C99)*   `<complex.h>`

```
double complex csinh(double complex z);
```
csinhf `float complex csinhf(float complex z);`
csinhl `long double complex csinhl(long double complex z);`

Returns Complex hyperbolic sine of z.   27.4

---

csqrt *Complex Square Root (C99)*   `<complex.h>`

```
double complex csqrt(double complex z);
```
csqrtf `float complex csqrtf(float complex z);`
csqrtl `long double complex csqrtl(long double complex z);`

Returns	Complex square root of z, with a branch cut along the negative real axis. The return value lies in the right half-plane (including the imaginary axis). *27.4*	

`ctan` *Complex Tangent (C99)* `<complex.h>`

```
        double complex ctan(double complex z);
ctanf   float complex ctanf(float complex z);
ctanl   long double complex ctanl(long double complex z);
```

Returns   Complex tangent of z.   *27.4*

`ctanh` *Complex Hyperbolic Tangent (C99)* `<complex.h>`

```
         double complex ctanh(double complex z);
ctanhf   float complex ctanhf(float complex z);
ctanhl   long double complex ctanhl(long double complex z);
```

Returns   Complex hyperbolic tangent of z.   *27.4*

`ctime` *Convert Calendar Time to String* `<time.h>`

```
char *ctime(const time_t *timer);
```

Returns   A pointer to a string describing a local time equivalent to the calendar time pointed to by `timer`. Equivalent to `asctime(localtime(timer))`.   *26.3*

`difftime` *Time Difference* `<time.h>`

```
double difftime(time_t time1, time_t time0);
```

Returns   Difference between `time0` (the earlier time) and `time1`, measured in seconds.   *26.3*

`div` *Integer Division* `<stdlib.h>`

```
div_t div(int numer, int denom);
```

Returns   A `div_t` structure containing members named `quot` (the quotient when `numer` is divided by `denom`) and `rem` (the remainder). The behavior is undefined if either part of the result can't be represented.   *26.2*

`erf` *Error Function (C99)* `<math.h>`

```
       double erf(double x);
erff   float erff(float x);
erfl   long double erfl(long double x);
```

Returns   erf(x), where erf is the Gaussian error function.   *23.4*

`erfc` *Complementary Error Function (C99)* `<math.h>`

```
        double erfc(double x);
erfcf   float erfcf(float x);
erfcl   long double erfcl(long double x);
```

Returns   erfc(x) = 1 – erf(x), where erf is the Gaussian error function. A range error occurs if x is too large.   *23.4*

exit   *Exit from Program*   `<stdlib.h>`

`void exit(int status);`

Calls all functions registered with `atexit`, flushes all output buffers, closes all open streams, removes any files created by `tmpfile`, and terminates the program. The value of `status` indicates whether the program terminated normally. The only portable values for `status` are 0 and `EXIT_SUCCESS` (both indicate successful termination) plus `EXIT_FAILURE` (unsuccessful termination).

9.5, 26.2

_Exit   *Exit from Program (C99)*   `<stdlib.h>`

`void _Exit(int status);`

Causes normal program termination. Doesn't call functions registered with `atexit` or signal handlers registered with `signal`. The status returned is determined in the same way as for `exit`. Whether output buffers are flushed, open streams are closed, or temporary files are removed is implementation-defined.

26.2

exp   *Base-e Exponential*   `<math.h>`

`double exp(double x);`
expf   `float expf(float x);`
expl   `long double expl(long double x);`
Returns   *e* raised to the power x. A range error occurs if the magnitude of x is too large.

23.3

exp2   *Base-2 Exponential (C99)*   `<math.h>`

`double exp2(double x);`
exp2f   `float exp2f(float x);`
exp2l   `long double exp2l(long double x);`
Returns   2 raised to the power x. A range error occurs if the magnitude of x is too large.

23.4

expm1   *Base-e Exponential Minus 1 (C99)*   `<math.h>`

`double expm1(double x);`
expm1f   `float expm1f(float x);`
expm1l   `long double expm1l(long double x);`
Returns   *e* raised to the power x, minus 1. A range error occurs if x is too large.   *23.4*

fabs   *Floating Absolute Value*   `<math.h>`

`double fabs(double x);`
fabsf   `float fabsf(float x);`
fabsl   `long double fabsl(long double x);`
Returns   Absolute value of x.   *23.3*

fclose   *Close File*   `<stdio.h>`

```
int fclose(FILE *stream);
```

Closes the stream pointed to by `stream`. Flushes any unwritten output remaining in the stream's buffer. Deallocates the buffer if it was allocated automatically.

Returns   Zero if successful, `EOF` if an error was detected.   *22.2*

fdim   *Positive Difference (C99)*   `<math.h>`

```
double fdim(double x, double y);
```
fdimf
```
float fdimf(float x, float y);
```
fdiml
```
long double fdiml(long double x, long double y);
```

Returns   Positive difference of x and y:

$$\begin{cases} x - y & \text{if } x > y \\ +0 & \text{if } x \leq y \end{cases}$$

A range error may occur.   *23.4*

feclearexcept   *Clear Floating-Point Exceptions (C99)*   `<fenv.h>`

```
int feclearexcept(int excepts);
```

Attempts to clear the floating-point exceptions represented by `excepts`.

Returns   Zero if `excepts` is zero or if all specified exceptions were successfully cleared; otherwise, returns a nonzero value.   *27.6*

fegetenv   *Get Floating-Point Environment (C99)*   `<fenv.h>`

```
int fegetenv(fenv_t *envp);
```

Attempts to store the current floating-point environment in the object pointed to by envp.

Returns   Zero if the environment was successfully stored; otherwise, returns a nonzero value.   *27.6*

fegetexceptflag   *Get Floating-Point Exception Flags (C99)*   `<fenv.h>`

```
int fegetexceptflag(fexcept_t *flagp, int excepts);
```

Attempts to retrieve the states of the floating-point status flags represented by `excepts` and store them in the object pointed to by `flagp`.

Returns   Zero if the states of the status flags were successfully stored; otherwise, returns a nonzero value.   *27.6*

fegetround   *Get Floating-Point Rounding Direction (C99)*   `<fenv.h>`

```
int fegetround(void);
```

Returns   Value of the rounding-direction macro that represents the current rounding direction. Returns a negative value if the current rounding direction can't be determined or doesn't match any rounding-direction macro.   *27.6*

feholdexcept	*Save Floating-Point Environment (C99)*	`<fenv.h>`

`int feholdexcept(fenv_t *envp);`

Saves the current floating-point environment in the object pointed to by `envp`, clears the floating-point status flags, and attempts to install a non-stop mode for all floating-point exceptions.

Returns   Zero if non-stop floating-point exception handling was successfully installed; otherwise, returns a nonzero value.   *27.6*

feof	*Test for End-of-File*	`<stdio.h>`

`int feof(FILE *stream);`

Returns   A nonzero value if the end-of-file indicator is set for the stream pointed to by `stream`; otherwise, returns zero.   *22.3*

feraiseexcept	*Raise Floating-Point Exceptions (C99)*	`<fenv.h>`

`int feraiseexcept(int excepts);`

Attempts to raise supported floating-point exceptions represented by `excepts`.

Returns   Zero if `excepts` is zero or if all specified exceptions were successfully raised; otherwise, returns a nonzero value.   *27.6*

ferror	*Test for File Error*	`<stdio.h>`

`int ferror(FILE *stream);`

Returns   A nonzero value if the error indicator is set for the stream pointed to by `stream`; otherwise, returns zero.   *22.3*

fesetenv	*Set Floating-Point Environment (C99)*	`<fenv.h>`

`int fesetenv(const fenv_t *envp);`

Attempts to establish the floating-point environment represented by the object pointed to by `envp`.

Returns   Zero if the environment was successfully established; otherwise, returns a nonzero value.   *27.6*

fesetexceptflag	*Set Floating-Point Exception Flags (C99)*	`<fenv.h>`

`int fesetexceptflag(const fexcept_t *flagp,`
`                    int excepts);`

Attempts to set the floating-point status flags represented by `excepts` to the states stored in the object pointed to by `flagp`.

Returns   Zero if `excepts` is zero or if all specified exceptions were successfully set; otherwise, returns a nonzero value.   *27.6*

fesetround	*Set Floating-Point Rounding Direction (C99)*	`<fenv.h>`

`int fesetround(int round);`

Attempts to establish the rounding direction represented by `round`.

Returns Zero if the requested rounding direction was established; otherwise, returns a nonzero value. *27.6*

---

fetestexcept *Test Floating-Point Exception Flags (C99)* `<fenv.h>`

```
int fetestexcept(int excepts);
```

Returns Bitwise *or* of the floating-point exception macros corresponding to the currently set flags for the exceptions represented by `excepts`. *27.6*

---

feupdateenv *Update Floating-Point Environment (C99)* `<fenv.h>`

```
int feupdateenv(const fenv_t *envp);
```

Attempts to save the currently raised floating-point exceptions, install the floating-point environment represented by the object pointed to by `envp`, and then raise the saved exceptions.

Returns Zero if all actions were successfully carried out; otherwise, returns a nonzero value. *27.6*

---

fflush *Flush File Buffer* `<stdio.h>`

```
int fflush(FILE *stream);
```

Writes any unwritten data in the buffer associated with `stream`, which points to a stream that was opened for output or updating. If `stream` is a null pointer, `fflush` flushes all streams that have unwritten data stored in a buffer.

Returns Zero if successful, EOF if a write error occurs. *22.2*

---

fgetc *Read Character from File* `<stdio.h>`

```
int fgetc(FILE *stream);
```

Reads a character from the stream pointed to by `stream`.

Returns Character read from the stream. If `fgetc` encounters the end of the stream, it sets the stream's end-of-file indicator and returns EOF. If a read error occurs, `fgetc` sets the stream's error indicator and returns EOF. *22.4*

---

fgetpos *Get File Position* `<stdio.h>`

```
int fgetpos(FILE * restrict stream,
            fpos_t * restrict pos);
```

Stores the current position of the stream pointed to by `stream` in the object pointed to by `pos`.

Returns Zero if successful. If the call fails, returns a nonzero value and stores an implementation-defined positive value in `errno`. *22.7*

---

fgets *Read String from File* `<stdio.h>`

```
char *fgets(char * restrict s, int n,
            FILE * restrict stream);
```

Reads characters from the stream pointed to by `stream` and stores them in the array pointed to by `s`. Reading stops at the first new-line character (which is stored in the string), when `n` − 1 characters have been read, or at end-of-file. `fgets` appends a null character to the string.

Returns `s` (a pointer to the array in which the input is stored). Returns a null pointer if a read error occurs or `fgets` encounters the end of the stream before it has stored any characters.   *22.5*

`fgetwc`   *Read Wide Character from File (C99)*   `<wchar.h>`

```
wint_t fgetwc(FILE *stream);
```

Wide-character version of `fgetc`.   *25.5*

`fgetws`   *Read Wide String from File (C99)*   `<wchar.h>`

```
wchar_t *fgetws(wchar_t * restrict s, int n,
                FILE * restrict stream);
```

Wide-character version of `fgets`.   *25.5*

`floor`   *Floor*   `<math.h>`

```
double floor(double x);
```
`floorf` `float floorf(float x);`
`floorl` `long double floorl(long double x);`

Returns Largest integer that is less than or equal to `x`.   *23.3*

`fma`   *Floating Multiply-Add (C99)*   `<math.h>`

```
double fma(double x, double y, double z);
```
`fmaf` `float fmaf(float x, float y, float z);`
`fmal` `long double fmal(long double x, long double y,`
`                long double z);`

Returns $(x \times y) + z$. The result is rounded only once, using the rounding mode corresponding to `FLT_ROUNDS`. A range error may occur.   *23.4*

`fmax`   *Floating Maximum (C99)*   `<math.h>`

```
double fmax(double x, double y);
```
`fmaxf` `float fmaxf(float x, float y);`
`fmaxl` `long double fmaxl(long double x, long double y);`

Returns Maximum of `x` and `y`. If one argument is a NaN and the other is numeric, the numeric value is returned.   *23.4*

`fmin`   *Floating Minimum (C99)*   `<math.h>`

```
double fmin(double x, double y);
```
`fminf` `float fminf(float x, float y);`
`fminl` `long double fminl(long double x, long double y);`

Returns Minimum of `x` and `y`. If one argument is a NaN and the other is numeric, the numeric value is returned.   *23.4*

fmod	*Floating Modulus*	`<math.h>`

```
double fmod(double x, double y);
```
fmodf `float fmodf(float x, float y);`
fmodl `long double fmodl(long double x, long double y);`

Returns Remainder when x is divided by y. If y is zero, either a domain error occurs or zero is returned.   *23.3*

fopen	*Open File*	`<stdio.h>`

```
FILE *fopen(const char * restrict filename,
            const char * restrict mode);
```

Opens the file whose name is pointed to by `filename` and associates it with a stream. `mode` specifies the mode in which the file is to be opened. Clears the error and end-of-file indicators for the stream.

Returns A file pointer to be used when performing subsequent operations on the file. Returns a null pointer if the file can't be opened.   *22.2*

fpclassify	*Floating-Point Classification (C99)*	`<math.h>`

```
int fpclassify(real-floating x);
```                                                                                         *macro*

Returns Either `FP_INFINITE`, `FP_NAN`, `FP_NORMAL`, `FP_SUBNORMAL`, or `FP_ZERO`, depending on whether x is infinity, not a number, normal, subnormal, or zero, respectively.   *23.4*

fprintf	*Formatted File Write*	`<stdio.h>`

```
int fprintf(FILE * restrict stream,
            const char * restrict format, ...);
```

Writes output to the stream pointed to by `stream`. The string pointed to by `format` specifies how subsequent arguments will be displayed.

Returns Number of characters written. Returns a negative value if an error occurs. *22.3*

fputc	*Write Character to File*	`<stdio.h>`

```
int fputc(int c, FILE *stream);
```

Writes the character c to the stream pointed to by `stream`.

Returns c (the character written). If a write error occurs, `fputc` sets the stream's error indicator and returns `EOF`.   *22.4*

fputs	*Write String to File*	`<stdio.h>`

```
int fputs(const char * restrict s,
          FILE * restrict stream);
```

Writes the string pointed to by s to the stream pointed to by `stream`.

Returns A nonnegative value if successful. Returns `EOF` if a write error occurs. *22.5*

fputwc	*Write Wide Character to File (C99)*	`<wchar.h>`

```
wint_t fputwc(wchar_t c, FILE *stream);
```

Wide-character version of `fputc`.   *25.5*

fputws	*Write Wide String to File (C99)*	`<wchar.h>`

```
int fputws(const wchar_t * restrict s,
           FILE * restrict stream);
```

Wide-character version of `fputs`.   *25.5*

fread	*Read Block from File*	`<stdio.h>`

```
size_t fread(void * restrict ptr, size_t size,
             size_t nmemb, FILE * restrict stream);
```

Attempts to read nmemb elements, each `size` bytes long, from the stream pointed to by `stream` and store them in the array pointed to by `ptr`.

Returns   Number of elements actually read. This number will be less than nmemb if `fread` encounters end-of-file or a read error occurs. Returns zero if either nmemb or `size` is zero.   *22.6*

free	*Free Memory Block*	`<stdlib.h>`

```
void free(void *ptr);
```

Releases the memory block pointed to by `ptr`. (If `ptr` is a null pointer, the call has no effect.) The block must have been allocated by a call of `calloc`, `malloc`, or `realloc`.   *17.4*

freopen	*Reopen File*	`<stdio.h>`

```
FILE *freopen(const char * restrict filename,
              const char * restrict mode,
              FILE * restrict stream);
```

Closes the file associated with `stream`, then opens the file whose name is pointed to by `filename` and associates it with `stream`. The mode parameter has the same meaning as in a call of `fopen`. *C99 change:* If `filename` is a null pointer, `freopen` attempts to change the stream's mode to that specified by mode.

Returns   Value of `stream` if the operation succeeds. Returns a null pointer if the file can't be opened.   *22.2*

frexp	*Split into Fraction and Exponent*	`<math.h>`
frexpf		
frexpl		

```
double frexp(double value, int *exp);
float frexpf(float value, int *exp);
long double frexpl(long double value, int *exp);
```

Splits `value` into a fractional part f and an exponent n in such a way that

$$value = f \times 2^n$$

f is normalized so that either $0.5 \leq f < 1$ or $f = 0$. Stores *n* in the object pointed to by exp.

Returns   *f*, the fractional part of value.   23.3

---

fscanf   *Formatted File Read*   <stdio.h>

```
int fscanf(FILE * restrict stream,
           const char * restrict format, ...);
```

Reads input items from the stream pointed to by stream. The string pointed to by format specifies the format of the items to be read. The arguments that follow format point to objects in which the items are to be stored.

Returns   Number of input items successfully read and stored. Returns EOF if an input failure occurs before any items can be read.   22.3

---

fseek   *File Seek*   <stdio.h>

```
int fseek(FILE *stream, long int offset, int whence);
```

Changes the file position indicator for the stream pointed to by stream. If whence is SEEK_SET, the new position is the beginning of the file plus offset bytes. If whence is SEEK_CUR, the new position is the current position plus offset bytes. If whence is SEEK_END, the new position is the end of the file plus offset bytes. The value of offset may be negative. For text streams, either offset must be zero or whence must be SEEK_SET and offset a value obtained by a previous call of ftell. For binary streams, fseek may not support calls in which whence is SEEK_END.

Returns   Zero if the operation is successful, nonzero otherwise.   22.7

---

fsetpos   *Set File Position*   <stdio.h>

```
int fsetpos(FILE *stream, const fpos_t *pos);
```

Sets the file position indicator for the stream pointed to by stream according to the value pointed to by pos (obtained from a previous call of fgetpos).

Returns   Zero if successful. If the call fails, returns a nonzero value and stores an implementation-defined positive value in errno.   22.7

---

ftell   *Determine File Position*   <stdio.h>

```
long int ftell(FILE *stream);
```

Returns   Current file position indicator for the stream pointed to by stream. If the call fails, returns -1L and stores an implementation-defined positive value in errno.   22.7

---

fwide   *Get and Set Stream Orientation (C99)*   <wchar.h>

```
int fwide(FILE *stream, int mode);
```

Determines the current orientation of a stream and, if desired, attempts to set its orientation. If mode is greater than zero, fwide tries to make the stream wide-oriented if it has no orientation. If mode is less than zero, it tries to make the stream byte-oriented if it has no orientation. If mode is zero, the orientation is not changed.

Returns   A positive value if the stream has wide orientation after the call, a negative value if it has byte orientation, or zero if it has no orientation.   *25.5*

---

fwprintf   *Wide-Character Formatted File Write (C99)*   <wchar.h>

```
int fwprintf(FILE * restrict stream,
             const wchar_t * restrict format, ...);
```

Wide-character version of fprintf.   *25.5*

---

fwrite   *Write Block to File*   <stdio.h>

```
size_t fwrite(const void * restrict ptr, size_t size,
              size_t nmemb, FILE * restrict stream);
```

Writes nmemb elements, each size bytes long, from the array pointed to by ptr to the stream pointed to by stream.

Returns   Number of elements actually written. This number will be less than nmemb if a write error occurs. In C99, returns zero if either nmemb or size is zero.   *22.6*

---

fwscanf   *Wide-Character Formatted File Read (C99)*   <wchar.h>

```
int fwscanf(FILE * restrict stream,
            const wchar_t * restrict format, ...);
```

Wide-character version of fscanf.   *25.5*

---

getc   *Read Character from File*   <stdio.h>

```
int getc(FILE *stream);
```

Reads a character from the stream pointed to by stream. *Note:* getc is normally implemented as a macro; it may evaluate stream more than once.

Returns   Character read from the stream. If getc encounters the end of the stream, it sets the stream's end-of-file indicator and returns EOF. If a read error occurs, getc sets the stream's error indicator and returns EOF.   *22.4*

---

getchar   *Read Character*   <stdio.h>

```
int getchar(void);
```

Reads a character from the stdin stream. *Note:* getchar is normally implemented as a macro.

Returns   Character read from the stream. If getchar encounters the end of the stream, it sets the stream's end-of-file indicator and returns EOF. If a read error occurs, getchar sets the stream's error indicator and returns EOF.   *7.3, 22.4*

---

getenv   *Get Environment String*   <stdlib.h>

```
char *getenv(const char *name);
```

Searches the operating system's environment list to see if any string matches the one pointed to by name.

Returns	A pointer to the string associated with the matching name. Returns a null pointer if no match is found.	*26.2*

gets   *Read String*   `<stdio.h>`

```
char *gets(char *s);
```

Reads characters from the `stdin` stream and stores them in the array pointed to by `s`. Reading stops at the first new-line character (which is discarded) or at end-of-file. `gets` appends a null character to the string.

Returns   `s` (a pointer to the array in which the input is stored). Returns a null pointer if a read error occurs or `gets` encounters the end of the stream before it has stored any characters.   *13.3, 22.5*

getwc   *Read Wide Character from File (C99)*   `<wchar.h>`

```
wint_t getwc(FILE *stream);
```

Wide-character version of `getc`.   *25.5*

getwchar   *Read Wide Character (C99)*   `<wchar.h>`

```
wint_t getwchar(void);
```

Wide-character version of `getchar`.   *25.5*

gmtime   *Convert Calendar Time to Broken-Down UTC Time*   `<time.h>`

```
struct tm *gmtime(const time_t *timer);
```

Returns   A pointer to a structure containing a broken-down UTC time equivalent to the calendar time pointed to by `timer`. Returns a null pointer if the calendar time can't be converted to UTC.   *26.3*

hypot   *Hypotenuse (C99)*   `<math.h>`

```
double hypot(double x, double y);
```
hypotf
hypotl
```
float hypotf(float x, float y);
long double hypotl(long double x, long double y);
```

Returns $\sqrt{x^2 + y^2}$ (the hypotenuse of a right triangle with legs x and y). A range error may occur.   *23.4*

ilogb   *Unbiased Exponent (C99)*   `<math.h>`

```
int ilogb(double x);
```
ilogbf
ilogbl
```
int ilogbf(float x);
int ilogbl(long double x);
```

Returns   Exponent of `x` as a signed integer; equivalent to calling the corresponding `logb` function and casting the returned value to type `int`. Returns `FP_ILOGB0` if `x` is zero, `INT_MAX` if `x` is infinite, and `FP_ILOGBNAN` if `x` is a NaN; a domain error or range error may occur in these cases.   *23.4*

imaxabs   *Greatest-Width Integer Absolute Value (C99)*   `<inttypes.h>`

```
intmax_t imaxabs(intmax_t j);
```

Returns	Absolute value of j. The behavior is undefined if the absolute value of j can't be represented.	*27.2*

imaxdiv | *Greatest-Width Integer Division (C99)* | `<inttypes.h>`

`imaxdiv_t imaxdiv(intmax_t numer, intmax_t denom);`

Returns	A structure of type imaxdiv_t containing members named quot (the quotient when numer is divided by denom) and rem (the remainder). The behavior is undefined if either part of the result can't be represented.	*27.2*

isalnum | *Test for Alphanumeric* | `<ctype.h>`

`int isalnum(int c);`

Returns	A nonzero value if c is alphanumeric and zero otherwise. (c is alphanumeric if either isalpha(c) or isdigit(c) is true.)	*23.5*

isalpha | *Test for Alphabetic* | `<ctype.h>`

`int isalpha(int c);`

Returns	A nonzero value if c is alphabetic and zero otherwise. In the "C" locale, c is alphabetic if either islower(c) or isupper(c) is true.	*23.5*

isblank | *Test for Blank (C99)* | `<ctype.h>`

`int isblank(int c);`

Returns	A nonzero value if c is a blank character that is used to separate words within a line of text. In the "C" locale, the blank characters are space (' ') and horizontal tab ('\t').	*23.5*

iscntrl | *Test for Control Character* | `<ctype.h>`

`int iscntrl(int c);`

Returns	A nonzero value if c is a control character and zero otherwise.	*23.5*

isdigit | *Test for Digit* | `<ctype.h>`

`int isdigit(int c);`

Returns	A nonzero value if c is a decimal digit and zero otherwise.	*23.5*

isfinite | *Test for Finite Number (C99)* | `<math.h>`

`int isfinite(real-floating x);` | *macro*

Returns	A nonzero value if x is finite (zero, subnormal, or normal, but not infinite or NaN) and zero otherwise.	*23.4*

isgraph | *Test for Graphical Character* | `<ctype.h>`

`int isgraph(int c);`

Returns	A nonzero value if c is a printing character (except a space) and zero otherwise.	*23.5*

isgreater | *Test for Greater Than (C99)* | `<math.h>`

`int isgreater(real-floating x, real-floating y);` | *macro*

Returns	(x) > (y). Unlike the > operator, isgreater doesn't raise the *invalid* floating-point exception if one or both of the arguments is a NaN. 23.4	

isgreaterequal | *Test for Greater Than or Equal (C99)* | <math.h>

```
int isgreaterequal(real-floating x, real-floating y);                macro
```

Returns   (x) >= (y). Unlike the >= operator, isgreaterequal doesn't raise the *invalid* floating-point exception if one or both of the arguments is a NaN.   23.4

isinf | *Test for Infinity (C99)* | <math.h>

```
int isinf(real-floating x);                                          macro
```

Returns   A nonzero value if x is infinity (positive or negative) and zero otherwise.   23.4

isless | *Test for Less Than (C99)* | <math.h>

```
int isless(real-floating x, real-floating y);                        macro
```

Returns   (x) < (y). Unlike the < operator, isless doesn't raise the *invalid* floating-point exception if one or both of the arguments is a NaN.   23.4

islessequal | *Test for Less Than or Equal (C99)* | <math.h>

```
int islessequal(real-floating x, real-floating y);                   macro
```

Returns   (x) <= (y). Unlike the <= operator, islessequal doesn't raise the *invalid* floating-point exception if one or both of the arguments is a NaN.   23.4

islessgreater | *Test for Less Than or Greater Than (C99)* | <math.h>

```
int islessgreater(real-floating x, real-floating y);                 macro
```

Returns   (x) < (y) || (x) > (y). Unlike this expression, islessgreater doesn't raise the *invalid* floating-point exception if one or both of the arguments is a NaN; also, x and y are evaluated only once.   23.4

islower | *Test for Lower-Case Letter* | <ctype.h>

```
int islower(int c);
```

Returns   A nonzero value if c is a lower-case letter and zero otherwise.   23.5

isnan | *Test for NaN (C99)* | <math.h>

```
int isnan(real-floating x);                                          macro
```

Returns   A nonzero value if x is a NaN value and zero otherwise.   23.4

isnormal | *Test for Normal Number (C99)* | <math.h>

```
int isnormal(real-floating x);                                       macro
```

Returns   A nonzero value if x has a normal value (not zero, subnormal, infinite, or NaN) and zero otherwise.   23.4

isprint | *Test for Printing Character* | <ctype.h>

```
int isprint(int c);
```

Returns   A nonzero value if c is a printing character (including a space) and zero otherwise.

23.5

ispunct   *Test for Punctuation Character*   <ctype.h>

```
int ispunct(int c);
```

Returns   A nonzero value if c is a punctuation character and zero otherwise. All printing characters except the space (' ') and the alphanumeric characters are considered punctuation. *C99 change:* In the "C" locale, all printing characters except those for which isspace or isalnum is true are considered punctuation.   *23.5*

isspace   *Test for White-Space Character*   <ctype.h>

```
int isspace(int c);
```

Returns   A nonzero value if c is a white-space character and zero otherwise. In the "C" locale, the white-space characters are space (' '), form feed ('\f'), new-line ('\n'), carriage return ('\r'), horizontal tab ('\t'), and vertical tab ('\v').

23.5

isunordered   *Test for Unordered (C99)*   <math.h>

```
int isunordered(real-floating x, real-floating y);    macro
```

Returns   1 if x and y are unordered (at least one is a NaN) and 0 otherwise.   *23.4*

isupper   *Test for Upper-Case Letter*   <ctype.h>

```
int isupper(int c);
```

Returns   A nonzero value if c is an upper-case letter and zero otherwise.   *23.5*

iswalnum   *Test for Alphanumeric Wide Character (C99)*   <wctype.h>

```
int iswalnum(wint_t wc);
```

Returns   A nonzero value if wc is alphanumeric and zero otherwise. (wc is alphanumeric if either iswalpha(wc) or iswdigit(wc) is true.)   *25.6*

iswalpha   *Test for Alphabetic Wide Character (C99)*   <wctype.h>

```
int iswalpha(wint_t wc);
```

Returns   A nonzero value if wc is alphabetic and zero otherwise. (wc is alphabetic if iswupper(wc) or iswlower(wc) is true, or if wc is one of a locale-specific set of alphabetic wide characters for which none of iswcntrl, iswdigit, iswpunct, or iswspace is true.)   *25.6*

iswblank   *Test for Blank Wide Character (C99)*   <wctype.h>

```
int iswblank(wint_t wc);
```

Returns   A nonzero value if wc is a standard blank wide character or one of a locale-specific set of wide characters for which iswspace is true and that are used to separate words within a line of text. In the "C" locale, iswblank returns true only for the standard blank characters: space (L' ') and horizontal tab (L'\t').   *25.6*

| ***iswcntrl*** | *Test for Control Wide Character (C99)* | `<wctype.h>` |

`int iswcntrl(wint_t wc);`

Returns   A nonzero value if `wc` is a control wide character and zero otherwise.   *25.6*

| ***iswctype*** | *Test Type of Wide Character (C99)* | `<wctype.h>` |

`int iswctype(wint_t wc, wctype_t desc);`

Returns   A nonzero value if the wide character `wc` has the property described by `desc`. (`desc` must be a value returned by a call of `wctype`; the current setting of the `LC_CTYPE` category must be the same during both calls.) Returns zero otherwise.
    25.6

| ***iswdigit*** | *Test for Digit Wide Character (C99)* | `<wctype.h>` |

`int iswdigit(wint_t wc);`

Returns   A nonzero value if `wc` corresponds to a decimal digit and zero otherwise.   *25.6*

| ***iswgraph*** | *Test for Graphical Wide Character (C99)* | `<wctype.h>` |

`int iswgraph(wint_t wc);`

Returns   A nonzero value if `iswprint(wc)` is true and `iswspace(wc)` is false. Returns zero otherwise.   *25.6*

| ***iswlower*** | *Test for Lower-Case Wide Character (C99)* | `<wctype.h>` |

`int iswlower(wint_t wc);`

Returns   A nonzero value if `wc` corresponds to a lower-case letter or is one of a locale-specific set of wide characters for which none of `iswcntrl`, `iswdigit`, `iswpunct`, or `iswspace` is true. Returns zero otherwise.   *25.6*

| ***iswprint*** | *Test for Printing Wide Character (C99)* | `<wctype.h>` |

`int iswprint(wint_t wc);`

Returns   A nonzero value if `wc` is a printing wide character and zero otherwise.   *25.6*

| ***iswpunct*** | *Test for Punctuation Wide Character (C99)* | `<wctype.h>` |

`int iswpunct(wint_t wc);`

Returns   A nonzero value if `wc` is a printing wide character that is one of a locale-specific set of punctuation wide characters for which neither `iswspace` nor `iswalnum` is true. Returns zero otherwise.   *25.6*

| ***iswspace*** | *Test for White-Space Wide Character (C99)* | `<wctype.h>` |

`int iswspace(wint_t wc);`

Returns   A nonzero value if `wc` is one of a locale-specific set of white-space wide characters for which none of `iswalnum`, `iswgraph`, or `iswpunct` is true. Returns zero otherwise.   *25.6*

iswupper	*Test for Upper-Case Wide Character (C99)*	`<wctype.h>`

`int iswupper(wint_t wc);`

Returns   A nonzero value if `wc` corresponds to an upper-case letter or is one of a locale-specific set of wide characters for which none of `iswcntrl`, `iswdigit`, `iswpunct`, or `iswspace` is true. Returns zero otherwise.   *25.6*

iswxdigit	*Test for Hexadecimal-Digit Wide Character (C99)*	`<wctype.h>`

`int iswxdigit(wint_t wc);`

Returns   A nonzero value if `wc` corresponds to a hexadecimal digit (0–9, a–f, A–F) and zero otherwise.   *25.6*

`isxdigit`	*Test for Hexadecimal Digit*	`<ctype.h>`

`int isxdigit(int c);`

Returns   A nonzero value if `c` is a hexadecimal digit (0–9, a–f, A–F) and zero otherwise.   *23.5*

labs	*Long Integer Absolute Value*	`<stdlib.h>`

`long int labs(long int j);`

Returns   Absolute value of `j`. The behavior is undefined if the absolute value of `j` can't be represented.   *26.2*

ldexp	*Combine Fraction and Exponent*	`<math.h>`

`double ldexp(double x, int exp);`
ldexpf   `float ldexpf(float x, int exp);`
ldexpl   `long double ldexpl(long double x, int exp);`

Returns $x \times 2^{exp}$. A range error may occur.   *23.3*

ldiv	*Long Integer Division*	`<stdlib.h>`

`ldiv_t ldiv(long int numer, long int denom);`

Returns   An `ldiv_t` structure containing members named `quot` (the quotient when `numer` is divided by `denom`) and `rem` (the remainder). The behavior is undefined if either part of the result can't be represented.   *26.2*

lgamma	*Logarithm of Gamma Function (C99)*	`<math.h>`

`double lgamma(double x);`
lgammaf   `float lgammaf(float x);`
lgammal   `long double lgammal(long double x);`

Returns $\ln(|\Gamma(x)|)$, where Γ is the gamma function. A range error occurs if `x` is too large and may occur if `x` is a negative integer or zero.   *23.4*

llabs	*Long Long Integer Absolute Value (C99)*	`<stdlib.h>`

`long long int llabs(long long int j);`

Returns	Absolute value of j. The behavior is undefined if the absolute value of j can't be represented. *26.2*

---

lldiv   *Long Long Integer Division (C99)*   `<stdlib.h>`

```
lldiv_t lldiv(long long int numer,
              long long int denom);
```

Returns   An lldiv_t structure containing members named quot (the quotient when numer is divided by denom) and rem (the remainder). The behavior is undefined if either part of the result can't be represented. *26.2*

---

llrint   *Round to Long Long Integer Using Current Direction (C99)*   `<math.h>`

```
          long long int llrint(double x);
llrintf   long long int llrintf(float x);
llrintl   long long int llrintl(long double x);
```

Returns   x rounded to the nearest integer using the current rounding direction. If the rounded value is outside the range of the long long int type, the result is unspecified and a domain or range error may occur. *23.4*

---

llround   *Round to Nearest Long Long Integer (C99)*   `<math.h>`

```
           long long int llround(double x);
llroundf   long long int llroundf(float x);
llroundl   long long int llroundl(long double x);
```

Returns   x rounded to the nearest integer, with halfway cases rounded away from zero. If the rounded value is outside the range of the long long int type, the result is unspecified and a domain or range error may occur. *23.4*

---

localeconv   *Get Locale Conventions*   `<locale.h>`

```
struct lconv *localeconv(void);
```

Returns   A pointer to a structure containing information about the current locale. *25.1*

---

localtime   *Convert Calendar Time to Broken-Down Local Time*   `<time.h>`

```
struct tm *localtime(const time_t *timer);
```

Returns   A pointer to a structure containing a broken-down local time equivalent to the calendar time pointed to by timer. Returns a null pointer if the calendar time can't be converted to local time. *26.3*

---

log   *Natural Logarithm*   `<math.h>`

```
       double log(double x);
logf   float logf(float x);
logl   long double logl(long double x);
```

Returns   Logarithm of x to the base *e*. A domain error occurs if x is negative. A range error may occur if x is zero. *23.3*

log10	*Common Logarithm*	`<math.h>`

```
        double log10(double x);
log10f  float log10f(float x);
log10l  long double log10l(long double x);
```

Returns   Logarithm of x to the base 10. A domain error occurs if x is negative. A range error may occur if x is zero.   *23.3*

log1p	*Natural Logarithm of 1 Plus Argument (C99)*	`<math.h>`

```
        double log1p(double x);
log1pf  float log1pf(float x);
log1pl  long double log1pl(long double x);
```

Returns   Logarithm of 1 + x to the base *e*. A domain error occurs if x is less than –1. A range error may occur if x is equal to –1.   *23.4*

log2	*Base-2 Logarithm (C99)*	`<math.h>`

```
        double log2(double x);
log2f   float log2f(float x);
log2l   long double log2l(long double x);
```

Returns   Logarithm of x to the base 2. A domain error occurs if x is negative. A range error may occur if x is zero.   *23.4*

logb	*Radix-Independent Exponent (C99)*	`<math.h>`

```
        double logb(double x);
logbf   float logbf(float x);
logbl   long double logbl(long double x);
```

Returns $\log_r(|x|)$, where *r* is the radix of floating-point arithmetic (defined by the macro `FLT_RADIX`, which typically has the value 2). A domain error or range error may occur if x is zero.   *23.4*

longjmp	*Nonlocal Jump*	`<setjmp.h>`

```
        void longjmp(jmp_buf env, int val);
```

Restores the environment stored in env and returns from the call of setjmp that originally saved env. If val is nonzero, it will be setjmp's return value; if val is 0, setjmp returns 1.   *24.4*

lrint	*Round to Long Integer Using Current Direction (C99)*	`<math.h>`

```
        long int lrint(double x);
lrintf  long int lrintf(float x);
lrintl  long int lrintl(long double x);
```

Returns   x rounded to the nearest integer using the current rounding direction. If the rounded value is outside the range of the `long int` type, the result is unspecified and a domain or range error may occur.   *23.4*

lround	*Round to Nearest Long Integer (C99)*	`<math.h>`

```
         long int lround(double x);
lroundf  long int lroundf(float x);
lroundl  long int lroundl(long double x);
```

Returns   x rounded to the nearest integer, with halfway cases rounded away from zero. If the rounded value is outside the range of the `long int` type, the result is unspecified and a domain or range error may occur.   **23.4**

malloc	*Allocate Memory Block*	`<stdlib.h>`

```
void *malloc(size_t size);
```

Allocates a block of memory with `size` bytes. The block is not cleared.

Returns   A pointer to the beginning of the block. Returns a null pointer if a block of the requested size can't be allocated.   **17.2**

mblen	*Length of Multibyte Character*	`<stdlib.h>`

```
int mblen(const char *s, size_t n);
```

Returns   If s is a null pointer, returns a nonzero or zero value, depending on whether or not multibyte characters have state-dependent encodings. If s points to a null character, returns zero. Otherwise, returns the number of bytes in the multibyte character pointed to by s; returns –1 if the next n or fewer bytes don't form a valid multibyte character.   **25.2**

mbrlen	*Length of Multibyte Character – Restartable (C99)*	`<wchar.h>`

```
size_t mbrlen(const char * restrict s, size_t n,
              mbstate_t * restrict ps);
```

Determines the number of bytes in the array pointed to by s that are required to complete a multibyte character. ps should point to an object of type `mbstate_t` that contains the current conversion state. A call of `mbrlen` is equivalent to

```
mbrtowc(NULL, s, n, ps)
```

except that if ps is a null pointer, the address of an internal object is used instead.

Returns   See `mbrtowc`.   **25.5**

mbrtowc	*Convert Multibyte Character to Wide Character – Restartable (C99)*	`<wchar.h>`

```
size_t mbrtowc(wchar_t * restrict pwc,
               const char * restrict s, size_t n,
               mbstate_t * restrict ps);
```

If s is a null pointer, a call of `mbrtowc` is equivalent to

```
mbrtowc(NULL, "", 1, ps)
```

Otherwise, `mbrtowc` examines up to n bytes in the array pointed to by s to see if they complete a valid multibyte character. If so, the multibyte character is converted into a wide character. If `pwc` isn't a null pointer, the wide character is stored in the object pointed to by `pwc`. The value of `ps` should be a pointer to an object of type `mbstate_t` that contains the current conversion state. If `ps` is a null pointer, `mbrtowc` uses an internal object to store the conversion state. If the result of the conversion is the null wide character, the `mbstate_t` object used during the call is left in the initial conversion state.

Returns   0 if the conversion produces a null wide character. Returns a number between 1 and n if the conversion produces a wide character other than null, where the value returned is the number of bytes used to complete the multibyte character. Returns `(size_t)(-2)` if the n bytes pointed to by s weren't enough to complete a multibyte character. Returns `(size_t)(-1)` and stores `EILSEQ` in `errno` if an encoding error occurs.   *25.5*

`mbsinit`   *Test for Initial Conversion State (C99)*   `<wchar.h>`

```
int mbsinit(const mbstate_t *ps);
```

Returns   A nonzero value if `ps` is a null pointer or it points to an `mbstate_t` object that describes an initial conversion state; otherwise, returns zero.   *25.5*

`mbsrtowcs`   *Convert Multibyte String to Wide String – Restartable (C99)*   `<wchar.h>`

```
size_t mbsrtowcs(wchar_t * restrict dst,
                 const char ** restrict src,
                 size_t len, mbstate_t * restrict ps);
```

Converts a sequence of multibyte characters from the array indirectly pointed to by `src` into a sequence of corresponding wide characters. `ps` should point to an object of type `mbstate_t` that contains the current conversion state. If the argument corresponding to `ps` is a null pointer, `mbsrtowcs` uses an internal object to store the conversion state. If `dst` isn't a null pointer, the converted characters are stored in the array that it points to. Conversion continues up to and including a terminating null character, which is also stored. Conversion stops earlier if a sequence of bytes is encountered that doesn't form a valid multibyte character or—if `dst` isn't a null pointer—when `len` wide characters have been stored in the array. If `dst` isn't a null pointer, the object pointed to by `src` is assigned either a null pointer (if a terminating null character was reached) or the address just past the last multibyte character converted (if any). If the conversion ends at a null character and if `dst` isn't a null pointer, the resulting state is the initial conversion state.

Returns   Number of multibyte characters successfully converted, not including any terminating null character. Returns `(size_t)(-1)` and stores `EILSEQ` in `errno` if an invalid multibyte character is encountered.   *25.5*

`mbstowcs`   *Convert Multibyte String to Wide String*   `<stdlib.h>`

```
size_t mbstowcs(wchar_t * restrict pwcs,
                const char * restrict s, size_t n);
```

Converts the sequence of multibyte characters pointed to by s into a sequence of wide characters, storing at most n wide characters in the array pointed to by pwcs. Conversion ends if a null character is encountered; it is converted into a null wide character.

Returns   Number of array elements modified, not including the null wide character, if any. Returns (size_t) (-1) if an invalid multibyte character is encountered.   *25.2*

mbtowc   *Convert Multibyte Character to Wide Character*   <stdlib.h>

```
int mbtowc(wchar_t * restrict pwc,
           const char * restrict s, size_t n);
```

If s isn't a null pointer, converts the multibyte character pointed to by s into a wide character; at most n bytes will be examined. If the multibyte character is valid and pwc isn't a null pointer, stores the value of the wide character in the object pointed to by pwc.

Returns   If s is a null pointer, returns a nonzero or zero value, depending on whether or not multibyte characters have state-dependent encodings. If s points to a null character, returns zero. Otherwise, returns the number of bytes in the multibyte character pointed to by s; returns –1 if the next n or fewer bytes don't form a valid multibyte character.   *25.2*

memchr   *Search Memory Block for Character*   <string.h>

```
void *memchr(const void *s, int c, size_t n);
```

Returns   A pointer to the first occurrence of the character c among the first n characters of the object pointed to by s. Returns a null pointer if c isn't found.   *23.6*

memcmp   *Compare Memory Blocks*   <string.h>

```
int memcmp(const void *s1, const void *s2, size_t n);
```

Returns   A negative, zero, or positive integer, depending on whether the first n characters of the object pointed to by s1 are less than, equal to, or greater than the first n characters of the object pointed to by s2.   *23.6*

memcpy   *Copy Memory Block*   <string.h>

```
void *memcpy(void * restrict s1,
             const void * restrict s2, size_t n);
```

Copies n characters from the object pointed to by s2 into the object pointed to by s1. The behavior is undefined if the objects overlap.

Returns   s1 (a pointer to the destination).   *23.6*

memmove   *Copy Memory Block*   <string.h>

```
void *memmove(void *s1, const void *s2, size_t n);
```

Copies n characters from the object pointed to by s2 into the object pointed to by s1. Will work properly if the objects overlap.

Returns   s1 (a pointer to the destination).   *23.6*

| **memset** | *Initialize Memory Block* | `<string.h>` |

```
void *memset(void *s, int c, size_t n);
```

Stores c in each of the first n characters of the object pointed to by s.

Returns   s (a pointer to the object).   *23.6*

| **mktime** | *Convert Broken-Down Local Time to Calendar Time* | `<time.h>` |

```
time_t mktime(struct tm *timeptr);
```

Converts a broken-down local time (stored in the structure pointed to by `time-ptr`) into a calendar time. The members of the structure aren't required to be within their legal ranges; also, the values of `tm_wday` (day of the week) and `tm_yday` (day of the year) are ignored. `mktime` stores values in `tm_wday` and `tm_yday` after adjusting the other members to bring them into their proper ranges.

Returns   A calendar time corresponding to the structure pointed to by `timeptr`. Returns
`(time_t)(-1)` if the calendar time can't be represented.   *26.3*

| **modf** | *Split into Integer and Fractional Parts* | `<math.h>` |

```
double modf(double value, double *iptr);
```
modff   `float modff(float value, float *iptr);`
modfl   `long double modfl(long double value, long double *iptr);`

Splits `value` into integer and fractional parts; stores the integer part in the object pointed to by `iptr`.

Returns   Fractional part of `value`.   *23.3*

| **nan** | *Create NaN (C99)* | `<math.h>` |

```
double nan(const char *tagp);
```
nanf   `float nanf(const char *tagp);`
nanl   `long double nanl(const char *tagp);`

Returns   A "quiet" NaN whose binary pattern is determined by the string pointed to by
`tagp`. Returns zero if quiet NaNs aren't supported.   *23.4*

| **nearbyint** | *Round to Integral Value Using Current Direction (C99)* | `<math.h>` |

```
double nearbyint(double x);
```
nearbyintf   `float nearbyintf(float x);`
nearbyintl   `long double nearbyintl(long double x);`

Returns   x rounded to an integer (in floating-point format) using the current rounding direction. Doesn't raise the *inexact* floating-point exception.   *23.4*

| **nextafter** | *Next Number After (C99)* | `<math.h>` |

```
double nextafter(double x, double y);
```
nextafterf   `float nextafterf(float x, float y);`
nextafterl   `long double nextafterl(long double x, long double y);`

Returns	Next representable value after x in the direction of y. Returns the value just before x if y < x or the value just after x if x < y. Returns y if x equals y. A range error may occur if the magnitude of x is the largest representable finite value and the result is infinite or not representable.	*23.4*

---

nexttoward   *Next Number Toward (C99)*   `<math.h>`

```
                double nexttoward(double x, long double y);
nexttowardf     float nexttowardf(float x, long double y);
nexttowardl     long double nexttowardl(long double x, long double y);
```

Returns   Next representable value after x in the direction of y (see `nextafter`). Returns y converted to the function's type if x equals y.   *23.4*

---

perror   *Print Error Message*   `<stdio.h>`

```
void perror(const char *s);
```

Writes the following message to the `stderr` stream:

string : *error-message*

string is the string pointed to by s and *error-message* is an implementation-defined message that matches the one returned by the call `strerror(errno)`.   *24.2*

---

pow   *Power*   `<math.h>`

```
        double pow(double x, double y);
powf    float powf(float x, float y);
powl    long double powl(long double x, long double y);
```

Returns   x raised to the power y. A domain or range error may occur in certain cases, which vary between C89 and C99.   *23.3*

---

printf   *Formatted Write*   `<stdio.h>`

```
int printf(const char * restrict format, ...);
```

Writes output to the `stdout` stream. The string pointed to by `format` specifies how subsequent arguments will be displayed.

Returns   Number of characters written. Returns a negative value if an error occurs. *3.1, 22.3*

---

putc   *Write Character to File*   `<stdio.h>`

```
int putc(int c, FILE *stream);
```

Writes the character c to the stream pointed to by `stream`. *Note:* `putc` is normally implemented as a macro; it may evaluate `stream` more than once.

Returns   c (the character written). If a write error occurs, `putc` sets the stream's error indicator and returns EOF.   *22.4*

---

putchar   *Write Character*   `<stdio.h>`

```
int putchar(int c);
```

Writes the character c to the `stdout` stream. *Note:* `putchar` is normally implemented as a macro.

Returns	c (the character written). If a write error occurs, putchar sets the stream's error indicator and returns EOF.	*7.3, 22.4*

puts   *Write String*   `<stdio.h>`

```
int puts(const char *s);
```

Writes the string pointed to by s to the stdout stream, then writes a new-line character.

Returns	A nonnegative value if successful. Returns EOF if a write error occurs.	*13.3, 22.5*

putwc   *Write Wide Character to File (C99)*   `<wchar.h>`

```
wint_t putwc(wchar_t c, FILE *stream);
```

Wide-character version of putc.   *25.5*

putwchar   *Write Wide Character (C99)*   `<wchar.h>`

```
wint_t putwchar(wchar_t c);
```

Wide-character version of putchar.   *25.5*

qsort   *Sort Array*   `<stdlib.h>`

```
void qsort(void *base, size_t nmemb, size_t size,
           int (*compar)(const void *, const void *));
```

Sorts the array pointed to by base. The array has nmemb elements, each size bytes long. compar is a pointer to a comparison function. When passed pointers to two array elements, the comparison function must return a negative, zero, or positive integer, depending on whether the first array element is less than, equal to, or greater than the second.   *17.7, 26.2*

raise   *Raise Signal*   `<signal.h>`

```
int raise(int sig);
```

Raises the signal whose number is sig.

Returns	Zero if successful, nonzero otherwise.	*24.3*

rand   *Generate Pseudo-Random Number*   `<stdlib.h>`

```
int rand(void);
```

Returns	A pseudo-random integer between 0 and RAND_MAX (inclusive).	*26.2*

realloc   *Resize Memory Block*   `<stdlib.h>`

```
void *realloc(void *ptr, size_t size);
```

ptr is assumed to point to a block of memory previously obtained from calloc, malloc, or realloc. realloc allocates a block of size bytes, copying the contents of the old block if necessary.

Returns	A pointer to the beginning of the new memory block. Returns a null pointer if a block of the requested size can't be allocated.	*17.3*

`remainder`   *Remainder (C99)*   `<math.h>`

```
double remainder(double x, double y);
```
`remainderf` `float remainderf(float x, float y);`
`remainderl` `long double remainderl(long double x, long double y);`

Returns $x - ny$, where n is the integer nearest the exact value of x/y. (If x/y is halfway between two integers, n is even.) If $x - ny = 0$, the return value has the same sign as x. If y is zero, either a domain error occurs or zero is returned.   *23.4*

`remove`   *Remove File*   `<stdio.h>`

```
int remove(const char *filename);
```

Deletes the file whose name is pointed to by `filename`.

Returns   Zero if successful, nonzero otherwise.   *22.2*

`remquo`   *Remainder and Quotient (C99)*   `<math.h>`

```
double remquo(double x, double y, int *quo);
```
`remquof` `float remquof(float x, float y, int *quo);`
`remquol` `long double remquol(long double x, long double y,`
               `                    int *quo);`

Computes both the remainder and the quotient when x is divided by y. The object pointed to by `quo` is modified so that it contains n low-order bits of the integer quotient $|x/y|$, where n is implementation-defined but must be at least three. The value stored in this object will be negative if $x/y < 0$.

Returns   Same value as the corresponding `remainder` function. If y is zero, either a domain error occurs or zero is returned.   *23.4*

`rename`   *Rename File*   `<stdio.h>`

```
int rename(const char *old, const char *new);
```

Changes the name of a file. `old` and `new` point to strings containing the old name and new name, respectively.

Returns   Zero if the renaming is successful. Returns a nonzero value if the operation fails (perhaps because the old file is currently open).   *22.2*

`rewind`   *Rewind File*   `<stdio.h>`

```
void rewind(FILE *stream);
```

Sets the file position indicator for the stream pointed to by `stream` to the beginning of the file. Clears the error and end-of-file indicators for the stream.   *22.7*

`rint`   *Round to Integral Value Using Current Direction (C99)*   `<math.h>`

```
double rint(double x);
```
`rintf` `float rintf(float x);`
`rintl` `long double rintl(long double x);`

Returns   x rounded to an integer (in floating-point format) using the current rounding direction. May raise the *inexact* floating-point exception if the result has a different value than x. *23.4*

---

round | *Round to Nearest Integral Value (C99)* | `<math.h>`

```
double round(double x);
```
roundf `float roundf(float x);`
roundl `long double roundl(long double x);`

Returns x rounded to the nearest integer (in floating-point format). Halfway cases are rounded away from zero. *23.4*

---

scalbln | *Scale Floating-Point Number Using Long Integer (C99)* | `<math.h>`

```
double scalbln(double x, long int n);
```
scalblnf `float scalblnf(float x, long int n);`
scalblnl `long double scalblnl(long double x, long int n);`

Returns $x \times \text{FLT\_RADIX}^n$, computed in an efficient way. A range error may occur. *23.4*

---

scalbn | *Scale Floating-Point Number Using Integer (C99)* | `<math.h>`

```
double scalbn(double x, int n);
```
scalbnf `float scalbnf(float x, int n);`
scalbnl `long double scalbnl(long double x, int n);`

Returns $x \times \text{FLT\_RADIX}^n$, computed in an efficient way. A range error may occur. *23.4*

---

scanf | *Formatted Read* | `<stdio.h>`

```
int scanf(const char * restrict format, ...);
```

Reads input items from the `stdin` stream. The string pointed to by `format` specifies the format of the items to be read. The arguments that follow `format` point to objects in which the items are to be stored.

Returns Number of input items successfully read and stored. Returns `EOF` if an input failure occurs before any items can be read. *3.2, 22.3*

---

setbuf | *Set Buffer* | `<stdio.h>`

```
void setbuf(FILE * restrict stream,
            char * restrict buf);
```

If `buf` isn't a null pointer, a call of `setbuf` is equivalent to:

```
(void) setvbuf(stream, buf, _IOFBF, BUFSIZ);
```
Otherwise, it's equivalent to:

```
(void) setvbuf(stream, NULL, _IONBF, 0);
```
22.2

---

setjmp | *Prepare for Nonlocal Jump* | `<setjmp.h>`

```
int setjmp(jmp_buf env);
```
macro

Stores the current environment in `env` for use in a later call of `longjmp`.

Returns Zero when called directly. Returns a nonzero value when returning from a call of `longjmp`. *24.4*

---

setlocale   *Set Locale*   `<locale.h>`

```
char *setlocale(int category, const char *locale);
```

Sets a portion of the program's locale. `category` indicates which portion is affected. `locale` points to a string representing the new locale.

Returns   If `locale` is a null pointer, returns a pointer to the string associated with `category` for the current locale. Otherwise, returns a pointer to the string associated with `category` for the new locale. Returns a null pointer if the operation fails.

25.1

---

setvbuf   *Set Buffer*   `<stdio.h>`

```
int setvbuf(FILE * restrict stream,
            char * restrict buf,
            int mode, size_t size);
```

Changes the buffering of the stream pointed to by `stream`. The value of `mode` can be either `_IOFBF` (full buffering), `_IOLBF` (line buffering), or `_IONBF` (no buffering). If `buf` is a null pointer, a buffer is automatically allocated if needed. Otherwise, `buf` points to a memory block that can be used as the buffer; `size` is the number of bytes in the block. *Note:* `setvbuf` must be called after the stream is opened but before any other operations are performed on it.

Returns   Zero if the operation is successful. Returns a nonzero value if `mode` is invalid or the request can't be honored.   *22.2*

---

signal   *Install Signal Handler*   `<signal.h>`

```
void (*signal(int sig, void (*func)(int)))(int);
```

Installs the function pointed to by `func` as the handler for the signal whose number is `sig`. Passing `SIG_DFL` as the second argument causes default handling for the signal; passing `SIG_IGN` causes the signal to be ignored.

Returns   A pointer to the previous handler for this signal; returns `SIG_ERR` and stores a positive value in `errno` if the handler can't be installed.   *24.3*

---

signbit   *Sign Bit (C99)*   `<math.h>`

```
int signbit (real-floating x);
```
macro

Returns   A nonzero value if the sign of `x` is negative and zero otherwise. The value of `x` may be any number, including infinity and NaN.   *23.4*

---

sin   *Sine*   `<math.h>`

```
double sin(double x);
```
sinf   `float sinf(float x);`
sinl   `long double sinl(long double x);`

Returns   Sine of `x` (measured in radians).   *23.3*

---

sinh   *Hyperbolic Sine*   `<math.h>`

```
double sinh(double x);
```

sinhf	`float sinhf(float x);`
sinhl	`long double sinhl(long double x);`
Returns	Hyperbolic sine of x. A range error occurs if the magnitude of x is too large. *23.3*

---

snprintf   *Bounded Formatted String Write (C99)*   `<stdio.h>`

```
int snprintf(char * restrict s, size_t n,
             const char * restrict format, ...);
```

Equivalent to `fprintf`, but stores characters in the array pointed to by s instead of writing them to a stream. No more than n – 1 characters will be written to the array. The string pointed to by `format` specifies how subsequent arguments will be displayed. Stores a null character in the array at the end of output.

Returns   Number of characters that would have been stored in the array (not including the null character) had there been no length restriction. Returns a negative value if an encoding error occurs.   *22.8*

---

sprintf   *Formatted String Write*   `<stdio.h>`

```
int sprintf(char * restrict s,
            const char * restrict format, ...);
```

Equivalent to `fprintf`, but stores characters in the array pointed to by s instead of writing them to a stream. The string pointed to by `format` specifies how subsequent arguments will be displayed. Stores a null character in the array at the end of output.

Returns   Number of characters stored in the array, not including the null character. In C99, returns a negative value if an encoding error occurs.   *22.8*

---

sqrt   *Square Root*   `<math.h>`

```
double sqrt(double x);
```
sqrtf	`float sqrtf(float x);`
sqrtl	`long double sqrtl(long double x);`
Returns	Nonnegative square root of x. A domain error occurs if x is negative. *23.3*

---

srand   *Seed Pseudo-Random Number Generator*   `<stdlib.h>`

```
void srand(unsigned int seed);
```

Uses seed to initialize the sequence of pseudo-random numbers produced by calling rand.   *26.2*

---

sscanf   *Formatted String Read*   `<stdio.h>`

```
int sscanf(const char * restrict s,
           const char * restrict format, ...);
```

Equivalent to `fscanf`, but reads characters from the string pointed to by s instead of reading them from a stream. The string pointed to by `format` specifies the format of the items to be read. The arguments that follow `format` point to objects in which the items are to be stored.

Returns	Number of input items successfully read and stored. Returns `EOF` if an input failure occurs before any items could be read.	*22.8*

strcat   *String Concatenation*   `<string.h>`

```
char *strcat(char * restrict s1,
             const char * restrict s2);
```

Appends characters from the string pointed to by `s2` to the string pointed to by `s1`.

Returns   `s1` (a pointer to the concatenated string).   *13.5, 23.6*

strchr   *Search String for Character*   `<string.h>`

```
char *strchr(const char *s, int c);
```

Returns   A pointer to the first occurrence of the character `c` in the string pointed to by `s`. Returns a null pointer if `c` isn't found.   *23.6*

strcmp   *String Comparison*   `<string.h>`

```
int strcmp(const char *s1, const char *s2);
```

Returns   A negative, zero, or positive integer, depending on whether the string pointed to by `s1` is less than, equal to, or greater than the string pointed to by `s2`.   *13.5, 23.6*

strcoll   *String Comparison Using Locale-Specific Collating Sequence*   `<string.h>`

```
int strcoll(const char *s1, const char *s2);
```

Returns   A negative, zero, or positive integer, depending on whether the string pointed to by `s1` is less than, equal to, or greater than the string pointed to by `s2`. The comparison is performed according to the rules of the current locale's `LC_COLLATE` category.   *23.6*

strcpy   *String Copy*   `<string.h>`

```
char *strcpy(char * restrict s1,
             const char * restrict s2);
```

Copies the string pointed to by `s2` into the array pointed to by `s1`.

Returns   `s1` (a pointer to the destination).   *13.5, 23.6*

strcspn   *Search String for Initial Span of Characters Not in Set*   `<string.h>`

```
size_t strcspn(const char *s1, const char *s2);
```

Returns   Length of the longest initial segment of the string pointed to by `s1` that doesn't contain any character in the string pointed to by `s2`.   *23.6*

strerror   *Convert Error Number to String*   `<string.h>`

```
char *strerror(int errnum);
```

Returns   A pointer to a string containing an error message corresponding to the value of `errnum`.   *24.2*

strftime	*Write Formatted Date and Time to String*	`<time.h>`

```
size_t strftime(char * restrict s, size_t maxsize,
                const char * restrict format,
                const struct tm * restrict timeptr);
```

Stores characters in the array pointed to by s under control of the string pointed to by `format`. The format string may contain ordinary characters, which are copied unchanged, and conversion specifiers, which are replaced by values from the structure pointed to by `timeptr`. The `maxsize` parameter limits the number of characters (including the null character) that can be stored.

Returns   Number of characters stored (not including the terminating null character). Returns zero if the number of characters to be stored (including the null character) exceeds `maxsize`.   *26.3*

strlen	*String Length*	`<string.h>`

```
size_t strlen(const char *s);
```

Returns   Length of the string pointed to by s, not including the null character.   *13.5, 23.6*

strncat	*Bounded String Concatenation*	`<string.h>`

```
char *strncat(char * restrict s1,
              const char * restrict s2, size_t n);
```

Appends characters from the array pointed to by s2 to the string pointed to by s1. Copying stops when a null character is encountered or n characters have been copied.

Returns   s1 (a pointer to the concatenated string).   *13.5, 23.6*

strncmp	*Bounded String Comparison*	`<string.h>`

```
int strncmp(const char *s1, const char *s2, size_t n);
```

Returns   A negative, zero, or positive integer, depending on whether the first n characters of the array pointed to by s1 are less than, equal to, or greater than the first n characters of the array pointed to by s2. Comparison stops if a null character is encountered in either array.   *23.6*

strncpy	*Bounded String Copy*	`<string.h>`

```
char *strncpy(char * restrict s1,
              const char * restrict s2, size_t n);
```

Copies the first n characters of the array pointed to by s2 into the array pointed to by s1. If it encounters a null character in the array pointed to by s2, strncpy adds null characters to the array pointed to by s1 until a total of n characters have been written.

Returns   s1 (a pointer to the destination).   *13.5, 23.6*

`strpbrk`	*Search String for One of a Set of Characters*	`<string.h>`

`char *strpbrk(const char *s1, const char *s2);`

Returns A pointer to the leftmost character in the string pointed to by `s1` that matches any character in the string pointed to by `s2`. Returns a null pointer if no match is found.

23.6

`strrchr`	*Search String in Reverse for Character*	`<string.h>`

`char *strrchr(const char *s, int c);`

Returns A pointer to the last occurrence of the character `c` in the string pointed to by `s`. Returns a null pointer if `c` isn't found.

23.6

`strspn`	*Search String for Initial Span of Characters in Set*	`<string.h>`

`size_t strspn(const char *s1, const char *s2);`

Returns Length of the longest initial segment in the string pointed to by `s1` that consists entirely of characters in the string pointed to by `s2`.

23.6

`strstr`	*Search String for Substring*	`<string.h>`

`char *strstr(const char *s1, const char *s2);`

Returns A pointer to the first occurrence in the string pointed to by `s1` of the sequence of characters in the string pointed to by `s2`. Returns a null pointer if no match is found.

23.6

`strtod`	*Convert String to Double*	`<stdlib.h>`

```
double strtod(const char * restrict nptr,
              char ** restrict endptr);
```

Skips white-space characters in the string pointed to by `nptr`, then converts subsequent characters into a `double` value. If `endptr` isn't a null pointer, `strtod` modifies the object pointed to by `endptr` so that it points to the first leftover character. If no `double` value is found, or if it has the wrong form, `strtod` stores `nptr` in the object pointed to by `endptr`. If the number is too large or small to represent, it stores ERANGE in `errno`. *C99 changes:* The string pointed to by `nptr` may contain a hexadecimal floating-point number, infinity, or NaN. Whether ERANGE is stored in `errno` when the number is too small to represent is implementation-defined.

Returns The converted number. Returns zero if no conversion could be performed. If the number is too large to represent, returns plus or minus HUGE_VAL, depending on the number's sign. Returns zero if the number is too small to represent. *C99 change:* If the number is too small to represent, `strtod` returns a value whose magnitude is no greater than the smallest normalized positive `double`.

26.2

`strtof`	*Convert String to Float (C99)*	`<stdlib.h>`

```
float strtof(const char * restrict nptr,
             char ** restrict endptr);
```

strtof is identical to strtod, except that it converts a string to a float value.

Returns The converted number. Returns zero if no conversion could be performed. If the number is too large to represent, returns plus or minus HUGE_VALF, depending on the number's sign. If the number is too small to represent, returns a value whose magnitude is no greater than the smallest normalized positive float. *26.2*

---

strtoimax *Convert String to Greatest-Width Integer (C99)* <inttypes.h>

```
intmax_t strtoimax(const char * restrict nptr,
                   char ** restrict endptr, int base);
```

strtoimax is identical to strtol, except that it converts a string to a value of type intmax_t (the widest signed integer type).

Returns The converted number. Returns zero if no conversion could be performed. If the number can't be represented, returns INTMAX_MAX or INTMAX_MIN, depending on the number's sign. *27.2*

---

strtok *Search String for Token* <string.h>

```
char *strtok(char * restrict s1,
             const char * restrict s2);
```

Searches the string pointed to by s1 for a "token" consisting of characters not in the string pointed to by s2. If a token exists, the character following it is changed to a null character. If s1 is a null pointer, a search begun by the most recent call of strtok is continued; the search begins immediately after the null character at the end of the previous token.

Returns A pointer to the first character of the token. Returns a null pointer if no token could be found. *23.6*

---

strtol *Convert String to Long Integer* <stdlib.h>

```
long int strtol(const char * restrict nptr,
                char ** restrict endptr, int base);
```

Skips white-space characters in the string pointed to by nptr, then converts subsequent characters into a long int value. If base is between 2 and 36, it is used as the radix of the number. If base is zero, the number is assumed to be decimal unless it begins with 0 (octal) or with 0x or 0X (hexadecimal). If endptr isn't a null pointer, strtol modifies the object pointed to by endptr so that it points to the first leftover character. If no long int value is found, or if it has the wrong form, strtol stores nptr in the object pointed to by endptr. If the number can't be represented, it stores ERANGE in errno.

Returns The converted number. Returns zero if no conversion could be performed. If the number can't be represented, returns LONG_MAX or LONG_MIN, depending on the number's sign. *26.2*

---

strtold *Convert String to Long Double (C99)* <stdlib.h>

```
long double strtold(const char * restrict nptr,
                    char ** restrict endptr);
```

strtold is identical to `strtod`, except that it converts a string to a `long double` value.

Returns   The converted number. Returns zero if no conversion could be performed. If the number is too large to represent, returns plus or minus `HUGE_VALL`, depending on the number's sign. If the number is too small to represent, returns a value whose magnitude is no greater than the smallest normalized positive `long double`.   *26.2*

---

strtoll   *Convert String to Long Long Integer (C99)*   `<stdlib.h>`

```
long long int strtoll(const char * restrict nptr,
                      char ** restrict endptr,
                      int base);
```

strtoll is identical to `strtol`, except that it converts a string to a `long long int` value.

Returns   The converted number. Returns zero if no conversion could be performed. If the number can't be represented, returns `LLONG_MAX` or `LLONG_MIN`, depending on the number's sign.   *26.2*

---

strtoul   *Convert String to Unsigned Long Integer*   `<stdlib.h>`

```
unsigned long int strtoul(const char * restrict nptr,
                          char ** restrict endptr,
                          int base);
```

strtoul is identical to `strtol`, except that it converts a string to an unsigned `long int` value.

Returns   The converted number. Returns zero if no conversion could be performed. If the number can't be represented, returns `ULONG_MAX`.   *26.2*

---

strtoull   *Convert String to Unsigned Long Long Integer (C99)*   `<stdlib.h>`

```
unsigned long long int strtoull(
    const char * restrict nptr,
    char ** restrict endptr, int base);
```

strtoull is identical to `strtol`, except that it converts a string to an unsigned `long long int` value.

Returns   The converted number. Returns zero if no conversion could be performed. If the number can't be represented, returns `ULLONG_MAX`.   *26.2*

---

strtoumax   *Convert String to Unsigned Greatest-Width Integer (C99)*   `<inttypes.h>`

```
uintmax_t strtoumax(const char * restrict nptr,
                    char ** restrict endptr,
                    int base);
```

strtoumax is identical to `strtol`, except that it converts a string to a value of type `uintmax_t` (the widest unsigned integer type).

Returns   The converted number. Returns zero if no conversion could be performed. If the number can't be represented, returns `UINTMAX_MAX`.   *27.2*

---

strxfrm   *Transform String*   `<string.h>`

```
size_t strxfrm(char * restrict s1,
               const char * restrict s2, size_t n);
```

Transforms the string pointed to by s2, placing the first n characters of the result—including the null character—in the array pointed to by s1. Calling `strcmp` with two transformed strings should produce the same outcome (negative, zero, or positive) as calling `strcoll` with the original strings. If n is zero, s1 is allowed to be a null pointer.

Returns   Length of the transformed string. If this value is n or more, the contents of the array pointed to by s1 are indeterminate.   *23.6*

---

swprintf   *Wide-Character Formatted String Write (C99)*   `<wchar.h>`

```
int swprintf(wchar_t * restrict s, size_t n,
             const wchar_t * restrict format, ...);
```

Equivalent to `fwprintf`, but stores wide characters in the array pointed to by s instead of writing them to a stream. The string pointed to by `format` specifies how subsequent arguments will be displayed. No more than n wide characters will be written to the array, including a terminating null wide character.

Returns   Number of wide characters stored in the array, not including the null wide character. Returns a negative value if an encoding error occurs or the number of wide characters to be written is n or more.   *25.5*

---

swscanf   *Wide-Character Formatted String Read (C99)*   `<wchar.h>`

```
int swscanf(const wchar_t * restrict s,
            const wchar_t * restrict format, ...);
```

Wide-character version of `sscanf`.   *25.5*

---

system   *Perform Operating-System Command*   `<stdlib.h>`

```
int system(const char *string);
```

Passes the string pointed to by `string` to the operating system's command processor (shell) to be executed. Program termination may occur as a result of executing the command.

Returns   If `string` is a null pointer, returns a nonzero value if a command processor is available. If `string` isn't a null pointer, `system` returns an implementation-defined value (if it returns at all).   *26.2*

---

tan   *Tangent*   `<math.h>`

```
double tan(double x);
```
tanf   `float tanf(float x);`
tanl   `long double tanl(long double x);`

Returns   Tangent of x (measured in radians).   *23.3*

tanh	*Hyperbolic Tangent*	`<math.h>`

```
       double tanh(double x);
tanhf  float tanhf(float x);
tanhl  long double tanhl(long double x);
```

Returns Hyperbolic tangent of x.   *23.3*

tgamma	*Gamma Function (C99)*	`<math.h>`

```
        double tgamma(double x);
tgammaf float tgammaf(float x);
tgammal long double tgammal(long double x);
```

Returns $\Gamma(x)$, where Γ is the gamma function. A domain error or range error may occur if x is a negative integer or zero. A range error may occur if the magnitude of x is too large or too small.   *23.4*

time	*Current Time*	`<time.h>`

```
time_t time(time_t *timer);
```

Returns Current calendar time. Returns `(time_t)(-1)` if the calendar time isn't available. If `timer` isn't a null pointer, also stores the return value in the object pointed to by `timer`.   *26.3*

tmpfile	*Create Temporary File*	`<stdio.h>`

```
FILE *tmpfile(void);
```

Creates a temporary file that will automatically be removed when it's closed or the program ends. Opens the file in `"wb+"` mode.

Returns A file pointer to be used when performing subsequent operations on the file. Returns a null pointer if a temporary file can't be created.   *22.2*

tmpnam	*Generate Temporary File Name*	`<stdio.h>`

```
char *tmpnam(char *s);
```

Generates a name for a temporary file. If s is a null pointer, `tmpnam` stores the file name in a static object. Otherwise, it copies the file name into the character array pointed to by s. (The array must be long enough to store `L_tmpnam` characters.)

Returns A pointer to the file name. Returns a null pointer if a file name can't be generated.   *22.2*

tolower	*Convert to Lower Case*	`<ctype.h>`

```
int tolower(int c);
```

Returns If c is an upper-case letter, returns the corresponding lower-case letter. If c isn't an upper-case letter, returns c unchanged.   *23.5*

toupper	*Convert to Upper Case*	`<ctype.h>`

```
int toupper(int c);
```

Returns	If c is a lower-case letter, returns the corresponding upper-case letter. If c isn't a lower-case letter, returns c unchanged.	*23.5*

---

towctrans   *Transliterate Wide Character (C99)*   `<wctype.h>`

```
wint_t towctrans(wint_t wc, wctrans_t desc);
```

Returns	Mapped value of wc using the mapping described by desc. (desc must be a value returned by a call of wctrans; the current setting of the LC_CTYPE category must be the same during both calls.)	*25.6*

---

towlower   *Convert Wide Character to Lower Case (C99)*   `<wctype.h>`

```
wint_t towlower(wint_t wc);
```

Returns	If iswupper(wc) is true, returns a corresponding wide character for which iswlower is true in the current locale, if such a character exists. Otherwise, returns wc unchanged.	*25.6*

---

towupper   *Convert Wide Character to Upper Case (C99)*   `<wctype.h>`

```
wint_t towupper(wint_t wc);
```

Returns	If iswlower(wc) is true, returns a corresponding wide character for which iswupper is true in the current locale, if such a character exists. Otherwise, returns wc unchanged.	*25.6*

---

trunc   *Truncate to Nearest Integral Value (C99)*   `<math.h>`

```
         double trunc(double x);
truncf   float truncf(float x);
truncl   long double truncl(long double x);
```

Returns	x rounded to the integer (in floating-point format) nearest to it but no larger in magnitude.	*23.4*

---

ungetc   *Unread Character*   `<stdio.h>`

```
int ungetc(int c, FILE *stream);
```

Pushes the character c back onto the stream pointed to by stream and clears the stream's end-of-file indicator. The number of characters that can be pushed back by consecutive calls of ungetc varies; only the first call is guaranteed to succeed. Calling a file positioning function (fseek, fsetpos, or rewind) causes the pushed-back character(s) to be lost.

Returns	c (the pushed-back character). Returns EOF if an attempt is made to push back EOF or to push back too many characters without a read or file positioning operation.	*22.4*

---

ungetwc   *Unread Wide Character (C99)*   `<wchar.h>`

```
wint_t ungetwc(wint_t c, FILE *stream);
```

Wide-character version of ungetc.		*25.5*

---

va_arg   *Fetch Argument from Variable Argument List*   `<stdarg.h>`

    type `va_arg(va_list ap,` *type* `);`   *macro*

Fetches an argument in the variable argument list associated with ap, then modifies ap so that the next use of va_arg fetches the following argument. ap must have been initialized by va_start (or va_copy in C99) prior to the first use of va_arg.

Returns   Value of the argument, assuming that its type (after the default argument promotions have been applied) is compatible with *type*.   *26.1*

---

va_copy   *Copy Variable Argument List (C99)*   `<stdarg.h>`

    `void va_copy(va_list dest, va_list src);`   *macro*

Copies src into dest. The value of dest will be the same as if va_start had been applied to dest followed by the same sequence of va_arg applications that was used to reach the present state of src.   *26.1*

---

va_end   *End Processing of Variable Argument List*   `<stdarg.h>`

    `void va_end(va_list ap);`   *macro*

Ends the processing of the variable argument list associated with ap.   *26.1*

---

va_start   *Start Processing of Variable Argument List*   `<stdarg.h>`

    `void va_start(va_list ap,` *parmN* `);`   *macro*

Must be invoked before accessing a variable argument list. Initializes ap for later use by va_arg and va_end. *parmN* is the name of the last ordinary parameter (the one followed by `, ...`).   *26.1*

---

vfprintf   *Formatted File Write Using Variable Argument List*   `<stdio.h>`

```
int vfprintf(FILE * restrict stream,
             const char * restrict format,
             va_list arg);
```

Equivalent to fprintf with the variable argument list replaced by arg.

Returns   Number of characters written. Returns a negative value if an error occurs.   *26.1*

---

vfscanf   *Formatted File Read Using Variable Argument List (C99)*   `<stdio.h>`

```
int vfscanf(FILE * restrict stream,
            const char * restrict format,
            va_list arg);
```

Equivalent to fscanf with the variable argument list replaced by arg.

Returns   Number of input items successfully read and stored. Returns EOF if an input failure occurs before any items can be read.   *26.1*

---

vfwprintf   *Wide-Character Formatted File Write Using Variable Argument List (C99)*   `<wchar.h>`

```
int vfwprintf(FILE * restrict stream,
              const wchar_t * restrict format,
              va_list arg);
```

Wide-character version of `vfprintf`.   *25.5*

---

vfwscanf   *Wide-Character Formatted File Read Using Variable*   `<wchar.h>`
               Argument List (C99)

```
int vfwscanf(FILE * restrict stream,
             const wchar_t * restrict format,
             va_list arg);
```

Wide-character version of `vfscanf`.   *25.5*

---

vprintf   *Formatted Write Using Variable Argument List*   `<stdio.h>`

```
int vprintf(const char * restrict format, va_list arg);
```

Equivalent to `printf` with the variable argument list replaced by `arg`.

Returns   Number of characters written. Returns a negative value if an error occurs.   *26.1*

---

vscanf   *Formatted Read Using Variable Argument List (C99)*   `<stdio.h>`

```
int vscanf(const char * restrict format, va_list arg);
```

Equivalent to `scanf` with the variable argument list replaced by `arg`.

Returns   Number of input items successfully read and stored. Returns `EOF` if an input fail-
            ure occurs before any items can be read.   *26.1*

---

vsnprintf   *Bounded Formatted String Write Using Variable Argument*   `<stdio.h>`
                List (C99)

```
int vsnprintf(char * restrict s, size_t n,
              const char * restrict format,
              va_list arg);
```

Equivalent to `snprintf` with the variable argument list replaced by `arg`.

Returns   Number of characters that would have been stored in the array pointed to by `s` (not
            including the null character) had there been no length restriction. Returns a nega-
            tive value if an encoding error occurs.   *26.1*

---

vsprintf   *Formatted String Write Using Variable Argument List*   `<stdio.h>`

```
int vsprintf(char * restrict s,
             const char * restrict format,
             va_list arg);
```

Equivalent to `sprintf` with the variable argument list replaced by `arg`.

Returns   Number of characters stored in the array pointed to by `s`, not including the null
            character. In C99, returns a negative value if an encoding error occurs.   *26.1*

---

vsscanf   *Formatted String Read Using Variable Argument List (C99)*   `<stdio.h>`

```
int vsscanf(const char * restrict s,
            const char * restrict format,
            va_list arg);
```

Equivalent to `sscanf` with the variable argument list replaced by `arg`.

Returns   Number of input items successfully read and stored. Returns `EOF` if an input failure occurs before any items can be read.   *26.1*

---

vswprintf   *Wide-Character Formatted String Write Using Variable*   `<wchar.h>`
Argument List (C99)

```
int vswprintf(wchar_t * restrict s, size_t n,
              const wchar_t * restrict format,
              va_list arg);
```

Equivalent to `swprintf` with the variable argument list replaced by `arg`.

Returns   Number of wide characters stored in the array pointed to by s, not including the
null wide character. Returns a negative value if an encoding error occurs or the
number of wide characters to be written is n or more.   *25.5*

---

vswscanf   *Wide-Character Formatted String Read Using Variable*   `<wchar.h>`
Argument List (C99)

```
int vswscanf(const wchar_t * restrict s,
             const wchar_t * restrict format,
             va_list arg);
```

Wide-character version of `vsscanf`.   *25.5*

---

vwprintf   *Wide-Character Formatted Write Using Variable Argument*   `<wchar.h>`
List (C99)

```
int vwprintf(const wchar_t * restrict format,
             va_list arg);
```

Wide-character version of `vprintf`.   *25.5*

---

vwscanf   *Wide-Character Formatted Read Using Variable Argument*   `<wchar.h>`
List (C99)

```
int vwscanf(const wchar_t * restrict format,
            va_list arg);
```

Wide-character version of `vscanf`.   *25.5*

---

wcrtomb   *Convert Wide Character to Multibyte Character – Restartable*   `<wchar.h>`
(C99)

```
size_t wcrtomb(char * restrict s, wchar_t wc,
               mbstate_t * restrict ps);
```

If s is a null pointer, a call of `wcrtomb` is equivalent to

```
wcrtomb(buf, L'\0', ps)
```

where `buf` is an internal buffer. Otherwise, `wcrtomb` converts `wc` from a wide character into a multibyte character (possibly including shift sequences), which it stores in the array pointed to by `s`. The value of `ps` should be a pointer to an object of type `mbstate_t` that contains the current conversion state. If `ps` is a null pointer, `wcrtomb` uses an internal object to store the conversion state. If `wc` is a null wide character, `wcrtomb` stores a null byte, preceded by a shift sequence if necessary to restore the initial shift state, and the `mbstate_t` object used during the call is left in the initial conversion state.

Returns   Number of bytes stored in the array, including shift sequences. If `wc` isn't a valid wide character, returns `(size_t)(-1)` and stores `EILSEQ` in `errno`.   *25.5*

---

wcscat   *Wide-String Concatenation (C99)*   `<wchar.h>`

```
wchar_t *wcscat(wchar_t * restrict s1,
                const wchar_t * restrict s2);
```

Wide-character version of `strcat`.   *25.5*

---

wcschr   *Search Wide String for Character (C99)*   `<wchar.h>`

```
wchar_t *wcschr(const wchar_t *s, wchar_t c);
```

Wide-character version of `strchr`.   *25.5*

---

wcscmp   *Wide-String Comparison (C99)*   `<wchar.h>`

```
int wcscmp(const wchar_t *s1, const wchar_t *s2);
```

Wide-character version of `strcmp`.   *25.5*

---

wcscoll   *Wide-String Comparison Using Locale-Specific Collating*   `<wchar.h>`
Sequence (C99)

```
int wcscoll(const wchar_t *s1, const wchar_t *s2);
```

Wide-character version of `strcoll`.   *25.5*

---

wcscpy   *Wide-String Copy (C99)*   `<wchar.h>`

```
wchar_t *wcscpy(wchar_t * restrict s1,
                const wchar_t * restrict s2);
```

Wide-character version of `strcpy`.   *25.5*

---

wcscspn   *Search Wide String for Initial Span of Characters Not in Set*   `<wchar.h>`
(C99)

```
size_t wcscspn(const wchar_t *s1, const wchar_t *s2);
```

Wide-character version of `strcspn`.   *25.5*

---

wcsftime   *Write Formatted Date and Time to Wide String (C99)*   `<wchar.h>`

```
size_t wcsftime(wchar_t * restrict s, size_t maxsize,
                const wchar_t * restrict format,
                const struct tm * restrict timeptr);
```

Wide-character version of `strftime`.   *25.5*

| **wcslen** | *Wide-String Length (C99)* | `<wchar.h>` |

`size_t wcslen(const wchar_t *s);`

Wide-character version of `strlen`.   *25.5*

| **wcsncat** | *Bounded Wide-String Concatenation (C99)* | `<wchar.h>` |

```
wchar_t *wcsncat(wchar_t * restrict s1,
                 const wchar_t * restrict s2,
                 size_t n);
```

Wide-character version of `strncat`.   *25.5*

| **wcsncmp** | *Bounded Wide-String Comparison (C99)* | `<wchar.h>` |

```
int wcsncmp(const wchar_t *s1, const wchar_t *s2,
            size_t n);
```

Wide-character version of `strncmp`.   *25.5*

| **wcsncpy** | *Bounded Wide-String Copy (C99)* | `<wchar.h>` |

```
wchar_t *wcsncpy(wchar_t * restrict s1,
                 const wchar_t * restrict s2,
                 size_t n);
```

Wide-character version of `strncpy`.   *25.5*

| **wcspbrk** | *Search Wide String for One of a Set of Characters (C99)* | `<wchar.h>` |

```
wchar_t *wcspbrk(const wchar_t *s1,
                 const wchar_t *s2);
```

Wide-character version of `strpbrk`.   *25.5*

| **wcsrchr** | *Search Wide String in Reverse for Character (C99)* | `<wchar.h>` |

`wchar_t *wcsrchr(const wchar_t *s, wchar_t c);`

Wide-character version of `strrchr`.   *25.5*

| **wcsrtombs** | *Convert Wide String to Multibyte String – Restartable (C99)* | `<wchar.h>` |

```
size_t wcsrtombs(char * restrict dst,
                 const wchar_t ** restrict src,
                 size_t len,
                 mbstate_t * restrict ps);
```

Converts a sequence of wide characters from the array indirectly pointed to by
src into a sequence of corresponding multibyte characters that begins in the conversion state described by the object pointed to by ps. If ps is a null pointer,
wcsrtombs uses an internal object to store the conversion state. If dst isn't a
null pointer, the converted characters are then stored in the array pointed to by
dst. Conversion continues up to and including a terminating null wide character,
which is also stored. Conversion stops earlier if a wide character is reached that
doesn't correspond to a valid multibyte character or—if dst isn't a null pointer—

when the next multibyte character would exceed the limit of `len` total bytes to be stored in the array pointed to by `dst`. If `dst` isn't a null pointer, the object pointed to by `src` is assigned either a null pointer (if a terminating null wide character was reached) or the address just past the last wide character converted (if any). If the conversion ends at a null wide character, the resulting state is the initial conversion state.

Returns   Number of bytes in the resulting multibyte character sequence, not including any terminating null character. Returns `(size_t)(-1)` and stores `EILSEQ` in `errno` if a wide character is encountered that doesn't correspond to a valid multibyte character.   *25.5*

---

wcsspn   *Search Wide String for Initial Span of Characters in Set (C99)* `<wchar.h>`

```
size_t wcsspn(const wchar_t *s1, const wchar_t *s2);
```

Wide-character version of `strspn`.   *25.5*

---

wcsstr   *Search Wide String for Substring (C99)*   `<wchar.h>`

```
wchar_t *wcsstr(const wchar_t *s1, const wchar_t *s2);
```

Wide-character version of `strstr`.   *25.5*

---

wcstod   *Convert Wide String to Double (C99)*   `<wchar.h>`

```
double wcstod(const wchar_t * restrict nptr,
              wchar_t ** restrict endptr);
```

Wide-character version of `strtod`.   *25.5*

---

wcstof   *Convert Wide String to Float (C99)*   `<wchar.h>`

```
float wcstof(const wchar_t * restrict nptr,
             wchar_t ** restrict endptr);
```

Wide-character version of `strtof`.   *25.5*

---

wcstoimax   *Convert Wide String to Greatest-Width Integer (C99)*   `<inttypes.h>`

```
intmax_t wcstoimax(const wchar_t * restrict nptr,
                   wchar_t ** restrict endptr,
                   int base);
```

Wide-character version of `strtoimax`.   *27.2*

---

wcstok   *Search Wide String for Token (C99)*   `<wchar.h>`

```
wchar_t *wcstok(wchar_t * restrict s1,
                const wchar_t * restrict s2,
                wchar_t ** restrict ptr);
```

Searches the wide string pointed to by `s1` for a "token" consisting of wide characters not in the wide string pointed to by `s2`. If a token exists, the character following it is changed to a null wide character. If `s1` is a null pointer, a search begun by a previous call of `wcstok` is continued; the search begins immediately after the null wide character at the end of the previous token. `ptr` points to an object of type `wchar_t *` that `wcstok` modifies to keep track of its progress. If `s1` is a null pointer, this object must be the same one used in a previous call of `wcstok`; it determines which wide string is to be searched and where the search is to begin.

Returns   A pointer to the first wide character of the token. Returns a null pointer if no token could be found.   *25.5*

---

wcstol   *Convert Wide String to Long Integer (C99)*   `<wchar.h>`

```
long int wcstol(const wchar_t * restrict nptr,
                wchar_t ** restrict endptr, int base);
```

Wide-character version of `strtol`.   *25.5*

---

wcstold   *Convert Wide String to Long Double (C99)*   `<wchar.h>`

```
long double wcstold(const wchar_t * restrict nptr,
                    wchar_t ** restrict endptr);
```

Wide-character version of `strtold`.   *25.5*

---

wcstoll   *Convert Wide String to Long Long Integer (C99)*   `<wchar.h>`

```
long long int wcstoll(const wchar_t * restrict nptr,
                      wchar_t ** restrict endptr,
                      int base);
```

Wide-character version of `strtoll`.   *25.5*

---

wcstombs   *Convert Wide String to Multibyte String*   `<stdlib.h>`

```
size_t wcstombs(char * restrict s,
                const wchar_t * restrict pwcs,
                size_t n);
```

Converts a sequence of wide characters into corresponding multibyte characters. `pwcs` points to an array containing the wide characters. The multibyte characters are stored in the array pointed to by `s`. Conversion ends if a null character is stored or if storing a multibyte character would exceed the limit of n bytes.

Returns   Number of bytes stored, not including the terminating null character, if any. Returns `(size_t)(-1)` if a wide character is encountered that doesn't correspond to a valid multibyte character.   *25.2*

---

wcstoul   *Convert Wide String to Unsigned Long Integer (C99)*   `<wchar.h>`

```
unsigned long int wcstoul(
    const wchar_t * restrict nptr,
    wchar_t ** restrict endptr, int base);
```

Wide-character version of `strtoul`.   *25.5*

---

wcstoull   *Convert Wide String to Unsigned Long Long Integer (C99)*   `<wchar.h>`

```
unsigned long long int wcstoull(
    const wchar_t * restrict nptr,
    wchar_t ** restrict endptr, int base);
```

Wide-character version of `strtoull`.   *25.5*

wcstoumax	*Convert Wide String to Unsigned Greatest-Width Integer* `<inttypes.h>` *(C99)*	

```
uintmax_t wcstoumax(const wchar_t * restrict nptr,
                    wchar_t ** restrict endptr,
                    int base);
```

Wide-character version of `strtoumax`.   *27.2*

wcsxfrm	*Transform Wide String (C99)* `<wchar.h>`

```
size_t wcsxfrm(wchar_t * restrict s1,
               const wchar_t * restrict s2, size_t n);
```

Wide-character version of `strxfrm`.   *25.5*

wctob	*Convert Wide Character to Byte (C99)* `<wchar.h>`

```
int wctob(wint_t c);
```

Returns   Single-byte representation of `c` as an `unsigned` char converted to `int`. Returns `EOF` if `c` doesn't correspond to one multibyte character in the initial shift state.

25.5

wctomb	*Convert Wide Character to Multibyte Character* `<stdlib.h>`

```
int wctomb(char *s, wchar_t wc);
```

Converts the wide character stored in `wc` into a multibyte character. If `s` isn't a null pointer, stores the result in the array that `s` points to.

Returns   If `s` is a null pointer, returns a nonzero or zero value, depending on whether or not multibyte characters have state-dependent encodings. Otherwise, returns the number of bytes in the multibyte character that corresponds to `wc`; returns –1 if `wc` doesn't correspond to a valid multibyte character.   *25.2*

wctrans	*Define Wide-Character Mapping (C99)* `<wctype.h>`

```
wctrans_t wctrans(const char *property);
```

Returns   If `property` identifies a valid mapping of wide characters according to the `LC_CTYPE` category of the current locale, returns a nonzero value that can be used as the second argument to the `towctrans` function; otherwise, returns zero.

25.6

wctype	*Define Wide-Character Class (C99)* `<wctype.h>`

```
wctype_t wctype(const char *property);
```

Returns   If `property` identifies a valid class of wide characters according to the `LC_CTYPE` category of the current locale, returns a nonzero value that can be used as the second argument to the `iswctype` function; otherwise, returns zero.   *25.6*

wmemchr	*Search Wide-Character Memory Block for Character (C99)* `<wchar.h>`

```
wchar_t *wmemchr(const wchar_t *s, wchar_t c,
                 size_t n);
```

Wide-character version of `memchr`.   *25.5*

---

wmemcmp   *Compare Wide-Character Memory Blocks (C99)*   `<wchar.h>`

```
int wmemcmp(const wchar_t * s1, const wchar_t * s2,
        size_t n);
```

Wide-character version of memcmp.   *25.5*

---

wmemcpy   *Copy Wide-Character Memory Block (C99)*   `<wchar.h>`

```
wchar_t *wmemcpy(wchar_t * restrict s1,
            const wchar_t * restrict s2,
            size_t n);
```

Wide-character version of memcpy.   *25.5*

---

wmemmove   *Copy Wide-Character Memory Block (C99)*   `<wchar.h>`

```
wchar_t *wmemmove(wchar_t *s1, const wchar_t *s2,
            size_t n);
```

Wide-character version of memmove.   *25.5*

---

wmemset   *Initialize Wide-Character Memory Block (C99)*   `<wchar.h>`

```
wchar_t *wmemset(wchar_t *s, wchar_t c, size_t n);
```

Wide-character version of memset.   *25.5*

---

wprintf   *Wide-Character Formatted Write (C99)*   `<wchar.h>`

```
int wprintf(const wchar_t * restrict format, ...);
```

Wide-character version of printf.   *25.5*

---

wscanf   *Wide-Character Formatted Read (C99)*   `<wchar.h>`

```
int wscanf(const wchar_t * restrict format, ...);
```

Wide-character version of scanf.   *25.5*

APPENDIX E
ASCII Character Set

	Escape Sequence										
Decimal	Oct	Hex	Char	Character							
0	\0	\x00		nul	32		64	@	96	`
1	\1	\x01		soh	(^A)	33	!	65	A	97	a
2	\2	\x02		stx	(^B)	34	"	66	B	98	b
3	\3	\x03		etx	(^C)	35	#	67	C	99	c
4	\4	\x04		eot	(^D)	36	$	68	D	100	d
5	\5	\x05		enq	(^E)	37	%	69	E	101	e
6	\6	\x06		ack	(^F)	38	&	70	F	102	f
7	\7	\x07	\a	bel	(^G)	39	'	71	G	103	g
8	\10	\x08	\b	bs	(^H)	40	(	72	H	104	h
9	\11	\x09	\t	ht	(^I)	41	)	73	I	105	i
10	\12	\x0a	\n	lf	(^J)	42	*	74	J	106	j
11	\13	\x0b	\v	vt	(^K)	43	+	75	K	107	k
12	\14	\x0c	\f	ff	(^L)	44	,	76	L	108	l
13	\15	\x0d	\r	cr	(^M)	45	-	77	M	109	m
14	\16	\x0e		so	(^N)	46	.	78	N	110	n
15	\17	\x0f		si	(^O)	47	/	79	O	111	o
16	\20	\x10		dle	(^P)	48	0	80	P	112	p
17	\21	\x11		dc1	(^Q)	49	1	81	Q	113	q
18	\22	\x12		dc2	(^R)	50	2	82	R	114	r
19	\23	\x13		dc3	(^S)	51	3	83	S	115	s
20	\24	\x14		dc4	(^T)	52	4	84	T	116	t
21	\25	\x15		nak	(^U)	53	5	85	U	117	u
22	\26	\x16		syn	(^V)	54	6	86	V	118	v
23	\27	\x17		etb	(^W)	55	7	87	W	119	w
24	\30	\x18		can	(^X)	56	8	88	X	120	x
25	\31	\x19		em	(^Y)	57	9	89	Y	121	y
26	\32	\x1a		sub	(^Z)	58	:	90	Z	122	z
27	\33	\x1b		esc		59	;	91	[	123	{
28	\34	\x1c		fs		60	<	92	\	124	|
29	\35	\x1d		gs		61	=	93	]	125	}
30	\36	\x1e		rs		62	>	94	^	126	~
31	\37	\x1f		us		63	?	95	_	127	del

BIBLIOGRAPHY

*The best book on programming for the layman is
"Alice in Wonderland"; but that's because it's
the best book on anything for the layman.*

C Programming

Feuer, A. R., *The C Puzzle Book*, Revised Printing, Addison-Wesley, Reading, Mass., 1999. Contains numerous "puzzles"—small C programs whose output the reader is asked to predict. The book shows the correct output of each program and provides a detailed explanation of how it works. Good for testing your C knowledge and reviewing the fine points of the language.

Harbison, S. P., III, and G. L. Steele, Jr., *C: A Reference Manual*, Fifth Edition, Prentice-Hall, Upper Saddle River, N.J., 2002. The ultimate C reference—essential reading for the would-be C expert. Covers both C89 and C99 in considerable detail, with frequent discussions of implementation differences found in C compilers. Not a tutorial—assumes that the reader is already well versed in C.

Kernighan, B. W., and D. M. Ritchie, *The C Programming Language*, Second Edition, Prentice-Hall, Englewood Cliffs, N.J., 1988. The original C book, affectionately known as K&R or simply "the White Book." Includes both a tutorial and a complete C reference manual. The second edition reflects the changes made in C89.

Koenig, A., *C Traps and Pitfalls*, Addison-Wesley, Reading, Mass., 1989. An excellent compendium of common (and some not-so-common) C pitfalls. Forewarned is forearmed.

Plauger, P. J., *The Standard C Library*, Prentice-Hall, Englewood Cliffs, N.J., 1992. Not only explains all aspects of the C89 standard library, but provides complete source code! There's no better way to learn the library than to study this book. Even if your interest in the library is minimal, the book is worth getting just for the opportunity to study C code written by a master.

Ritchie, D. M., The development of the C programming language, in *History of Programming Languages II,* edited by T. J. Bergin, Jr., and R. G. Gibson, Jr., Addison-Wesley, Reading, Mass., 1996, pages 671–687. A brief history of C written by the language's designer for the Second ACM SIGPLAN History of Programming Languages Conference, which was held in 1993. The article is followed by transcripts of Ritchie's presentation at the conference and the question-and-answer session with the audience.

Ritchie, D. M., S. C. Johnson, M. E. Lesk, and B. W. Kernighan, UNIX time-sharing system: the C programming language, *Bell System Technical Journal* 57, 6 (July–August 1978), 1991–2019. A famous article that discusses the origins of C and describes the language as it looked in 1978.

Rosler, L., The UNIX system: the evolution of C—past and future, *AT&T Bell Laboratories Technical Journal* 63, 8 (October 1984), 1685–1699. Traces the evolution of C from 1978 to 1984 and beyond.

Summit, S., *C Programming FAQs: Frequently Asked Questions*, Addison-Wesley, Reading, Mass., 1996. An expanded version of the FAQ list that has appeared for years in the Usenet *comp.lang.c* newsgroup.

van der Linden, P., *Expert C Programming*, Prentice-Hall, Englewood Cliffs, N.J., 1994. Written by one of the C wizards at Sun Microsystems, this book manages to entertain and inform in equal amounts. With its profusion of anecdotes and jokes, it makes learning the fine points of C seem almost fun.

UNIX Programming

Rochkind, M. J., *Advanced UNIX Programming,* Second Edition, Addison-Wesley, Boston, Mass., 2004. Covers UNIX system calls in considerable detail. This book, along with the one by Stevens and Rago, is a must-have for C programmers who use the UNIX operating system or one of its variants.

Stevens, W. R., and S. A. Rago, *Advanced Programming in the UNIX Environment,* Second Edition, Addison-Wesley, Upper Saddle River, N.J., 2005. An excellent follow-up to this book for programmers working under the UNIX operating system. Focuses on using UNIX system calls, including standard C library functions as well as functions that are specific to UNIX.

Programming in General

Bentley, J., *Programming Pearls*, Second Edition, Addison-Wesley, Reading, Mass., 2000. This updated version of Bentley's classic programming book emphasizes writing efficient programs, but touches on other topics that are crucial for the professional programmer. The author's light touch makes the book as enjoyable to read as it is informative.

Kernighan, B. W., and R. Pike, *The Practice of Programming,* Addison-Wesley, Reading, Mass., 1999. Read this book for advice on programming style, choosing the right algorithm, testing and debugging, and writing portable programs. Examples are drawn from C, C++, and Java.

McConnell, S., *Code Complete,* Second Edition, Microsoft Press, Redmond, Wash., 2004. Tries to bridge the gap between programming theory and practice by providing down-to-earth coding advice based on proven research. Includes plenty of examples in a variety of programming languages. Highly recommended.

Raymond, E. S., ed., *The New Hacker's Dictionary,* Third Edition, MIT Press, Cambridge, Mass., 1996. Explains much of the jargon that programmers use, and it's great fun to read as well.

Web Resources

ANSI eStandards Store (*webstore.ansi.org*). The C99 standard (ISO/IEC 9899:1999) can be purchased at this site. Each set of corrections to the standard (known as a Technical Corrigendum) can be downloaded for free.

comp.lang.c Frequently Asked Questions (*c-faq.com*). Steve Summit's FAQ list for the *comp.lang.c* newsgroup is a must-read for any C programmer.

Dinkumware (*www.dinkumware.com*). Dinkumware is owned by P. J. Plauger, the acknowledged master of the C and C++ standard libraries. The web site includes a handy C99 library reference, among other things.

Google Groups (*groups.google.com*). One of the best ways to find answers to programming questions is to search the Usenet newsgroups using the Google Groups search engine. If you have a question, it's likely that someone else has already asked the question on a newsgroup and the answer has been posted. Groups of particular interest to C programmers include *alt.comp.lang.learn.c-c++* (for C and C++ beginners), *comp.lang.c* (the primary C language group), and *comp.std.c* (devoted to discussion of the C standard).

International Obfuscated C Code Contest (*www.ioccc.org*). Home of an annual contest in which participants vie to see who can write the most obscure C programs.

ISO/IEC JTC1/SC22/WG14 (*www.open-std.org/jtc1/sc22/wg14/*). The official web site of WG14, the international working group that created the C99 standard and is responsible for updating it. Of particular interest among the many documents available at the site is the rationale for C99, which explains the reasons for the changes made in the standard.

Lysator (*www.lysator.liu.se/c/*). A collection of links to C-related web sites maintained by Lysator, an academic computer society located at Sweden's Linköping University.

INDEX

Note: In C99, some `<math.h>` functions have three versions (one each for `float`, `double`, and `long double`). This index contains a single entry for such functions, using the name of the `double` version. For example, there's only one entry (under `acos`) for the `acos`, `acosf`, and `acosl` functions. The `<complex.h>` functions, which also come in three versions, are treated in a similar fashion.